DEATH OR VICTORY

*The Battle of Quebec
and the Birth
of an Empire*

DAN SNOW

ALLEN LANE
CANADA

ALLEN LANE CANADA

Published by the Penguin Group

Penguin Group (Canada), 90 Eglinton Avenue East, Suite 700,
Toronto, Ontario, Canada M4P 2Y3 (a division of Pearson Canada Inc.)

Penguin Group (USA) Inc., 375 Hudson Street, New York, New York 10014, U.S.A.
Penguin Books Ltd, 80 Strand, London WC2R 0RL, England
Penguin Ireland, 25 St Stephen's Green, Dublin 2, Ireland (a division of Penguin Books Ltd)
Penguin Group (Australia), 250 Camberwell Road, Camberwell, Victoria 3124, Australia
(a division of Pearson Australia Group Pty Ltd)
Penguin Books India Pvt Ltd, 11 Community Centre, Panchsheel Park,
New Delhi – 110 017, India
Penguin Group (NZ), 67 Apollo Drive, Rosedale, North Shore 0745, Auckland, New Zealand
(a division of Pearson New Zealand Ltd)
Penguin Books (South Africa) (Pty) Ltd, 24 Sturdee Avenue, Rosebank,
Johannesburg 2196, South Africa

Penguin Books Ltd, Registered Offices: 80 Strand, London WC2R 0RL, England

Published in Canada by Penguin Group (Canada), a division of Pearson Canada Inc., 2010.
First published in Great Britain by HarperPress, an imprint of HarperCollins*Publishers*,
77–85 Fulham Palace Road, Hammersmith, London W6 8JB, 2009.

1 2 3 4 5 6 7 8 9 10 (RRD)

LIBRARY AND ARCHIVES CANADA CATALOGUING IN PUBLICATION

Snow, Dan, 1978–
Death or victory : the battle for Quebec and the birth of an empire / Dan Snow.

(History of Canada)
ISBN 978-0-670-06737-4

1. Québec Campaign, 1759. I. Title. II. Series: History of Canada series

FC386.S66 2010   971.01'88   C2010-903068-0

British Library Cataloguing in Publication data available

Visit the Penguin Group (Canada) website at **www.penguin.ca**

Special and corporate bulk purchase rates available; please see
www.penguin.ca/corporatesales or call 1-800-810-3104, ext. 2477 or 2474

To Mum and Dad

CONTENTS

INTRODUCTION
to
THE HISTORY OF CANADA SERIES

Canada, the world agrees, is a success story. We should never make the mistake, though, of thinking that it was easy or foreordained. At crucial moments during Canada's history, challenges had to be faced and choices made. Certain roads were taken and others were not. Imagine a Canada, indeed imagine a North America, where the French and not the British had won the Battle of the Plains of Abraham. Or imagine a world in which Canadians had decided to throw in their lot with the revolutionaries in the thirteen colonies.

This series looks at the making of Canada as an independent, self-governing nation. It includes works on key stages in the laying of the foundations as well as the crucial turning points between 1867 and the present that made the Canada we know today. It is about those defining moments when the course of Canadian history and the nature of Canada itself were oscillating. And it is about the human beings—heroic, flawed, wise, foolish, complex—who had to make decisions without knowing what the consequences might be.

We begin the series with the European presence in the eighteenth century—a presence that continues to shape our society today—and conclude it with an exploration of the strategic importance of the Canadian Arctic. We look at how the mass movements of peoples, whether Loyalists in the eighteenth century or Asians at the start of the twentieth, have profoundly influenced the nature of Canada. We also look at battles and their aftermaths: the Plains of Abraham, the 1866 Fenian raids, the German submarines in the St. Lawrence River during World War II. Political crises—the 1891 election that saw Sir John A. Macdonald battling Wilfrid Laurier; the snap election that resulted in John Diefenbaker's massive 1958 landslide; Pierre Trudeau's triumphant patriation of the Canadian Constitution—provide rich moments of storytelling. So, too, do the Expo 67 celebrations, which marked a time of soaring optimism and gave Canadians new confidence in themselves.

We have chosen these critical turning points partly because they are good stories in themselves but also because they show what Canada was like at particularly important junctures in its history. And to tell them we have chosen Canada's best historians. Our authors are great storytellers who shine a spotlight on a different Canada, a Canada of the past, and illustrate links from then to now. We need to remember the roads that were taken—and the ones that were not. Our goal is to help our readers understand how we got from that past to this present.

Margaret MacMillan
Warden at St. Antony's College, Oxford

Robert Bothwell
May Gluskin Chair of Canadian History,
University of Toronto

LIST OF ILLUSTRATIONS

Major General James Wolfe, by George Townshend, 1759 © McCord
Museum M245

Louis-Joseph, Marquis de Montcalm. By kind permission of the Library
and Archives Canada, Acc. No. 1991-209-1/c027665

Vice Admiral Sir Charles Saunders, by Richard Brompton, 1772–3
© National Maritime Museum, Greenwich, London

Brigadier Robert Monckton © Mary Evans Picture Library

Brigadier General George Townshend, by Samuel William Reynolds, 1838
© National Portrait Gallery, London

Brigadier General James Murray © Mary Evans Picture Library

James Wolfe, by Joseph Highmore, c.1749. By kind permission of the
Library and Archives Canada, Acc. No. 1995-134-1

James Peachey's view of Quebec, 1784 © British Library Board. All Rights
Reserved. Maps K.Top 119.39.d

Peachey's Montmorency falls, 1765 © British Library Board. All Rights
Reserved. Maps K.Top 119.44-c

March of the Guards to Finchley, by William Hogarth, 1750 © The
Foundling Museum, London, UK/The Bridgeman Art Library

An Indian of ye Outawas Tribe and his Family going to War, by George
Townshend, 4th Viscount and 1st Marquess Townshend, 1751–1758
© National Portrait Gallery, London

An Indian war chief completely equipped with a scalp in his hand, by
George Townshend, 4th Viscount and 1st Marquess Townshend,
1751–1758 © National Portrait Gallery, London

Portrait of a male Native American, by William Hodges © The Royal
College of Surgeons of England

Portrait of an Inuit woman from Labrador, 1772 © The Royal College of
Surgeons of England

War club, pipe of peace and dagger © British Library Board. All Rights
Reserved. 980.i.28.

General James Wolfe, at Quebec, by George Townshend, 1759 © McCord
Museum M1794

Journal of James Wolfe, Quebec Expedition, 1759 © McCord Museum M255

ix

LIST OF MAPS

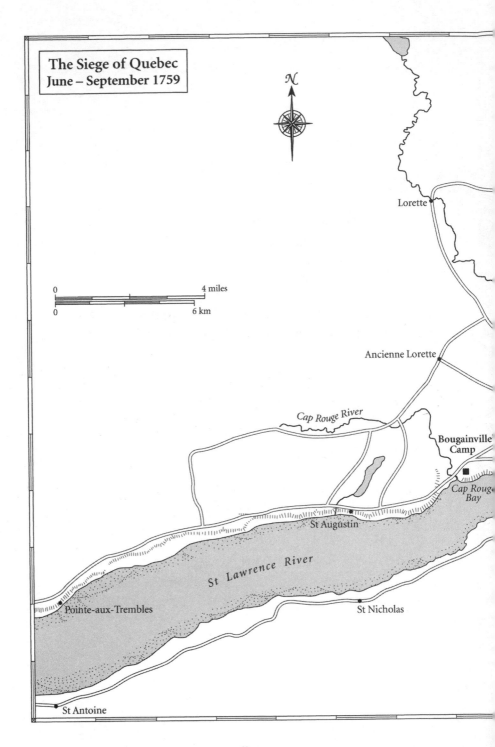

The Siege of Quebec
June – September 1759

N

0   4 miles
0   6 km

Lorette

Ancienne Lorette

Cap Rouge River

Bougainville Camp

Cap Rouge Bay

St Augustin

St Lawrence River

Pointe-aux-Trembles

St Nicholas

St Antoine

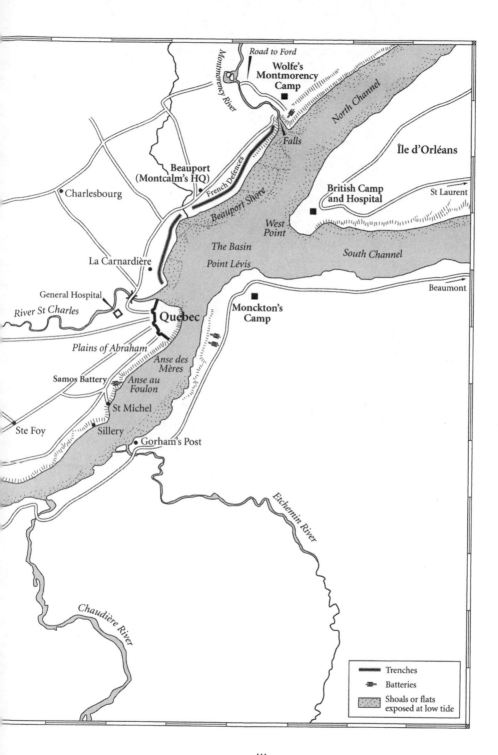

Road to Ford

Wolfe's
Montmorency
Camp

Montmorency River

North Channel

Falls

French Defences

Île d'Orléans

Beauport
(Montcalm's HQ)

Charlesbourg

Beauport Shore

British Camp
and Hospital

St Laurent

West
Point

La Carnardière

The Basin

Point Lévis

South Channel

General Hospital

Beaumont

River St Charles

Quebec

Monckton's
Camp

Plains of Abraham

Anse des
Mères

Samos Battery

Anse au
Foulon

St Michel

Ste Foy

Sillery

Gorham's Post

Etchemin River

Chaudière River

	Trenches
	Batteries
	Shoals or flats exposed at low tide

xiii

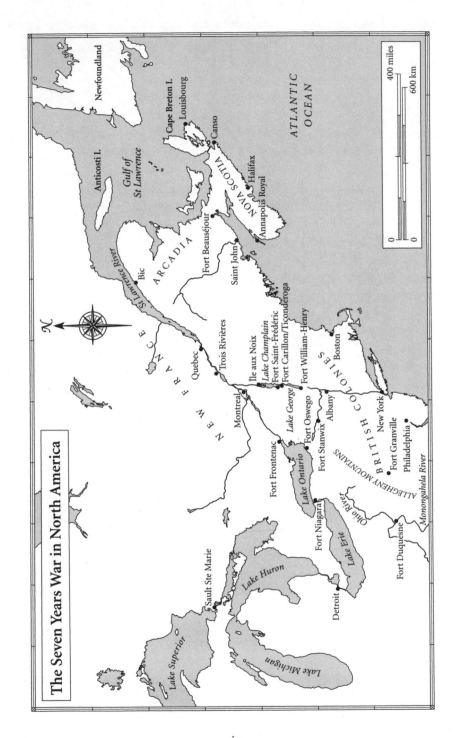

The Seven Years War in North America

Lake Superior

Lake Michigan

Lake Huron

Sault Ste Marie

Detroit

Lake Erie

Lake Ontario

Fort Niagara

Ohio River

Monongahela River

Fort Duquesne

ALLEGHENY MOUNTAINS

Fort Frontenac

Fort Stanwix

Fort Granville

Philadelphia

Fort Oswego

Albany

New York

BRITISH COLONIES

Lake George

Fort William–Henry

Fort Carillon/Ticonderoga

Fort Saint-Frédéric

Lake Champlain

Île aux Noix

Montreal

Boston

Trois Rivières

Quebec

NEW FRANCE

St Lawrence River

Bic

ARCADIA

Fort Beauséjour

Saint John

Annapolis Royal

NOVA SCOTIA

Halifax

Canso

Louisbourg

Cape Breton I.

Gulf of St Lawrence

Anticosti I.

Newfoundland

ATLANTIC OCEAN

0   400 miles

0   600 km

N

xiv

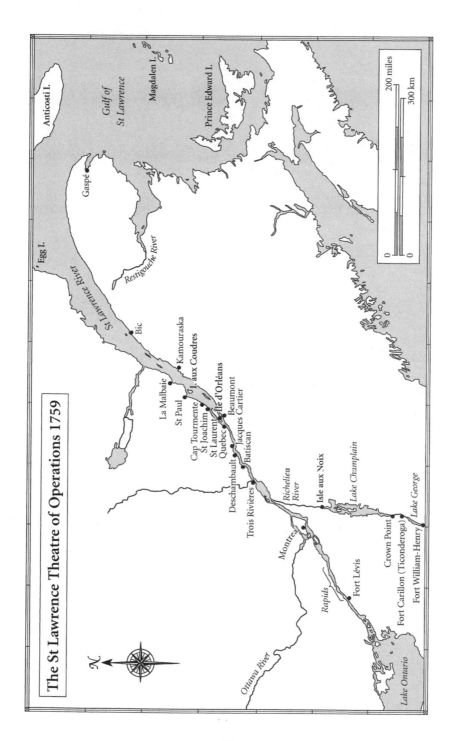

The St Lawrence Theatre of Operations 1759

Anticosti I.

Egg I.

St Lawrence River

Gulf of St Lawrence

Magdalen I.

Prince Edward I.

Gaspé

Restigouche River

Bic

Kamouraska

La Malbaie

St Paul

I. aux Coudres

Cap Tourmente

St Joachim

St Laurent

Île d'Orléans

Quebec

Beaumont

Jacques Cartier

Deschambault

Batiscan

Trois Rivières

Richelieu River

Isle aux Noix

Lake Champlain

Montreal

Crown Point

Fort Carillon (Ticonderoga)

Fort William-Henry

Lake George

Fort Lévis

Rapids

Ottawa River

Lake Ontario

200 miles

300 km

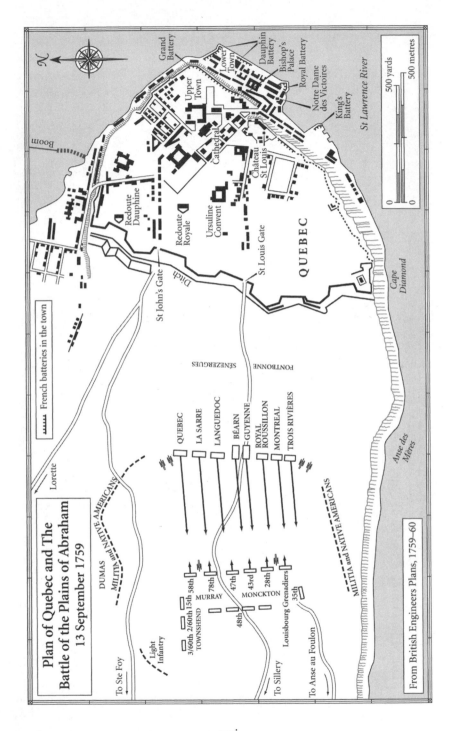

Plan of Quebec and The Battle of the Plains of Abraham 13 September 1759

From British Engineers Plans, 1759–60

AUTHOR'S NOTE

'One of the great battles of the world.'
FIELD MARSHAL MONTGOMERY

BATTLES CAN CHANGE the course of history. The fighting in North America that culminated with the battle James Wolfe fought outside the walls of Quebec on 13 September 1759 altered the world in a dramatic and lasting way. The dominance of the Anglo-Saxon model with its ideas of government, manners, trade, and finance was built on the British victory in what was truly a world war. Appropriately, I wrote this book during the course of a busy year spent all over the world. In Auckland, New Zealand, I wrote for a few hours every day and then took a fast stroll down to the glistening waters of the Hauraki Gulf to restore my energy. Every time I passed Wolfe Street I smiled; the shabby city street seemed to have little to do with the lanky, chinless, volatile commander of the British army at Quebec. It was, however, a powerful reminder of the enduring significance of the Seven Years War. Those events in the mosquito-ridden woods of New England and Canada, on the foaming seas off Western Europe, and in the shadow of the grand architecture of Quebec still matter. There are Wolfe Streets in cities in every corner of the world: Cape Town, Canberra, Baltimore, Houston, London, Liverpool, and Little Rock, Arkansas. On reflection it is not surprising that Auckland, a city that sprang into life during this time of Anglo-Saxon cultural supremacy, should have a reference, however small, to a man who helped to bring that supremacy about.

The raising of the Union Flag over Quebec and the destruction of French power in North America were far more significant for world history than the subsequent American Revolution. The revolution was merely a squabble for control over the fruits of the British victory over France and her Native allies. At the end of the Seven Years War a continent rich in farmland, minerals, and raw materials fell into the lap of the Anglo-Americans. In time, this continent would become the engine of an international system based on the rule of law, commercialism, representative institutions, and the English language. In the twentieth century North America would play the key part in defending that system as it was challenged by militarism, fascism, and communism. It was the armourer, paymaster, granary, and provider of millions of troops to defend the world order that had been born as a result of the Seven Years War.

Britain defeated France in the Seven Years War because she was able to assemble a crushing advantage in men and ships, paid for by an unprecedented level of government borrowing. By the mid-eighteenth century the French crown was unable to mobilize the country's superior wealth or manpower nearly as effectively as its smaller neighbour, Britain. The underfunded French navy was swept from the seas by a supremely professional British Royal Navy, while its army remained bogged down in a European war against enemies kept in the field by British loans. British victory owed much to favourable credit ratings. Yet the muskets still needed firing, the ships of the line still needed expert handling, the armies and raids still needed leadership, and the men who trudged along the frontiers of empire still needed to bear the heavy burden of campaigning, fighting, and surviving. The campaign and battle at Quebec in 1759 is a reminder that it was also a victory of flesh, blood, and grit. Indeed, the battle fought on the Plains of Abraham outside Quebec, brief though it was, demonstrates that individuals and the choices they make matter hugely even in vast conflicts. British financial might may have projected Wolfe and his army deep into enemy territory and kept them fed and supplied but the capture of Quebec was not bound to follow.

A battle is celebrated, remembered, and studied not just because it is a decisive event, but because it looks and sounds like one. We cannot help but to be fascinated by its violent crescendos, its sounds, smells, and extremes of emotion, and the flight of one side or another. The mass of British subjects, at the time and since, could not understand or even picture a bond market and were unlikely to name streets after one, but battles can fill imaginations. To English-speaking peoples the victory at Quebec came to be seen as a milepost that marked their rise to global hegemony. Quebec symbolized, and still does, the seismic geo-political shift that occurred in the middle of the eighteenth century. A shift that changed the world for ever.

In attempting to tell the story of that summer in 1759 I have been assisted by friends, colleagues, and family in at least four countries. The book would not have existed were it not for my agent, Caroline Dawnay, and my auntie, Margaret MacMillan, a historian who I can only dream of emulating. Another historian I have always respected and to whom I now owe a debt of gratitude is Professor Robert Bothwell, an expert editor who helped me to avoid terrible mistakes and improve the book in no small measure. Arabella Pike at HarperCollins provided the unflagging support that one would expect from the latest in a line of martial types. It was a privilege to be allowed to renew my partnership with Martin Redfern when Arabella left on maternity leave. Carol Anderson was stunningly efficient. Sarah Hopper was her usual brilliant self on the pictures and Sophie Goulden had the patience of a rock as she steered the project home.

Museums and libraries all over the world have been unstintingly generous with their time and advice. Dorian Hayes at the British Library was a great source of suggestions. Valerie Adams at the Public Record Office in Belfast could not have been more helpful. Pieter Van der Merwe at the National Maritime Museum was very good to give up a morning to fire volley after volley of brilliant, if totally unrelated facts and ideas at me. Richard Kemp at the Somerset Military Museum went so far beyond the call of duty that I was embarrassed. Lizzy Shipton at the Rifles Museum, Salisbury, was a great help and Alan Readman, the assistant country archivist, West Sussex, Nora Hague at the McCord Museum, Montreal, Odile Girard at the Library and Archives Canada, and the team at Harvard all made research that little bit easier.

I was blessed with researchers, translators, and givers of advice. The book would not have been written without Gwyneth MacMillan in

Quebec. She was efficient, intelligent, generous, and cheerful. Eddie Kolla in Paris was enormously helpful. Michael Manulak was very helpful in the opening stages. My sister, Rebecca Snow, is an expert in her own right and Roger Nixon and David Mendel were stalwarts; the latter walked me around Quebec bringing the eighteenth century alive on every street. Glen Steppler, Laurence Westgaph and Erica Charters were very good to me while Isabelle Pila and Brigitte Sawyer were vital translators.

Shuna and Katie Snow encouraged me and made me laugh through the process. My parents, Peter Snow and Ann MacMillan, were as unfailingly supportive as they have been of all my projects through the years. They read every word and, more importantly, they have always told me I could do it.

PROLOGUE

AN HOUR BEFORE SUNRISE the hated drummers marched along the rows of tents. Their sticks beat the 'General', driving a clear message into the sleeping brains of the men. Even those befuddled by 'screech', cheap rum brewed by boiling the sediment from molasses barrels, were dragged from their slumbers. Men clambered over their drowsy comrades and emerged into the open air. Their feet squelched in the urine-soaked ground, for soldiers invariably eased themselves at the entrance to their tents or even inside where they slept. For an hour a mass of figures in the semi-darkness jostled and cursed. But as the light grew so did their regularity. By the time the drummers beat the 'Assembly' at 0500 hours the tents had been struck, kit packed, weapons retrieved and the men bundled onto the assembly area to line up by company and regiment, ready for inspection, colours unfurled, sharp new flints securely fastened in the jaws of their muskets. Companies of between 50 and 100 men were commanded by a captain who knew every one of them by name. When he was happy that his men were properly attired, their weapons clean and thirty-six rounds in their cartridge cases he reported to the major or lieutenant colonel and soon the whole force was ready to march.

Groups of light infantrymen and rangers set off first. The British force had been in the heart of Canada for less than a week and they had been given a shocking immersion into the world of insurgency, sniping, ambush and Native American warfare. Bodies of soldiers that strayed from the riverbank were found horribly killed and mutilated, their scalps taken as trophies by Native Americans and the Canadians who had learnt their way of war from them. Civilians in this populous part of Canada were trapped in between. Their farmhouses ransacked, their provisions confiscated by hungry warriors. That very morning a patrol of British light troops had searched one house and finding no one set it on fire. A British officer reported that 'they were alarmed with bitter shrieks and cries of women and children'. They had, apparently, 'foolishly concealed themselves among some lumber in a cellar'. British troops 'very humanely exerted themselves for the relief of those miserable wretches, but their best endeavours were ineffectual ... these unhappy people perished in the flames'. The officer wrote in his diary that 'Such alas! are the direful effects of war.'[1] By the end of the summer an incident like this would barely raise a comment as atrocity fed atrocity and the campaign became a nightmare of terror, retribution, and disease.

This was the first serious push away from the beaches where the British had landed just days before. Major General James Wolfe, their commander, had ordered this force to move west, away from the comforting presence of the fleet anchored in the river, to tighten the noose around Quebec, a fortress said to be impregnable, capital of the vast French North American empire. They were to seize a prominent piece of ground called Point Lévis from where British guns could fire across the river into Quebec. The soldiers knew the French would not let this probing force march with impunity. The terrain favoured the defence with thick woodland and a steep rise overlooking the track. One British officer described the route as 'no regular road' but 'only a serpentine path with trees and under-wood on every side of us'.[2]

Rangers led the column. They looked more like Native Americans than Christian subjects of King George with tomahawks at their waists, moccasins and powder horns, while a few even carried scalps of fallen enemies hanging from their belts. They were nearly all Americans recruited from the frontiers and despite their appearance and their unruly reputation (the French dubbed them 'the English savages') their skill in this kind of conflict meant that they could command twice the pay of red-coated regular infantrymen. Some carried the long, accurate rifle but most thought that the Brown Bess musket, possibly with a few inches sawed off the end to make it lighter, was a better weapon for close quarters bush fighting. It was quicker to reload and capable of firing buckshot. Alongside them was a new brand of British regular, the light infantryman. They had been introduced by innovative officers to try to improve the British army's woeful performance in the wilderness fighting of North America. They were picked men who had been selected for having a sharp mind, an ability to improvise and a true aim. Major General Wolfe had written careful instructions. The light troops were to 'post detachments in all the suspected places on the road to prevent the columns from being fired at, from behind trees, by rascals who dare not show themselves'. As the column marched past the light troops would then fall in as the rear guard.[3] They had not advanced far before the woods echoed to the bangs of muskets and rifles, the howls of wounded and the shriek of the Native Americans, allies of the French.

The men of the North American tribes were bred as warriors. Martial prowess was highly prized and even in times of peace young men picked fights with neighbouring groups in order to win acclaim. Prisoners, in Native cultures, could replace relatives who had fallen in battle or could be tortured expertly so that their pain assuaged that of the family of a fallen brave. In the two centuries since Europeans had introduced gunpowder into North America the Native Americans had mastered the musket and rifle and men had honed their marksmanship for hunting as well as war. At close quarters they were just as skilled with tomahawk or knife. Their terrible reputation for savagery, together with expert bushcraft, exotic tattoos, and haunting war cries, had all conspired to send many British units into total panic at even the prospect of an encounter. The Canadians of European descent were no less fearsome. Canada had only just survived in the face of an unforgiving climate and constant hostility from some tribes. Her young men had adapted to the North American way of war and to many outsiders they were indistinguishable from the Native warriors. As the British force pushed along the track the biggest challenge was overcoming the massive psychological inferiority that years of ambush, slaughter, and defeat had bred in the men. The redcoats were edgy. One officer reported an unfortunate 'friendly fire' incident in which a light infantryman shot one of his corporals, and the wounded man had to be carried on 'a blanket with skewers to two poles'. It took six men to carry the casualty and they were 'relieved every quarter of an hour'.[4]

Wolfe would report to his political masters in London that the force had 'two or three skirmishes' but the evidence from those who actually sweated up to Point Lévis, clutching their muskets and scanning the unfamiliar woodland for any movement, suggests that it was not as casual as Wolfe made it sound.[5] A Highlander who acted as his regiment's bard gives a graphic description in a Gaelic song: 'the marshalling was under Beaumont/ those ranks were handsome/ sent up to Pointe Levis/ to test the warriors;/ Indians and Frenchmen/ were very close to us in the bushes/ wrecking the heads/ and the legs that belonged to us!'[6] As the soldiers skirted the shore many caught their first horrifying glimpses of this new kind of war. One young Scotsman was horrified at the sight of several British corpses, 'all scalped and mangled in a shocking manner'. He wrote that, 'no human creature but an Indian could be guilty of such inhuman cruelty,' but changed his journal to read, 'no human creature but an Indian or Canadian could be guilty of such inhumanity as to insult a dead body'.[7] His men were uncowed though, if the Gaelic war song is to be believed: 'when we were fully drawn up/ in line of battle/ and watching them/ to see if they would wait and give us satisfaction/ they sprayed fire into our faces/ but they got it back in return;/ they took fright/ when they recognised us'.[8] The hit and run tactics of the Canadians and Native Americans could slow the British advance but not stop it. In a series of mini engagements, the light infantry and the rangers edged forward towards Point Lévis. One sergeant called it a 'sharp skirmish of near two hours' and said 'we sustained a considerable loss of killed and wounded'.[9] An officer wrote that in the end the French forces could not 'withstand our fire and numbers' and put the casualty figure at 'thirty killed and wounded'.[10] The fighting had been intense enough to make their commander think about turning back.

As the exhausted men fought their way onto the cleared ground around Point Lévis they gazed across the St Lawrence River in awe. There, around half a mile away, was Quebec. It occupied one of the most powerful natural positions of any town or city in the world. Fine buildings with tall sloping roofs and churches with high spires sat above cliffs which soared out of the St Lawrence. The walls atop the cliffs bristled with cannon and beyond the city a great army was camped along the shoreline. Those with telescopes scanned its defences knowing that they could very well be asked to storm its walls. One was dismayed by what he saw: 'their situation appears to be very strong by nature, and ... they are very numerous'. Even from this far away he could pick out lines of trenches and redoubts and, also, 'throughout their camp there are a continued chain of houses, the windows of which are logged up for the service of musketry'.[11]

It had been a bloody morning. The men who now gazed on Quebec and its defenders realized that it was simply a prologue. Before the waters of the mighty river froze in winter the British force would have to capture Quebec or face an ignominious retreat that could derail the entire British war effort not just in North America but in distant Europe too. Defeat was not an option, yet the soldiers staring out at Quebec knew that they could well pay a terrible price for victory.

ONE

Assault on New France

THERE WERE SHIPS in the St Lawrence. Not an armada, but a squadron powerful enough to dominate the river. Around ten in all, seven of them were obviously warships; their hulls were chequered with gun ports. The largest was a fine man of war with eighty guns, a match for any craft afloat. The air was heavy with fog. The vessels drifted in and out of banks of cloud and cohesion was maintained by the largest ship firing one of its cannon at regular intervals. Sharp-eyed officers of the watch saw an eruption of white smoke with a momentary stab of fire at its centre, seconds later came the deep sound of the explosion, echoing back off the banks of the river as the shore-lines slowly converged.[1]

The river had grown narrower. After days of sailing up the Gulf of St Lawrence where the land was barely visible on either side, the crews could now see clearly either shore. On the north side it was spectacular: high, near vertical slopes, covered with spruce trees, broken only by the occasional section of cliff, damp with water that gave them a bright sheen during rare bursts of sunshine. On the south side, only twenty-two miles away, the coastline was flatter but beyond it, another mountain range reminded the crews of the vast, wild nature of the country.

There was a large island, separated from the south shore by a gap of just over three miles. With a good natural harbour the Île du Bic had, for centuries, been an easily defensible haven for ships on the passage up or down the river and home to a small community of priests and pilots. Here the largest ship broke out a large plain white flag, or ensign, at its mizzen. It was the 'Bourbon Banner', symbol of the Bourbon kings of France. On the shore the inhabitants, who had been keenly examining the ships for clues as to their nationality, broke out into 'the greatest rejoicing imaginable'.[2]

This was the gateway to Canada, the jewel in the crown of New France, a vast French empire that stretched from the North Atlantic to the Rocky Mountains and down to New Orleans at the mouth of the Mississippi. But its great size was matched by its vulnerability and especially now that France was at war. Her ancient rivalry with England, inherited in 1707 by the newly created Britain, had been revived at the end of the seventeenth century and they had fought a series of wars, each greater than the last, separated by periods of unconvincing peace. No longer did Englishmen strive to carve out dynastic empires in France itself; instead, the fighting surged across the almost limitless horizons of newly discovered continents, dragging in the settlers of the adolescent colonial empires. For four years New France had been fighting the British whose colonies in North America clung to the Atlantic Ocean from Massachusetts down to Georgia. At the beginning of each campaigning season when the ice melted in the St Lawrence River, the artery of Canada, the settlers, or *habitants*, waited nervously to see what help France would send to her North American possessions. This year, it seemed, France had been generous in her aid. The people of Bic rushed into canoes and paddled out to greet the ships, which they assumed were carrying the food, gunpowder, soldiers, and gold which New France so desperately needed to hold back the British and their American colonial allies.

The enthusiastic Canadians scrambled up the towering sides of the hulls on slippery, shallow steps that formed a vertical ladder. But as soon as they reached the deck, their euphoria was instantly extinguished. Rather than receiving a warm welcome from fellow subjects of the Most Christian King, Louis XV of France, they found themselves with British oak beneath their feet, and the muskets and cold steel of red-coated marines pointed at their bellies. The ships were British. It was 23 May 1759: the war had arrived in the heart of the French empire. This Royal Naval squadron under the command of

2

Rear Admiral of the Red, Philip Durell, had been given the task of blockading Canada; to cut it off from any help that France might send, and hasten its capitulation.

On shore the joy of the *habitants* turned to confusion as they waited for the canoes to return, then to 'consternation, rage and grief' as they saw 'the White colours struck, and the British flags, hoisted in their place'. Apparently, a priest who had been avidly watching the proceedings with a telescope clamped to his eye, 'dropped down and instantly expired'.[3] With an age-old *ruse de guerre* Durell had lured experienced Canadian pilots on board, men he desperately needed to complete his mission.

The squabbles of European monarchs had poisoned relations between their colonies in the Americas since those continents had been discovered 250 years before. The ambitions of Louis XIV in Germany, the Low Countries, and Spain had pushed England into armed opposition. Fighting had spread from Western Europe to the wildernesses of the Carolinas or northern New Hampshire as it had to West Africa and Asia. But the current conflict was different. Long the victims of Europe's wars, the colonies now became their instigators. As their size, populations, and economies had all swelled they developed their own ambitions, interests, and points of friction with the colonies of other powers. While Europe would never lose its primacy in policymakers' minds, by the mid-eighteenth century French and British politicians found themselves increasingly impelled by colonial considerations. In the late 1740s ambitious British colonials had crossed the Allegheny Mountains and started trading with the Native American inhabitants of the Ohio valley. The British colonies had always claimed the entire continent as far as the Pacific but the barrier of the Alleghenies and the hostility of the Native Americans beyond them had prevented them from ever making these claims a reality. Now these adventurers hoped to sell vast swathes of this fertile land to migrants from the colonies, who would then provide a market for manufactured goods that they would supply. Little attention was paid to French assertions of sovereignty in the area, and none at all to those of the Native Americans.

The French regarded these encroachments as an unacceptable violation of the strategic corridor that linked Canada, along the St

Lawrence, to Louisiana, a colony that was growing along the length of the Mississippi. New France moved troops into the Ohio valley and started building a chain of forts. This represented a threat not only to the individual British colonies, who believed it their destiny to expand west to the Pacific, but also to British North America as a whole which faced being surrounded by an unbroken ring of French forts from the Gulf of Mexico to the St Lawrence River. Even the British Prime Minister, Thomas Pelham Holles, Duke of Newcastle-upon-Tyne and Newcastle-under-Lyme, probably the least belligerent man in George II's government and no friend to rascally marauders on the fringes of empire, believed that this was intolerable. 'No war,' he wrote to the British ambassador at Versailles, 'could be worse than the suffering of such insults.' Britain would lose its entire position in America if her colonies were confined to the narrow coastal strip of the eastern seaboard. 'That,' he wrote emphatically, 'is what we must not, we will not, suffer.'[4]

With only a handful of British regular troops in North America it was left to the colonies to counter the French threat. Virginia took up the challenge and in true British style wrote a strongly worded letter to the French commander in the Ohio valley. It was delivered by eight men. Their leader was in his early twenties, a tall, hardy, rather conservative officer in the Virginia militia who owed his appointment to his connections to Lord Fairfax of Cameron, one of Virginia's leading landowners. His name was George Washington. Given his later titanic reputation it is perhaps surprising that he stumbled rather than strode onto history's stage. There was little sign of future greatness, indeed he was lucky to survive. He delivered his letter but the French commander was contemptuous. The following year Washington led a motley force over the mountains, planning to use gunpowder and steel where ink had failed. The first shots of the Seven Years War were fired in a glen near present-day Uniontown in Fayette County, Pennsylvania. In an action that did him no credit, on 28 May 1754, Washington ambushed a small force of French troops who were coming to warn him away from French land. Ensign Joseph Coulon de Villiers de Jumonville and nine of his men were killed. The French responded quickly, defeated Washington, sending him limping back across the

Alleghenies. His actions had made war inevitable. He and his men were fortunate that they did not spend the whole of it as prisoners.

The fighting triggered the sending of reinforcements to North America by both the British and the French. Britain moved first by lunging into the Ohio country, trying to capture Fort Duquesne at the Forks of the Ohio River. A force under General Braddock was cobbled together from different units and sent out from Britain. It was raw, unused to American conditions and its men were utterly terrified of the Native Americans. Braddock made some attempt to adapt to local conditions but was unwilling to listen to colonial advice and as far as Native Americans were concerned, he told Benjamin Franklin that 'it is impossible that [they] should make any impression' on his disciplined troops.[5] Braddock's men wilted as they hacked their way through thick forest, travelling between three and eight miles a day. The supply train collapsed as wagons broke up on the brutal road and horses dropped dead. Dysentery tore through the ranks. It was hugely impressive that the expedition got as far as it did. On 9 July 1755, the British force of approximately fifteen hundred men crossed the Monongahela River, nine miles short of the French Fort Duquesne. Their reward for such grit was blundering straight into a terrible ambush by 108 Canadian colonial troops, 146 militiamen, and 600 Native Americans. Braddock's force was utterly routed. The French poured fire into the thickly packed column, while sharpshooters picked off the officers. Without leadership, the men simply herded together like terrified animals desperately seeking a false sense of security in numbers. The column eventually broke and flooded back along the road they had made. Native Americans swooped down on the wounded, killing many, saving others to torture later, and claiming others as prisoners to induct into their tribes and replace fallen family members. Braddock was mortally wounded, Washington was hurt and had several horses shot from under him. Two-thirds of the British force were killed or captured. The French suffered less than fifty dead and injured. Of the 150 men in the colonial Virginia Regiment 120 became casualties. Monongahela ranks with the battle of Isandlwana of the Anglo–Zulu War and the massacre of the British army between Kabul and Jalalabad during the First Anglo–Afghan War as an epic tragedy in the military history of the British Empire. The French captured money, supplies, and artillery but the psychological consequences of the defeat were the most serious. It shook the confidence of the British army in North America for years to come and created a myth of the Native American as a superhuman savage.

The war in North America continued to go badly. In Europe the news was scarcely better. The British were forced to shoot one of their admirals, John Byng, on his own quarterdeck to, in Voltaire's memorable words, 'encourage the others'. A court martial determined that Byng had been insufficiently aggressive when he withdrew his fleet after an indecisive battle off Minorca, allowing a French force to capture the vital island. On the Continent Britain's woes were added to not by an absence of aggression but by a surfeit. Britain's ally, Frederick II of Prussia, ignited a general war by invading Saxony, thus triggering a series of alliances that united Russia, Austria, and France against him, all three determined to punish Prussia's temerity with annihilation. King George II's hereditary possession in Germany, his beloved Electorate of Hanover, was rapidly overrun by French troops.

Britain's fortunes did slowly improve from this nadir. French colonies were picked off in West Africa and the Caribbean. The French army was driven out of Hanover and then held at bay by an allied army paid for by London but commanded by a Prussian, Frederick's brother-in-law, Ferdinand of Brunswick. Frederick won a series of stunning victories that would earn him the epithet 'the Great' but even so Prussia was never far from dismemberment. There was unequivocally good news from India where Robert Clive routed the Nawab of Bengal and his French allies at the battle of Plassey in 1757. This battle turned the British East India Company's zone of influence into an empire. Fighting moved to the Carnatic where British forces sought to wipe out French power as they had in Bengal. But in North America there were years of defeat. Regular troops were trounced as they struggled with unfamiliar terrain and enemies while the civilians of the frontier were murdered, tortured, or captured by war parties of Native Americans and Canadians. 1758 had finally seen some success when a British amphibious force had seized the French stronghold of

Louisbourg perched on the rocky Atlantic coast of Cape Breton Island.

Everything suggested that 1759 would be the decisive year. Britain was to make a massive push for victory in North America. Austria and Russia seemed to have Frederick on the brink of defeat and France, frustrated by her lack of progress in Germany, was assembling an invasion force to cross the Channel and knock Britain out of the war. She would then regain those colonies lost on the battlefield at the negotiating table.

For Britain the year began in crisis. London's financial community were terrified by the spectre of invasion. Everyone knew that Le Havre was awash with shipwrights, its harbour filling inexorably with shallow-draught invasion barges. Forty thousand soldiers had been moved to France's north-west coast. Lord Lyttelton, an opposition politician, wrote from London that 'we talk of nothing here but the French invasion; they are certainly making such preparations as have never before been made to invade this island since the Spanish Armada'.[6] Government bonds sold at the steepest discounts of the war. The national debt was larger than anyone could have imagined possible and any new taxes had little chance of getting through a House of Commons packed with country gentlemen who, while patriots, had no wish to fund a perpetual war for the benefit of London financiers, merchants, and American prospectors. The cost of the navy alone jumped from £3.3 million in 1758 to £5 million in 1759. In all the Duke of Newcastle would have to find £12 million in 1759, over half of which he would need to borrow and as the markets lost confidence in the progress of the war the cost of that borrowing crept up.

The campaigning season opened with defeats for Ferdinand in Germany. He was driven back to the borders of Hanover itself. Frederick suffered sharp setbacks and later in the year he was so badly beaten by the Russians and Austrians at Kunersdorf that he thought the war lost. In Britain, by the start of summer the Chancellor of the Exchequer had asked to resign, government stock had plunged, and Newcastle was thinking about suspending seamen's wages. The Prime Minister wrote a memorandum in which he admitted that 'we are engaged in expenses infinitely above our strength ... expedition after expedition, campaign after campaign'. He suggested that Prussia should be warned that Britain might not be able to continue the war for another year.[7]

Attempts were made to fortify strategic points in southern England. Chatham, Portsmouth, Dover, and Plymouth were given earthworks and batteries were erected along the coast. They were futile gestures. The country was stripped of regular troops. The commander in chief of the British army told his colleagues that only 10,000 men would be available to meet an invasion on the south coast. So many of Britain's Royal Engineers had been sent to America there were only five qualified engineers left in the country.[8] The only other troops available were a half-assembled militia of amateur soldiers. In a clash with veteran French infantrymen there would be no doubt as to the result. In desperation the population clung to reassuring jingoism. A great favourite was 'Rule, Britannia', with words by James Thomson and music by Thomas Arne, a song which had become wildly popular during Charles Edward Stuart's Jacobite uprising of 1745–6. Another hit at the time was 'Great Britain For Ever'.

Defiance alone never repelled an invasion. Britain's real defence was her fleet. But her politicians had left little margin for error. The First Lord of the Admiralty reported to a small de facto war cabinet in February that the majority of British battleships had been dispatched around the globe to poach French possessions. Forty-one were left in home waters. The French were thought to have forty-three, although some of these were in her southern ports in the Mediterranean. The number of French ships that were in a condition to get to sea, let alone last long in the Channel, would be far smaller but the Royal Navy was also weaker than its paper strength, lacking nearly ten thousand men; many of its capital ships were hardly able to weigh their anchors.[9]

The government had taken a terrible gamble. Britain itself was at risk and yet men, ships, and treasure had been sent abroad. Vast resources were committed to the invasion of Canada, the most important operation yet undertaken in the war. Failure would place the North American colonies in danger, threaten the creditworthiness of the British government, and almost certainly destroy Newcastle's administration. The fate of the expedition would be felt from the log cabins of the American frontier to the palaces of Whitehall and Versailles.

If Durell's Royal Naval squadron in the St Lawrence could block French supplies to Canada the prospects for the British attack would be rosy indeed. But he also had another task, almost as important. The river was unknown to British seamen. With its reefs, currents, rocks, and other hazards it was Canada's first and, many thought, strongest line of defence. Durell was charged with finding a route up the river. The French authorities had made desultory attempts to chart the river but the results were unimpressive and, it seems, at best only partially available to the British. For generations the French had relied on pilots, each expert in a small stretch of river. So important was their knowledge that one British officer discovered that 'it is a rule with the inhabitants of Quebec not to let any pilots have the whole navigation of this river'.[10] Durell had tricked these men aboard by showing them the Bourbon Banner. It was a perfectly legitimate ruse according to the rules that governed eighteenth-century warfare, and it had brought these vital pilots straight to him.

Durell was typical of the fighting admirals of the mid-century navy. He was 52 years old and had been at sea since he was 14. Like so many naval officers he had joined a ship thanks to the patronage of a family member, his uncle Captain Thomas Durell of the *Sea Horse*, although rather more unusually he had joined as an ordinary seaman. Serving his time on the lowest rung of the Georgian navy had given him an unbeatable training in what it took for men to sail and fight a ship. He had spent the rest of his teenage years in North American waters and was made an officer at 24 and a captain by his early thirties. War had made him rich. In the maelstrom of battle naval officers could fight for something more tangible than honour: prizes. Naval officers were incentivized by the guarantee that they would receive a proportion of the value of any enemy ship captured. In the 1740s he had helped take two French merchantmen, returning from the East Indies packed with valuable goods. But wealth had not dampened his ambition; he had continued at sea and had fought in large fleet actions against the French in European waters until returning to North America for good in 1758.[11]

Durell had had an awful winter. He had written to the Admiralty in London in March 1759 from the British naval base of Halifax in Nova Scotia telling them that 'the winter has been the severest that has been known since the settling of the place', vessels attempting to get up the coast 'have met with ice eighteen or twenty leagues from the land, so were obliged to return, after having had some of their people froze to death, and other frost bitten to that degree, as to lose legs and arms'.[12] Durell had stationed one of his quickest, most manoeuvrable ships, the frigate *Sutherland* under Captain John Rous off Canso, to bring him news of the ice melting. Rous was also in his fifties and knew the waters off the coast of Newfoundland and the Gulf of St Lawrence as well as any Briton or American. He had been a New England privateer, preying on French merchantmen, before a commodore in the Royal Navy recruited this 'brisk, gallant man' for the King's Service.[13] When planning his campaign Durell had decided not to risk taking his full squadron into the gulf to lie in wait for the enemy. He had spent years in these waters, time which included a vain search for the French in similar conditions in 1755, and reckoned that his chances of finding them at sea were small and the cost to his crews and ships from the cold too high. Far better, he decided, to wait for the ice to melt in Halifax, and then sail up the St Lawrence and intercept the French in the confined waters of the river.

But Durell had been unable to leave Halifax until 5 May, trapped by ice and contrary winds. By the time he had arrived at Bic he had found out that his gamble had failed. As one British officer on the ships wrote,

> near the isle of Bic we took a small sloop ... who gave us the disagreeable news of the arrival of many transports and some frigates from Old France, which they left early in March and were deeply loaded with provisions and warlike stores. Had we sailed at the time you so earnestly wished, we had most certainly intercepted them, as they were not more than 10 days before us.[14]

This was a disaster; the bold attempt to sever the umbilical cord to France had failed and with it any prospect of an easy campaign of conquest. These French supplies would enable Canada to fight on and nothing short of a full military campaign would bring the colony to its knees. Another British officer wrote, 'this, you may imagine was mortifying news to us'.[15]

It was mortifying enough for the sailors on the ships, but Durell would have known that for one man in particular it would be the most unwelcome news imaginable. The man whose job it was to command the soldiers that would do the fighting once the fleet delivered them up the St Lawrence into the heart of Canada, whose army would attempt to bring about the ruin of New France, to kill, capture, or scatter its defenders and batter its strongholds into submission. For this man, it would be by far the greatest test of his short career but he had been confident of success, as long as the British ships could stop French supplies from reaching the Canadians. Now his plan had misfired before he had even entered the St Lawrence. This commander was Major General James Wolfe.

While Durell secured pilots and intelligence, James Wolfe had spent the spring chafing to follow him up the river. Wolfe was charged with threatening, and ideally capturing, the principal towns of Canada, particularly its capital, Quebec, perched on a plateau, protected by cliffs which plunged down to the St Lawrence. Quebec was a great prize that had eluded British soldiers for generations. On paper he had a considerable force but his chances were lessening by the day as the expedition suffered delay after delay. The campaign season in North America was short; the onset of winter put a stop to any military activity as the river froze and the temperatures plunged far below zero. Every minute counted.

Even as Wolfe and many of his senior officers had met in Portsmouth, in southern England in February 1759 there was already a sense of great urgency. Previous attacks on Canada had petered out as the gales and frosts of September and October had heralded the onset of the terrible winter. Surviving letters to these officers from the bureaucrats and politicians in London are laced with exhortations of speed. On 1 January the Admiralty Secretary had written to the port admiral at Portsmouth telling him 'in the most pressing manner' to get the ships ready for service in North America, 'with all the expedition that is possible'.[16] Wolfe was in overall command of the army; Rear Admiral Charles Saunders would command the fleet, including Durell's ships as soon as he arrived in North American waters. Saunders assured the government that 'the least delay' was unacceptable.[17]

The red-coated soldiers who would do the bulk of the fighting were already in America, but Wolfe and Saunders were bringing civilian ships hired by the navy to act as transports to get the men and supplies up the St Lawrence. There were 20,000 tons of shipping in all, each ton costing 12s. 9d. and was 'victualled' or supplied with food for four months. Many of these ships came straight from the collier trade that brought the coal from north-east England down to London, a city which even by 1759 was insatiable in its appetite. Over Christmas officers were sent up the Thames to chase dawdling ships carrying powder and shot. The Admiralty demanded an account of the readiness of the transports 'every other day'.[18]

Accompanying these transports and protecting them from French interference, Saunders commanded an overwhelmingly powerful naval task force. The Royal Navy was the strongest on the planet. It outnumbered the French navy, enjoying an advantage in battleships or 'ships of the line' of approximately 120 to 55. But whereas Britain had naval commitments across all of the world's oceans, France was concentrating her ships to launch an invasion of Britain. Despite this threat Saunders was given fourteen battleships to protect the convoy of troop ships across the Atlantic, supported by six smaller frigates, three bomb vessels, and three fireships. These would join Durell's American squadron of ten ships of the line and four frigates which had wintered in North America. This vast concentration of naval firepower would then be the strongest single fleet in the world.[19]

Portsmouth was booming. It was the crucible of Britain's naval effort and was packed with sailors, many with spare cash from enlistment bounties and their share of the prize money awarded for capturing enemy ships. The navy was larger than it had ever been before, with unprecedented investment being poured into ships and shore facilities like the Haslar Hospital in Gosport, opened in 1753, with a capacity for 2,000 patients, four times greater than Guy's and St Thomas's in London, the next biggest in the country. For years to come Haslar would be the largest brick building in Europe. A visitor to Portsmouth in 1759 commented that, 'The streets are not the cleanest, nor the smells most savoury; but the continuous resort of seamen &c makes it always full of people, who seem in a hurry.'[20] It was here that Wolfe was joined by his subordinate, Brigadier George Townshend, who recorded the event in his journal, 'I embarked on the *Neptune*, the Admiral's ship, on the 13th of February on board of which was also the General.'[21]

On 15 February Saunders sent an advance party of fifteen warships, a mix of ships of the line and frigates, plus sixty-six transports to New York to round up the troops who had wintered in the American colonies and collect fresh supplies.[22] The same day he received a promotion. He was made Vice Admiral of the Blue, and the *Neptune* immediately raised a blue ensign.[23] The next day Saunders was able to 'acquaint the Lords Commissioners of the Admiralty that I am now working out between the Buoys, with the wind at East'.[24] Townshend confirmed the journey's auspicious start, writing that 'we had a fine wind down the channel'.[25] Given that the prevailing winds in the Channel are south-west it must have seemed like a happy omen for the Atlantic crossing that lay ahead.

It did not last. After hitting calms off Cornwall the weather turned rough. Although ships could make the eastern seaboard of America in around a month,[26] the large convoy was held up by the pace of the slowest vessels. Thanks to 'strong gales and thick hazy weather' they lost contact with the *Dublin* with 'three of the victuallers, two transports and a bomb tender'. Even though Saunders had 'no doubt of their getting safe to America', these incidents were pushing the operation into ever greater delays.[27] Other ships lost masts and spars in the heavy weather.

Navigation was an imperfect art. Fixing a ship's longitude with any accuracy in 1759 was impossible. Seven years before, the University of Göttingen in Hanover had published a longitudinal table which allowed a careful navigator to work out his longitude to within sixty nautical miles but it is not known how many of the British ships carried the means to use even this rudimentary method. Cracking longitude was the great civilian and military challenge of the time, what the race to jet engines and harnessing the power of the atom was to the twentieth century. The Royal Navy was edging closer to a solution; two years later in 1761 the *Deptford* would sail for Jamaica with John Harrison's chronometer on board and would stun his detractors by arriving just over one nautical mile out from her calculated position.[28]

Such a revolution was a distant dream for the officers of Saunders' fleet as they lined the quarterdeck every day at noon, praying for a gap in the clouds to get their reading from the position of the sun. Meanwhile ships lost topmasts, sails were shredded, and many of the transports parted company. In these northern latitudes they came across 'floating islands of ice'.[29] They were aiming for Louisbourg, until the year before a French possession on Cape Breton Island that had guarded the mouth of the St Lawrence. It had fallen after a siege in the summer of 1758 and would now be a base for attacking Canada rather than defending it. Two miserable months after leaving Portsmouth the fleet neared Louisbourg but as it did so it ran into a thick shelf of ice miles wide that stretched out from the shore. The harbour at Louisbourg was completely enclosed. Saunders dispatched smaller boats to try to find passages through the ice but to no avail.

Saunders had no choice. Working the ships in these conditions was unimaginably tough. The sails were 'stiff like sheets of tin', making them impossible to furl, while the 'running ropes freeze in the blocks'. The 'topmen' were suffering the most. These young, agile seamen were responsible for the setting and furling of these highest sails and faced frequent climbs up into the frozen rigging. The weather made this impossible. Durell reported to London that, in conditions such as these, 'the men cannot expose their hands long enough to the cold to do their duty'.[30] Having been buffeted with 'contrary winds and hard gales' and now 'stopped with a body of ice' from getting into Louisbourg, Saunders had to head south-west, away from the Gulf of St Lawrence and towards the British base at Halifax.[31] The risks to his fleet from a further period at sea in the blizzard conditions waiting for the ice to melt were too great. He was already undermanned and the grim realities of eighteenth-century seafaring were further depleting his crews.

Lack of access to fresh provisions, the freezing weather, and physical exertion left the men, who slept in hammocks fourteen inches apart slung across a gun deck, prone to debilitating sickness. The year before HMS *Pembroke* had sailed from Portsmouth to Halifax and due to a rather circuitous route the voyage had lasted seventy-five days. Twenty-six men had died on the passage and a large number were put in hospital as soon as she arrived; five desperate men deserted in one of her small boats just after they dropped anchor.[32] Things were not as bad for Wolfe on the flagship, *Neptune*, but even so he chafed at the delays. He was a very poor sailor. The year before he had written to his father, 'You may believe that I have passed my time disagreeably enough in this rough weather; at best, the life, you know, is not pleasant.'[33] On this crossing he wrote to a senior officer that 'your servant as usual has been very sensible of the ship's motions'.[34]

As the battered fleet entered the bay at Halifax on 30 April Wolfe's frustration turned into rage. There sitting at anchor was Durell's North American squadron which should by now have been blockading the St Lawrence. The seamen of the fleet would have noticed immediately that Durell's ships were riding at just one anchor and were therefore clearly ready to sail on the first fair breeze but the landsman Wolfe was livid. To his political superiors in London he was measured but to Major General Jeffrey Amherst, the senior British commander in North America, he wrote that, having arrived in 'tolerable good order, the length of our passage considered', he was 'astounded to find Mr Durell at anchor'.[35] This was positively diplomatic compared to comments recorded in a remarkable and recently discovered private journal written by one of Wolfe's close ring of aides. This straight-talking account, the so-called 'Family Journal', is more outspoken in its condemnation of Durell and his late departure from Halifax: 'Nothing could astonish Wolfe more than on our arrival at Halifax' to discover Durell riding at anchor, and 'nothing could be more scandalous than their proceedings' when 'all the bellowing of the troops at Halifax could not persuade them to leave that harbour for fear of the ice'. The diarist writes that Wolfe, who 'knew the navy well', had feared since leaving Britain that they would be late to leave thanks to 'an aversion to run the hazards of the river'. He went on to say that 'much time, according to custom was spent in deliberation, and at length they determined that it would be more agreeable to sail up the river when the spring was well advanced than during so cold a season'. The 'Family Journal' makes it clear that Wolfe believed this was a setback of the most serious kind: had they got into the river when they were supposed to have done 'supplies [would have] been intercepted' and 'the enemy would not have been able to fire a gun'. In short, concludes the journal, 'Canada would certainly have been an easy conquest, had that squadron gone early enough into the river.'[36]

Saunders, for whom sadly little personal correspondence exists, was kinder to his subordinate, writing to London on 2 May that he found Durell 'unmoored, and ready to sail … He waits only for a wind, and, I hope, will sail tomorrow.'[37] He did sail on 3 May but 'the wind proved contrary' and 'they were obliged to anchor' just outside the harbour until 5 May.[38] As a result Durell entered the St Lawrence just days after the precious convoy from France. Wolfe would never forgive his naval colleagues for this failure. It was the first crack in a relationship upon which combined operations depended and the resultant schism was almost as detrimental to the British cause as the arrival of succour to his enemies.

The hysteria of Wolfe's circle is perhaps attributable to the slow realization of the scale of the challenge and the paucity of their resources. Troop ships from New York trickled in slowly. The first to arrive was the *Ruby*, on 1 May, carrying ordnance, gunpowder, and shot. She told of storms, dismastings, and delays afflicting the rest of the fleet.[39] As the other ships did start to arrive it soon became clear that they were carrying numbers of men who were consistently below what Wolfe had been expecting. In Britain, he had been promised battle-hardened regiments of the British army in North America; however, nobody had considered that winter would leave these units decimated. Three thousand reinforcements were supposed to have been sent out from Britain, a mix of new recruits and soldiers drafted in from other regiments.[40] However, these men had been diverted to bolster a bogged-down campaign in the French-owned Caribbean islands of Martinique and Guadeloupe. Vague promises were made to transfer these men back up to Wolfe's army after they had conquered the islands, but these assurances must have rung hollow to Wolfe. It was a fact that service in the Caribbean ruined any unit sent there. Microbes broke armies in the Indies more surely than enemy steel. From 1740 to 1742 a British and colonial American army outside the walls of Cartagena had lost 10,000 of its 14,000 men, about one in ten of them as a result of enemy action, the rest from disease. Wolfe, as a boy soldier, had been earmarked for the expedition but had been saved from an almost certain death by a delicate constitution that was so overwhelmed by the germs of Portsmouth that he was sent home to recuperate with his mother. The Spanish boasted that disease provided a surer defence than ships, forts, and men. They morbidly celebrated yellow fever, as *fiebre patriótica*, 'patriotic fever', because it attacked outsiders with such jingoistic fervour.[41] Criminals were granted a reprieve from the death penalty in Britain if they agreed to serve in the tropics. Soldiers were often given the choice when being punished for a grave offence: 1,000 lashes or service in the Caribbean; they usually chose the former.[42]

Wolfe would have known it would be a miracle if the troops arrived back in the North Atlantic in time to be of any use even if they were not eviscerated by disease. He would have to make do with the regiments already in theatre. At least every regiment had seen action. British regular soldiers had been fighting in North America since 1755. Each summer's fighting had been on a larger scale than the year before. Early in the war the men had been so raw that many of them had been taught how to use muskets on decks of transports by officers who had learnt their trade through reading manuals. Now every unit had served through at least one operation and had survived one tough winter. On the downside the campaigns and climate had exerted a powerful attritional effect. Men had used the dispersal to billets over the winter as an opportunity to desert and disappear along the vast and unregulated frontier. Disease could be just as bad among the snow as it was in the tropics. The absence of fresh fruit and vegetables over the winter meant that men lacked vitamin C and scurvy was a constant threat. The year before Wolfe had written at the start of the campaigning season that 'some of the regiments of this army have 3 or 400 men eaten up with scurvy'.[43] This terrible disease appeared first as liver spots on the skin and then quickly led to spongy gums and haemorrhaging from all mucous membranes. Sufferers became listless and immobilized and the advanced stages saw the loss of teeth and suppurating wounds. It is famously associated with long sea journeys, but such was the isolation of garrisons in the backcountry during the winter, that it was just as common along the frontier.

Wolfe wrote a barrage of letters to superiors in London and New York, describing the condition of the four battalions that had spent the winter in Halifax. They were 'in good order', but 'are at a very low ebb'. Measles had recently 'got amongst them', and they would have suffered far worse had it not been for the 'more than common care of the officers that command them'. Their officers had attempted to obtain fresh provisions where possible, maintain good hospitals, and lay on plenty of the local anti-scorbutic, 'spruce beer', a mildly alcoholic drink brewed from molasses and spruce tips and a good source of vitamin C. These precautions, combined with strict discipline, had 'preserved these battalions from utter ruin', without them, 'these regiments would have been utterly annihilated'. Even so, Wolfe warned that their numbers were still well below expectations. Many of the battalions at Halifax numbered around five hundred men each, just over half their ideal complement. Wolfe feared that the two battalions left further north in Louisbourg, cut off from the outside world over the winter, were 'in a worse condition'. He stated glumly that 'the number of regular forces can hardly exceed the half' of 12,000 that London had promised him during the planning phase. Any losses during the sail up the St Lawrence or a bad outbreak of disease during the campaign would result in 'some difficulties', and Wolfe was convinced that the risky nature of this amphibious assault meant that they were 'very liable to accidents'. He would fight this campaign with no reserve, no margin for error. However, he told his superiors in London, 'our troops, indeed, are good and very well disposed. If valour can make amends for want of numbers, we shall probably succeed.'[44]

Wolfe set about preparing his army for the expedition with the relentless energy for which he had become famous. At 32 he was young for so important a command. In a letter to his uncle he blamed his appointment on 'the backwardness of some of the older officers', which 'in some measure forced the Government to come down so low'.[45] As so often the pre-war hierarchy had failed to shine in the first few years of combat and promising young officers had been rapidly promoted. Wolfe certainly had shown potential but he was not Achilles reborn. He was exceptionally tall at six foot, but thin and ungainly, with pale skin, long red hair that looked fine and lank, a pointy, fragile nose, and a weak, receding chin: in all a strange 'assemblage of feature'.[46] He had piercing blue eyes but they could not detract from an overall sense of physical infirmity, reinforced by his own constant commentary on his ill health. He suffered from 'the gravel', a painful condition caused by the build-up of crystals in the urinary tract, which he tried to douse with regular doses of liquid soap. It no doubt aggravated a pronounced tendency to hypochondria; he often described himself as a broken man. He wrote to his mother that 'folks are surprised to see [my] meagre, consumptive, decaying figure'. He blamed hard campaigning that 'stripped me of my bloom' and brought him 'to old age and infirmity'. A repeated lament of his letters is that 'I am perhaps somewhat nearer my end than other of my time.'[47] To his uncle he wrote, 'If I have health and constitution enough for the campaign, I shall think myself a lucky man; what happens afterwards is of no great consequence.'[48]

Wolfe is strangely inaccessible. He was certainly melodramatic, sensitive, and prone to self-pity. Many of his letters drip with disapproval for fellow officers and contain an almost puritanical adherence to duty. As a result he is often portrayed as aloof and uneasy among his peers, and yet there are hints of a more relaxed side to him. One officer under his command recorded that 'his gestures [were] as open as those of an actor who feels no constraint' and he displayed 'a certain animation in the countenance and spirit in his manner that solicited attention and interested most people in his favour'.[49] He certainly had a very loyal group of close friends. His attitude to the men under his command varied wildly depending on his mood and their performance in battle. But he was unwavering in his strong paternalism and the men in return seemed to harbour a genuine affection for their commander. He was certainly visible, his claims of physical infirmity are belied by his behaviour on campaign; he was always where the action was hottest and had the scars to prove it. He never shrank from the rigours of active service and it is possible that his maladies were exaggerated for effect.

His grandfather and father had both been soldiers. He was commissioned an officer aged 14, thanks to his father's influence, first into the marines and then into an army regiment destined for service on the Continent. He tasted action for the first time at 16 against the French at the battle of Dettingen, where he caught the eye of a powerful patron, the 22-year-old Prince William Augustus, Duke of Cumberland, second and favourite son of King George II. With Cumberland's support, plus his own impeccable family and social army network and his real talent, he ascended quickly through the ranks. He proved himself an excellent regimental commander; his battalions were disciplined and drilled to the highest standards that the army's peacetime penury would allow. He also thought and wrote with genuine insight on tactics in the age of musket, bayonet, and cannon.

Wolfe's plan had been to leave Louisbourg and sail up the St Lawrence on 7 May. This was wildly optimistic; the sea ice and the slow Atlantic crossing had delayed operations but so too had the sheer scale of North America and the inadequacy of eighteenth-century communications. Some regiments which had wintered in the colonies only heard about their inclusion in the amphibious force in April. Many were scattered across swathes of country to minimize the impact on the community of the number of extra mouths to feed during the long winter. Four companies of the 78th Regiment had been garrisoning Fort Stanwix over the winter, two-thirds of the way between Albany and Lake Ontario. They had suffered terribly from scurvy, been the target of a daring and bloody Native American raid and were only relieved on 10 April. They were buffeted by blocks of ice on the Mohawk River as they made their way to Albany, then bundled on ships to take them to New York City where, without being allowed to land, they were transferred onto transports and shipped to join Wolfe's army. It is impressive that they arrived at all. Provisions for the operation arrived from the rich pastures of Pennsylvania, shipped over seven hundred miles from Philadelphia. These were huge logistical achievements on a continent which had not witnessed warfare on this scale before.

On 13 May the *Neptune*, with Wolfe and Saunders on board, loosed her main course and fired two guns, the prearranged signal for the fleet to weigh anchor.[50] Then she stood out to sea and made for Louisbourg 'with all the ships that were in readiness'.[51] Two days later they arrived off Louisbourg. 'The coast was still full of ice'[52] but this time there were sufficient gaps for Saunders to be able to thread his ships into the harbour.

Perched on a barren landscape, Louisbourg was a squat, grey fortress that commanded the mouth of the St Lawrence and was the key to Canada as well as providing French fishermen on the Grand Banks, the most lucrative fishing grounds in the world, with a secure harbour. It had been captured the year before, but had held out long enough to deny the British the chance to enter the St Lawrence and attack the heart of New France. Wolfe had commanded a brigade in the besieging force and his energy and courage had won him a reputation and a promotion back in Britain. Chevalier Johnstone, a Scottish exile serving with the French forces, had painted a bleak picture of life in this desolate stronghold: 'the climate, like the soil, is abominable at Louisbourg: clouds of thick fogs, which come from the southwest, cover it, generally from the month of April until the end of July, to such a degree that sometimes for a month together they never see the sun'. The surrounding countryside had little to recommend it either, 'miserable soil – hills, rocks, swamps, lakes and morasses – incapable of producing anything'.[53] It was the most modern of all the French fortifications in North America, and looked to visitors like a textbook Flanders fortress. Indeed, some of the cut stone had been shipped out from the Rochefort area of France, used as ballast on vessels crossing the Atlantic.[54] The defences had been battered during the previous summer's siege, many of the houses and the 'King's Bastion', or citadel, had been reduced to rubble by British cannon and a large breach had been smashed in the curtain wall. As Wolfe had predicted the regiments that had occupied this broken city over the winter were in a parlous state. Scurvy had crippled hundreds of men; recruiting parties sent to the American colonies had proved unsuccessful at persuading young men to surrender their independence in return for a precarious existence at the former French fortress courtesy of King George. So desperate was the need for recruits that no less than 131 former French soldiers were absorbed into British units. Amherst, the senior British officer in North America, expected them to 'immediately desert' to their former masters, 'as soon as we come near to the enemy'.[55]

There was still snow on the ground in the hollows and Saunders reported to London that 'the harbour was entirely filled up with ice, that for several days it was not practicable for boats to pass'. The weather would cause further delays; in fact, its severity 'has, by much, exceeded any that can be remembered by the oldest inhabitants of this part of the world'.[56] Another senior officer wrote that there was so much ice 'for several days that there was no getting on board or ashore without a great deal of trouble and some danger'.[57] The sailors were undeterred. Lieutenant John Knox, of the 43rd Regiment, who left the liveliest and most detailed of all the journals of the campaign, arrived in Halifax with his regiment to find 'foolhardy seamen' getting from ship to shore and back again using the floating ice as stepping stones, 'stepping from one to another, with boat-hooks … in their hands; I own I was in some pain while I saw them, for, had their feet slipped from under them, they must have perished'.[58]

Knox was Irish, the third son of a Sligo merchant with an uncle who had attended Trinity College, Dublin and became a priest. He was typical of the educated, 'middling' sort of men who considered themselves gentlemen but lacked the money or connections to scale the heights of eighteenth-century society. The army offered men like Knox an honourable career path, with possibilities of glory, reward, and advancement. As was normal he joined as a 'volunteer', a civilian given permission to serve with a regiment with a view to obtaining a vacancy in the officer corps when disease or a bullet created one. They carried muskets and served as ordinary soldiers but ate and socialized with the officers. Gallant conduct was the surest way to gain attention and throughout the eighteenth century these young men would show suicidal bravery on countless occasions. Knox's moment came at the defeat at the battle of Lauffeld, after which Cumberland awarded him an ensigncy (the most junior officer's rank) in the 43rd Regiment of Foot.

He seems to have made a good marriage to a wealthy woman but her money was held by a trustee who went bankrupt. It was clearly to be on the field of battle that Knox would have to make his fortune.[59]

Knox and his men had spent nearly two lonely years in Nova Scotia around Annapolis and Fort Cumberland. His experience of frontier life was typical: extraordinary seasonal extremes of hot and cold weather, long periods of boredom punctuated with moments of utter terror. He was honest about the realities on the ground that belied the carefully coloured maps of Whitehall,

> though we are said to be in possession of Nova Scotia, yet it is in reality of a few fortresses only, the French and Indians disputing the country with us on every occasion, inch by inch, even within the range of our artillery; so that, as I have observed before, when the troops are not numerous, they cannot venture in safety beyond their walls.[60]

Seventeen fifty-nine was to be different; the 43rd was finally going to take part in active campaigning. There was a sense of excitement as Knox's ship fell in with the other transports and arrived at Louisbourg, with its narrow entrance, passed the large naval ships and anchored under the walls of the town. The ice and thick fog forced many of the supply ships to wait off the coast for days at a time before attempting to enter the port, their crews straining their ears for the sound of breakers on the rocky beach to let them know when they were too close to shore.[61] A cannon roared from a battery on the island in the middle of the bay to give navigators and lookouts a reference point. Despite the conditions Knox was thrilled to be a part of the gathering force: 'every person seems cheerfully busy here in preparing for the expedition'.[62] Wolfe noted the arrival of Knox and his fellow soldiers in Kennedy's 43rd Regiment in his journal: 'Webb's, Kennedy's, part of Lascelles's Artillery and Military from Boston arrived. A ship with Webb's Light Infantry ran upon the rocks in Gabarus Bay. Coldness on that occasion. The troops got safe on shore.'[63] Knox hoped to catch a glimpse of his young commander and he managed to watch as General Wolfe made inspections. On 25 May Knox reports that Wolfe 'was highly pleased' with the 'exactness and spirit' of some troops who were demonstrating their 'manoeuvres and evolutions'. So impressive were these particular troops that other commanding officers apologized to Wolfe in advance, saying that the long period in winter quarters had limited their abilities to drill the men and implement a new exercise, which Wolfe favoured, of firing musket volleys. According to Knox, Wolfe cheerfully dismissed their concerns, '"Poh! Poh! – new exercise – new fiddlesticks; if they are otherwise well disciplined and will fight, that's all I shall require of them."'[64]

The peacetime British army was small, scattered, and poorly trained. Even the existence of a standing army in peacetime was controversial. The British political class revelled in its perceived freedoms and could become hysterical in defending their 'ancient liberties'. A standing army was seen as a buttress of tyranny. The Stuart kings of the seventeenth century, Charles I and his two sons, and Cromwell, the imperial anti-king, had demonstrated dangerously autocratic tendencies, epitomized by their maintenance of large standing armies. Across the Channel Europe provided a multitude of examples of arbitrary government, regimes whose existence rested on the muskets of conscripted peasants. A central plank of the 'Glorious Revolution' settlement of 1688–9 was the passing of the Mutiny Act which stated clearly that it was illegal to recruit and maintain a standing army without the consent of Parliament. From then on numbers of troops depended entirely on Parliament's willingness to pay for them.

By the 1750s the peacetime British army numbered just under thirty thousand men, well below half the size of the Prussian army and equivalent to that commanded by the King of Sardinia. King George could also call on the 12,000 men of the Irish army paid for by his Irish subjects but the Parliament in Dublin got nervous when more than two thousand of these men were sent to serve abroad. The Westminster Parliament proved itself unwilling to impose taxes to maintain even the small British army properly. There were virtually no purpose-built barracks with facilities to allow whole regiments, let alone brigades or bigger units, to train together. Instead regiments were broken up and billeted upon reluctant landlords in pubs and hostelries across wide areas. The resulting lack of tactical cohesion, not to mention deep antipathy of the civilian population, is not hard to imagine. Wartime was really the only opportunity to concentrate several regiments in single encampments and drill them together. Camp commanders could then enforce a standard drill, equalizing the length and speed of pace, imposing uniform musketry practice and recognizable command signals. As soon as Knox had landed in North America in 1757 his regiment was to join the others and 'take all opportunities for exercise'. Entrenchments were built 'in order to discipline and instruct the troops, in the methods of attack and defence'. This would 'make the troops acquainted with the nature of the service they are going upon; also to render the smell of powder more familiar to the young soldiers'.[65] For many it would be the first time they had trained with anything other than their own company of, at most, a hundred men.

At Louisbourg Wolfe's army got the opportunity to make up for the scarcities of peacetime. Gunpowder and musket balls were issued to every soldier; the daily crackle of musket volleys echoed around the bay. Malcolm Fraser was a 26-year-old subaltern. He was an unlikely redcoat. His father had been 'out' for Charles James Stuart in the '45 rebellion, when Bonnie Prince Charlie had attempted to seize the throne of Britain back from his distant cousin George II. Charles' depleted, exhausted, and starving army was annihilated on Drumossie Moor, a battle known to history as Culloden. With suicidal bravery the Highlanders had charged into withering British musketry and artillery fire, leaving the moor heaped with dead. Among the fallen was Malcolm Fraser's father. The rebellion lingered on long enough to give the Duke of Cumberland an excuse to launch a systematic and brutal campaign of counter-insurgency throughout the Highlands. Settlements were burnt, men transported to the New World, and Highland dress, weapons, and bagpipes were all banned. Wolfe had served during the campaign and remained in Scotland long afterwards as part of what was effectively an army of occupation.

Now, only a decade later, the British government's need for troops forced them to swallow their mistrust of the Highlanders and acquiesce to some recruitment among the more loyal clans. The prospect of economic and social advancement as well as the chance to don traditional Highland garb and assemble with their fellow clansmen on the field of battle ensured that the new Highland regiments were inundated with volunteers. Men begged to serve in the army that had recently slaughtered their fathers and uncles. Malcolm Fraser appears at ease with his inverted allegiance. Loyalty to the family and clan were far more important than the external allegiance of their chief. It mattered little to him which descendant of James VI and I sat on the throne in London. Men like him were happy if they were among their peers, a brace of pistols and a long Highland sword at the waist, accompanied by the clan piper playing traditional airs. Fraser described this period of intensive training after a long winter of isolation with excitement in his journal. 'We are ordered ashore every day while here,' he wrote, 'to exercise along with the rest of the Army.'[66] On 31 May four regiments 'performed several manoeuvres in presence of the General Officers, such as charging in line of battle, forming the line into columns, and reducing them; dispersing, rallying ... Which were all so well executed, as to afford the highest satisfaction to the generals.'[67]

While Fraser, Knox, and the other soldiers trained, Wolfe continued in his attempts to scrape together every last man for the expedition and ensure that they were fed and kept as healthy as possible. The garrison at Louisbourg was under the command of the Governor, Brigadier Edward Whitmore. It consisted of four regiments, one of which, Colonel Bragg's 28th, was ordered to join Wolfe's army. Each regiment in the British army also had a grenadier company. This was made up of the elite of each regiment, physically fit and experienced veterans, distinguished by different uniforms and headwear. Wolfe was given the three grenadier companies from the remaining regiments of the Louisbourg garrison, who would make up a small but crack regiment in his army known as the 'Louisbourg Grenadiers' consisting of thirteen officers and 313 men. Wolfe wanted more; as well as a grenadier company, regiments in North America had recently formed companies of 'light infantry'. It was hoped that these units would give the British army more flexibility when fighting in the woods of North America. Ideally, they were the regiment's best marksmen and the quickest witted, agile men who were encouraged to fight in a more open, irregular style than the classic infantryman.

Wolfe begged Whitmore for all of his light infantrymen as well as his grenadiers. 'We are disappointed of the recruits which were intended to be sent from the West Indies to join us,' he wrote, 'and as several regiments are much weaker than they were thought, in England, to be, I must further represent to you that good troops only can make amends for the want of numbers in an undertaking of this sort.' He reminded him of the strategic situation: 'upon the success of our attacks in Canada, the security of the whole continent of north America in a great measure depends'.[68] Wolfe did not hold Whitmore in high esteem; they had both served as brigadiers in the siege of Louisbourg the year before, and with Whitmore approaching his seventieth birthday, Wolfe had described him as a 'poor, old, sleepy man', and claimed that 'he never was a soldier'.[69] It is possible that Wolfe's difficulty to hide his contempt for people contributed to Whitmore's refusal. He would not part with any more men than London had specifically ordered. Whitmore had sailed on Quebec as a young man in 1711 and had seen the fleet wrecked on the river and hundreds of men drowned; his duty was to protect Louisbourg not send his finest troops on a dangerous mission to satisfy the thirst for glory of the lanky young Major General. Wolfe informed London, 'I applied to Mr Whitmore for three companies of light infantry of his garrison ... If Brigadier Whitmore did not consent to my proposal it has proceeded from the most scrupulous obedience to orders, believing himself not at liberty to judge and act according to circumstances.'[70]

Wolfe's disappointment at Whitmore's defiance did not interfere with his furious activity. He and his staff were busy planning the next phase of the operation: getting the army on board transports and up the St Lawrence as far as the city of Quebec. Daily orders were issued concerning every aspect of the men's lives. It was 'particularly necessary' that a large stock of shoes was provided, given the difficulty of getting them during the campaign. Axes, picks, shovels, and bill hooks were handed out in proportion to the numbers of men in each regiment. Fraser's large 78th Regiment with its 1,000 men was given 100 pick axes, Amherst's smaller 15th was only issued with fifty. Regimental quartermasters, the all-important officers responsible for a unit's equipment, were to go and claim for 'one hundred and forty tents' per regiment from the *Fair American* transport. Every man was issued thirty-six rounds of ammunition as well as musket balls and spare flints, a vital part of the firing mechanism on their 'flintlock' muskets. More powder and balls were stored in casks aboard each transport. It was a reminder that as soon as the fleet left Louisbourg they were in hostile waters. Every attempt was also made to obtain 'as much fresh provisions as can be procured'; each regiment would send a party daily to the barren ground to the north-east of the town, Pointe de Rochefort, at half an hour intervals to receive their daily supply. On 4 June the *Neptune*'s log recorded that she 'received on board six live bullocks'.[71] Although eighteenth-century medical knowledge was sketchy they had certainly grasped that fresh meat was better than salted. Meanwhile 'lines and hooks' were placed aboard the transports so that they could eat fresh fish on the way up the river. 'To prevent the spreading of distempers in the transports, the hospital ship will receive any men that may fall ill on the voyage,' Wolfe ordered. Transports would raise a flag at the mizzen peak, the end of the yard that carried the mizzen sail, to notify the fleet that they had sick men on board who needed hospitalization, while the hospital ships themselves flew a red banner from the top of their foremast. The men were not to be 'too much crowded' and each commander was to report on the state of their transport and whether it was fit to proceed. Officers were told that 'a quantity of spruce beer ... would be of great use to their men'. Any men who were already 'weak and sickly' were 'not to embark with their regiments'. But they were not to worry: 'measures will be taken to bring those men to the army as soon as they are perfectly recovered'.[72]

By 1 June, Wolfe could be stayed no longer. He was almost a month behind schedule already and he still had to brave the treacherous waters of the St Lawrence before he could even lay his eyes on the enemy. His order for the day stated that 'the troops land no more'. Flat-bottomed boats, innovations designed specifically for amphibious operations, were 'to be hoisted in' and 'washed every day to prevent leaking'. The ships and crews must now be ready to 'sail at the first signal, when three guns are fired from the saluting battery, all officers to repair on board'.[73] The next day the sick were finally sent ashore and those men too old or disabled to have a hope of recovery were sent aboard a transport for the crossing back to Britain. Wolfe and Saunders announced that they were intent on 'sailing on the first fair wind'. Instructions were left at Louisbourg for any latecomers to follow the fleet into the St Lawrence.[74]

The laborious process of weighing anchor began in the early morning of 4 June. On the biggest ships like the *Neptune* it was a Herculean task. Ten sailors worked each of fourteen wooden bars that slotted into a giant winch or 'capstan' on the middle gun deck just forward of the mainmast. Below them another ten men worked each of twelve bars on a 'trundlehead', essentially another capstan working on the same axis. These teams, 260 strong, could lift approximately ten tons. Depending on the length of cable, the wind and tide, an anchor could take six hours to raise. In emergencies, the captain could order the crew to 'let slip' and simply leave the anchor and cable behind on the seabed. The twenty-four-inch cable was made from the intertwining of three regular ropes and was too wide for the capstan and so a smaller 'messenger' rope was attached to the cable with 'nipper' cords that had to be slid along at regular intervals as the cable came in. To lighten the load on the seamen, if the wind favoured it, ships could set some sail to bring them 'a-peek', a point at which they were vertically above the anchor. Once it was raised almost out of the water, it had to be 'catted': another team of men hauled on a tackle which brought it up out of the water, while keeping it away from the hull, making sure the heavy flukes did not puncture the wood, and lashed it to the side of the forecastle. Meanwhile, the cable was stored right down in the bottom of the ship, below the waterline. When it dried off the soft manilla rope made an excellent mattress and sleeping in the cable tier became a perk of the senior members of the ship's company.

Knox watched the operation from the 337-ton, London-based transport ship, the *Goodwill*, under its colourful master, Thomas Killick. One hundred and seventy-nine officers and men of the 43rd Regiment were on board. He watched the transports as they 'got their anchors a-peek', with the soldiers on board sweating at the capstans alongside the seamen. The time it took to get the entire fleet out of the harbour meant that the brief window of favourable weather was missed. It turned 'foul, with a thick fog [and] little or no wind'. Those ships not already out of the harbour had to drop their anchors again and wait for the weather to change. One of Wolfe's senior officers recorded that the wind remained 'contrary' until the sixth, 'during which time the Admiral kept in the offing', sailing backwards and forwards off Louisbourg until the rest of the fleet could get out of harbour.[75]

At 0400 hours on 6 June it was the *Goodwill*'s turn to crawl out of Louisbourg. By 1000 hours she joined the waiting fleet. The weather was fair, with a variable, light breeze. 'Now that we are joined, imagination cannot conceive a more eligible prospect,' enthused Knox. 'Our whole armament, naval and military, were in high spirits,' he recorded, and despite the grave challenges ahead he had no doubt that under 'such Admirals and Generals' together 'with so respectable a fleet' and 'such a body of well-appointed regular troops' there would be 'the greatest success'. He reported that 'the prevailing sentimental toast among the officers is – British colours on every French fort, port, and garrison in America'.[76] Not everyone shared Knox's enthusiasm. Fraser made an ominous entry in his diary: 'I hear a Lieutenant on board one of the men of war has shot himself – for fear I suppose the French should do it.' Fraser was surprised to hear of the suicide given the dangers that certainly beckoned. 'If he was wearied of life, he might soon get quit of it in a more honourable way.'[77]

Wolfe was relieved to be underway and finished a dispatch that day on board the *Neptune* in which he was upbeat about the prospects for the operation. He attached a return of the troops embarked at Louisbourg and wrote that he expected 'to find a good part of the [French] force of Canada at Quebec', but his army was 'prepared to meet them. Whatever the end is, I flatter myself that his Majesty will not be dissatisfied with the behaviour of his troops.' A senior member of Wolfe's staff wrote that the 'whole force was now assembled' and 'amounted to 8,535 soldiers, fit for duty, officers included'. It was far short of the 12,000 that Wolfe had been promised and it would almost certainly be fewer men than the French could muster to defend Canada.[78]

It was the largest naval expedition in North American history: forty-two men of war, fourteen of which carried sixty guns or more and were known as 'ships of the line'. In the eighteenth century, the weight, accuracy and range of cannon meant that ships were designed to carry many of them firing at ninety degrees to the direction of the vessel. As a result action was joined when the enemy was alongside rather than in front or behind. The mighty capital ships of powers like Britain and France would form lines and exchange crashing broadsides with their opponents. The *Neptune,* on whose quarterdeck Wolfe and his staff took their daily exercise, was one of the most powerful ships of the line in the world. Weighing nearly two thousand tons, she was 171 feet long and crewed by just under eight hundred officers and men. She had twenty-eight cannon on her lower gun deck, each firing a thirty-two-pound ball, termed 32 pounders, and on her middle and upper deck another sixty 18 and 12 pounders. In a second the *Neptune* was capable of blasting a ton of lead into the hull and rigging of an enemy ship. Other warships had different roles; lighter, quicker frigates could harass an enemy's merchant fleet or provide support for land forces in shallower waters. Some ships carried mortars or acted as scouts. Saunders was well supplied with all varieties.[79]

The main role of the naval vessels was to protect the vast array of civilian vessels on which the success of the operation relied. In all there were between one hundred and twenty and one hundred and forty transport ships of all rigs and sizes. They were carrying not just the troops but all the supplies that would allow the force to sail deep into enemy territory. It had to be assumed that no food would be available around Quebec and so the expedition was forced to bring every sack of flour as well as every spade and ounce of gunpowder with it. The *Hunter, Resolution*, and *Scarboro* from Boston carried cattle; ships like the *Phoenix, Martha*, and *Hannah* had all the paraphernalia associated with artillery in their holds: siege guns, spare carriages and ramrods, in all 163 pieces of artillery of all shapes and sizes. Other ships carried just powder and shot. The expedition's 75,000 cannonballs sat low in the holds, providing extra ballast. The *Industry* and *Sally* from the south coast of England carried some of the 65,000 shells for the mortars. There were 1.2 million musket cartridges, 10,862 barrels of powder, and even 250 primitive rockets. The New England-based *Good Intent* and *Peggy & Sarah* weighing in at just over a hundred tons were designated sounding vessels: shallow-draught ships that could go ahead of the main fleet and check the depth of water by taking regular soundings using a lead weight thrown over the side and measuring the depth on a marked line.[80]

Such a massive fleet needed tight organization if it was to avoid the twin perils of getting scattered across the North Atlantic or of crashing into each other. Saunders had issued a long set of sailing instructions at Louisbourg.[81] The fleet would travel in three divisions: white, red, and blue. Wolfe's army had been divided into three brigades and appropriately enough, each brigade was assigned to one of the divisions. Every single ship would fly 'vanes' (long, thin flags) denoting which division they were in and exactly what or who was on board. The twenty-eight-gun frigate *Lowestoft* would command the lead, white division and would 'wear a white broad pendant' during the day and a light on the stern of her poop deck and another at the top of her mainmast at night. All the transports in the division were distinguished by smaller white vanes. Each regiment had a slight variation. Ships carrying Knox and his fellow soldiers of the 43rd had white vanes with one red ball. Malcolm Fraser in the 78th sailed in a ship with a white vane with two blue balls. Next, was the red division, commanded by Captain Schomberg on the *Diana* flying a red pendant and trailed by transports with the second brigade on board all flying red vanes. This was followed by the blue division with the third brigade of Wolfe's army on board. Ships carrying artillery flew red-and-blue striped flags; those carrying provisions, blue-and-yellow. Saunders used a series of intricate signals using flags and cannon fire to maintain command and control of his unwieldy fleet. He could summon all the key personnel on board, masters of transports, regimental commanders and staff. If he or Wolfe wished to see Knox's commanding officer, Major Robert Elliot, for example, a blue-and-white chequered pendant would be flown from the head of the main topmast. The masters of the transports had been unambiguously told to obey orders, they were 'as far as they are able to keep their respective divisions, and carry sail when the men-of-war do, that no time may be lost by negligence of delays'. Saunders emphasized that 'the regular and orderly sailing of the fleet' was 'of the utmost consequence'. The master of every transport was 'strictly enjoined to look out for and punctually obey' all the signals that his divisional commander made. Alarmingly for the transports, if they failed to notice or act on a signal, 'the Captains of his Majesty's ships are directed to compel them to a stricter observance of their duty by firing a shot at them'. The cohesion of the fleet was vital. The most vulnerable phase for any amphibious force was before it had the chance to deploy on land. The greatest threats to the expedition were the treacherous waters of the St Lawrence, French ships and summer storms. These had the capacity to defeat Wolfe more surely than French muskets outside Quebec.[82]

The soldiers found themselves in a different world, with its own language, hierarchy, mores, and even calendar. They had to know how to behave. To save their red coats from the harsh climate they wore them inside out. On the passage across the Atlantic Knox had almost been fired upon by an American privateer when they saw a deck full of men wearing off-white coats, the colour worn by the French infantry. Wolfe had ordered the soldiers to 'be as useful as possible in working their ships'. Wooden ships carried great quantities of pitch, tar, gunpowder, and canvas, and were, as a result, horribly vulnerable to fire. Soldiers who were unused to life afloat had to be made aware of this threat. An order to men crossing the Channel to Flanders during the previous war stated that 'a sergeant, a corporal and 12 men of each transport to be as a guard to keep things quiet and to place sentries on the officers' baggage and to suffer no man to smoke between decks'.[83] Wolfe was equally careful to ensure discipline and fire prevention on board ship and zealous in the preservation of his men's well-being: 'when the weather permits the men are to eat upon deck, and be as much in the open air as possible. Cleanliness in the berths and bedding and as much exercise as their situation permits, are the best preservatives of health.'[84]

For a landsman, his first passage in a tall ship was extraordinary. Upon entering this new realm for the first time one young man wrote: 'Nor could I think what world I was in. Whether among spirits or devils. All seemed strange; different language and strange expressions of tongue, that I thought myself always asleep or in a dream, and never properly awake.'[85] Their lives were now regulated by 'watches'. Every half hour a petty officer would turn the hourglass and strike the bell. At 'eight bells' the four-hour watch had come to an end and half of the crew could go below and sleep. All the watches were four hours, apart from two watches of two hours each, known as the 'dog watch', between 1600 and 2000 hours. At four bells in the morning watch, 0600 hours, the bosun would pipe, 'Up Hammocks', at which point the watch below roused themselves and brought up their hammocks on deck to stow in the netting which ringed it. There was no chance of a lie-in. The bosun patrolled the gun deck with a knife and would simply slice through the ropes holding a hammock to the deck beams if its occupant was slow to wake up. The ships were cleaned every morning. The bilges were pumped out, and the decks washed with seawater and holystones. Hours of maintenance and odd jobs followed until the bosun's pipe signalled dinner, a large meal in the early to mid-afternoon followed by the doling out of the grog ration. In the evening the crew would practise 'Beating to Quarters' or going to their action stations. Rich captains, who had supplemented the ship's gunpowder supplies out of their own pocket, would practise the crew at firing their cannon at this time; those of more moderate means had less opportunity to do this since the navy was stingy with its powder allocation and it had to be hoarded in case of an action with the enemy.

Sailing as part of a massive fleet, close to the shore, in largely unknown waters was a challenge to those in command. Constant adjustments to the course of the ship and the sail plan were made as winds varied, or other transports came too close. Collisions were not unusual. Knox's religious observations were interrupted when on Sunday, 10 June, 'as we were going to prayer, about ten o'clock, we got foul of another transport, which obliged us to suspend our devotions'.[86] Other accounts are full of near misses. Exhausted captains could expect not to leave their quarterdecks for days in such conditions.

Soldiers provided useful muscle on the passage. Under the command of a quartermaster they formed teams to 'attend to the braces', pulling the yards around to optimize the position of the sails in relation to the wind. They could not be forced to climb the rigging and work aloft. That was the province of the topmen, men with a fixed conviction in their own immortality. A seaman wrote that this job 'not only requires alertness but courage, to ascend in a manner sky high when stormy winds do blow ... the youngest of the topmen generally go highest'.[87] They handed and made sail, reefed and carried out repairs, all while balancing precariously up to one hundred and fifty feet above the deck. Inshore waters demanded the keeping of a good lookout, which along with extensive use of a line with a lead weight on the end to measure the depth, was the basis of all navigation. Sharp-eyed members of the crew stayed high in the rigging reporting every sighting to the deck. Rewards were given to those with the keenest eyes.

Since the days of Drake there had been an informality born of intimacy on board naval ships; he had always emphasized that officers should lend a hand and haul on ropes. The eighteenth-century navy was a far more harmonious community than has often been assumed; examples of hanging and flogging were exceptional. Many officers had started their careers as common seamen and were promoted, if not always to the highest ranks, through aptitude. The safety of the ship and the lives of everyone who sailed in her depended on officers knowing their business. There was far less opportunity than in the army for venality or the well-connected incompetent. Intruders from the more hierarchical army world were often surprised. Knox was shocked to hear the master of his transport crossing the Atlantic using 'some of the ordinary profane language of the common sailors'.[88]

By the second week of June the expedition had reached the Gulf of St Lawrence, the largest estuary in the world. It was named by explorer Jacques Cartier who had arrived here for the first time on the feast day of St Lawrence. Nearly two thousand miles inland lay its furthest headwater in today's Minnesota. It drains nearly four hundred thousand square miles, an area which includes the Great Lakes, the world's largest system of freshwater lakes. Underneath Saunders' ships 350,000 cubic feet of water a second discharged into the North Atlantic.

The St Lawrence is the greatest tidal river in the world. It is hugely difficult to sail up thanks to the torrent of water surging to the sea, south-westerly winds that tend to prevail in the summer months and a vast amount of local variation in conditions caused by shallows, reefs, and islands. The amount of deviation that compasses will experience from true north varies and squalls regularly tear down off the high ground. Even the easterly winds that Saunders was praying for were often a mixed blessing as winds from that direction were often accompanied by rain and fog.

Captain John Montresor was a 23-year-old engineer on the expedition. He was the son of an engineer and had been raised on that rocky outcrop of empire, Gibraltar, where he had learnt his trade from his father. They had both been sent to America on the outbreak of hostilities and he was already the veteran of several abortive operations, picking up a wound in the Pennsylvanian backcountry at the hands of the Native Americans. Although his age belied his experience, Wolfe had been unimpressed when he had met him the year before during the Louisbourg expedition, describing him, rather hypocritically, as just a 'boy'.[89] Engineers were scarce in the British army and even scarcer in North America and Wolfe would have to tolerate Montresor's youth. The young engineer kept a careful journal of the passage up the St Lawrence, recording the weather each day and all the important landmarks, headlands, and islands that guided the expedition into the river mouth. On the evening of 11 June, a gale blowing hard out of the Gulf of St Lawrence scattered the fleet. The gale continued until dusk on 12 June when the ships were suddenly becalmed, left to drift east-north-east with the tide. By the fourteenth the fleet saw land in the distance on both sides. On the north shore it was 'very craggy, irregular' while the south was 'very high being mountains of Notre Dame'. The ships took frequent soundings with eighty fathoms of line (480 feet) and 'found no bottom'. Montresor could tell because the depth, like everything else, was communicated to the fleet. If an ensign fluttered at the main topmast of the *Neptune* the depth was over forty fathoms (240 feet); if a yellow pendant was hoisted in its place the depth was five fathoms (thirty feet), if it was hoisted twice in succession the depth was six fathoms (thirty-six feet), three times, seven fathoms (forty-two feet), and so on.[90]

It was clear to the British that the St Lawrence was a formidable barrier. One marine officer wrote that 'the whole of this channel is exceedingly dangerous, and the passage up so nice, that it might with some propriety be considered as the principal outwork of Quebec, and in ordinary attacks more to be depended upon, than the strongest fortifications or defences of the town'.[91] The further the expedition progressed up the Gulf of St Lawrence the more challenging it became. The strength of the tide grew more pronounced. Knox's host, Killick, described the flood tide as 'extremely curious' and the winds 'perverse'. Montresor reported typical gulf weather on 15 June. The wind was 'small and very changeable never continuing long in the same quarter. We observed several vessels having a fresh breeze when others within a quarter of a mile have been becalmed, this circumstance is very frequent, owing to the eddies of the wind from off the high lands.' Few British subjects had ever ventured into these waters; there is an other-worldly tone to the accounts of both men as they watched the shores close in on the fleet. Knox noticed that 'the low as well as the high lands are woody on both sides'. The water had gone a 'blackish colour' with weird ripples and swirls. Montresor thought 'the land on the south shore very mountainous and romantic, forming in some parts a kind of table land, its appearance was very green. The trees seemed to be of Birch-Beach [sic] and fir.'[92]

The sixteenth of June saw the fleet smothered in a heavy fog which tested the admiral's sailing instructions. The bigger ships tacked in the middle of the channel to avoid shallow water, the *Neptune*'s cannon roaring out, seven times if she was going to port, nine if starboard and with additional guns after four minutes to notify the fleet by how many degrees. The smaller ships risked shallower waters, some sailing 'within a league of the shore'.[93]

The winds had so far favoured the expedition. Progress had been swift down the Gulf of St Lawrence but not fast enough for the young commander. Wolfe's frustration is palpable in his journal entries. On 10 June he records, 'Fog and contrary wind obliged the Fleet to anchor. I intimated my design of going up with the very Troops to the Admiral, and hinted the pushing on of the Transports, leaving the men-of-war to come up at leisure.'[94] The Admiralty in London had assumed that Saunders would keep the larger ships at the mouth of the St Lawrence to lie in wait for any French fleet that dared to interfere with Wolfe's expedition or threaten Louisbourg and Halifax.

Instead, Saunders obviously intended to push as much of his fleet as far up the river as possible. It may have slowed progress up the St Lawrence but Saunders no doubt believed that his ships with, in all, nearly two thousand cannon and approximately thirteen thousand five hundred officers and men on board could play a decisive role not just in transporting Wolfe's army safely to the target but an active one in operations once they had arrived.

On 18 June, with Île du Bic eight miles to the south-west, a sail was sighted. Five days before Durell had sent Captain Hankerson and his frigate *Richmond* with many of the captured French pilots on board to wait for Saunders. Wolfe was about to get his first news from Durell since he had sent him packing from Halifax.[95] Knox records that the *Richmond* sent a midshipman aboard his transport to inform them that Durell had occupied the Île aux Coudres further upstream where the river was very narrow. The fleet finally learnt that although he had managed to take three prizes with 'flour and other provisions' on board, dozens of other French ships 'had escaped them' laden with 'provisions, especially bread, that are scarce in the French army'.[96] Wolfe's journal oozes a barely controlled rage, it records that letters were captured on some of the prizes which 'mention the most extreme want of everything at Quebec' before the supply ships arrived, 'so that if Mr Durell had come up the river in time every one of the ships might have been taken and Quebec obliged to surrender in a very few days, instead of which they now have plenty of everything'. He repeats himself the next day, 19 June, saying that he had 'read a number of [captured] letters from Quebec, painting their distress in the liveliest manner. All in general agree that they must have starved if the succours from France had not arrived.' To cap it all, 'Captain Hankerson told Mr Saunders that there had been no ice in the River these two months.'[97]

The *Neptune* raised its 'jack' on the ensign staff on its stern and fired one gun. It was the signal for the ships to anchor. The jack was the Union Flag of Great Britain with the red cross of St George superimposed on the white saltire on a blue background of St Andrew and usually flew at the bows of naval ships. Three ships had gone ahead of the fleet, one flying the British jack, the second a French flag, and the last displaying the Dutch colours. They were the marker ships and the ships of each division anchored as close to them as possible. The anchorage was in the sheltered water provided by Bic. At the last minute each helmsman turned the bows into the wind and as the ship slowed the final stopper was yanked off and the heavy iron anchor crashed into the water taking the cable whipping after it. As the anchor held, the ship turned to face the direction of the strong St Lawrence tidal flow. In tightly packed anchorages like this one another anchor was rowed out on the ship's boat and released so that when the tide turned the ship would be held in position and not swing around and risk hitting neighbouring ones. The complexity of the operation was bound to produce the odd accident. Montresor watched one of the transports run afoul of a smaller naval ship and break her bowsprit off. She had to be rescued by the seventy-gun *Orford*.[98]

The next day the fleet was underway again but from now on, as one senior officer recorded, 'we were, for the most part, obliged to take advantage of the flood-tides, and daylight, as the currents began to be strong, and the channel narrow'.[99] The fleet would now anchor every night, the treacherous waters, fast tides, and squalls of wind being far too dangerous to press on in the dark. They often anchored during the ebb tide as well. Strengthened by the waters of the St Lawrence flowing downstream the ebb can reach six knots today. Knox reported that he witnessed 'nine or ten knots' and called it 'the strongest rippling current I ever saw'.[100] As the tide turned and the sea advanced up the St Lawrence the fleet would weigh anchor and creep another few miles into the heart of the continent. Progress was achingly slow, even if the wind and tide were kind. The sounding vessels had to go ahead and feel their way along the rocky bottom of the river with their lead lines to measure the depth of water. As a result the ships were constantly dropping and weighing anchor.

Brigadier Townshend wrote that 'the river above Bic is about 7 leagues [around twenty-two miles] in breadth. Both shores very high: the southern very beautiful. Though of a most wild and uncultivated aspect, save where a few straggling French settlements appear. We could now upon this fine river view the whole fleet in three separate Divisions.' Smaller schooners and sloops dashed between the larger ships carrying messages and personnel, desperately trying to maintain the cohesion of the fleet. This new land had plenty to amuse the soldiers packed on board; Montresor reports a 'great number of white whales and many seals'. Knox recalls seeing 'an immense number of sea-cows rolling about our ships ... which are as white as snow'. He estimated that their exposed backs were twelve to fifteen feet in length and when he and his men fired muskets at them, the balls bounced off. All the journals make numerous references to collisions and groundings that were becoming more frequent as the channel narrowed. On 21 June a transport struck a shoal and fired three guns, to be towed off. Townshend tells of near disaster when five of the largest warships were 'nearly running on board each other, the current being strong' and 'few would answer the helm at first'. The *Diana* was 'ungovernable for a long while' and there was very nearly a collision with the *Royal William* and the *Orford*. Just as the situation reached the 'critical' point, 'a breeze sprung up which ... saved us from that shock which but a few moments before seemed inevitable. Had the least fog prevailed or had it been a little later, nothing could have prevented disaster.'[101]

At 0200 hours on 23 June the *Stirling Castle*, one of Durell's squadron which had pushed up the river and now waited for Saunders and the main body of the fleet, anchored off the Île aux Coudres, heard the noise of cannon downriver. As dawn broke her log records that she 'saw a fleet to the east' sailing with the wind up the St Lawrence. The captain ordered his ship cleared for action and the shrill noise of the bosun's whistle sent the watch below tumbling out of their hammocks and 'to their quarters'.[102] A flurry of signalling ensued and it was soon established that this was Saunders' fleet. Gradually all the ships caught up and anchored in a protected bay on the north coast. The island was bleak; the 400-feet-high cliffs on its north side presented a defiant aspect to the ships as they sailed under them.

Quebec was about fifty miles ahead. But between the fleet and the French stronghold lay by far the most dangerous stretch of river. A passage through 'the Narrows' separated Île aux Coudres from the north shore and beyond that the St Lawrence was scattered with low lying islands and reefs just below the surface. A number of channels led through this natural barrier but they were ever-changing because of silting. The ebb tide tore down the river and in certain wind conditions could create steep, short waves that could swamp open boats and even small ships. They were a fearsome physical barrier. To make matters worse as the British fleet approached the heart of Canada, French intervention grew ever more likely. There was every possibility that the defenders of Quebec would take up positions to augment the natural barricades with ships, men and cannon. So far the enemy had hardly shown himself; the odd crack of a musket from the trees along the shoreline had been a fine gesture of defiance but held little menace. However, after years of desperate battles against the French and their Canadian colonists, no one in Wolfe's army doubted that they would fight to the last extremity to protect their land from invasion. The all-too-visible progress of the fleet ensured that they would have plenty of notice of the British advance and although, as Knox commented, they saw no Canadians, they did see 'large signal fires everywhere before us'.[103] The French knew they were coming.

TWO

'The enemy are out to destroy everything that calls itself Canada'

AT DUSK ON 22 MAY 1759 the keel of a small boat crunched into the sand and mud of the beach and a group of Frenchmen clambered over the sailors, who had shipped their oars, and jumped over the bows. They had made the 150-mile trip from Montreal in just thirty-six hours. With great urgency the group walked into the so-called *Basse Ville* or Lower Town. They passed a battery of ten cannon, huddled behind a three-feet-thick stone wall with wide embrasures lined with less brittle red brick, and into the chaotic huddle of buildings, clustered at the base of the cliff and penned in by the sweep of the river. On every side of them were the houses of prosperous merchants squeezed in among the storehouses that held their fortunes and numerous taverns that dotted the unpaved roadsides. The houses were all brick built, and nearly all were three storeys or more. Every one of them was coated in whitewashed mortar to protect the brick and give them a veneer of respectability. All had imposing, tall, sloping roofs to keep the winter snow from crushing them. Their windows were large but tightly latticed; made up of many small panes of glass that were easier to ship from France than large squares. Not an inch of land was wasted; the only real open space was the marketplace that dated back almost to the foundation of the city. There was a bust of Louis XIV in the middle and at its southern end a fine church: Notre Dame des Victoires, 'Our Lady of Victories', built and named to celebrate earlier failed attempts by the hereditary Anglo-American enemy to seize the town.

After just 100 paces the Lower Town ended abruptly at an almost vertical face of rock with only two real roads winding up it, besides a couple of paths that were almost too steep for carts. At the top of the slope, more than two hundred feet high, two principal batteries of fifty cannon and ten squat mortars perched on the edge, their mouths threatening the St Lawrence River. Up here, in the *Haute Ville* or Upper Town, the aspect of the buildings changed. The very wealthiest inhabitants had built magnificent homes, almost palaces, designed to the latest French architectural styles but with substantial adaptations to allow their inhabitants to survive one of the most extreme climates in the world. For months every winter Canada froze. The arterial St Lawrence, link to the outside world, was sheathed in ice. Temperatures plunged to minus thirty degrees. Generations of Canadians had feared the climate more than the English. In early summer, however, the horrors of winter could be forgotten. Formal gardens abounded in the Upper Town, giving it a fragrant, spacious, genteel ambience. Without the pressure for space of the Lower Town the houses were lower to the ground, usually only one or two storeys high. As the group of men ascended the steep road they passed the Bishop's palace on the right, perched on the cliff; straight ahead was the cathedral and to their left the Château St Louis, the Governor's palace. Cannon, Catholicism and Command: the pillars on which French power in North America rested. From the magnificence of the buildings, the dress and manners of the people in the street, visitors could have been in one of the finest towns in France. In fact, they were in Quebec, stronghold of empire, capital of the vast territories of New France.[1]

Quebec was the nucleus of Canadian life. It had been the very first seed of settlement planted in the barren turf of Canada and it had flourished. It was Canada's political, religious, educational, and social centre, its link to the outside world, the depository for the wealth of an empire. It occupied the best natural defensive position in North America and it was the continent's most powerful fortress. One of Canada's greatest governors, Louis de Buade, Comte de Frontenac, wrote to Colbert in France in 1672 that 'nothing has seemed to me so beautiful and magnificent as the site of the city of Quebec, it cannot be better situated, and is destined to one day become the capital of a great empire'.² That prophecy had certainly come true.

Louis-Joseph, Marquis de Montcalm-Gozon, Seigneur of Saint-Véran, Candiac, Tournemine, Vestric and Saint-Julien-d'Arpaon, Baron de Gabriac, Lieutenant General in the army of Louis XV, and commander in chief of French forces in Canada, had arrived in Quebec. He was short, stocky, and energetic. Within minutes of the group installing themselves in Montcalm's accommodation on the north of Upper Town overlooking the St Charles River, messages, requests, and orders started pouring out. An already febrile city was stirred up to new heights. Since 10 May the ships that had evaded Durell had been arriving from France. They represented salvation. The vast cereal producing areas of modern Canada were not settled in the eighteenth century. The land of the populated valley of the St Lawrence was far from ideal for growing wheat, and while enough was grown to feed the civilian population, the addition of several thousand hungry and unproductive soldiers brought the colony to the edge of starvation. New France had a slim industrial base, there was only one iron forge and the dawning of total war overwhelmed indigenous capabilities. The ships' holds were packed with food, alcohol, and the stuff of war, including barrels of gunpowder and cannonballs that acted as ballast. Not least, the convoy had also brought news of Wolfe's expedition, gleaned from intelligence sources in Europe and papers found aboard a captured British ship. Montcalm had spent the winter in Montreal, where he was better placed to strike out in the direction of the first attack that the British would launch on the colony. It was now clear that, despite threats on other fronts, he would be needed in Quebec.

Montcalm was 47 years old. His dark brown eyes were full of life and he had a passionate drive that could occasionally tip into a fiery temper. Contemporaries called him a typical southerner. He was born in the ancestral chateau of Candiac near Nîmes in southern France and his was an impeccably aristocratic, if not a wealthy line. His ancestors had been raised, lived and killed on the battlefield. Few of the Montcalms had died in their beds. He had been commissioned an officer at the age of 9 and by 17 was a captain. He saw active campaigning in the 1730s under the great Marshal de Saxe and was left in no doubt as to the dangers of high command when he was close to the Duke of Berwick as he was blown to pieces by a cannonball at Philippsburg in Germany in 1734. He had made the all-important advantageous marriage to Angelique Louise Talon de Boulay, daughter of the Marquis de Boulay, a well-connected colonel. Their marriage was a love match and of ten children six had survived, two boys and four girls. His poignant letters to his wife, enquiring after his children and full of longing for his native Provence, have made him an attractive figure to later biographers.

He had bled for France. Montcalm had been wounded during the defence of Prague in his late twenties and then almost starved to death on the infamous retreat from Bohemia during the War of Austrian Succession. As a colonel he had led his men from the front and twice rallied his fleeing regiment during the crushing French defeat at Piacenza. He ended the battle a pathetic prisoner in Austrian hands, his unit annihilated and his body savaged with no less than five sabre cuts. He was exchanged for an Austrian prisoner of equal rank only to be wounded in another French defeat in a ravine in the Alps. Just after the inconclusive peace that ended the War of Austrian Succession he petitioned the Minister of War for a pension, citing his thirty-one years, eleven campaigns, and five wounds. He was given an annual stipend of 2,000 livres in 1753.[3] He could have easily seen out his days as a stout provincial nobleman, a pillar of Montpellier society, finding good matches for his daughters and regiments for his boys, but that was never the fate of the Montcalms.

Given the jingoistic enthusiasm for empire that swept across the world in the late nineteenth century, it is perhaps surprising that the idea of trans-oceanic empire was unfashionable and unpopular for much of the time since its inception in the sixteenth century. Colonies were often seen as expensive millstones around the neck of the mother country, enriching bourgeois merchants or propping up royal egos. Colonies were lethal to the health of Europeans, peopled by new men on the make who sought opportunities denied them in the stratified societies of Europe. They were crucibles of immorality. Colonists often proved willing to adopt the habits and the women of the Natives. 'Civilized' values were eroded and social barriers scaled as turbulent young societies coalesced and fragmented. Above all, for military men, there was nothing glorious about a war of ambush, stockades, river cross-ings, and forests. The eighteenth-century officer regarded the plains of northern Europe as the natural theatre for war. Here honour was to be won, in battles of foot, cavalry, and artillery which were fought as their fathers, and grandfathers, had done, under the eyes of royal dukes or perhaps even the sovereign himself. Even Wolfe dreamt about commanding a cavalry regiment on the Continent, in the Anglo-Pruss-ian force that was defending George II's small German Electorate of Hanover from the armies of Louis XV. French policymakers and mili-tary men also regarded this as the primary theatre. Traditionally British gains in West Africa, India, the Caribbean, or North America were wiped out at the peace table as long as French armies occupied strate-gically important Channel ports or German cities.

The capture of the Baron Dieskau, commander of French forces in Canada, in a skirmish on the banks of Lake George at the very fringe of empire was a case in point. Few senior officers were willing to replace him and serve in the New World. It was a forgotten theatre of war, and one in which the imbalance was slowly increasing as every spring more reinforcements were sent from Britain than from France. Montcalm's name was chosen from the list of junior field officers. It was 'a commission that I had neither desired nor asked for', he recorded in his journal. But 'I felt I had to accept this honourable and delicate commission', because it 'ensured my son's fortunes'. Like many a proud, noble but impecunious family, the Montcalms depended solely on the crown for patronage. Part of the package was a promise that 'the King would give my regiment to my son'. He was also promoted to *Maréchal de camp*, a Major General in British parlance, with a 25,000 livres salary, resettlement money, and living expenses. He would receive a pension of 6,000 livres a year, and half for his wife if he failed to return. This last provision was 'dear to my heart', he wrote and 'touched me because I owe Madame de Montcalm so much'. On 11 March 1756 he had gone to Versailles, to collect his commission and present his son to the King, who duly made the teenager a colonel. Having guaranteed the social, military, and financial stability of his line, he had ridden for Brest on the fifteenth where he met his staff and boarded ship for Canada.[4]

The crossing had taken five weeks. Like Wolfe, he tired of being cooped up aboard ship and he disembarked as soon as he could, below Quebec, travelling up the last thirty miles of the St Lawrence to the town on horseback. As he rode he no doubt cast his practised eye over the shoreline, placing artillery batteries and forts in his mind's eye to impede the progress of the British fleet that he knew one day would try to penetrate up the river. He had arrived in Quebec in May 1756 and stayed a week. Long enough to realize that this was 'a country and a war where everything is so different from European practice'.[5] It was not a compliment.

Three years later he had not changed his mind. He never came to love Canada nor its rugged inhabitants. The deeply conservative aristocrat could not bring himself to embrace the mobility of Canadian culture. Skilled labourers or fur traders could amass fortunes, buy enough land to become seigneurs, obtain military commissions for their sons, who could then build the family's reputation on the battlefield and eventually acquire noble rank. Soldiers could make fortunes from the massive funds that were earmarked for the colony. Montcalm complained that Le Mercier, the commandant of the artillery for Quebec, 'came out twenty years ago a simple soldier, [but] will soon be worth about six or seven hundred thousand livres, perhaps a million if these things continue'.[6] 'He does not care for much,' Montcalm confided to his journal, 'other than his own interest.'[7] One of his aides wrote that 'one must agree that this spirit of greed, of gain, of commerce, will always destroy the spirit of honor, of glory, and military spirit'. He worried about the effect of this brave new world on the men under their command. 'Soldiers,' he wrote, 'corrupted by the great amount of money, [and] by the example of the Indians and Canadians, breathing an air permeated with independence, work indolently.' He concluded that 'this country is dangerous for discipline'.[8]

The art of war was another area in which Montcalm found himself deeply at odds with Canadian thinking. He saw warfare only through the lens of a regular officer, unable to escape the mindset in which he had been immersed all his life. He regarded war in America as barbaric. For generations Canada had defended herself from the Native Americans and British settlers alike by adopting the tactics of the former.

Raids, ambushes, massacres, and farm burning were the norm for Canadians, much to the horror of regular officers sent out from France. In Europe the behaviour of armies was tightly circumscribed. Rules and conventions protected women, civilians, the wounded, and prisoners of war. Enemy commanders wrote shocked letters to each other, always in impeccable French, if any of their subordinates broke this code. No commander could ever ask a junior officer to obey an order that conflicted with his duty as a gentleman. Indeed, the officers of all the *ancien régime* armies counted themselves as members of a supranational group espousing the principles of honour and gentility. They would even socialize freely during the regular truces or breaks in fighting. The prospect of total war was anathema; it was believed that it would destroy religion and property, and invert the social order. Anarchy of this sort threatened to be catastrophic for the combatant powers and would certainly outweigh any short-term military advantage gained.

In North America war had none of this refined veneer. War was total, and cold-blooded slaughter was common. Communities, French or British, white or Native, faced utter annihilation at the hands of the enemy. Native Americans routinely enslaved prisoners or tortured them to death with excruciating exactness. Settlers on both sides faced an existence of scarcity and brutality with no reward for civility. Faced with the bloody realities of life on the frontier Montcalm was appalled. Yet Canadians were certain that their strongest weapon against the encroachments of the far more populous British settlers from the south had always been their Native American allies. Native raids could throw back British colonists almost to the coastal cities, as time and again they were hopelessly outmatched by tribes bred to fight among the rivers, lakes, and forests of the backcountries of New York, Pennsylvania, and Virginia. Armed with French muskets, powder, and knives, fed when necessary with French provisions and paid in brandy and gold, the Native war parties terrorized vast swathes of frontier. Among them were handfuls of Canadian colonial soldiers, fluent in their language, dressed and painted like Natives so that it was hard to tell the difference. These men attempted to channel Native American aggression along avenues that would serve the cause of New France.

Montcalm and many French officers regarded the Native Americans with at best suspicion, but usually utter disdain. As for the Canadians who served alongside them, men who chose to live like the 'savages' even when presented with the opportunities of Christian civilization, they were worse than the 'savages' themselves. Traders, the *voyageurs*, travelled to the far west adopting the attitudes, dress, language, and women of the Natives. Louis Antoine de Bougainville, one of Montcalm's aides-de-camp, wrote of these men, that 'one recognizes them easily by their looks, by their size and because all of them are tattooed on their bodies with figures of plants or animals'. Tattooing in New France was a 'long and painful' process with burning gunpowder poured into holes pricked in the skin. Bougainville observed that 'one would not pass for a man among the Indians of the Far West if he had not had himself tattooed'.[9]

Montcalm argued strongly that a new era of warfare had dawned in North America. No longer would small numbers of tough, tattooed fighters and their Native American allies protect New France. Since the outbreak of this round of fighting, the scale of the resources sent by the French and the British had brought modern warfare to the continent. 'The war had changed character in Canada,' he wrote to France in the spring of 1759, 'the vast forces of the English' meant that the Canadian way of making war was obsolete. Previously, 'the Canadians thought they were making war, and were making, so as to speak, hunting excursions'. Once, 'Indians formed the basis; now, the accessory.' He made little attempt to disguise his disdain; apparently he had tried to tell the Canadians, 'but old prejudices continue'.[10] In 1758, he asserted that 'it is no longer the time when a few scalps, or the burning [of] a few houses is any advantage or even an object. Petty means, petty ideas, petty councils about details are now dangerous and waste material and time.'[11] Bougainville loyally agreed with his commander. 'Now war is established here on the European basis,' he wrote. 'It no longer is a matter of making a raid but of conquering or being conquered. What a revolution! What a change!' The effect of Montcalm's dismissal of the traditional tactics of Native Americans and Canadians was malignant. As the war progressed rifts between French regulars sent out from Europe and the home-grown defenders of New

France grew ever wider. Regular troops robbed the *habitants* and their officers snubbed their opposite numbers in the militia. Both Montcalm and Bougainville were withering in their criticism of Canadians. New France 'will perish' predicted Bougainville, 'victim of its prejudices, of its blind confidence, of the stupidity or of the roguery of its chiefs'.[12] To Montcalm, one man personified Canadian attitudes, and, in his view, failings. He sat at the pinnacle of New French society: the Canadian-born Governor and Lieutenant General, Pierre de Rigaud de Vaudreuil de Cavagnial, Marquis de Vaudreuil.

Vaudreuil's father had been sent out from France at the end of the seventeenth century to command the royal troops in the colony, and had then been appointed Governor General of New France. Vaudreuil had been enrolled as an ensign at the grand old age of 6, was a captain at 13, and a major at 27. He had campaigned in the west against the Fox Indians during the 1720s and from 1743 to 1753 he was Governor of the portion of New France called Louisiana: the lands from New Orleans at the mouth of the Mississippi up the river to the Great Lakes. He was appointed Governor General in 1755, the first to have been born in Canada. In 1759 he was 60.

Vaudreuil was proud, indecisive and deeply defensive about the abilities of Canadians. Like many colonial soldiers, he was extremely keen not to be seen as inferior to French-born officers. Vaudreuil had tried to convince the Minister of Marine in France that he did not need to send out a commander for the regular troops. Vaudreuil himself knew how to save Canada; he just needed an infusion of regular troops. But the army were having none of it. French regulars would fight under their own officers, not Canadians.

Vaudreuil was disliked by the influx of French officers. Montcalm regarded him as a meddling amateur. Bougainville described him as a 'timid man and who neither knows how to make a resolution nor to keep one once made'.[13] For three years Montcalm and Vaudreuil had clashed over strategy. In 1758 Bougainville noted in his journal: 'I see with grief the growing misunderstanding between our leaders.'[14] Vaudreuil lacked the stomach for direct confrontation but his letters to his masters at the French court in Versailles are full of complaints about Montcalm and reveal a great sensitivity over his position within the colony. At the end of the campaigning season of 1758 he informed Versailles of the 'indecent observations made by the officers of the regular troops of which I had the largest share'. He feared they had 'even become so public that they form the conversation of the soldiers and the Canadians'. He knew full well who was to blame: Montcalm, who had given 'too great liberty' to his officers who were 'giving an unrestrained course to their expressions'. The situation was clearly grave, but 'I pass the matter by in silence, I even affect to ignore it, in the sole view of the good of the king's service, already aware of the consequences which might attend an open rupture with the Marquis'.[15] In this Vaudreuil was right, Montcalm made no secret of his dislike of the Governor General. He talked openly of it with his junior officers and his official journal is littered with snide comments. It was unprofessional and deeply harmful to relations between the French and the Canadians.

Vaudreuil's policy of raids deep into British-held territories had proved remarkably successful in the first few years of the war. A smattering of French officers brought gold, trade goods, and brandy to the Native Americans along the British frontier from the Great Lakes down to Georgia, to encourage them to hurl back vulnerable British settlements. The British sphere of influence had been shrunk by a hundred miles as Native raids had burnt homes and scalped farmers deep into Pennsylvania, Massachusetts, and New York. Fort Granville, in modern Lewistown, Pennsylvania, just over one hundred miles from Philadelphia, was captured and burnt by Native Americans and Canadians. All the resources, manpower, and treasure of the wealthy and populous central colonies, in particular of Virginia and Pennsylvania, were poured into protecting their own frontiers, largely without success.

In northern New York, the other front between the British and French zones of influence in North America, along the traditional invasion route of Lake George, or Lac du Saint-Sacrement as the French called it, the lumbering red-coated armies of King George II had been fought to a standstill over three consecutive campaigns. Raids by the mixed war parties of Natives and Canadians had slowed British movements to a crawl, terrified the British soldiers and commanders alike and destroyed convoys of supplies on which any thrust up towards

Canada depended. In 1756, Vaudreuil had sent a reluctant Montcalm to attack the British fort of Oswego, their toehold on Lake Ontario. It had fallen but Montcalm was appalled by the behaviour of the Natives who massacred some of the British prisoners after the surrender of the fort. In 1757, a massive force of Native Americans from as far away as the western prairies gathered south of Montreal, recruited by the promise of scalps, slaves, and plunder on a huge scale. Montcalm took Fort William Henry at the foot of Lake George and desperately tried to prevent an even larger massacre by Native Americans furious that the Europeans had made peace between themselves, while not a scalp had been taken. He was only partially successful; despite his personal intervention and that of Bougainville and other officers, unarmed British soldiers were enslaved or slaughtered and their corpses maimed. This infamous incident, gruesomely exaggerated in the British press at the time, poisoned relations between the British and French. Montcalm could have followed up his success with a drive towards Albany but blamed the Canadians' desire to return to collect the harvest and withdrew. In 1758, a British attack on Fort Carillon at the north end of Lake George ended in slaughter as the British threw themselves time and again on a barricade through which the French kept up a regular, terrible musketry. The British commander, Abercrombie, squandered a very favourable situation with this bizarre head-on attack, and then compounded his mistake by panicking and retreating south in headlong flight, leaving much heavy equipment behind. Again Montcalm was cautious. Rather than march south to pursue his stricken enemy he stayed put. He did not want to risk his small force on offensive operations so for the third year running there was no follow-up to a successful encounter.

In the winter of 1758/9 reports from prisoners suggested that the relentless build-up of British forces for an assault on Canada was continuing. The British seemed likely to strike in no less than three places. There was Wolfe's attack up the St Lawrence. A major overland invasion would move up Lake George, aiming for Montreal. Last, there would be a strike at the forts of the west, with Fort Niagara being the most obvious target. Niagara was the vital link in the chain that led from the main body of the colony on the St Lawrence River to the

vast hinterland of forts and trading posts that stretched to the Mississippi and up into present-day Alberta. This was the *pays d'en haut*,
the upper country, an area under the strong influence, if not the
control, of France. Both the French and the Native Americans regarded
themselves as sovereign. The Natives accepted French forts as a necessary evil to ensure the flow of gunpowder, muskets, and metal work
which the French exchanged for furs and without which life was inde-
scribably hard. Were the Frenchmen guests or masters? The answer
could wait until after the common British enemy was defeated.

Faced with this triple attack the debate over strategy grew ever
fiercer. Vaudreuil wanted to hold the British everywhere; every yard of
his precious Canada ceded to the British was too great a sacrifice. He
urged the use of irregular troops, Native Americans and Canadians,
to launch pre-emptive attacks to sow confusion among the British as
they prepared for the invasion. Montcalm took entirely the opposite
view. 'Considering our inferiority,' he wrote to Versailles, they ought
to 'contract our defensive [perimeter], in order to preserve at least, the
body of the colony, and retard its loss'. He was thinking as a European
statesman of bargaining chips on an eventual peace table, not of hunting and fishing grounds that were part of the Canadians' DNA. He
was fatalistic about Canada's chances, and increasingly melodramatic
about his own role: 'prejudice' or 'councils of quacks are followed', he
complained, but he would play the martyr, 'I shall none the less exert
myself, as I have always done' even if it meant he must 'sacrifice myself
for the [public] good'.[16]

Montcalm and Vaudreuil had reached such an impasse that at the
end of 1758 the French court was petitioned to arbitrate. In case
Versailles doubted the seriousness of the issue Montcalm effectively
offered his resignation by requesting his own recall to France. Two
emissaries were sent, one from the Governor, the other from the
General. Both carried letters and dispatches brimming with oppro-
brium towards the other and pleas to ignore whatever they wrote.
Montcalm made the wiser choice of messenger; his letters were carried
by his 29-year-old aide-de-camp, Captain Bougainville. The young
ADC had enjoyed an unusual career. Born into a glittering family he
showed an early aptitude for mathematics and in his mid-twenties had

published a treatise on integral calculus for which he was elected to the Royal Society in London. He had also established a reputation as a brilliant lawyer. On first meeting Bougainville, Montcalm described him as 'witty and well educated'.[17] This bright, young star would prove an able diplomat for Montcalm, while Vaudreuil's emissary was ignored.

Bougainville had joined the army at the age of 21, which was far too old to get ahead. However, his unusual talents secured him a series of appointments as ADC to senior officers. He had been assigned to Montcalm and had joined him in Brest before they had sailed for Canada together in 1756. He did not look like a soldier; he was short, overweight, and asthmatic. But he did not flinch during his first battle, at Oswego, where he served alongside Montcalm, and subsequently proved himself an able student of war. Montcalm wrote that his young ADC,

> exposes himself readily to gunfire, a matter on which he needs to be restrained rather than encouraged. I shall be much mistaken if he does not have a good head for soldiering when experience has taught him to foresee the potential for difficulties. In the meantime there is hardly a young man who, having received only the theory, knows as much about it as he.[18]

He was an adept handler of the Native Americans too. He sat on councils, sang the war songs and had even been adopted into the Nipissing tribe. Despite being wounded during the French victory at Carillon in the summer of 1758, Bougainville was the obvious choice to return to France that winter to plead for more military assistance for Canada. Bougainville's passage was not a pleasant one. Battered by gales as soon as they left the St Lawrence he wrote that 'we suffer in this wretched machine beyond anything words can express. The rolling is horrible and unceasing ... an imagination most prolific in troublesome ideas could not come within a hundredth of outlining the unbearable details of our position.'[19] In fact, their actual position was worse than he thought; the captain was mistaken in his navigation and sailed his ship into the Bristol Channel, home to a nest of privateers. Luckily, they realized their mistake, turned round and soon arrived in Morlaix. Within hours Bougainville was on the road to Paris.

In the French capital he received compliments, promotions, and fine parties but little substance. Louis XV's armies had been defeated in Europe and his fleet was being slowly strangled at sea. The state was rudderless. France was still an autocratic monarchy. All lines of government converged only in the person of the king. Louis' great-grandfather, the mighty Louis XIV, had created this system and he alone had had the self-discipline and intelligence to control it. Despite insisting that, 'in my person alone resides the sovereign power, of which the essence is the spirit of counsel, wisdom, and reason ... to me alone belongs the legislative power, independent and entire ... public order emanates from me; I am its supreme guardian,' Louis XV was unequal to the task.[20] He was a man of honour who genuinely desired to do good, but he lacked the charisma and the confidence to defend his policies when they came under criticism, and the gargantuan work ethic of his great-grandfather. He hated confrontation and attempted to rule by stealth, becoming ever more secretive and suspicious. He also found it difficult to apply himself to hard work, preferring the company of his many lovers or indulging his passion for hunting. A government that was designed to respond to a forceful central figure slowly became paralysed. Ministers competed to fill the void. There were constant changes of personnel. One dominant figure was Jeanne-Antoinette Poisson, Marquise de Pompadour, once the King's favourite mistress; she now supplied women of low status for the King's bed, who would satisfy his lust without challenging her political power. Beautiful and clever, cultured and astute, she played a much debated role in French government throughout the war. Although accused at the time, and subsequently by some historians of dominating the affairs of state, she was not a shadowy dictator. A weak and inconstant king ensured that no one figure was able to amass that much power in the dysfunctional hierarchy of the French government. Pompadour did, though, have a powerful voice in policymaking, in particular the appointment and dismissal of key officers in the army and the state. She kept up correspondences with many of the field commanders although the letters consisted mainly of encouragement and promises to look after any family members that wanted jobs.

Had Pompadour or any other strong figure emerged to usurp the power of the King, it may well have been better for France. Instead, half-hearted royal government staggered on. Louis' great enemy, the energetic, commanding Frederick II, 'Frederick the Great', of Prussia wrote in his memoirs that his adversary's 'zeal was extinguished within a few days, and France was governed by four subaltern kings, each independent of the other'. France was 'a vessel sailing without a compass on a stormy sea, simply following the impulsion of the wind'. A contemporary French historian famously commented that ministers changed 'like scenery at the opera'. During the war France would get through four ministers of foreign affairs and five ministers of marine, who had responsibility for the colonies and the navy. Just before Bougainville's visit in November 1758 Pompadour had secured the appointment of one of her favourites, Nicolas-René Berryer, as Minister of Marine; he was the fourth man to take the job. His qualifications for the position were dubious. He had been the Chief of Police of Paris and he treated his new job as an investigation into what would happen in Canada should it fall to the British rather than throwing himself into its defence.[21]

Bougainville quickly realized that Versailles was preparing itself for the worst in Canada. Attention was fixed on central Europe where Frederick II had inflicted a stunning series of defeats on the forces of Austria, Russia and France. The threat to the colonies could wait. The honour of France's armies and the situation in Europe were more important. French policy for 1759 was to drive into western Germany to threaten King George II's Electorate of Hanover and Frederick's western front, while conserving its naval resources for an all-out invasion of Britain. King George's government would be forced to negotiate. British subsidies which were the lifeblood of Frederick's war effort would be cut off, and any losses overseas could be restored to Louis with the stroke of a pen. In the meantime Canada would have to look to her own defence. In the words of Berryer in his audience with Bougainville, 'Sir, one does not try to save the stables when the house is on fire.' Bougainville shot back bravely, 'Well, sir, at least, they cannot say that you speak like a horse.'[22] Meetings with Pompadour and other key figures proved just as fruitless. The pessimism seeping out of Montcalm's and Bougainville's own depositions only convinced government belief that the situation in Canada was hopeless. Montcalm's one, rather odd request was that Canada could be saved by an amphibious assault on the Carolinas. The French fleet would meet no opposition since the British ships would be concentrating on northern waters. Montcalm informed Versailles that the Cherokee would join the French as would the German settlers throughout the central colonies. The Quakers of Pennsylvania would not fight and the huge slave populations would rise up and support the French, hoping for their freedom. Ministers praised the plan and shelved it.

A king in want of ships, guns, and men was generous with the one resource in which he was rich. Promotions, honours, and decorations flowed to the personnel in Canada. Bougainville was made a colonel, Montcalm, a lieutenant general, with a salary of 48,000 livres, and Vaudreuil received the Grand Cross of the Order of Saint Louis. The newly promoted Montcalm now outranked Vaudreuil. Rather than resolving the crisis of leadership, Versailles had exacerbated it. Over the winter the court seems to have wavered over a solution to this bitter quarrel. Ministerial minutes record that they were well aware of the problem, acknowledging that 'the Marquis de Vaudreuil and the Marquis de Montcalm lived on such indifferent terms ... This estrangement had exercised an influence over all minds.'[23] They recognized that Montcalm wished to be brought home, especially now that it would be beneath the dignity of a lieutenant general to answer to a governor.

Montcalm's second in command, who had also received a promotion, was the very able *Maréchal de camp*, François-Gaston de Lévis, who was on good terms with Vaudreuil and had in the past praised Canadian military commanders for their skill. He would have been an ideal candidate to succeed Montcalm in an attempt to reconcile the French army with the Canadian colonial soldiers and militiamen. Having discussed this plan the document ends with an entry on 28 December 1758 saying simply, 'on mature reflection, this arrangement cannot take place, as M de Montcalm is necessary at this present conjuncture'. Montcalm would stay on; Vaudreuil would defer to him in decisions relating to the defence of the colony, although he would continue to command the colony's militia.[24] It was a disastrous compromise. Instead of a firm decision, the bickering over precedence was to continue. Montcalm was instructed to get along with Vaudreuil; meanwhile, 'M. Berryer writes to the same effect to M. Vaudreuil and directs him to conduct himself with the greatest harmony towards you; you must both feel all its necessity and all its importance.' Strategically at least the French court had sided unambiguously with Montcalm; the focus of operations was to defend the core of the colony, forces should be stationed so as to be 'always enabled mutually to help one another, to communicate with and to support each other. However trifling the space you can preserve, it is of utmost importance to possess always a foothold in Canada, for should we once wholly lose that country, it would be quite impossible to enter it again.' In conclusion Montcalm was told that, 'the recollection of what you have achieved last year makes His Majesty hope that you will still find means to disconcert their projects. M Berryer will cause to be conveyed to you as much provisions and ammunition as possible; the rest depends on your wisdom and courage, and on the bravery of the troops.'[25]

Ships of the line would be hoarded in France to prepare to knock Britain out of the war by direct invasion. Instead, frigates were sent and fast private ships paid for at exorbitant rates to take supplies out to Canada. Bougainville travelled to Bordeaux where a flotilla of ships was being assembled. Even though France's army was at least twice the size of that of Britain, no new units of regulars were sent out. There was a fear, partly thanks to Montcalm's gloomy predictions, that they would be intercepted by the British. There was also the consideration that if they did arrive in Canada they would place too much strain on the colony's limited food supply. Montcalm was informed that, 'you must not expect to receive any military reinforcements'.[26] Altogether around four hundred recruits, of mixed quality, were sent to bring the regular units up to strength together with sixty specialists such as engineers and sappers. Apart from the men, the ships carried food, gunpowder, and other provisions to Quebec. Bougainville boarded the frigate, *La Chézine*, and set sail on 20 March. A few ships crept out from other ports; in mid-March the *Atalante*, thirty-four guns, and the *Pomone*, thirty, left the Channel. All the captains hoped they would enter the gulf before the blockading squadron.

La Chézine sailed into the basin of Quebec on 10 May, the first of twenty-three supply ships from France to do so. Its arrival provoked a blizzard of rumours in a town cut off from supplies and news for months. Nearly all of the rest of the fleet trickled in over the next week. The vast majority of ships sent had beaten Durell's British blockade. Montcalm's pessimism had been misplaced. There was huge rejoicing by the townspeople who had been haunted by the prospect of starvation. One diarist, Jean-Claude Panet, who had arrived in New France as a 20-year-old soldier and was now approaching his fortieth birthday as a notary in a Quebec court, wrote that, 'you cannot doubt the joy that this news gave to us'.[27] Canada had been jolted by a series of poor harvests, partly caused by the inclement weather and partly by the absence of the farmers who had been called into the colony's militia and sent to distant frontiers. To add to the discomfort of the Canadians, the winter had been awful. The same low temperatures suffered by the men at Halifax and Louisbourg had been felt right across Canada as well. 'The winter has been one of the coldest ... the ice has backed up to such an extraordinary degree and with such violence, as to throw down a house,' wrote one officer.[28] Now the arrival of the supplies ensured that Canada could fight another campaign. Vaudreuil had told Versailles that 'of all enemies the most redoubtable is the famine to which we are exposed'. This had been averted although the man responsible for feeding the army and the colony, François Bigot, the short, red-haired, ugly *Intendant*, calculated that he had received about eighty days' rations for the regular army, 'at the rate of half a pound of flour and half a pound of pork per head', which was less than 'the proper ration'. Canada received about a third of the food that the colonial authorities had asked for.[29] She would have to find the rest herself: cows were requisitioned; two families would have to share one beast to pull their ploughs. Montcalm dramatically announced to Vaudreuil that despite the disappointing supplies from France, 'trifles are precious to those who have nothing ... I shall entirely devote myself towards saving this unfortunate country and if necessary, die in the attempt.'[30]

The many threats to Canada had meant that Montcalm had spent the winter in Montreal near the centre of the colony and best placed to react to whichever proved to be the most pressing. He had informed the aged Duc de Belle Isle, the Minister for War, that 'the rest of the troops remain in their quarters; they hold themselves in readiness to march on the first notice'. He would stay in Montreal until it became clear 'to what point it will be necessary to proceed; that will depend on the enemy's movements; their superiority forces us to receive the law from them in regard to our movements'.[31] Early rumours brought to him at the beginning of May by 'several English prisoners ... unanimously concurred in reporting, that great preparations were in making in the British colonies for the invasion of the whole of Canada; and that the intention of making three simultaneous attacks was spoken of, in which more than 60,000 men were to be employed'.[32] These wildly inflated reports were swallowed whole by Montcalm and did nothing to lighten his sense of doom.

The arrival of the intelligence which was brought by the flotilla from France had left him in no doubt that Quebec was where his duty now lay. Within hours of arriving in Quebec, Montcalm, in his own words had 'already given activity to many necessary arrangements'. He went to bed on 24 May but was awoken at midnight with the first reliable intelligence of the British movements. The couriers informed him 'of the arrival of 15 large ships of the line', an exaggerated account of Durell, and Montcalm rightly assumed that 'it's assuredly the vanguard of the English army destined to attack Quebec'. He finished his letter in typical style, half bellicose, half defeatist, 'I fear not tell you, My Lord, that our arrangements here are somewhat tardy ... whether strong or weak, we shall fight somewhere or other, and perhaps be fortunate.'[33]

The news was corroborated by beacons which burnt brightly on the southern bank across the narrows from the city of Quebec. The chain of beacons ended with the 'fires on Point Lévis', which pierced the darkness. The guns of the town fired as if in receipt of the signal. Their deep booms rolled across the basin of Quebec; it was a grim augury.[34]

There was consternation. It was a universally embraced axiom of Canadian life that the St Lawrence was an impenetrable obstacle. Vaudreuil had airily assured Versailles that 'I do not presume that the enemy will undertake coming to Quebec.' One journal records flatly

that, 'the rumour in regard to [an attack on] Quebec was not generally credited; because the river, from the difficulty of its navigation,
was considered an impenetrable barrier'. Yet here were the British little
more than fifty miles from the town. It was 'astounding' to launch 'an
enterprise apparently so daring, and at a time when the season was so
little advanced'. The diarist blamed the 'North East wind, which had
constantly blown for several days'. With a 'favourable wind' the 'whole
of the enemy's fleet ... might be before Quebec, in less than three days'.
He describes the sense of helplessness: 'the alarm was general throughout the country – there was no troops in Quebec – the town was open
on every side – no plan of operation, or of defence had been formed;
– every body hastened to pack up, and to place their effects in security
by sending them to Trois Rivières, or to Montréal'.[35]

Montcalm threw himself into preparing Quebec for a siege. The
winter before Governor General Vaudreuil had rather pompously
informed Versailles of his plans: 'on the first news I shall receive of the
enemy being in the river, I shall provide for the security of the frontiers of this government. I shall go down, in person, to Quebec.' He
would take with him the militias of Montreal and Trois Rivières to get
them building defences. He assured Versailles that 'I shall always feel
great pleasure in communicating to them [Montcalm and Lévis] all the
movements I have ordered, and even in making use of such reflections
as place and circumstances will suggest to them.' This does not suggest
that Vaudreuil was preparing himself for a campaign season of
constructive cooperation. News from France of Montcalm's promotion
and orders to defer to him in military matters cannot have improved
his attitude.[36]

True to his word Vaudreuil hurried to the capital where he and
Montcalm would spend the rest of the summer bickering over who
was responsible for what. Montcalm wrote to his second in command,
Chevalier de Lévis, that 'I have still less time, my dear Chevalier, for
writing since the arrival of the Marquis de Vaudreuil, for I have to
allow him to play the role of general. I act as secretary and major for
him, and greatly long to have you with us.' At least one journal agreed,
'in the midst of this chaos, M le Marquis de Vaudreuil arrived, council upon council was held, at which every person who chose to assume

airs of importance was invited to assist – but at these councils no decisive measures were resolved upon'. They were unruly affairs, people
crushed in 'pell mell … whatever may be their stations'. Whatever
Vaudreuil's strengths or weaknesses as a strategist he was certainly no
chairman. The councils were chaotic with people 'squeezing [and]
elbowing – and where persons of low stature, slip under the arms of
taller ones to gain the front row; – where they all scream and interrupt
each other's speeches; and talk loudly all at the same time, and upon
matters, totally irrelevant to the subject of the debate – such is the
council chamber – such the form of the council!' [37]

One of Vaudreuil's priorities was the well-being of the civilian
subjects of Louis XV. With the British fleet already at Bic he needed to
decide quickly how he would respond to the calls for assistance from
the Canadian settlers along the banks of the river. Everyone had a plan;
many of them involved aggressive counter-attacks aimed at the British
ships. However, as Vaudreuil made clear right away, 'owing to the position of the enemy and lack of provisions', it was impossible to move
a serious body of troops down the river. Instead of waiting for succour
the *habitants* must evacuate. Vaudreuil's commands raced down the
extensive postal network, carried by horse and carriage, typically nine
miles between each post. They ordered old men, women and children
to retreat as far as Quebec. Forage was to be destroyed in the evacuated areas and valuables left behind in caches. Cattle were to be
brought with them, to feed the hungry mouths of Quebec. An officer,
de Léry, was sent to instil the necessary urgency and to arrest those
who refused to cooperate. Two scouts each with three fast horses
would stay behind from every deserted parish to report on British
movements. The young men would form militia units and oppose
enemy attempts to land; anyone capable of bearing arms was to be
included, 'none must be left from 15 years upwards'.[38] Unsurprisingly
many of the *habitants* proved unwilling to abandon their land, cattle,
and crops to the British. It took a lifetime of toil to clear the strip of
land on which families depended for their survival. For generations
Canadians had defended it tenaciously against all comers. Abandonment was a grave decision. Vaudreuil was forced to compromise. On
31 May he acknowledged that 'the difficulties made by the inhabitants

have multiplied to that degree that he has been obliged' to allow them to take to the woods, staying with their possessions and cattle and lying low. Despite this concession he told de Léry to impress upon the *habitants* the gravity of the situation and the importance of denying the British anything that could be of use to them. By early June Vaudreuil was recommending exemplary punishment to those *habitants* who resisted his orders.[39]

De Léry's journal hints at the struggle involved in prising Canadians from their farms. They 'refused to believe' him at first, then told him that they had not started 'seeding the oats' yet and they declined to leave. By 6 June he records that large numbers of Canadians were deserting the ranks of the militia.[40] Back in Quebec, Vaudreuil's letters grew more hysterical. While cursing the unseasonable regularity of the north-east wind that was pushing the British ships closer to the city, he threatened everyone with disciplinary action. He apologized for having to use such language but men and food were required to save Quebec. De Léry had to make it clear to the foot-dragging *habitants* that 'the enemy are out to destroy everything that calls itself Canada'.[41]

The author of one journal was scathing about the evacuation: 'these hurried and ill-judged orders … caused much greater injury to thousands of the inhabitants, than even the enemy could have inflicted upon them – numbers of families were ruined by these precipitate measures – three fourths of the cattle died'.[42] The whole operation was far too hurried; the British ships, of course, had been only the advance guard and had not pushed on towards Quebec. But in the rushed flight supplies of grain and herds of cattle were abandoned. Panet commented that the operation was conducted 'with such a haste that no honour can be given to those who were charged with its execution'.[43] Marguerite Gosselin lived on the tip of the Île d'Orléans on a prosperous farm and had a horde of children. She obeyed orders to evacuate, which turned out to be a 'real nightmare'. 'If it had been more carefully planned,' she wrote, 'we would never have lost our cattle.'[44] Another journalist wrote that 'several of the inhabitants, women and children unhappily perished … Without any means having been previously taken of providing food for their sustenance, boats for their conveyance or places to which they could retire.'[45]

Around Quebec huge preparations were underway to prepare the city for a siege. Montcalm hoped that 'the navigation of the River St Lawrence, often difficult, may afford him time to take those precautions which have been neglected, and might, in my opinion, have been taken beforehand'.[46] He had a large body of soldiers of many different varieties available for its defence. Every kind from the grenadiers of his regular army battalions, who had stood motionless on battlefields in Europe as muskets and cannon tore down their comrades beside them, to young boys with no training, scarcely strong enough to carry a firearm. He had eight battalions of French regular troops, *troupes de terre*, which roughly translates as 'soldiers of the land'; so named because French battalions were raised from certain geographical parts of France. They had been shipped over since the outbreak of hostilities and now numbered in all 3,200 men. There were also full-time colonial soldiers or 'regulars', the *Compagnies franches de la marine*, so called because they were provided by the Ministry of Marine which oversaw the colonies. They were largely recruited in France and answered to Canadian-born officers. They served in Canada for their whole careers and usually settled in the colony when they were discharged. Montcalm calculated that they could put 'at most, fifteen hundred men in the field'. As well as these full-time, professional regulars, every Canadian man was made to serve in the militia. Many nations had some kind of arrangement for raising amateur soldiers in times of crisis. These part-time warriors were generally despised by professional officers all around the world for their inexpert fumbling. But in Canada, despite Montcalm's sneering, things were different. Wolfe himself, the arch professional snob, wrote that 'every man in Canada is a soldier'.[47] Generations of warfare, combined with the tough life of a trapper or hunter, had produced a strong military ethos among all Canadians that was unique.

Canada was vast but empty. Although the European population was doubling every generation, in 1759 it numbered just over seventy thousand people. The prospect of a dangerous North Atlantic crossing, cold winters, isolated settlements, and almost continual war had discouraged mass migration. Nor were conditions suitable for growing a cash crop like tobacco which had financed the population explosions in British colonies like Virginia and Pennsylvania. Montcalm estimated at the beginning of the campaign that 12,000 Canadians were capable of bearing arms. He deducted from this figure those away trapping furs on the frontier and those involved in the movement of supplies by road and boat and estimated that he could muster around five thousand militia. But even if he was able to, it would take too many people away from the land, nothing would get planted and 'famine would follow'. In all he expected to face the enemy with just over ten thousand troops. 'What is that,' he wailed, 'against at least fifty thousand men which the English have!'[48]

Typically Montcalm underestimated his own strength and exaggerated that of his enemy. The British had 20,000 regular soldiers in North America but they were parcelled out in different groups. Wolfe's army was one of these but it was badly understrength; most of his battalions numbering between five hundred and eight hundred men. Colonial levies would be mobilized but the British colonies showed little enthusiasm, especially if the men were to be used outside their native colony. Virginia raised one rather than two battalions, and the other southern colonies did not come close to recruiting their quota of men. In all less than twenty thousand British Americans signed up for the campaign of 1759.

Montcalm would face less than forty thousand men, and these were divided into three major thrusts. The French force was outnumbered but not overwhelmingly so. They had many other advantages too. Warfare in the vast, inhospitable spaces of North America was quite unlike anything that the British had encountered in their campaigns at home or in the Low Countries. Every European soldier was struck by the scale and majesty of the terrain. Bougainville wrote while travelling through the lands above Montreal that 'the navigation is very difficult, but there is the most beautiful scenery in the world'.[49] It was a glorious spectacle indeed, but a logistical nightmare, especially for anyone seeking to invade Canada. Separated by hundreds of miles of virtually impenetrable forest and lakes, each thrust was unsupported and each risked being defeated in detail by French forces operating over internal lines of communications, using familiar routes along rivers that could see huge numbers of men transferred from front to front with great speed. Vaudreuil had summed it up during the winter by saying that if the enemy attempted to attack Quebec they must be defeated quickly, 'a single battle gained saves the colony; the fleet departs, and we return to oppose the enemy's progress'[50] up through Lake George. One British marine officer pondered the challenges of attacking 'so remote, uncultivated, inhospitable a country as that of Canada; where rivers, woods, and mountains break off all communication'. It was a land 'where the very face of nature is set against the invader, and is strong as the strongest barrier; where uncommon heats and cold are in alliance with and fight for the adversary'.[51] And that was in the summer. Between November and March or April all sizeable military operations of whatever kind had to be suspended. Troops fought hard merely to stay alive. During Bougainville's first winter he wrote, 'it is impossible to conceive of a viler sort of weather ... one could not understand how frightful this country is if he has not been here'.[52]

Montcalm enjoyed all the advantages of geography but he was also stronger than he had assumed, even though not every one of his men was available for the protection of Quebec. Montcalm was forced to send three of his eight French army battalions to protect the southern invasion route into the colony, which was threatened by General Amherst from Lake George. Joining them were eight companies of colonial regulars and 1,200 militiamen; about three thousand men in all. He also had to send troops to garrison Fort Niagara to protect the gateway to Canada's vast western lands. For the defence of Quebec, one officer estimated that there were the five battalions of the French army, 'about 1600 men', 'about 600 colonial' regulars and '10,400 Canadians, and sailors distributed throughout the batteries'. New France could also call upon allied groups of Native Americans, from the Christianized Abenaki of St François to the more mercenary distant tribes from the west who joined for money, adventure, and booty. Estimates differ on the number of Native Americans present during the summer of 1759, and no doubt the number fluctuated as they came and went much as they pleased, but the same officer counted '918 Indians of different nations'. Last, there was 'a troop of cavalry composed of 200 volunteers taken from different corps and to be posted promptly wherever the enemy should show themselves, to be attached to the general's suite and to convey orders'. In all he gave the rather precise figure of 13,718 men. The journal comments that

> so strong an army was not anticipated, because it was not expected that there would be so large a number of Canadians ... but such an emulation prevailed among the people, that old men of 80 and children of 12 and 13 were seen coming to the camp, who would never consent to take advantage of the exemption granted to their age.[53]

A witness comments that the *habitants* 'assembled themselves with so much activity and zeal that, on the field, we make up a body of eleven to twelve thousand men'.[54] The people of New France were flocking in unprecedented numbers to help with the defence of their capital.

It was an empire dependent on its capital. Montcalm had told Versailles during the winter, that Canada would fall 'without a doubt' if Quebec did. 'There is not' he wrote, 'a second line any place of strength, any spot having in depot any warlike stores or provisions'. Nor could Canada 'sustain herself by herself and without succours from France', and Quebec was Canada's only port. Montcalm was as clear as Wolfe that it was in front of the walls of Quebec that the decisive clash for domination of the North American continent would take place.[55]

Quebec was derived from *Kebec*, which in the local Native American dialect meant 'narrows'. At Quebec the St Lawrence River rapidly shrinks from being more than ten miles wide to just two-thirds of a mile. Here also the St Charles River joins the St Lawrence and in between the two there is a promontory of land surrounded on three sides by steep cliffs and water and on the fourth by an open patch of scrub known as Les Plaines d'Abraham or the Plains of Abraham. On this natural bastion sat the Upper Town of Quebec. Below it a thin strip of land at the bottom of the cliff was, in some places, around a hundred yards wide and was the site of the Lower Town, a few crowded blocks of buildings. Downriver from the narrows the St Lawrence widens out into a basin, the edges of which are very shallow. Large ships were unable to get close in; Quebec was not a natural harbour.

In 1535 the French explorer Jacques Cartier arrived and immediately realized that this was the place to dominate this vast new continent and, he hoped, the route to China. Large ocean-going ships could penetrate this far but little further, and the river was narrow enough to control who came and went. Added to this the site was almost impregnable. Cartier named the cliff which soared more than two hundred feet out of the river, Cap Diamant or Cape Diamond. It is still easy to see why he chose to spend his first winter in Canada on top of this peak. The small French party held out through a vicious Canadian winter in a little stockade protected by a moat built on top of Cap Diamant, the first European fort in Canadian history. Decimated by scurvy and threatened by Native attacks, Cartier abandoned the site in the spring. Several more attempts were made to settle the area, each of which was abandoned as the failure to find valuable raw materials or the hoped for sea-routes to China meant that the will evaporated to overcome the challenges of distance, climate, and the local inhabitants. A permanent settlement was finally established on 3 July 1608 by the father of Canada, Samuel de Champlain, who landed and built a trading post where the Lower Town of Quebec now stands. He promised his king that Quebec was the gateway to the continent and possession of it would make France the most powerful nation on earth.

The experiment in global supremacy did not get off to a great start. The early town was blockaded and captured without a fight in 1629 by the Kirke brothers, two English corsairs who ransacked the town so that when it was returned to the French in the treaty of 1632 it had to be rebuilt again from scratch. In 1690 when the Acadian town of Port Royal, near modern-day Annapolis Royal in Nova Scotia, fell to an English fleet, it was decided that Quebec needed a wall on its western landward side to protect the town from its only vulnerable approach, on the Plains of Abraham, the raised plateau of rolling ground to the west. A wooden palisade was built, protecting the city from an enemy simply capturing it *coup de main* with the simplest of attacks.

The building work could not have been timelier. On 16 October 1690, thirty-four New English ships arrived off Quebec with around two and a half thousand men on board. They were led by Sir William Phips, an adventurer who had become fabulously wealthy after he salvaged the wreck of a Spanish galleon. These New Englanders were flushed from successes against the French settlements on the Atlantic seaboard and were now intent on conquering New France. Massachusetts had optimistically paid for the expedition on credit to be redeemed with the booty from Quebec. Few, if any, New Englanders had ever seen the stronghold before the expedition; its dominant position must have come as an unpleasant surprise. A messenger was sent to issue an ultimatum to the French governor. The Comte de Frontenac, a proud, aristocratic soldier of France, had to be restrained from hanging him for his impertinence. He gained control of his temper and told the messenger, 'Tell your master I will answer him with the mouth of my cannons!' This message of defiance against the piratical New English seamen became a Canadian motto for the next hundred years.

Phips' assault carried vital lessons for future operations against Quebec. The obvious place for a force to land was along the north shore of the St Lawrence, east of the town on its downriver side. From the St Charles River, which marked the town's eastern edge, the shore-line ran for five miles to the Montmorency River with its spectacular waterfall. In the centre lay the village of Beauport; the Beauport shore offered numerous low lying coves and beaches on which to land men. This is where Phips sent his troops. They were carried from their transports in ships' boats, the sailors pulling hard at the oars. As they waded ashore the New Englanders were harassed by Canadians and allied Native Americans. Both of these two groups were highly skilled in the arts of bush fighting and used the woodland as cover from which to launch lightning attacks. Meanwhile, the larger ships attempted to batter the defences of Quebec with their cannon but came off distinctly second best in their duel with the batteries on shore.

Having landed, the New Englanders attempted to march westward along the Beauport shore towards the St Charles River, force a crossing and storm the town. They never made it to the riverbank. The Canadian and Native irregulars kept up a withering fire from the cover of the woods and so demoralized the New Englanders that they retreated in near panic back to the beaches and onto their ships.

Around one hundred and fifty of them were killed or wounded, while the Canadians suffered nine dead and perhaps fifty wounded. Sickness swept through the fleet and the shortening nights terrified the sailors of the expedition, who imagined being trapped by ice in the St Lawrence. On 23 October Phips and his fleet weighed anchor and made for Boston. They suffered heavy losses at sea on the way back. It would take more than a fortnight and more than a handful of ships and men to take Quebec.[56]

Frontenac knew that his defences would not prove as impregnable against a force armed with modern siege artillery; cannon that could hurl a thirty-two-pound ball at 485 yards per second would brush aside a wooden stockade half a mile away as if it were paper. Work started on modern fortifications but soon got bogged down into a bewildering quagmire caused by shortage of funds and a rapid succession of engineers who all without fail utterly condemned their predecessor's work. Nothing dramatic was achieved until war broke out again with the British in 1744. Louisbourg fell in the summer in 1745 and the government of New France was once again faced with an urgent need to protect their capital. Every able-bodied man from 14 to 60 within forty miles of the city was forced to help with the construction. They built a modern stone wall, with an earth filling, designed to withstand cannon fire. Four half octagonal bastions jutted out from the wall, allowing the cannon on them to produce an 'enfilading' fire – sideways down the length of the wall. At either end the wall was anchored on the top of the cliffs that surrounded the city with another demi-bastion. On the southern end a redoubt was built on the very highest point of Cap Diamant.

It was advanced for North America but war on the continent was changing fast. New forts were being built to the latest European designs. For any fortress to survive the hammering of an artillery bombardment it had to be surrounded by low lying stone and earth walls yards thick arranged in geometric patterns to allow cannon to sweep every angle. Soon North American fortifications would look more like state of the art complexes in Flanders than the old stockades of just a generation before. Quebec never reached this level of sophistication. There were a couple of serious drawbacks. High ground on the rolling Plains of Abraham allowed cannon to be placed that would look down on the wall. Also the cost and effort of completing the landward defences was simply too much. When Britain and France made peace in 1748 Louisbourg was returned to Louis in exchange for Madras in India, which had been captured by a French expedition. The work petered out at Quebec. The all-important ditch with a 'glacis' or gently sloping, raised earthwork to stop artillerymen getting a clear line of sight to the walls was never completed. One observer later wrote that because the walls were 'constructed before any ditch was sunk and the soil is of a slaty rock, the blowing of it for that purpose must undoubtedly shake the whole mass of the works'.[57] Blasting a ditch would have brought the walls down. Instead, a shallow ditch and a glacis seem to have stretched down from the north end for only a quarter of the wall. In addition the fifty-two cannon on the wall were mounted on the flanks of the bastions to produce a lethal enfilading fire at attacking infantry but this meant they could not fire out over the Plains of Abraham directly away from the city.

By the Seven Years War it was widely accepted, especially by the disdainful French regulars, that if a large modern force could get troops to the west of the city and bring their large siege cannon to bear on the wall it would be only a matter of days before they had pounded a breach and poured infantry into the city itself. The 42-year-old Chief Engineer of New France, Nicolas Sarrebource de Pontleroy, described by Montcalm as 'an excellent man' declared that the city 'is not capable of useful defence in case of siege, having neither ditches, nor counterscarps nor covered way, and being dominated by heights behind which there is cover facilitating the approaches'. Bougainville wrote that Quebec 'was without fortifications ... if the approaches to the city were not defended, the place would have to surrender'.[58] Montcalm agreed, a journal relates that 'he was persuaded that an army, which can get near to the walls of a town, is sure, sooner or later to compel its surrender, whatever may be the numbers engaged in its defence; and must in an especial manner be the case with Quebec, which not being fortified, was merely secured against being taken by surprise'.[59] With his usual vitriol for Canadians, he described de Pontleroy's predecessor as Chief Engineer as 'a great ignoramus in his profession (you need only look at his works) who robbed the king like the others'. The defences at Quebec, he wrote, were 'so ridiculous and so bad that it would be taken as soon as besieged'.[60]

Montcalm's simple solution was to do everything he could to stop the enemy seizing the Plains of Abraham to the west of the city. The best way to do that was to stop them landing on the north shore at all. As he had written to Versailles that winter, 'all our hopes depend on preventing the landing'.[61] To this end he erected temporary fortifications right along the Beauport shore, ensuring that Wolfe's men would be unable to simply march ashore as Phips' men had. One French officer recorded, 'Quebec, the only barrier of this colony on the river side, being, from the nature of its fortifications, incapable of sustaining a siege, attention was directed ... to putting it at least beyond the danger of a *coup de main*.' Some work had been progressing over the winter but the news that the British were in the river 'roused the men from their languor'.[62] Montcalm did not let his pessimism erode his determination to prepare Quebec for a siege. He threw himself into improving the defences with huge energy and in the words of one officer, 'made the necessary dispositions for a vigorous defence'.[63] He made his headquarters at the village of Beauport and spent his time inspecting every inch of riverbank with Pontleroy and together they sited cannon batteries, redoubts, and lines of trenches. They both knew that in the open field their part-time soldiers could not face Wolfe's trained killers on equal terms, but positioned behind fixed defences they could be relied upon to stand firm. Also they would be supported by a massive amount of firepower. In all '234 pieces of cannon, 17 mortars, and 4 howitzers' were available to Montcalm and if even some of these could be brought to bear at the critical moment Wolfe's army could be pulverized.[64] Bougainville was more optimistic than his general. Two years before he had written that 'defensive lines ... which three or four thousand men could hold, would ... make the city entirely safe'. Any British attempt on the city would be 'foolish'.[65]

Jean Baptiste Nicholas Roch de Ramezay was the King's Lieutenant (*Lieutenant de Roi*) in Quebec. He was 50 years old, born in Canada and an embodiment of New France's interconnected web of military and trading oligarchs. Since the age of 11 he had campaigned for his king against the Fox in Illinois and the British in Acadia. He was now paid 18,000 livres a year to protect Quebec, or more correctly, the Upper Town. Only a year into the job, he was now about to earn his salary as no other King's Lieutenant had ever done. His account of the siege describes how men hammered stakes into the ground to enclose open areas and placed 'some cannon on the top of the road that leads from the Lower to the Upper Town'.[66] For two weeks thousands of men, the sailors from the merchant and naval ships, regular soldiers and members of the militia, carried, dug, and hacked at the earth. Houses along the Beauport shore were evacuated, barricaded, and had loopholes punched through the walls. Montcalm made it clear that the entire colony would be involved in a supreme effort to ensure its survival; 'the monks, priests, civil officers and women will perform the field labor'. Women were allowed to stay for the time being but Montcalm did not want to feed the extra mouths when the siege began and gave orders that all the 'women, children, magistrates and all those persons that embarrass the defense [were to] be immediately sent to Trois Rivières'.[67] Angélique Renaud d'Avène des Méloizes de Péan was the wife of one of New France's richest, and most corrupt, merchants. She wrote that 'most of the nobles and gentry of Quebec have taken refuge at Trois Rivières or Montreal, but I refused to follow their lead. I will not leave my dear husband.' The beautiful Madame Péan had less to fear than most. François Bigot was entirely smitten with the young woman and, as she admitted, 'my house has been transformed into a veritable fortress because he fears for my safety'. 'Those of an envious disposition,' she continued gaily, 'say that all available resources should rather be used to improve the city's fortifications.'[68] There were other young women rather less fortunate than Madame Péan. Quebec had no less than three nunneries, the Ursuline Convent, the Hôtel Dieu, and the General Hospital. The majority of nuns were of noble birth and the rest were from well to do merchant families. Families paid a huge 3,000 livres for the privilege of installing a daughter in the nunnery so only the wealthy could even dream about joining. This was more than fathers paid in all but the most fashionable convents in France.[69] The nuns would stay through the siege and provide vital healthcare to the wounded. One kept a journal of the summer and

73

describes the flight of 'all the families of distinction, merchants, etc' who were 'capable of sustaining themselves'. They were 'removed to Three Rivers and Montreal, thereby relieving the garrison during the siege'.[70]

Some people stayed, many left. One French officer recorded that 'all persons who could be of no service in the siege, such as ladies and others, were desired to withdraw from the city; this request being considered by most people as an order, was submitted to, but not without reluctance'.[71] In fact, many ignored it; there were certainly women left in Quebec right through the summer. Those who remained helped the soldiers and militiamen as they carried out Montcalm's orders. Two fully armed ships were scuttled in the mouth of the St Charles River to act as forts and block the entrance. A wooden boom was also run across the mouth, attached with chains to either side, to prevent raids by small boats. The two sides of the river were connected by a bridge of boats with either end protected by an earthwork. Beyond them on the Beauport shore work continued 'to line the crested bank from the River St Charles to the Falls of Montmorency with entrenchments'.[72] Every few hundred metres, a redoubt was built containing three or four cannon each, with infantry positions dug in alongside and behind. In all just under forty cannon swept the coastline. In the city itself new batteries were constructed along the waterfront of the Lower Town. These guns, numbering over a hundred in all, would have the absolutely vital task of stopping the British ships getting through the narrows of the St Lawrence and upriver or 'beyond' the town. Once there they could cause havoc with Quebec's communications with the rest of the colony and potentially land troops on the all-important north shore. It was imperative that the British fleet was kept below the town. Just as the Beauport entrenchments covered the French position to the east, the cannon of the town would stop the British opening a front to the west. A French officer noted in his journal that 'batteries were erected on the Quay du Palais, and those on the ramparts, and in the lower town, were repaired, completed, and considerably enlarged'.[73] Four shore batteries called 'Royal', 'King's', 'Queen's', and 'Dauphin's' (the heir to the French throne) were all either built or augmented. As a result, although some defences were built further upriver, in places like L'Anse des Mères and Sillery, 'that quarter was deemed inaccessible'. Houses that backed onto the water had their walls strengthened. Passageways from the Lower to the Upper Town were barricaded. The Scottish Jacobite, Chevalier Johnstone, was given this job; 'I was employed for three weeks upon it with miners and other workmen, to render all the footpaths impracticable.'[74] His work made a direct assault on the Lower Town with a view to storming the Upper a very difficult prospect. Cannon were mounted in small boats designed to harass any ships who ventured into the basin of Quebec. Innovative new ideas jostled for funding. Panet describes 'two boats, armed with four 24 pound cannon', which he says were called *tracassiers*, literally 'harassers'.[75] Monsieur Duclos, captain of the frigate *Chézine* which had brought Bougainville back from France, 'proposed the construction of a floating battery'. It was agreed to and he was given command. Known as *La Diable*, 'The She-Devil', she was described as a 'pontoon of a hexagonal figure; capable of bearing 12 guns of large calibre'. Six 'gunboats each carrying a 24 pounder' were built and each placed under the command of one of the captains of the merchant ships recently arrived in Quebec. Finally, eight small boats were each given an eight-pound gun. All these boats were able to oper-ate in the shallow water off Beauport and would serve 'the purpose of preventing the landing of the English'. An officer records that these boats would 'send bark canoes ahead, which patrolling throughout the night, would be able to give notice of the slightest movement on the part of the enemy'.[76]

Councils of war were held and radical ideas debated. One was to destroy the Lower Town to allow clear fields of fire if the British tried to assault it directly. A diarist says that this plan was dismissed because Quebec was 'in fact nothing if the Lower Town was destroyed'.[77] Montcalm did knock down the odd warehouse to improve fields of fire for his cannon and deny any assaulting force cover as they tried to land but he was against wholesale destruction. 'If the success of the colony could be assured by the destruction of the houses, we should not hesitate,' he wrote to his artillery commander, Le Chevalier le Mercier, 'however there is no point destroying houses and ruining poor people without good cause.'[78]

The Plan of Operations for the army stated that the 'general disposition' of the troops was to 'oppose a landing between St Charles River and Montmorency falls, as well as for retirement behind this river in case the landings were effected'. Troops were spread out along the north shore of the St Lawrence. They were supported by the Native Americans although one diarist points out that 'the savages were dispersed according to their own inclinations, it being found impossible to reduce them to any state of subordination or discipline'. Montcalm ordered his force to 'entrench itself along its whole front for protection against cannon fire, and work will be set about to fortify the places which appear to offer the readiest facilities for landing'. In the city itself he left 800 militiamen, just over a hundred colonial regulars, and all the seamen who had come over with the fleet, perhaps seven hundred men. They manned the all-important artillery batteries which would shut off the upper river.[79]

If the British did try to bludgeon their way ashore, 'no precise directions can be given for such a time. Everything will depend on the circumstances and the manner in which the enemy attacks. The army leaders must apply themselves to use every means to repel the enemy, and not to expose themselves to a total defeat by failing to secure a path for retreat.' If withdrawal became necessary, cannon which were too heavy to drag away in a hurry should be 'spiked', rendered useless by driving a nail through the touch-hole on top of the barrel, so that the British could not use French cannon against them. If the French retreated across the St Charles then that line must be held at all costs; once it was crossed then the weaknesses of Quebec's western fortifications would be exposed. In fact, if the British crossed the St Charles, Montcalm signalled his intention to abandon Quebec, rather than endure a siege. If Quebec was abandoned, the orders warned, 'the colony is in extremis'. However, the tone of the orders was upbeat, and the commanders assured the troops that 'in the situation in which we are, it is the only position we can take. It is both audacious and military.'[80]

As for the town, the command of the garrison in the Upper Town was given to de Ramezay, the King's Lieutenant, and the Lower Town had a subordinate commander because Ramezay 'could not be everywhere at once'. One French officer said there were 'in all about 2000' men in the garrison of the town, 'composed of the Burghers and seamen'. But he claimed that they were 'relieved every four days from the camp'. It is possible that Montcalm tried to keep his troops alert by rotating them through various positions.[81]

For those who were worried about the British braving the cannon fire and pushing through the narrows to probe above the town, the Plan gave contained reassurance. The combination of the town's batteries and the French frigates above the town was being counted on to hold back the British: 'there is no reason to believe that the enemy is thinking of attempting to pass in front of the town and landing at L'Anse des Mères, and so long as the frigates are active, we have at least nothing to fear on that side'.[82]

In this febrile fortnight Montcalm made several decisions that would have a momentous impact on the defence of Quebec and Canada. While he strengthened the fortifications he also planned for defeat. Canada clung to the banks of the St Lawrence. At many places the colony merely stretched inland the length of one farm. Nearly every settlement had river frontage and all the major towns were sited along the river. A gap of 110 miles separated Quebec from the next principal town, Trois Rivières, and Montreal was almost exactly the same distance further upriver. As a result the contingency for defeat was obvious: to withdraw along the St Lawrence. A journal recorded that 'it was doubtful what might be the issue of a battle; after the English had made good a landing, it was determined to construct ovens, all the way up from Quebec to Trois Rivières; and to establish storehouses, and small magazines in different places, for securing a retreat'. Troops were also 'ordered to retain the smallest quantity of baggage possible and to send the rest away into the interior'. Despite Montcalm's insistence that Canada was lost if Quebec fell, he was clearly preparing for continued resistance should Wolfe capture the town, in accordance with the instructions from the French court to keep hold of a scrap of territory no matter how small. One decision in particular was to have a major impact on the campaign. He decided that ships carrying much of the essential supplies for the colony would be moved just over fifty miles upriver from Quebec to Batiscan. This was above the Richelieu rapids, which only very shallow-draught ships could negotiate and only at certain times. Here the ships and stores would be safe from Saunders. It also meant that if Quebec fell, the colony's entire supply of food and powder would not fall with it and there was hope for further resistance. Montcalm's army would be supplied by a regular flow of food and stores that would come in small boats down the St Lawrence from Batiscan to Quebec. It was a long supply line and therefore vulnerable. The danger was that in planning for the aftermath of the fall of Quebec he risked weakening his position and thus hastening that eventuality. His plan for the defence of Quebec now relied on the assumption that he could stop the British from passing the narrows and operating above the town, where they would be able to intercept his supplies.[83]

Having waited in vain for the mighty river to swallow up the British fleet, the French resorted to that other traditional instrument of salvation, the raid and ambush. On 30 May, as so often before in the bloody history of Canada, a party of between two hundred and fifty and three hundred Canadians and Native Americans 'was sent ... to the coast of the Ile aux Coudres to skirmish with the English who had landed there, and to lay in ambush for them under cover of the woods, with which the island was almost wholly overgrown'. A French army officer, with a scorn of their Native allies typical of his class, said that on seeing the British the Native Americans refused to continue 'and the expedition had to be abandoned'. But it seems that a small group of Canadians insisted on pressing on and lay in wait on the island. Three young British naval officers blundered into the trap and triggered the first contact of the 1759 campaign. It was a quick and easy Canadian success. The war party 'killed the horses which they rode, without hurting the riders who they brought away'. The three men were midshipmen, the most junior naval officers, and they had been 'placed as sentinels to make signals when they described any vessels to the southward'. They were brought back to Quebec. Another journal recorded that they were as young as 14. No less than three sources agree that, remarkably, one of the teenagers was a relative of Rear Admiral Durell, probably a grandson. According to Panet they 'were treated honourably' during their time in Quebec where they spoke freely about the British fleet, somewhat exaggerating its size, and of the British expectation that Quebec would fall without too much resistance. Indeed, Panet thought they sounded like 'they considered this operation already accomplished'. After just over a week they were sent further inland to Trois Rivières, to keep them out of mischief but not before they had 'praised the skill of the Canadians for having killed their horses without having harmed them'.

Despite the unorthodox methods of the Canadians and Native Americans they proved on this first foray that they had huge potential as irregular troops, in this instance gaining the first real intelligence about the British fleet. Our scornful French officer refused to be impressed. In his journal he pointed out that the midshipmen told their captors that another 600 men were unarmed and milling about on the beach. He regretted this missed opportunity, writing that they could all have been 'destroyed' by the 'smallest detachment'.[84]

Even so, it was no doubt a morale-boosting success. By the beginning of June a cautious optimism had replaced the panic occasioned by the fiery beacons. A journal recounted that 'by the end of the month [May] the palisades were fixed, the batteries completed, and Quebec secured against a coup de main'.[85] The number of men present for the defence of the city was far greater than people had dared hope for. The walls of the city and the north bank of the St Lawrence bristled with cannon. Supplies of food and powder were sufficient, if not plentiful. In fact, there was an odd feeling of anticlimax. The whole population had believed that the British would land within days of their appearance at Bic. They had thrown themselves into the task of protecting the city but as June plodded on there was no sign of the British and 'the delay ... gave leisure for that ardour to cool'. After all, the Canadians were 'by nature impatient'.[86]

Their desire to meet the enemy stemmed from a conviction that they would beat any British force. Importantly, people believed that Quebec would hold out. The history of Canada, from Cartier's first pathetic attempts to survive the winter, was one of struggle against the climate, the Native Americans, and invasions by land and sea. Time and again grave threats to the colony had been overcome. Quebecers believed that their town was impregnable and had been protected by the Virgin Mary herself against pagans and heretics for hundreds of years.

One myth fast being demolished, however, was that of the impassable St Lawrence. While Montcalm's men dug, built, and sweated under the increasingly warm early summer sun it seemed to them that the north-east wind blew with depressing regularity. This is not entirely corroborated by the more objective logs of the British ships but the British were certainly blessed with fairly benign conditions. The news that the British ships had arrived at the Île aux Coudres 'renewed the consternation, for no doubt was now entertained, that the whole English fleet was closely following'. It was particularly embarrassing for the French sailors: 'our seamen, who had always represented the navigation of the river to be extremely difficult (which indeed the very frequent accidents that befell our ships, gave every reason to believe was true) had cause to blush at seeing the English ships accomplish it, without incurring any loss or danger'.[87] Voices in the colony had for some time demanded manmade defences for suitable points on the river. Despite everyone blaming each other it seems the main reason for these not being put into action was simply the vast cost and considerable logistical effort in building forts and batteries on inaccessible headlands and islands. The French were not totally downcast, however. They knew that the toughest stretch of navigation in the whole river still lay ahead of the British. Although the river was still around fourteen miles wide at the Île aux Coudres, the navigable channel was narrow and ran tight along the north shore, between Coudres and the awesome Cap Tourmente, thirty miles away, with its steep, heavily wooded sides. From here the passage crossed diagonally to the south between rocks, sand spits, and reefs. The ebb tide tears through the passage at up to six knots, even with a light contrary wind it will kick up such steep waves that small boats can be swamped and lost. It was uncharted, had never been passed by a large ship and the French had removed all the navigation marks. It was the final and most formidable navigational hurdle before the fleet reached Quebec. It was known simply as 'the Traverse'.

THREE

Mastering the St Lawrence

FOR DAYS THE SMALL BOATS bobbed around on anchor or crept forward under oar and sail whenever wind and tide permitted. During the halts the sailors leant on their blades, readying themselves for the next burst of activity. In the stern the master took frequent soundings, noted down the results, and used compass and landmarks to fix their position. The current ebbed and flowed under them at a giddy speed of up to six knots. Only men who had crept cautiously around Alderney in the Channel Islands or knew the Bristol Channel would have seen anything like it before. Frequent squalls soaked the crews and the red-coated soldiers and marines tried to wrap the breeches of their muskets in rags to keep their powder dry. Every day they edged slightly further along the channel close to the north shore, but when they ventured too close puffs of smoke would billow out from the treeline accompanied by the sharp crack of a musket. Each attack would provoke a pointless game of cat and mouse as guard boats carrying infantrymen pulled hard at their oars, heading for the shore. But by the time they arrived the shadowy Canadian marksmen had melted further into the thick forest where the redcoats feared to follow.

One man who spent more time in the sounding boats than any other was the master of the *Pembroke*, James Cook. The man who was to become the first European to explore the east coast of Australia, Hawaii and great swathes of the Pacific was 30 years old and a newcomer to the navy. He had grown up in a family of landlubbers, twenty miles from the North Sea in Yorkshire. His father had worked his way up to farm manager and the farmer paid for young James to go to school. After a brief stint as a shopkeeper's boy, he went to sea at age 18. He served Mr Walker, a Quaker from Whitby, who made his money delivering coal from north-east England down to London where a nascent industrial revolution was firing a demand for coal that employed 400 ships a year making the dangerous journey from the Tyne to the Thames. Treacherous enough with GPS, charts, weather forecasts, navigation marks, and engines, the east coast of England was a harsh nursery of seamanship. If Cook could learn how to avoid the East and West Barrow in the Thames Estuary, the sandbanks off Ipswich, the North Sea fogs and the violent squalls he could face any waters in the world. It was a ruthless meritocracy which ensured only the competent survived. Cook became a talented seaman. Walker offered him command of a ship in his late twenties but Cook made a surprising decision. Perhaps driven by a thirst for adventure he elected to join the Royal Navy as a lowly able seaman. War had just broken out with France and Cook would have his fill of action. Within a month his skills were recognized and he was promoted to Master's Mate. He faced the enemy for the first time in May 1757 on board the *Eagle*; she captured a valuable French merchantman but only after a stiff fight in which she was shot to pieces. Skill was prized above birth in the navy, for the same reason as it was on the colliers, and promotion beckoned if he could pass his exams. Cook sat and passed for the position of Master in late 1757. The next year he was in North American waters, Master of the sixty-four-gun ship *Pembroke*. The job has no modern equivalent and was already dying out in Cook's time. Traditionally the King's government had hired ships to fight in times of war. The Master came with the ship to sail it. The officers were gentlemen put on board to fight it. The post had survived into the age of full-time naval ships and it still had responsibility for navigation, pilotage, log keeping, and other technical aspects of being at sea. Masters did not wear uniforms but their high degree of technical know-how made them one of the most important men on the ship even if they lacked the lace of an officer.

The *Pembroke* had supported the operations off Louisbourg during the siege in the summer of 1758. During a trip ashore Cook had a chance meeting with Samuel 'Holland' that was to change his life. Holland was a Dutch engineer and excellent draughtsman. He had been sent to map parts of the coastline. With his skipper's permission Cook set about learning the art of mapmaking. He produced his first chart in the autumn of 1758 and during the winter of 1758/9 together with Holland he tried to build a picture of the St Lawrence from existing, fragmentary French charts found at Louisbourg and the results of their own soundings on an autumnal cruise along the north shore of modern New Brunswick and into the Gulf of St Lawrence itself. Holland wrote years later, 'during our stay in Halifax, whenever I could get a moment of time from my duty, I was on board the *Pembroke* where the great cabin, dedicated to scientific purposes and mostly taken up with a drawing table, furnished no room for idlers'. Together they produced a chart and Holland claimed that 'these charts were of much use, as some copies came out prior to our sailing from Halifax for Quebec in 1759'.[1]

After arriving off Bic, Durell had ordered Captain William Gordon of the *Devonshire* to take with him the *Pembroke*, *Centurion*, *Squirrel*, and three transport ships and press on up the St Lawrence. Cook has traditionally been given all of the plaudits for the pilotage, but although his role was to grow as the summer went on, at this point he was just one of the several masters who all share the credit for providing information about where the channel lay. Men like Hammond, Master of Durell's flagship, the *Princess Amelia*, spent long days in the open boats with sounding equipment. This was essentially a long line with a twelve-pound lead weight on the end. Along the line were coloured markers at intervals of one fathom (six feet), allowing the men to gauge the depth. The bottom of the lead was hollowed out and filled with rendered beef or mutton fat, tallow, which collected a sample of the riverbed. Slowly they developed an accurate idea of the depth of water and whether the bottom was rock, sand or shale.[2]

This advance guard moved up the St Lawrence, feeling their way and praying their anchors would hold through the ebb tide and frequent squalls. The routine of shipboard life continued. The logs went on recording the state of the stores and the frequent occasions on which the ships 'exercised great guns and small arms'.[3] By the afternoon of

8 June 1759 the mighty Cap Tourmente loomed on their starboard bows and they were at the start of the Traverse, the most treacherous part of the St Lawrence. On the ninth the *Devonshire* signalled 'for all boats manned and armed in order to go and sound the channel of the Traverse'. Cook and the other masters, with their mates, plus sailors to row them and soldiers to protect them, spent their time feeling out the bottom of the river with their lead lines. On the tenth Cook in his tiny, neat hand wrote in the *Pembroke*'s log, 'all the boats went a sounding as before'.[4]

To the astonishment of the officers the legendary Traverse was found to be wider than expected. By 11 June it seems that Cook 'returned satisfied with being acquainted with the Channel'.[5] On 13 June the *Centurion* weighed anchor at 1700 hours and three hours later dropped it on the eastern tip of the Île d'Orléans on the far side of the Traverse, becoming in the process the largest ship to have ever passed through it. The final, supposedly impassable barrier to Quebec had been penetrated in less than a week. Buoys were laid and, together with the anchored boats, were used to guide the following ships and the process of getting the rest of the fleet through could now commence.

As the first British ships anchored off the Île d'Orléans some French officers had begged to be allowed to try to take the fight to the invaders. Groups of Canadian and Native American troops were sent out to lie in ambush for British landing parties and met with mixed success. A request was made by François-Marc-Antoine le Mercier, the commander of the artillery around the city, to place cannon on the island. The confused chain of command meant that he was dispatched by Vaudreuil without Montcalm's knowledge.

He took four cannon with him to the Île d'Orléans. It was a small battery but he would have stood a chance of doing real damage to the British ships if he had been able to fire red-hot shot. This was a complicated business. To make the shot red hot the iron cannonballs were heated in a portable forge. A charge of gunpowder was placed in the mouth or muzzle of the cannon and then rammed all the way down the barrel to the breech at the end. Then a 'wad' was put in, made of wood to separate the powder from the red-hot shot which was placed in next after some wet rags to protect the wood and prevent the heat of the shot immediately igniting the powder. Last, the shot was picked out of the forge with a 'scoop' and placed in the muzzle, where it rolled down and came to rest on the wadding. The powder charge was pricked by prodding it through a touch-hole on top of the barrel with a sharp priming iron, more powder was tipped into the touch-hole and then a linstock or portfire, essentially some lit match, was applied to the powder in and around the touch-hole, which burst into flame and in turn ignited the main charge which blasted the shot out of the muzzle of the cannon. The shot could do fatal damage to a wooden ship. As well as the physical destruction of the iron projectile passing through the ship, the heat of the iron shot meant that if it lodged in the hull it would almost definitely start a fire on board. Fire was a dreadful prospect on the wooden ships packed with flammable materials. Many eighteenth- and early nineteenth-century fleet actions were illuminated by an inferno as one or two unlucky ships caught fire and burnt down to the waterline.

Saunders' ships would not face this threat at least. In a bitterly critical tone, one of the leading French journals recounted that 'in the whole corps of artillery belonging to the colony, not one man could be found who was capable of showing the way in which the balls were to be made red hot'. The diarist concluded that the situation was 'almost too ludicrous to mention'.[6] Even so the cannon represented a threat to the ships especially since any damage to the hull or rigging was especially serious when the ship was thousands of miles deep in enemy territory. Le Mercier made his way across to the island arriving on 16 June just in time to witness Captain Gordon of the *Devonshire* dispatching the boats from his vanguard to 'cut out' or capture a French ship that lay in the channel to the north of the Île d'Orléans. Crowded with marines and sailors, the boats rowed towards their prey. Suddenly there was a volley of fierce 'musketry from the shore' and twenty-five canoes emerged from the cover of the island. Native Americans paddled furiously, propelling the canoes at a surprising speed. The young Master and Commander of the *Porcupine* sloop, John Jervis, a promising young officer destined for great things, attempted to bring his vessel into the shallower water and use his fourteen guns to send the Native American attack packing. A sudden dearth of wind left him dead in the water. The sails hung limply and the crew watched impotently as the British open boats clumsily turned around and fled. One boat was unable to escape. The cutter of the frigate *Squirrel* was designed for sailing with two stowable masts. Its small crew would not have been able to row the boat as fast as some of the others, having just one man on each oar, whereas a 'pinnace', for example, had two men straining on the same blade. With hundreds of sailors and troops watching the cutter was overhauled and captured. The crew of eight were taken prisoner and provided the French with valuable intelligence.

The next morning Le Mercier opened fire on the ships. *Centurion*'s log records that she 'received several shot' from the French, which 'cut away a bobstay and the clue of our maintopsail'. Both she and the *Pembroke* kept up a heavy fire on the battery all night but at 0700 hours on 18 June according to Cook's log, 'we and the *Centurion* shifted our berths further off; afterwards the firing ceased'. This first large skirmish in which Native Americans in canoes had complemented the artillery barrage under Le Mercier had resulted in a sharp French victory. It was a potent lesson in the limitations of sailing ships when operating close to enemy shores in variable winds. Although the French lacked the seagoing firepower of the British fleet, if they could utilize their advantage in fast moving, small, oar and paddle powered boats and their large arsenal of artillery they could mount a serious challenge to the control of the water on which any British plan depended.[7]

As the first real blows were being exchanged, the rest of the fleet, further downstream, was following slowly. The weather was getting 'hot and sultry'. In light airs, the gun decks would have been getting uncomfortable to sleep on. On the night of the 22/23 June the tide had ebbed at a stunning 6.5 knots and Montresor's ship, like several others, had dragged its anchor. Luckily the wind was blowing from the east and they could stem their drift. Both Montresor and Knox commented on the great increase in the number of habitations on the banks as the fleet edged past the Île aux Coudres. Knox wrote that there were 'settlements now on each side of us'. The landscape grew ever more dramatic. Knox commented that 'the land [is] uncommonly high above the level of the river'. Another British officer reported, 'towering among the clouds, the most noble and awful ridges of mountains that I ever saw: they give one a highly finished image of the grandeur and rude magnificence of nature'. The woods were thick, green blankets of trees 'of every genus' and the steep valleys that cut through the mountainous rampart often had 'surprising cascades' running down their centre. He also noticed more and more evidence of human settlement: 'The inhabitants have cleared and levelled some few spots around their dwellings, which form a delightful terrace.' The officers had plenty of time to observe the shores because the ships were advancing up the river at a crawl, but Knox reports that 'the reason for our not working up with more despatch does not proceed from any obstructions in the navigation, but in the necessity there is of sounding as we advance; for which purpose, a number of boats are out ahead'. Saunders was taking no chances. Despite the route finding of Durell's ships and the presence of French pilots, each division was still feeling its way.[8] Behind Knox's transport, the 15th Regiment of Foot had taken to their ship's boats to attempt to suppress musketry coming from the banks but a greater threat than the nuisance of the Canadian militia on the banks were still the other ships. A combination of fast currents and light breezes, especially if combined with poor seamanship, was deadly. Knox was involved in two collisions in as many days. Neither, he reported thankfully, with fatal consequences.

Montresor heard that Wolfe, their thrusting young commander, had pushed ahead in the *Richmond* frigate to join the vanguard of the fleet. Wolfe had been bridling for some time and had eventually lost his patience. His frustration can only be guessed at, but anyone who has sat at anchor all day with limp sails drying in the sun, buffeted by a contrary current, can probably empathize. Wolfe returned again to his theme of leaving the larger ships behind. On 19 June he confided in his journal that Saunders was 'running all the great Ships of War in amongst the Divisions of the Transports threatening some danger & a good deal of Disorder, as the Wind blew fresh'. It was the arrival of the news of 'some cannonading from that Island [d'Orléans] on the shipping' that determined him to get up the river and put himself at the very front of the expedition. On 22 June his journal says that he sent his aide-de-camp with a 'memorandum to Mr Durell and inform him that I proposed to go on the next morning if possible'. He also 'enquired what troops Mr Durell had detained and desired they might be forwarded'. Wolfe wanted every man and ship up to the Île d'Orléans as soon as possible.[9]

The next day he boarded the *Princess Amelia* to demand in person that Durell push more ships up the river. Durell acquiesced, sending the two warships ahead and instructing the Captain of the *Richmond* to 'proceed with General Wolfe up the Traverse, and land him when he shall think proper'.[10] There is more than a hint here of frustration with an army officer who clearly did not understand the complexities of the passage. On 25 June Wolfe was again disagreeing with the naval officers over how many ships should be pushed ahead. His journal says that the suggestions of Captain Mantell of the *Centurion* 'nearly drove me into expressing my mind with some Freedom'. Only the 'good sense and management' of Wolfe's good friend, the expedition's Quartermaster General, Colonel Guy Carleton 'averted this'.[11] The growing tension was not helped by soaring temperatures. Knox's journal says again that it was getting 'inconceivably hot' and mosquitoes were 'very troublesome to us'. Such is the remarkable transition from winter to summer in that part of the world. A journey that had begun with sailors risking frostbite now threatened them with sunstroke.

Wolfe demanded that the transports with the troops on board be prioritized. It was midsummer and not a British boot had touched the soil around Quebec. Saunders attempted to mollify his frustrated army counterpart. He ordered the larger warships carrying seventy to ninety guns and drawing more than twenty feet to stay behind and attempt the Traverse in their own time. He 'switched his flag' or moved ship from the *Neptune* to the smaller *Hind*, which proudly recorded in her log that she 'made new pole topgallant masts to accommodate Admiral Saunders for hoisting his flag'. Sadly for the *Hind* the next day he switched again, this time to the *Stirling Castle,* a sixty-four-gun ship which was small enough to push quickly through the Traverse. By the afternoon of the twenty-seventh the *Stirling Castle* was through with three warships and 'several transports'. The log reports that Saunders had left the ship in his cutter, so it is possible that as parts of the fleet passed the Traverse, Saunders was personally racing to and fro, shouting instructions to his captains on how to get the ships through.[12]

The *Goodwill* attempted the Traverse on 25 June. On board Knox and the others were left in no doubt as to the danger of the operation. They watched as 'a trading schooner struck on a rock, near to the place where we first anchored, and instantly went to pieces; the weather being moderate the crew were saved, and some casks of wine'.[13] Knox finally got a look at one of the French pilots who had been lured on board the British fleet by such dirty tricks.[14] The *Goodwill*'s captain, Killick, and this pilot did not get on. The former considered it an insult, the latter, 'gasconaded at most extravagant rate, and gave us to understand it was much against his inclination that he was become an English Pilot'. Knox goes on to describe the pilot's dark predictions:

> The poor fellow assumed great latitude in his conversation; said, 'he made no doubt that some of the fleet would return to England, but they should have a dismal tale to carry with them; for Canada should be the grave of the whole army, and he expected in a short time to see the walls of Quebec ornamented with English scalps.' Had it not been in obedience to the Admiral, who gave orders that he should not be ill used, he would certainly have been thrown over-board.[15]

An hour later the *Goodwill* was in the Traverse, 'reputed a place of the greatest difficulty and danger'. Knox was fascinated by the terrible Cap Tourmente on the north shore, 'a remarkably high, black looking promontory', as the ship glided past on the flood tide. Meanwhile the relationship between Killick and the pilot had not blossomed. 'As soon as the pilot came on board today, he gave his direction for the working of the ship.' A mistake clearly; Killick's word alone was law on the *Goodwill*. The captain 'would not permit him to speak; he fixed his mate at the helm, charged him not to take orders from any person except himself, and, going forward with his trumpet to the forecastle, gave the necessary instructions'. Knox's commanding officer protested to Killick and the pilot 'declared we should be lost, for that no French ship ever presumed to pass there without a pilot'. Killick replied casually, 'Aye, aye my dear, but damn me I'll convince you, that an Englishman shall go where a Frenchman dare not show his nose.' Knox joined the captain at the bows where Killick pointed out the discolorations of the water, ripples and swirls that showed him the best route. Before one gives Killick too much credit for his supernatural ability to see what lay beneath the surface, it is worth remembering that Saunders had placed ships' boats to act as navigational markers. As Knox reported, 'soundings boats ... lay off each side, with different coloured flags for our guidance'. Even so Killick's seamanship is commendable, the product of a lifetime spent in the Thames Estuary. 'He gave his orders with great unconcern' and even 'joked with the sounding boats'. He said wryly, 'aye aye my dear, chalk it down, a damned dangerous navigation – eh, if you don't make a sputter about it, you'll get no credit for it in England'. Having brought the *Goodwill* safely through the channel, which Knox said 'forms a complete zig-zag', he shouted to his mate, 'Damn me, if there are not a thousand places in the Thames fifty times more hazardous that this; I am ashamed that Englishmen should make such a rout about it.' The pilot asked Knox if Killick had ever sailed these waters before; 'I assured him in the negative, upon which he viewed him with great attention, lifting, at the same time, his hands and eyes to heaven with astonishment and fervency.'[16]

Not all the ships were as lucky as the *Goodwill*. At least three ships grounded in the approaches or in the Traverse itself. Bad weather would have wrecked them as certainly as the trading schooner that Knox watched break up. The next day it was the *Lowestoft*'s turn to get through the Traverse. After lending one of her anchors to the transport *Ann and Elisabeth* who had lost all hers during the passage, she was forced to go to the assistance of one sloop and one schooner who both hit ledges. Cargo would have been loaded into the ships' boats and the drinking water pumped over the side. The lightened ships then refloated as the tide rose. The Traverse took three hours to clear. By the end the *Lowestoft* fired a gun to catch their attention and signalled the rest of its division to make more sail and increase speed, seemingly in an attempt to clear the passage before the weather changed. Both on the twenty-fifth and twenty-sixth the onset of evening was marked with 'violent' squalls, 'incessant rain, thunder and lightning'.[17]

At 0400 hours on 26 June Saunders ordered the last division of the fleet to weigh, but they had to anchor again almost immediately. By the afternoon they were ready to take on the Traverse. Montresor commented on the boats moored with flags to mark the route. 'Boats were appointed with red flags and white ones to guide the fleet – directions to keep the red flags on the starboard and the white ones on the larboard sides.' This was exactly as laid down by Saunders before leaving Halifax. In Montresor's blue division the wind turned unfavourable and it was 'obliged to make several tacks within it'. It was a stunning display of seamanship.[18]

The British were ecstatic. Journals, letters, and accounts are virtually unanimous in their praise for the seamen and a swaggering pride in their achievement. One senior officer boasted that although the Traverse was 'reckoned dangerous', the British ships were not only able to sail through it but even did so into the teeth of a 'contrary wind'. He wrote that 'this piece of seamanship surprised the enemy a good deal, for we were perhaps the first that ever attempted to get through in that manner'. He concluded that 'it must be observed that we found the navigation of the river much less difficult than we could expect from the accounts given of it'.[19] A marine officer paid tribute to 'the great abilities, required of a British admiral to steer his squadrons with safety in so intricate a navigation as that of the River St Lawrence, and so little known to Englishmen'.[20] Another officer wrote that 'the French account of the navigation of the river St Lawrence we found to be a mere bugbear'.[21] Another described it as 'an entertaining navigation'.[22] Captain Killick, of course, told Knox that having sailed up all the principal rivers of Europe, 'he esteems the River St Lawrence to be the finest river, the safest navigation, with the best anchorage in it, of any other within his knowledge; that it is infinitely preferable to the Thames or the Rhone, and that he has not yet met with the least difficulty in working up'.[23] It comes across as a bravado born of enormous relief. Interestingly the only person who makes no mention of the navigational feat is Wolfe. His diary and subsequent letters and dispatches to London are all silent on the matter. He was desperately impatient. He had pushed ahead to be in the vanguard of the fleet and clearly regarded Saunders' methodical creep up the St Lawrence as overly cautious. The anonymous 'Family Journal' written by someone close to Wolfe, contains a scathing indictment of the support he received from the navy. In the very last lines of the journal the author writes that the foremost ships could not be persuaded to 'go up to the basin of Quebec' because 'fire ships, rocks and floating batteries had taken such possession of them, that there was an universal tremor among them'. It ends with the phrase 'how much is the General to be pitied whose operations depend on naval succour'.[24] This was a grossly unfair critique of the navy. Saunders had brought hundreds of ships up an unknown and hugely treacherous river, in which one Anglo-American expedition and countless other ships had been lost in the past. It was one of the epics of eighteenth-century maritime history, an achievement that was to help cement Britain's reputation as the world's foremost naval power for centuries to come. Wolfe's total lack of understanding of the sea and his impatience to get his men onto dry land made him a poor commander of an amphibious operation which was dependent for its transport, supply, command and control, and much of its firepower on the ships of the Royal Navy.

Unlike Wolfe and his clique, the French were in no doubt about the scale and importance of the achievement. Bougainville had written two years before with utter certainty that 'the shoals, with which the river is filled, and the navigation, the most dangerous there is, are Quebec's best defense'.[25] Now this certainty was shattered. It was humiliating that, in the words of one officer, 'the traverse, a channel so difficult to cross, if our pilots are to be credited, was cleared without any trouble by the English squadron'.[26] 'It was truly a matter of surprise and astonishment,' reports one journal.[27] Vaudreuil was incredulous, 'the enemy have passed sixty ships of war where we durst not risk a vessel of a hundred tons by night and day'.[28] A French naval officer, de Foligné, who now commanded one of the town batteries, was disgusted with the Canadian seafarers. Having assured everyone that the Traverse would be, 'of itself, a sufficient obstacle to the enemy', they should now, he hoped, 'blush with shame for having waited for the enemy's arrival before finding out to the contrary'. They had 'deceived the court and laid the king's forces and the whole colony open to attack, because they would not take the trouble to get proper soundings'.[29] Montcalm was withering in his journal about French sailors, 'liars and show-offs' who refused to sail in bad weather and insisted that the Traverse was 'an invincible obstacle'.[30]

The French had thought about making a belated attempt to block the channel. A journal records that when it was heard that the British were at Île aux Coudres, the decision was taken to sink 'three large merchant ships' in the Traverse, 'which our seamen boldly affirmed was only 100 feet wide'. Before condemning the three ships, 'the precaution was taken of sending proper persons to sound the Traverse, and ascertain its breadth'. To the astonishment of the entire colony, 'it was found to be nine hundred toises [one mile] wide, and that a whole fleet might pass it abreast'.[31] An 'officer of the port of Quebec' was summoned to explain himself and he admitted that 'it was 25 years since he had sounded the traverse'. Recently, 'he had proposed its being done; he was refused payment of the expenses which would have attended its execution'.[32]

As a result of this revelation, no action had been taken to block the passage. Nor was there much point building a hurried gun emplacement as the British ships would be able to pass outside the effective range of the cannon. It was a devastating admission of ignorance for the colony. The only real mystery is why the French frigates did not attempt to obstruct the Traverse. They would have been able to play havoc with the little open boats with Cook and the other Masters on board. To fight them off larger British ships would have been forced into the Traverse with no preparatory sounding and it would have made the whole operation a lot more dangerous for the British. There is one slightly curious reference to this idea in one French journal which suggests that the frigate captains refused and demanded some kind of security if their vessels were lost, which was not forthcoming.[33] Any active defence of the Traverse would have been better than the dismay and detachment with which the French watched the advance of the British fleet. Any delay, even for just a couple of days, increased the chances of a storm catching the British in a bad anchorage, or of sickness breaking out between the crowded decks. The French had lost a serious opportunity to derail the advance of the British force.

By 27 June in clear weather and a fair breeze, the final division of transports anchored 'within a mile and a half' of the Île d'Orléans. To one of Wolfe's officers, it had been a 'tedious, but pleasant navigation up this vast river, unused to British keels'.[34] It had been anything but tedious to the naval officers responsible for keeping those British keels away from French rocks and reefs but they had managed to do so and now after twenty days the remarkable voyage was over. Ramezay was astonished to see '120 or 130 sails along Île d'Orléans ... among them there were a few Men O'War and frigates to provide support for the invasion'.[35] Nothing like it had ever been seen in the river before. The siege was about to begin.

FOUR

Beachhead

AT FIRST LIGHT a red-and-white chequered flag was raised on the main topgallant masthead of the *Lowestoft*. As it caught the breeze the thud of a cannon demanded the fleet's attention. Saunders had given the order for the landings to commence on the Île d'Orléans. A carefully choreographed marine dance now commenced. From all the ships of the fleet small boats detached themselves and made ready to ferry men and equipment ashore according to a carefully prepared schedule. For the first time in the campaign the specially designed flat-bottomed boats were winched out of the ships' waists and lowered into the water. Four of them were put afloat from the *Richmond* alone. They had been husbanded by Wolfe and Saunders until now, their use forbidden for mundane tasks, so vital were they to the success of the operation. Smaller ships, schooners and sloops, with shallow draughts crept in close to shore. The flat-bottomed boats all rendezvoused at the *Lowestoft* and then made for these small ships where light infantrymen and rangers, carrying the minimum of kit, clambered down the sides of the hulls and sat in tightly packed rows, some of them helping the crew of twelve sailors with the oars. By 0500 hours on 27 June the rangers were splashing ashore on the Île d'Orléans, their muskets raised high to keep their powder dry in case the inhabitants or Native Americans were lying in wait. The men moved quickly off the beach and through the empty village of St Laurent, on their backs they carried only a rolled-up blanket and just two days' worth of food: biscuit and salted meat. Their pouches contained thirty-six rounds of ammunition.[1]

The boats backed their oars to clear the shallows and headed out to the ships where they collected the regular infantry. They would land in strict seniority; the regimental numbers denoted the notional order in which they had been established, the smaller the number the older the unit. Amherst's 15th Regiment of Foot was the senior unit of Wolfe's army and its men would have the honour of landing first. As the flat-bottomed boats picked up the men of the 15th from the *Employment,* a London-based transport, other boats made for *Blackett, Three Sisters*, and *Fortitude* where the men of the 28th scrambled down into them.

It was the start of the largest military operation in North American history. Not only were vastly more ships and men involved on either side than ever before but the total number of soldiers, sailors, Native Americans, townsfolk, and rural *habitants* within a ten-mile area of Quebec represented by far the largest concentration of humanity in North America at that time, outnumbering the biggest city, Philadelphia, with its population of 24,000 by quite some distance.[2]

Previous amphibious operations had relied upon getting the troops to shore in the ships' existing boats, which were small having been designed for tasks like ferrying supplies to and from shore, laying an anchor, or transporting officers to the flagship when summoned. This had put a major restriction on the number of men that could be sent ashore in the first wave. It also tended to mean that they arrived in a disorderly rabble. In the event of a contested landing, success depended on as many troops getting ashore as quickly as possible, ideally in a condition to fight when they arrived. Good generalship, at its simplest, is the ability to deploy as many soldiers as possible, where you want them, at top speed. The flat-bottomed boats could each hold seventy soldiers, vastly more than the biggest of the ships' boats. Two prototypes had been built at Woolwich after a failed amphibious assault on the French coast and tested on the Thames in April 1758. The *London Evening Post* noted that 'on Wednesday last two boats of a new construction, built for landing His Majesty's Forces in shallow waters, were launched, and sailed down the Thames. They ... are rowed by twenty oars, and go much swifter than any other vessels on the river.' The First Lord of the Admiralty, George Anson (a brilliant seaman turned politician who had made his name circumnavigating the globe in the early 1740s in the *Centurion*, with Charles Saunders as his first lieutenant) was watching from a barge and was sufficiently impressed to order as many as could be built within the space of a month.[3] They were now employed on the front line for the first time. Every effort had also been made to maximize the number of other types of shallow-draught boats available to the operation. As well as seventeen purpose-built flat-bottomed boats there were thirteen roomy whale boats, sturdily built and designed to be beached, and cutters, around thirty feet in length, which could be rowed or sailed. There were also 104 small ships that could be used. All together Wolfe could count on 134 small craft of all varieties that could deliver 3,319 men to the landing place in one go.[4] As the boats crossed the mile and a half gap between the fleet and the shore an army officer, a drummer, and a corporal sat in the stern of each alongside the boat's coxswain, who steered. The soldiers sat three or four abreast on benches or 'thwarts' between the rowers. In the bows naval petty officers attached the boats to the side of transports or secured the boats on the shore while the soldiers jumped into the shallows.

Knox and the 43rd Regiment sailed in the white division, which was the first to land its troops. His men were more heavily loaded than the light infantrymen and rangers, with 'knapsacks, tools, camp neces-saries, and 1 blanket of their ship bedding, besides their own blankets, 36 rounds of ammunition … and four days provisions'. Knox would have to forgo some of the luxuries that his rank entitled him to. Wolfe had strictly ordered that the officers 'must be contented with very little baggage for a day or two'.[5] Knox had spent the previous day scanning the shore and as he set foot on dry land his positive impressions were confirmed. Île d'Orléans is a long thin island, 21 miles by 5 miles. Along the centre of the island there is a ridge that runs right along the spine, with a continuous, gentle slope leading down to the river on either side. The farms were, and still are, long thin strips on this slope providing every farm with a river frontage. Indeed, there was hardly a farm or settlement in Canada that was not within yards of the St Lawrence or tributary rivers. Well-built farmhouses tended to be posi-tioned near the water so there was an almost continuous band of settle-ment around the shore with the fields in neat, narrow strips stretching off up the hill behind them. The island appeared 'fertile and agreeable' and the 'delightful country' was dotted with 'pleasant villages' and 'windmills, water-mills, churches, chapels and compact farm houses, all built with stone and covered some with wood and others with straw'. Knox was 'inclined to think we are happily arrived at the place, to all appearance, will be the theatre of our future operations'.[6]

The soldiers were extremely pleased to be disembarking from the crowded ships, on which they had been unwelcome interlopers, and finally set their feet on dry land. John Johnson was the Quartermaster and Clerk of the 58th Regiment. Like most sergeants he was literate but he was unusual in that he wrote an account of the campaign. (The vast majority did not.) He described the land as 'the most agreeable spot I ever saw ... it is a bountiful island and well cultivated, and produces all kinds of grain, pasture and vegetables [and] is full of villages'.[7] The most explicit were the Highlanders. A remarkable song composed by the regimental bard Iain Campbell during the campaign, in his native Gaelic, recounts that, 'we were glad to be on the land,/ each one of us,/ with a good deal of haste/ went into the long boats/ to go to the island of Orleans'.[8]

The island was deserted. The previous day on the south shore Knox had spotted 'the country-people ... removing their effects in carts' and being escorted to a place of safety, far from the British invaders.[9] They crossed the river to the north bank where they sought shelter with friends or relatives. The sheer concentration of British ships caused panic around the Quebec basin, not just on the Île d'Orléans: 'At the sight of so many English ships,' recorded one French journal, 'terror again seized upon the women, most of whom left the town as soon as possible, and retired into the country.'[10]

There was certainly no resistance to the landing. Amphibious assaults are terribly vulnerable when the attacking troops are cooped up in small boats just before landing. Wolfe's men were unable to fire their muskets effectively while afloat and boats full of defenceless men made tempting targets. The French, however, made no move to defend the coast. With such a huge shoreline the Île d'Orléans was impossible to protect while still maintaining their positions along the all-important Beauport shore. Montcalm had to accept that Wolfe would be able to land his army in the area around Quebec. He just had to stop them landing in a place that gave them a springboard for attacking the city itself. The Île d'Orléans was indefensible and Montcalm was content to cede the island knowing that Wolfe would have to make yet another amphibious assault before he could get his forces up to the walls of the city. That next assault, Montcalm planned, would receive a lethal reception.

The night before, on the evening of 26 June, Wolfe had sent Captain Joseph Gorham ashore with forty of his men to scout out the landing place. Gorham was a tough New England ranger who had fought alongside his father and older brother since he was a teenager, protecting the isolated settlements of Nova Scotia against Native American raids. Not encountering any opposition the rangers pushed on to the north side of the island. Here they stumbled upon a large party of the inhabitants who were hiding their valuables in the woods and there was a skirmish. Gorham and his men retreated to the south shore and barricaded themselves into a farmhouse. They had lost a man and when they searched for him the next day they found the corpse 'scalped and butchered in a very barbarous manner'. They followed a grim trail of blood to the water's edge on the north shore and realized that the Canadians had made their escape.[11] It was a first, gruesome signal that the summer's fighting was to be conducted along very different lines to what the men could expect on the battlefields of Europe.

For the moment, though, the British troops were told to conduct themselves according to the European norm. Non-combatants were to be protected; Wolfe issued strict orders that 'no insult of any kind be offered to the inhabitants of the island'. Wolfe also forbade the landing of the numerous bands of women that always accompanied eighteenth-century armies. These soldiers' wives made themselves useful on campaign, doing all sorts of jobs such as laundry, nursing, and cooking, but Wolfe regarded them as a nuisance. He did not want them getting in the way of what could be a sharp fight to get ashore. They would be allowed to disembark only after order had been established.[12]

After landing, the infantrymen marched inland for about a mile and pitched their tents in a long line facing to the north, the direction from which trouble was likeliest. Knox had grabbed the opportunity of having a look around the church in the village of St Laurent, 'a neat building with steeple and spire'. Inside, 'all the ornaments of the altar were removed' and there was a charming note from the local priest addressed to the '"Worthy Officers of the British Army"', begging them 'from their well known humanity and generosity they would protect his church and its sacred furniture, as also his house and other tenements adjoining to it'. In a very Christian gesture the priest concluded that 'he wished we had arrived a little earlier, that we might have enjoyed the benefit of such vegetables, viz. asparagus, radishes, etc etc as his garden produced, and are now gone to seed'. Knox commented on the distinctive tone, 'he concluded his epistle with many frothy compliments, and kind wishes etc consistent with that kind of politeness so peculiar to the French'.[13]

While his officers were sightseeing, pitching the camp, and bringing men and supplies ashore, Wolfe, as always, was pushing forward. Finally giving his curiosity free rein he and a small group of men crossed the island to catch a glimpse of the prize which he had travelled thousands of miles to claim. By his side was one of his most important colleagues: his Chief Engineer, Patrick Mackellar. The 42-year-old engineer was the perfect man for the job. Not only had he served more than twenty years in the Ordnance, the body responsible for the army's engineering and artillery as well as its logistical and technical support, but he had also been stationed in North America from the beginning of the current war. He had accompanied the ill-starred General Braddock on his drive deep into the Pennsylvania backcountry in 1755, where he was badly wounded in the fiasco on the Monongahela. Mackellar's war had not improved. He had been captured while attempting to defend the woefully inadequate fort at Oswego the following year. After languishing as a prisoner in Quebec itself for a few months he was exchanged for an officer of equal rank. He had then accompanied Amherst and Wolfe to Louisbourg where the Chief Engineer had been wounded and Mackellar inherited the role. The French fortress fell and Mackellar was now uniquely qualified for the Quebec job. Not only had he proved his ability to conduct a formal siege in North American conditions but he was one of the few living British men who had actually seen Quebec. He wrote a detailed report on the city, but his strict imprisonment had meant that he had been unable to see the landward walls. He had picked up hints from servants and had seen a copy of an old map. These combined with the 'difficulty they made of our seeing it' seemed to Mackellar to confirm 'that the place must be weak towards the land'. An attack from this quarter 'is the only method that promises success'. Wolfe had so far followed the recommendation in his engineer's report to the letter. Mackellar had suggested seizing the Île d'Orléans and reorganizing there, threatening the whole north bank of the St Lawrence. This, he wrote, will 'probably make the enemy more doubtful where the landing is intended, which may be a very considerable advantage'.[14]

Wolfe had met Mackellar the year before at the siege of Louisbourg and was, at first, unimpressed by what he saw. At the beginning of the Quebec campaign he had written to his uncle saying that 'it is impossible to conceive how poorly the engineering business was carried on' at Louisbourg. The French fortress 'could not have held out ten days if it had been attacked with common sense'. He bemoaned that his engineers were 'very indifferent, and of little experience; but we have none better'.[15] It was not the first time Wolfe was unkind in his judgement, nor would it be the last time he would be forced to revise it.

Mackellar's diary for June 1959 reports that 'while the troops were disembarking, the General went to the point of Orleans with an escort'. Wolfe, Mackellar, and a company of rangers walked along the road that circles the island and after six miles arrived at the western tip. There Wolfe finally saw Quebec for the first time. From that vantage point Quebec looked spectacular, as it still does. The cliffs are clearly visible, about four miles away across the basin. To the south of the town the narrows can be distinctly seen, with steep wooded hills on either side, looking almost like a gorge. Mackellar would have pointed out the landmarks, identified the massed batteries, and also explained the difficulty of assaulting the Upper Town from the Lower. Quebec looked impregnable enough but Wolfe must have prepared himself for that. What he had not gambled on was the scale of the French defences that stretched along the north shore of the St Lawrence. Mackellar wrote that he and Wolfe 'saw the enemy encamped along the North shore of the basin in eight different encampments, extending from the

River St Charles to within a mile of the Falls of Montmorency, and the coast fortified all along'.[16] The author of Wolfe's 'Family Journal' writes that 'from the falls of Montmorency to Beauport (which is four miles) the banks are very high and steep'. While 'from Beauport to the river St Charles the banks are low and level the shore winds here in the form of an amphitheatre'. But this ideal landing place was 'deeply entrenched, and batteries of cannon at small distances for the whole way'.[17] Wolfe reported to London that 'we found them encamped along the shore of Beauport ... and entrenched in every accessible part'.[18] His heart sank. He would later describe it as 'the strongest country perhaps in the world to rest the defence of the town and colony upon'.[19] Both he and Mackellar also noticed the small gunboats and floating batteries, providing more mobile firepower.

While crossing the Atlantic and sailing up the St Lawrence Wolfe had come up with a plan of operations. He had lightly assumed that 'to invest the place and cut off all communication with the colony it will be necessary to encamp with our right to the river St Lawrence, and our left to the river St Charles'. This meant landing on the Beauport shore fighting 'a smart action at the passage of the river St Charles' and then surrounding the town on the landward side. This plan, like so many others, was predicated on the total inactivity of the enemy. Disobligingly the French commander had fortified the Beauport shore to such an extent that any landing would have to take place in the teeth of a terrible crossfire. Wolfe had written to his uncle that if he found the enemy was 'timid, weak, and ignorant, we shall push them with more vivacity'. If, however, 'I find that the enemy is strong, audacious, and well commanded, I shall proceed with the utmost caution and circumspection'.[20] In that case the best he could hope for was to pin down as many defenders of Canada as possible and thereby limit the number of men that General Amherst would face on his push north towards Montreal. From his first view of the dispositions of the enemy it looked decidedly like the latter scenario was more likely.

Later in the summer Wolfe would write in his report to the Secretary of State, William Pitt, that 'the natural strength of the country, which the Marquis de Montcalm seems wisely to depend upon', had presented him with 'obstacles' which were 'much greater than we had reason to expect, or could forsee'. It was abundantly obvious as he and Mackellar peered through their telescopes and beheld the sheer scale of the trenches, bastions, and batteries and also the numbers of defenders that the French were in a 'very advantageous situation'. Stunningly, Wolfe, hitherto so eager to get to grips with the defenders of Quebec, even admitted in the report that 'I could not flatter myself that I should be able to reduce the place.'[21] His sudden pessimism demonstrated his inexperience as a commander. Word seems to have spread quickly throughout the army. Knox wrote in his journal that he had heard about the strength of the enemy position and that the French are employed 'in adding every kind of work, that art can invent, to render it impenetrable'.[22] It is interesting that even the French journals seem to have got wind of the rumours in the British camp. One goes so far as reporting that 'we have since learned that as soon as he [Wolfe] had taken an exact reconnaissance ... he did not conceal from his principal officers of the army who accompanies him, that he did not flatter himself with success'.[23] The only man on the French side who was not cheered by these rumours was Montcalm; ironically, he was equally disconsolate. 'It seems like everything points to failure,' he wrote in his journal as he wrestled with the lack of munitions and the slow pace of constructing his fortifications.[24]

'After taking a full view of all that could be seen from this place,' Mackellar reported that he and Wolfe 'returned to St Laurent'[25] where the army was disembarking and making camp. The hill above the village was seething with activity. Men cleared trees and stumps, others dug trenches for latrines and quartermasters marked out spaces on which their regiments would camp. Parties of men scoured the countryside for fresh hay; Knox reports that they returned with 'excellent hay to lie upon'.[26] That was not all, days later he comments on the 'great quantities of plunder, that they found concealed in pits in the woods'.[27] The arrival of thousands of men, with a sizeable hardened criminal minority, was like a plague of locusts. Not a cupboard, shed, or even suspiciously fresh piece of earth was left unsearched. Meanwhile, the hillside was alive with the noise of hundreds of mallets tapping away at pegs. Neat rows of tents were appearing on the south-facing slope. The British army always pitched them according to the same pattern. The comforting and familiar shape of the camp attempted to create some normality for soldiers who found themselves in utterly alien surroundings. The army would camp 'in one line', Knox tells us, 'with our front to the north-ward'.[28] On the northern edge of the camp were around five tents per regiment to house the quarter guard, a security force which men would rotate through to provide a twenty-four-hour watch. A wide avenue separated them from just over ten 'Bells of Arms', painted tents where the men's muskets and bayonets were stored. Wolfe ordered his men not to leave any loaded muskets in these tents as it was known to cause 'frequent mischiefs [sic]'.[29] Behind these were neat double streets of tents for the men of the regiment. The dwellings of officers, non-commissioned officers, and the men were naturally strictly segregated. All the tents were dipped in salt water to stop them getting mildewed but when they eventually reached the end of their useful lives they would be turned into trousers and gaiters for the soldiers. Privates slept with comrades of their own rank, usually six to a tent, but Wolfe had ordered the day before landing that 'as the months of July and August are generally very warm in Canada, there are to be no more than 5 men to a tent, or if the commanding officer likes it better and has camp equipage enough he may order only four'.[30] Most of the officers slept alone but only because they were forced to buy their own tents. The most junior officers, struggling to survive on their tiny salaries, slept two to a tent.

Behind this mass of canvas were the tents of the majors and lieutenant colonels, closest to the river. Each regiment was easily identifiable, their uniforms and equipment bore their distinctive colour. The linings of the men's jackets, the drums, the colours the regiment carried in battle would all be in this colour. White was the so-called 'facing colour' of Kennedy's 43rd. Knox wore white cuffs and had white facings on his red jacket. The little camp colours that fluttered above their tents were white. These were little flags, eighteen inches square, on which was also emblazoned the number of the regiment. They were flown on poles that the regulations very precisely specified were to be seven feet six inches long except those by the quarter guard which were to be nine feet tall. They were erected by the Quartermaster to mark out where the tents should be pitched and from then on distinguished the regiment from the others in the encampment. The Bells of Arms were painted in the facing colour too and emblazoned with the royal cipher, the crown, and the number of the regiment.

Throughout his career Wolfe had been notably conscientious. His professionalism had won him many admirers in a peacetime army in which units were often left to go to seed. He had always insisted on strict discipline and sartorial correctness from his men. But he was just as hard on officers. He took the patriarchal duties of leadership very seriously indeed and expected his fellow officers to do likewise. In his writings on military life, gathered together and published years later, there are constant reminders to subalterns to pay attention to the welfare of their men. Much of it reads like a very modern manual with the emphasis on leading men into battle rather than driving them. When it came to setting up camp Wolfe insisted 'that all colonels and commanding officers see their regiments encamped before they quit them: and all captains and subalterns to see their men be encamped before they pitch their own tents'.[31] It was an influential work in the late eighteenth and early nineteenth centuries, read by young men desperate to learn their trade in the absence of any comprehensive training.[32]

From the road Wolfe and Mackellar would have been able to get a very good sense of the size of the army. The larger regiments like Fraser's Highlanders or Webb's 48th had many more tents than the understrength 15th or 28th. Wolfe wrote to his uncle just before entering the St Lawrence and said quite plainly that 'the army under my command is rather too small for the undertaking'. However, he believed it was 'well composed'. The troops were 'firm' having been 'brought into fire' at the siege of Louisbourg the year before.[33]

These regiments were the basic building blocks of the British army. Bigger units, such as brigades, existed only as ad hoc tactical formations. The regiment recruited the men, trained them, clothed, armed, and disciplined them and occasionally even paid them. Each one had a colonel at its head. Colonels had once literally owned the regiment, paying for its recruitment and weapons and hiring it out to the crown. By the eighteenth century a prolonged assault on this ramshackle late medieval system by Georges I and II had modernized the British army and the colonels' role had been circumscribed. By 1759 they tended to be senior army officers, and occasionally important politicians, who kept an eye on the regiment on behalf of the crown. It was very rare for one of these colonels to command a regiment in the field. Instead lieutenant colonels or even majors would lead the unit on campaign, where they were known as battalions. A few regiments had second or even third battalions. Two of Wolfe's battalions belonged to the same regiment, the 2nd and 3rd Battalions of the 60th Royal American Regiment. Traditionally regiments had simply been known by the names of their colonels. During the 1740s the regiments had been given numbers which, in theory, reflected their seniority. Numbers and colonels' names were interchangeable throughout the 1750s, although technically the number had become the official method of labelling the regiment.

Nine battalions had disembarked and were putting up their tents; one, the 3rd Battalion of the 60th Royal American Regiment (the 3rd/60th), had stayed on board the ships to give Wolfe the option of striking a blow at another point on the St Lawrence. Wolfe also had a force of marines. Lieutenant Colonel Hector Boisrond commanded twenty-five officers and 577 of these sea soldiers. There could have been as many as a thousand others divided up between the naval ships. They hung their hammocks between the officers and the men, guarded the supplies of rum and the door to the captain's cabin. Serving at sea prevented them from becoming fully effective soldiers. Crack infantrymen had to be able to run unthinkingly through a set of complicated drills for marching, loading and firing their muskets. Drill was practised again and again until it was second nature. At sea opportunities for this kind of training were limited. There was neither the space nor the numbers to replicate training on land. These marines did, however, represent a reservoir of semi-trained manpower which could free up army units for other duties. Wolfe feared that the shortage of regular troops meant that he could well be forced to stand them in the line of battle. To prepare for that eventuality orders in Wolfe's army frequently included instructions to the marines to 'be out at exercise as often as they conveniently can'.[34]

Alongside the regular infantry Wolfe had a force of rangers. These were Anglo-American colonial troops who had been recruited from frontiersmen, who, it was hoped, would have the necessary skills to challenge the Native Americans in irregular warfare. Unlike Canada the British colonies in America were not brimming with hardened backcountry men. Anglo-Americans were farmers and tradesmen, not hunters and trappers. Perhaps as a result, the rangers had rarely delivered on some of the more extravagant promises of their advocates. Wolfe was utterly dismissive of his rangers, full of a regular officer's contempt for his more unorthodox colleagues. The year before he had watched them in action and wrote that 'the Americans are in general the dirtiest most contemptible cowardly dogs that you can conceive. There is no depending on them in action. They fall down dead in their own dirt and desert by battalions, officers and all. Such rascals as those are rather an encumbrance than any real strength to an army.'[35] The following year had not given him cause to adjust his rather unambiguous position. He wrote from Louisbourg before departing for Quebec that he had 'six new raised companies of North American Rangers – not complete, and the worst soldiers in the universe'. To Pitt he wrote that 'they are in general recruits, and not to be depended upon'.[36] Like so many other British officers sent to North America Wolfe underestimated both the threat posed by the Canadians and Native Americans and the potential utility of irregular troops to combat them. The siege of Louisbourg had largely been a conventional, European-style campaign with limited involvement by the Native troops. The forests, rivers, and hills around Quebec held very different challenges.

On leaving Louisbourg Wolfe had divided his army into three brigades each commanded by a brigadier general. He had written to his uncle describing them as being 'all men of great spirit'.[37] But it had not been his choice of team. When he had been given command of the expedition Wolfe had rather petulantly demanded that he should appoint these three key officers. He had written to the commander in chief of the British army, Lord Ligonier, saying that unless, 'he would give me the assistance of such officers as I should name to him he would do me a great kindness to appoint some other person to the chief direction'. He attempted to usurp London's power of appointment because of his experience at Louisbourg the summer before. He blamed the lack of certain key people as the reason for the length of time it had taken to capture the French stronghold. He wrote that 'so much depends upon the abilities of individuals in war, that there cannot be too great care taken in the choice of men, for the different offices of trust and importance'.[38] But as so often London was not prepared to surrender its vital powers of patronage to the commander in the field. It was one of the few ways in which the high command could influence the course of a campaign before the advent of telegraph, steamships, and railways. Wolfe moaned in a letter that his demand 'was not understood as it deserved to be'.[39]

But he had little cause for complaint. Two of his three suggestions had been acceded to. One of them was his second in command, Robert Monckton, who was six months older than his commander. Monckton was the second son of the 1st Viscount Galway and had joined the prestigious aristocratic bevy of the 3rd Foot Guards as a boy of 15. Like Wolfe he had fought at Dettingen and he had seen action at Fontenoy as well. He had entered the House of Commons in 1752 and his strong political connections may have helped gain him a command in North America where it was clear that war could not be long avoided. When hostilities did break out he moved swiftly against two French forts on Chignecto Isthmus, Beauséjour and Gaspereau, which he captured in June 1755. It was the only real victory for British arms in three barren years of failure.

That summer Monckton carried out his orders to forcefully remove French-speaking Catholic Acadians from modern-day Nova Scotia after their refusal to take the oath of allegiance to King George II. France had ceded Acadia to Britain at the Treaty of Utrecht in 1713 but the loyalties of the French settlers had remained understandably Francophile and their new British masters lacked the means or the desire to grasp the issue and coerce their allegiance. With the outbreak of war in 1755 and the arrival of troops from Britain the Governor of Nova Scotia finally had the military means to solve the problem by a wholesale removal of the settlers. Monckton's men burnt villages, rounded the inhabitants up and herded them on board ships which transported them to the British colonies on the Atlantic coast or back to France. Some Acadians made their way to Canada where their harrowing tale of ethnic cleansing put iron into the souls of the Canadians, who now doubly feared the consequences of defeat. Some Acadians made their way to the French colony of Louisiana where their name would eventually be corrupted and become Cajun.

Monckton had gained the reputation as a serious, efficient professional. Wolfe seemed genuinely pleased to have him as second in command and wrote to him that 'I couldn't wish to be better supported, your spirit and zeal for the service will help me through all difficulties – I flatter myself that we set out with mutual good inclinations towards each other, and favourable opinions. I on my side shall endeavour to deserve your esteem and friendship.'[40]

The most junior brigadier was also the oldest. James Murray was 39 years old and had soldiered for well over half his life. He was short, his eyes burnt brightly as if with a constant grievance and he had a fiery temper. He and Wolfe had known each other for some time and that winter Wolfe requested that Murray command a brigade on the St Lawrence expedition. He was the fifth son of Lord Elibank but his aristocratic family had harmed rather than advanced his career thanks to some impolitic choices made by his brothers. Two of them had embraced the cause of the House of Stuart and ruined the family reputation. Murray's family was one of many throughout Britain which had been split down the middle when in 1688 the Catholic Stuart King James II had been forced from the thrones of England, Ireland, and Scotland by his nephew and son-in-law William of Orange. Ever since then he and his male descendants had been barred from the throne and had launched a series of violent attempts to press their claim. Brothers had faced each other across the field of Culloden, the last stand by the Jacobite cause in Britain which saw hundreds of stunningly brave Highlanders slaughtered on a sleet-blasted moor outside Inverness in April 1746.

Wolfe had been at that battle and had stayed on afterwards as part of an army of occupation. Many of the men fighting under him at Quebec had served with the rebels or had family members who had. Murray's brother was a close adviser to Charles Edward, the mercurial Bonnie Prince Charlie, the grandson of James II. Murray believed that his brother's treason had stalled his career. He had joined a Scottish regiment in the Dutch army at the age of 15 and regarded it with pride as the tough crucible of his professionalism. He liked to boast that there he had 'served in all ranks except that as a drummer'.[41] He had enrolled in the British army and had served on the ill-fated Cartagena expedition in 1740. The disease that tore through British ranks helped Murray by clearing the next few rungs on the ladder of advancement and he returned a captain and still only 20 years old. He campaigned in the West Indies, Flanders, and France and by the early 1750s was a lieutenant colonel in the 15th Regiment. The size of the British army meant that most officers knew or knew of each other. Wolfe referred to Murray when they served alongside each other on the Louisbourg campaign as 'my old antagonist', possibly because of a falling out in Scotland in the 1740s or an altercation after the failed amphibious operation against the French town of Rochefort, the post mortem of which had divided the officer corps. However, Wolfe praised Murray during the Louisbourg campaign, writing that he 'acted with infinite spirit. The public is indebted to him for great services in advancing by every method in his power the affairs of the siege.'[42]

For his final brigadier Wolfe had requested the Yorkshireman Ralph Burton, commanding officer of Webb's 48th Regiment. Like Murray and Monckton he was a lifelong, professional soldier, although not nearly so well heeled. Both the place and exact date of his birth are unknown but he was an old friend of Wolfe's and had served in North America from the beginning of the current war. At Monongahela he had been wounded, unsurprisingly given that only six out of twenty-four officers of the 48th had survived the battle unscathed. Lord Loudoun, a previous commander in chief in North America, had written of him: 'Burton I did not know before, but he is a diligent sensible man, and I think will be of great use here.'[43] Wolfe valued his professionalism; his 'Family Journal' describes him as 'a good officer, and is esteemed a man of spirit and sense'.[44]

Instead of Burton, Wolfe was given a very different man altogether. A man who stood at the very socio-political zenith of the oligarchic British state: George Townshend. No man outside the Royal Family had a more illustrious name or connections. George I himself had been one of the sponsors at his baptism in 1725. His great uncle was the current Prime Minister, the Duke of Newcastle. His grandfather, Charles 2nd Viscount Townshend, had been one of the chief architects of the Georgian Whig supremacy in the early eighteenth century that had established forty years of unassailable one-party rule. The 2nd Viscount had been the closest ally of the man who had become Britain's first Prime Minister, the mighty Sir Robert Walpole. They were so close he had even married Walpole's sister. One of Townshend's uncles had been an MP; the other was still one, as was he and his younger brother Charles, who would become Chancellor of the Exchequer.

Unlike his brother, George had chosen a predominantly military career, with politics as a sideline. In 1743, age 19, having breezed through Eton and Cambridge, he went on a tour of Europe which he interrupted to join the British army in Flanders as a gentleman volunteer. He saw action at Dettingen and possibly Fontenoy. His regiment was summoned back to crush the Jacobite uprising in 1745–6 and he was present at Culloden, alongside his future commanding officer, James Wolfe. He returned to Europe in the privileged role of aide-de-camp to George II's son, the Duke of Cumberland. He saw yet more action at the battle of Laffeldt on 21 June 1747 and was given the honour of carrying the dispatch back to London, which by tradition conferred an immediate promotion. As well as receiving a captaincy in the 1st Foot Guards he was elected to the House of Commons to represent Norfolk. His military career had been brought to an end not by the onset of peace in 1748 but by disagreements and a full falling out with Cumberland. The Hanoverians never forgot and rarely forgave. Townshend resigned from the army in 1750 finding that Cumberland had not only vetoed any promotion for him but also for his youngest brother Roger.

Cumberland had fallen from grace and been removed as commander in chief of the British army after a catastrophic defeat on the Continent in 1757. Townshend meanwhile had been establishing friendly relations with the rapidly ascending politician William Pitt. They shared a belief in placing the defence of Britain in the hands of the militia rather than expensive regular troops. Pitt, now Secretary of State for the Southern Department, one of the most powerful jobs in government and one which gave him responsibility for North America, ensured that Townshend was reinstated into the army in May 1758 with the rank of Lieutenant Colonel and the job of aide-de-camp to George II. Later that year Pitt helped to secure him a job on the Quebec campaign.[45] The gossip and prolific letter writer Horace Walpole wrote that, 'the expedition, called to Quebec, departs on Tuesday next, under Wolfe, and George Townshend, who has thrust himself again into the service, and as far as wrongheadedness will go, very proper for a hero'.[46]

Wolfe sent a distinctly ungenerous note to Townshend on his appointment. There was some very faint praise: 'such an example in a person of your rank and character could not but have the best effects upon the troops in America and indeed upon the whole military part of the nation'. There was condescension: 'what might be wanting in experience was amply made up, in an extent of capacity and activity of mind, that would find nothing difficult in our business'. This was more than mildly offensive to a man who had stood on more battle-fields than Wolfe himself. There was an attempt to play the role of inti-mate but stern commanding officer: 'I persuade myself that we shall concur heartily for the public service – the operation in question will require our united efforts and the utmost exertion of every man's spirit and judgement.'[47] Wolfe was clearly not pleased by having this 'polit-ical general' foisted upon him. It is true that Townshend's military experience had mainly been in staff jobs, and he had spent limited time actually commanding units. But Wolfe, who had served on the staff of a general, ought to have known better than denigrate Town-shend's experience. Furthermore to resent a man for advancing swiftly through political connection is curious for Wolfe whose entire career was shaped by his father's influence and those of powerful mentors, not least the son of the King, the Duke of Cumberland, but also Lord John Sackville, the colonel of the 20th Foot which Wolfe had commanded as Lieutenant Colonel. Wolfe wrote to the latter in syco-phantic terms and never hesitated to bring friends to the notice of this powerful patron. Wolfe was no radical, he did not seek to change the rules governing advancement in the eighteenth-century army; he was just piqued that someone else was better placed to take advantage of them.

Townshend and Wolfe had shared the quarterdeck of the *Neptune* from Portsmouth to the St Lawrence. Their journals, however, remain distinctly silent on the subject of the other. It is likely that as the troops landed on the Île d'Orléans the relationship between the two men was at best, formal.

At 1400 hours of the day of the landing the gentle easterly breeze suddenly strengthened and veered violently. It seemed like the prayers of the French and Canadians might be answered. Within minutes the ships were hit by a full westerly gale. Montresor says vividly that it 'rose with great violence together with a great swell which occasioned almost all the fleet to drive from their anchorage and running foul of one another'. He remembers it lasting between three and four hours, during which time, 'there was nothing but cutting of cables – ships running one against the other, others driving and bearing away before the wind in order to run aground on the island of Orleans if possible which several ships were obliged to do'.[48] Anchor cables parted, others were desperately jettisoned by their crews as the anchors dragged or loose ships threatened to collide with them and drive them ashore or tear away rigging. In a letter to his father Montresor wrote that 'several vessels lost their masts'.[49]

Small boats, heavily loaded with stores for the landed army, were caught in the open. Many were swamped by the waves or driven inexorably into the shallows, their rowers unable to combat the gale. The crews of the warships worked quickly to 'strike' or dismantle their exposed yards and topmasts and then, where possible, sent men to the transports to help them avoid destruction. The transports were particularly vulnerable having fewer sailors on board than the men of war. The log of the *Lowestoft* gives us a glimpse of the pandemonium. Early in the gale she was hit by a 'transport that came foul of us' and tore away her 'gibb boom sprit sail yard', and one of her catheads, used to secure the anchor when raised (often decorated with the face of a cat), which sent their best anchor to the bottom. But there was still more damage as the afternoon wore on; two hours later she 'came foul of another transport which carried away our spare anchor, larboard main chain and our barge cutter, and one flat bottomed boat, all lost'. At 2200 hours a schooner drifted onto the *Lowestoft*'s anchor cable and then got entangled with her, ripping away some timbers from the outside of the hull and the hand-rails around the most forward part of the ship. The schooner lost her mast in the encounter. It took an hour and a half to separate the two ships.[50] The Third Lieutenant of the *Diana* recorded 'hard gales' in his log and reported 'a great deal of damage done among the shipping' especially the loss of 'yards and topmasts'.[51]

The damage could have been catastrophic. Countless amphibious operations throughout history had been destroyed by storms which grateful defenders attributed to divine intervention. The expedition suffered real damage but it was not terminal. *Pembroke*'s log reports that 'in the height of the gale seven sail of transports parted from their anchors and run on shore upon the island'. Wolfe's journal agrees that the wind 'drove several ships on shore'.[52] All but two seem to have been refloated. The journeys of the vulnerable boats packed with troops, most of whom could not swim, were immediately suspended according to Wolfe's 'Family Journal'. It records that 'at this time the debarkation of the army was not completed; by good fortune none of the troops were lost; the remaining troops landed the succeeding day'. The loss of a few empty transports, and damage to many others, was unimportant. Several accounts mention the loss of anchors, which would limit shallow-water operations. One says that the storm caused 'great damage to many of the transports; they lost above ninety anchors and cables'.[53] But the real blow to the expedition was the loss of many of the small open boats and flat-bottomed craft. Some had been swamped, others had been washed ashore and their fragile frames stove in on the rocks. The *Pembroke*'s log says that 'several of the flat bottomed boats and others belonging to the transports broke adrift and drove on the south shore, and was afterwards burnt by the enemy'.[54] The engineer Mackellar, who had accompanied Wolfe to the end of the Île d'Orléans that morning, wrote in his journal that, although there was a 'good deal of damage among our transports ... the only loss we felt sensibly was that of our boats, which affected our motions throughout the whole campaign'.[55] Other reports all agree that the loss of flat-bottomed boats was potentially very serious.

Wolfe seems to have regarded the unfortunate episode as yet another example of naval incompetence. Despite the heroic efforts of Saunders' men to keep the vast majority of the ships from running aground Wolfe, in his journal, criticizes the navy. He described a 'multitude of boats lost and strange neglect of the men-of-war's crews'.[56] It is almost impossible to believe that the naval crews had showed neglect. On the contrary it is almost certain that a greater disaster was avoided only by the attention and skill of Saunders' sailors. Saunders himself wrote to the Admiralty telling them that he had sought to give the transports the 'best assistance in my power'.[57] Given his extremely impressive record both before and after the gale it is very likely that he spoke the truth.

The French were euphoric as the gale tore down the St Lawrence valley. The first reports in Quebec were that there had been huge losses. Montcalm wrote in his journal that he hoped the British fleet would be badly damaged. He noted bitterly that a French fleet would have 'perished' in such conditions.[58] When 'the truth came to be ascertained' reported a diarist in Quebec, and it appeared that the only damage was 'two small vessels wrecked, and five or six of the same size driven on shore' which 'were easily pulled off', there was enormous disappointment. The diarist bemoaned that, 'if the gale of wind had lasted only one hour altogether, perhaps two thirds of the English fleet would have been destroyed'. Apart from the fickle wind he blamed the French leadership. He wrote that there had been 'upon this island 1200 men, Canadians and Savages, who undoubtedly might have been extremely troublesome to the English during their debarkation, and particularly whilst the tempest lasted', because the British 'were in a state of disorder and dismay'. However, the force was no longer there thanks to orders, 'sent the preceding night from the Marquis de Vaudreuil for it to evacuate the island and pass over to the Beauport coast'. An equally good opportunity was missed, 'in not having kept upon the South Shore 3 or 400 Savages, who remained in Quebec, where they did nothing but create disturbances and who might with the greatest ease have destroyed vast numbers of the English left upon the shore, in consequence of the stranding of their vessels upon the coast'.[59] A British account hints at guerrilla activity that was progressing as the storm caused havoc among the fleet, recording that 'a ranger killed and scalped, and a stake drove through his body'.[60]

Montcalm had no intention of fighting a guerrilla war of hit and run. He regarded operations involving the Canadian irregulars and Native Americans as worthless and beneath his dignity. He was determined to wait in his fixed positions and let Wolfe break his army on them. Yet again, however, this conservatism had caused him to miss an opportunity to strike at the British when they were vulnerable. The French would not remain totally inactive, though. In the meantime they would deploy yet another weapon against the British. Their invasion force had overcome the treacherous St Lawrence with its rocky banks and irresistible currents. They had survived the gale. There was a further elemental force that could destroy their ships, one that the French were able to control: fire.

FIVE

First Skirmishes

THE LOOKOUTS KNEW what to watch for. Wolfe's Chief Engineer, Patrick Mackellar, had warned his fellow officers that the French would attempt to burn the British fleet. He knew that the French would prepare sacrificial ships and were planning to use them as huge floating bonfires. During his captivity in Quebec he had heard the constant boasts of his jailers and had even been shown a local variation on this tactic, the *radeaux à feu*, rafts packed with combustibles, which the French assured him would burn any fleet that showed itself before Quebec.[1] So it was no surprise when just after midnight on the night of 28/29 June the dark Quebec basin was pricked by a flash of light. Soon other lights appeared until from a distance it looked like a procession of blazing torches. The glow from the dancing flames illuminated the woods on the south shore, the shadows of the trees quivering as the fire rose in intensity. The British fleet was spread along the south shore of the Île d'Orléans and the easternmost ships could see the clear silhouettes of the upriver ships against the light cast by the fires and their reflections off the surface of the St Lawrence. The French were sending fireships towards the heart of the British fleet. Men of war cleared for action, bells rang and the watch below came sprinting up through the hatches and prepared to slip anchors and make sail. The British were ready: the ships' boats had been standing by and their crews heaved on the oars, domes of white water atop the end of each blade. In the bows bosun's mates prepared grappling hooks and lines, carefully coiling the rope to ensure that they would not snag.

Fireships were something of an anachronism by 1759. In fact, this was the only example of their use during the Seven Years War. Two hundred years before they had been a battle-winning weapon but their use had declined as ships and tactics had progressed. They were most famously used by Lord Howard of Effingham and Sir Francis Drake against the Spanish Armada as it sat at anchor off Calais in 1588. On that occasion eight ships of the English fleet were sacrificed; their helms lashed in place, their hulls filled with gunpowder and pitch and they were sent into the Spanish fleet with a following wind. The Spanish panicked, cut their anchors, and abandoned their formation. The scattered Spanish ships were attacked and defeated in the battle of Gravelines the following day. In the sixteenth and seventeenth centuries fleets fought in tightly packed formations and the aim of an admiral was to break up that of his enemy and in the melee destroy or capture the isolated ships. Fireships were ideally suited for this role. But by the eighteenth century cannon fleet actions were more spread out as ships fought gunnery duels sailing in long lines. Fireships had no part to play.

In very specific circumstances, however, they could still be very useful. In August 1666 English Admiral Sir Robert Holmes had launched a devastating attack on a mass of Dutch merchantmen lying off the coast in the Vliestroom, which destroyed over one hundred and fifty ships.[2] It was in these conditions, a narrow channel, with a following wind and a strong ebb tide, that they could be sent into a crowded anchorage and cause mayhem among an enemy fleet. Conditions like those off Quebec in late June 1759.

The French had been preparing for weeks. At vast expense merchant ships were purchased and made ready. To ensure that the fire was fed by a constant stream of fresh air the gun ports were hinged at the bottom rather than the top so they would fall open when their retaining ropes burnt through. Funnels were bored to provide a clear updraught from below decks to the rigging above. The masts were strengthened to make sure they did not collapse too soon. Barrels of gunpowder and anything flammable were packed on board. Cannon were loaded with double shot.[3] It was a delicate process; one of the eight ships burst into flame in the harbour according to a French officer, 'through the imprudence of the men who were preparing it'.[4]

Another journal says that 'either from inattention or ignorance' the ship caught fire 'at the very moment of its completion'. In all, 'twelve men were killed by the fire' and for a terrifying moment 'the most serious apprehensions were entertained' of it setting the other ships or even the town itself aflame. It was a terrible demonstration of the potency of fire in a wooden world.[5]

The wind was blowing from the south-west. The logs agree that it was a squally night with a bit of rain in the air. It was as dark as 'sable' according to Knox, with 'no light but what the stars produced'.[6] The ebb tide was running and with conditions close to perfect the French decided to deploy their fireships. They had high hopes. One journal speculated that 'if they acted effectually, [they] would completely put an end to the enterprise of the English'.[7] Success depended on the crews being brave enough, first, to sail their ships towards an enemy fleet carrying hundreds of cannon and, second, to set fire to the ships at the last possible minute. A length of quick match ran along a trough from barrels of gunpowder and resin to the escape hatch in the ship's side. The minute that was lit the crew would clamber down into the longboats which the fireships towed and make their escape. It required nerves of steel and a good deal of luck.

The French crews lacked both. Nearly all the sources agree that the French fired their ships too soon. This advertised their presence to the British and gave them vital extra minutes to prepare. One journal records that the day before the French captains 'differed widely in their opinions and even some indications were perceptible of want of courage and resolution'. Perhaps as a result, at 2200 hours as they headed to the ships, they had only a vague plan to follow the example of the commander 'who was to take the lead, and was to fire two musket shots, as the signal that each captain was to set fire to his ship'. This author then blames the commander, 'a cowardly man of no reputation', for taking fright and setting his ship alight far too early. They were still miles away from the British fleet but 'a panic had seized on all the captains', and they insisted on copying their leader and fired the charges early.[8] There is the possibility that one ship blew up prematurely and the other crews panicked, fired their ships, and leapt into the waiting longboats.

Wolfe believed that the carefully posted guard ships, the *Centurion*, *Sutherland*, and *Porcupine*, anchored furthest upstream, firing 'on the fire ships obliged them to set their matches earlier than they should have done'.[9] Certainly from the log of the *Centurion* we hear that she 'fired several guns in order to alarm the fleet that lay 3 or 4 miles below us'. This gave the rest of the fleet time to prepare their response. However, she and the *Sutherland* had to take immediate evasive action. The fireships were close enough to force them to 'cut our best bower [main] cable' and get out of the way as soon as possible.[10] The rest of the fleet watched intently. The *Stirling Castle* was moored much further down the river and in her log reported that 'at half past 12 [we] saw 7 large fires floating down from Point Levis towards [us]'. It was a whole half hour later that the crew 'observed them to be fire ships'.[11]

Knox watched from the Île d'Orléans: 'as they drew near to the west end of the island, some cannon that had been loaded, on board the vessels, with round and grape shot' were ignited by the flames and sprayed their shot at the island. It 'rattled about the shore and trees' and 'so disconcerted some small detached parties, and our sentries, that they quitted their posts, and in retiring towards the camp, fell in upon each other in a confused manner and alarmed the army'. The men rushed to their arms, were ordered to load muskets and lined up in battle formation.[12]

Knox provides a vivid description:

> nothing could be more formidable than these infernal engines were on their first appearance, with the discharge of their guns, which was followed by the bursting of grenades, also placed on board in order to convey terror into our army ... they were certainly the grandest fireworks (if I may be allowed to call them so) that can possibly be conceived, every circumstance having contributed to their awful, yet beautiful, appearance.

Another eyewitness watched them floating towards the British fleet with topgallant sails and topsails set, making good progress with 'a fresh breeze and a strong ebb tide'.[13] The fire that was slowly consuming them, 'running almost as quick as thought up the masts and rigging', and 'profuse clouds of smoke' billowed from the ships, illuminated by the flames below them. The noise carried to the men on the island across the water. The shouts of the seamen, 'the firing of cannon ... the crackling of the other combustibles', all 'reverberated through the air, and the adjacent woods'.[14]

If the army panicked the navy most definitely did not. After the *Stirling Castle* had watched the *Sutherland* and the *Centurion* let off a few shots at the fireships and cut their anchor cables she 'sent all boats manned and armed to tow them off'.[15] Other ships did the same. With remarkable bravery and cool-headedness the sailors threw grappling hooks at the fireships and took them under tow. Even Wolfe was impressed. The 'vigilance and dexterity of the seamen' prevented the fireships 'from doing any harm'.[16] His mariner-phobic 'Family Journal' also praises the seamen, 'as the channel near St Laurent is narrow and the ships were numerous there was a great probability of their doing mischief, the expertness of the seamen that were sent in boats to tow them aside, hindered their having any effect'.[17] Knox listened to 'the sonorous shouts, and frequent repetitions of *All's well*, from our gallant seamen on the water'.[18] One by one the fireships either drifted onto the shore of their own accord or were pulled away from the fleet. There was a bit of confusion as some ships like the *Hunter* or the *Porcupine* had to slip their anchors and move out of the way, the latter briefly tangling with a transport during the process. But the damage to the fleet was negligible. The *Stirling Castle* rewarded the men in the boats with a half pint of brandy each.

Mackellar wrote in his journal that the fireship attack 'managed so as to entertain us instead of annoying us. They set them on fire and left them to the direction of the current before they got within half a mile of our headmost ship, which gave our boats time to grapple and tow them ashore, though in flames, and they there burnt down without touching a single ship.'[19] A sergeant in the Louisbourg Grenadiers simply wrote that 'thank God, they did no damage'.[20] Their impact had almost been greater on the shore. Knox advises that in future commanders should let the men know 'all expectant occurrences of this nature'. The army had been terrified and if Montcalm had appeared at the head of 'three or four thousand choice veterans, or perhaps half that number, at so critical a juncture, it is difficult to say what turn our affairs might have taken'.[21]

A night attack on the British camp on the Île d'Orléans to coincide with the fireship attack was probably beyond even the organizational skills of Alexander the Great. Uncertain winds, strong tides, bad paths, and pitch darkness made it virtually impossible to coordinate the fire-ships and a sizeable attack by thousands of men. But yet again the British had showed that their army was vulnerable. The men on the shore were nervous and all too easily spooked. Montcalm, however, absolutely refused to attempt a bold stroke. He had never expected anything of the operation. His journal condescendingly refers to 'our dear fireships' and he describes the night's action as if it was nothing to do with him. His tone is one of smug sarcasm. 'They were set on fire,' he claimed, 'three leagues [around nine miles] from the enemy'; they were nothing more than 'bad jokes'. Expensive ones too; he esti-mated that 'they cost 15 to 18,000 francs'.[22] Montcalm was deter-mined to keep the great mass of his men rooted to their defensive positions. He would not risk his men on daring raids at night across difficult country. He would build his trenches, redoubts, and block-houses and then, as at Fort Carillon the year before, he would let the enemy break themselves on them.

Few appeared to share his strategic vision in Quebec where there was a, by now, depressingly familiar post mortem. At dawn the next day 'the whole river was covered with a thick smoke'.[23] Yet nothing had been achieved. Again, high hopes had been dashed. Panet thought that 'the project was good, but was very badly executed'. The ships, he wrote, were set on fire, 'in such a way that the English who were, at first concerned, cried Hurray! and mocked our operations'.[24] The army, according to one of its officers, was 'indignant' at the 'conduct of the commanders of those fireships'. Everybody blamed the crews for setting the fires too soon. He also pointed out that, 'these fireships were not chained two by two, as had been agreed on'. That would have made it harder for small boats to tow them. This officer was furi-ous that 'M de Vaudreuil was unwilling to say anything disagreeable to them' and gave them jobs with the other sailors at the various batter-ies. He estimated that the 'experiment cost the king about a million'.[25]

Quebecers had tasted enough failure. The author of one journal wrote in the margin that, if this fiasco had occurred in the British camp and the commander had fired the ships too early, 'he would have been beheaded at least, which would have been too great an honour for a man who deserved nothing less than the scaffold'.[26] Another journal describes Vaudreuil's attempt to ascertain what exactly had gone wrong. The following day the captains appeared in front of him, and all promptly blamed the commander of the expedition, de Louche. One of them made a brave speech in which he suggested that all of the captains should act as common seamen and take one final fireship into the heart of the British fleet to wipe clear the stain on their honours or die in the attempt. The unimpressed author of the journal writes that 'the speech was prodigiously applauded, but no further notice was taken of an affair that had proved so very disgraceful to the colony'.[27] The officers and men took their places at the cannon of the town along with all the other sailors.

Wolfe had been dismayed by the behaviour of the troops the night before when they had panicked at the sight of the fireships. He ordered that the officer commanding one outpost be 'put under arrest and will be tried by a General Court Martial as soon as it can be conveniently assembled'.[28] It was another unwelcome symptom of nerves in an army that was clearly coming to terms with its situation as a small force deep inside enemy territory.

The day before Wolfe had announced that the army 'must hold itself to fight in constant readiness, either to march or fight, at the shortest warning'. The French could attack the camp at any time and stragglers could be ambushed by the enemy's impressive Native Americans or Canadian irregulars. He ordered that 'no detachments, either with or without arms are to be sent to any distance from the camp without the knowledge of the brigadier general of the day'. He also chided the soldiers, telling them that they 'are to keep close to their encampment, [and] are not to pass without the guards or wander through the country in the disorderly manner that has been observed here'.[29] The 'detachments and outposts' outside the camp were to 'fortify themselves in the best manner they can' by digging trenches, building stockades, and cutting down trees to provide cover. Wolfe assured his men that 'in this situation a small party will be able to defend itself till succour arrives'. After only a day or two ashore the lurking danger of the forest was clear. Enemy marksmen lurked among the trees. Snipers picked off anyone who made himself a target. Wolfe specified that 'No sentries are ever to be planted within point blank of musket shot of a wood, unless behind stones or trees, so as not to be seen in woody country.' If passing through the woods was a necessity, 'all imaginable care and precaution' should be taken when doing so and 'detachments must never halt or encamp in the little openings'. Above all, he told his men, 'next to valour the best quality in a military man are vigilance and caution'.[30]

After the fire Wolfe and Saunders determined to seize the initiative. Monckton was sent to the commanding Point Lévis where Saunders had 'reason to think that the enemy had artillery and a force'.[31] Wolfe's 'Family Journal' also noted another reason for wishing to possess this dominant site. From Point Lévis he could 'bombard the town from that side'.[32] Carleton, the Quartermaster General, was sent with the grenadier companies of the army to occupy the western tip of the Île d'Orléans. Wolfe believed that it was 'absolutely necessary to possess these two points' because if the enemy occupied either of them they would 'make it impossible for any ship to lie in the basin of Quebec, or even within two miles of it'.[33]

Guy Carleton was 34 and a product of that stable for British army officers, the younger sons of the Anglican Irish. He was an old friend of Wolfe's, having served under him as a company commander when Wolfe was running the 20th Foot.[34] Wolfe's 'Family Journal' is, typically, rather backhanded in its praise, describing Carleton as 'not of a quick capacity but solid, proper for a Quartermaster General'.[35] His career had been blighted by some indiscreet remarks he had made about the quality of George II's troops from his cherished native Electorate of Hanover. George had come to hear of these jibes and hell hath no fury like an elector scorned. Carleton was virtually proscribed. Wolfe wrote to his mother twice before the siege of Louisbourg complaining about the King's intransigence: 'the King has refused Carleton leave to go, to my very great grief and disappointment, and with circumstances extremely unpleasant to him'. 'Prejudices against particular people often hurt the common cause ... princes of all people, see the least in to the true characters of men.'[36] He was not impressed by the army's leadership at Louisbourg and he told his mother that 'we want grave Carleton for every purpose of the war'.[37] Wolfe had requested him for the Quebec mission and the King had crossed his name off the list. Ligonier and Pitt both had to intercede with the King before he reluctantly agreed.

Carleton would now lead the grenadier companies from all the regiments and secure the headland 'from whence' Wolfe expected 'our operations are likely to begin'.[38] A regiment was made up of ten companies, one of them being a grenadier company. Grenadiers were an elite, the finest men in the regiment gathered together. Their forebears had used primitive grenades as a shock weapon when assaulting the enemy but their use had died out and now they shouldered muskets like the rest of the regiment.[39] Cumberland's *Standing Orders* of 1755 stated that these units 'be completed out of the best men of their respective Regiments, and to be constantly kept so'. They were often the oldest troops in the regiment and by 1759 these veterans had seen a fair bit of action. The rest of the men referred to them as 'grannies'. They were instantly recognizable. Lace-covered shoulder ornaments called 'wings' jutted out from their jackets and made them appear wider. In deference to their ancient role they carried on their right shoulder a perforated brass tube in which the lighted match for the grenades used to be stashed. Unlike the black felt tricorne hats worn by the rest of the infantry they sported an imposing mitre cap that added eight inches to their height, surmounted by a tuft in the regimental colour. The front panel was beautifully embroidered with wool. On it was the royal cipher, 'G. R.' for George Rex, surmounted by a crown and underneath, the white horse of George's beloved Hanover. Designs differed slightly from regiment to regiment. The grenadiers who fought alongside Knox in the 43rd had a grenade stitched into the back as well as the regimental number. On the inside the sweat and grease of years of service turned the linen brown. Emblazoned just above the eyes was '*NEC ASPERA TERRENT*', 'Difficulties Be Damned'.

Carleton led the grenadiers off to the end of the Île d'Orléans. According to one contemporary estimate they would have carried sixty-five pounds twelve ounces of kit, which included their muskets, ammunition, other equipment, and rations.[40] They started the march early to cover six miles before the sun became unbearably hot. Next Wolfe sent Monckton's force to occupy the dominant heights of Point Lévis. This headland sat across the narrows from Quebec itself. Mackellar recorded that Monckton's force left 'in the evening'. They crossed 'the south channel from St Laurent to the village of Beaumont with four battalions, three companies of light infantry, and some rangers'.[41] They camped by the shore but were ready to move early the next morning. Knox claims that the ebb tide was exhausted by the time his regiment came to cross and they were forced to spend the 'excessively cold' night sleeping without tents by the shore, huddled around fires to keep warm.[42]

The following day they set off for Point Lévis, the column of redcoats preceded by a screen of light infantrymen and rangers. As they edged away from the safety of their ships they entered the world of the Native Americans and Canadians. From invisible positions in the undergrowth marksmen opened fire on the British and the march quickly turned into a rolling skirmish with an elusive foe.

Native Americans inspired both hatred and admiration from Europeans. Their physical appearance immediately struck newcomers to North America. In 1756 Captain Charles Lee wrote home telling his sister of the tall, athletic Mohawks: 'I assure you that if you were to see the young Warriors dressed out and armed you would never allow that there was such a thing as gentility amongst our finest gentlemen at St James's!'[43] The diaries of Louis Antoine de Bougainville, Montcalm's erudite aide-de-camp, are one of the finest sources on Native Americans in the eighteenth century. They were, he says, 'curious to the eye of a philosopher who seeks to study man in conditions nearest to nature'. He agreed with the British Captain that 'in general these are brawny men, large and of good appearance'. Their appearance was 'more suited to terrify than to please' as they 'were naked save for a piece of cloth in front and behind, the face and body painted, feathers on their heads'. In their hands they carried 'the symbol and signal of war, tomahawk and spear'. On another occasion he describes a Native American war party as moving 'through the woods in several files, the Indians almost naked, all in black and red war paint'.[44]

The eventual subjugation and near extermination of the Native peoples of North America by industrial societies armed with repeating rifles and shrapnel shells distorts the reality of a conflict that was, in fact, fought over centuries and had, at times, promised a very different outcome. The first English and French colonies in North America in modern-day Virginia and Quebec respectively were abandoned in the face of Native American hostility. French Canada had teetered on the verge of destruction at the hands of her Native enemies for a century after its foundation. Right up until the large deployments of European troops during the Seven Years War the Iroquois Confederation represented the most powerful military entity on the eastern half of the continent. Their one lethal vulnerability was the lack of a developed industrial base to produce their own weapons and powder, on which they had become utterly dependent. But as long as European powers competed for North America then this weakness was hidden as all sides supplied muskets and ammunition in an attempt to gain favour or at least ensure neutrality.

French power relied on the acquiescence of the Native tribes west of Quebec. New France was more of an alliance than an empire. Native Americans took every opportunity to signal their independence. Bougainville recorded the speech of one Iroquois from La Presentation: 'we have not renounced our liberty or the rights we hold from the Master of Life,' he insisted. 'It is only we who can give ourselves chiefs.'[45] New French defence against the more populous British colonies had always depended on mobilizing Native warriors to pin British colonials back behind the Alleghenies. Many Native tribes were willing to fight for the French against the British because the French offered the prospect of coexistence whereas the British model of colonization clearly did not. A pro-French Native American spoke to his comrades in 1754 about the difference between the British and French:

Brethren, are you ignorant of the difference between our father [the French] and the English? Go and see the forts our father has created, and you will see that the land beneath their walls is still hunting ground, having fixed himself in those places we frequent only to supply our wants; whilst the English, on the contrary, no sooner get possession of a country than the game is forced to leave; the trees fall down before them, the earth becomes bare.[46]

The British came in vast numbers as farmers, hungry for land. The French, as the Governor of Massachusetts, Thomas Pownall, realized, 'have insinuated themselves into an influence with the Indians'. They had achieved this 'by becoming hunters and creating alliances with the Indians as brother sportsmen ... [behaving] according to the true spirit of the Indian laws of nations'. [47] Frenchmen and Canadians travelled great distances with Native Americans in search of furs. It was not unusual for these men to take a Native wife and settle among them.

Scotsman Robert Kirk was captured in 1759 by Native Americans and was forcibly assimilated into a tribe to replace a lost relative. He asked his Native 'brother' 'what was the reason, he and the rest of his nation had so much regard for the French, and such an antipathy to the English, and why they acted with so much inhumanity towards the settlers'. The Native American replied that 'the French were kind to them, and dealt in everything towards them with honesty, whereas the English used them quite otherwise, several having wronged and in short given them nothing in return for their goods'. He added 'that the lands now possessed by the English, formerly belonged to them, and that the French promised they should be restored; he remarked that the English instead of making this restitution were daily encroaching, and curtailing them of what was left'. When Kirk pointed out that God was not at all pleased 'about all this murder', the Native American pointed out that the Lord 'was certainly angry with the white people for taking their lands'. It was particularly unfair since God 'had given them [the Europeans] some things easy, their cows and other cattle coming home quiet and tame, whereas the Indians had great trouble in hunting and bringing home their provisions, and were frequently in extreme want when the snow fell deep'. This hostility to the British was bolstered by French gold. Kirk's 'brother' admitted that the French 'paid them well for all the scalps they took, which induced them more'. This payment was vital 'as by that they were enabled to provide themselves with many necessaries, which they should otherwise be in want of'. The Native Americans had become reliant on European manufactured goods, scalps were one of the few commodities they could offer in return.[48]

There is a disagreement over the origin of scalping. Recent finds at Vindolanda, a Roman fort just south of Hadrian's Wall in the north of England, suggest that Roman legionaries from Gaul, modern France, may have practised it.[49] So it is possible that the habit was brought over with the French to Canada. Wolfe's 'Family Journal' explained that 'there is no method of certifying their [Native American] services but by their producing some tokens of their exploits, the scalp is the most portable'. This led to 'an inveteracy [that] has fathered all degrees of cruelty' and meant that 'inhumanity is inseparable from an Indian war'.[50] Scalps became receipts for payment and tokens of military prowess. Warriors carried dried, stretched scalps on hoops on their belts. Bougainville wrote that 'these are their trophies, their obelisks, their arches of triumph; the monuments which attest to other tribes and consign to posterity the valor [and] the exploits of the warriors'.[51]

Despite routinely referring to the Native Americans as 'savages', Vaudreuil regarded their friendship and support as central to the defence of New France. 'We shall never be able to make those Indians move according to our desires,' he wrote to Versailles at the beginning of 1759, 'if we be not in a situation to relieve at least their most urgent wants.'[52] Relations varied from tribe to tribe. Some Native Americans had settled in communities close to Quebec and adopted Christianity and European dress. These were the so-called 'Mission Indians' such as the Huron of Lorette. Others lived at St François and Sillery; they were the remnants of New England Algonquian who had found shelter among the Mahican, western Abenaki, and Mohegan, and smaller tribes of the Hudson River all of whom shared a hatred of the British colonists who had devastated their ancestral lands and driven the survivors into exile. The Abenaki of St François, in particular, were New France's greatest allies. For years they had halted the expansion north of Massachusetts and were determined to protect their land, containing the bones of their ancestors, from annexation. Native Americans from further west were less subject to French control. The

Missisaugas of Toronto, Ottawas and Potowatomis from Detroit, the Iowas, Foxes and Delawares from even further west came and went as they pleased. They would defend New France but only if they were well rewarded.

Bougainville's diaries are dominated by descriptions of attempts by his general to keep the Native Americans onside. On one occasion he notes that the 'Indians determine the route, the halts, the scouts, and the speed to make, and in this sort of warfare it is necessary to adjust to their ways'. It was certainly not how the officers of Louis' army had expected to conduct operations. Bougainville never lost his distaste for it. Bending Native American troops to one's will required 'authority, brandy, equipment, food and such. The job never ends and is very irksome.' Their different outlook proved exasperating for regular officers brought up to regard speed and decision as the greatest of virtues. On one occasion Bougainville lamented that 'the caprice of an Indian is of all possible caprices the most capricious'.[53]

Yet despite the groaning of the regulars they were not just tolerated but actively encouraged because every man was a hunter and a warrior. At a time and in a situation of their choosing they could annihilate an enemy and put so great a fear in the hearts of the survivors that they never wanted to take to the field ever again. The Vikings, who briefly touched on the east coast of Newfoundland in the early eleventh century, recorded tales in their sagas of constant Native attacks from all sides, which forced them to retreat. Centuries later little had changed apart from the weapons. Native Americans were absolutely at home in the thick woodland, patient in pursuit of a quarry, masters of their weapons, and Bougainville remarks that 'one could not have better hearing than those people'.[54] One of the Christian Native Americans told de Lévis that 'thou hast brought into these places the art of war of this world which lies beyond the great ocean'. 'We know that in this art you are a great master,' he continued, 'but for the science of the craft of scouting, we know more than thee. Consult us and thou will derive benefit from it.'[55] Wise French commanders took his advice. Native Americans had to be left to fight in their own manner.

A Mohawk chief, Tecaughretanego, defined their doctrine just before the Seven Years War; 'the art of war,' he said, 'consists in ambushing and surprising our enemies and in preventing them from ambushing and surprising us'.[56] Throughout skirmishes with Native Americans they would remain unseen. At Monongahela one survivor wrote that 'if we saw of them five or six at one time [it] was a great sight and they either on their bellies or behind trees or running from one tree to another almost on the ground'.[57] They always strove to surround their enemy, spaced out so that every man had a clear field of fire. When pressed they withdrew and took up positions further back. If the terrain allowed, a blundering enemy could be drawn into their concave line, caught in a withering crossfire. Five years later William Smith was 'attacked by savages'. He describes the sense of bewilderment: 'He cannot discover them, though from every tree, log or bush, he receives an incessant fire, and observes that few of their shots are lost.' If the defender attempts to counter-attack, 'he will charge in vain. For they are as cautious to avoid a close engagement, as indefatigable in harassing his troops.' 'Notwithstanding all his endeavours,' he concluded, 'he will still find himself surrounded by a circle of fire, which, like an artificial horizon, follows him everywhere.'[58] These tactics could destroy the morale of an enemy. Bougainville watched one encounter in 1757 in which 'the English, terrified by the shooting, the sight, the cries and the agility of these monsters, surrendered almost without firing a shot'.[59]

John Johnson leaves a vivid description of a Native American's method of attacking. They began 'concealed behind some tree ... in which station they continue with the utmost secrecy'. When the victim approaches, 'they fire and very often kill him dead on the spot; for they seldom miss their aim, being excellent marksmen'. Without waiting to see the effect of their shot, 'they immediately spring up to him, and with their butt, strike at his head and endeavour to beat out his brains'. If there is fight left in the victim, they will not close for the kill but stand off and 'taking a cool and deliberate aim, they throw their Tomahawk ... which they throw with great certainty for a considerable distance and seldom miss'. 'No sooner have they delivered the Tomahawk,' he reports, 'but they spring up to him, with their scalping knife; which is made in every respect like our Kitchen carving knives, and generally at the first approach rip him open, and sometimes take out his heart.'

Finally, 'they cut round the top of the crown, to the skull bone, and raising up one side of the skin, with the knife, with a jerk they tear it off by the hair, and the work is done; upon which they set up the Indian whoop, as a signal to their barbarous companions that the work is finished, as also a shout of triumph'.[60] Bougainville relates atrocities performed by the Native Americans in battle, 'even the recital of which is horrible'. 'The cruelties and insolence of these barbarians is horrible,' he wrote, 'their souls are as black as pitch. It is an abominable way to make war; the retaliation is frightening, and the air one breathes here is contagious of making one accustomed to callousness.' At the fall of Fort William Henry he watched as 'they put in the pot and ate three prisoners'. 'All have become slaves unless they are ransomed,' he continued. 'A horrible spectacle to European eyes.'[61] Warriors wore scalps on their belts to demonstrate their military prowess or sold them to the French in return for gold. For both these reasons huge importance was attached to them, and securing them became an obsession which could derail an attack as Native Americans forgot the objective in an orgy of scalp taking. In 1755 a French commander ordered that 'the Indians were not to amuse themselves scalping until the enemy be entirely defeated, inasmuch as ten men can be killed whilst one is being scalped'.[62] The prospect of slaves and plunder also undermined their obedience, vague at the best of times. As a result the warriors were capable of frustrating their French superiors as much as they terrified the enemy. They inspired admiration and horror in equal measure, but despite their weaknesses Bougainville insisted that 'in the midst of the woods of America one can no more do without them than without cavalry in open country'.[63]

It seems as though the fighting against the Native Americans and the Canadians, who stalked the British column along the track, was tough enough to make Brigadier Monckton reconsider the advance. Wolfe's 'Family Journal' was scathing. It claimed that Monckton gathered his senior officers around him and held 'a kind of council' at which they each 'gave their opinion whether the post was tenable'. The journal reports that Wolfe 'was amazed when he heard that such a counsel had been held, as he had given positive orders to occupy the post [Point Lévis], which he knew would be highly essential in his future operations'.[64]

Across the river Vaudreuil and the people of Quebec had been watching, quite literally, the course of the battle. Many had gathered by the batteries in the Upper and Lower Towns to squint at the column of red coats as it moved haltingly towards Point Lévis about two thousand yards away. Vaudreuil regarded the dogged performance of his beloved Canadians and Native Americans as justification for his high opinion of them. He wanted to reinforce the men on the south shore with '1000 or 2000 men, Canadians and Savages'. Advocates of this plan pointed out that the broken terrain was 'most congenial to the habits and inclinations of Canadians and savages, who passed their lives in the woods, and forests; and their local knowledge would afford them many means of annoying the enemy, and give them so decided a superiority, as must ensure their defeating the English however numerous they might be'.[65] A journal, written by a usually disparaging French regular officer, agreed. He records that the Native Americans arrived back on the north bank with thirty scalps, a figure that roughly tallies with Knox's estimate. In the light of this success, he writes that 'had a more considerable force been ordered out upon this service, sufficient to have brought on a serious affair, and to have ended it to our advantage, it certainly had been more for the interest of our generals'. He mentions that it 'was proposed', but 'did not tally with the plan of defence agreed on' so it was 'rejected and dropped'.[66]

Confusingly Montcalm's journal suggests that he agreed with the proposal. It states that 'Montcalm went to the town to confront Vaudreuil with the need to send more troops to Lévis before the English settled in.'[67] The reason for French hesitation on this occasion, apart from an ambiguous command structure which choked bold decision making, was that they were thoroughly tricked by a newly arrived British prisoner captured by the Native Americans. His name is lost to history although his impact on the campaign was substantial. Prisoners and deserters were by far the most effective source of information available to either general, one of the only ways to get a sense of what was happening in their enemy's camp. Generals would very often carry out the interrogations themselves, such was their value. Montresor recorded that three prisoners were captured by Monckton's men during the course of their march and they 'were brought over to Major General

Wolfe and were examined'.[68] A French journal records that during the interrogation this British prisoner insisted that the 'landing at the Point Levis, was merely a stratagem to veil the real designs of the English' and instead Wolfe 'intended that very night making an attack upon Beauport with 10,000 men'.[69] This was utter fantasy. Not only did Wolfe not have 10,000 men, he had absolutely no intention of throwing his army in a night attack against an impregnable French position on the north shore of the river, especially not when he regarded the naval situation in the basin as unacceptable thanks to the timidity of his fleet. It was a stunning bluff but Vaudreuil and the French fell for it completely. A French officer wrote that the news 'disconcerted a plan which had been formed, to convey a large body of troops across the river to drive the enemy from that quarter before securing the position there'. Vaudreuil countermanded his orders to the Canadian militiamen who were preparing to cross. Instead, every man who could shoulder a musket spent the night armed and ready in the town and the camp having taken 'all possible precautions to give them a warm reception on landing'.[70] Canadians, French regulars, and cavalrymen waited at their battle-stations. One Canadian journal records that 'everybody was under arms during the night' and 'the gates of the town were closed for the first time'.[71] Montcalm and Bougainville inspected the army's positions with an engineer in tow. Montcalm's journal says scornfully that Vaudreuil and Bigot were present but were ready in a flash 'to jump on their horses and save themselves'.[72]

The attack never came. Panet lamented that 'nothing could have been so untrue'.[73] The expectant French troops were overwhelmed by nerves and exhaustion. They mistook a ripple, a seabird, or a friendly sentry for a landing. A French officer wrote that 'it happened at break of day; by some misunderstanding, the origin of which could not be discovered, the militia of the right fired without any cause, a general discharge of musketry; we thought ourselves attacked in that quarter; the whole army flew to arms and rushed thither'.[74] The noise was enough to catch the attention of Wolfe, who noted in his journal that there was 'great firing ... a little before daybreak'. He assumed it was 'an attack upon some post of Br. Monckton's corps'. In fact, 'it turned out to be a false alarm in the French camps on the Beauport side'.[75]

Little did he know that he had a British soldier to thank that it was the latter rather than the former.

Wolfe's relations with Monckton were battered at the first sniff of serious action with the enemy. They would plunge still further the next day when the French sent their gunboats across the St Lawrence to harass Monckton's force and lend some support to the Native Americans and the Canadians who still lurked around the fringes of his camp. Malcolm Fraser records how 'the French sent some floating batteries from the other side of the river to play on us'. Monckton appears to have believed that it was an amphibious force of French troops about to land and Fraser and his men 'were ordered to stand to their arms'. They lined up two deep on the beach preparing to unleash volleys of musketry into the French soldiers but none came. Instead, the floating batteries simply sat there and fired at the British. 'They cannonaded us for about half an hour.' Infantrymen hated being on the receiving end of artillery more than anything else. Twenty-four-pound cannonballs tore down groups of men and there was nothing they could do about it except wait for an order from an officer to lie down or withdraw. Fraser's regiment had 'four ... killed and eight wounded' while 'one Sergeant of the 15th Regiment and eight of the colour's company were knocked down with one ball, behind the colours, and all wounded, two, I believe, mortally'.[76]

Sergeant Thompson of Fraser's regiment mentions the incident too, and confirms the grizzly death of the sergeant from the 15th. He criticizes Monckton openly for making the men line up and present themselves for destruction. It was particularly foolish he says since 'there was a ridge of rocks where we could have been formed under shelter from the effect of the enemy's shot'. Unpleasant though it was for the men it could have been a lot worse according to Thompson, 'if they had only the sense to have fired canister at us'. Canister was named after the metal canister in which was packed scores of smaller balls. The canister was fired out of the cannon and disintegrated sending out a cloud of balls. It was as if the cannon had been turned into a giant shotgun. Canister was devastating at close range. Thompson writes that 'they would have mowed us down like grass for our brave general had paraded us in the best manner possible for that purpose'.[77]

Wolfe was losing faith in his second in command. In his official journal he records that he was 'very surprised' to see the men exposed to the fire of the 'contemptible boats'.[78] His 'Family Journal' is scathing. It relates how Monckton lined up his entire brigade on the beach, ripe targets for the French cannon and says that 'fourteen soldiers were killed'. Apparently 'it was a matter of conversation in the army, what could be his reason for exposing the soldiers in that manner, 'twas said that it could not be from an apprehension that the enemy would land to attack his brigade as there were not above eight or ten men in each of the floating batteries'. Several pages later, unfortunately at the bottom of a damaged one, the author passes a libellous judgement on Monckton, saying that he has a 'dull capacity, and may be properly called fat headed, timid and utterly unqualified'. The journal claims that 'a month of his command would be sufficient to ruin that excellent ...' and here the words become sadly indistinguishable but no doubt refer to the units under Monckton's command. If, as seems likely, these words reflect the feelings of Wolfe, then the expedition's high command suffered from as great a schism as their French enemy across the basin of Quebec.[79]

Wolfe's anger was no doubt compounded by what he regarded as the failure of his navy. Montresor tells us that Wolfe had attempted to cross from the Île d'Orléans to the south shore to observe the fighting himself. But he had been forced to turn back because his boat was attacked by the 'floating battery' which was an 'oblong stage with 4 embrasures and a great flag'. This was presumably part of the flotilla of boats that was bombarding Monckton's men. As Wolfe's boat retreated, the French, pleased with their little victory, 'gave several cheers'. However, one of the British frigates came to Wolfe's rescue and made the French gunboats retreat 'with great precipitation'.[80] The disappearance of the floating batteries was also a blessed relief for Monckton's men. Knox praised the 'good conduct of our naval friends'.[81] But, of course, Wolfe blamed the navy for having let the French craft get close to the south bank at all. On 30 June his 'Family Journal' records that 'none of our men of war' had yet 'ventured into the basin of Quebec (though some were bold enough to peep into it)'.[82]

He and his close staff clearly regarded the naval officers as nothing short of cowards.

The next week was spent fortifying, consolidating, entrenching, and planning. Of primary importance was the securing of the two sites at the tip of the Île d'Orléans and Point Lévis. Wolfe's Adjutant General, Isaac Barré, wrote huge numbers of notes to the brigadiers and subordinate commanders transmitting Wolfe's orders. Barré is another example of the workings of patronage. Like Carleton, the Quartermaster General, Barré was a personal friend of Wolfe's. He had been born to French Huguenot parents in Dublin thirty-two years before. Although prodded towards the law, he chose the army instead. The theatre had also beckoned. Horace Walpole reports that 'in his younger days he had acted plays with so much applause that it was said [David] Garrick had offered him a thousand pounds a year to come upon the stage'.[83] Barré spoke with the composure and eloquence of an actor. He had served with Wolfe on two previous expeditions. In 1758 he had been Wolfe's Brigade Major, a staff officer who helped run the brigade and transmit Wolfe's orders. In 1759 despite his lowly rank of Captain and his tender age Barré was given the vital job of Adjutant General doing much the same thing but this time for the whole army. Wolfe's 'Family Journal' describes Barré, who was an intimate member of the 'Family' of staff officers, as 'a worthy good man, with a great share of understanding and humour – brave, but still better qualified for the cabinet than the field – and very proper as an adjutant general'.[84]

Barré wrote to Monckton to encourage him in his work: 'the general has ordered me to acquaint you, that you immediately fortify your camp with all possible despatch and precaution, by constructing redoubts in open places, and making abatis in such as are woody'. Redoubts were small strongpoints enclosed by a mound of earth to provide cover from enemy muskets and light guns while an abatis is a vicious natural form of barbed wire which is still occasionally used by modern armies. They are made from felled trees with sharpened branches. In keeping with Wolfe's habit of assuming that his subordinates were halfwits the letter explicitly states that 'you should fortify your flanks in the strongest manner', advice that Monckton, a seasoned campaigner, would have possibly found insulting. Of some real use, though, was Wolfe's dispatch of some marines, 'who you may employ as Pioneers'.[85]

Wolfe shuttled between the points of Île d'Orléans and Lévis regularly. He was pleased by the range from Lévis to Quebec. The 'weak' Lower Town would be an 'easy bombardment'. However, he was still concerned by the performance of Monckton. On his first visit to Point Lévis, Wolfe was 'amazed at the ignorance in the construction of the Redoubts'. He was never one to hide his disapproval and now he immediately 'directed some new works'.[86] His journal does hint at other reasons for his prickly mood. Not only was he directing his first major operation against a much stronger enemy than he had expected but he was doing so a good month behind schedule. His health was also a nagging problem. His journal on 2 July notes, 'bladder painful. A good deal racked.' His solution was to ignore it; that evening he 'studied plans'.[87]

Monckton's men felled trees, hacked at the ground, and started dragging artillery up from the shore. They did so in full view of the town. One French journal reports that 'with the aid of telescopes' the author and other Quebecers watched in horror as 'at least 5000 men and a great quantity of artillery had been landed there'. There was no question what all the work was trying to achieve, 'it was apparently the intention of the enemy to erect batteries along the heights opposite the town'.[88] The town's batteries fired off round after round to try to interrupt or possibly even to halt the proceedings. Despite the odd ball ploughing into working parties, the French could not bring the construction to a halt. After a few minutes the British soldiers would pick up their tools and resume their work. A few losses to the French cannon were borne with stoicism. These men had served at Louisbourg the year before and long range, random death was an inevitable feature of sieges. A French source was, unsurprisingly, frustrated; 'some shell and shot were fired at these workmen, who appeared to suffer, but did not abandon their occupation'.[89] By the end of the week on 8 July Wolfe reports in his journal that the batteries were 'in some forwardness' even though there was a 'warm fire of the enemy upon the workmen'.[90]

On the Île d'Orléans Townshend's brigade was ordered to follow Carleton and the grenadiers to the tip of the island. Montresor says that they 'Marched from their first encampment on the island to the Point, the following regiments – Bragg's, [28th] Lascelles', [47th] Anstruther's, [58th] commanded by Brigadier Townshend with the camp equipage and four days of provision each man being provided with either spade or pickaxe.' Again a screen of light infantrymen and rangers watched the van and the rear as they marched. As always the regimental quartermasters and the 'camp colourmen' pushed ahead with the foremost troops. Their job was to arrive at the destination a few hours before the main body of the troops and mark out, with the camp colours, where the regiments were to pitch their tents. Yet again the light troops found themselves in action. Only a mile into the march the rear of the column was 'fired on by a party of Indians who discharged 6 shot and wounded 3 men'. Major Scott led seven of his rangers 'into the woods after the enemy'. Montresor records that the column halted for an hour and an officer led some regular infantry into the woods to support the rangers. The rest of the men must have waited in the shade, or poked about on the verges for wild fruit and vegetables to augment their dinner. Occasionally the sharp crack of a musket shot alerted them to the deadly skirmishing that simmered among the trees.[91]

The men arrived at the tip of the Île d'Orléans and started constructing a strong camp. Wolfe's engineer Mackellar records that it was 'fortified for a place of arms and an hospital … here the general, for the present, fixed his Headquarters'.[92] Artillery was landed in the boats to protect the new camp but also to try to bar French gunboats from entering the north channel between the Île d'Orléans and the Beauport shore. To help man the artillery Wolfe ordered that 'a sergeant and 15 men from each regiment in camp are to parade at magazine, to receive orders from an artillery officer and remain with that corps'.[93] The Royal Artillery provided only the specialist officers and men, while the hard, unskilled work was done by infantrymen. This was especially true as more naval guns were brought into service on shore. There were far too many to be manned by the artillerymen and sailors were kept on land to operate them.

Brigadier Murray brought the rest of the troops to the tip of the Île dOrléans the following day. The army was now in two camps, one on the tip of the Île d'Orléans and the other on Point Lévis. In the words of Wolfe's 'Family Journal' both were 'strongly fortified, [with] hospitals and magazines established at each'.[94] Having secured his bases and brought ashore a huge amount of supplies, Wolfe could apply himself to the tricky problem of getting across to the north shore of the St Lawrence and bringing Montcalm to battle. Clearly his original plan of romping ashore at Beauport, crossing the St Charles, and laying siege to Quebec was not such an easy prospect as it had been from the panelled splendour of Whitehall or the swaying admiral's cabin on the *Neptune* during the Atlantic crossing. Especially not now that talks with Saunders revealed that there was a wide area of shallows, the 'Beauport Bank', which would stop the large ships getting close to the shore to provide gunfire support to the landing troops. The massive firepower of the ships was one of Wolfe's trump cards yet, as he recorded in his journal, the 'admiral was of opinion that none of the ships could be the least use in an attempt on the Beauport side'.[95] Instead, all their thoughts turned to another option, one that Wolfe had laid out in a letter from Louisbourg. He had always regarded an attack below the town as the most practicable solution to getting ashore on the north bank, 'unless,' he wrote, 'we can steal a detachment up the river St Lawrence, and land them three, four, five miles, or more, above the town, and get time to entrench so strongly that they won't care to attack'.[96] Wolfe, Saunders, and the senior officers knew that when attacking it was always best to go where the enemy was not. Montcalm's army was ready for them downriver of Quebec; the north shore above the town was unprotected. Pushing above the town was an attractive option but to do so the ships carrying the men would have to brave the narrows, with its firewall of French artillery, and swarms of gunboats.

Wolfe decided that these were less threatening than the defences of Beauport and his journal states that 'our notions agreeing to get ashore if possible above the Town we determined to attempt it. Troops and ships prepared accordingly.'[97] Having taken this momentous decision, Murray was sent to reconnoitre the north shore of the St Lawrence by walking along the south bank upriver of Point Lévis towards the Etchemin River. Mackellar records that 'some rafts for ferrying the troops across were ordered to be made'.[98] Meanwhile Monckton was to push ahead with the batteries on Point Lévis, in order to begin 'a warm bombardment' on Quebec, and Townshend prepared his brigade for a feint. Wolfe himself was to land on the north shore of the St Lawrence but downstream of Montcalm, beyond the virtually impassable Montmorency falls. This, according to Wolfe's journal, would 'draw the enemy's attention that way and favour the projected attempt' above the town.[99]

It was left to Saunders to ensure that all these operations were transported, fed, supplied, communicated with, and protected at the same time. As the army commanders schemed, a very real battle was going on for control of the basin of Quebec. Sadly, it is one for which the sources are thin. We get only snapshots of the action: canoes and boats ambushing each other in the dawn or twilight, the frustration of the frigates as they felt their way into the shallows to follow French gunboats, the perverse winds of the St Lawrence threatening all the mariners with a sudden squall that could drive them onto the shore. Each night the guard boats stayed afloat waiting for more fireships or incursions by Canadians and Native Americans in their silent canoes. The ships' logs contain watchwords which edgy sailors demanded of shadowy boats or at the sound of a churning paddle and the drips of water from a hovering oar. The watchwords were always patriotic, an attempt to give heart to the shivering guards, wrapped in darkness. On 6 July it was 'Boscawen' one of Britain's foremost fighting admirals, the following day it was 'Pitt'. Later that summer 'Marlborough' was used, the name of Britain's greatest general who had destroyed the imperial ambitions of Louis XIV, the Sun King.[100]

During the day the French would use the currents and light conditions which they knew so well to dart out and attack any vulnerable British ships, boats, or infantry detachments on the shoreline. Wolfe's frustration deepened; he noted in his journal that 'the Enemy [are] permitted to insult us with their paltry boats carrying cannon in their prows'.[101] The small boats presented a huge problem for the large ships. Operating in confined waters with fickle wind they simply could not get close enough to the French to bring their guns to bear. The French chose the time and place of the attacks, only venturing out if conditions gave them an advantage over the sail-powered vessels. Ramezay wrote on one occasion in early July that 'despite the fact that the English maintained not to have suffered from our fire, the frigates have retreated a little closer to the shore of Ile d'Orléans'.[102] The gunboats had to be taken on by the small British guard boats. Many of these boats had been destroyed in the storm at the end of June and the remaining ones were already gravely overstretched ferrying supplies and men as well as with their combat tasks. The *Stirling Castle*, Saunders' temporary flagship, 'sent several flat bottomed boats and longboats to carry troops from Orléans to Point Levis' on the early afternoon of 5 July. A short time later she 'sent 4 barrels of powder' ashore. At 1700 hours she dispatched 'several boats manned and armed to row guard above Point Levis to ward off any fire ships or stages that the enemy may send down'. While 'at 4 AM sent several boats to board transports to carry provisions on shore to the army'.[103] The hands of the exhausted sailors became hard with calluses as they rowed their boats endlessly to and fro.

It was the kind of opportunistic, autonomous action that appealed to the Canadians and the Native Americans. They fought only when they stood an overwhelming chance of success and never pressed an attack home if the odds changed. Their canoes were faster than the British oared boats. An eyewitness described them measuring 'from ten to twenty eight feet long'. The smallest of them 'hold but two persons ... as in a coffin'. They took a great deal of skill to use as they 'are apt to over set; if the passengers move to one side or the other'.[104] These canoes were the technology on which French power in North America relied. What roads were to Rome, canals and railways to nineteenth-century Britain, so rivers were to Canada. It was an empire of waterways. 'The lakes and rivers are the only outlets,' wrote Bougainville, 'the only open roads in this country.'[105] The tentacles of French power crossed the continent along the vast galaxy of tributaries that flow into the Great Lakes, Hudson Bay, the St Lawrence, and the Mississippi, the watersheds between all these systems being easy to traverse. Journeys of immense distances could be completed in surprisingly short times. New Orleans, 2,000 miles away on the Gulf of Mexico, took around six months to reach by river, and was quite simply impossible over land. Canoes could be fashioned from birch bark with only a knife and an axe; they could float along the shallowest trickle of a stream. A European eyewitness described them as 'safe and steady' and 'very convenient upon the account of their extreme lightness and drawing of very little water'.[106] They were also exclusive to Canada; to the south the birch did not grow to the same size and there the Native Americans and British frontiersmen had to use elm, which was heavier, far less durable, and rougher. The Canadian canoes could carry a decent load. *Voyageurs* paddled hundreds of miles into the *pays d'en haut* armed with gifts and trade goods, knives, beads, brandy, muskets, and gunpowder to buy the friendship of the Native tribes. They returned to Quebec with mounds of furs, the only Canadian product sold with any success in the markets of Europe.

Now these canoes were demonstrating their utility for war as well as trade. On 7 July a British barge was attacked in the north channel between the Île d'Orléans and the Beauport shoreline. A French source says that the Native Americans 'saw a barge making soundings between the North Shore and the Île d'Orléans. They set about preparations to go there in their canoe, and pursued the barge right onto the island. They fired on the barge, killing several of the English, who were managing it and made a prisoner of an engineer.'[107] A British source confirms that 'one of Admiral Saunders' barges was taken by canoes with armed men in them, the sailors for so near on shore that they leaped into the water and escaped, excepting one wounded man who was taken'.[108] The British on the island sprang into action and rushed down to the beach, firing wildly as they charged. The French journal claims that '700 or 800 musket shots' were fired, 'which wounded one Indian'. The British prisoner proved reluctant to go with them and so they 'split his head open, and returned in triumph having the barge in tow'.[109] Both sides always maximized the number of combatants and casualties on the other side and minimized their own. But the loss of a barge could not be denied. There was more to come. Later that afternoon one ship's log records that some gunboats exchanged cannon fire with the frigates *Richmond* and *Baltimore*. So slippery were these gunboats that the rest of the fleet had to send 'flat bottomed boats manned and armed to assist our frigates'.[110]

Wolfe's 'Family Journal', as ever, blames the navy. According to it, the snatched barge was 'not being supported by other boats'.[111] Thomas Bell, Wolfe's young aide-de-camp, mimics the tone of his boss in his own journal, saying that British shipping was 'insulted every day' and crews taken prisoner while nothing was being done to prevent it. Around the same time he wrote, 'our fleet all retired within the Point of Orléans for fear of Bombs. The Passage from Montmorency to Levy for Boats very dangerous, the floating Batteries still reigning triumphant.'[112] Wolfe was openly contemptuous of his fleet; in his journal on 8 July he noted, 'disposition of the Frigates & Bomb Ketches – their prodigious distance from the Enemy – Amazing backwardness in these matters on the side of the Fleet'.[113] The 'Family Journal' goes much further: in one section it describes the 'difficulties' Wolfe was faced with in terms of the terrain and Montcalm's dispositions, and then comments that 'with regard to our own fleet he had not a few'. Saunders is described as 'a worthy gentleman and a brave man' but lacking 'an understanding framed for such an enterprise'. Apparently, 'he had been taught to look on Mr Wolfe as a rash madman that would lead into scrapes'. That idea was reinforced, says the journal, 'by the frozen cold council of some of the captains of the fleet had benumbed every nerve of enterprise'. While entrenched conservatism and timidity paralysed the fleet, 'the enemy's floating batteries with impunity insulted our posts, and often cut the communications'. The journal relates how Wolfe attempted to stimulate naval activity, but claims that 'it was not possible to invigorate' with ideas 'to defeat the enemies floating batteries, or to cut them away during the night. The whole were benumbed and dead. Wolfe urged every motive, but in vain.' Wolfe was in no doubt that it was a failure of the higher leadership: 'I must assert that the boats for the army were ill commanded, there was only a master and commander to command the whole, whereas there should have been a captain of authority and experience to each division of boats.' He did at least acknowledge that 'many of the lieutenants commanding boats were brave and did their duty from motives of honour and regard to the service of their country'. Although the journal noted that, 'some skulked, authority would have restrained them'.[114]

What these landlubbers could not realize was that just as they did on shore, where Canadians and Native Americans could harass the much more powerful British regiments with what were essentially guerrilla tactics, the same was true on the water. The large sailing ships were vulnerable to hit and run attacks that could not destroy the fleet but could certainly exhaust it, depress its morale, and delay it from carrying out its other tasks. Ultimately Wolfe and his staff, who had all almost exclusively been army officers since puberty or just before, had no understanding of naval warfare. There was no centralized, formal officer training in the Georgian army, except for the engineers and artillerymen, and certainly no defence academy to prepare men for higher command. Army officers learnt their trade in their regiment; any abstract or wider thinking about military affairs was left to the individual officer's personal interests.

There was one particular feature of naval custom that drove army officers mad with envy. The sailors of the 'senior service' returned from war with vast fortunes gained through prize money; financial rewards derived from the value of any enemy ships they captured. It was a perk hardly ever available to their marching brethren. It was 'curious enough' states the 'Family Journal' that while 'death and wounds were rife in the several posts of the army', the navy was safe on board their ships, far from the expert Canadian marksmen or the tomahawks of the Native Americans. Worse still the fleet were apparently 'in deep dispute about sharing a prize that was taken in the chops of the river'. The naval officers were bickering about the spoils of war paid for by the blood of Wolfe's men.[115]

Wolfe's diatribe against the fleet that had brought his force so efficiently to Quebec is impossible to excuse but easier to understand. Progress was slow; frustratingly slow, given the overwhelming preponderance of naval power in the basin of Quebec. But Wolfe's dismissal of his navy's contribution is not reflected by the French sources. They are universally in awe of the British naval effort. Time and again writers praise the skill and temerity of the British sailors, such as on one occasion when 'an English frigate ... [was] seen in the north channel, engaged in trying to penetrate about a mile and a half beyond the falls of Montmorency, which excited the surprise of our pilots; who had always declared, that there was not in that part even water sufficient for a vessel of ten tons'.[116]

The fleet faced an attritional struggle. It would take time to sweep the French boats from the St Lawrence. The immediate consequence of the navy's inability to dominate the waters around Quebec by early July was the forced suspension of Wolfe's thrust upriver. The General's journal records that Murray had returned from his reconnoitre 'satisfied with the practicability of the attempt'.[117] Mackellar records that 'upon his return there was a plan fixed for landing there', and, because the French still blocked the narrows and the purpose-built flat-bottomed boats would not be able to get above the town, 'some rafts, for ferrying the troops across the river were ordered to be made at Point de Levis'. However, he confirms in the same entry that 'that plan was soon afterwards laid aside'.[118] The scenario that haunted Wolfe was that if he did push a force ashore, the French small boats would block the river and his men would be cut off from reinforcement. He was also nervous about French counter-measures. The French had not remained supine as groups of British troops ranged around on the south shore. Already a force of 300 Canadians had been sent to Anse des Mères just above the town. A French journal tells of a cunning plan to carry 'a quantity of tents sufficient for a much larger body of troops, in the hope of deceiving the English'.[119]

Instead of sending grenadiers splashing through the shallows into the enemy's positions Wolfe sent a strongly worded letter. At midday on 4 July, in the midst of a hail storm, the first of many official messages passed between the commanders of the two belligerents.[120] Truces were entirely normal though their protocol was tightly proscribed. If the British initiated the truce a white flag would be waved, while since the French fought under the white Bourbon flag they used a red one to ask for a ceasefire. Emissaries would then emerge. Quick-witted men like Bougainville were often used so that they could engage the enemy in verbal jousting, which would both dampen the spirits of, and glean information from, the enemy officers. Truces were also an opportunity to have a look at the condition of the enemy defences. To prevent this Amherst ordered his army in 1759 that any messenger was to be kept outside the camp's defences so 'that they cannot see any of the post outworks or camps till the answer from the general is returned'.[121]

The French in Quebec were keen to deny Wolfe's emissary a good look at their defences. A French journal relates that as the British sloop with its white flag made for the Lower Town, 'there was some reason to suspect that this was a pretext for sending an engineer, disguised as a common seaman, to take a closer survey of the state of Quebec'. To prevent this, a French boat was sent out to receive the letter, 'without allowing a nearer approach of the English vessel'.[122] Another journal claimed that 'there were three or four officers or engineers who were disguised as sailors but they were recognized by their look and their hands being white and not used to hard labour'.[123]

Wolfe's letter declared his intention to attack Quebec. This chivalrous, if spectacularly superfluous, announcement also contained a threat. It warned that 'it was his Majesty's express command to have the war conducted without practising the inhuman method of scalping, and it was expected the French troops under [Montcalm's] command to copy the example, as they shall answer the contrary'. Wolfe was trying to impose the norms of European warfare on a campaign that stubbornly refused to comply. Le Mercier carried Vaudreuil's reply to the British 'taking two or three captains with him, dressed as sailors, to look at the state of the enemy fleet'.[124] Vaudreuil attempted to conjure up some of the defiant rhetoric of his forebear, Frontenac, who had so haughtily dismissed a previous British surrender demand. He intimated his 'surprise' that 'with so few forces [Wolfe] would attempt the conquest of so extensive and populous a country as Canada'.[125] He also let Durell know that his grandson, snatched on the Île aux Coudres, was in good health and that he 'had treated the prisoners with honour, and that as soon as the Admiral will have the kindness to inform him of his departure, that he will send them back to him'.[126]

Vaudreuil's defiant words projected a unity that was in reality absent from the French high command. Internecine squabbling split the French decision makers just as it had set Wolfe against his naval officers and at least one brigadier. Many felt that the French had let the British come ashore and consolidate their positions. Crowds gathered and demanded to be sent to attack the enemy, who were even now preparing batteries which would unleash a terrible bombardment on their town.[127] Every civilian diarist became a tactical genius, advocating ambushes and assaults that would surely drive the British back into the Atlantic. One stated that 'it is evident that had there been 500 or 600 savages at the isle of Orléans, and as many at the Pointe de Lévis, they would have been able, at the moment of the debarkation of the English, or on their penetrating into the woods, to have killed a great number, and perhaps have entirely defeated them'. The reason for this being that 'the English were all regular troops, who marched in close ranks, and would not have dared to engage where the woods were so thick as to be almost impervious'.[128] Another account pointed out that even if these kinds of attacks were beaten off, 'a secure retreat was always to be found in the woods in the rear, where the Canadian and Indian, 'tis known, possess so great an advantage over regulars'.[129] The problem for the interventionists was working out where best to aim the blow. The British 'were endeavouring to mislead us', complained one journal, 'it was also difficult for us to judge in which place they had their largest body of troops'.[130]

In early July the first resupply convoy sailed up the St Lawrence and delivered food to the British forces. Knox tasted 'fresh provisions' for the first time since landing.[131] The unglamorous business of resupplying the British army would determine whether Quebec would stand or fall. No troops, however brave, skilled, motivated, or well led, could survive without food in their bellies and powder in their cartridge cases. The army and fleet would not be forced to raise the siege due to a shortage of food. This remarkable logistical achievement was the bedrock on which Wolfe could make his next moves.

SIX

A New Kind of War

THE SUN WAS LOW in the western sky, and Quebec was etched in a bright golden backlight. The long sloping roofs of the Upper Town and the spires of the cathedral flashed as the sun reflected off into the basin below. On the tip of Île d'Orléans the hour had arrived. Wolfe's 'Family Journal' relates how they had been waiting all day for the light to dip, and 'at 8 O'clock in the evening, when the enemy could not see our motions, the general began his march'.[1] Half of the tents in the camp had been struck and were now on carts; the other half stood to lull the enemy into thinking that nothing was afoot. First to leave the camp, of course, were the light infantrymen and the rangers. Wolfe's harsh criticism of the latter, so violent before the campaign started, was now muted. His constant use of them as scouts and to secure the flanks of his army on the march suggested that they had won his grudging respect. These men left camp in a loose formation, dressed in a roguish assortment of gear, their unit denoted only by the dark green jackets that had been found for them. Tomahawks dangled from straps at their waists. Filthy rolled-up blankets were wrapped around their torsos. In their arms most cradled their muskets, while a minority carried longer rifles, which they had carefully loaded before leaving camp. Their flints were good and sharp, the powder and ball rammed home, the frizzen snugly in position, protecting the priming powder. On their heads was a highly irregular assortment of caps and hats made from leather and fur and many were decorated with flowers and feathers, like young boys playing at soldiers. Behind them, marching in columns to a regular drumbeat, came the red-coated men of Wolfe's infantry. Their muskets were strictly sloped on their left shoulders, forming the longest side of a triangle with their left arm supporting the butt, a forearm's length away from the body. The rhythmical crunch of their studded shoes on the earth, the rattle of the drummer's sticks on the tight skin of the drumhead, the jangling of thousands of pans and kettles in backpacks, the clink of flask, and the soft thud of bayonets which swung and bounced against their thighs as the men trudged along, all combined to form the instantly recognizable soundtrack to the men's lives.

It was twilight on 8 July 1759 and over two thousand soldiers were on the march. Wolfe's 'Family Journal' says 'the corps was composed of the Grenadiers of Louisbourg, the light infantry of the line, the grenadiers of the 1st brigade, General Townshend's Brigade and [Captain] Dank's Rangers'.[2] Unable to land forces upriver of Quebec, Wolfe was looking elsewhere to break the stalemate on the St Lawrence. Earlier that day, Wolfe had found time to reply to an acquaintance, Captain Henry Parr, who had written to him hoping for a job. Wolfe told him that 'I have little time for letter writing as you can well fancy at present' and a sense of his frustration is palpable. 'Thus far,' he continued, 'we have done little, although M de Montcalm has suffered badly from our cannon and mortar.' However, 'tomorrow, all being well, we move a little closer, changing camp to the north bank of the river'.[3] To that end the column made its way towards the north shore of the Île d'Orléans, 'to that part of the island opposite the falls of Montmorency'.[4] Here they would be met by the flat-bottomed boats which would ferry them across to the north bank of the St Lawrence to the east of the Montmorency falls.

There would be an impressive deception campaign, planned by Wolfe to stop the French concentrating their forces and attempting to repel the landing. 'In order to draw the enemy's attention elsewhere the camp was struck at Levis, and the boats of the fleet assembled there; and Lawrence's battalion [3rd/60th] that were aboard the transports threatened Beauport.'[5] This carefully synchronized ballet of all the disparate parts of Wolfe's force should paralyse the French response until the landings were beyond their most vulnerable early stages.

The French spent the night, as they had spent every other since the landings on Île d'Orléans, awake and in their trenches, redoubts, and batteries, expecting a British assault. One journal records that, 'every night had been passed under Arms, both in the camp, and in Quebec; from the apprehension that each succeeding night was to be that of the intended disembarkation'.[6] As Saunders' ships escorted the transports closer to Beauport and around Point Lévis, one French officer commented that there was 'a doubt in our camp, whether this motion of the enemy had any real object or design'. This officer suggested that the high command regarded this latest movement as another feint and 'under this false persuasion, that nothing could be attempted on that side, no measures were taken, either to prevent or disconcert their operations, or to make them purchase their success at a dear rate'.[7]

Another admirable deception ploy on the part of Wolfe was, as a French journal noted with dismay the next day, to send his 'flat bottomed boats to make a great circuit, all round the east of the Isle d'Orléans'.[8] They arrived on the north side of the island, unseen by the French, and just before dawn they took the men across. While the soldiers established a beachhead, Saunders sent ships to provide fire support. Montresor saw the *Captain*, sixty-four guns, get as close to the north bank as possible to pound French shore positions. New Englander Captain Rous with his fifty-gun *Sutherland* also risked the shallow waters on an ebb tide to add his support. A bomb ketch lobbed mortars at the shore, although Montresor was unimpressed, 'bombs fired on the enemy's three encampments near the falls of Montmorency, with little effect as most of the fires were short and the distance great'.[9] The mortars were actually more effective than he gave them credit for. One French journal writes that 'the English sent a bomb ketch near to the falls of Montmorency, which fired incessantly throughout the whole night, bombs, and balls … till they forced the Canadians to retire to a less exposed situation'.[10]

Whatever the damage caused by the naval gunfire Wolfe's troops were able to splash ashore and start seizing key ground, with no sign of opposition. The light infantry were in the first flat-bottomed boats, then the grenadiers, led by those from Monckton's brigade, next those of the Louisbourg garrison and finally those from Townshend's brigade. Last, the three regiments, Bragg's 28th, Monckton's 2nd Battalion of the 60th Royal Americans, and then Lascelles' 47th. Wolfe was one of the first ashore; his 'Family Journal' comments, 'the descent was effected without firing a shot'.[11] In front of them was a very steep escarpment while a few hundred yards to the west the Montmorency River crashed over a spectacular waterfall 280 feet high. When Knox had first spotted it he described it as 'a stupendous natural curiosity'.[12]

The falls had been named by Samuel de Champlain after Henri, Duc de Montmorency who served as a viceroy of New France in the early seventeenth century. Today tourists clamber up a dubious-looking wooden staircase, slippery with spray. Above the falls the river was 'narrow but deep with high and steep woody banks', according to an officer in Wolfe's army.[13] It is a description that still rings true. It is no more than one hundred and fifty feet wide but the banks are thickly wooded. There are fords where men and animals could wade across, but these would take time for Wolfe to scout out. They were known to the Canadian defenders and like narrow passes in a range of mountains they were easy for small groups of crack troops to defend. In addition, the journey to the fords on either side was along tracks through thick woodland. By risking a battle in the woods, the British would be, at best, unable to fight in the manner that most suited them, that of fast, massed volleys in the open against an enemy they could see. At worst, they risked another Monongahela. As Wolfe and his officers took in the land with their practised eyes, none of them would have been without any doubt that although they had reached the north shore of the St Lawrence, they still had a river to cross.

In the next few hours, however, there were far more immediate threats to the force than the prospect of a tricky river crossing at some stage in the future. The landing force was vulnerable: the men were unsure of their new surroundings, no defences bolstered their position, supplies were yet to be landed, the sun was up and the enemy now clearly aware of the move, which the night before had been shrouded by deceit. Wolfe hurried to make camp, no easy task, 'having five pieces of ordnance to drag up a very difficult hill, and the weather bad'.[14] In his haste, according to Brigadier Townshend, who was bringing his brigade ashore next, Wolfe led the grenadiers and light infantry off the beach and left the following troops no indication of where they had gone. As Townshend landed he found

> no one sent to show me the road the rest had taken though it was dark. And found all the baggage of the different grenadiers and light infantry left in a long string in the meadows at considerable distances. No officer to command the whole, and no where more than five men together, so that 10 savages might have plundered the whole and massacred the men one by one.

The horrified Townshend immediately organized a guard and led his men blindly up the slope, assuming that was where Wolfe had led the vanguard. On catching up with his general, he was shocked to find himself reprimanded: 'upon my arrival at the headquarters the general gave me a hint that he thought I had not passed – suggesting I suppose that I had been dilatory'. Townshend's journal brims with righteous indignation; in it he swears that 'I had never waited a moment but for the mounting of the cannon'.[15]

Sadly we do not have Wolfe's side of the account but there is plenty of evidence to suggest that his relationship with Townshend was not a happy one. Previous generations of historians cast Townshend as the villain of the piece, a scheming aristocratic soldier of no worth who tirelessly undermined the flawless Wolfe. This no longer rings true but in place of certainty we have only conjecture. We know that Wolfe believed Townshend to be a political general and not a professional soldier. This can only have been reinforced by Townshend's curious choice of uniform while on the campaign. He wrote to his wife, saying, 'I wear my militia regimentals at Quebec, and trust that if occasion draws them out I shall see more glorious days with that uniform.'[16] This flaunted his belief in amateur soldiering in front of Wolfe, the ultimate professional to whom the militia was nothing but an ineffective waste of money. Wolfe was also not allowed to forget Townshend's unmatchable political connections. Although they were in the depths of a wild continent, they were by no means free from the tentacles of the Georgian state. Orders shouted in the heat of battle could reverberate through the halls of Westminster in months to come. Wolfe's journal refers to one fascinating example of this. Two days before, on 7 July, he records that there has been 'some difference of opinion upon a military point termed slight and insignificant and the Commander in Chief is threatened with parliamentary inquiry into his conduct for not consulting an inferior officer and seeming to disregard his sentiments!'[17] This is all the more tantalizing because this is the only mention of the incident in any surviving material. It is fairly likely that this 'inferior officer' was Townshend and we can be absolutely certain that wearing a militia uniform and threatening his commanding officer with a parliamentary inquiry every time he was not consulted was not the way for Townshend to win Wolfe's trust and friendship. Wolfe's 'Family Journal' gives us a typically cutting critique of Townshend's character, suggesting there were personal as well as political and professional differences between the two. It says that he was 'of a fickle and inconsistent mind, his line of life not directed by any fixed principles, and as he is exceedingly subject to very high and very low spirits'. The author objected to the company he kept, 'his favours are not directed by merit, he is always surrounded by the most indifferent subjects in the army'. There is perhaps a hint that Wolfe's more serious circle found the charismatic Townshend's popularity threatening: 'he has a great deal of humour well sustained with bawdy, and may be esteemed an excellent tavern acquaintance; in matters respecting the movements and conduct of an army he is without a scale. The circle is too large for his capacity to embrace.'[18]

Their time together in the new Montmorency camp did not lead the two men to bond. In fact, their relationship deteriorated still further. Townshend was appalled when Wolfe appeared to tease him about the strength of his fortifications. Despite being almost surrounded by woods in which hostile forces lurked, Townshend's journal records that Wolfe 'went round the front and disapproved of it saying I had indeed made myself secure, for I had made a fortress'.[19] Another of Townshend's documents records that he 'was almost reprimanded for the strength and form of my fortification', even though the 'insecurity of our disposition and outposts had brought the enemy's savages into the very centre of our quarters'.[20] Next they argued about the orientation of the camp and its vulnerability to French cannon across the

Montmorency River. Matters came to a head when Townshend heard on 13 July that Wolfe was going to visit the camp at Point Lévis, 'leaving me the first officer in the camp, not only without orders but also even ignorant of his departure or time of return'. He rushed down the St Lawrence 'as fast as I could' and caught Wolfe just before he was about to embark. Townshend recorded that Wolfe received him 'in a very stately manner; not advancing five steps'. Townshend 'told him that if I had suspected his intention of going over I had waited on him for his Commands which I should be very glad to receive and execute to his satisfaction'. '"Sir,"' Wolfe replied 'very dryly, "The Adjutant General has my orders, permit me, Sir, to ask are the troops to encamp now on their new ground or not to do it until the enemy's battery begins to play."' With this witheringly rude remark, made in public, Wolfe took his leave. Townshend wrote, 'I must observe that he must have had an uncommon disposition to find fault with me.'[21] Wolfe's clipped journal makes no mention of these disagreements that Townshend records in such detail. Yet again, however, Wolfe's 'Family Journal' helps to fill in the gaps. Around the middle of July the author of that journal wrote, 'I was sorry to see the seeds of sedition here, which afterwards grew into a great tree, and spread its branches over Townshend's and Murray's tables; to account for it, one needs only enquire into the characters of the two men, and you there find a soil that must produce such fruit.' The author is clear, however, that 'the officers of the army instead of being seduced by their conversation, took offence at it, so gross were their reflections, and so well established the character of Wolfe'.[22]

The new camp was surrounded on its landward side by woodland with the Montmorency River and the St Lawrence at their backs. It was a threatening position. Through the morning of the British landings Montcalm's irregulars dropped into the Montmonrency River and waded across the fords that they knew well. Panet says 200 'Ottawa savages moved there willingly' alongside a number of Canadians.[23] A party of rangers, commanded by Captain Benonie Dank, was stationed during the morning around three hundred yards from the new encampment nervously checking the woodland for any threats as working parties cut wood with which to build stockades and other defences. At

1000 hours the silence of the woods was broken by a crash of musketry
and the scream of Native American warriors as they followed their
volley with a lightning attack. Leaping through the undergrowth they
fell upon the rangers, finishing off the wounded, scattering the rest of
the stunned company. The dead and dying were scalped with a swift
flash of the knife and then the tomahawk was taken to the survivors
before they had time to rally. Dank was hit and the rangers had lost
around 20 per cent of their strength in a few seconds. Wolfe comments
simply that they were 'defeated' and suffered, 'so many killed and
wounded as to be almost disabled for the rest of the campaign'.[24]
Townshend's account in his private papers is somewhat different to
the picture of calm security that he painted for his wife and mother in
regular letters home. He wrote that 'a number of their savages rushed
suddenly down upon us from the rocky woody height, drove a few
Rangers that were there down to my quarters for refuge, wounded
both their officers, and in an instant scalped 13 or 14 of their men'.
He found himself directly in harm's way as one ranger 'was wounded
at my door and the other close by it'. The grenadiers of Bragg's 28th
stood to arms and threw themselves into a counter-attack. 'Had it not
been for Bragg's grenadiers,' Townshend records, 'who attacked the
Indians very bravely, whilst some inclined round to the right to
surround them – they [would have] spread confusion everywhere.'[25]

As so often the Native Americans seemed, according to Panet, to
have become 'preoccupied with taking scalps' and had lost their cohesion. This left them vulnerable to the grenadiers' attack and they wisely
avoided a pitched battle and disappeared into the woods as quickly as
they had struck.[26] Some of the wounded were saved by this quick
counter-attack. The grenadiers pressed on to the banks of the Montmorency where a withering fire from marksmen on the far bank pinned
them down as the Native Americans swam and waded back to safety.
Wolfe later reported to Pitt that 'the enemy also suffered in this affair'
and his 'Family Journal' records that 'by accounts since the Indians
lost six killed, 30 wounded, two only were left on the field'.[27] The
Native Americans always made every effort to carry off their wounded
with them so it was difficult to know the scale of their casualties; this
led the British to always wildly exaggerate the number of enemy dead

and wounded. Panet says that they lost only three men and five injured. The raid was merely the first in a series of vicious encounters in and around the camp at Montmorency. Situated so close to the enemy camp, across usable fords that were well known to the locals, the defenders spent every day feeling like they were under the barrel of an enemy gun, and could only leave the fortifications in force. John Johnson recalled that 'it was generally reckoned by all, that the duty at Montmorency far exceeded all the rest, both for difficulty and danger', with his time there punctuated by frequent 'sharp skirmishes'.[28]

After it was over Wolfe's wounded could look forward to an uncomfortable transfer to the field hospital, which was now set up at the Île d'Orléans camp. Planning for a hospital with a capacity of 400 had been made during the winter. Neat lists of everything required from the two surgeons to '1000 wooden spoons' bear witness to the minute care taken over the preparations for every aspect of the operation. The surgeons were supported by an apothecary, ten surgeon's mates, a clerk, storekeeper, and a steward. Five hundred beds were brought up the St Lawrence, with 1,500 blankets and 500 sheets. The hospital had its own designated cows and twenty barrels of oatmeal. 'Particular care' was taken 'that there is a sufficiency of medicine'. Two items on the list remind us of the macabre realities of eighteenth-century medicine: the surgeons' tools, '2 Chopping Knives' and '2 Flesh Forks'.[29] If the wounded men survived the tender mercies of the surgeons, but were unable to carry on soldiering, then their only safety net was one of two Royal Hospitals.

The Francophile Charles II had founded a Royal Hospital, in faraway Chelsea, upstream along the Thames from London, in 1681, after apparently being deeply impressed by reports of Louis XIV's Hôtel des Invalides on the south side of the Seine in Paris for the worn-out victims of his self-aggrandizement. Its aim was, and still is, to provide 'succour and relief of veterans broken by age and war'. Luckily enough Christopher Wren was on hand to build it and the magnificent building was finished in 1692, complete with formal gardens with canals and summer houses that stretched down to the Thames. A full house of 476 pensioners was assembled within a few months. Those seeking residence or simply a monthly stipend had to report in person to Chelsea or the hospital in Dublin, built for the King's Irish subjects. No system of examination by proxy officials existed. This made it a trying process for Scottish or American veterans who would have to make the arduous journey to appear before the board.

Pensioners were maintained by a 'poundage' paid by serving soldiers, a stoppage of a day's pay per year from every man in the army. Clearly the nascent British Empire generated more broken old soldiers than the hospital could cater for. Not everyone was as lucky as John Johnson, one of the most detailed chroniclers of the Quebec campaign, who was an 'in-pensioner', 'lodged in safety, basking under the bright beams of His Most Gracious Majesty, in Chelsea Hospital'. As a resident he was 'plentifully provided with every comfortable necessity of life, by the benevolence of his country'. Thus looked after, 'and having too much leisure time, and no profitable employment he set himself down; and for the amusement of himself, as also such of his comrades, who were partakers with him in the toils and dangers mentioned in the following memoirs'.[30] Most old soldiers were considerably less lucky. They were given a slip of paper which they could present to a magistrate every three months for a pension, usually 5d. a day, less than an agricultural wage, and were otherwise left to fend for themselves.

Hugh Smith had arrived in Chelsea in March 1759 and instantly excited the pity of the board. The register records that he was 'scalped by the Indians in America'. Room was found for him even though as a 30-year-old he had not served the twenty years that he should have done in order to qualify. Once ensconced he could look forward to two pints of beer a day, a pound of meat and one of bread, and enough tobacco to puff on while he no doubt argued with John Johnson about the ideal length of a musket barrel or whether rifling was any use in the close quarters woodland battles of North America. He is not the only example of a man who survived scalping. The admission rolls bear witness to two or three others who carried this most American of wounds back to the leafy towns and villages west of London.[31]

A pattern was now clearly emerging. Using their irregular Canadians and Native Americans in small raiding parties, the French would swoop on the British and hand them a small but eye-catching defeat. There would then be a round of recriminations in the French camp as to why these successes were not followed up. One French officer says that during this last raid, the Native Americans had sent to 'Chevalier de Levy for assistance', but he was too slow in responding and 'arrived too late'. The officer saw this as typical; 'this was not the only instance, in which the slowness of our motions was a service to the enemy'.[32] Another officer was furious that the attack was not pressed home, given that 'never was more ardor visible than was manifested on this occasion by the soldier, the Canadian and Indian'; many of his fellow officers 'appeared to despair on seeing such happy arrangements neglected'.[33] It was understandable frustration but to a great extent the duration and scale of these raids was determined by the nature of the Native societies from whence these warriors emerged. Their small populations limited the number of available men and also imposed a very conservative understanding of 'acceptable losses'. Native Americans fought on their own terms, when they found the enemy weak. If they returned to the British camp with reinforcements they would have found a quite unsuitable situation waiting for them. British troops lined up, with shouldered arms and bayonets fixed. Wolfe realized this better than anyone and returned to the subject time and again in his orders to the army. Just days earlier he had told his men that he would order 'some of the light troops to retire before the enemy at times, so as to draw them nearer to the army, with a view either to engage them to fight at a disadvantage, or to cut off their retreat'.[34] In this situation the Native Americans would have thought it worthless pressing home any attack.

This was why Montcalm regarded these raids as militarily insignificant. His main concern was to avoid sending his regulars, needed for the defence of the city and the Beauport shore, to reinforce or rescue every Canadian group of adventurers who crawled off to have a dig at the British. If he sent regulars into these situations, they risked becoming entangled in a slogging match which he feared the more numerous British infantry would win.

However, he underestimated the utility of this kind of warfare in two ways. Since he believed hugely inflated accounts of British strength he did not give this irregular warfare enough credit for its attritional effect. The loss of every musket-carrying infantryman was very serious to Wolfe. Dank's company of rangers had been virtually put out of action for the rest of the campaign by the briefest of fights. Mackellar was to write a little later in the summer that although on the occasion of each raid 'we always repulsed the enemy' it was 'seldom without some little loss, which in the end amounted to a pretty considerable number'.[35] Losses of key personnel like officers, engineers, and NCOs would seriously erode Wolfe's ability to carry out complex operations. The death of a commander might prove decisive. History is littered with examples of campaigns that have been totally derailed following the death of a leader. Just the year before a confused skirmish in the woodlands outside Fort Carillon had led to the death of George Augustus, 3rd Viscount Howe, the young, dashing second in command of Abercrombie's ill-fated army. His death was widely held, in Britain, France, and their respective colonies, to have been the cause of Abercrombie's subsequent dithering and defeat.

Second, Montcalm seems to have ignored the psychological impact of these raids. In the same entry Mackellar says that the British troops 'soon began to despise' the Canadians and Native Americans. It was a hatred born out of sheer terror. This was one of Montcalm's most potent weapons and he did little to exploit it. A more adaptable, free-thinking commander would have spent time considering how to use the techniques of ambush and raiding to inflict greater casualties on the British and grind down their morale.

Despite Montcalm's hesitancy, throughout July the British troops were faced with brutal fighting that bordered on full-scale insurgency. On coming ashore Wolfe had taken steps to try to ensure the neutrality of the Canadian *habitants* in his confrontation with the forces of France. Orders were issued to the British troops forbidding the endemic looting that accompanied the passage of soldiers: 'any soldier who is found with plunder in his tent, or returning with plunder to the army of any kind not taken by order, shall be sent directly to the provost in irons, in order to be tried for his life'. These failed to stem the habit, which soldiers seem to have regarded as one of their official perks. Knox reports that the light infantry returned from one patrol 'well loaded with plunder of various kinds'.[36] Wolfe issued constant threats throughout the summer to try to stop it. One of these stated that 'no churches, houses, or buildings of any kind are to be destroyed or burned without orders. The peasant that remains in their habitations, their women and children are to be treated with humanity; if any violence is offered to a woman, the offender shall be punished by death.'[37]

Wolfe had notices attached to church doors that informed Canadians that 'The King, my master, justly irritated against France and resolved to lower her insolence and revenge the insults offered to the English Colonies, has at length determined to send to Canada the formidable sea and land armament which the people of Canada now behold in the heart of their country.' He assured them that 'the King of Great Britain wages no war against industrious Colonists and peasants, nor against women and children, nor the sacred ministers of religion; he foresees their distressful circumstances, pities their lot and extends to them offers of protection'. Provided that they 'take no part directly or indirectly in the contest between the two crowns', he assured them that they 'can, without fearing the least molestation, there enjoy their property, attend to their religious worship; in a word, enjoy, in the midst of war, all the sweets of peace'.[38]

It was spectacularly naive to believe that the *habitants* would remain as disinterested observers watching the British, whose 'object' the proclamation admitted was to 'totally deprive the French crown of its most valuable settlement in north America'. This was not Flanders where the people were happy to provide a picturesque backdrop to the formalized military posturing of *ancien régime* Europe, their rights as non-combatants protected carefully by each successive commander, the armies differing only in the colour of their coats. This was Canada, where generations of *habitants* had fought wars for its very existence, time and again, against enemies who had sought its, and their, total annihilation. Even today stories of shocking violence, of last ditch defences of stockades, of families butchered by the Mohawk are still part of the popular consciousness. In 1759 people only had to look to the miserable fate of the exiled Acadians, thrown off their burnt farms by the British, and now living among them, trying to rebuild shattered lives. The name, nationality, and religion of the resident of the Governor General's palace mattered to the people of Canada.

Even if they had wanted to remain neutral, they had no choice. Every man who could bear arms was in the militia. His duty was to fight the invaders. If he proved hesitant his enthusiasm was boosted by Native American war parties that Vaudreuil sent out to remind Canadians where their loyalties lay. Colonel Williamson, Wolfe's chief artillery officer, wrote to a colleague during the summer that 'the sharp lookout of Vaudreuil's Indians alone kept the peasant militiamen from stealing home to their farms, wives and children'.[39] Williamson was unfair in suggesting that force alone kept the Canadians with Montcalm's army, many did not need the encouragement. As the accounts on both sides all attest, many Canadians were keen to kill redcoats. Any British soldier who left camp alone or found himself isolated while on patrol or with work parties risked a horrible death. Ramezay reports that 'every day, we saw them walking up and down around the dwellings at Point Levis with self-assurance, even though the inhabitants who retreated into the woods are harassing them constantly, and every day they kill some of them as soon as they wander away from their detachments'.[40] Even the camp on the Île d'Orléans was not immune. One journal records that two of the Louisbourg Grenadiers 'were scalped, and most cruelly mangled on the east end of the island of Orléans by three lurking Indians'.[41] They had paddled over from the north shore and lain in ambush. Johnson records a typical incident, in which three men took themselves into the woods to have a poke around for any wild vegetables 'to eat with their salt meat; and which are good for several disorders, and with which the woods abound in the summer season'. No sooner had they entered the wood but 'they were surprised by a party of these Canadian savages, and butchered in the most cruel and barbarous manner; being first killed and scalped, then ripped open and their heart taken out and themselves left on the spot where they had committed this horrid barbarity'.[42] Such savage violence led to a steep spiralling in relations between the British troops and particularly their Canadian and Native American enemy. Atrocity sparked atrocity.

Wolfe issued order after order trying to keep wandering redcoats, accustomed to augment their diets when on campaign by purchasing victuals from the locals or roaming the forests, strictly in their camps or with their detachment at all times. 'The first soldier who is taken beyond the out-guard, either in the front, rear, or flanks of the army, contrary to the most positive orders, shall be tried by a general court martial,' he ordered. The camps would be made impregnable, fortified 'in such a manner to put it entirely out of the enemy's power to attempt any thing by surprise, and that the troops may rest in security after their fatigues'. Even with their stockades and breastworks, 'the safety of an army depends in great measure upon the vigilance of the out-guards, any officer or non-commissioned officer who shall suffer himself to be surprised by the enemy, must not expect to be forgiven'.[43]

It was not just Britons who were suffering. Despite attempting to shelter the innocents of the St Lawrence, inevitably their blood was spilt. Malcolm Fraser was appalled by an incident involving a group of rangers operating on the south bank of the St Lawrence. Nearly every day the rangers would be out disputing control of wooded no-man's-land and looking for prisoners to provide valuable intelligence. It was a parallel campaign to the more formal machinations of Wolfe and, sadly, is far less well chronicled. But for much of the summer it was the rangers and light infantry who were doing the bulk of the fighting. On one such raid Fraser heard that a group of rangers had captured a Canadian *habitant*. The prisoner had two young sons who followed the raiders crying out in distress. Fraser wrote that they were both 'murdered by those worse than savage Rangers, for fear, as they pretend, they should be discovered by the noise of the children'. He knew the cause: 'cowardice and barbarity ... seems so natural to a native of America, whether of Indian or European extraction'. Knox relates the story only slightly changed. He said the ranger officer was mortified by what he had been forced to do; apparently, 'the officer declared to me that it was with the greatest reluctance that can be conceived'.[44]

The rangers also provided protection to the infantrymen who were hard at work on defences for the camp on Point Lévis and new batteries with which to bombard the town. Every day, according to Knox, the sharp-eyed rangers 'took post on all the adjoining hills, which command the road' that ran along the coast and joined the batteries to the encampment. On each hilltop perched 'small parties [of rangers] with breastworks about them'.⁴⁵ Below them work on the batteries was proceeding apace.

Wolfe had written to Monckton, whose brigade was labouring on the construction on and around Point Lévis, saying that he intended the batteries to unleash 'such a tremendous fire, that no human head can venture to peep up near it'. Wolfe had given Saunders and the navy long enough to deal with the enemy's gunboats and floating batteries, now he intended to take matters into his own hands. 'I think it the greatest misfortune, that so much water business interferes with us,' he told his second in command before outlining his solution. He would blast them off the surface of the St Lawrence. The heavy but scarce thirty-two-pound cannonballs should not be fired at the town but at 'the boats and every swimming thing', all of which 'must be shattered'.⁴⁶

A mile down the coast, where the river was at its absolute narrowest, were the batteries at Pointe aux Pères. They were connected to the camp by a road with fortified strongpoints at regular intervals. The ever cheery and observant Knox enjoyed even this drudgery, 'Being on a working party this morning at our batteries, I had a most agreeable prospect of the city of Quebec for the first time.' But he looked on the town not as a tourist but as a demolition specialist. After his inspection he decided that 'it is a very fair object for our artillery particularly the lower town whose buildings are closer and more compact than the upper'.⁴⁷

Knox and his men worked hard on the necessary batteries. Vast amounts of hardware were disgorged by the naval ships and transports: 'mortars, guns, shells, shot, and all manner of artillery stores, are landing at every tide'. Sailors rowed backwards and forwards with the cannon suspended underwater beneath the boats. Once ashore they were hauled into a 'park of artillery and stores adjoining to our camp'. It was no mean task. Knox tells us that 'the heaviest guns on shore are 32 pounders and largest mortars are 13 inches'.⁴⁸ This was firepower on an industrial scale, an extraordinary contrast to the ancient warfare of war parties and knives that was being fought by Native Americans and rangers only yards away. Thirty-two-pound cannon were around three yards long and weighed three tons. Even the much smaller nine-pounder guns weighed more than a ton each. Only the Royal Navy could carry this weight of firepower into the heart of North America. The *Neptune* and the *Princess Amelia* alone had around the same number of cannon on board as the entire Anglo-German force fighting France in Europe at the time and far more than Wellington commanded at any time during the Peninsula War.[49] The artilleryman, Colonel Williamson, made great use of this vast reservoir of firepower. He later wrote that in early July, 'we marked out batteries for five 13 inch mortars and six 32 pounders borrowed from the navy to save our 24s'.[50] The navy did not just lend the guns, it sent its sailors to manhandle them into position. A British officer, two years later, witnessed sailors doing exactly this kind of work on another expedition and he wrote that

you may fancy you know the spirit of these fellows, but to see them in action exceeds any idea that can be formed of them ... a hundred or two of them, with ropes and pullies, will do more than all your dray horses in London. Let but their tackle hold and they will draw you a cannon or a mortar on its proper carriage up to any height, though the weight be never so great. It is droll enough to see them tugging along with a good 24 pounder at their heels; on they go huzzaing and hullooing, sometimes up hill, sometimes down hill; now sticking fast the brakes, presently floundering in the mud and mire; swearing, blasting, damning, sinking as if careless of everything but the matter committed to their charge as if death or danger had nothing to do with them.[51]

It was dangerous work. Not only did stragglers and strays risk death by tomahawk or knife, the French batteries across the river attempted to put a stop to the British building works by pounding them furiously with their own artillery. On 10 July Knox spent five hours under bombardment. He estimated that the French fired 122 shots and twenty-seven exploding shells, 'yet we had not a man killed or wounded'. Montresor confirms that on 10 July for the 'great part of the day the enemy kept a constant cannonading from the town on our works constructing under the command of Brigadier Monckton'. Panet also mentions this cannonade, which he watched from the walls of Quebec, although he laments that it 'did not appear that this impeded their operations at all, even though we continued firing at night'.[52] Siege warfare was the one area of eighteenth-century warfare which bore a strong resemblance to the massive industrial struggles of the twentieth. The men who built the batteries and the artillerymen who worked the guns lived in a world of trenches, sandbags, and sudden, arbitrary death from afar. Knox and his men avoided casualties in part because of the sensitivity shown by his superiors, particularly Wolfe who on one particular occasion won undying gratitude for showing 'great attention to the preservation of the men'. He ordered them to 'lie down or get under cover as soon as a flash was perceived'.[53] Back in Britain Walpole heard a similar story about Wolfe in which the General came across a soldier who was shot through the lungs. Wolfe 'stopped to press his hand ... praised his services, encouraged him not to abandon the hopes of life – assured him of leave of absence and early promotion'. Walpole concluded that Wolfe 'gave the most minute attention to the welfare and comfort of his troops; and instead of maintaining the reserve and stateliness so common with other commanders of that day, his manner was frank and open, and he had a personal knowledge of perhaps every officer in his army'.[54] Despite his abysmal relationships with his senior officers, it was these acts of thoughtfulness together with a genuine concern for the men's welfare that seem to have earned Wolfe respect and even great affection from the lower ranks of his army.

The steady progress of the batteries was too much for the people of Quebec watching from across the St Lawrence. Through telescopes they could see exactly the quantity and type of artillery that the British were assembling opposite their beloved city and nobody doubted the terrible destruction that was about to be rained down on them. A French journal describes how 'the enemy at the Point Levis was now seen to be busily employed in conveying in carts, with several yoke of oxen, mortars and cannon to the batteries opposite the town'. It reports that 'the alarm became very great, and the expectation general of the town being reduced to ashes during the night, without any place of shelter to which the inhabitants could retire safely against the bombs'. Before the British had arrived the same journal had commented that 'the strongest reliance' was being placed on the sailors who manned the French batteries and who 'were encamped under tents, pitched, each close to his battery'.[55] Now, despite their heavy fire on the British, it was clear that this confidence had been misplaced. Counter-battery fire could slow the British down but it was a nuisance rather than a serious threat. The mood was grim. Knox talked to a French prisoner brought in by the rangers and asked what the general situation was in the French camp. The prisoner replied that 'I cannot tell you any particulars being too young to judge of these matters: this I know, that we are all in great distress for bread, both army, garrison and country.'[56] Every man, whether a private citizen or a combatant, was given a soldier's ration while any woman who had insisted on staying could only buy bread from the bakery at exorbitant prices. Scarcity of food made Montcalm's army even more ungovernable. A static army is an unruly one. Young, aggressive men become easily bored. Morale is almost always higher among troops on active operations even if they face greater dangers. By deciding that his men were no match for the British in open warfare and, as a result, adopting a totally defensive posture, rooted to the redoubts and trenches, Montcalm condemned thousands of his soldiers to months of dull monotony. Restive Native Americans and Canadians roamed around looking for food and trouble. At the beginning of July the French journal commented that 'an evil was noticed today which had already existed a considerable time, this was, the desertion of the Canadians'. It blamed it on 'either from their timidity, or from their not being accustomed to restraint and regular habits, or of remaining for a length of time inactive, encamped in a plain'. Their commanders took active measures to put a stop to it and apparently these 'succeeded ... in checking its daily recurrence'.[57]

They may have been frustrated and hungry, but according to the official account, they were still 'full of ardor'. Canadians were worried by 'the progress of the enemy's works' and were desperate to strike a blow. Many of them 'renewed their representations to the Marquis de Vaudreuil for permission to form a strong detachment, with which they proposed to cross to Point Lévis and destroy the enemy's works'.[58]

Another journal says that it was particularly 'the principal merchants and tradesmen of Quebec (the persons who were the most interested in the preservation of the houses and other buildings)' who met and decided to take a petition to Vaudreuil.[59] This time permission was given for the operation to go ahead. As usual every source assigns credit and blame differently to every conceivable actor in the drama but is hard to believe, though, that Vaudreuil was not an enthusiastic advocate of offensive action by his beloved Canadians and Native Americans. Meanwhile the journals of the regular officers such as de Lévis and Montcalm have the unmistakable tone of cynical disengagement with the whole project. A source close to Vaudreuil records that 'the General [Vaudreuil], who was acquainted with the intrepidity of the farmers, consented, notwithstanding the remonstrances which reached him from other quarters, and promised to send that detachment'.[60] Ramezay reports that 'this manoeuvre was not approved of by M. le Marquis de Montcalm'.[61] The latter's journal laments that 'there is fermentation in the heads of the citizens of Quebec, they want to govern themselves and make their own decisions about military operations'.[62] One source, which has the ring of truth to it, suggests that Montcalm eventually gave his grudging acquiescence, 'to avoid discouraging the town's people'.[63] The expedition would be led by Jean-Daniel Dumas, who immediately volunteered his services. His name must have inspired confidence. Dumas had fought in Germany and Italy in the French army before transferring to the colonial service and arriving in Acadia in 1750. He immediately took to North American warfare, and proved adept at securing the services of Native American allies. He was transferred to the Ohio valley in time to march out to stop Braddock's column reaching Monongahela. During the first volleys of that battle, the French commander had been killed and Dumas had seized control, directing the rest of the fighting which resulted in a stunning victory. He was showered with praise and honours and distinguished himself on his next post as Adjutant for all the militia units on the expedition to take Fort William Henry. Vaudreuil, always relentlessly positive about the militia, claimed that 'because of his diligence, our troops, and even our Canadians, yielded nothing to the *troupes de terre* in the most precise execution of military duties'. Now he was Adjutant General for all the colonial forces in Canada, responsible for their drill, discipline, and administration. He combined bravery under fire with a personal probity almost unique in the rotten administration of New France. A later report into corruption in the colony commented that 'everywhere the Sieur Dumas was in command, expenses diminished by half on the day of his arrival, and upon his departure rose again to their normal level'.[64]

The chance to drive the British from Point Lévis under one of Canada's most dashing officers led to a surge of willing recruits. One French officer noted that 'men of all ranks, even to the mere schoolboy, volunteered in crowds for the detachment'. As a regular officer he was concerned that this 'mob of militia, without discipline' would have no chance against 'regular troops in their entrenchments'. But he was ambivalent. Although it appeared 'imprudent', it would 'cease to be so considered when it is known that those entrenchments were commanded by woods whence they could be fired on'. This was an important consideration because, as he was generous enough to admit, the militia were expert marksmen. It was a skill at which they 'excel incomparably' to the regular troops.[65]

Montcalm remained unconvinced. He was a regular officer and believed that the outcome of the campaign would be decided by regular troops. Since he had fewer than Wolfe he assumed that he would lose a straight fight. His only chance of success, he believed, lay in using his fortifications as a force multiplier. The strength of his positions would cancel out Wolfe's greater numbers. Operations like Dumas' raid were, to Montcalm, a waste of precious professional soldiers. He sent a token number of men. Only one company of *troupes de terre*, at most one hundred and fifty men, was earmarked. The rest was to be made up of a similar number of *troupes de la marine*, Canadian militiamen, and Native Americans. Around a thousand men and boys were taken on, including a gaggle of students from the Jesuit college who were given the nickname the 'Royal Syntax'. Ramezay reports that Dumas 'would have had an even larger number if we had permitted all of those to go with him who had earnestly entreated to do so. There were even some Magistrates who volunteered themselves eagerly.'[66]

Just before the departure of the motley force a deserter from the British arrived to tell them that the magazine was in an entrenchment by the church on Point Lévis. Armed with this useful intelligence they left Quebec on the evening of 12 July. They marched upstream half a mile to the Anse des Mères. A crowd of townspeople apparently 'flocked to the heights to see the embarkation'. The men of the expedition were in fine fettle, 'all manifesting the greatest ardour and full of confidence, and impatient to surprise and attack an enemy much inferior to them in number'.[67] They crossed the St Lawrence, and now in total darkness, assembled on the south bank. Dumas divided his men into three columns to advance in tandem, 'so that they might cover a larger area in their effort to find out whether the English have an outpost'.[68] Dumas was using a well-tried technique for fighting in the woods. If one force came up against a British strongpoint, the other two could outflank it and attack from behind. Any force that attempted to stop the French attack could find itself encircled and trapped.

Unfortunately, Dumas was not with a war party of Abenaki, or other hardened veterans of countless raids along the frontier. He was with a scratch rabble of amateurs who staggered and crashed through the woods, their veins fizzing with adrenalin. Perhaps inevitably elements of the various columns stumbled upon each other, saw silhouettes of men with muskets and fired blindly at them. Panet blames 'schoolboys' and 'scatterbrains' who 'fired upon their friends'.[69] As musket balls whined overhead and thumped into tree trunks the pulse of every novice raced and suddenly every shadow became a British grenadier. Muskets rang out through the woods. A couple of men were hit and like wildfire the Canadians panicked. 'They imagined themselves surrounded by the enemy,' wrote a French officer, 'fired at their own men and went tumbling over one another down the hill to get back to the canoes.'[70] Men threw away their weapons and ammunition pouches as they sprinted back to the water's edge. The accounts are as confused as the men were that night. Dumas may have managed to rally his men once or even twice only for the same thing to happen. Tantalizingly the Native Americans who had gone on ahead reported 'that the enemy were not making any movement'.[71] Panet says that

Dumas joined these Native Americans and they came 'within a rifle's range and a half' of the 'English entrenchments'.[72] If Dumas could have launched an attack he would have done so with complete surprise. In fact, the British had no idea that there had been a hostile force on the south side of the St Lawrence until days later. But Dumas was unable to rally more than a couple of hundred of his terrified flock. Trying to re-establish command and control in the dark, among a crowd of petrified, inexperienced volunteers, was an impossible job. A journal relates that 'neither the entreaties, the prayers, nor the threats of the officers had the slightest effect in reanimating their courage'.[73] At least two men were dead, others were wounded, many had discarded their weapons, and the vast majority were worthless with fright. As Dumas walked from group to group he was left in no doubt that his only option was to get back to the north side of the river. It had been an utter failure. A French officer wrote simply that the mission demonstrated 'all the extravagances a panic is capable of producing'.[74]

It was more than an embarrassing failure, it was a missed opportunity. One diarist wrote that 'this misadventure caused us the loss of one of the most favorable opportunities to strike a blow on the enemy, which the singular uneasiness we have since learned they were continually in, might have rendered of so much the greater advantage ... they had as yet only some imperfect entrenchments'.[75] A journal called it a 'disgraceful, and voluntary overthrow', and stated that it 'flung all who remained in the Town into the greatest consternation and almost into despair'.[76] Montcalm and his fellow French regulars must have had their worst snobberies confirmed about the uselessness of Canadian troops and irregular forays in general. Yet much of the blame for the failure of the expedition lies with him. Night attacks through woodland towards unreconnoitred enemy positions are one of the hardest operations to accomplish even today. Dumas' force should never have been allowed to go. The fact that it was suggests that Montcalm regarded a large proportion of his force as quite superfluous and cared not how they passed the time. Despite Montcalm's dismissal of the entire venture, it had represented a significant opportunity. By splitting the British force into three different camps Wolfe had opened himself to the possibility of one portion of it being defeated in detail. A well-led, experienced force could have administered a nasty shock to Monckton's men on Point Lévis. As well as taking a heavy toll in British men and supplies this might have retarded the construction of the batteries, thus stealing still more of Wolfe's most scarce resource: time.

There was yet more woe for the French that night. As Dumas' force blundered around in the woods the cannon in Wolfe's batteries on Point Lévis finally roared out. Shot and shell hurtled across the St Lawrence. Dumas' farce would have tragic consequences for the town and people of Quebec.

SEVEN

'Trust me, they shall feel us'

THE TRENCHES WERE ALIVE with activity. Blue-coated artillerymen mixed with infantrymen in red and pioneers in an array of ragged smocks. In front of them sat the squat outlines of cannon in a regular line, each behind a neat embrasure of packed earth or bulging, earth-filled baskets known as 'gabions'. The north-west corner of the sky was still bright. The sun had set twenty minutes before but the outline of Quebec was perfectly silhouetted. If the gunners looked to their right they would have seen British ships manoeuvring in the basin, 'bomb ketches' each carrying a giant mortar, which could fire an exploding bomb in a high, looping trajectory. To have any hope of hitting anything the ship had to be stable, and for some time the ketches had been trying to set their anchors at their bows and stern to keep themselves steady. They had spent the afternoon getting into posi-tion and had been attacked by French gunboats. Royal Navy frigates had sailed to support them and Knox watched as for an hour there was a 'smart cannonading' but without 'any damage being sustained on either side, the enemy scarce venturing to come near enough for execution'. Eventually he judged that 'the ketches got into a good situ-ation, and kept it'.[1]

At a command from the artillery officer in charge of each group of guns, the crews stepped forward. Five men surrounded each gun, two on either side and a sergeant to the rear. Four more stood further back ready to feed the iron cannon with more gunpowder from a store a safe distance away. The sergeant commanded; his rank obvious by the sash tied around his waist, his long blue jacket with broad red lapels. Each gun had been 'searched' for any cracks in the barrel that would weaken the cannon and risk it exploding, and also carefully 'wormed' to remove any impurities. After the gunpowder had been pushed down the barrel as far as it would go, a wad of hay or rag was placed between it and the cannonball, which was rolled in last. A quadrant was inserted into the mouth of the cannon which enabled the aiming officer to calculate the correct elevation. Since these cannon would be firing at near their 'utmost' range the mouths were raised to about forty-five degrees above the horizontal, by adjusting the 'elevating screw' beneath the belly of the gun, an invention less than ten years old which replaced crude wedges shoved underneath the breech. With the cannon aimed and loaded the team waited for the order to fire. Between two cannon, with its sharp point buried in the mud, was a long pole which held slow match, a 'linstock'. The match was three loosely woven hemp strands prepared with old wine and saltpetre which burnt very slowly.

At 2100 hours on 12 July, as Dumas' unlucky force was muddling through the woods towards the batteries, a rocket flew up vertically; it exploded like a firework and cast an unnatural light on the waiting men and their cannon. It was the signal to open fire. At each of the six cannon, the sergeant barked an order and the 'ventsman' stepped forward and stabbed a sharp tool down into the vent on top of the barrel, which pricked the fabric enclosing the main charge of powder in the breech below and made ignition more certain. Then he filled up the vent with a fine gunpowder. Next he stepped well back and the sergeant turned to his left and said 'fire'. The ventsman had already used the linstock to light a stiff tube of layered paper around half a yard long, which burnt at an inch a minute. He plunged this 'portfire' into the powder in the vent. There was a bright flash, and milliseconds later an almighty crash as the main charge ignited. The cannon and its carriage sprang back as if it weighed only a few pounds. Thick smoke totally engulfed the gun crew as they automatically began the reloading drill as if it was second nature. The ventsman rushed to cover the vent to stop any air getting in and igniting any residual powder. If he failed to do this properly the spongeman could lose his arms in the resulting explosion. Traditionally the spongeman had the right to hit the ventsman over the head with his staff if he thought the latter was not doing his job. When he was satisfied with his colleague's effort, the spongeman plunged a fleece attached to the end of a wooden rod into a bucket or cask of water and then rammed it dripping into the muzzle to douse any red-hot traces of powder or wadding. To the left of the barrel a gunner had a charge of powder ready, and as soon as the spongeman was finished he pushed it into the barrel. The spongeman twirled his rod around and inserted the other end into the barrel where he rammed the powder home. Next the ball was rolled down and the gun was ready to fire again. The whole team heaved at the wheels of the carriage and moved it back into position.

On board the stoutly built bomb ketches the four-ton mortars roared as they sent their gunpowder-filled bombs, thirteen inches in diameter, into a high arc above the city. Each ship was built around the mortar, it took up the entire mid-section and there were no continuous decks. The officers slept huddled at the stern, the crew at the bows while the artillerymen who fired the mortar often slept on shore or even in the ship's open boats along with their supplies. That night the decks had been soaked with river water, through a little valve in the bottom of the ship, and drenched curtains screened off the captain's cabin where artillerymen prepared fuses. The bombs were lowered in on a pulley, the fuse lit and then fired as quickly as possible. The recoil was enormous, it was absorbed by the network of massive wooden beams that cradled the mortar, but it shook every man on board to the bone.

The bombardment of Quebec had begun. Initially as Wolfe's chief artilleryman, Colonel Williamson, reported, it was carried on by the mortars on board the ships in the basin, joined by 'five 13 inch mortars and six 32 pound' cannon on Point Lévis. Interestingly Williamson says that the cannon in question were 'borrowed from the navy to save our 24 [pounder]s'. He wanted to avoid too much wear and tear on the barrels of his twenty-four pounders which were the most efficient weapons for battering down the walls of Quebec whenever the British army could get itself across to the north shore and start the close siege. The guns were operating at long ranges, firing at targets 'from 1100 to 2000 yards' away.[2]

With cold barrels and a new target Knox reports that the first and second volleys 'fell rather short' much to the rejoicing of the enemy, 'who put forth many triumphant shouts on the occasion'. Their laughter was soon stilled as 'we immediately got to the proper distance and changed their mirth'.[3] It was terribly cruel on the Quebecers who saw the first balls splash harmlessly in the river only to see the range creep forward with every subsequent discharge. Soon solid round cannonballs were smashing into the stone houses of the Lower Town. Perhaps even worse were the 'carcasses', iron baskets reminiscent of skeletons, hence the name, packed with a potent mix of whatever flammable materials were at hand such as pitch and mealed gunpowder. They were primitive incendiary bombs; rather than exploding on detonation they would burn intensely. As they arched across the sky they left a flowing tail of fire like a shooting star.

Jean-Felix Récher, the 35-year-old parish priest of Quebec, left a detailed journal of the siege. In the previous few days, he wrote, the noise of the French cannon blasting the British batteries 'caused me to become partially deaf'. On the night the British opened fire the congregation met in the cathedral at 2100 hours for a 'last meeting' and 'then the cannon started'.[4]

Panet reports that the cannon and mortars fired a volley every half an hour. Other French sources estimate that around two or three hundred projectiles of different kinds landed in Quebec that night and 'inflicted considerable damage'.[5] Ramezay claims that the town for which he was responsible 'received more than 200 bombs, which caused considerable damage'.[6] Another eyewitness records that 'the bombs were directed against the upper town and towards those parts of it where there were the largest buildings and the greatest assemblage of Houses; changing their aim at every volley'. It became clear to the people of Quebec that Wolfe's aim was not to 'dismount the batteries' that protected the narrows and the town but to 'frighten the people and make them abandon the town'. This was not a bombardment with a specific, clinical military objective; the total destruction of Quebec could have only very marginal military usefulness. Instead, it was an attack on the psychology of everybody in and around the town; an application of raw terror. On that basic level it certainly succeeded.

The same source describes the explosions and the collapsing buildings and says that 'not any quarter of Quebec afforded shelter against so tremendous a fire – the people all fled from their homes and sought for refuge upon the ramparts, on the side next to the country'.[7] Récher wrote that his residence was hit by two cannonballs. 'The whole town was terrified,' he recorded, 'in particular the women and children who were gathered in a big group by the citadel, crying, lamenting and praying continually, huddled in small cliques to recite prayers using their beads.'[8] As the sun rose, the town gates were thrown open and 'women and children were seen flying in crowds along the fields'.[9] Pontleroy, the engineer, was 'concerned about the unfortunate people and opened up all the water tanks to women and children'. Both Montcalm and he deeply regretted that they had no bread to give these miserable fugitives.[10]

Wolfe made no attempt to disguise the nature and purpose of the attack. He regarded terror as an entirely appropriate weapon for this war. On setting out upon the campaign he had assured Amherst that, even if he failed to capture Quebec, 'trust me, they shall feel us'.[11] The French, their settlers, and Native allies were to be punished. The year before he had written another chilling letter to Amherst, then his commander during the siege of Louisbourg, saying that when 'the French are in a scrape, they are ready to cry out on behalf of the human species; when fortune favours them, none more bloody, more inhuman'. He believed that 'Montcalm has changed the very nature of war, and has forced us, in some measure, to a deterring and dreadful vengeance.'[12] Wolfe wrote around the same time, in similar terms, to a friend and patron justifying the bombardment of Louisbourg on the grounds that 'the American war was different from all others'. The French had 'thought fit to establish' a type of combat that was in defiance of civilized norms. Thanks to the 'unheard of, and unprecedented, barbarities exercised by the French, Canadians and Indians, upon such of our people as had the misfortune to fall into their hands', Wolfe regarded the destruction of their capital as straight revenge, punishment for the scalping, abductions, and murder that had terrorized the British American frontier for years. Under Wolfe's command were men who had served at Monongahela where prisoners were burnt alive and even eaten, or at Fort William Henry where even the dead had been dug up to be scalped. As a result they were every bit as cold blooded as their commander. In the same letter Wolfe says that he was 'extremely sorry' that Louisbourg surrendered because if the town had been assaulted by British troops, 'we might at one blow [have given] the troops the revenge they wished for'.[13]

Even the most hardened and unflinching enemy of New France would have been satiated by the avalanche of destruction that now engulfed its capital. Starting on the evening of 12 July the guns were hardly ever completely silent for the rest of the summer. Day and night the batteries pounded the city. Wolfe added to them until thirty-nine guns and mortars were hurling death and destruction into the town.[14] By the middle of August British gunners were rearranging the rubble of what had been the finest town in North America. Quebec, like all towns and cities, always struggled with fire. Tightly packed buildings and high winds had regularly led to devastating blazes that swept through the Lower Town in particular. As a result successive governors had attempted to ban wood buildings and insist on 'fire-walls' that separated each house from its neighbour. These jutted up a yard beyond the roofline and still give Quebec's terraced houses their unmistakable shape. Cheap wood-shingle roofs were banned and expensive imported French slate encouraged. Heavy wooden planks were tolerated, although flammable, at least they would not catch fire and fly around in the wind as the shingles had done. In theory, all houses were supposed to have a stone floor in their attic, so that the house might be saved if the roof burnt; many did although this was obviously hardest to police.

The British were ingenious in their destruction. Incendiary devices would start fires that the gunners would then target with their cannonballs to stop the townspeople dousing the flames before they could get out of control. On several occasions firestorms swept through the city. The bombardment differed widely in intensity. In the heat of action as two ships of the line pounded each other to destruction a gun crew could fire one shot in just over a minute, but this soon placed the barrel under extreme pressure and continuing that rate of fire for longer than a few minutes risked the gun itself blowing up. As a result the bombardment would oscillate between a few lazy shots a day and great crescendos of fire. At the siege of Havana three years later a British officer was impressed by the sailors:

> our sea folks began a new kind of fire, unknown, or at all events, unpractised by artillery people. The greatest fire from one piece of cannon is reckoned by them from eighty to ninety times in twenty-four hours; but our people went on the sea system, firing extremely quick, and with the best direction ever seen, and in sixteen hours fired their guns one hundred and forty five times.[15]

Rarely would the British batteries in Quebec have fired with that intensity. The greatest brake on the bombardment there was not the tolerance of the gun barrels. It was the consumption of powder, shot, and shell, all of which had to be rowed in from the ships anchored in the river, while resupplying the ships meant a long and hazardous journey from Britain or her American colonies.

Thousands of men and women around the basin of Quebec watched the destruction in awe. The unofficial chronicler of the Highlanders, Iain Campbell, provides a glimpse of what the soldiers must have seen night after night: 'With bombs detonating/ and with huge explosions/ setting fire to every wall/ in that fair city;/ it was difficult to look upon,/ let alone relate again,/ the dead in their slumber/ being thrown up into the air.'[16]

By 15 July Panet says that the Lower Town was 'riddled with cannon shots' and the church of Notre Dame des Victoires had received 'several cannonballs'.[17] Récher wrote that one of his parishioners, an elderly and infirm woman, was killed. 'She had,' he noted, 'been to confession, fortunately, the day before.'[18] On 16 July a French source records that the Point Lévis battery, 'which had not hitherto very considerably damaged the town, was now productive of prodigious destruction. Several houses fell down, and the fire which caught in the centre of the town entirely consumed five or six of the finest houses in it – the enemy strove to augment this fire, by redoubling the discharges from their battery.' Three thousand bushels of flour were lost and 'several persons crushed this day by the bursting of shells'.[19] The following day Panet reported that 'Collet, a merchant, officer of the battery of M. Parent, which is in front of his house, was killed by a cannonball, as well as Gauvreau, a cooper. One named Pouliot, from Ste. Foye, was hit by a bomb that annihilated him. Two men were hurt.'[20] Alongside the guns already firing, sweating pioneers were digging out new trenches for more weapons. While the batteries on Point Lévis were wreaking havoc in Quebec the bomb ketches, anchored in the river, had not been a success. Wolfe, obviously, blamed this on the timidity of the crews. His journal for 12 July says, 'the Bomb Ketches who were to have joined their fire would not be induced to go near enough for the purpose: so that their fire ceased immediately'. Wolfe clearly complained about this publicly because it also records that 'the Admiral displeased with me for speaking harshly upon the subject of the irregularities committed by the seamen'.[21] In fact, hitting a target from a tossing bomb vessel was very difficult. Mortars were fired at a high trajectory but that did mean they had to be fairly close to their target. It may have been that enemy gunboats were too threatening to go close enough to the city to make their fire tell. A French journal records that the British bomb ketches 'were unable to reach so far; and not daring to approach any nearer, ceased to fire and retired'.[22] However, the real culprit was almost definitely the limitations of the ships and difficult conditions. The rigging restricted the field of fire; the mortar could only fire at targets which were at right angles to the direction of the ship, sending its bomb up between the two masts. This meant anchoring the ship across the tide which would have buffeted it around and made a mockery of any attempts to keep the ship stable and direct its fire accurately. Wolfe's engineer Mackellar is more generous than his boss: in his journal he records that a ketch, 'could not lay her broadside to the town for the strength of the current', it was decided that they should be 'employed by land'.[23]

Any guns that were situated on stable, if muddy, ground found the target presented by the town was too good to imagine. Quebec's founders had looked upon Point Lévis as a view, not a threat. The magnificent palaces and religious buildings all offered themselves up for destruction. The first 'considerable' fire on 22 July was, according to Mackellar, started by a carcass and it 'burnt the Cathedral and ten or twelve good houses in the neighbourhood'.[24] The French accounts are more emotive; to one diarist the night 'was made memorable by the horrors of a prodigious number of bombs, which fell in the town, and set it on fire in two or three different places; there was no possibility of extinguishing the flames, the conflagration soon became dreadful, burnt all the centre of the town, and entirely consumed the cathedral'.[25] Marguerite Gosselin had fled from her farm on the Île d'Orléans where she had raised sixteen children. She was now a refugee living in the woods to the north of Quebec. There she received some terrible news. 'What sorrow!' she wrote. 'My son Joseph is dead. He was only 22.' Her son had been killed during the bombardment 'when he tried to rescue an old lady who refused to leave her house'. 'My heart is heavy when I look at my other children, sleeping around me, so far from our home.'[26]

Notre Dame de Quebec was seat of the diocese of Quebec, the oldest see in the New World north of Mexico. It was built in the 1630s and was the first Roman Catholic cathedral in North America. It was 'entirely consumed' according to the log of the *Stirling Castle*, which like all the other ships' logs kept a careful note of the nightly devastation.[27] The cathedral's stone walls remained standing but now without windows, doors, or a roof, like an ancient ruin. Until hours before it had been the thriving heart of Canadian spiritual life. Many of its treasures, collected over a century, were lost. Some survived: a magnificent model of a French frigate, the *Brézé*, had been donated by a French soldier, de Tracy, as an ex-voto, fulfilling a promise he had made God if He delivered him and his crew from a particularly rough crossing. It was suspended from the ceiling of the cathedral. A British cannonball sent it crashing to the floor where the pieces were scooped up and preserved by a monk.

Nearby, at the Ursuline Convent, the chapel with its two naves, one for the nuns and their young novices, the other for members of the public, both of which could see the priest in the pulpit but not each other, contained magnificent wood-carved ornamentation. This was made by colonial craftsmen at the beginning of the eighteenth century in a spirited attempt to imitate high baroque style. St Joseph and the Christ child gazed down on the congregation while the altar had an image of the sacred heart and was surrounded by relics. During the bombardment the chapel lost its roof and had holes punched in the sturdy walls yet somehow the carvings survived. The nuns fled to the General Hospital, a convent situated half a mile outside the city walls to the west, where one sister who kept a diary commented that the cannons fired 'in a manner to excite the greatest alarm in our unfortunate Communities of religious ladies'. The Ursulines were not the only ones who flooded west. She writes that 'as our house was beyond the range of the enemy's artillery, the poor people of the city did not fail to seek refuge there. All the out-houses, stables, barns, garrets, etc. were well filled.'[28]

The nuns of the Hôtel-Dieu took shelter in the strong vaulted cellars under the convent where they prayed around makeshift altars that are still down there today. Other Quebecers were less pious. One journal recounts that, 'during these disasters, the persons who were left in the town for the defence, became, for the most part, robbers; no sooner had the bursting of a bomb shattered the doors or windows of a house during the night, than it was pillaged and stripped'. The authorities forbade plunder on pain of death and 'to strike greater terror by menace, than reality, a double gibbet was erected near the ramparts'.[29] A few days later, on the twenty-sixth, a sailor manning the cannon batteries was hanged for looting. On the thirtieth Récher describes 'two soldiers ... one of them 20 the other 16, who stole a barrel of eau de vie from a cellar and rolled it from St Roch'. They bottled and sold it. 'They were discovered at 6 in the morning. Prosecuted at 10. At 4 o'clock in the afternoon they are hanged.'[30]

Falling bombs destroyed huge numbers of houses and killed and wounded 'many persons' as fires spread throughout the packed dwellings. One added consequence 'of the devastation of the fire and the continual falling of the bombs' was that 'all the ovens in the town ceased to bake; and people were obliged to eat only biscuit, till ovens could be built in the suburbs'.[31]

The fires started on the night of 22 July carried on for 'all the next day' in the words of a watching British sergeant.[32] Three bells in a parish church melted so intense was the heat.[33] As usual the British did everything they could to stop the French dousing the flames. One journal reports that 'much terror was caused by the large number of bombs which the enemy threw to prevent the extinguishment of the fire'.[34] During these 'terrible' nights up to six bombs would rain down on the city at once. Another French diarist wrote that the population was 'astonished' at 'so very harsh [a bombardment] pursued against inanimate objects'. No one could understand why Wolfe was 'acting so contrary to the ordinary uses of war'.[35]

There was no let-up. The night of 8/9 August witnessed an unimaginable fire in the Lower Town. Panet wrote that it was 'fateful for me and for many others'.[36] The Dauphin Battery, a hundred yards north of the Royal Battery, took a direct hit. A British eyewitness says that this 'blew up their magazine, platforms, and burnt with such violence that some of the garrison were obliged to get into boats to save themselves from the flames'.[37] The rest of the Lower Town was totally consumed in a fire that, according to a French diarist, 'destroyed the greater part of it, as well as the Dauphin Battery. The fire lasted about 80 hours, without our being able to extinguish it.'[38] According to Mackellar, 'by eight o'clock [p.m. on 9 August] it was burnt to ashes, all but four or five houses'.[39] French sources say that no less than '152 houses were reduced to ashes there' and that many of them belonged to 'persons heretofore accounted very rich' who now had their 'whole property reduced to ashes'.[40] Among the victims was Panet, whose house in the Lower Town took a direct hit from a carcass and was totally destroyed. 'In vain did we try,' he wrote, 'to cut off and put out the fire at my house, when there came a small wind from the north-east, and soon the lower-city was nothing more than an inferno'.[41]

Knox heard that it was begun by a British shell that 'forced its way into a vaulted cellar, hitherto deemed bomb proof'. As a result of this false designation the French had packed the cellar with brandy and 'several smaller casks of other spirituous liquors'.[42] The British saw the fire catch and redoubled their efforts to stop the French putting it out. The flames 'attained to such a height that there was no possibility of putting a stop to its progress; no sooner had the flames broke out in any place than the troops retired from it'. The heart had been ripped out of Quebec, the Governor General's palace, the Bishop's palace, the cathedral, even more worryingly for the superstitious

Quebecers, the church of Notre Dame des Victoires, all lay in ruins.[43] By early September Saunders could report to Pitt that 'the town of Quebec is not habitable, being almost entirely burnt and destroyed'.[44]

Surviving British accounts exude satisfaction at a job well done. One journal blamed this 'dismal consequence to Quebec, the pride of America, who now sits mourning in ashes' on the 'delusive hopes of her aspiring monarch'.[45] Not one diary or letter mentions the people of Quebec; instead the entire bombardment is treated as a technical exercise. After the August fire, the chief artilleryman, Colonel Williamson, reported to London that 'about 300 of their homes are burned down ... among which is almost all of the eastern part of the lower town which makes a wretched appearance indeed'. His batteries 'have done infinite damage to the houses remaining many of them are in a tottering condition and more which cannot be repaired'.[46] In a neat calculation of the expenditure and the remaining supplies of ammunition Williamson drew up on 18 August 1759 he records that the thirty-two-pound guns in the Lévis batteries had fired 1,589 cannonballs, and the mortars had fired 2,326 thirteen-inch shells and 1,590 ten-inch shells. Two hundred and ninety destructive thirteen-inch carcasses had been fired at the town and 125 of a ten-inch variety. In the column for supplies he scribbled 'nil'. There were no carcasses left, but had they known it would have given the French little cause to cheer; across the river there was nothing left for them to burn.[47] The people of Quebec had moved to suburbs or nearby woodland, packed together in lean-to shelters. A few people lived among the ruins of the town, sleeping in basements surrounded by grotesque, mangled masonry.

The vehemence of the bombardment and the satisfaction that British officers took from it were closely linked to their frustrations elsewhere. As the days passed they were no closer to landing in a place which would threaten to capture the town and thus force Montcalm's army to fight them. Wolfe remained fixated by a frontal attack on the Beauport shore. He would bludgeon his way onto the beach in the teeth of opposition from Montcalm's waiting forces. On 16 July he wrote to Monckton telling him to prepare his men to take to some hurriedly constructed rafts, unless they were 'defective'. In which case 'we must make the best shift we can, with the long boats of the fleet'. Despite the strength of the enemy entrenchments he was confident that heavy fire from the British cannon 'will make the enterprise easy'.[48] Yet again the grenadiers of the various regiments would be massed together and used as shock troops. Wolfe ordered that 'the six Grenadier companies of the line are to be at the water side tonight at 9 O'clock with all their baggage'; a staff officer would 'attend on the opposite shore and provide them with carts'.[49]

They may have been glad to leave Montmorency. Wolfe's 'Family Journal' gives an impression of life deep within enemy territory. The reality for the men was grim. Daily parties were sent out to cut firewood and 'fascines' or bundles of wood to strengthen the fortifications, and armed men would be deployed to watch them. Inevitably one or two would be picked off. There were 'constant skirmishes between our working parties and the Indians, and the enemy's fire across the river killed and wounded a good many men'. They were watched constantly, 'the enemy always observing when our parties cut fascines every third or fourth day used to lay ambuscades for them of large parties of Indians and Canadians'. It was miserable for the men but this member of Wolfe's inner circle found positives even in this situation. The low level violence 'had the good effect of inuring the men to fighting with the Indians, and explained to them more than precepts what resolution will effect'. The author insists that 'on all occasions a most determined spirit showed itself among the troops, which ever happens where the general has great qualities, for I believe they always receive his stamp'.[50]

Wolfe's orders for 17 July were very specific in requiring that any detachments sent to cut fascines were to 'have escorts of light infantry' and that 'the working parties are not to go into the woods until the light infantry are posted'.[51] However, the shortcomings of these new precautions were shown up that very day. Wolfe's journal records that 'the savages attacked the centre of a covering party, killed 5 men and wounded others, carried off three prisoners'. Almost as an afterthought is scribbled the thought 'cruelty of these savages'.[52] Perhaps it was the same attack as that recorded by one of the Louisbourg Grenadiers. In his journal he wrote that 'we went out fascining, and to make oars, with a small party to cover us; – five were killed of which four were scalped, and we was obliged to quit the woods directly; the Indians came up very close, and killed and scalped one man close by us'.[53] John Johnson records that there was nothing unusual in this vicious encounter. 'There was scarcely a day passed,' he wrote, 'without our working parties being surprised, and very often routed by the skulking parties of Canadians and Indians, they often being three or four times our number; and would sometimes pursue them to the very skirts of our camp; and very often sharp skirmishes would happen between them, which would sometimes be attended with considerable loss, both of killed and wounded.'[54] Ramezay describes one ruse used by these French irregulars in a raid on the Montmorency camp. He says that 'only the three Canadians approached the camp, pretending to flee as soon as they saw a small enemy detachment leave the camp'. The Canadians led the detachment into a trap, a group of Native Americans waiting in ambush: 'when the Savages were within range, they fired a complete discharge upon them, killing numerous Englishmen, and taking three prisoners'.[55]

Actions like this one demonstrated that, especially at Montmorency, the British controlled only the territory enclosed within their ramparts. Beyond was French. Throughout the summer Wolfe issued almost daily orders trying to force his men not to stray beyond the camp and remain vigilant at all times. Obviously the long sojourn aboard ship had led the claustrophobic soldiers to embrace their new freedom because he had to insist that 'soldiers are to keep close to their encampment, are not to pass without the guards or wander through the country in the disorderly manner that has been observed here'. Despite the danger, the men were kept in the camp only with great difficulty, even by the middle of August when he was still issuing threats: 'any soldier who passes the out-sentries on any pretence whatever, shall be brought to a court-martial and punished'. The reason for this was the 'enemies light troops' which were 'continually hovering about the camp in hopes of surprising some small guard or some of the sentries'. Things were so bad that 'for an hour before day, and at least half an hour after broad day light, the whole [force stationed at Montmorency] are to be under arms'.[56] The entire British army in North America existed in a state of perpetual tension. Years of warfare with unseen Canadians and Native Americans had forced commanders to keep their men in a constant state of readiness. Hundreds of miles away at Fort Edward as Amherst's army prepared for the push up through Lake Champlain towards Montreal, the diary of an American colonial officer William Henshaw reflected this heightened security. His men were forbidden from leaving camp after the drummers had Beat Retreat, typically about ten minutes after sunset. The evening's guards were 'to lie in the front tents that they may be ready to turn at any time at a moment's notice'. It took his regiment three minutes to be 'drawed up' once the alarm was sounded.[57]

It was a very different war from one fought in Europe. There it was seen as murder to kill a sentry in cold blood. Wolfe and the other officers used terms such as 'assassinate' when they described such attacks during the summer of 1759. The men in Europe would wander freely through the countryside after a day's march and buy fresh provisions off the local inhabitants. If they bumped into scouting parties of the enemy they would almost certainly live and let live. Their officers might exchange a few complimentary words of French. Here in North America every soldier that attempted to augment dull rations or explore the surrounding country risked ending up as a mutilated corpse.[58]

The defences of the camps were slowly augmented until all three were veritable fortresses, a tribute to the effectiveness of Canadians and Native Americans. A French source records that the Montmorency camp, in particular, was massively fortified: '[Wolfe] lined his camp with eleven redoubts, almost all entrenched, fraised and palisaded.'[59] At Point Lévis Knox describes a ditch, an abatis, and 'an excellent palisade-work, with loop-holes for musketry'.[60] But defences are worthless without determined defenders manning them. Wolfe tried to bolster the men's aggression and morale with rewards for good service. On 17 July he sent 'two sheep and some rum' to one company for 'the spirit they showed this morning in pushing those scoundrels of Indians'. However, he also warned against overconfidence, recommending to the officers that they should 'preserve their people with caution, least they should be drawn too far into the woods and fall into an ambuscade'.[61] It is possible to detect in the surviving sources the terror of the sentries as they peered out night after night into the dark; the forest beyond the ramparts alive with threats, real and imagined. Wolfe issued one order that 'no man should leave his post, under pretence that all his cartridges are fired', after all, he assured his nervous men, 'in most attacks by night, it must be remembered, that bayonets are preferable to fire'. No single sentries were posted in the woods, in the usual fashion of the British army, since it gave 'the enemy frequent opportunities of killing single men at their posts'.[62] Groups of no less than eight men would patrol instead, and they must never stray out of hailing distance from the guards at the camp. Wolfe was very precise in his instructions, telling his men that while on guard they did not need to show the customary marks of respect to a passing officer. He also set down precise drills to be followed if they spotted someone in the trees. 'When any sentry,' he ordered, 'challenges and is answered "friend" he is to say, with a clear voice, "Advance with the countersign"; when the person advances, the sentry is to receive him in the proper posture of defence. Surprises may be prevented without risking the lives of our own soldiers.'[63] Monckton's Order Book gives the challenge and countersign or 'parole' (like most military terms this one was borrowed from the French, meaning 'spoken word') each day for the camp at Point Lévis. On 4 September the shouting of 'Middlesex' and a reply shortly after of 'Bristol' ringing through the North American woodland must have seemed peculiar to those who stopped to think about it.[64]

Despite the hovering menace just outside the camp's walls the soldiers had a remarkable ability to create a recognizable normality within. Again the tents were laid out in regulation streets. Despite Wolfe's initial ban on women leaving the camp on the tip of the Île d'Orléans, a few resourceful types had made their way across the St Lawrence to be with their men. Women were an integral part of eighteenth-century armies, present on every campaign no matter how harsh the surroundings. From the sweltering heat of India to the fever ridden islands of the Indies and the frozen outposts of North America women followed their men in war as well as peace.

Wolfe disapproved of their presence. He believed that they eroded discipline, sold illegal spirits, and poisoned relations with the locals thanks to their relentless scavenging. Books containing collections of all the military orders for the North American campaigns are replete with, what one suspects, are largely unheeded orders to curb the behaviour of wives, girlfriends, and other female camp followers. Wolfe had limited the number that each regiment was officially allowed to bring; on other campaigns ten women per company was normal. For the Quebec expedition, Wolfe had insisted that a company of seventy men was allowed only three wives, while a company of 100 men could bring one more.[65] By this calculation around ninety women should have sailed with the army and received a half ration of food daily. It is certain that several times this number actually did so. They found their way on board transports or even paid for their passage from New England merchants who supplied the fleet. They were a fact of military life, even here in the heart of enemy territory.

Soldiers were wedded to the army and most commanding officers did not approve of a 'bigamous' relationship with an actual woman at the same time. Wolfe wrote early in his career that he 'recommends to the soldiers not to marry at all; the long march, the embarkation that will soon follow, must convince them that many women in the regiment are very inconvenient, especially as some of them are not so industrious, nor so useful to their husbands as a soldier's wife ought to be'. He told his officers at the same time that they were to 'discourage matrimony among the men as much as possible; the service suffers by the multitude of women already in the regiment'. He clearly regarded them as a pernicious influence; on garrison duty in Dover he worried that the local ladies were 'women of loose and disorderly conduct' and he banned his men from seeing them.[66] His repeated efforts to keep women away from his men suggest that he had little success in doing so; women tested the mythical coercive mechanisms of the Georgian army well beyond their limits.

Occasionally permission was given to formally marry a woman. Wolfe granted it reluctantly and only if the soldier had 'consult[ed] his officer before his marriage, that the woman's character may be enquired into'.[67] But even this legal relationship did not guarantee that the wife would be allowed to follow the husband on campaign. Before departure, in a terrible ritual the phrases 'to go' or 'not to go' were written on scraps of paper and placed in a hat. The women of the regiment drew them out. Screams of joy or utter despair attended the embarking of the men, as this grim task was often left to the last minute on the quayside in an attempt to postpone the pain as long as possible. Crying men were dragged from their families, there were even a few examples of those who killed themselves on the spot rather than say goodbye to wives and children who faced destitution.[68]

Some women hid themselves on board; others disguised themselves and marched on in the ranks. There is one example of a woman, Hannah Snell, who hid her sex and served four and a half years in the marines. An extraordinary feat, especially given that during the siege of Pondicherry in 1748 she was wounded and extracted the musket ball with thumb and forefinger. In 1750 she left the army, received a pension from the Royal Hospital Chelsea, and then revealed her sex. A fellow soldier instantly proposed to her, they married, and she made money performing infantry drills on stage.[69]

Other women were scarcely less involved in the fighting than Snell. Martha May's husband was in the 1st/60th Royal Americans serving in Pennsylvania. She wrote to the commanding officer begging his pardon after she had publicly hurled abuse at him. She pointed out that 'I have been a Wife 22 years and have Traveld with my Husband every Place or County the Company Marcht too and have workt very hard ever since I was in the Army.' She hoped that she would be able to 'go with my Poor Husband, one time more to carry him and my good Officers water in ye Hottest Battle as I have done before'.[70] Half a century later, at Waterloo, the wife of Sergeant Major Edwards in the Hussars rode a pony through her husband's unit asking the men what was the matter with them and lambasting them as cowards. Women like May and the formidable Mrs Edwards played an important and overlooked role in a campaign. They cooked, nursed the ill, and made good money selling food to the soldiers and washing their limited wardrobe. Still more surprisingly women lined the edge of battlefields, some carrying water and ammunition to their men, others waiting to pounce on the wounded for a chance of plunder. Casualties were cared for by women nurses in the hospital on the Île d'Orléans. Wolfe tolerated women as long as they carried out their more necessary functions.

But he tried to limit their ability to sell alcohol and loosen the strict bonds of regimental discipline. He also attempted to limit their ability to spread disease. 'If any woman in the regiment,' he had ordered years before, 'has a venereal disorder, and does not immediately make it known to the surgeon, she shall upon the first discovery be drummed out of the regiment.'[71]

Whether Wolfe liked it or not, women played a key role in the logistics of any campaign. Without them acting as cooks, suppliers, nurses, and laundry workers the infantry of the army would have been put under much greater pressure. They were a key part of the most impressive logistical organization in the world. It was founded on the deep pockets of the British government backed by the financial community in the City of London. Rather than raising taxes to pay for everything directly, the government was able to borrow on a previously unimaginable scale while the tax revenue serviced these loans. Thanks to its reliable repayment record and the trust that the City had in the Prime Minister, the Duke of Newcastle, the British government was able to raise more money at much better interest rates than the French, despite Britain's smaller population and economy. This paid for men, supplies, and the ships to carry them up the St Lawrence. Increasingly, professional government officials ran the system with far more efficiency than their counterparts across the Channel. British taxpayers complained but their money was being spent with greater effectiveness than ever before.

In an age where the glittering signs of McDonald's and Pizza Hut adorn US army bases from Korea to Iraq, the diet of Wolfe's army seems far from extravagant. But it was enough to keep calories flowing into the bellies of his hard-pressed men. Each week a soldier could expect to receive seven pounds of all-important bread, which could be eaten straight or boiled with lard and other ingredients to make a soup. One piece of salted pork and one of beef was issued, as well as a pint and a half of oatmeal, the same amount of peas, and half a pound each of butter and cheese, or if these were in short supply, half a pint of oil. Men typically pooled their rations with their tent mates, the men they trained, laboured, and fought beside. If one of them was lucky enough to have his wife in camp, she would often do the cooking, while groups of bachelors could pay another man's wife to do theirs. They ate off simple plates of pewter or even wood. To swill this down the men were given a quarter of a pint, a 'gill' of rum per day, which they would mix with water, thus making 'grog'.[72] Officially sanctioned wives were on half rations, children on quarter. Spruce beer was brewed in huge quantities to keep scurvy at bay. Knox was cautiously positive about his diet. All in all, they were 'tolerably well provided with the conveniences of life'. He goes on to say that although 'at times butcher's meat is scarce' other food supplies can fill the void such as 'young horse flesh' or 'a loin of a colt' both of which 'eat well'. In addition he concludes, 'there are many other parts of the carcass, which, if disguised in the same manner that one meets with other victuals at table, may deceive the nicest palate'.[73] These rations may be unappealing to the modern gastronome but they provided the men with the energy required to work, march, and fight for the whole summer. Keeping the men fed was a massive achievement; the limiting factor in most pre-nineteenth-century military campaigns was logistical. The lack of easily transportable, long-lasting provisions had destroyed many more armies than enemy action. In 1757, after the fall of Fort William Henry, the entire New York northern frontier lay at Montcalm's feet. A shortage of supplies ruled out a drive towards Albany even if the cautious Montcalm had wished to take advantage of this opportunity.

Frenchmen did, and still do, regard the British diet as tasteless and monotonous at best. In the eighteenth century Franco–British competition infected all aspects of life: religion, trade, political economy, and even food. Britons revelled in eschewing French sauces and delicacies. Plain meat was the price of liberty. A song heard in taverns across the land stated bluntly, 'Down, down with French dishes, up up with roast beef.' It ended with a roar: 'Here's Liberty, Loyalty – aye – and Roast Beef.' The same was true of beer drinking. Necessity was celebrated. The gloomy British climate did not support grapes, so they and the wine that came from them were despised. 'Beer drinking Britons can never be beat' ran another popular song. The link between diet and patriotism could not have been clearer: 'beef-eating, beer-drinking Britons are souls/ who shed their last blood for their country and King'.[74]

The simplicity of the food in Wolfe's army therefore fitted neatly into a pre-existing culture of patriotic self-denial. Even so the soldiers did try to augment their diets slightly. In Europe they could add to their rations by buying, or pilfering, fresh food from civilians. Soldiers were paid 8*d*. a day, about the same as an agricultural labourer in one of the poorer counties of England and only a third of what a labourer might make in London. From this there were all sorts of deductions for replacement kit, food, surgeon's equipment, and a contribution to the Royal Hospital. In some regiments the men found themselves permanently trapped by debt as unscrupulous officers or NCOs contrived ways of stopping the men's pay for an array of real and imagined reasons. Good officers tried to prevent this happening, knowing full well its corrosive effect on morale. When running a regiment in Scotland in 1750 Wolfe had ordered that 'no recruit at exercise to be stopped more than six pence per week; this to be a standing order'.[75]

In Canada there was less opportunity to augment rations. Not only did men take their lives and their scalps in their hands whenever they left camp but the local farmers and their families were short of food themselves and often unwilling to sell it to men who had arrived to conquer their homeland. Some markets were organized. By the camp at Point Lévis a few Canadians were joined by the swarm of New England 'sutlers', men and women who followed the army looking to sell directly to the soldiers. These market days must have given the men a welcome relief from a hard campaign. Despite constant threats from Wolfe, alcohol was readily available and for some Canadians pragmatism trumped patriotism as they realized that the salt meat that the soldiers offered for barter would help them survive a cruel winter. By the end of August one officer noted that 'the face of the camp at Point Levis [has] entirely changed owing to the great encouragement given to vendors of all kinds'.[76]

Knox recorded a comprehensive list of all the items for sale by the sutlers. A pound of beef cost a little more than a day's pre-stoppages wage at 9*d*. A reasonable loaf of 'good soft bread' came in at 6*d*. Alcohol is prominent in his reckonings. Madeira was the priciest drink at 36*d*. (or 3*s*.) a quart; good New England rum was available at 30*d*. (2*s*. 6*d*.) per quart. Dark, strong beer, known as 'Porter' because the men who heaved loads around the docks and streets of eighteenth-century London used it to refresh themselves, cost 12*d.* (1*s.*) per quart.[77] If all these tipples proved too much for the hard-up redcoat a 'bad malt drink from Halifax' came in at 9*d.* a quart and cheapest of all was New England cider at as little as 6*d.* a quart.[78]

Sutlers were needed to supply the army but their propensity to sell anything to anyone had to be curbed. A lieutenant in Amherst's army recorded the strict conditions under which they operated. They required official sanction in the form of passes; they had to encamp in one place, while the 'provost guards shall encamp around them to keep good order'; 'No lights are suffered at night' and, most importantly, 'none of the soldiers are allowed or permitted to be there after the retreats beating'.[79] Wolfe was 'determined to allow no drunkenness or licentiousness in the army'. He ordered that 'if any sutler has presumption to bring rum on shore in contempt for the general's regulations, such sutler shall be sent to the provost in irons, and his goods confiscated'. The commanders of the regiments were warned that they 'were answerable that no rum or spirits of any kind be sold in or near the camp when the soldiers are fatigued with work or wet upon duty'.[80]

None of Wolfe's men starved during the course of the long summer but a diet of dried biscuit and salted meat, replaced occasionally by horse flesh, presented a real challenge. Men grew desperate to supplement their diets, particularly with fresh food. Deserters brought tales of British shortages to the French who listened with glee. Others took matters into their own hands. On 7 August Knox recorded that 'some sailors and marines strayed today into the country, contrary to repeated orders, to seek for vegetables'; they were attacked 'by a party of the enemy' which left three of them 'killed and scalped' and another two were slightly wounded.[81]

Wolfe did what he could by sending out strong parties of men to forage. On 10 August he sent a detachment of light infantry along with Bragg's 28th Regiment to leave the camp early and 'supply themselves with peas and other greens'.[82]

Wolfe's men earned their meagre rations. At any one time it seems like a third of the men were improving the defences of the various camps by building redoubts, widening ditches, and eternally cutting firewood and fascines. During Amherst's advance north such was the fear of Native American raids that when a working party was ordered into a trench they were told to 'take their arms with them'. They were even instructed that 'when they work to the right they will order their arms to the right; and when they work to the left they will lodge their arms to the left'.[83] We can be certain that Wolfe's exposed force, particularly at Montmorency, was similarly cautious.

Another third of the army, according to Montresor, was kept busy 'hauling cannon and carrying stores in the artillery park'. Yet again Montmorency was the scene of the hardest work because here the cannon had to be manhandled 'from the beach to the encampment about 100 feet from the level of the water' and 'the declivity very sudden'.[84] Work began early and paused during the hottest hours of the middle of the day when temperatures could regularly break 30°C. Wolfe ordered that 'men are to begin work at six O'clock in the morning … and continue till ten, then leave off till two (or perhaps three O'clock) in case of excessive heat, and work from that time till six or seven'.[85] Years before, when stationed in Scotland, Wolfe had insisted that 'soldiers cannot better employ themselves in the intervals of duty than in some sort of work, and would by all means encourage labour and industry, as the best way to preserve their healths, and enable them to undergo fatigue whenever they shall be called upon'.[86]

There was to be no sunbathing or swimming in the St Lawrence for those who were not working. A different grenadier company each day would have the honour of guarding Wolfe himself. Other small groups, headed by a corporal or perhaps a sergeant, would guard stores or patrol the camp keeping an eye on discipline. For the rest of the men if they were not hauling supplies or digging trenches, they drilled. Some days Wolfe ordered just the 'recruits and awkward men of each company' to practise.[87] At other times whole battalions were ordered to go through their paces. On 6 August 'the battalions of the Americans [60th Regiment] give no men for work this afternoon, that they may be under arms at 6 O'clock to exercise'. The following day it was the turn of Otway's 35th to have the morning free from work 'that they may have leisure to exercise'.[88]

There was a brief pause on Sundays when Wolfe ordered 'divine service will be performed ... at 10 O'clock in the forenoon' for some regiments and 'at four in the afternoon' for the others.[89] For this church parade and in fact at all times 'when the soldiers are not employed in work', the men were to 'dress and clean themselves, so as to appear under arms and upon all occasions in the most soldierlike fashion'.[90]

If the troops worked particularly hard extra provisions were given to them and sometimes an extra ration of rum. Wolfe's orders stated that he would allow 'such refreshment as he knows will be of service to them' and he would 'reward such as shall particularly distinguish themselves'. 'On the other hand,' the orders warned, 'he will punish any misbehaviour in an exemplary manner.'[91]

Throughout July the men sweated by day: harnessed like pack animals to carts, digging trenches, and building redoubts. At night they shivered in their lookout posts, peering over earth ramparts into the black woodland beyond. Fighting flared up around the fringes of the camp and on patrols through the countryside when patriotic Canadians took potshots at British troops. None of this skirmishing brought the British army any closer to the walls of Quebec. Wolfe obstinately stuck to his plan to smash through French defences on the Beauport shore. But on the evening of 18 July a daring action threatened to break the stalemate and presented him with several new opportunities.

At 2230 hours the flood tide was running at its maximum speed. Although the St Lawrence normally swept past Quebec towards the Atlantic for a few hours a day the incoming tide reversed the flow of the river and provided blessed assistance to sailors attempting to make their way upstream. The wind, usually stubbornly south-west, blew from the north-north-east. Conditions were favourable to make the attempt to get past the guns of the town.

Five British ships heeled over under a good press of canvas as the wind caught them just behind the beam. They were moving fast despite the darkness of the night and the proximity of land. Leading the squadron was the *Sutherland* with Captain Rous on the quarterdeck. Following his ship were others commanded by some of the finest captains in Saunders' fleet. Alexander Schomberg in the frigate *Diana* had won praise the year before at Louisbourg, as had the smaller *Squir-rel*. All three ships had served as a unit the summer before; sailing as close to the shore as possible to pound French positions while Wolfe had led in the amphibious assault. Two armed sloops and two transports carrying a battalion of the Royal Americans completed the little flotilla.

The ships were cleared for action as they approached the town. Deep in the hold of the *Sutherland* the carpenter prepared plugs of various diameters, ready to thrust them into any jagged holes torn in the hull of the ship by Quebec's many cannon. Around the magazine decks and bulkheads had been wetted. Damp fabric screens covered the doors to prevent sparks; light trickled in through glass windows from candles in a next-door room. The men who worked in the magazine, surrounded by barrels of gunpowder, crept around without shoes or anything that risked causing a spark. Above their heads the gun deck was cleared of any unnecessary obstruction. Gone were the elaborate wooden bulkheads that usually divided the ship into a warren of little spaces, each occupied according to status and rank. Instead, now there was just a vast open space, centred around the needs of the cannon. The true purpose of the ships was starkly obvious: they were giant floating gun batteries. The starboard side cannon were loaded and run out of the gun ports in anticipation. Beside each of the cannon eight men crouched ready. The only light came from modified lanterns, one per gun crew, which provided a trickle of light, just enough for them to operate the guns. There were also red glowing pin-pricks at regular spaces along the deck where one of the gun crew knelt, facing away from the cannon, blowing gently on a length of slow-match, ready for the gun captain to use it to ignite the powder and fire the weapon. All the other tools needed to aim, reload, clean, and fire the guns were stashed above their heads in iron cradles. Every gun was trained forward as far as possible. Each gun captain crouched, peering along the barrel, his hand covering the priming powder to stop it blowing away, waiting until the Lower Town came into his field of vision. In the middle of the deck beside the gaping hatches that led to the orlop deck below stood red-coated marines, making sure that no one let their terror overcome their sense of duty.

On the upper deck men huddled around twelve-pound and six-pound guns, lighter than the twenty-fours below them. These sailors would fire the lighter armament if the town came in range but would also carry out running repairs on the rigging. A lucky French shot could carry away a yard or topmast which might slow the ship to a crawl as mangled rigging dragged in the water like a sea anchor. These men had to be ready for anything, to repair or rebuild the rig or chop away debris. Above their heads netting was slung to protect the crew from any blocks or chunks of wood knocked loose.

On the quarterdeck four helmsmen gripped the large steering wheel while below them men were poised to steer the ship by emergency steering gear near the rudder should the helm be shot away. In front of the helm stood Captain Rous, with his 1st Lieutenant, his Master, and some midshipmen poised to carry his instructions to parts of the ship or signal the other vessels following him. Rous had something to prove. The night before the same group of ships had been ordered above the town and they had not sailed. Wolfe's journal stated that 'the wind [was] fair, night seemingly favourable to their wish, but yet Capt. Rous did not go there'. Thomas Bell, Wolfe's aide-de-camp, went further, saying that despite wind and tide in his favour Rous 'did not stir'. Bell reports that 'The Admiral was going to supersede him and sent Capt. Everett on board at 12 to know the reason of his not getting under way. His excuse was that there was not wind enough', even though, says Bell, 'it positively blew a hot gale'.[92] Yet again Wolfe and his close staff were effectively accusing naval officers of cowardice. Yet again they obviously did not do so entirely behind closed doors and tent flaps. The lowly Montresor heard that the *Sutherland* was ordered to sail above the town 'but did not proceed'.[93] It was clearly the talk of the army. The 'Family Journal' as ever gives a sense of the feeling of Wolfe's intimate group. It says, 'Mr Wolfe had long wished to see some of our ships of War above the town ... but he found the blood chilled in the naval veins.' It reports that the captains were 'deaf to all that he could say to them: eighty pieces of cannon of the enemies' ramparts towards the river, reasoned with more conviction to their ears than the breath of honour'. It concludes that the 'operation in the end was saddled on old Rous a man whom they thought was of little consequence what became of'.[94] The following night Wolfe had again ordered Rous and his squadron to pass the town. The General had gone to Point Lévis to watch the squadron make the attempt and this time Rous was leading his ships for the narrows without flinching.

On shore the French sailors manning the batteries rushed to their guns as the ships came into view. One by one the cannon roared as the French desperately sought to slam the door of the upper river shut. The British ships hugged the Point Lévis bank. An hour before the attempt a naval cutter had dropped anchor off Point Lévis in four and a half fathoms, or twenty-six feet, of water. She shone a light to show the ships just how close to the bank they could steer. The town's cannon fired from about a half a mile away. This was well within their theoretical range but accuracy and effectiveness were difficult at this distance. If any French rounds did find their target the effect could still be hideous. A ball could punch through thirty inches of oak at half a mile. It would kill anyone it hit but just as terrifying were the shower of splinters that could be sent flying from the point of impact. Spinning through the air, these shards of wood caused horrific tearing, ripping injuries that were harder to treat than musket ball wounds. Injured men were taken down below to the orlop deck where the surgeon stood by with newly sharpened saws and knives. Men killed outright were unceremoniously tipped through the opened gun ports.

The ships swept through the narrows, firing back at the shore as their guns came to bear. To a novice the gun deck would have been a vision of utter havoc. The noise of the guns in the confined space made men's ears bleed after a few discharges. The bright muzzle flashes blinded the men whose eyes were used to the low flickering light of shielded lanterns. Every time a gun roared it illuminated only a bank of thick smoke, which the north-easterly breeze blew back into the gun deck. The guns sprang backwards three yards after every firing, brought to a halt by thick ropes which went hard as iron as they absorbed the shock. Without this restraint the cannon would not have stopped for fifteen yards. The crew leapt forward to swab the gun down and reload it. When flat out the teams could fire one aimed shot less than every two minutes. The insatiable demand for powder was met by the powder boys, one per gun, who stumbled along the deck to fetch charges of powder from the magazines below. Each charge had to be brought up individually as it was obviously unacceptable to have excess gunpowder sitting near the cannon. The temperature on the gun deck soared. The scalding iron barrels heated the summer air and the men were soon soaked in sweat.

The *Sutherland* made it through without serious damage. A French journal suggests that it was 'unmolested' because it was not 'noticed till it was too late to fire upon it'.[95] Montcalm wrote in his journal that the French cannon fired 'without effect' because it was 'a very dark night'.[96] The *Sutherland*'s log reports that the French opened fire late, when the British ships were already 'abreast of the town'. Perhaps in the dark night they did not see them any sooner. The log claims that all the French shot 'went over us, except one which struck our wall [hull] about a foot from the water'. The *Squirrel* also swept through, the most serious damage was a cannonball through her mizzen topsail.[97] There was also a good deal of confusion about the British intentions. The French journal records that 'the alarm became general – the drums beat to arms, and it was believed, that the enemy was about to make an attack upon the town'.[98] This fear of an assault on the Lower Town meant that although the French had a huge number of cannon, not many of them were perfectly sited to fire on the narrows. Many were positioned so as to pour fire on a force as it attempted to assault the Lower Town or threatened to sail up the St Charles River. The Royal Battery, for example, on the corner of the Lower Town had only perhaps four of its cannon able to engage the British ships as they passed through the narrowest part of the river. With three knots of tide, and a very conservative estimate of three knots of speed through the water, the British ships would have covered the most risky two-mile stretch in only twenty minutes, allowing even a highly skilled crew to fire little more than ten aimed shots.[99]

The first few ships had made it through without a scratch but any celebrations were premature. As the people of Quebec and the soldiers on Point Lévis looked on, the *Diana* and one of the sloops became entangled. A lieutenant's log from the *Diana* records that 'in going abreast of the town a sloop fell athwart us'. The *Diana* took dramatic evasive action, but in the narrowest part of the river this led to disaster. 'Endeavouring to get clear of her,' wrote the Master, '[we] got into the eddy of the tide and little wind and unfortunately run on shore.'[100] With a terrible shudder the *Diana* ran aground. Her Captain, Schomberg, wrote later that 'I could not disengage myself from [the sloop] till I was forced into an eddy tide, which carried me on the rocks.'[101] The *Diana* stuck fast. She was stranded, vulnerable. Quebecers rejoiced; 'we think that it will not be able to move off,' wrote Panet in his diary.[102] Luckily for the crew they were just out of range of Quebec's cannon. But as Schomberg related, the French responded by 'sending the floating batteries out to insult us'.[103] They blasted away at the beached ship, which stubbornly refused to respond to the crew's attempts to refloat her. As the tide fell more of her hull became exposed. French gunboats beetled out and fired their cannon at the tempting target. A lieutenant on the *Diana* recorded that they 'received some damage'.[104] Schomberg feared the worst. Later he wrote that 'had they been more enterprising I think they might at first have destroyed us'.[105] Had the *Diana* been alone the French boats would have edged closer and pounded her to pieces, but she was far from alone; various Royal Naval warships immediately sailed into the narrows to protect one of their own. The *Pembroke* and the *Richmond* both crowded on sail and they anchored near the *Diana* daring the French rafts and gunboats to come closer. Carpenters and spare hands were sent in a flotilla of boats to help the *Diana*'s crew get the ship off the rocks. Together the sailors 'did what we could to lighten her'. They threw various bits of rigging over the side, 'hove 13 guns overboard', and sent powder, shot, and ballast after it.[106]

At sunrise, according to her log, the *Diana* was 'still aground'. More guns were thrown overboard, pushed out through the gun ports. Various attempts were made to attach hawsers to the other ships and eventually, just after midnight the following night, as the flood tide forced more water under her keel the *Diana* responded to the tow ropes and refloated. She was aground for just over twenty-four hours. At 0300 hours her exhausted crew dropped anchor by the western tip of the Île d'Orléans. Lacking most of her artillery, and damaged by rocks and enemy gunboats, she was in no shape to continue operations in the St Lawrence and was soon sent back to Boston for repairs accompanied by around twenty-five empty American transport ships, ones that had been most seriously damaged by the storm at the end of June.

Despite costing one of the frigates, the operation to get British ships up the St Lawrence beyond Quebec was an important success. Wolfe had broken out of the prison that was the basin in front of the town. Miles of undefended coastline beckoned. The opportunity now existed to get ashore on the north bank of the St Lawrence and march over-land to threaten the town's weakest, landward side. The attack on the Beauport shore was called off and Wolfe and his commanders pondered their expanded list of options. The threat was clear to the French. Montcalm visited the batteries the following morning and noted that the most exposed had 'lost a lot of people' from the fire of the British ships. Then, in one of the most candid sections of his jour-nal, he admitted that the passing of the enemy squadron caused 'consternation'. 'Were we wrong?' he desperately asked himself. 'If the enemy decides to go up the river and land at any point they will block our supply route for food and munitions.'[107]

EIGHT

Competing Ideas

IT WAS EVENING, and Major General James Wolfe was 'cheerful' according to Tom Bell, his aide-de-camp.[1] They had spent the day after the ships had passed the narrows reconnoitring the banks of the river beyond Quebec, which the navy had now brought within striking distance of Wolfe's army. The shore was steep on either side. The river was just under a mile wide, with both banks heavily wooded. At various points on the north side small roads or paths ran down from the plateau above to the foot of the cliffs. Any attempt to land would have to be made up one of these. It would be no easy task to push men up these tracks, let alone drag cannon, and it would be a hundred times more challenging if they were defended by a group of determined soldiers. At present though there was only a sprinkling of Canadians and Native Americans along the bank.

Wolfe regretted that he had not followed through with his planned attack above Quebec in the first few days of July. In his own diary he noted that 'if we had ventured the stroke that was first intended we should probably have succeeded'. The word 'infallibly' was originally written instead of 'probably' but Wolfe, reining in his excitement, crossed it out and made the more sober judgement.[2] He remained excited enough to write to Monckton and tell him that the blow that was to have fallen on the Beauport defences below the town would now be redirected above the town. Monckton was to row upriver in flat-bottomed boats, 'until you perceive three lanterns, hanging abreast' from the *Sutherland*. The force would then push ashore on the north bank and capture the high ground above the bank along which the road to Quebec ran and start building fortifications. Artillery would be rushed ashore to turn the outpost into yet another impregnable fortress. As Wolfe wrote, 'if we can take four or five good posts and keep them till our friends arrive, it may bring on a very decisive affair'.[3] On the way back to Point Lévis Wolfe halted where a small river, the Etchemin, entered the St Lawrence. He looked long and hard at one particular encampment of Native Americans and Canadians on the north shore. There was a steep path leading down to a small indentation that hardly deserved the title of *l'anse* or cove. Wolfe used a spy glass to watch people climb up and down and saw people washing and doing laundry in the St Lawrence. As they trudged into the camp at Point Lévis later in the day, Wolfe said to a young engineer lieutenant, Samuel Holland, who had accompanied him on the reconnoitre, 'There, my dear Holland. That will be my last resort.' The cove's name was L'Anse au Foulon.[4]

Monckton was busily preparing his men for the new assault but by that very afternoon Wolfe's confidence deserted him. He penned another note to Monckton saying that 'Particular circumstances make it necessary to delay our attempt for a few days, and to keep it secret. In the mean while we shall make all the diversion we possibly can.'[5] Yet again the French had forestalled him. Refusing to play the passive part allotted to them in Wolfe's plan, they rushed men above Quebec to defend the shoreline.

The French had watched with horror as British ships had passed Quebec. Yet another pre-war certainty had been shown up as a mirage. The cannon of the town had signally failed to block the narrows. Suddenly there were British ships and men upriver of the town, where they were a step closer to Quebec's most vulnerable side and potentially able to strike at her supply route from the rest of the colony. One diarist appreciated the full menace of this development: '[the British] could, at pleasure, make excursions on either of the two coasts; and thus become Masters of the entire navigation of the river, whilst awaiting the opportunity of disembarking the whole of their army at this place, which it was now in their power to effect'.[6] Montcalm responded quickly to this new threat. Dumas was sent with 600 men and Native

Americans to keep an eye on the British ships. Le Mercier, the artillery-man, followed with two 18-pound cannon and a mortar. Montcalm, who despised him, was disparaging about his efforts. 'He pretends to have strongly inconvenienced a frigate,' he wrote sneeringly in his journal.[7] But British accounts suggest that his guns were successful in driving off their ships. The *Squirrel*'s log records that while she and the other British ships 'cut out' or captured two small French ships near the bank, the French 'began firing from a gun and bomb battery which they erected on the hill and haled [put pressure on] us'. They shot through a key piece of rigging and 'wounded our main mast'.[8] They moved further upriver out of range. One French journal confirms that the French 'set up a fine battery which compelled the ships to go some distance down the river'.[9]

Wolfe was dismayed by these French moves. He later reported to Pitt that on reflection the shoreline above the town presented the same 'great difficulties' as it did below owing to the 'same attention on the enemy's side ... the nature of the ground, and the obstacles to our communication with the fleet'. 'But what I feared most,' he admitted, 'was that if we should land between the town and the river Cape Rouge, the body first landed could not be reinforced before they were attacked by the enemy's whole army.' The few ships above the town were incapable of landing enough men to take on Montcalm's entire force. To do that more and more transports would have to pass the narrows and this would require the confluence of darkness, wind, and tide. Essentially, reported Wolfe, Monckton's attack had been called off because 'the enemy were jealous of the design, were preparing against it, and had actually brought artillery and a mortar ... to play upon the shipping'. The whole attack 'seemed so hazardous that I thought it best to desist'.[10]

Murray was furious about the decision to abandon this attack. He was certain, he wrote in a letter to Wolfe, that it was possible to 'strike a decisive blow in that quarter' because of the 'enemy's inattention to every thing above the town'. He assured Wolfe that 'I as ardently wish you success, as if you had done me the honour to employ me in procuring it, I am too much a Briton to be insincere in this respect, and am too much a soldier to grumble that I am left here inactive.' He finished by saying, 'however strong my inclinations to quit this place may be, I shall check it, and as patiently as I can remain at the post you are pleased to assign to me, I should have thought myself very fortunate had it been a more active one'.[11] Wolfe soothed Murray who was clearly desperate to thrust himself into the middle of the action. He wrote that communications between the fleets above and below the town were uncertain and 'the admiral is of opinion that the flat boats cannot pass the town without danger and difficulty and the night tides do not favour us for the present'. In short Wolfe cautiously asserted that 'I chose to look about me a little before we undertook.'[12]

Wolfe's indecision might have been poor leadership but his caution was not. It was justified a few days later when two ships, the frigate *Lowestoft* and the sloop *Hunter*, attempted to pass the town but were forced to turn back by a combination of wind and enemy gunfire. The log of the *Dublin* asserted that a 'floating battery fired on one of our frigates which attempted to go above the town'. The battery managed to put 'one shot in the hull, and damaged some of her rigging'. It was not fatal but 'little wind obliged her to come back'.[13] The *Hunter*'s log says that they waited until 0300 hours to pass the narrows but 'when abreast of the town the wind took us short and the French firing at us from their quarters in the town, we could not sail to windward of Point Levy; was obliged to put back'.[14] Malcolm Fraser on the shoreline described it as such a 'smart cannonade'[15] that he was certain it would damage them badly while a sergeant wrote that the French 'fired so hot at them, they were obliged to turn back'.[16] It was a welcome success for the French. 'Our fire this day was well served'[17] records one journal while another said that 'no sooner were they within range of our cannon, than all the batteries played upon them so vigorously, as compelled them to tack about, and return to their former stations'.[18] Neither French source makes any mention of the part played by the dying breeze.

The force upriver was not strong enough to take on the French army by itself and clearly reinforcing it was going to be difficult. It could make itself useful, though, as Wolfe described to Pitt, to 'divide the enemy's force, and to draw their attention as high up the river as possible, and to procure some intelligence'. To do this Wolfe sent Colonel

Carleton 'to land at the Pointe aux Trembles, to attack whatever he might find there, bring off some prisoners, and all the useful papers he could get'.[19] Carleton landed there, twenty miles above Quebec, on 21 July, drove off some Native Americans, searched in vain for military stores to destroy and left, taking with him a haul of civilian prisoners, including, according to a French source, '200 women'.[20] Montcalm sneered that he only detained the 'pretty ladies'.[21]

It was a rare skirmish with the Native Americans that did not produce a worrying butcher's bill and this was no exception. The commander of the 3rd/60th Major Augustin Prevost was shot in the head and had to be immediately evacuated to New York. Remarkably he survived a trepanning and carried the scar on his forehead the rest of his life, earning the nickname 'bullet-head' from his family. He was exactly the kind of man Wolfe could not afford to lose. Few knew more about warfare in North America. Along with his brother, Colonel Jacques Prevost, he had been integral to founding the 60th Royal Americans. The two brothers had constantly drilled their men in the skills suitable for North America such as scouting and sharpshooting. Wolfe needed men like Prevost to provide that irreplaceable backbone of expertise and experience which could make useful soldiers out of novices.[22] On this occasion Wolfe let his delight at the arrival of a boat load of women overcome his sorrow at losing Prevost. He personally debriefed them. A French journal reports that 'His Excellency', as the officer referred to Wolfe, the enemy commander, with impeccable etiquette, 'received his prisoners very graciously, entertained them for two days, and then sent them back, greatly charmed with his politeness, and the genteel treatment they had met with'.[23] Having been released, the ladies were full of praise for Wolfe. Some had dined with him, and he had 'joked considerably about the circumspection of our generals'. He had told the ladies that 'he had offered very favorable opportunities for an attack [by Montcalm] and had been surprised that no advantage had been taken of them'. The women 'spoke equally well of the treatment they had received from the English officers'.[24]

Panet says that these well-born Quebec women, including 'Madames Duchesnay, De Charney, her mother, her sister, mademoiselle Couillard, the family, Joly Mailhot, Magnan', were 'treated with all the possible politeness'. In return the women paid Wolfe 'many compliments'. Indeed, the British come out of things far better than the allies of New France. According to Panet, 'the saddest part of this story is that the English did not do them any wrong, but the savages pillaged their houses and almost all of the goods of these refugee families'.[25]

The women were sent into Quebec under the terms of a six-hour truce, during which time Wolfe received Montcalm's permission to bring his sick and wounded from Montmorency and Point Lévis to the hospital on the western point of Île d'Orléans. The women were landed at 1500 hours, 'brought back', according to Panet, 'with much politeness'. He says that 'each officer had given his name to the beautiful prisoners that they had taken. The English had promised not to cannon or bombard until nine o'clock at night to give the women time to retreat back to where they judged necessary, but that, past this time, they would fire with ease.' 'They kept their word,' he wrote, 'at nine o'clock; they fired, each quarter of an hour, ten to twelve bombs, some of which were filled with explosives. They set fire to the Parish Church and M. Rotot's house, as well as the houses from M. Duplessis until M. Imbert, and all of the houses behind, including mine ... were consumed by the flames.'[26]

It was a curious moment, gentility entwined with barbarism. This uneasy relationship could not last. In a fascinating snippet one journal hints at the erosion of traditional military values between the two sides. It claims that 'Captain Smythe, aide de camp to General Wolfe, [was] not politely used by the French in town' as he escorted the civilians back.[27] As a messenger Smythe should have been treated with respect and dignity. Yet the inhabitants of Quebec, their homes incinerated, were losing patience with the niceties of European warfare. The bonds of civilization were weakening for those who remained in the shattered town. Frustrated 'with the considerable theft that is going on in Quebec, committed equally by the sailors, soldiers and militia', Panet began to lobby Vaudreuil and Bigot to 'create an Ordinance in order to hang the thieves without delay'. The suggestion was approved, a commission was established and Panet was named the Secretary. His associate, François Daine, was given the power to have looters hanged the same day they were caught. On 29 July a man was hanged for theft.[28]

Wolfe experienced the brutal realities of North American warfare just days after his pleasant dinner with the French ladies. Tales of fords across the Montmorency had sparked his interest. If these were 'practicable' then he could march across the river and drive the French troops from the Beauport shore altogether. It is easy to see how his frustration with the navy boosted his enthusiasm for finding one of these fords. A straightforward attack across the Montmorency would be an army operation alone. There would be no need for the kind of cooperation with the navy that he obviously found so irksome. On 26 July, therefore, Wolfe set out to look for the ford. Mackellar records that he took 'Brigadier Murray, with Otway's 35th Regiment, five companies of Light Infantry, and one of the Rangers, and two field pieces'. The two cannon were probably six pounders which were more mobile than the heavier pieces. Even so, Mackellar continues, 'after we had gone about a mile and a half the field-pieces were sent back to camp, the road being too bad to get them on'.[29]

It was thick woodland. As they pushed further upstream the roar of the falls grew ever quieter. This was the terrain which suited the Canadians and Native Americans perfectly. The latter's relationship with the French had been strained by their inactivity. Around that time Vaudreuil wrote to de Lévis describing them as 'too lively' and hoping that the latter had found a way to make them 'less impatient'.[30] Now Wolfe was offering a solution. His men had marched well before dawn and in the semi-darkness, at 0400 hours, with the sunrise still an hour away, the sound of muskets and high-pitched war cries heralded a first attack on the column. Wolfe's 'Family Journal' describes it as a 'skirmish with about 20 Indians'.[31] They fell upon the lighter troops who were to the front and flanks of the main column. These light infantrymen and rangers skirmished tenaciously and allowed the march to continue.

The column reached the ford a few hours later. On the far side there was 'a breast work of considerable extent'.[32] Wolfe tried to get a good look at the practicality of crossing it but was forced to stay under cover by a withering fire from the far bank. 'As the river is narrow here,' his 'Family Journal' says, 'the enemy's fire galled our left from their entrenchments.'³³ It was harrowing but worse was to follow. At 0900 hours another attack from across the river threatened to overwhelm Wolfe's column completely.

'A strong body of Indians passed over to attack us,' reported Wolfe's 'Family Journal' and the outcome was 'doubtful for some time'.³⁴ Mackellar estimated that no less than fifteen hundred men now attacked the British. They had crept up the riverbank from a ford higher up and now hurled themselves at a company of light infantry who retreated under the onslaught. The French attack then crashed into two companies of Otway's 35th Regiment. As always this assault relied on speed, surprise, and accuracy with the musket or rifle. These lightning tactics were supposed to spread panic in the enemy and make them scatter, allowing the attackers to hunt down the isolated individuals. The psychological impact was paramount. Against novices these tactics were awesomely effective.

The 35th were no novices. They were no longer the men who, two years before at Fort William Henry, had surrendered to Montcalm's army and naively expected safe passage to the nearest British fort. On that terrible occasion the Native allies of the French, furious that not a scalp had been taken and the enemy were allowed to march away, could not be restrained and had fallen on them. The wounded in the infirmary had been slaughtered and soldiers initially robbed and then beaten and killed. In desperation the British soldiers had offered the Natives their own rum ration, only to fan the flames as the alcohol-crazed attacks became more and more brutal. Even fresh graves were dug up and corpses scalped. French officers had intervened, appalled that the terms of surrender were being broken. Around two hundred men, women, and children were killed, and many others captured. These latter were ransomed and returned to the British by a contrite French colonial administration. Many survivors scattered into the wilderness and stumbled back to British-held territory days later. It was denounced as a war-crime throughout the English speaking world. Now on the banks of the Montmorency the men of the 35th were taking their revenge.

The unit was vastly changed to the one that had arrived in New York in June 1756. The battered and discoloured orange cuffs and facings on the men's red coats still paid tribute to their roots as a Protestant Irish regiment originally raised in 1701 in Belfast by a wealthy landowner who paid for it out of his own pocket. They were granted permission to wear orange facings by King William of England, Scotland, and Ireland, who came from a family whose origins had been in Orange, a principality in northern Provence. He was seen as a hero by Protestant British settlers in Catholic Ireland for defending the Protestant ascendancy and to this day the colour orange is closely associated with the Protestant Irish identity. But years of service in North America had changed the ethnic mix of the regiment.

Only Protestants were supposed to serve in the British army, but during times of war Catholic Irishmen were regularly found in the ranks, especially of Irish regiments. Fresh recruits were sent out from Ireland and no questions asked, especially given that Otway's regiment was chronically short of men. At 500 officers, NCOs, and privates, it was at around half-strength. All the regiments had made great efforts to recruit in North America. After all, the colonials were subjects of George II and in the mid-eighteenth century regiments had none of the regional affiliations that were assigned to them a few decades later. It has been suggested that over ten thousand redcoats in the North American army throughout the Seven Years War were American born.[35]

Their appearance and the way they fought had changed just as much as their nationalities. Gone was the parade ground perfection. One North American veteran wrote that

> the art of war is much changed and improved here. I suppose by the end of the summer it will have undergone a total Revolution … Our hair is about an inch long … Hats … are worn slouched … coats are docked … The Highlanders have put on breeches … swords and sashes are degraded, and many have taken up the hatchet and wear Tomahawks.[36]

A year and a half before, Knox had watched a detachment that had been sent out to gather firewood return from the woods. They looked like a 'detachment of Hungarian or Croatian irregulars'.[37] Another officer wrote to a friend saying, 'you would laugh to see the droll figure we cut ... You would not distinguish us from common plough men.'[38] Beards were left to grow, clothes chosen for utility not martial appearance. The man who had pioneered these changes had been the unfortunate George Augustus, Viscount Howe, older brother of William who now commanded the light infantry of Wolfe's army. Time spent at Westminster School, Eton College, and the backbenches of the House of Commons had not prevented George Augustus from embracing this new kind of warfare. According to one witness he 'laid aside all pride and prejudice, and gratefully accepted counsel from those whom he knew the best qualified to direct them'. He eschewed the 'pedantry of holding up standards of military rules where it was impossible to practise them'.[39] On his instructions hair, coats, and hats were cropped so as to limit anything that could get snared on undergrowth. In the early engagements of the war officers had paid a terrible price for the signs of seniority that they wore. Native Americans and Canadians prided themselves on their worth as marksmen and they knew exactly whom to aim for on the battlefield. Officers in Europe wore a sash over one shoulder as well as gorgets, a decorative symbolic accessory that hung loosely around the throat; both were discarded after the first brush with enemy sharpshooters. As was the lace that bedecked rich officers' coats once it was found that it attracted Abenaki snipers as surely as it did the ladies of St James's.

This relaxation of dress code was reflected in the hunt for new tactics, better suited to the tough conditions. Before it left Ireland, the 35th had been trained for war in Europe. Volume of fire was more highly prized than accuracy. Here in North America shots had to count. Robert Rogers, the pioneering ranger, had made enemies at the commissariat by insisting on using up valuable ammunition to practise firing at targets. The 60th Regiment was founded in North America and from the beginning its doctrine was different from regiments raised in Britain and Ireland. Soldiers were

> sent to fire at Marks [targets], and in order to qualify for the service of the woods, they are to be taught to load and fire, lying on the ground and kneeling. They are to be taught to march in order, slow

and fast, in all sorts of ground. They are frequently to pitch and fold their tents, and to be accustomed to pack up and carry their necessities in the most commodious manner.[40]

The commander of the 1st battalion, 60th Royal American Regiment was a Swiss-born professional soldier who had served in at least two continental armies, Lieutenant Colonel Henry Bouquet. A Highlander serving alongside his battalion commented that 'every afternoon he exercises his men in the woods and bushes in the manner of his own invention, which will be of great service in an engagement with Indians'.[41] He issued his sixteen best marksmen with rifles. These were weapons with grooves, or 'rifling', cut into the barrel. These grooves spun the ball which meant that it left the muzzle with greater speed and accuracy, which is why rugby and American football players attempt to achieve the same effect on a long pass. Other units imitated the 60th although the rangers preferred the smooth bore musket for fighting in woodland since the thickness of the foliage ensured that they rarely got a clear shot at over fifty yards. They found a musket was more useful than an accurate rifle which took longer to load. Some even chopped a few inches of barrel off their muskets to make them lighter and easier to handle. The newly raised Highland regiments were issued with shorter muskets, or carbines, anticipating the close combat they would face in North America.

Wolfe had written brilliantly about the kind of tactics required in 'strong enclosed country' as a battalion commander hungry to see more action in 1755. He told his men that 'every inch of ground that is proper for defence' should be 'disputed with the enemy'. They should 'without confusion or disorder' move from 'place to place' to 'fall on the enemy with advantage, or retire when it is proper to do so' thus drawing 'the enemy into a dangerous position'. Always, they should remember to make every shot count by 'levelling their pieces properly'.[42] Passages like these demonstrate a strikingly modern way of thinking about fire and movement. Nothing could be further from the old cliché of eighteenth-century soldiers as unthinking criminals firing volleys in stiff ranks, kept there only by the threat of flogging and hanging. His writings suggest that while he may have been poor

at maintaining good relations with his subordinates and could be indecisive, Wolfe was a hugely gifted tactician.

Wolfe's army had spent months training for this type of warfare.
Knox relates how at the beginning of campaigns the men were
'constantly employed in forming and dispersing in the woods, and in
other exercises adapted to the peculiar method of carrying on war in
close-covered countries'.[43] They were encouraged to spread out in open
order, and in the event of an ambush, the shout went out to 'Tree All',[44]
upon which everybody would dive for cover behind trees. Ultimately
Native attacks had to be met with aggression and determination.
Montcalm's ADC, the Chevalier Johnstone, wrote a curious and unre-
liable account of the summer in which he puts words into the mouths
of the protagonists like a classical historian. There is one particular
passage that has the ring of truth, in which Johnstone visualized Wolfe
describing the fierce skirmish on the Montmorency. 'There is no other
method,' Johnstone imagined Wolfe saying, 'for troops to defend themselves against the Indians than what I practised with success, when I
was surprised by them at the ford of Montmorency: the soldiers, with
fixed bayonets, dispersed themselves, rushed on in disorder towards
the places where they perceived the smoke of the Indians' discharge;
and by these means my detachment in the woods chased away your
nine hundred Indians.'[45]

The redcoats would never master the Native Americans but skirmishes like this one showed that at least it was a more even contest
than the horrific early years of the war had been. The men of Otway's
with support from the light infantry stabilized the British position and
seem to have chased the Native and Canadian troops back to the ford.
Despite the eventual victory it had been a vicious fight. Mackellar
records that they 'had 55 men killed and wounded, officers included'.[46] In his journal Wolfe blames most of the casualties on fire from
the other side of the river which caught the British during their 'indiscreet pursuit' of the enemy.[47] Among the wounded was Wolfe's aide-
de-camp, Thomas Bell, who wrote, 'I got my arm broke by the
Rascals.'[48]

On the French side there were mixed feelings. The British army had
been bloodied but again many felt that it had been an opportunity lost.

One officer wrote that the attack 'was so impetuous that according to what we since learned ... The English, obliged to fall back, retired more than two hundred paces from the field of battle in order to rally, and the alarm extended as far as the camp.' He says that reinforcements were sent to follow up the initial success but they were too late and 'the entire army regretted the loss of so fine an opportunity'.[49] Panet, a Canadian by outlook, if not by birth, was deeply dissatisfied. He insisted that 'the consternation was so great among the English that they were crying: "all is lost"', but yet again, 'we did not take advantage of this blow'. He blamed the fact that de Lévis had felt obliged to check with Montcalm before leading reinforcements to the river and as a result 'arrived too late'.[50] Yet again the discussions following the operation exacerbated divisions between Frenchmen and Canadians. The latter were, on the whole, more inclined to pursue a forward policy. In the middle of July Montcalm noted in his journal that the Canadians are 'disgusted' and 'discouraged' by the 'slowness' of this campaign. They preferred, he wrote, to make a sudden aggressive blow and then return home. 'It is regrettable that circumstances do not permit us to risk the fate of the colony on a single blow.'[51] Relations did not improve; at the end of July Montcalm wrote to de Lévis saying that 'they are all crazy, and, because I have to deal with them, soon, I will not be any wiser than them'.[52]

There is also a sense in both Johnstone's cryptic text and Mackellar that the way the redcoats had rallied after their initial wobbles showed that they were no longer as terrified of the Native Americans as they had been. Johnstone imagines Montcalm talking to Wolfe in Hades saying, 'the Indians told me on your return, that it was now no more possible to fight you as formerly since the English had learned their way of fighting'.[53] This is obviously fanciful but Mackellar mentions in his diary that 'the Indians were dispirited from that day's loss for the rest of the campaign'.[54] Ramezay puts that loss at only twelve men killed and injured. It seems likely that this was a conservative estimate.[55]

Even if the Native Americans were unhappy that the British no longer ran at the merest whoop, the British were hardly euphoric. They had been made to pay a bloody price for simply looking at the ford.

The next day Wolfe wrote to Monckton informing him of the skirmishes, 'in which our people were victorious but lost more than the enemy'.[56] No one had any desire to take another march through the woods.

He reported to Pitt that 'in reconnoitring the river Montmorency, we found it fordable at a place about three miles up; but the opposite bank was entrenched, and so steep and so woody, that it was to no purpose to attempt a passage there'.[57] Wolfe's attempts to threaten Montcalm's two flanks had come to nothing. The ships above the town needed reinforcing before they could achieve anything and pushing across the Montmorency involved a dangerous passage through thick woodland and a river crossing guarded by strong entrenchments. Many in the British force found Wolfe's apparent lack of a coherent strategy grating. A naval officer wrote to Governor Lawrence in Halifax at the beginning of August. The letter provides a glimpse into a deep pool of frustration. 'Within the space of five hours we received at the general's request, three different orders of consequence, which were contradicted immediately after their reception,' wrote the officer. Nor was this an isolated incident; in fact, it had been 'the constant practice of the General ever since we have been here to the no small amazement of everyone who has the liberty of thinking'. The officer was damning: 'Every step he takes is wholly his own; I'm told he asks no one's opinion, and wants no advice.'[58] Townshend confided in his journal at this time that 'the general seemed to be at a stand which place to make his attack'.[59] News and rumour were inseparable fellows as they swept around the shores of the Quebec basin from mouth to mouth. Knox recorded in his journal that 'many new projects are talked of; but, I believe, from no other motive than to amuse the enemy, in order that false intelligence may be circulated throughout their camps, should any of our soldiers desert, a practice common in all armies'.[60]

The French command was no more unified. Deeply frustrated by his fellow officers, like Vaudreuil and Le Mercier, Montcalm wrote in his journal at the end of July: 'In whose hands are we? What kind of outcome can we expect from such people?'[61] He, like many on the British side, was utterly confused about Wolfe's intentions. On 20 July his journal says simply, 'this whole thing becomes every day more obscure'.[62] News of skirmishes beyond either flank, new batteries being erected in Montmorency, ships passing the town to threaten his right: it was an impenetrable intelligence picture. He spent the whole of that night on the ramparts of Quebec peering into the murk ready to unleash the town's artillery at the merest glimpse of a British ship heading upriver to join her comrades. There was no movement. During the days he wrestled with increasing shortages of powder, for which he blamed corruption, and food, which he suspected the inhabitants were hiding. At the beginning of June the authorities had requisitioned all oxen and bulls in the Quebec area. Now, at the end of July, this order was extended to Trois Rivières.

As July came to a close Wolfe had determined to make a serious attempt at breaking into the enemy's position. Having been frustrated on either flank Wolfe's gaze had drifted back to where it had first fallen: the Beauport shore.

Before Wolfe could land his blow the British fleet found themselves on the receiving end of yet another terrifying attack. There was a strong ebb tide on the night of 27/28 July and, according to the log of the *Stirling Castle*, 'at midnight saw a sky rocket from the French camp which proved a signal for setting on fire a large raft of fire stages which they sent down upon us'.[63] One naval lieutenant described his terror in a letter, 'I was hugely alarmed with a most dreadful sight. The enemy had linked together 100 fire stages, which spread a full 400 yards in length.'[64] Rather than sending down a squadron of fireships the French deployed an ingenious line of rafts which Mackellar had got a glimpse of when a prisoner in Quebec. He called them *radeaux à feu* or 'fire rafts' and described them as platforms stacked with timber and other flammable materials 'tied together by the ends so as to form a chain, and coated over with a strong composition, they are to be set on fire when the ships are near'. Ideally they would then wrap themselves around the bows of ships and set them on fire.[65] Other accounts estimate that there were two or three hundred of these fire rafts. Knox wrote that 'it could not be less than an hundred fathoms [600 feet] in length, and was covered in grenades, old swivels, gun and pistol barrels loaded up to their muzzles, and various other inventions and combustible matters'.[66]

The French were desperate to avoid a repetition of the futile sacrifice of their fireships. This time they were commanded by Courval, 'an intelligent, skilful man' and 'a Canadian, who had given these last years proofs of his bravery'. He guided the chain of rafts to within 'musket range of the first ship' before setting them on fire.[67] The *Lowestoft*'s log reported that they were 'so contrived that they were all in a flame in one minute'.[68] However, the British fleet was prepared for their sudden appearance. An officer on board the *Lizard* reported in a letter that 'we have a number of boats lie on guard every night under the walls of the town, ready to receive any fire machines that may be sent down'.[69] These were armed with 'grapnels and chains fitted a purpose to grapnel them and tow them clear of the fleet'.[70] They pulled hard on their oars, aiming for the rafts, while the most upriver frigate slipped her anchor and calmly signalled to the rest of the fleet. The French seem to have anticipated this interdiction by the guard boats. Attached to the fire rafts was a large platform around five yards square. It sat about two feet high out of the water and was not on fire. Thinking it was a good base from which to throw a grapnel a midshipman from the *Dublin* leapt aboard, his boat being 'nigher and brisker than the rest'. No sooner had he done so than the raft exploded, having been booby trapped to detonate when 'the least weight falls on it'. He was killed and three of his crewmen injured. The *Lizard*'s officer commented that it 'was very fortunate that there were no more boats near'.[71]

Eventually more boats joined the *Dublin*'s and, according to Knox, 'our gallant seamen, with their usual expertness, grappled them before they got down above a third part of the basin, towed them safe to shore and left them at anchor'.[72] The basin was full of boats all towing a collection of rafts, in the words of one witness, 'each separately representing a lofty pillar of solid fire'.[73] Knox could hear the shouts of the sailors across the water. They continually reassured each other with calls of 'All's Well!' He also heard one 'remarkable expression from some of these intrepid souls to their comrades' which he felt 'I must not omit on account of their singular uncouthness.' One voice yelled, 'Damn me Jack, didst thee ever take hell in tow before?'[74]

The rafts may have caused the odd, easily extinguishable fire, depending on which source is to be believed, but overall the damage to the British by the rafts was negligible. The French were satisfied with their performance, and the leadership of Courval, even if the 'success did not correspond with his zeal'. He was 'hotly pursued' and had to be rescued by French gunboats. The general tone of the French sources was that he had been unlucky, on account of 'progress [being] extremely slow and the night not being very dark'.[75] The British were very pleased with the night's work. The *Stirling Castle* 'served the boatmen for the above service ½ a pint of brandy each'.[76] They had earned it.

Wolfe was furious. The next day a flag of truce was sent to the town and a stern message delivered to the French commanders. Wolfe was bored with repeated attempts to incinerate his ships, his men, and his lifeline. According to Knox the message said that 'If the enemy presume to send down any more fire-rafts, they are to be made fast to two particular transports, in which are all the Canadian and other prisoners, in order that they may perish by their own base inventions.' Knox reported that this threat was, however, 'only looked upon as a menace'.[77] Montcalm told de Lévis that Wolfe's letter was 'pretty stupid' and did not 'necessitate a response'.[78]

NINE

Defeat at Montmorency

EARLY IN THE MORNING of 31 July 1759 Lieutenant Colonel Howe led the light infantry and another regiment north out of the British camp at Montmorency and followed the river inland. They made no secret of their march. They wanted to be seen. Above them the sky was clear and the men were hot well before the sun had even fully cleared the tops of the trees. Howe's march was part of an intricate plan. The camp they left was bustling. Every cannon in the area was being hauled to the very edge of the steep cliffs, overlooking the roaring waterfall. Townshend wrote in his journal that this was done 'in order to rake the French entrenchments'.[1] Across the St Lawrence the camps at Point Lévis and on the tip of the Île d'Orléans were also buzzing. Flat-bottomed boats were drawn up on the shoreline; the grenadiers of the army were rechecking their equipment before boarding. Sharp new flints were carefully screwed into the jaws of the cock. To keep pebbles out of their shoes as they splashed through the shallows gaiters, white regulation ones or slightly more waterproof black linen ones if the soldier could afford it, were properly fastened. The company officers were busy. Before any attack it was the job of lieutenants and captains to 'see that the balls fit in the men's guns so that they may run down their barrels' and 'all their arms are clean and in good order' as one British officer of the time recorded in his journal.[2] Each soldier wore his light buff leather shoulder strap over his left shoulder supporting his cartridge box on his right hip. The box contained a wooden block with holes drilled for pre-prepared cartridges containing gunpowder and a musket ball. The black leather flap was supposed to keep the rain out. Cartridge boxes were not supplied by the government but by the regiment's colonel, who was paid a lump sum to do so by the crown. Many colonels provided shoddy cartridge boxes and were slow to replace defective ones, choosing instead to pocket the leftover money. 'Those that have not cartridge boxes' were told by their officers to 'break their cartridges and put their powder into horns' while keeping the musket balls loose in a pocket or pouch.[3] Bayonets were sharpened and then sheathed in a scabbard on a waistbelt that could also carry a sword, although on this campaign most grenadiers had dispensed with these cumbersome weapons. Since they were shock troops, the first wave was carrying the lightest possible load. Rations and blankets would be sent after them. Those in the second wave wore knapsacks on their backs with rolled-up blankets on top.

The brick-red coats, waistcoats, and breeches were so bright when new that the tailors who made them often went blind. A new coat was supposed to be issued every year on the anniversary of King George II's accession, 11 June, whether at home or on campaign. But the men about to climb into the flat-bottomed boats would not have been a mass of blinding colour. The new uniforms were often kept for formal occasions and if men could get away with it they patrolled, worked, and fought in their older, more comfortable coats. On their heads their tall mitre caps contributed to the sweat which poured off their brows. The grenadiers of Fraser's 78th Highlanders had embellished their caps with bear fur which within a few years would be the regulation for all grenadiers.[4]

Most officers, like Wolfe himself, wore their simple 'red clothes', an undecorated red frock coat without lace or even the distinctive colours of their regiments. On their feet were well-worn boots. These were not the dandies of fable. They were nearly all tough professionals who had grown up in the army. Most of them were country stock and they had been toughened by a childhood of tramping through the woods, moorland, and marshes of Britain and Ireland in pursuit of deer, grouse, and pheasant.

At 0800 hours the grenadier companies filed onto the flat-bottomed boats. As they did so British ships pushed into the north channel between the Île d'Orléans and the Beauport shore. Extensive sound-ings had been carried out by James Cook and others to ascertain just how close the warships could get to the north bank. These had been performed at night and under the constant threat of being snatched by a group of Canadians or Native Americans in their canoes. The fifty-gun *Centurion*, nearly thirty years old, crept as close to land as she dared and began thundering away at the most easterly French posi-tions on the north shore, the ones that sat alongside the Montmorency River and falls. Wolfe later reported to Pitt that 'the ship was of great use, as her fire was very judiciously directed'.[5] As it did so Townshend's fifty cannon began blasting the same positions from across the river.

Next, to the astonishment of the French defenders, two 'Cats', chunky coastal craft like the colliers on which Cook had learnt his trade, crowded as much sail on as possible and, at full speed, ran ashore. They grounded in the shallows about five hundred yards from the French shore defences. They were the *Russell* and the *Three Sisters* and Mackellar says that they were both 'mounting 14 guns each'.[6] These ships were 'remarkably strong built' according to the eighteenth-century *Universal Dictionary of the Marine* and with their broad beam and shallow draught they were designed to 'take the ground' rather than avoid it at all costs like most ships.[7]

As their keels ran hard into the mud of the St Lawrence at 1000 hours it became immediately clear that the plan had gone wrong. Wolfe had been told by Cook and other naval officers that the Cats would be able to get much closer to the French positions. He had been hoping to use them as forts or bunkers from which his grenadiers would assault the shore while others remained on board to supply them with covering fire from the shelter of their heavy oak timbers. On board were four companies of grenadiers, under the command of Wolfe's friend Lieutenant Colonel Murray of the 15th Regiment, some artillerymen, two light cannon designed to be dragged ashore to support the infantry, and 1,000 entrenching tools. Wolfe's 'Family Journal' states that 'the water being very shallow, they could not get so near the redoubts as the general had been informed was practica-ble. T'was said that at the top of the tide they could get within fifty yards, instead of which their distance was six hundred.'[8] An added frustration was that as the tide had dropped, the *Three Sisters*, which was closest to the shore, had swung around and could not even bring her cannon to bear on the French positions. Instead, she was vulnerable to 'raking' fire from the French artillery which set about blasting her from stem to stern. Montresor reported to his father that the French floating batteries joined their colleagues on the shore in pouring a withering fire on the Cats with 'almost every shot taking place'.[9]

With typical bravery Wolfe immediately demanded to be rowed out to the Cats so he could make a decision on whether his attack was still realistic. He had originally intended to land troops and seize a redoubt on the shore. From his careful scrutiny from the Île d'Orléans he thought he had spotted, as he later told Pitt, one particular redoubt which was 'detached' and 'appeared to be out of musket shot of the entrenchments upon the hill'.[10] This would be his toehold on the heavily fortified Beauport shore. Montcalm would be forced to drive him out and this, Wolfe hoped, would bring on the general engagement that he wished so much to precipitate.

On 28 July he had written to Monckton and outlined his intentions. He told his second in command that 'The Master of the Pembroke [James Cook] assures the Admiral that a Cat can go within less than 1000 yards of the Redoubt – if so, it will be a short affair. The business will be to keep it.' Wolfe made sure his most trusted subordinates held the key positions. Lieutenant Colonel Murray would command the grenadiers on the two Cats, while his favourite, Burton, 'would have direction' of the main body of the amphibious forces. Monckton was told to prepare the assault force with 10,000 musket cartridges, 200 shovels, fifty pick axes, and twenty 'felling axes'.[11] A couple of days before he had written again, on a scrap of paper for which he apologized, saying, 'I have no better.' In this letter he had emphasized that he wanted to stir Montcalm into action. It was infinitely possible that the French commander should attack a 'corps of ours with superiority of numbers, than that we should attack his whole army entrenched, with what we can put on shore at one landing'. He was feeling very bullish. He promised Monckton that 'If the Marquis gives Burton and I only two hours we shall knock his battalions about most furiously.'[12]

An attack on the isolated redoubt on the very eastern extremity of the French line also gave Wolfe the chance to concentrate his forces. His 'Family Journal' explained his thinking:

> he could act with his whole army at once, for during the time that the troops from Levis and the Point of Orléans were passed over in boats, the troops from our camp to the east of the falls could march down and pass the Montmorency below the falls (which were fordable at low water); add to this that he hoped to shake the enemy's line by the power of his artillery across the falls, and by that favour our attack.

Townshend's men could march across the bottom of the falls and support the amphibious landing. If Wolfe had aimed further towards the centre of Montcalm's position where the beach was more favourable to an assault, all the troops would have to be landed by boat and 'as the boats could not contain the half of the army the first debarkation would have been crushed before they could be sustained, particularly as the descent there must be in the presence of the main body of the French army'.[13]

The decision to attack the very edge of Montcalm's army surprised the French commander as much as anyone. Only six days before he had written to de Lévis, his second in command, and responsible for the left of the French line, saying that he 'did not believe the English will attack the left'. In fact, he was beginning to believe they would not attack at all, 'but will try to intercept French supplies and destroy the countryside'.[14]

Four days later four companies of grenadiers had boarded the two Cats. The attack was planned for 30 July but there had not been a breath of wind. Wolfe's Journal recorded that 'calm made it impossible to attack the Redoubt'. Slightly later the journal gives us another indication of disagreements within the highest echelons of the British forces. There is an entry that says, 'dislike of the General Officers and other to this business – but nothing better proposed by them'.[15] On 31 July there was just enough breeze and Wolfe had ordered the attack to start.

As Wolfe arrived at the *Russell* it was already coming under heavy fire from the shore. Two companies of the Louisbourg Grenadiers, just over one hundred and fifty men, were packed on board. All infantrymen hate being cooped up in an alien environment, passively enduring a heavy bombardment. The heat of the sun was being augmented by the ship's gunners, who, Mackellar wrote, were 'firing as fast as their guns would allow'; the infantrymen's situation was close to being unbearable.[16] They had begun taking casualties. Wolfe was risking his life by going aboard. He told Saunders later that 'I was no less than three times struck with the splinters in that ship and had my stick knocked out of my hand with a cannonball while I was on board reconnoitring the position and movements of the enemy.'[17]

Wolfe's bravery was laudable and no doubt boosted his popularity with the huddled redcoats whose danger he shared, but his job was to make a decision. He was now close enough to the shore to realize that his assumptions about the French defences were wrong. The redoubt that he had hoped to capture was not isolated; it was not out of range from the French entrenchments. He reported to Pitt that 'the redoubt was too much commanded to be kept without very great loss', meaning that if he seized it the French would be able to fire down onto it from their entrenchments on the hills above. The central idea that had underpinned the operation had turned out to be false. The question was: should he call off the attack?

Like all commanders in the thick of battle Wolfe found himself impelled towards action. Officers and men would have mentally prepared themselves to go into battle, their blood was up. From the shotblasted deck of a crowded ship, with wounded and dying men scattered around him, the idea of cancelling the operation must have seemed the cowardly rather than the wise option. The grenadiers had endured a summer of frustration, time and again being ordered into flat-bottomed boats for assaults that had been cancelled. Friends and comrades had been captured, tortured, and scalped while on patrol. Wolfe knew that these men were desperate for revenge, and desperate to get off this unfamiliar ship. Behind him on the St Lawrence more grenadiers were crammed onto flat-bottomed boats, bored and terrified at the same time, waiting for Wolfe's decision.

He later explained to Pitt that the 'enemy seemed in some confusion'. Since 'we were prepared for an action, I thought it a proper time to make an attempt upon their entrenchments'.[18] It was a convenient excuse. Having told Monckton that he did not want to launch a direct assault on the enemy trenches he was now about to do just that. Orders were sent to the brigadiers, the grenadiers were to be taken off the Cats and ferried ashore in small boats. Wolfe was about to command his first battle.

The tide was high when the Cats beached themselves, to allow them to get as close in as possible. Wolfe now realized, according to his 'Family Journal', that "twas necessary to let the ebb run e're he attempted to land the troops, otherwise the landing would be under the musketry of the enemy'.[19] Not only did he have to wait for the waters to recede and allow his men to deploy on the beach without being cut down by French musketry but he also had to wait for the ford below the Montmorency falls to become crossable by Townshend's men waiting on the far side. This would not be possible for about four or five hours. The grenadiers were taken off the Cats, and they joined their fellows in the flat-bottomed boats bobbing in the middle of the St Lawrence. Malcolm Fraser was in one of the boats and wrote that 'in this way we continued going sometimes up, sometimes down the river, the enemy throwing a shell at our boats almost every ten minutes, which luckily did no execution'.[20] The occasional soaking in river water caused by the cannonballs must have almost been welcome on such a hot day.

At around 1600 hours the tide was out. The retreating waters had uncovered a large strand on which Wolfe's attack could form up. He gave the signal for the boats to head for the shore: a red flag from the main topgallant mast of the *Russell*. When this signal had been noted he flew a blue-and-white striped flag from the same place to tell Townshend to start his march across the Montmorency. The sailors pulled hard on their oars. Suddenly the leading boats crunched onto a ledge that Wolfe described as being 'a considerable distance' from the shore. 'This accident put us in some disorder,' he reported. Wolfe's 'Family Journal' says that he immediately 'ordered the intermediate space twixt them and the enemies shore be sounded, to know if the troops could march it, without wetting their ammunition', but 'in many places the water was five feet deep'.[21] While the grenadiers and sailors heaved the boats off the ledge, with cannonballs slapping into the water around them, Wolfe sent a message to Townshend to delay the crossing of the Montmorency and then took one flat-bottomed boat and tried to find a passage through the shallows. After an hour he had done so and 'as soon as we had found a fit part of the shore' he ordered the troops to disembark, 'thinking it not yet too late for the attempt'.[22] Mackellar says that the time was about 1715 hours. Forty-five minutes later the boats grounded and the grenadiers jumped into the water, hoisting muskets and cartridge cases high out of it. A witness wrote that 'the grenadiers showed uncommon bravery in this affair; we got out of our boats and formed as well as we could in the water, which came up to our waistbelts'.[23] Clouds had suddenly blackened the sky and Knox described the weather as 'very gloomy'.[24]

Any sequence of events less likely to disguise his intentions from the enemy is hard to imagine. Knox watched all afternoon as French reinforcements drifted to the left of their line. Mackellar wrote in his diary that Montcalm's forces 'were now sufficiently apprised of our design, and had time enough to be prepared accordingly: their entrenchments upon the edge of the bank were fully manned for a considerable way'.[25] The French had watched the flat-bottomed boats attempting to find a path through the shallows, and one of Montcalm's soldiers wrote that 'we could no longer doubt the enemy's intention to attack us'. Once the French commander was certain that Wolfe was focusing on the far left of his line, commanded by de Lévis, he 'weakened' other parts and 'repaired in person to Chevalier de Levis' camp' at the head of the Guyenne Regiment.[26] When he arrived he found the troops there had been having a torrid time under the 'hottest fire imaginable' from the ships in the St Lawrence and the shore batteries on the other side of the Montmorency. One officer records that the fire from the latter 'galled our men more than the discharge from the shipping'.[27] Montcalm claims that the British fired in total '3000 shot'.[28] Against this maelstrom the French deployed 'only four pieces of cannon'. The British tried to knock them out but thanks to the strength of their earthworks they failed to do so and the French cannon fired all day.[29] Panet says that the French pierced the hull of just one of the Cats with more than thirty shot.[30] In the trenches the regulars and the Canadian militiamen stood side by side; their shared experience of being under British bombardment produced a rare moment of harmony between the two groups. One French officer recorded that even 'though it was the first time they had ever seen the face of an enemy', they remained 'unterrified, and stood to their arms with a steadiness, that greatly pleased our generals, and merited their applause'.[31]

The thirteen companies of grenadiers, supported by 200 men from the 2nd Battalion, 60th Royal American Regiment, waded up the beach, across slippery ground that until minutes before had been underwater. John Johnson remembered the ground as being 'covered with slimy mud, exceeding slippery, and broken into deep holes'.[32] Montresor wrote that it was 'about half a mile over to the redoubt' and another quarter of a mile beyond that lay the slope in which the French had their trenches.[33] Officers bellowed at the men to form up as soon as they found their footing. But the grenadiers were in no mood to be corralled. They had spent six hours in flat-bottomed boats, in roasting sunshine, under bombardment. They had no idea of the reason for the delays. As soon as they were ashore they slid their bayonets over the muzzles of their muskets and took matters into their own hands. One officer wrote, 'the general ordered the "Grenadiers March" to beat, which animated our men so much that we could scarce restrain them, we moved on through a very bad muddy beach and attacked the redoubt and battery which we carried'.[34]

Two years of ambush, skirmishing, sieges, and lonely sentry duty had produced such a desire to get to grips with the enemy that the grenadiers exploded into the French positions. Knox wrote that they must have been 'impatient for glory'.[35] Wolfe was amazed: 'whether from the noise and hurry at landing,' he wrote, 'or from some other cause, the grenadiers, instead of forming themselves as they were directed, ran impetuously towards the enemy's entrenchments in the utmost disorder and confusion, without waiting for the corps which were to sustain them, and join in the attack'.[36]

John Johnson looked back stoically and commented that 'it often happens that the best concerted plans get marred in the execution; so it happened here'.[37] Perhaps each grenadier company was keen to demonstrate its superiority to the others. One story has it that the 200 Royal Americans who landed with the grenadiers were keen to show off their prowess, especially because their commander, Captain David Ochterlony, had fought a duel the day before with a grenadier officer. Ochterlony shouted at the latter that although his men were not grenadiers they would be first to the redoubt. This may be myth but it illustrates the fierce competitiveness that existed between all these units, the proudest in Wolfe's army.

Sergeant Edward 'Ned' Botwood was a grenadier in Lascelles' 47th Foot. He had written a song called 'Hot Stuff!' to be sung to a well-known tune before the expedition left Halifax. It is a brilliant snapshot of the mood of the men, their language, their humour, and their pride in themselves, their leadership, and their units. It is a potent warning not to dismiss the otherwise anonymous redcoats as mindless, downtrodden, or unwilling.

Come, each death-doing dog that dares venture his neck,
Come, follow the hero that goes to Quebec;
Jump aboard of the transports, and loose every sail,
Pay your debts at the tavern by giving leg-bail;
And ye that love fighting shall soon have enough;
Wolfe commands us, my boys, we shall give them Hot Stuff.

Up the River St. Lawrence our troops shall advance,
To the Grenadier's March we will teach them to dance.
Cape Breton we've taken and next we will try
At the capital to give them another black eye.
Vaudreuil, 'tis in vain you pretend to look gruff,
Those are coming who know how to give you Hot Stuff.

With powder in his periwig, and snuff in his nose,
Monsieur will run down our descent to oppose;
And the Indians will come, but the Light Infantry
Will soon compel *them* to betake to a tree.
From such rascals as these may we fear a rebuff?
Advance, grenadiers, and let fly your Hot Stuff!

When the Forty-seventh Regiment is dashing ashore,
When bullets are whistling and cannon do roar,
Says Montcalm, 'Those are Shirley's, I know their lapels.'
'You lie,' says Ned Botwood, 'We are of Lascelles!
Though our clothing is changed, yet we scorn a powder-puff;
So at you, ye bitches, here's give you Hot Stuff!

With Monkton [sic] and Townsend [sic], those brave brigadiers,
I think we shall soon have the town 'bout their ears,
And when we have done with the mortars and guns,
If you please, Madam Abbess, a word with your nuns.
Each soldier shall enter the convent in buff
And then, never fear, we will give them Hot Stuff.[38]

Botwood was now on the beach, surrounded by a thousand men 'that love fighting', sprinting towards the French positions, all discipline forgotten. A British officer who was not present but heard the story first hand from many survivors wrote, 'the attack was impetuous, the French gave way and spiked their own cannon ... but the grenadiers flushed with success pursued violently huzzaing as they went along and nothing could stop them until they got among the French lines'.[39] The French abandoned the redoubt and the artillery battery on the beach and scrambled back up to their trenches. The grenadiers hardly paused at the redoubt and surged onwards up the slope. A sergeant in one of the companies of the Louisbourg Grenadiers wrote that as they charged up the beach the French 'cannon played very briskly on us; but their small arms, in their trenches lay cool'. However, when the French 'were sure of their mark; then they poured their small shot like showers of hail, which caused our brave grenadiers to fall very fast'.[40]

At least several hundred muskets fired as quickly as they could be reloaded. Panet gives the credit to his fellow Canadians for such a hot fire, but says they were 'supported' by French regulars.[41] Alongside the men in the trenches, cannon fired 'grape shot', sacks of small lead balls, possibly mixed with scraps of metal and nails. The British grenadiers pushed forward into this firestorm. A witness paints a picture of them 'labouring up the hill, sinking in the sand and entangled in the pickets'. As they clambered up the slope, they were engulfed in 'a shower of musketry as is not to be described, which continued without intermission for the space of twenty minutes'.[42] Several of the sources use the same words, 'extraordinary' and 'incessant', to describe the deluge of fire. It was too much. An officer who arrived in Quebec a month later wrote a letter when he got there saying that he had heard that the men 'behaved with the greatest courage imaginable ... but there were such lanes made through them by the small shot and grape from the enemy that they were obliged to retreat'.[43]

They withdrew down the hill but rallied and attacked again. Knox, who was watching, wrote that they 'made many efforts, though not with the greatest regularity, to gain the summit, which they found less practicable than had been expected'. 'Their ardour,' he wrote, 'was checked by the repeated heavy fire.'[44] One sergeant claimed that he could see Montcalm riding along his lines high above them. More believably he recorded that enemy fire 'killed a good many of our men, I don't recollect how many'. He also wrote that the struggling grenadiers did not even have the satisfaction of returning fire. 'We did not fire, for it would have been no use, as they were completely entrenched, and we could see only the crown of their heads.'[45] In a private letter Wolfe later raged that the 'blockhead' grenadiers ruined his attack with their 'strange behaviour'.[46] The cream of his army was tearing itself to pieces in front of his eyes. He curbed his language when he wrote to Pitt, prob-ably recognizing that it was difficult to criticize men for hurling them-selves enthusiastically into enemy fire. He said simply that they were 'unable to form under so hot a fire' while praising their leadership saying the grenadiers had 'many gallant officers wounded, who (care-less of their persons) had been solely intent on their duty'.[47]

Captain Schomberg whose ship, the *Diana*, was lying at anchor, heavily damaged, had been assigned a role in organizing the amphibi-ous operation. He watched the slaughter and wrote that 'the fire was very extraordinary, nor did I imagine that the fire of musketry could have been kept up so uninterruptedly'.[48] Dead and wounded men lay thick on the ground. Many grenadiers tried to find shelter from the hail of gunfire in the abandoned French redoubt but even here musket balls found them.

As if to match the ferocity of battle, nature now unleashed a storm of its own. The roar of thunder was audible even over that of the cannon and lightning forked across the sky. Seconds later rain fell in such a deluge that it turned the ground beneath the grenadiers' feet to slurry and soaked the ammunition of every soldier on the battle-field. The log of the *Stirling Castle* records that the 'very heavy squall of wind and rain ... rendered the mounting a high and very steep hill to come at the enemy's lines impracticable'.[49] Knox, as always, gives it a memorable description. He wrote that it was the 'dreadfullest thunderstorm and fall of rain that can be conceived', adding that the 'violence of the storm exceeded any description I can attempt to give of it'.[50]

The shattered grenadiers looked at the slope ahead of them. Rivulets poured down over mud and grass that had been slippery even before the downpour. The men's shoes were hardly made for these conditions. They were cut square to fit on either foot and grip was provided by hobnails through the bottoms. Above them the French troops waited for them with gleaming bayonets atop their muskets, while Native Americans and Canadians gripped hatchets and scalping knives in their wet hands. There was nothing to be gained by continuing their attack.

The bedraggled survivors trudged back to the shoreline where Monckton's brigade was now landing in the second wave. These regiments, Wolfe reported, were 'drawn up on the beach, in extreme good order' and the grenadiers took shelter behind the ranks of their comrades as their officers attempted to form them up. Wolfe took stock. His shock troops had been decimated. His ammunition was unusable. Nightfall was approaching and now the tide 'began to make'. Townshend's brigade could only cross the ford at the foot of the Mont-morency falls at low tide. They had done so during the grenadiers' attack and now stood ready a couple of hundred yards from where the boats were landing Monckton's brigade. Wolfe wrote that 'in case of a repulse' the retreat of Townshend's men 'might be hazardous and uncertain'. Wolfe finally made a brave decision: 'I thought it most advisable, not to persevere in so difficult an attack.'[51] His 'Family Journal' says that with the 'tide now flowing [in], from that consideration alone [he] ordered the troops to retire'.[52]

Townshend's men had only just arrived on the beach. Panet was impressed that they marched 'with solemn step, and in good order', and he grew nervous as they advanced 'to within double the range of a musket'. At this point 'they saw those from the barges re-embark' and then they received the message to turn around and recross the ford.[53] Monckton's corps climbed back onto the flat-bottomed boats with the grenadiers while Wolfe covered the retreat, marching back across the ford at the head of Fraser's 78th Highlanders. They witnessed a grim spectacle that shocked even those veterans who were hardened to war in the Americas. As soon as the grenadiers had withdrawn from the battlefield the Native Americans and Canadians descended on it like vultures. Malcolm Fraser watched the 'men coming down from the trenches where some of our people lay killed; we imagined they were Indians who were sent to scalp them'.[54] He was right. As John Johnson left the beach he was distraught that the army was 'leaving behind them, a vast number of killed and wounded to the mercy of those barbarous cannibals, whose chief thirst is after blood ... who massacred and scalped them in our own sight, it not being in our power to help them, nor deliver them out of their savage and barbarous hands'. The whole army was 'filled with horror at the barbarous cruelty of the savages committed on their brother soldiers'. One incident became a cause célèbre in the British army. Captain Ochterlony, the officer of the 60th Royal Americans who had apparently been so competitive when his men landed, was left wounded in the mud. By him lay his friend and comrade Ensign Peyton. They were approached by a group of the enemy. They tried to surrender to a Frenchman who relieved Ochterlony 'of his watch and money, and taking his hat, which was gold lace'. He then moved off and left Ochterlony to 'the care, and tender mercy of the two Indians'. One clubbed the captain, the other shot him. Peyton then grabbed a musket off the ground and shot one of them and tackled the other. It was a brutal death match: 'Mr. Peyton was fearful who would have the advantage, but at length he prevailed, and got uppermost, and with his dagger killed him outright.' The fracas attracted a group of Native Americans who made their way towards him as he attempted to reload his solitary musket. Luckily it also got the attention of some of the Highlanders who had not yet left the beach and they rushed over and dragged Peyton off. Ochterlony, with three bullets lodged in his body, was, incredibly, rescued by a combination of French soldiers and some nuns who bravely threw themselves in the way of the blood lust of their Native allies.[55] One nun left an account praising the bravery of her sisters. They 'conveyed [the British] wounded to our hospital, notwithstanding the fury and rage of the Indians'.[56]

The Highlanders were the last men off the beach. Townshend reports that 'two companies of the highlanders would not retire' until they had checked that not a single wounded Highlander lay at the mercy of the enemy. By the time they were satisfied that no living Highlanders breathed on the west side of the Montmorency 'the tide of flood was so high' that they 'could scarcely wade over the ford and the enemy had time to bring their guns to rake them in their retreat'.[57] Schomberg watched the army retreating and noted that the troops did so with a 'sullen pride and in good order'.[58] Montresor was particularly impressed by the Highlanders, who 'with the commander in chief at their head [crossed] the ford and to give them their due merit they passed it as regularly as at a review or exercising a manoeuvre of that kind, notwithstanding they were not 400 yards from a battery of 3 guns that bore on them the whole time'.[59]

Behind them they left the body of Sergeant Ned Botwood. The lyricist was just one of around four hundred and fifty casualties. Sources disagree on the numbers of dead; Barré's calculation suggests that there were around fifty men killed outright, while many of the wounded would have died a lingering death in the hospital.[60] Wolfe was furious; despite his anger at the grenadiers he could not deflect the blame for the defeat. His journal is sombre and he concludes the day's account by calling the whole attack a 'foolish business'. He noted grimly that 'many excellent officers hurt'.[61] Among the injured were his two favourites, Burton, whom Wolfe had intended should win the laurels of the day's fighting, and Lieutenant Colonel Murray. A few sources hint that the British got away lightly; Mackellar was unimpressed by the French artillery, saying that they 'must have done a good deal of execution had they been well served'.[62] Both Schomberg and Montresor thought that although the musketry was on a tremendous scale, the range was slightly too far to inflict maximum casualties and the steep angle down which the French had to fire meant a lot of musket balls were going high. It was scant consolation.

The two Cats were dreadfully battered. No attempt was made to refloat them as the tide came in and Saunders ordered them to be burnt. Townshend's journal tells us that the orders were carried out, 'in rather too much of a hurry as all the guns and two brass field pieces that the general had ordered to be put on board was destroyed'.[63] The French were thrilled to see the two burning hulks in front of their lines. One story circulated through the French army that in their hurry to leave the ships the British abandoned their wounded on board and incinerated them.

A frustrating month for Wolfe had been crowned with a sharp defeat in the largest action of the campaign thus far. One French officer wrote that 'the good order he observed in our troops, probably inclined the English general to lay aside all thoughts of succeeding in this attack, and induced him to give up'.[64] Another said that the storm 'opened Mr Wolfe's eyes to the temerity of his undertaking'.[65] Nearly all of them describe the storm as an unwelcome intermission in the slaughter of redcoats. A French officer wrote, 'certain it is that had he attempted to have forced our lines, his whole army would have run the risk of being cut to pieces'.[66] However, a few voices are far less bullish. One French journal, while praising the 'plunging fire' which was 'so hot and destructive that it obliged' the British to pull back, does say that 'our safety that day was owing to a storm coming on at the very moment of the attack'. 'Nothing,' it continues, 'could not have been more well timed, for we were in want of powder, of balls, and for a very long time there had not been any matches for the cannon.'[67] Panet says that it 'was very singular, [but] there were almost no bullets at the camp'. 'Fortunately,' the British grenadiers, 'were so well received that they re-embarked on their barges with the same haste with which they had left them.' However, 'what happiness [it was] that they did not know that there were no bullets at the camp! What negligence that there were none there, and what misfortune there would have been, if the English had been able to continue their attack.'[68]

Fortune had not smiled on the French thus far but now a dose of luck had delivered a considerable victory. According to the priest Jean-

Félix Récher, the victory 'caused us great joy'.[69] Vaudreuil believed Quebec had been saved for the year. 'The day was brilliant,' he wrote to de Lévis, 'and would certainly have been decisive for us if the British had been a bit less prudent.' He had 'the greatest hopes for the campaign'. In a calculated snub to Montcalm, Vaudreuil showered praise on de Lévis, telling him that 'the happy events of the day are due to your conjectures'.[70] De Lévis himself was particularly pleased by the lack of casualties among his men. He wrote in his journal that the French had lost '20 to 30 soldiers and just a few wounded officers'.[71] Montcalm was cheered by the 'fine shooting' of his troops and their 'very good composure' but he remained typically pessimistic. He worried that the British would be thirsting for revenge.[72] The real lesson for the French commanders was that when they were used properly Native Americans and Canadians could take their place alongside regular troops. One French officer said that they 'exhibited, on this occasion, all the firmness that could be expected'.[73] Joyful men broke out white French flags all along their trenches. Vaudreuil summed up the mood in a letter two days later, saying it 'is to be hoped that the English want to engage in a general affair', believing that another defeat would send the British back down the St Lawrence.[74]

Wolfe tried to cut the figure of a defiant leader in public. The next day he scolded his hot-headed men, telling them that

> the check which the grenadiers met yesterday will, it is hoped, be a lesson to them for the future. They ought to know that such impetuous, irregular, and unsoldier-like proceeding destroys all order, and makes it impossible for the commander to form any disposition for an attack, and puts it out of the general's power to execute his plan. The grenadiers could not suppose that they alone could beat the French Army.

However, he continued, 'the loss ... is inconsiderable; and may, if the men show a proper attention to their officers, be easily repaired when a favourable opportunity offers'.[75] In private, though, he seems to have let this defeat blacken his entire outlook. Later he admitted that 'if the attack had succeeded, our loss must certainly have been great, and theirs inconsiderable'. After all, 'the river of St Charles still remained to be passed, before the town was invested'.[76] He wrote a weak, apologetic letter to Saunders. In it he attempted to blame Cook for his assurances that the Cats could get close in; however, he does not push the point. He wrote dramatically that the 'blame' for 'that unlucky day ... I take entirely upon my own shoulders, and expect to suffer for it. Accidents cannot be helped; as much of the plan as was defective falls upon me.' 'The great fault of the day,' he thought, was 'in putting too many men into boats, who might have been landed the day before and might have crossed the ford with certainty, while only a small body remained afloat; and the superfluous boats of the fleet employed in a feint that might divide the enemy's force'. He ended by telling Saunders that 'a man sees his error often too late to remedy'.[77] His 'Family Journal', predictably, found fault with others. As well as blaming the grenadiers, it could not resist a dig at the navy. The fire-support from the *Centurion* and others 'annoyed' rather than 'hurt' the enemy. While 'a mistake by the regulating captain of the boats', it says, 'in some measure occasioned' the disorder that befell the force when they landed: 'The unavoidable delays that naturally present themselves in so complex an affair gave the enemy a full discovery of the place intended to be attacked and time to draw their troops there.'[78] Defeat corroded still further his damaged relations with the navy and his subordinates. One of them, his Chief Engineer, Patrick Mackellar, confided to his journal that he had a very negative outlook. At the beginning of August he wrote, 'there is little or no chance of landing upon a coast naturally strong and fortified, and defended by superior numbers, so that the capture of the city had now become doubtful'.[79]

History places blame and finds excuses. The shallows, weather, and tide had conspired to frustrate Wolfe, his grenadiers had shown too much spirit, and the French defences were more imposing than they had looked from the Île d'Orléans. But failure in battle is always so obvious in retrospect. Had he been victorious Wolfe's plan would have been 'bold'; but in defeat it was 'foolhardy'. What mattered in the days and weeks following was not the strength or weakness of Wolfe's plan but that the French had not administered a crushing defeat. Wolfe's army was intact, if battered. It was in his own mind that he would have to find the resources to overcome defeat. Fought on the last day of July it fell precisely on the half way point of the summer campaigning season which ran from June to the beginning of October. Stalemate beckoned; only inspired generalship could avoid it. But would disappointment at Montmorency dent Wolfe's belief in himself and stop him showing the leadership required to defeat his enemy?

TEN

'It is war of the worst shape'

AN EIGHTEENTH-CENTURY ARMY had procedures for everything, even death and defeat. After the battle, neat lists of killed and wounded were compiled by every regiment on both sides. Quick burial of the dead was essential to prevent the spread of disease. French troops set to work burying the corpses of friend and foe alike, scattered all over the beach and the redoubt on the west side of the Montmorency falls. Before they went into the ground every pocket and fold of clothing was rifled through for food and valuables. The British also buried the slow trickle of men who succumbed to their wounds. Over the next few days possessions were auctioned off to pay off the debts that the dead owed the living.

Two officers of Otway's 35th Regiment who had been killed during Wolfe's reconnoitre along the Montmorency a week before had their effects auctioned off on 8 August. They had both led a spirited counterattack during the heavy skirmishing. Wolfe's 'Family Journal' says their leadership 'gave a turn to the day', but their courage had cost them their lives.[1] The army was informed on the fourth that if anyone was owed money by either of the two men they should go and see a Major Morris of the 35th to stake their claim. On the seventh it was announced that 'part of the effects of Captain Fletcher and Lieutenant Hamilton, late of Otway's regiment, to be sold tomorrow at ten o'clock in the rear of said regiment'.[2] Soldiers lived in debt. What little they did receive in payment was often recklessly gambled away. When men were killed their creditors asked their commanding officers for payment out of their wages. If more money was required then the dead man's property was auctioned off. In the fortnight after the defeat at Montmorency there were many such auctions. It was an excellent opportunity to buy replacement kit. In particular, sergeants and 'volunteers' who were given commissions in the field found them an invaluable chance to buy items of their new uniform that would otherwise be far beyond their means. Dead men were not just stripped of their assets; if their wives had accompanied the army their allocation of rations could stop, depending on the attitude of the regimental commander, on the day their husbands died. The severity with which this was implemented varied from one unit to another but there were numerous cases of widows being forced to remarry just hours after the death of their husbands.[3]

Wolfe made sure his men remained busy. He ordered a massive bombardment of Quebec from the Point Lévis batteries on the night of 1/2 August as if rearranging the rubble of the destroyed town would make up for his setback. The camp at Montmorency was to be further strengthened; Wolfe wanted to be sure, as he wrote in his journal, that 'we may receive no insult from an enemy impatient to decide their fate by an action'.[4] He wrote to Monckton saying, 'This check must not discourage us, the loss is not great. Keep the men in gentle exercise, drive away all your superfluous sutlers and prepare for another and, I hope, a better attempt.'[5]

Messengers flitted between the armies under flags of truce. Both sides attempted to paint themselves as the guardians of civilized values during the arcane exchange of letters. Wolfe was notified that his dead had been given Christian burial and that his wounded, including the mauled Captain Ochterlony who was still clinging to life, were being looked after by the nuns of the General Hospital. Le Mercier, the artilleryman, who was the usual choice as courier, carried a note from Ochterlony which Townshend's journal reports as saying 'he owed his life to a French Grenadier, who saved him from the cruelty of the Indians, [and] that he is taken good care of'.[6] In a covering letter Vaudreuil wrote to Wolfe telling him that he would ensure good treatment of all prisoners. The French would furnish Ochterlony with any money he should require in accordance with established practice; the two staffs would settle everything up at the end of the campaign. Vaudreuil also asked Wolfe to stop locking up women and children on transports, as they were non-combatants.[7] Meanwhile, Le Mercier brought 'refreshments' for the prisoners to try to alleviate their suffering while cooped up aboard British ships.[8] It was a good opportunity to pick up scraps of information. Le Mercier talked to a frigate captain who told him that Wolfe was 'a very brave man but he is not a general'. Another officer told him that the Native Americans were terrifying and the French seemed to have a lot of them.[9]

While his officers gossiped with the enemy, Wolfe wrote to Vaudreuil and with it he sent a twenty-guinea reward for the grenadier who had saved Captain Ochterlony's life. Vaudreuil sent the money back saying that the man was simply doing his duty. Wolfe then wrote to the Mother Superior of the General Hospital and promised her that he would protect her community of nuns, out of gratitude for their care for the British wounded. This goodwill remained undimmed even after the death of the unfortunate Ochterlony in mid-August, whom even twenty-first-century medicine would have struggled to save. A message was sent to the British to inform them, according to Panet, that he had left everything he had to the French grenadier who had saved his life.[10] These exchanges are remarkable, but so is the extent to which everyone in either army seemed to know the contents of each message. Even the most junior ranks seem to have known the details of their generals' correspondence. Sources on both sides are in remarkable agreement. One thing the British sources did not pick up on was the effect of Wolfe's promise of protection to the nuns. A French journal tells us that 'this letter made the General Hospital be considered as a place of perfect security, and everybody was hurrying to deposit in it, whatever they had that was most valuable'.[11]

Quite apart from the rhetorical sparring, truces were an opportunity for all sorts of other activities. The defenders of Quebec had used the ceasefire on 24 July to rebuild their batteries. One French journal says that the 'real motive was to obtain time for employing 3 or 400 men to clean the streets, which were filled with the ruins of the buildings demolished by the cannon of the besiegers, for no person had dared to attempt working in the streets whilst the cannonading continued'.[12] Perhaps strangest of all is a note in another French journal which reports that during the third truce in as many days in the first week of August 'many of the English embraced this opportunity to visit Quebec and some of the French also visited the enemy'.[13]

The year before Bougainville had become very friendly with General Abercrombie's nephew, a captain by the same name. They had exchanged views on North America and Abercrombie had been able to fill the Frenchman in on all the news from the other theatres of the war. Bougainville received a 'basket of Bristol beer' and in return he sent the British officer several bottles of 'Pacaret wine'. Bougainville had written in his diary that this was 'a necessary and good example to set in this barbarous country, not only on account of humanity but because of politeness between enemies at war'.[14]

The inhabitants of Quebec did not regard the bombardment of their houses as polite. Night after night they endured the sound of cannon-balls tearing through masonry and carcasses thundering through wooden roofs. On the night of 16 August Panet watched as townspeople tried to douse the flames that were consuming a widow's house near to one of Quebec's many monasteries. It had been hit by one of 'many bombs and fireballs'. Two priests and two carpenters 'prevented the spread of the fire, by climbing on top of the neighbouring house' and stripping it of flammable material. This was 'despite the bombs and the cannonballs which were being aimed at the fire'. Panet 'left in fear' after 'two cannonballs grazed' him and one board from the roof of the monastery, 'detached by a cannonball', crashed to the ground between him and a monk.[15] The parish priest, Jean-Félix Récher, becoming so used to the bombardment, wrote in the middle of August that 'these kind of cannonades occur so often, nearly every day, that I do not even notice'.[16]

Wolfe's disappointments on either side of the Montmorency River renewed his interest in the river above Quebec. Murray, his ambitious and impatient junior brigadier, was to be given an independent command to head upriver and cause trouble. Wolfe's instructions allowed plenty of latitude. Murray was to attempt to attack French shipping and supplies towards Trois Rivières. This would 'divide and distract' them and might just even open a channel of communication through to Amherst, whom Wolfe hoped might be marching up the Lake George–Lake Champlain corridor by now. Above all, as Wolfe wrote to Murray, he should do what 'mischief' he could and 'oblige the enemy to divide his force and carry his attention to the upper river'. Wolfe also encouraged him 'to endeavour to bring any of their detachments to an engagement, if their numbers do not so far exceed your own, and you may take the most effectual measures in your power by burning some of their houses or taking their women prisoners to engage them to fight'.[17]

Murray would be given around twelve hundred men. Knox watched as the chosen units 'marched into the woods' in order to receive specialist training. They 'performed several manoeuvres which were showed them, in case of being attacked in front, rear, right, left'.[18] The force was composed of Amherst's 15th Regiment, 300 Royal Americans of the 3/60th, 200 light infantrymen, and 200 marines. Among the light infantrymen was the light company of Fraser's 78th Highland Regiment, now widely seen as one of the finest units in the army. There were also twenty rangers whose job it would be to try to get through to Amherst. The force marched along the south bank of the St Lawrence and were met on 6 August by twenty flat-bottomed boats, which the night before had used rainy and squally conditions to pass the narrows. The French heard the sound of oars too late and barely fired a shot as they slipped past.

Montcalm's outlook was not greatly brightened by his success at Montmorency. His journal and letters to de Lévis are pessimistic. Both his and Vaudreuil's letters contain constant references to sleep deprivation, caused by the constant flow of messengers updating them on the fluid situation across the wide theatre of operations. 'I did not sleep last night,' Vaudreuil wrote to de Lévis at the end of July, 'and likely will not have the time during the day.'[19] The exhausted Montcalm was now deeply unhappy about all this activity across what he had viewed as his secure lines of communication. He had reinforced the first detachments he had sent to guard the upper river until he had quite a formidable force there. When Murray made his move Montcalm sent his protégé Bougainville to keep an eye on him with 'a company of grenadiers, a light company of regulars, and one of militia'. Bougainville's journal also speaks of a force of 150 'volunteer cavalry under the command of M de la Rochebeaucourt ... Instructed and disciplined by this officer, who has served with the greatest distinction.'[20] This force would grow until by the end of August Bougainville had the elite from Montcalm's five French infantry regiments, their grenadier and light companies, in all 500 men. He also had, according to one senior officer, 'five hundred picked Canadians, and about six hundred selected at random'.[21] Bougainville's unenviable job was to shadow the British flotilla as it sailed or simply drifted back and forward with the tide in order to oppose any landing that Murray might make. He set the men to work fortifying various points at which a force could land on the north shore. A French journal says that 'although Anse des Mères, Anse au Foulon, Sillery, and St Michel were regarded as inaccessible, nevertheless the engineers were sent thither for the purpose of having ditches and abatis constructed in the slopes leading thereto'.[22]

Murray's force sailed about forty-five miles upriver of Quebec at which point 'the pilots would not take even the Cats farther'. On the shore he wrote to Wolfe that he could see 'a considerable body of foot' which 'kept pace' with their movements. From what he could make out 'they appeared to be regulars'. He also caught sight of the mounted troops. Murray was spoiling for a fight and within days he thought he had found a way to strike a blow. On 8 August he spotted two floating batteries and he thought it 'was very practicable to drive them on shore'. Then he would land troops and make the enemy 'fight in defence of their floating batteries'.[23]

Murray decided to wait for low water so that there would be a large open strand for his men to form up on, hopefully out of range of musket fire from the trees along the shoreline. His troops climbed into the ship's boats and waited for the command. The three companies of light infantry were to land first when 'the signal was made'. At 'a wave of the brigadier's hat' the boats surged forward towards 'a little point above Pointe au Trembles', about twenty miles upriver of Quebec, which was 'the only place within reach free from precipices, and wood'.[24] The *Sutherland* blasted the distant shore with its broadside but yet again the St Lawrence dashed the British plans. Boats ran into rocks and reefs which held them up exactly as they had done during the attack at Montmorency. The boats carrying the Highlanders got closest in to the beach and they clambered out and attempted to wade ashore. One eyewitness comments that they looked back and saw the other boats lagging and attributed 'the cause to shyness, when in reality it was owing to two boats running on the reef of rocks formerly mentioned'. They waited where they were for 'about 16 minutes' with most of the company 'three feet deep in water, being tide of flood which damaged part of their ammunition'.[25] The French had shadowed the *Sutherland* with her escorts as they sailed along the river. The length of time it took to load the British redcoats into boats gave the French ample warning of an attack and Bougainville summoned reinforcements and began lining the shore with infantrymen, safely ensconced among the trees. As soon as the British boats lumbered into range the French opened up. A 'pretty smart' enemy fire now came from the wooded banks, which caused casualties even though, in their excitement, the French troops were shooting 'at too great a distance'. Bougainville was in the thick of the action, marshalling the French troops. In his journal he records that his horse was hit under him.[26] Possibly it was hit by shot from a 'swivel gun', which were small cannon mounted in the bows of the British boats, small enough to be swivelled in a bracket. The sailors bombarded the shore in an attempt to support their hard-pressed comrades.

Murray later told Wolfe that he had 'imputed the retardment, the sunken rocks had occasioned, to fear' and, therefore, 'in hopes to animate the rest I instantly joined the Highlanders'. But his men had not lacked the will, simply the means. After hauling boats across shallows and splashing through deep pools, many of the troops finally caught up with their brigadier and the Highlanders. Murray looked ahead and saw Bougainville's men 'powering from all sides to reinforce the body defending the shore'. His attack had become disjointed; he saw that the tide was now on the flood and wide pools still needed to be negotiated before he reached dry ground. It was, he told Wolfe, 'the same situation you was in near the Montmorency' and Murray made the same decision: 'I beat the retreat.' Drummers, waist deep in water, rattled the instantly recognizable rhythm on their drums and the soaking men heaved themselves into the boats. Unlike his commander, Murray had nothing but praise for the naval support. 'Some of the boats gave us notable aid on this occasion with their swivels, and the behaviour of the men and officers cannot be too much commended,' he wrote.[27]

Yet again a British attack had been frustrated by the river and the alacrity of the French defence. Murray, however, was determined to make another attempt. 'I resolved to wait till near high water,' he wrote, 'then to attack them without any interruption to my boats.'[28] This time the boats made it into the shore, but the French were waiting for them and unleashed a terrible storm of musketry. The first attack had been met by about five hundred men but Mackellar, in his journal, records that for the second attack, 'the numbers of the enemy were greatly increased, the woods were everywhere lined, all the houses of the village occupied, a considerable body of regulars drawn up behind a church, and a body of cavalry dismounted near the shore'.[29] Murray admitted that he had been 'mistaken'. The defenders were 'everywhere in force and carefully concealed, till we were too far engaged'.[30] One British eyewitness saw 'an officer on horseback' on the shore, possibly Bougainville, coordinating the defence.[31]

Murray paints a gruesome scene. Yet again the brave landing force approached the shore but this time 'our boats were thrown into confusion, [and] many of the seamen killed and wounded'. Mackellar wrote that the fire was so 'heavy' that the 'sailors could not sit at their oars'. This 'obliged most of the boats of the light infantry to retreat, or lie an inactive object to the enemy's fire', reported Murray. Oarsmen lay dead or wounded in the bilges of their boats, survivors cowered in terror at the whine of musket balls speeding overhead. Showers of splinters were thrown up as others thumped into the gunwales. Yet again Murray had to make a tough decision. 'When I saw,' he reported, 'that they had lined the windmill, houses, church ... that the tide was now beginning to ebb, and would soon leave the boats dry, I gave it up and ordered the troops on board.' The soldiers in the boats 'did not hear' the signal, 'being under the fire of the enemy', but had taken matters into their own hands anyway; they had 'seized the oars, backed water, and drew off from the fire'. It had been a bloody repulse. Mackellar records that 'we had about 140 men killed and wounded including 30 seamen'.[32] Panet reports that Bougainville told him that 'he saw seven barges each of which could carry 50 men, and that he did not notice in each more than four or five capable to row'.[33]

The French had yet another victory to celebrate. One journal rejoiced that Bougainville had 'repulsed them vigorously'. It boasted that the British 'need not have taken the trouble' to attack the second time since it met with the same fate.[34] It was a depressingly familiar story for the British. At both Montmorency and Pointe aux Trembles the redcoats and seamen had behaved with exemplary courage. Both times, however, they were frustrated by a withering fire from defenders on the banks, in good strong positions. The tide was proving inflexible and troublesome. It was nigh impossible to organize complicated amphibious assaults at exactly the right moment of time, wind, and tide, in such a way that allowed the troops to even set foot on dry land, let alone achieve a modicum of surprise. Those hoping that the riverbank above Quebec was the soft underbelly of Montcalm's defences were cruelly disappointed. British blows had now been parried at various points along a thirty-mile front.

The French forces might have been holding on tenaciously to their positions around their capital, but elsewhere the defences of New France were finally penetrated. The day after the people of Quebec were cheered by reports of victory at Pointe aux Trembles, they were hit with dark tidings from the *pays d'en haut*. A messenger arrived from the upper country with the terrible news that Fort Niagara, the bridge to the massive expanse of French-dominated lands in the west, had fallen to the British.

In June Brigadier John Prideaux had led a British force to Oswego. There it had been met by Sir William Johnson, the infamous 'Mohawk Baronet'. Johnson was an Irishman, a native of County Meath, who had emigrated to North America at age 22. He had managed to build one of the largest fortunes in the colonies acting as a deal broker between the British and the Native Americans of the Iroquois Confederation, the most powerful Native grouping in eastern America. Iroquois lands formed a buffer between New York and Canada and stretched along the southern side of Lake Ontario. Johnson genuinely straddled the ethnic divide, sitting on the New York governing council while also glorying in his status as an honorary *sachem* or chief. He cohabited with a Mohawk princess and was as happy in the log house as he was in Manhattan. Johnson was one of the first self-appointed agents of imperial expansion, a Cecil Rhodes of his day, who created facts on the ground which dragged the crown further and further into the American interior. Through his career he would exploit both the British crown and the Native Americans to make vast amounts of money. He sold British metalwork and muskets to the Iroquois, and particularly the Mohawk, one of the six nations of the Iroquois Confederation, and in return bought up their agricultural surplus and turned Oswego into the principal fur-trading post in British America. He soon found himself in politics. During the War of Austrian Succession he had tried to encourage the Iroquois to drop their strict neutrality in wars between Britain and France. In 1755 as the two powers again went to war Johnson was made 'Sole Agent and Superintendant [sic]' of the Iroquois. His position was cemented by his relationship with Molly Brant, one of the most powerful figures in the matrilineal Iroquois Confederation, with whom he had several children. He had commanded the force which in 1755 fought an indecisive battle around Lake George, during which Montcalm's predecessor, Jean-Armand Dieskau, was wounded and captured. An empire starved of good news turned Johnson's skirmish into a major victory. He was feted as a hero in New York and made a baronet by the King. In spring 1759 he convinced around 940 Iroquoians to join Prideaux's expedition to Niagara. The Iroquois seem to have been persuaded to drop their neutrality believing that the British would support their claims of ownership over the Ohio valley and other lands south of Lake Ontario. Rolling back French influence would deal a serious blow to the Iroquois' competitors in these lands; the French-allied Miamis and the Munsees. Johnson met Prideaux at the head of his Native American troops and became second in command of the expedition.

Prideaux and his force of about 3,300 regulars, provincials, and Native allies paddled for four days along the south shore of Lake Ontario. They arrived at Fort Niagara, in present-day Youngstown,

NY, in the first week of July to the utter consternation of the defenders. Pierre Pouchot, the garrison commander, was an experienced officer, with a powerful fort, built along European lines. But he had made a fateful gamble. Relying on the local Native Americans to warn him of any approaching attack, he had sent the vast majority of his garrison to François-Marie Le Marchand de Lignery, French commander in the Ohio valley, to reassert French influence there, after the loss of Fort Duquesne, and launch renewed frenzied assaults on the frontiers of Virginia and Pennsylvania. This, it was hoped, would divert British men and supplies from the thrusts on New France. The French had then been hugely unlucky. Their Native American allies had not detected the British advance. Neither had the force bound for the Ohio which had just missed stumbling upon Prideaux's by a few days. Of the two French ten-gun ships on Lake Ontario, which could have blasted the hurriedly constructed British boats and rafts out of the water, one was out of service and the other did not spot them. Through a mixture of good luck, organization, diplomacy, and stealth Prideaux and Johnson had managed to get the British force into a position to start the siege. As they opened fire on 19 July a shell exploded prematurely at the mouth of a mortar and killed Prideaux. Johnson took over.

Despite its modern fortification, Niagara could not hold out against the hail of shot and shell that levelled its walls and outworks. Accounts of the siege tell of terrible French suffering. Defenders were overwhelmed by an avalanche of explosives and were unable to sleep for days on end. The only thing that could save the fort was a relieving force. On 23 July that force arrived: Lignery with the army of the Ohio. The British had anticipated them and had built a barricade across the road two miles south of the fort near a portage over the Niagara River. At 0800 hours on the twenty-fourth with enormous courage but little judgement 600 French *troupes de la marine* and Canadian militiamen threw themselves at the barricade. Behind it just under five hundred regulars and provincials fired volley after volley. Within seconds the ground was thick with corpses; the French force broke and was hunted down by the Iroquois. Only a hundred survivors lived long enough to be taken prisoner and most of them were wounded. Lignery died of his wounds three days later.

The fort's position was hopeless, Pouchot's men were driven to the point of mutiny, and he surrendered on 25 July. French links to the *pays d'en haut* were severed. Any heavy supplies going to the Illinois country or the Mississippi had to go via the portage route at Niagara; canoe routes further north were for transporting people only. The isolated outposts of New France were now cut off from any substantial succour. Worse still for Montcalm, British troops now threatened the heart of the colony from the west as well as the south and east.[35]

On 9 August news of the capitulation reached Quebec. It followed the news that French forces under Bourlamaque had carried out a controlled withdrawal in front of Amherst's army on Lake Champlain, blowing up Forts Carillon and St Frederic before making a stand at the Île aux Noix on the Richelieu, which was uncomfortably close to Montreal. A journal records that the fall of Niagara 'increased considerably the dejection which the news of the evacuation of Carillon and St Frederic had already spread among the people ... Montréal ... was at the moment bare of every sort of defense.'[36]

Montcalm was forced to dispatch de Lévis with around a thousand men, mainly Canadians but with a sprinkling of regular troops. Ramezay wrote that 'we witnessed M. Le Chevalier leave with great sadness, as we have the highest confidence in him'.[37] As they marched west one journal commented that 'a force so superior in three different places, and the comparatively small number that we had to oppose them, created an exceeding great dread that the fatal moment was fast approaching, when the whole colony would pass under the yoke of the English'.[38] Other witnesses were cheered by the recent victories and believed the inexorable onset of winter would save New France.

Montcalm and de Lévis decided to take advantage of the latter's move upcountry by attacking Murray's unsuspecting force on the way. French observers had spotted that Murray's men did not bother fortifying their camp because they were certain the French would never attempt to cross the river, since it was guarded by the ships of the navy. Yet again luck intervened to save the British detachment from the horrors of a night attack. One French officer wrote that 'nothing was better combined, but the bad weather deranged all'.[39] A period of 'very heavy rain', a journal explained, 'put a stop to the execution of this project'.⁴⁰ With the river running too fast to risk a crossing, de Lévis reluctantly abandoned the plan and marched his troops west.

Montcalm could cope with the loss of men. Supplies were a much bigger problem than manpower. Now that the British controlled the river between Batiscan and Quebec 'no course was left but to have them brought by land, which was still not unattended by difficulties'. This was achieved with the aid of 'young children, women [and] old men', who were the only people still living in the countryside, the men of military age all having been called up. Despite a bad road and a shortage of vehicles, '700 barrels of pork or flour were conveyed on 271 carts from Batiscan to the army', a distance of well over fifty miles. This brought around two weeks of supplies into the town but 'from that moment, alarm was felt at the difficulties that service would eventually encounter; a number of carts were already broken; the women and children who guided them, rebuffed by such rude labor, left no hope of being able to support it long'. Unsurprisingly 'regret was begun to be felt at having placed the army's stores at so great a distance'.⁴¹ Appeals were made for all Quebecers to hand in specie in return for bills of exchange. This hard currency allowed the government to buy wheat from farmers, who were otherwise hiding it. One report states that 'beef was never wanting ... This the farmers could not hide as they did their wheat.'⁴² Even in Montreal de Lévis witnessed terrible shortages. There was an 'extreme state of famine', he wrote in his journal. 'To survive they had to utilise the crops which had not yet been harvested.' To do this he sent 400 of his own troops into the fields 'because there was no one else to bring in the harvest'. He ordered 'women, nuns, priests, and everyone in the town' to help 'directly or indirectly with this work'.⁴³

While Canada attempted to avoid starvation, Brigadier Murray cruised the upper river looking for an opportunity to win laurels. His force was encamped on the south shore of the river near the church at St Antoine. He wrote to Rear Admiral Holmes, the commander of the little flotilla above Quebec, explaining 'that the enemy are stronger than I am' and, therefore, 'what I attempt against them must be by surprise'. However, 'I can never surprise them by moving with the fleet or in the day' because 'their motions on shore must be quicker than yours by the tide'.[44]

One of his patrols was shot at while patrolling. Mackellar confirms that 'a captain and four men [were] wounded'. In accordance with Wolfe's announcement at the beginning of the campaign Murray put a notice on the church door saying that 'since they had fired several times upon our troops ... All the houses in the parish should be burnt.'[45] On 12 and 13 August the entire parish was destroyed. This act of brutal retaliation was not isolated. The huge column of smoke billowing from St Antoine joined several others. Along the length of the St Lawrence valley palls of smoke hung in the hot, motionless August air. Wolfe had lost patience with the people of Canada. His efforts frustrated near the town, his troops harassed by insurgents, he lashed out against Canadians in a vicious campaign of terror designed to punish them for their loyalty to France and undermine their way of life to the point of utter destruction.

On 25 July Wolfe's rage was fanned by a terrible rumour. He wrote to Monckton saying that three grenadiers had been captured by the enemy and apparently burnt alive by the Native Americans. Burning was a common punishment for prisoners of Native warriors, who prided themselves on their ability to burn someone just slowly enough that it would inflict the maximum conceivable amount of pain before the victim eventually expired. It was a communal experience, members of the tribe gained solace for lost loved ones through the hideous suffering of one of their hated enemies. Wolfe, however, had no interest in the anthropological niceties of native society. Burning of prisoners of war was an unacceptable crime. He told Monckton that if these rumours be true, 'the country shall be one universal blaze'.[46] In a heated, but scrupulously polite, written exchange Barré wrote to Vaudreuil on behalf of Wolfe. The British general, he wrote, demanded 'to know what has become of [the captured grenadiers], so as to regulate his conduct in future accordingly'. He gave Vaudreuil a stark warning:

The British troops are only too much exasperated; the enormous cruelties already committed and especially the base infraction of the capitulation of Fort William Henry are yet fresh in their minds. Such

acts deserve, and if repeated will certainly meet, in future, the severest reprisals; all distinction will cease between Frenchmen, Canadians and Indians; all will be treated as a cruel and barbarous mob,
thirsting for human blood.[47]

Bougainville, on behalf of Vaudreuil, assured Wolfe that there was no
foundation in this report. 'Your Excellency ought to have regarded as
soldiers' gossip the tales related ... The fate of those three prisoners has
been the same as that of all the others taken by the Indians; the king
has ransomed them at considerable expense.' He concluded icily that
'the Marquis de Vaudreuil has not instructed me to respond to the
menaces, invectives and accusations with which that letter abounds'.[48]

This incident turned out to be a ghoulish camp rumour but Wolfe's
men were nevertheless suffering badly at the hands of the Canadians
and Native Americans. Hardly a day went by without the loss of
another sentry or another group of off duty soldiers rummaging
through the woods trying to supplement their diets. On 25 July Wolfe
issued a final proclamation to the local people. It announced that 'His
Excellency, indignant at the little regard paid by the inhabitants of
Canada to his proclamation ... is determined no longer to listen to the
sentiments of humanity which prompted him to solace people blind to
their own interests.' Sadly, 'the Canadians have, by their conduct,
proved themselves unworthy of the advantageous offers he held out to
them'. From now on 'he had issued orders to the Commanders of his
Light Infantry and other officers, to proceed into the country and to
seize and bring in the farmers and their cattle, and to destroy and lay
waste what they shall judge proper'.[49]

From that point on Wolfe unleashed a wave of destruction along
the length of the St Lawrence River. Many people at the time and since
have seen this as an admission of failure. One French officer wrote
that 'during the greatest part of the month of August, general Wolfe
remained inactive in his camp upon the Falls of Montmorency, and
confined his operations to the burning and plundering of what houses
there were in the country he was master of, waiting the arrival of the
forces under Mr Amherst, before he made any new attempts'.[50]
Vaudreuil also believed that Wolfe 'no longer makes a secret of saying

that the expedition to take Canada has failed'. He had given up hope of taking Quebec and the 'only resource he has found in his despair is to pillage, ravage and burn the settlements which are near his army'.[51] Wolfe did, indeed, have his doubts that he would take Quebec but his destruction of farms was not purely sadistic. He intended to weaken Canada so that its starving and demoralized inhabitants would fall easy prey to a British force in 1760. His own 'Family Journal' records that since his announcements 'had no effect in preventing the peasants from taking arms, and the acquisition of Quebec [was] very dubious, Mr Wolfe *au pis aller* [in the last resort] thought it would be a severe check on the colony to destroy the villages and settlements below'.[52]

Wolfe also justified the devastation by claiming that it was to 'engage the Marquis de Montcalm to try the event of a battle to prevent the ravage, and partly in return for the many insults offered to our people by the Canadians'.[53] Goading a well-fortified enemy to come out and fight by ravaging the countryside is a tactic so old that it is described in the *Iliad*. As to the second part, he now found himself fighting a full-scale counter-insurgency and acted accordingly. The guerrilla-style attacks on his men were destroying morale, sapping his manpower, and offending his sense of how war ought to be waged. Wars in north-west Europe, where Wolfe had served his apprenticeship, were altogether different. For generations peasants had watched competing empires, electorates, and kingdoms advance and recede. A change of regime made little impression on people's existence. Few were prepared to risk their family's lives in guerrilla attacks out of dynastic loyalty to the Habsburgs or Hohenzollerns. Armies traversed to and fro and tended to leave peasants enough grain to subsist on over the winter. There were notable examples of soldiers ravaging countryside but they were atypical, and condemned by all sides.[54]

North America was a different world. John Johnson wrote menacingly that when it became clear that the proclamations 'had produced no good effect, and in order if possible to intimidate the enemy, [Wolfe] found it absolutely necessary to connive at some irregularities which were committed by our soldiers, by way of retaliation'.[55] By the third week of August, Mackellar recorded wholesale destruction: 'We began to burn the habitations between St Joachim and the falls of Montmorency, agreeably to the manifesto lately published.'[56] British detachments roamed along the shoreline bringing destruction with them. The soldiers set to the task with undoubted enthusiasm. Montresor wrote to his father saying that the 'desolation will afford us no small diversion to our soldiery who are all in charming health'.[57] Wolfe shared his men's hatred of the Canadians; the previous summer he had written to a friend saying that 'though I am neither inhuman nor rapacious yet I own it would give me pleasure to see the Canadian vermin sacked and pillaged and justly repaid their unheard-of cruelty'.[58] He was particularly disappointed in them during the summer of 1759. He had offered them a generous bargain. He had promised to protect their property and allow the unrestricted practice of their religion. By their continued violence they had refused his offer. Now they would suffer the consequences.

Johnson outlines the instructions that he and the troops received from Wolfe. He was ordered to 'distress all in his power, all those who had thus set at naught his lenity, and tenderness towards them'. He and his comrades were to 'kill and destroy by every means they could' all the cattle, grain supplies, orchards and 'whatsoever else they found growing in the ground'. Johnson was even given permission to 'despoil them of whatever moveables they could find in their possession'. Wolfe was, however, very precise as to the limits of this orgy of destruction and theft. 'Churches, convents or places of public worship' were to be left alone 'under pain of death'. Almost as sacrosanct were the bodies of 'young women and virgins', the abuse of which would bring on 'the severest punishment'. Johnson was also warned off 'using ill the persons of ancient men or women, or helpless children'.[59] These restrictions may have salved Wolfe's conscience but they seem to have been only partially obeyed as his men swept along the banks of the river.

One of the first areas to feel the scourge was the parish of Baie St Paul, near the Île aux Coudres, about fifty miles downstream of Quebec. Joseph Gorham, the New England ranger, was the obvious choice as commander. The previous November he had helped the gifted Massachusetts soldier, George Scott, lay waste to the French settlements up the Petitcodiac River, and had submitted a report of the raid describing 'his party a-burning and destroying the enemy's substance'.[60] Now he commanded a mixed group of the best of the rangers and some regulars. Knox writes that all the redcoats were volunteers.[61] Gorham and his force, just under three hundred strong, were sent downriver. They were fired on by the British sloop *Zephyr*, possibly because its jumpy commander, Greenwood, had only just brought his little twelve-gun ship into the St Lawrence. Gorham rowed as close as he dared and roared at them to cease fire. Having corrected the mistake Greenwood accompanied Gorham further down the river. The first target was the bay of St Paul because of the 'presumption' the residents had shown by firing on the British as they had sailed up the St Lawrence over a month before.

At 0300 hours on the morning of 9 August Gorham's men attacked out of the early morning murk. A hail of musketry from the shore killed one man and wounded another eight, but while the *habitants* reloaded the British force stormed ashore. A sergeant in the Louis-bourg Grenadiers heard from a comrade who was on the raid that forty Canadians put up a stiff fight for two hours before being driven off. The British force then burnt the village, 'consisting of about 50 fine houses and barns', and killed their cattle.[62] Piles of plunder were carried off including 'books, apparel and household stuff of various kinds'.[63] Even fifty-five miles away Knox could tell that Gorham had been at work. He wrote that 'a great smoke is perceived this morning on the north side, at a distance below Orleans: this is supposed to be occasioned by Captain Goreham's detachment, who are burning the settlements abreast of the isle of Coudres'.[64] Having suffered only nine casualties in the attack Gorham pressed on. He moved east twenty miles to Malbaie, where the Louisbourg Grenadier tells us 'they destroyed a very pretty parish, drove off the inhabitants and stock without any loss'. Not satisfied Gorham crossed the St Lawrence, 'destroyed part of the parish of St Ann's [St Anne] and St Roan [St Roche], where were very handsome houses with farms, and loaded the vessels with cattle'.[65] Wolfe watched the smoke and tried to guess where Gorham had attacked next. He wrote to Monckton on 14 August saying that 'I hear Goreham has been at Mal Baye – and by the smoke on the south shore it is imagined that he has carried the terror of his arms even to that coast. I want him back.'[66] Sensitive to his general's every desire, Gorham returned on 15 August.

From this point both sides of the St Lawrence, containing some of the finest farmland in Canada, were put to the torch. On 15 August Wolfe wrote to Monckton saying, 'all the houses and barns between the Etchemin River and la Chaudiere may be burned whenever any opportunity offers'. The reason: 'It is to very little purpose to withhold the rod, seeing they are incorrigible, they have had Indians upon the Isle of Orleans, and have scalped four sailors very lately.'[67] Later in August Wolfe shifted his attention to the settlements on twenty miles of the north shore between Montmorency and St Joachim. In early September Major John Scott, no stranger to village burning after his part in the expulsion of the Acadians, was sent with a motley band of redcoat volunteers, marines, and rangers to destroy the entire south coast. He was accompanied by a frigate and an armed sloop. Knox watched them go and recorded that their orders were to go 'down the river, as far as there are any settlements' and then 'to lay waste to such parishes as shall presume to persist in their opposition'.[68] Panet is utterly disdainful, every day his journal notes which stretch of the St Lawrence shoreline has been burnt. On 21 August he noted that 'the English, following their laudable custom, have set fire to St Joachim'. Two nights later he could watch the ribbon of orange destruction stretching for miles from the walls of Quebec.[69]

Scott's expedition sailed down to Kamouraska and marched back burning as they went. Scott reported that 'upon the whole we marched fifty two miles, and in that distance, burnt nine hundred and ninety eight good buildings, two sloops, two schooners, ten shalloops and several batteaus and small craft, took fifteen prisoners (six of them women and five of them children), killed five of the enemy, had one regular wounded, two of the rangers killed and four more of them wounded'.[70]

We get only small glimpses of the suffering of the people of the St Lawrence that summer. Passing references in journals allude to the horror of this full-scale counter-insurgency. The people were trapped between the dictates of Vaudreuil, enforced by his lethal war parties of Native Americans, or of Wolfe with his equally vicious bands of rangers who struck with impunity all along the valley of the St Lawrence. Knox wrote that at the very beginning of September some letters of Vaudreuil's were intercepted, in which with 'great *hauteur*' he demanded that the priests of several of the downriver parishes 'pay more respect to his commands for the time to come on pain of incurring his highest displeasure'. They were to stop being so disobedient, help any of Vaudreuil's irregular soldiers, and hide their cattle more effectively in the woods, to deny them to the British.[71]

One priest who seems to have needed no encouragement from Vaudreuil was René Portneuf, the priest of St Joachim, on the north shore of the St Lawrence opposite the very eastern tip of the Île d'Orléans. He was Canadian born and had been responsible for the souls in this little community for twenty-four years. In spring 1759 the Quebec church had told its priests not to carry arms and had reminded them that their first duty was to their flocks, not to the regime. The Bishop, Henri Marie Dubreil de Pontbriand, was determined to preserve his church even if New France fell. He wrote to his priests in June and told them that if the British arrived in their parishes, they should greet them courteously and ask them to spare the lives of civilians and the property of the church. Most of the approximately two hundred priests in Canada obeyed this dictate. Historians have identified fifteen who did not and took up arms against the invader.

The most celebrated was René Portneuf. On 20 August Vaudreuil wrote to him thanking him for the intelligence that he was sending to Quebec about the British movements. He wrote that 'the proceedings of the British, although violent and contrary to the laws of man', did not surprise him as they 'are due to the recognition of the uselessness of the whole campaign'. The inhabitants must, however, continue to offer the 'liveliest opposition to the British'. He apologized that he could spare no reinforcements because of the need for every last man in Quebec.[72]

Three days later the curé appears in Knox's journal. He had heard that 'a priest, with about four score of his parishioners, have fortified themselves in a house a few miles to the eastward of our camp'. Knox had heard that 'they indiscreetly pretend to brave our troops'. Menacingly, he reports that 'a detachment of light infantry, with a field piece and a howitzer, are to be sent to reduce them'.[73]

This party was commanded by Captain Alexander Montgomery. When he landed he found a letter waiting for him from Portneuf. In it the Canadian priest acknowledged that Montgomery was fighting 'for his king and for glory' and as a result he hoped that Montgomery would understand that he was 'fighting for his poor parishioners, and defending his country'.[74] Portneuf had misjudged his adversary. One story goes that Montgomery was deeply embittered by the loss of a brother during the horrific frontier fighting of the previous few years and he, like his commander Wolfe, was in no mood to tolerate Canadian resistance.

The British officer moved a cannon into a position to bombard the priest's stronghold. In the meantime he placed his troops in the edges of the nearby woods to wait. Details are confused but it appears that after a short bombardment the Canadians were flushed out and ran straight into the ambush. There was a desperate hand-to-hand fight. Some of the Canadians surrendered, others were killed. Malcolm Fraser, who had already been shocked earlier in the summer by the brutality of British troops, wrote that 'the barbarous Captain Montgomery' ordered that the prisoners 'be butchered in a most inhuman and cruel manner'. Fraser was appalled; he could see 'no excuse for such an unparalleled piece of barbarity'.[75]

All the sources agree that their priest commander was killed and scalped along with the rest of them. Ramezay heard that Portneuf's men 'were treated very badly'. However, their leader, 'whom the English no doubt suspected of having stirred up this handful of men, was treated even more cruelly'. 'The English,' Ramezay reported, 'cut off his head in cold blood and in front of his miserable inhabitants.'[76] Three days later a burial certificate was drawn up by the priest of the neighbouring parish where Portneuf was interred; the church and presbytery of St Joachim having been destroyed in the fighting. It states that Portneuf was 'massacred by the British on the 23rd, being at the head of his parish to defend it against the incursions and hostilities which the enemy was carrying on against it'.[77]

Despite Wolfe's disgust at scalping when he had first arrived in the St Lawrence, the long brutal summer had clearly eroded his proscription of it. On 27 July he had issued a general order which stated that 'the General strictly forbids the inhuman practice of scalping, except when the enemy are Indians, or Canadians dressed like Indians'.[78] Knox suggests that this order was put into practice, claiming that the reason Portneuf's men were 'treated with such cruelty proceeded from the wretched parishioners having disguised themselves like Indians'.[79] By this point in the campaign that meant instant death. By August British troops regarded the Canadian people and their Native allies with utter hatred. As increasing numbers of friends and comrades fell to Canadian scalping knives or rifles, British troops lashed out in punitive raids against farms and communities, which embittered the *habitants* still further. Townshend records that by August Wolfe 'gave it out in orders that if any soldier chooses to go out in the Woods and lay in Ambush for the Indians and bring in an Indian Scalp [he] should have 5 Guineas reward'.[80] By the beginning of September one British soldier wrote that 'scalping is practised on both sides; as it is likewise by our ranging parties, who scour all the country'.[81]

Although there was a creeping acceptance of scalping, as long as the victims were the despised Native Americans, attempts were still made to protect civilians who were clearly non-combatants. Wolfe was determined that his men would not kill women or children. Amherst also prohibited scalping in certain circumstances. A soldier in his army recorded the policy for scalping: 'it is the general orders that no scouting party or others in the army under his command shall, whatsoever opportunity they may have, scalp any women or children belonging to the enemy'.[82] In both Amherst's and Wolfe's army these orders were interpreted flexibly by the rangers and redcoats who struck village after village in dawn raids. Women and children often suffered the same fate as their husbands and fathers. Montcalm was livid: 'The English, imitating the ferocity of our Indians, have scalped a few inhabitants of the south coast,' his journal reports. 'Are we to believe that a nation of laws is determined to mutilate corpses in cold blood? This barbarism would have been abolished among the Indians if they had proved themselves possible of correction.'[83]

One such Native American on the hunt for scalps was brought dripping in front of Townshend on 8 August when two sentries spotted the former swimming across the Montmorency. Knox suggested that the assassin was 'drunken' and trying to kill a British sentry to win favour with Montcalm.[84] Native Americans were well rewarded for services to New France. Bougainville wrote that 'those who distinguished themselves would receive medals and gorgets'. These medals hung on ribbons round the necks of the warriors. Bougainville tells us that 'on one side [was] the imprint of the King ... on the other a French warrior and an Indian shaking hands'.[85] Townshend's journal says that a soldier spotted the Native American and wasted no time in 'presenting his piece to his breast'. Whereupon the Native American 'got down on his knees threw away his knife and delivered himself up'. Wolfe was very pleased at the vigilance shown by the sentry and encouraged others to emulate it. A few days later he announced to the army that the sentry was to receive a five-guinea reward.[86] The Native American was brought before Townshend, who was keen to see one at close quarters. It made a change; 'most nights,' he noted in his diary, 'we hear the Indians hollow in the woods all about us' but could never see them. Townshend was unimpressed and described him as 'a very savage looking brute and naked all [apart from] an arse clout [loin cloth]'. Understandably, 'he seemed to be very apprehensive of [me] putting him to death'. He spoke a tongue which even those who spoke a few Native American languages could not understand so it is probable that he was from the far west.[87] The bedraggled prisoner was then loaded onto one of the larger warships to be taken to Britain as a curiosity. But he managed to dodge this strange fate. A French journal reports that 'one night, whilst the sentinels were asleep, he found means to disencumber himself of part of his irons and flinging himself out of a port hole into the water'. Quick-witted sentries on deck spotted him and 'fired several musket shots at random upon the water'. Knox says boats were launched in an attempt to find him but 'as the savages in general are dextrous in swimming and diving, their searches were fruitless'.[88] He made good his escape, though, and rejoined Montcalm's army, claiming that he was to have been given as a gift to the British king.[89]

By early September the lands bordering the St Lawrence had been laid to waste. Canadians and Native Americans had been slaughtered, others interred on British ships anchored in the river. A sergeant in the Louisbourg Grenadiers estimated that 'we have destroyed upwards of fourteen hundred fine farm houses'.[90] One Canadian historian has put the total number of farms destroyed as high as 4,000.[91] To some of the troops these operations were just punishment for Canadian inhumanity and a welcome chance to accumulate plunder. To many others it was war at its worst. Robert MacPherson wrote to his brother Andrew in Scotland describing the countryside as 'most cruelly wasted'.[92] Wolfe wrote a long report back to Pitt on 2 September, which was published in the *Annual Register*, a London newspaper, as was customary. Tellingly the paragraph relating to the laying waste of the countryside was not made public, as it did not show British arms in a positive light. Perhaps the toughest condemnation of all came from the pen of the third in command of the British army, Brigadier Townshend. In an emotional letter to his wife, which he began by saying, 'the happiness of writing to you is beyond all I know', he poured out his heart. 'My affection for you,' he continued, 'and your dear little ones convince me how unfit I am for this scene, which another month will thank god give conclusion to.' He told her that the sight of the captive women and children being brought into camp reminded him of his own loved ones back in Britain. Had he listened to his 'own nature more' he would 'not been now in a scene of ambition, confusion, and misery; and you oppressed as I know you must be, with terrors and affliction'. 'I never served so disagreeable a campaign as this. Our unequal force has reduced our operations to a scene of skirmishing cruelty and devastation. It is war of the worst shape. A scene I ought not to be in, for the future believe me my dear Charlotte I will seek the reverse of it.' He ended by telling her that 'I shall come back in Admiral Saunders' ship and in two months shall again belong to those I ought never to have left – Adieu. Your most affectionate husband and faithful friend.'[93] Townshend felt repugnance for a campaign that had brought little success. By August the British army had been sorely tried by the heat, Native attacks, French resistance, mosquitoes, and hard labour but the following months would bring greater tests yet.

Major General James Wolfe in a water-colour by his subordinate, Brigadier George Townshend. This is thought to be the most realistic portrait of the young general. Relations between Wolfe and Townshend deteriorated steadily throughout the summer.

Louis-Joseph, Marquis de Montcalm. Commander of the French forces in North America. He hated Canada and missed his family.

The forgotten hero of the Quebec operation: Vice Admiral Charles Saunders, commander of the naval side of operations. 'He was a pattern of the most sturdy bravery, united with the most unaffected modesty,' wrote Horace Walpole, 'no man said less, or deserved more.'

Brigadier General Robert Monckton.
He was Wolfe's second in command.

Brigadier General James Murray. Wolfe
and he became bitter enemies with one
of Wolfe's aides describing him as 'deadly
nightshade, the poison of a camp.'

Brigadier General George Townshend,
godson of George I, great-nephew of the
Prime Minister. He owed his appointment
to his impeccable political connections.

James Wolfe at around age 22.
By this stage he was a veteran of several
campaigns and already a major.

A view of the city of Quebec, the capital of Canada. James Peachey was an officer in the engineers who made a series of intricate images of Quebec in the 1780s. This is the view that would have greeted Wolfe's men as they fought their way towards Point Lévis.

The Montmorency falls in the eighteenth century. The spectacular landscapes of the Quebec campaign were on a different scale to operations in Europe. Many British and French soldiers were overwhelmed by the challenges the terrain and climate posed.

March of the Guards to Finchley by William Hogarth. The chaotic arrival of an infantry regiment in an English town. Drunkenness and gambling were constant companions to soldiers on the march. Contrary to the traditional view however, a redcoat was not simply a criminal in uniform, held in order by brutal discipline. The majority were volunteers, felt great pride for their unit and many left thoughtful journals and letters behind.

An Indian of ye Outawas tribe and his family going to war. Contemporary images of Native Americans are rare. That these were drawn by Brigadier George Townshend during the Quebec campaign makes them incredibly precious. Wives and children accompanied many of the participants whether European, Native American or colonial.

An Indian war chief completely equipped with a scalp in his hand. Another sketch by Townshend. Taking scalps was a sign of martial prowess but the gruesome practice enraged the British and ensured a brutal summer with little of the gentility that accompanied war in Europe.

An eighteenth-century Native American by William Hodges. The gorget around the neck was worn, as in the British and French armies, as a sign of rank.

A portrait of Caubvick, a Native American, in the late eighteenth century by an unknown artist. Caubvick was an Inuit woman from Labrador.

Accoutrements of war and peace. A collection of Native American objects; a war club, dagger and peace pipe assembled by a traveller through the interior in the 1760s. Some of the European diaries of the Quebec campaign double up as fascinating anthropological studies.

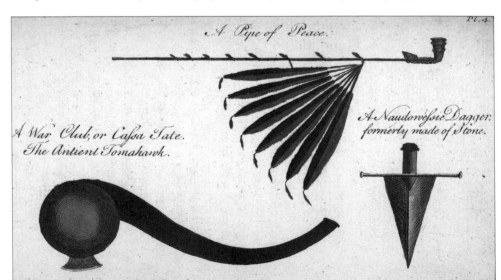

Sketch of Wolfe by Brigadier Townshend. Townshend drew a series of satirical sketches depicting Wolfe during the campaign. Here he is ridiculing his commander for his close attention to the digging of latrines. Wolfe is instantly recognizable by his long pony tail and weak chin. Despite constant orders concerning hygiene Wolfe could not prevent the outbreak of dysentery and typhus.

A page from Wolfe's journal. Its terse descriptions are punctuated by reports of declining physical health. Tellingly he destroyed his journal from 16 August onwards, possibly to obscure his own role in the event of an inquiry.

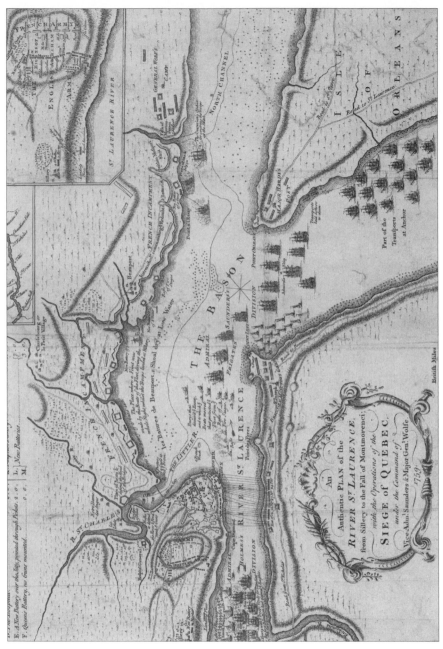

Plan of the operations at the taking of Quebec. The Quebec campaign immediately stimulated a massive demand for diaries, maps and paintings. This plan shows the dispositions of the troops and fleet and the intricate geography of the basin of Quebec. It is a powerful reminder of the amphibious nature of the campaign.

Spectacular but useless: the French send fireships against the British fleet. A wooden fleet in confined waters, packed with hemp, pitch and tar, with tons of gunpowder stored in holds was terribly vulnerable to fire.

Cap Rouge Bay by Hervey Smyth. A sizeable British man of war floats with impunity where the Cap Rouge River enters the St Lawrence. The bay was just one of many possible landing sites. The total command of the river by the Royal Navy was the decisive factor in the summer's fighting.

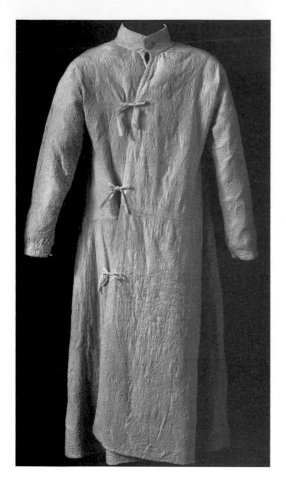

Wolfe's quilted cotton dressing-gown, held at Quebec House. It was used to wrap Wolfe's body during its journey back to Britain.

A French musket from 1717. A skilled infantryman was expected to fire at least three shots a minute.

A model of the flat-bottomed landing craft used at Quebec. These specially constructed craft were brand new at Quebec having been trialled on the Thames the winter before.

A *view of the launching place above the town of Quebec.* This etching dates from 1761 and was widely replicated for the popular market after the fall of Quebec. The artist has elided events to portray a simultaneous version of the landings at Anse au Foulon on 13 September 1759 and the battle that followed. Flat-bottomed boats and other craft bring in wave after wave of infantrymen from transports and naval vessels. The troops advance up the ravine to the Plains above but further downstream the light infantry can be seen scaling the cliff. The battle on the Plains is also depicted, with neat lines of infantry and clouds of smoke from their musket volleys.

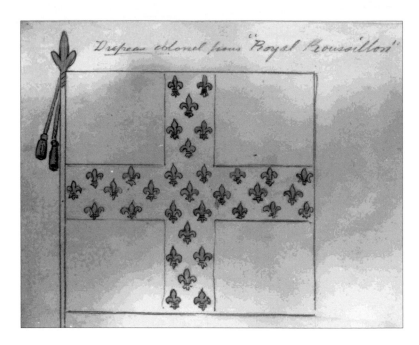

The 'Colonel's Colour'. On either side, every regiment had two colours. One was a 'King's Colour' and the other was particular to the unit. This is the latter, the so-called 'Colonel's Colour' of the Royal Roussillon regiment. The fleurs-de-lis denote royal favour.

A gaudy colour of the Royal American Regiment. To lose the colours in battle was unimaginable. They were defended to the last and always provided a rallying point in the heat of battle.

The Death of General Wolfe by Benjamin West. West's fanciful portrayal of Wolfe's death became the most reproduced piece of art in eighteenth-century Britain. It is wildly ahistorical – most of the figures were nowhere near Wolfe at the time and no Native Americans, whom Wolfe despised, accompanied his expedition. Interestingly, Townshend is absent, while Murray refused to sit for it, such was his dislike of Wolfe. None of this stopped it capturing the imagination of a country coming to terms with its status as the new global hegemon.

The Death of General Wolfe by Edward Penny. Penny painted an altogether more realistic version of Wolfe's last minutes. He was attended not by generals but by two Louisbourg Grenadiers, one of whom, James Henderson, apparently advised Penny on the painting.

The Death of Montcalm by Watteau. Refusing to be outdone, the French artist Watteau produced a painting of Montcalm's death even more inaccurate than West's of Wolfe's. Contrary to this portrayal, tents, palm trees and Polynesians were all absent at the moment of Montcalm's passing. Despondent in the face of death and defeat, Montcalm succumbed to his wounds in the dead of night in a bomb-damaged convent.

A view of the Church of Notre Dame des Victoires. A series of engravings made by a British eyewitness just after the fall of Quebec shows the terrible damage caused by the indiscriminate British shelling of the town.

A view of the inside of the Recollet Friars Church. British officers inspect the damage caused by their cannonballs and incendiary devices. This church suffered less than many other buildings.

A view of the Bishop's palace with the ruins, as they appear up the hill from the Lower to the Upper Town. Once the most magnificent vista in North America, this shocking image shows damage on a scale more associated with the twentieth century than the eighteenth.

A New Map of the Province of Quebec according to the Royal Proclamation on 7 October 1763, by Jonathan Carver. France decided that the sugar producing island of Guadeloupe was more valuable than the whole of Canada and in early 1763, at the Peace of Paris, she signed over the heartland of her American empire. The menacing presence on the northern and western frontiers of Britain's North American colonies was forever calmed. Yet few of King George's rejoicing subjects on either side of the Atlantic could have guessed just how divisive this victory would prove.

ELEVEN

'We find ourselves outnumbered and we fear, out generaled'

IN THE LONG MONTH of burning, crop destruction, and plunder one raid alone had a notable military purpose. Brigadier Murray commanded a detachment upriver of the city. Here the northern bank of the river towered out of the water and an army was only able to land at a small number of creeks or inlets which were protected by the French. Twice he had attempted to land and twice he had been repulsed with hardly a soldier ever having even stood on dry land. Murray was determined to learn from his failures above the city and on 17 August he began an operation designed to confuse the enemy and avoid their roving patrols on the north bank of the St Lawrence. Chief Engineer Patrick Mackellar reported that at 2000 hours Murray's redcoats boarded the flat-bottomed boats while the marines stayed in their camp at St Antoine on the south coast, 'with the order to make the usual number of fires that night and all the show they could the next day'.[1] The boats pushed off and rode the flood tide around fourteen miles upriver to Port Neuf on the north shore. Thanks to Murray's insistence that they take the boats rather than the ships, with their towering masts silhouetted even against the night sky, the French had not noticed the move. An hour after sunrise, according to one of the British soldiers, they landed, 'to our surprise, without opposition'.[2] Knowing that no sojourn on the hallowed north shore would be left untroubled for long Murray rapidly formed his little force into a column, with light infantry at the front and Fraser's 78th Highlanders bringing up the rear. The target of the expedition was the village of Deschambault three miles upstream. Intelligence reports had informed the British that there was a sizeable magazine of military supplies at Deschambault, which Murray meant to destroy.

They marched 'without molestation' until they got within sight of the church of St Joseph. Churches were the most solidly constructed buildings in these parishes and had become the focal point for military operations. Detachments of British soldiers regularly barricaded themselves inside churches when patrolling through hostile country. Now from out of this church poured the garrison of Deschambault, 'a captain of De La Sarre's regiment … with about 60 regulars'. There was little honour to be won in certain death to defend a heap of supplies and these outnumbered men rapidly withdrew to the protection of the woods.[3]

Quickly Murray searched the village and found a mountain of kit in a fine house belonging to Quebec merchant Monsieur Payreau. Murray reported to Wolfe that 'it consisted of that clothing, spare camp equipage, arms etc of the regular troops in Canada and of the Marquis de Montcalm and Monsieur de Lévis personal baggage'. Another British witness made a quick estimate that in all it was worth about ninety thousand pounds sterling. Murray ordered his men to set fire to the lot of it. 'There were many explosions,' the report continued, 'whence I conclude some of the casks in the cellar were gun powder or cartridges.' He destroyed 'all that could be of service to the enemy'.[4] Mackellar wrote that 'there were above forty different explosions of gunpowder, by which two neighbouring houses were unintentionally destroyed'.[5] The British troops had to hurry, for as the morning progressed French rapid reaction troops were arriving in the outskirts of the village, drawn by the pillar of smoke.

The French regarded the raid as extremely serious. A journal reports that

> this was the finest part of Canada; it was from the harvest at Deschambault that we expected our largest supply; and it was much to be apprehended, that the English, who had laid waste more than a mile and half of the country upon the side of the river opposite to the Pointe aux Trembles, either by fire or by sword, would do the same at this place.

But it also lay astride Montcalm's supplies from the heart of Canada: 'at the same place a large convoy was expected, of corn and of bullocks, the loss of which would inevitably be followed by that of the colony'. Perhaps the greatest fear of all was that 'the enemy would form an establishment there, take the post of Jacques Cartier in the rear, establish himself at both places, and cut off all communication between Quebec, Trois Rivière and Montréal'. This, the journal concluded, 'must cause the loss of the colony'.[6]

Montcalm was seriously concerned. When he heard of the landing he mounted and 'left immediately with the grenadiers to join M. de Bougainville'. Vaudreuil, his journal says, 'regarded the event as being of little importance' but, dramatically, Montcalm believed it was 'the greatest threat to the continuance of the colony'. He force marched his men to Pointe aux Trembles, where he heard that the British had withdrawn and returned to Beauport. His diarist asked, 'What would have happened if [Wolfe] had established himself at Deschambault?' The answer was that 'it would not have been easy to eject him'. Montcalm's aide wrote that 'we all feared this, and M. de Montcalm felt the importance of this position so strongly that he left there intending to attack it, strong or weak, entrenched or not. Little communication with our magazines, little food here, the country open to the enemy; the colony was lost or is going to be.'[7]

French forces arrived on horseback and on foot. Murray reported that 'they fired constantly upon us for two or three hours' but 'never came near enough to hurt a man of my detachment'. The reason he supposed for this was 'the dread they had of the English Musket'. He then says that he was forced to order his men to fire back 'in their way, at a distance'. Typically the British liked to save their fire until the enemy were very close, at a range where the musket's inaccuracy mattered little. By 1800 hours Murray realized that time would only bring more French troops and he began the tricky process of disengaging from the enemy and embarking on the boats, taking stolen sheep with them. The light infantry brought up the rear and not a man was lost. Bougainville took dubious credit for their evacuation saying that 'I forced them to re-embark.'[8] Murray learnt two key lessons: the first was that the tides could be harnessed to great effect and were not just a malignant force; the second was about the Canadians, who 'will never attack us but in woods or when we are in the boats, their arms and order will not admit of it'.[9]

One French officer dismissed the attack claiming that 'all these transactions were attempted with no events of consequence, and in no shape forwarded the main design of General Wolfe'.[10] True, the loss of spare equipment and personal baggage, though no doubt galling to the moody Montcalm, did not hasten the fall of Canada; however, a more perceptive eyewitness realized that allowing the British to operate with impunity in the river above Quebec was a mistake. The journal claims that 'all judicious persons ... maintained, that the king's two frigates well armed, ought to have been stationed immediately above Quebec; which would have prevented the English flat bottomed boats from appearing on that side, and would have secured to us the navigation of the river'.[11]

Murray continued his raids above Quebec, but below the town Wolfe was growing increasingly impatient to have some of his best troops back with him. He wrote to Monckton on 19 August saying, 'I wish we had Murray's Corps back, that we might be ready to decide it with 'em.'[12]

A combination of adverse winds, heavy rainfall adding to the flow of the St Lawrence, and French small boat activity had severed Wolfe's communication with Murray altogether. A series of letters survive from Wolfe to his junior brigadier, each angrier than the last. On 13 August he wrote,

> I have written two letters to you, if they get to your hands, I conclude we shall see you down ... the Light Infantry and Amherst's regiment, your own person ... are much wanted here, and if you have no very great stroke in mind I shall be glad to see you back. The Light Infantry must get into the Isle of Orleans as soon as possible.[13]

By 22 August he was using Murray as a, possibly rather convenient, excuse for taking no offensive action against Montcalm. He wrote to Monckton, his second in command, saying that Murray was putting 'an entire stop' to his operations. By his 'long stay above' and 'detaining all our boats' he was 'master of our operations'.[14]

Wolfe's letters were not finding their way to Murray. As Knox reported, thanks to the enemy's floating batteries, 'our boats cannot pass up or down'.[15] In the slow battle of attrition for naval supremacy in the narrows, British might was beginning to tell but it was taking time. A French journal recorded that 'great advantages' were derived from these 'small boats mounted with cannon' but of the original fourteen 'half of them had been destroyed or were unfit for service' and there was no time or money to build more.[16] The remaining craft were still enough to close the narrows to British boats. A detachment of Knox's regiment, the 43rd, attempted to get through to Murray by marching along the south shore but the Etchemin River was so swollen that as they tried to ford it one man was drowned and others swept away and forced to swim back to the shore. Knox added that 'to complete the disagreeableness of their situation, the enemy fired at them' from their battery across the St Lawrence at Sillery.[17]

On 24 August Wolfe ordered Monckton to fire rockets from Gorham's post, 'so our ships above may see them: this will be a hint to the people above that we want something'.[18] This finally seemed to work. Murray returned to Point Lévis on 25 August bringing with him the first news of the other British thrusts into Canada. The situation he returned to in the Quebec basin was far from happy. The town and surrounding lands were smouldering wrecks, no progress had been made towards capturing the capital of Canada, and the army he rejoined was dejected, divided, and, worst of all, diseased.

French attacks on the British camps at Lévis and Montmorency had been kept up with a terrible constancy. Wolfe wrote to a government minister in London that in this 'woody country, so well known to the enemy, and an enemy so vigilant and hardy as the Indians and Canadians are ... scarce a night passes that they are not close in upon our posts, waiting an opportunity to surprise and murder. There is very little quarter given on either side.'[19] It was often the most enterprising who died first. Losses fell heavily among promising young officers or seasoned NCOs who sought to stop the flight of their men or led spirited counter-attacks. Wolfe wrote to Monckton informing him of one such death. He concluded that 'we are particularly unlucky in the loss of officers – it has fallen upon the most deserving'.[20] Knox himself had a close shave. The enterprising young officer was sent to Montmorency on an errand and took the opportunity of making a full and conscientious reconnoitre of the fortifications and the enemy positions across the river. As he stood there making notes and sketches, 'I was hastily called to by one of our sentinels, when, throwing my eyes about, I saw a Frenchman creeping under the eastern extremity of their breast-work, next to the main river, to fire at me; this obliged me to retire as fast as I could out of his reach.' When Knox thanked the sentry, 'he told me the fellow had snapped his piece twice, and the second time it flashed in the pan'. Thanks to damp powder or perhaps an obstruction in the touch-hole Knox survived to furnish posterity with the most detailed and colourful account of the Quebec campaign.[21]

Wolfe's men were gaining experience but not enough to staunch the inexorable flow of losses. Townshend recorded in his journal that 'there have been parties every night in ambush for the Indians since the order was given out but has met with no success'.[22] There was a particular incident on 11 August that showed the utter terror which was often the result of Native American attacks. Knox describes how a 'body of Indians' crept towards a party out cutting wood, 'whereupon they ran in confusion to their arms, and, without any kind of order, fired impetuously at everything they saw, whether friends or enemies'.[23] Wolfe himself rushed into the fray with the camp guards followed by two six pounder cannon which chased the Native Americans away. He was livid. In his orders for the day he let it be known that 'the general was extremely surprised to see the disorder that seemed to run through the working party this morning; and foresees that if a stop is not immediately put to such unsoldierly proceedings, they may have very dangerous consequences'. From this point forward, any man who leaves the platoon without orders shall be made 'an immediate example' of by the officers.[24] By this Wolfe meant summary execution. While commanding a battalion in Canterbury a few years before Wolfe had written that 'a soldier who quits his rank, or offers to flag [surrender], is instantly to be put to death by the officer who commands that platoon, or the officer or sergeant in rear of that platoon; a soldier does not deserve to live who won't fight for his king and country'.[25] Wolfe was no sadist. His views were a commonplace among military officers of the day regardless of nationality. The nature of military authority, and the necessity for survival on a battlefield, dictated a rough and obvious discipline. This ferocity simply reflects the effect which wavering men could have on their fellows. A smart line of soldiers could become a disorderly, panicked rabble in a flash if just one of them lost heart and turned tail.

Punishments for any misdemeanour in the Georgian army could be harsh. Cowardice was regarded as totally unacceptable. If the perpetrator escaped execution he may well have been forced to walk 'the gauntlet'. Stripped to the waist he had to walk between lines of troops who beat him with sticks, a practice that often resulted in death. Some officers preferred a more psychological punishment. On 22 August Thomas Darby and George Everson were named and shamed in the General Orders that went out to the entire army for 'having behaved in a scandalous and unsoldierlike manner upon their post last night'. Darby's crime was 'screaming out and firing his piece', while they had both given 'the most evident tokens of fear'. They were ordered to stand for an hour by the latrine 'each with a woman's cap upon his head this evening, as a small punishment for the dishonour they have brought upon the corps and their brother soldiers'. When the army moved in future they were ordered to 'march in front of all other parties without a grain of powder in their pieces, where they may have the opportunity to wipe off the infamy they now lay under'. Wolfe ended the order by saying that he did 'not suppose there is another man in the regiment who is afraid of the French or their contemptible allies; but if there should be any such, they are desired to give their names into the adjutant that they may be properly posted in time of service'.[26]

Knox reports that these punishments could have the required effect. A few seasons before a soldier of his regiment was found by court martial to be 'a notorious coward'. He was forced to ride a contraption called the 'wooden horse', a cruel instrument in the form of a bench raised too high off the ground for a soldier to rest his feet, which meant that as he sat astride it, his body weight bore down on his testicles. He rode the wooden horse for half an hour a day for six days, 'with a petticoat on him, a broom in his hand, and a paper pinned to his back, bearing the inscription: Such is the reward of my merit'. The punishment aroused the 'inexpressible mirth of the whole garrison, and of the women in particular'. In this particular case humiliation led to redemption; from then on the poor man apparently proved himself a 'remarkable gallant soldier'.[27]

Contrary to the depiction of this period in florid historical novels and films, the British soldiery was not a cabal of rapacious criminals, never far from mutiny and held in check only by the threat of Draconian punishment. They certainly had their moments; constant immersion in destructive violence and the prolonged exposure to life-threatening situations mixed with strong alcohol is enough to loosen the hold of civilization over anyone. There was also a small minority of actual criminals who had escaped a long, rotting prison sentence or the gallows by 'volunteering' for the army. On the whole, though, it is surprising just how willing the men were to be led into battle, showing great courage and devotion to their officers throughout years of campaigning.

The massive concentration of men of fighting age in any one place requires strict regulation. Discipline was very harsh but it should be seen in the context of a society that still executed adults and children for a number of crimes and inflicted physical punishments for many others. The notorious 'Black Act' of 1723 increased the number of capital crimes by about fifty, most of which dealt with those who sought to interfere with the property of Britain's booming commercial classes. Large crowds turned out for executions, which in Britain were public until 1868, and the pillorying of homosexuals, who were sometimes stoned to death. Armies are, by their nature, composed of the younger, more aggressive, and often more brutalized members of the society from which they are drawn and it is not surprising that discipline was even more savage. In 1750 Wolfe had informed the soldiers of the 20th Regiment in which he was a major and effective commander that 'a want of honesty and fidelity will be attended with the worst consequences to themselves, and that whoever acts the part of the villain must expect the full rigour of the strictest justice'.[28]

Opposition to flogging and capital punishment could be found only in the very wings of radical opinion, the kind of Utopian dreamers who also believed in the abolition of slavery. One of the most daring acts of the French revolutionary government was to ban the thrashing of men only two generations after the Seven Years War. Floggings in the British army and navy happened regularly. On ship the captain judged whether to take 'the cat out of the bag' to punish a miscreant. On land the decision of five regimental officers gathered together in a court martial was enough to sentence a man to a savage whipping of up to three hundred strokes, but only with the consent of the commanding officer. Some were notable floggers, others rarely used the lash. If a man was to be flogged it happened in the centre of his regiment drawn up in a hollow square. He stripped to the waist, was tied to an iron frame while a drummer took the cat o'nine tails out of the bag. At a word from the commanding officer the drummer laid into the unfortunate offender. The sergeant major called out every stroke as the knotted rope whip with multiple tails cracked across the victim's back. Within a few strokes the back was a mass of blood and flayed skin. The commanding officer regularly interceded to reduce the number of blows. Partly as a result of their role as floggers, drummers were a caste unto themselves, paid as NCOs, fourpence more per day than privates, but widely shunned by the rest of the regiment.

The attack at Montmorency had demonstrated that, despite the existence of a terrible disciplinary code, the army was not simply motivated by fear. When well led, the Georgian redcoat was enthusiastic in battle. Morale differed vastly from unit to unit. Fraser's 78th Highlanders were a homogeneous group, commanded by traditional clan officers, and seemed to have a high self-imposed standard of behaviour. Flogging was virtually unknown. Other units were hastily assembled by poor officers who hoped to disguise their inability with repressive brutality. Some units with the worst records were assembled rapidly on the outbreak of hostilities by scraping the barrel of new recruits and being given drafts from other regiments, usually of their most dispensable men. As a result these units performed terribly. The 44th and 48th Regiments who found themselves on the receiving end of the Franco-Native American attack on the Monongahela were composite units, newly inducted men and the cast-offs from other regiments. They felt little loyalty to their new officers or the strangers around them in the ranks and the result had been utter rout.

A very different example is provided by Gentleman Volunteer Cameron on 16 August outside the Montmorency camp. Cameron, as a volunteer, was an aspirant officer with Lascelles' 47th Regiment. As he was leading a patrol of NCOs and eighteen men, they were attacked, Wolfe told Monckton, by 'at least 200 Indians'. Rather than panic and fly, Cameron led a 'gallant defence' in a farmhouse. The Native Americans pressed the attack so boldly that they even poked their muskets through the broken windows to fire at his men.[29] A message was sent back to the camp and Wolfe himself immediately set off with the grenadier company of Bragg's Regiment. They 'hastened to the assistance of their friends', Wolfe later announced to the army, 'with very great spirit'.[30] Meanwhile, Wolfe had ordered rangers and light infantry to plunge into the woods to cut off the Native Americans' retreat to the ford across the Montmorency.

The Native Americans withdrew at the advance of reinforcements and 'retreated to the spot the Light Infantry had orders to possess themselves of'. But as Wolfe's 'Family Journal' explained, 'the difficulties in marching through the woods prevented their being there quite time enough, 10 minutes earlier would have thrown them into their jaws: the enemy afterwards discovering the march of the Light Infantry, ran off'.[31] Wolfe told Monckton that the light infantry got within 150 yards of them, 'but they were off so precipitately that he could not get above 6 or 7 shot at them'.[32] Yet again the British force had not been quite quick enough through the unfamiliar woods to trap a sizeable body of Native Americans, but it was a heartening episode among a month of setbacks and disillusionment. Wolfe told Monckton, rather optimistically, that the Native Americans had met with 'a very severe check', while 'our little detachment brought off one scalp and a number of trophies'.[33]

Cameron was rewarded by being made an officer. In a letter written on 22 August Wolfe apologizes to Monckton for interfering with the latter's unit, the 2nd Battalion of the Royal American Regiment. As well as being a brigadier, Monckton was colonel of this unit and patronage was a jealously guarded prerogative of military command. Sons of friends and political allies could be rewarded with commissions. Wolfe was hugely apologetic for imposing Cameron on him. He explained: 'you know I promised Mr Cameron the first vacancy in the army, or no recommendation whatever should have interfered with yours in your own regiment'.[34]

Cameron joined the approximately one-third of officers in the British army of the eighteenth century who were promoted on merit without money changing hands. The other two-thirds bought their rank. The ability to purchase in this way did lead to the occasional warped situation where rich, well-connected young men rose extraordinarily fast. Lord John Lennox, second son of the Duke of Richmond, was made a Lieutenant Colonel at 20 years old in 1758. Arthur Wellesley, the future Duke of Wellington, was a Lieutenant Colonel at 25. Examples like these have helped earn the Georgian army its reputation for being led by wealthy amateurs, dull younger sons of the great aristocratic families. In fact, this rapidity was very unusual. The army was officered overwhelmingly by men who had served since their teens and had learnt their trade over years of campaigning or garrison duty. The purchase of commissions did not occur in an anarchic free market. There were firm controls on who was allowed to buy what rank; no one could purchase a rank more than one above his own, and a seller was supposed to offer it first to the next officer in seniority in his own regiment. There was a clear tariff for each commission. No man was supposed to become a captain without having served ten years as a subaltern. Above all the crown had the right to block any purchase of which it did not approve. George I, his son, George II, and grandson, the Duke of Cumberland, all took this aspect of their role very seriously. They made regular inspections, knew the names, strengths, and weaknesses of most of the just over two thousand officers in the army in 1755, and reacted ferociously when politicians attempted to interfere with this vast patronage machine.

The British political class actively approved of the purchasing of commissions. It ensured that the army was officered by men who held a stake in the status quo, men of land, property, and influence. Their interests were those of the state. These men would not play the role of a Cromwell, a low-born adventurer who stood to benefit from the subversion of King, Church and State. It also meant that officers had a powerful reason to behave well. In the event of them being thrown out of the army, or 'cashiered', they were not allowed to sell their commission.

Many though, like Cameron, faced the daunting challenge of scaling the ranks without money, connections, or political influence. This was not as hopeless in Britain and Ireland as it was in the French army where the nobility were fighting an aggressive campaign to exclude non-nobles from the officer corps entirely. By 1781 they had succeeded in getting the King to sign an ordinance making it impossible to rise beyond the rank of Captain unless you were a noble. It was a final act of hubris of a class that would soon face annihilation. There was snobbery in Britain, and senior ranks were dominated by nobles, but no attempt was made to mimic the French; partly because there were simply not enough aristocrats to go round. France had more than a hundred thousand nobles in the middle of the eighteenth century. Britain had less than three hundred peers. Well over half of the senior officers in the British army were made up of aristocrats or grand gentry but at a junior level they made up only a quarter.[35] The rest were sons of lesser gentry, churchmen, provincial merchants, and, of course, army officers. An officer from a modest background like Cameron could expect a widely differing reception by his fellow officers depending on the culture of the regiment. In some 'smarter' units men promoted from the ranks would be bullied; in others, particularly newly raised units, they would have found that they were among men in the same position as themselves. Chances of further promotion depended on the course of the war. Peace was an anathema. In wartime officers could cover themselves with glory; new units were raised whose officers were professionals, appointed by the crown rather than being open to purchase. War also vastly increased the turnover of officers as musket balls and disease made vacancies in the ranks which, in these circumstances, could not be sold but had to be filled by the next officer in the battalion in seniority. Cameron could reasonably hope to end his life as a major, and further progress was not out of the question. During the Seven Years War no less than 400 men were commissioned as officers having served in the ranks as soldiers.[36] War offered men like Cameron an opportunity to clamber a few rungs up the well-defined social ladder.

Wolfe made much of Cameron's escapade because it was unusual. August had brought little to be proud of. The weather added to the woes of the men. Periods of blazing heat were punctuated by summer storms which turned trenches and redoubts into baths of mud as the low clouds obscured the smouldering ruins of Quebec from Wolfe's wistful gaze.

Desertion, always the bane of armies in this period, rose to epidemic proportions. There was a vast array of reasons why men crept across to enemy lines including better rations and conditions or the fear of impending punishment. Many of the men were American settlers of mixed, German, or Dutch descent who felt no particular loyalty to either king and were happy to serve both. Some men were actually French. The Louisbourg Grenadiers, in particular, had recruited a number of the French defenders of Louisbourg, after its surrender the year before. These men now saw an opportunity to return to their old allegiance.

Not that crossing the lines was as easy as it could be in Europe. The forests between the two armies were alive with Canadian and Native American troops, who terrified the British. Townshend recorded in his journal that these irregulars were partly there to stop any French troops crossing the lines. He was told by one such deserter that the Native Americans were ordered to be on the lookout for any French deserters and to scalp them if they found them. Many others, he told Townshend, had met such a grizzly end and 'he himself was very nigh undergoing the same fate'.[37] Montcalm attempted to encourage British desertion by assuring potential turncoats with a proclamation in French, German, and English

> that all who would desert the English Army, should receive the greatest favour and encouragement, and would have nothing to fear from the barbarity of the Savages; – they were directed to observe a particular method of holding their Guns (by the stocks) and that at this particular signal, the savages would fly to succour them; fire upon their pursuers, and conduct them faithfully and in safety to the French Camp.[38]

This may well have worked as reports from both sides suggest that desertion increased throughout August. On the fourth a French officer recorded that 'five new deserters came over to us today'.[39] On the fifteenth no less than seven marines deserted from Point Lévis according to Townshend's journal.[40] Two days later 'such of the marines as are foreigners' were ordered aboard ship for the rest of the campaign to prevent any more desertion.[41] Other precautions were taken to stem the flow of men. On 25 August Wolfe issued a General Order to the army, telling 'the outposts and guards' to be 'more careful in the future in stopping all soldiers who are attempting to slip by them'.[42] The next day a particularly embarrassing desertion took place in full view of the army as a sergeant from Otway's 35th Regiment splashed across the ford at the foot of the Montmorency falls. One of the Louisbourg Grenadiers wrote that 'our people fired several grape-shots after him' but he dodged the hail of fire and 'got clear off to the enemy'.[43]

Not everybody was so lucky. A sailor from the *Dublin*, possibly one of the many foreigners serving with the Royal Navy, tried to swim the St Lawrence. But a British sergeant reported that 'the current ran so strong, that he was driven on shore on the island side'. Here he was captured by a Louisbourg Grenadier and 'carried on board his own ship again, stark naked'.[44] The penalty for attempted desertion was death. Commanding officers often commuted this to a hideous flogging or tried clemency if they thought that this would prove a more effective deterrent. Often a mixture of the two was employed. Lieutenant William Henshaw, marching up from the New York frontier with Amherst, describes how two men were about to be shot for desertion. The first was killed and the second pardoned at the last possible moment.[45] When a French prisoner was captured on the same front and he turned out to be a British deserter there was no chance of clemency. He was hanged, wearing his French coat with a label on his breast saying 'Hanged for desertion to the French.' He was then to be buried, 'and his French coat with him,' reported an officer on the expedition.[46]

Captive soldiers faced with being half starved to death as prisoners of war often chose reluctantly to serve in their enemy's ranks. These men then faced death if captured by their erstwhile masters or death if they attempted to desert during the campaign. It was a miserable plight endured by many, especially in North America where infantrymen were in short supply. Commanders could not just rely on savage coercion to keep their armies intact, however. Fair treatment of the men, acceptable rations, a tolerable workload, and at least occasional payment were the policies followed by the wiser generals.

Wolfe was very particular in his desire to personally interrogate enemy personnel. He ordered that 'when a deserter comes in from the enemy, the officer who commands the guard or post who takes him up, is immediately to send him to headquarters, and not permit him to be examined by any person whatsoever, until he is presented to the commander in chief'.[47] It is extraordinary just how porous both armies were through the summer. Deserters happily divulged the camp gossip and prisoners were just as garrulous. During truces officers would discuss the course of the campaign and of the war in general. Rumours whipped right around the Quebec basin and there is a bewildering number of journal entries and references in letters of imminent attacks at one point or another, of operations planned and cancelled. Wolfe's habit of never telling anyone anything, much to the frustration of his fellow officers, stemmed partly from the knowledge that nothing would stay secret on the St Lawrence for more than twelve hours.

The real reason for his secretiveness was not genius but paralysis. Wolfe spent the month casting around for ideas. On 11 August he wrote in his journal, with more hope than determination, that he proposed 'to undertake something of consequence in a few days'.[48] It came to nothing. Little is known about his thinking for the next month because he destroyed his own diary from 12 August onwards. We know, however, that he continued to look longingly at the Beauport shore while at the same time not ruling out an attack above the town, if Murray returned with news of weak points in Montcalm's defences there. He also wrote to Monckton thinking of an all-out assault on the Lower Town. Mackellar wrote in his journal that the General gave orders for augmenting the batteries across the narrows from Quebec 'to forty pieces of cannon; this was thought favourable to a storming of the town by water'.[49] Mackellar had always disapproved of such a desperate gamble. Knox heard that the Chief Engineer, 'who is well acquainted with all the interior parts of the place', believed it was 'an enterprise extremely dangerous, and without any prospect of succeeding, particularly as the fleet cannot assist us, their guns not having sufficient elevation to affect the upper town'. Even if the Lower Town was captured, 'we could neither carry our point nor continue in possession of it'.[50] The army would be trapped on the narrow strip of ground below the cliffs and face annihilation. Wolfe listened to his Chief Engineer. He reported to Pitt that because the few passages from the Lower to the Upper Town were so 'carefully entrenched' and covered by the batteries from above, Wolfe could not bring himself to attempt 'an undertaking of so dangerous a nature, and promising so little success'.[51] Knox heard on 21 August that 'the enterprise of storming Quebec' had been given up 'as too desperate'.[52]

Wolfe even started planning for failure. If he had to embark his army and disappear down the St Lawrence to winter in New England and Halifax he thought about leaving an outpost on the Île aux Coudres to dominate the river during the winter, until a new amphibious force was sent up in the spring. There are various references to this plan in Knox's journals until this plan too was abandoned. Knox reports that the planned fort, big enough to hold 3,000 men, 'is laid aside for want of proper materials, and the season being too far advanced for such an undertaking'.[53] Knox was well informed. Wolfe wrote to Pitt ten days later saying, 'I intended to fortify Coudres and leave 3000 men for the defence of it; but was too late in the season, to collect materials sufficient for covering so large a body.'[54]

As well as high levels of desertion, there are other clues that imply tumbling morale. On 18 August Wolfe was forced to remind his men that if any of them 'pretends to dispute the authority of an officer of any other corps under whose command he is, and if a soldier presumes to use any indecent language to the non-commissioned officers of his own, or of any other corps, such soldiers shall be punished in an exemplary manner'. On 26 August Wolfe ordered that since he supposed 'that all the officers and men are equally ready to march whenever the service requires it' if ever volunteers were lacking for an expedition he would send whichever unit was next up for duty. It seems that the men's enthusiasm for leaving camp and braving the perils of the Canadian woods was flagging.[55]

The general malaise spread from the bottom of Wolfe's army to the very top. The lack of a coherent plan articulated to his officers, coming off the back of his failure at Montmorency and his unwillingness to attempt anything in the weeks following led to serious whispering in the British camp. A naval officer wrote to a colleague saying that the attempt at Montmorency had been 'impracticable; which some General Officers scarcely hesitate to say'. He went on to describe how 'one of them of knowledge, fortune and interest I have heard has declared the attack then and there, was contrary to the advice and opinion of every officer; and when things are come to this, you'll judge what the event may be'. In short, he wrote, 'we find ourselves outnumbered and we fear, out generaled ... we imagine here that near 500 are killed, missing and wounded since our first arrival and we have not gained as I can perceive, any considerable advantage'.[56]

Captain Schomberg of the *Diana* wrote to a fellow officer saying that 'General Wolfe appears in his conduct more like [Fabius] Maximus than Achilles, notwithstanding what has been said of his impetuosity by his enemies and rivals.'[57] Fabius Maximus had been nicknamed 'Cunctator' or 'the Delayer' by Romans angry at his apparent refusal to attack Hannibal as the latter rampaged along the length of the Italian peninsula.

It was not just the naval officers who were questioning Wolfe's leadership. Bell's journal on 31 July contains a remarkable reference to 'Colonel Carleton's abominable behaviour to the General'.[58] What kind of behaviour, and what sort of abomination, were regrettably not specified. That even this favourite of Wolfe's was now becoming hostile is a shocking admission of his alienation from even his closest colleagues.

Wolfe's 'Family Journal' launches vitriolic attacks on nearly everyone during August. 'After the miscarriage of the attack on the lines of Montmorency,' it relates, the evil spirits began to show themselves more openly than before and form into parties, every person who had undergone censure during the campaign fled to the standard of discontent of Murray and Townshend, however their numbers were very few. They looked on the whole affair as over, and that no future attempt would be made, which is a tacit confession that would have been the case with themselves, had they commanded.

Unstintingly loyal to his idol, the author notes that 'they were little acquainted with the invincible spirit of Wolfe'. He wrote that 'Wolfe held their cabal very cheap, and as he acted from noble principles disregarded ill grounded opinions.'[59] Sometime during late July Murray had obviously overtaken the Royal Navy and Townshend as the chief object of Wolfe's disdain. His 'Family Journal' calls his junior brigadier 'deadly nightshade, the poison of a camp'. It continues, 'envy and ambition are the only springs that work him. The more brilliant and excellent any character is the more his envy is excited, and the more he detracts. Neither honour, gratitude – anything else that is binding among mankind, are bars to ambition.' It claims he was 'the very bellows of sedition and discord' and 'he has great artifice in setting evil spirits afloat in an army, and in persuading people that their merits are not rewarded'. It finishes with a vicious summary of his abilities: 'He is hot in action, brave from ambition not zeal – a tolerable good commander of a brigade – anything beyond that is too extensive for him.'[60] The author of the journal believed that there was a real reason for Murray's raid upriver: 'The only step [Wolfe] took was to separate Townshend and Murray by sending Murray to destroy the Magazine of Deschambault, and I afterwards heard him make this observation that Townshend was innocent when separated from Murray.'[61] The army may have been few in number, but it was not a happy few, nor a band of brothers.

Townshend's disgust with the brutality towards civilians further poisoned his respect for his commander in chief. He wrote to his mother and said, 'As to Mr Wolfe, I am convinced you knew him better than I did, and had I known him as well as you, I would not have been under his command in America.'[62] He did not just share his poor opinion of

Wolfe with his mother. It was widely known in the army. Wolfe's friend Lieutenant Colonel Murray of the Louisbourg Grenadiers wrote to a close friend on 8 August saying, 'Townshend is well but a malcontent. I meddle in no politics or party, am well with all.' He sounds rather pleased that he is apparently considered 'a favourite of the whole army; I go by the name of "the old soldier."'[63] Wolfe's tension with Townshend was nothing new, but the collapse in his relationship with the other brigadiers is fascinating. Monckton needed soothing after flying into a rage at Wolfe detaching various units from his force at Point Lévis, and, in his view, dangerously weakening it. Wolfe wrote an apologetic letter on 15 August. He explained that 'Barré, who esteems you much' had told him of Monckton's unhappiness and he insisted that 'I have all possible regard and esteem for you.' He made him 'hearty excuses' and promised that 'I never mean to disoblige – I am too well convinced of your upright sentiments, and zeal for the public service, not to set the highest value upon your friendship.' The next day he was forced to prostrate himself again: 'I do repeat to you, that I would avoid all occasion of offence ... and I heartily beg your forgiveness, for this last, or any other former error or mistake of mine.'[64]

Colonel Williamson, his artillery commander, also found Wolfe's behaviour perplexing. He wrote to Lord Ligonier saying, 'I am certain that as we are situated an addition of three or four thousand men to go and land at any convenient spot two or three miles above the town would finish our work in a fortnight's time.' Instead, the army did nothing while 'our shot and shells are destroying their capital'.[65]

Given the speed of news and rumour passing through and between armies, even the French found out about the schisms in the British high command. An officer in the French army heard from a deserter in late August that 'some misunderstanding existed between the land and naval commanders. We had already heard this, and it is since confirmed.'[66]

Just when frustration and indecision were plaguing the British camp a new threat emerged. One with more potential to do damage than the cautious Montcalm; a scourge which no pre-industrial army could hope to avoid for long: disease. In early August Knox observed the first signs of illness. 'The troops, on this side,' he wrote, 'begin to grow sickly, particularly the marines, who are therefore ordered to remove to the westward of the church, where they have room enough to render their camp more open and airy; the disorders prevailing among the men are fluxes and fevers, such as troops are usually subject to in the field.'[67] On 9 August Major Boisrond, the marines' commanding officer, sent a return to Monckton of the number of men under his command ashore and their condition. Of 1,001 men 150 were sick.[68] The casualty rate of 15 per cent would slowly climb through the rest of the month.

By 17 August news of the condition of the British troops was brought to the French camp. 'We learned by three new deserters from the enemy's army,' reports one journal, 'that a severe dysentery was prevailing there, which had already destroyed a great many people.'[69] Wolfe and the other commanders did what they could to halt the spread of disease. Orders were issued for the men to clean themselves properly. Latrines, trenches dug in the ground and covered over when full, were situated with great care. After at least a month of the camp being totally static, space was rapidly used up for opening new latrines within the tight confines of the defences. Wolfe took a close interest; near the beginning of the campaign he had ordered that 'in order to preserve the health of the troops, each regiment ... [is] to make new houses [outhouses] at least every third day, and throw some earth into them daily. They are to be made by the front line as far advanced as they conveniently can, and those of the 2nd line as far in the rear of the whole encampment.'[70] Townshend, in his series of witty but cruel caricatures, portrayed Wolfe as obsessed by the whole unglamorous business.

Human waste was not the only threat. As the camps grew dirtier by the end of July Wolfe ordered that 'butchers and others who kill meat, [must] always bury the offal'. A point emphasized a few days later when Wolfe announced that 'great care [is] to be taken by the Regiments within their respective encampments, and in their neighbourhood, that all offal and filth of every kind which might taint the air be buried deep under ground and the general recommends in the strongest manner to the commanders of the corps to have their camps kept clean and sweet'.[71]

Eighteenth-century camp life was a constant battle against the microbes. In the winter of 1758/9 the Highlanders stationed at one fort had been told in no uncertain terms to use the latrines: 'if any man is found to shite or otherwise nasty the fort he shall be obliged to clean it with his hands, and no other instrument shall be allowed, as it is a scandal and shame that so much nastiness should be seen in the fort already'. Also, 'pisspots, which are to stand at the door of the barracks, [are] to be carried out of the fort and cleaned every morning'.[72] Dealing with human and other waste is a central theme of any account of a campaign. As Wolfe tried to make his men use the relevant facilities, in Amherst's army a provincial major was issuing order after order to try to keep his men disease free. 'It is reported to me,' ran one such order,

> that some of the men are lousy, therefore it is expected that the captains or commanding officers of companies enquire into the affairs and if there is any that is so to order them cleaned otherwise they will louse the whole ... and examine the men's tents and see that they are kept clean and to see the men wash their shirts and stockings as often as needful.

Officers were also to check that 'all the filth [is] cleaned out and buried and new earth covered over'.[73]

Dysentery, known at the time as the flux or bloody flux, was spread through unsanitary water. Micro-organisms flourished in it and entered the body where they attacked the lining of the men's intestines. Sufferers experienced severe diarrhoea with blood in their faeces and possibly vomiting. Some victims could not keep down any liquids at all and died of dehydration. The other killer was typhus which was carried by the lice that feasted off the flesh of humans especially in tightly packed concentrations. The disease that devastated Athens during the Peloponnesian War is thought to have been typhus and during Napoleon's retreat from Moscow it killed more men than the pursuing Russians. In Britain it broke out in the dreadfully packed prisons and was known as 'gaol fever' which was estimated to carry off as much as a quarter of the prison population of London each year. In the twentieth century it would rip through the malnourished and filthy population of Bergen-

Belsen killing inmates long after it was liberated. Wolfe's men would have been struck by a headache, fever, and a rash. Then fall into a listless stupor and experience terrible delirium.

The tents were breeding grounds for lice. In June Wolfe had ordered five men maximum to a tent but ideally no more than four. The men slept head to toe; two men shared their two blankets using one as a ground sheet and the other to keep them warm. Initially fresh straw was laid on the ground of the tents but after a short time, Montresor reported to his father, 'the straw is grown bad'. As a result 'Parties are daily detached from this camp for boards for the men's tents, and also for corn to dry in the sun.'[74] At the end of July Wolfe admitted that such static camping was not ideal but 'as it is impossible at present to move to better ground, great care is to be taken to air the tents and dry the straw and ground'. He went on to say that 'as fresh straw cannot be conveniently got for the troops, it is recommended to the commanding officers to direct the cutting [of] spruce bows for that purpose'.[75] Days of heavy rain turned the camps into bogs, soaking the men's bedding and contaminating the whole area with overspill from shallow latrines. Knox reports that at one stage 'our encampment [was] under water'.[76] At the end of August he reports that spruce bows on the floor were not enough and the men 'were ordered to strip houses, boards being wanted to floor our men's tents for the preservation of their health'.[77] The houses of the *habitants*, already picked bare by looters, were now ripped apart and their planks used to floor the tents in an attempt to combat the filthy muddy conditions, the result of days of heavy rain.

Wolfe ordered the men to keep themselves clean and encouraged swimming in the river. Curiously he forbade them from doing so through the hottest hours of the day. Possibly to prevent sun burn and sun stroke they were only allowed to swim 'in the morning and evenings'. This order, of 19 July, does not seem to have been obeyed as the next day he ordered the 'guard near the water side to take up any soldiers that may be swimming between the hours of 9 in the morning and 5 in the evening'.[78]

Despite new flooring, swimming, and strict sanitation by the end of August the hospital in the church on the tip of the Île d'Orléans was full and the staff were overwhelmed. Wolfe pressed the women of the army into service. On the twentieth he announced that 'if any woman refuses to serve as a nurse in the hospital, or after being there leaves it without being regularly dismissed by order of the director, she shall be struck off the provisions roll; and if found afterwards in any of the camps, shall be turned out immediately'.[79] The women, many with no previous experience of the horror of a field hospital, must have had a terrible shock. Men with burns, gouges, and slash wounds from battle lay alongside those with chronic diarrhoea and vomiting. With no idea of microbiology the staff fought the diseases with a vague sense of the importance of cleanliness and slightly better rations than those provided to the healthy soldiers. Milk from captured dairy cows was earmarked for the patients. Any men who were lucky enough to survive the regimen of hospital were sent back to their regiments. Once they returned to their units, Wolfe ordered that 'they are to be kept off duty for a week or ten days, as the surgeons shall think best'.[80]

Scurvy was less of a threat given the availability of some fresh produce and the realization that spruce beer prevented it. It requires thirty days without any vitamin C in the diet for skin problems to appear followed by minor haemorrhages and lethargy. After eleven weeks the gums become soft and old wounds reopen. During the summer anti-scorbutics seem to have been available although there were still some sufferers. Treatments were more Iron Age than Enlightenment. Knox witnessed a remarkable attempt to cure a sufferer where a man was buried to his neck in sand and 'remained for some hours: this I am told is to be repeated every day, until his recovery is perfected'. Remarkably, 'the poor fellow seemed to be in good spirits, laughed and conversed with the spectators who were about him'.[81]

John Johnson paints a grim picture of the army at the end of August. He described the 'small number we are now reduced [to] fit for the field'. Many of his comrades had been 'lost by sickness, and rendered entirely useless through hard duty'. With more than a hint of melodrama Johnson says that this 'handful of men' in 'three very weak Brigades' had only a 'very small' chance of becoming 'masters of Quebec'.[82]

On 19 August Wolfe himself was struck down. He had always suffered from intestinal and other complaints and the microbes found a willing host in his weak body. His 'Family Journal' says simply that 'Mr Wolfe was taken ill of a fever' and 'was incapable of business'.[83] Wolfe wrote to a government minister in London and blamed 'the extreme heat of August and a good deal of fatigue'.[84] Rumours swept around the army for days until news of their commander's illness was confirmed on 22 August. It came as no surprise to Knox whose suspicions had been aroused by Wolfe's failure to visit the camp at Point Lévis for three or four days. Clearly until then he had visited every encampment of his far-flung army almost daily. This was only a small part of his gruelling routine. He inspected fortifications, batteries, and latrines. He led counter-attacks against Canadian and Native American raids. He interrogated deserters. Perhaps most stressful of all was the terrible responsibility for the success or failure of the mission. He had found the French much stronger than he had hoped. He had not heard a single thing from Amherst, supposedly the other half of a giant pincer attack. All his assaults had come to naught while his army was being whittled away by ambush and disease. Although only a sergeant, John Johnson showed great empathy for his commander, putting his illness down to stress. Wolfe was worried, Johnson explained, that 'he should be exposed to the contumelies [insults] of a harsh and unthinking populace, and that his military talents should be exposed to ridicule, after exerting every faculty of both body and mind, for the service of his country'. 'These perturbations of his mind,' he continued, 'affected his body to that degree, that he was for some days entirely unfit for public business.'[85]

His men took the news of their general's illness very badly. Knox reported that 'it is with the greatest concern to the whole army, that we are now informed of our amiable General's being very ill of a slow fever: the soldiers lament him exceedingly, and seemed apprehensive of this event'.[86] Whatever disagreements Wolfe may have had with his senior officers his popularity among the men had remained high. His attention to their well-being, his energy and presence in every corner of every British camp, and, perhaps above all, his determination to share the dangers of battle with his men had made him a popular commander. In the forests along the Montmorency or in the leading flat-bottomed boat feeling its way into the shore through the shoals during the attack on 31 July, Wolfe had been in the middle of some of the thickest fighting. His calm refusal to be intimidated by Native American tactics and his constant assurances that if the men trusted their comrades, their officers, and their muskets they would overcome, seem to have won their respect.

Wolfe was bedridden for at least a week. Knox crossed the river on 24 August to receive orders for Monckton's brigade at Point Lévis but Wolfe 'was so ill above stairs as not to be able to come to dinner'.[87] His headquarters were in 'a tolerable house', according to Knox, which survives until today although it is boarded up, surrounded by weeds, and in need of paint. It is little bigger than a cottage but considerably more comfortable than the tents of the men he led. Something of his lifestyle during his time there can be deduced from a will he wrote in June while aboard the *Neptune* sailing towards Quebec. He left his 'camp equipage, kitchen furniture, table linen, wine and provisions' to his successor in command of his army. He had a servant, François, who was to take half of his 'clothes and linen' while 'three footmen' would share the other half.[88] Wolfe would have been kept in clean, comfortable conditions with a regular supply of fresh food. These, rather than the close attention of the army's surgeons, with their belief in draining blood from the patient, gave him a decent chance of recovering. More so than the hundreds of men who lay crammed and filthy in the overflowing hospital on the Île d'Orléans.

Unable to leave his bed, his army depleted, and the nights gradually closing in, Wolfe was forced to break with habit and consult. The man who had taken no advice now sent from his sickbed instructions that, in the words of his 'Family Journal', his brigadiers should 'take what measures they thought most salutary'.[89]

In a letter to his three subordinates Wolfe wrote that he hoped that 'the public service may not suffer by the General's indisposition'. He begged that the 'Brigadiers will be so good to meet and consult together for the public utility and advantage, and to consider of the best method of attacking the Enemy, if the French army is attacked and defeated, the General concludes the town would immediately surrender, because he does not find they have any provisions in the place'.[90] He outlined three ways of attacking the enemy. The first suggestion involved 'fording the Montmorency 8 or 9 miles up' and attacking the French Beauport positions from the rear. Wolfe admitted that it would be hard to complete this march in secret, writing that 'it is likely they would be discovered upon their march on both sides of the river'. The second and third plans involved a force marching across the ford at the bottom of the falls and making an attack on a weak point in the Beauport defences while Monckton brought his men across in the flat-bottomed boats. This was, in effect, the same plan that had led to such a sharp defeat on the last day of July. It was not fresh thinking and neither was his final comment that 'the general thinks that the country should be ruined and destroyed as much as can be done consistent with a more capital operation'.[91]

Obviously Wolfe could not tear his gaze from the sprawling enemy camp along the Beauport shore. Despite his defeat at Montmorency he clearly still believed that the basic plan and objectives had been sound. His brigadiers disagreed. Townshend wrote to his wife during these days saying that 'General Wolfe's health is but very bad. His generalship in my poor opinion is not a bit better, this only between us.' Townshend appears to have given up hope. He concluded that 'the success of this campaign, which from the disposition the French have made of their force must chiefly fall to General Amherst and General Johnson'.[92] Despite this pessimism on 28 August the brigadiers met in the morning at Point Lévis to consider their commander's recommendations. Then they went on board the *Stirling Castle* to confer with Saunders, who had been overseeing the slow battle to drive the French gunboats from the St Lawrence basin as well as keeping the army fed and supplied with convoys of small boats passing to and fro between the British camps. Monckton returned to Point Lévis in the evening but Murray and Townshend stayed aboard overnight.[93] The next day they sent Wolfe their reply. It was not what he was expecting.

'Having met this day, in consequence of General Wolfe's desire to consult together for the public utility, and advantage, and to consider of the best method of attacking the enemy,' the brigadiers began, 'we ... considered some propositions of his with respect to our future operations, and think it is our duty to offer our opinion as follows.'[94] They dismissed Wolfe's obsession with the Beauport shore as politely as they could. 'The natural strength of the enemy's situation between the river St Charles, and the Montmorency, now improved by all the art of their engineers makes the defeat of their army if attacked there very doubtful,' they wrote. 'From late experience', they reminded Wolfe, the British boats would be unprotected by the fire of the ships. Nor were they impressed with Wolfe's other idea: the long flanking march which would cross the Montmorency miles inland and then attack the French from behind. 'It appears to us,' they told him, 'that, that part of the army which is proposed to march through the woods ... to surprise their camp is exposed to certain discovery, and to the disadvantage of a continual wood fight.' The long summer of fighting had convinced the brigadiers, and Saunders, that victory lay neither in frontal amphibious assaults nor in prolonged marches through woodlands teeming with Native American and Canadian skirmishers. Even if Wolfe's attacks on the Beauport defences did result in victory, the French would simply withdraw across the St Charles and 'dispute the passage' of that river, supplied, as he was, from his magazines further west.[95]

They begged Wolfe to banish thoughts of a battle for Beauport altogether. They were unanimously 'of the opinion that the most probable method of striking an effectual blow is by bringing up the troops to the south shore, and directing our operations above the town'. There was 'very little doubt' that the British could establish themselves on the north shore above the town as Murray had shown with his raid on Deschambault. In this event 'the Marquis de Montcalm must fight us on our own terms [because] we are betwixt him and his provisions, and betwixt him and their Army opposing General Amherst'. 'If he gives us battle,' they asserted, 'and we defeat him, Quebec and probably all Canada will be ours, which is an advantage far beyond any we can expect by an attack on the Beauport side.' Having totally rejected his plans and suggested a radically different strategy his brigadiers attempted to comfort him with declarations of their loyalty: 'we cannot conclude without assuring the General, that whatever he determines to do, he will find us most hearty, and zealous in the execution of his orders'.[96]

The brigadiers even went as far as to prepare a plan of operations which suggested the immediate abandonment of the Montmorency camp. A minimum of troops would be left at Point Lévis and the tip of Île d'Orléans and the rest of the army concentrated at the mouth of the Etchemin River around six miles above Quebec where it entered the St Lawrence. Troops would then be packed into as many transports as could get past the guns of the town and landed on the north shore. The best place, they thought, was 'half a league' above the Cap Rouge River, which was about ten miles upriver of Quebec. As soon as the first wave was landed, every boat available would ferry the remaining troops from the south shore across to join the first wave on the north. This plan would menace Quebec's least fortified side, it would threaten Montcalm's all-important communications and supply routes, and it would concentrate the diminished manpower of the British expeditionary force in one single thrust. Above all it would circumvent the two greatest obstacles to British arms encountered thus far: the irregular forces of Canada and the bristling shore defences of the St Lawrence.[97]

Saunders and the brigadiers spoke with huge confidence about operating above the town because, as they met to consider how to break the deadlock on the St Lawrence, the navy, after weeks of trying, had finally managed to get more ships past the town. Wolfe had made his usual insinuations that the navy were cowards as August had progressed and Saunders' ships had failed to get above Quebec. On 13 August Wolfe had written to Monckton demanding to know the reason for the 'delay of the ships and for their not attempting it yesterday when the weather was so favourable'.[98]

Time and again ships had tried to get through the narrows but the wind had failed them at the key moment and the town's cannon forced the almost stationary ships to return. It was not until 27 August, as Saunders reported to the Admiralty, that 'they got up, which was the fourth attempt they had made to gain their passage'. On the night of 27/28 August he continued, 'the *Lowestoft* and *Hunter* sloop with two armed sloops and two catts with provisions [are] to pass Quebec and join the *Sutherland*.[99]

One British officer watching from Point Lévis said that the French fired 200 shots at the ships.[100] A sergeant in the Louisbourg Grenadiers thought that the French batteries 'fired so hot at them with shot and bombs, that one would have thought it impossible for any vessel to pass; but they received little or no damage'.[101] A few of them did, in fact, find their target. The *Hunter*'s log reported that 'when abreast of the town, the French being at their quarters fired very hard for a space of time; we passed with the loss of two men and one wounded'. The day after the carpenters were 'repairing what was damaged by the shot' and the following day the 'sailmakers [were] mending the shot holes in the fore and mizzen topsails'. The *Lowestoft*'s log said that at 2045 hours she was 'abreast of the town of Quebec, from which we received a smart fire of shot and shells, at which we fired seven 9-pounders ... In passing the town received many holes through our sails and a deal of our running rigging shot away.' [102]

The upriver fleet was now turning into a powerful body capable of carrying and landing a large number of troops in one wave. Saunders made sure that more and more ships were sent to reinforce this growing force commanded by his subordinate, Rear Admiral Holmes. A sergeant in the Louisbourg Grenadiers recorded that on 29 August 'five sail went to pass the town'; the batteries 'fired very warm all the time of their passing, and I was very well informed that only 15 of their shot took place out of all their firing'. On the thirtieth 'four of our ships passed the town, where they kept a continual firing; but did us very little damage'.[103] Ramezay reports that 'we fired upon them, without being able to see the harm we caused'. 'But,' he continued, rather desperately, 'we have found some effects on the beach that led us to believe that we had sunk a few of them.'[104]

A few pieces of driftwood did not signify a sinking. The French batteries were simply unable to discourage the British ships from passing if they had a fair easterly breeze and a flood tide to get them past the town. By the end of August the shore batteries of the Lower Town had been thoroughly blasted by the British. A French journal records that 'it was no longer possible for anyone to remain' on the ramparts because 'the fire from the batteries on the Pointe Lévis was vigorously sustained by day and night'. They spent truces desperately building cannon-proof 'épaulements' or breastworks to try to protect their artillerymen but they still took terrible casualties. Over a single four- or five-day period the French journal recounts that thirteen men were 'killed or wounded passed recovery'.[105]

Typically when taking on batteries, ships would use a mixture of round shot to damage the fabric of the battery itself and grape to kill the artillerymen or at least scare them into abandoning their posts. Despite the seeming mismatch between lighter guns on an unstable ship firing at heavy, well-mounted cannon ensconced behind stone defences, ships often silenced shore batteries. Back on the coast of France Captain Hervey of the *Monmouth* embarrassed the French defenders of Brest by sailing in and capturing prizes under the mouths of the cannon of the shore batteries. A hail of grape shot sent the French gunners scurrying away from their guns. In January 1762 it took HMS *Dragon* only an hour to silence a shore battery in Martinique. Faced with aggressive British fire the guns of Quebec were not enough to block the narrows and as the wind blew fresh from the east Saunders crowded the upper river with British ships.

On the night of 31 August/1 September five more vessels, led by the frigate *Seahorse*, passed the town. A French journal bemoaned that 'the English had now 17 vessels above the town, of which, one of them was a two decker, two frigates, and the rest small vessels and transports – of these however several were mounted with cannon'.[106] Montcalm described their manoeuvres to Bougainville as being 'of the most alarming kind'.[107] It was the one threatening development in an otherwise better than expected month for the French. Great swathes of Canada had been burnt and its principal town had also been reduced to ashes but the British were no closer to taking possession of it. By the end of August the French even felt bullish enough to take some aggressive action against the fleet in the river above the town.

As soon as British ships had passed the town in July, Vaquelin, a naval officer who had won the respect of his peers fighting the British at Louisbourg the year before, had been sent up to look after the

French frigates that had been moored for safety a long way beyond Quebec, near Trois Rivières. Early in the summer he had sent a message to Quebec saying that if they sent him the ships' crews, who were manning the artillery batteries in the Lower Town, he would capture or destroy the British ships operating above the town. His suggestions were ignored. A French journal did not know 'whether it was that they did not like at that moment to unman the batteries, or that they would not render themselves responsible for the two frigates, in case of their failing in the attack'. Either way, 'a deaf ear was turned to his solicitations'.[108] In late August, however, his suggestion was finally taken up. One French journal records that 'a levy was made of 1,100 men, officers and sailors' in order to 'arm *Le Machau*, *Le Senectaire*, and some other ships to attack the enemy ship of 50 guns'.[109] Panet reports that two battery commanders from Quebec 'with the elite men' were to rearm the frigates.[110]

'When everything was in readiness for putting in execution the plan,' records one journal, 'they were preparing to sail … with a favourable wind; and in the opinion of all the seamen, success was infallible.' At that very moment a courier reached the crews. He had been sent from Quebec with an urgent summons for the sailors to return. It was 28 August and the night before more British ships had passed the town. Vaudreuil wanted the sailors back. Not only did he now fear an assault on the Lower Town, but the replacement artillerymen had proved woefully inadequate. They had failed to do much damage to the British ships; indeed, they were dangerous to themselves. 'Above 20 of our men were wounded,' records the journal, 'and not any from the fire of the enemy, but solely from their own unskilfulness in serving our guns at the batteries.' The sailors were deeply upset. 'Nothing could exceed their discontent, at being frustrated in their wish of prosecuting an enterprise, which they were assured would have afforded them the opportunity of signalizing, and perhaps enriching themselves.'[111] It was a cruel blow to another French plan that had great potential. Vaudreuil displayed poor leadership in not seeing the opportunity earlier. The small squadron of British ships above Quebec was isolated and vulnerable. An attempt should have been made against them before the end of August. By the time the French made their move the

British had advanced enough ships into the upper river to decisively fix the balance of power in their favour.

There was good news, though, from the other fronts. The cautious British had made no attempt to follow up the success at Fort Niagara and advance towards Montreal from the west. On 24 August an Abenaki unit had captured a small party carrying a dispatch from Amherst to Wolfe. The official message was swallowed but lots of letters from officers in Amherst's army to friends and colleagues in Wolfe's were taken and they made it clear that Amherst was not going to make a dash for Montreal before the end of this season. He had not heard from Wolfe and for all he knew the latter's force could have been defeated and he could find himself facing the whole army of Canada at the top of Lake Champlain.

In Quebec these reports were indistinguishable from rumour. Earlier in the summer Panet notes that people told each other that 'Louis-bourg had been taken back by the French, and that the English fleet was worried and was going to gather and leave'. Récher reports this and adds that a Spanish fleet was blockading Boston, the old king having died and his heir having allied himself with France. Another relentlessly upbeat story circulated which 'said that the King of Prussia had lost 20,000 men in battle; that the Queen of Hungary was mistress of Silesia and the French of the Hanover electorate'. Now, at the end of August, Quebecers cheered themselves with the entirely false news that 'we are masters of the large majority of Ireland'. Panet added fervently: 'I hope that this is so.'[112]

Perhaps the rumours grew more optimistic as their position remained deeply uncertain. Despite the lack of British progress it was difficult for the French to celebrate. Supplies seemed to be the biggest French problem. Vaudreuil wrote two affectionate letters to de Lévis in the middle of August in which he tells him how much he, and Madame Vaudreuil, miss him and also describes 'the pressing want in which we live'. Bigot had told Vaudreuil that by the middle of September 'we must live on the new flour of this autumn from Montreal'. 'What a hard situation!' Vaudreuil groaned. 'It is an absolute necessity that we plan in advance to cut, beat, and mill Montreal's autumn wheat. We have no time to lose, as the army will lack totally the means to live if we do not receive the flour in question.'[113] Later in the month Vaudreuil wrote again saying 'we must do everything possible to assure that we do not lose a kernel of wheat because we have basically no other resource other than the harvest of the government of Montreal for the colony to live on until next spring'. He ordered de Lévis to reduce the ration in Montreal, Île aux Noix, and Île aux Galops to one pound of bread. This was necessary because if the army knew there was a different ration to the one they were receiving around Quebec, 'it would be very unhappy'.[114] In reality, Récher wrote, Quebecers often received less than a pound a day as priority was given to the soldiers, who were also bolstered by 'half a pound of lard and a shot of eau de vie'.[115]

Montcalm remained pessimistic. At the end of August he noted in his journal that 'if we survive this year, the campaign will have been beautiful and glorious'.[116] But he clearly regarded that eventuality as unlikely. He wrote a letter near the end of August saying 'Mr Wolfe (if he understands his business) has nothing to do but bear the first fire – advance fast upon my army – stop at his discharge – my Canadians without discipline at the sound of the drum will get into disorder and fly – such is my deplorable situation.' Even so, he knew that time was running out for Wolfe and he told his correspondent that 'the campaign cannot last a month on account of the terrible autumn winds, which are totally against the fleet'. His adversary, he wrote 'can never succeed as long as he attacks from the other bank'. He knew that something dramatic was required and told his correspondent that 'Quebec must be taken by a *coup de main*.'[117]

On 31 August Knox reported that 'General Wolfe appeared in his camp today, for the first time since the late illness.' Rumours of his recovery had generated the 'inconceivable joy of the whole army'.[118] As Wolfe evaluated the situation he realized he had little choice but to embrace the plans of his subordinates. He wrote Saunders a morose letter in which he admitted that 'my ill state of health hinders me from executing my own plan; it is of too desperate a nature to order others to execute. The generals seem to think alike as to the operations.' Reluctantly, 'I, therefore, join with them, and perhaps we may find some opportunity to strike a blow.' At times this pessimistic letter descends into gloomy fatalism: he told his naval commander that 'I am sensible of my own errors in the course of the campaign; see clearly wherein I have been deficient; and think a little more or less blame to a man who must necessarily be ruined, of little consequence.' As to the future, he knew that 'Beyond the month of September I conclude our operations cannot go. We can embark the superfluous artillery; and Barré has a list ready for you of quarters for the troops, supposing (as I have very little hope of) they do not quarter here.'[119]

He was drafting his dispatch to Pitt, his first since arriving in Canada. Sent in the first few days of September it carried the first official account of the campaign to Britain and after it was digested by the official mind it was published in the newspapers to inform the burgeoning political class. On Wednesday, 17 October 1759, *The Public Advertiser* carried Wolfe's report. It was crammed onto an inside page, curiously juxtaposed beside an announcement about the latest 'Eau de Luce' which, despite the titanic struggle being fought between Britain and France, was 'just imported from Paris'. Even though they were mortal enemies nobody could deny the Frenchman's leadership in matters of fashion and modernity.[120] In this anodyne setting the British people read Wolfe's account, without, of course, the paragraph describing the destruction of the farms and settlements of the St Lawrence. This dispatch was only slightly more upbeat than his private letter to Saunders. He began by apologizing that 'I wish I could, upon this occasion, have the honour of transmitting to you a more favourable account of the progress of his majesty's arms; but the obstacles we have met with ... are much greater than we had reason to expect, or could foresee.' After a précis of the fighting thus far he ended by saying that his 'much weakened' army opposed by 'almost the whole force of Canada' meant that he was faced by 'such a choice of difficulties, that I own myself at a loss how to determine'. He acknowledged that 'the affairs of Great Britain' demanded the 'most vigorous measures' but he was unwilling to endanger more of his men. 'The courage of a handful of brave men,' he wrote, 'should be exerted only where there is some hope of a favourable event.' Gone is any expectation that he might take Quebec, instead he suggested that he would be 'happy if our efforts here can contribute to the success of his majesty's arms in any other parts of America'.[121] When this downbeat missive was published it caused widespread disbelief. Canada was seen as a wasteland of peasant Breton immigrants mixed with its 'savage' original inhabitants, infected with idolatrous papist religion. Across British possessions in North America and in Britain itself its fall was believed to be a matter of time. A friend wrote to Sir William Johnson, the 'Mohawk Baronet' who had taken Fort Niagara, with the news from New York. As well as informing him that 'we were very merry on [Johnson's] success' and cries of 'Johnson for ever' were on people's lips, he also informed him that 'General Wolfe and the army were furiously cannonading and bombarding [Quebec] and had burnt the one half of it – the French army entrenched near the walls on the other side of the town, we have not heard of one sally they made, nor any action between the armies whatsoever – we all expect Quebec will fall into our hands.'[122]

Wolfe's miserable report would come as a rude shock to those whose optimism was stoked by the cosy self-congratulation of New York, Bristol, or Edinburgh. His private correspondence was even more alarming. His almost total psychological as well as physical breakdown is confirmed in a letter to his mother written at the end of August. 'Dear Madam,' it began, 'My writing to you will convince you that no personal evils (worse than defeats and disappointments) have fallen upon me.'

> The enemy puts nothing to risk, and I can't in conscience put the whole army to risk, my antagonist has wisely shut himself up in inaccessible entrenchments, so that I can't get at him without spilling a torrent of blood, and that perhaps to little purpose. The Marquis de Montcalm is at the head of a great number of bad soldiers, and I am at the head of a small number of good ones, that wish for nothing so much as to fight him – but the wary old fellow avoids an action doubtful of the behaviour of his army.

He repeats his well-practised complaints about the 'uncommon natural strength of the country' before making a stark confession. During this miserable campaign, he has hatched a 'plan of quitting the service which I am determined to do at the first opportunity'.[123]

Weakened, depressed, and resigned to failure, Wolfe still had an army to command, for a few more weeks at least. He had endorsed the brigadiers' plan but he had no enthusiasm for it. His 'Family Journal' says that 'the brigadiers unanimously declined the execution of [Wolfe's suggested] attack and were of opinion to move the operations above the town, with what view I know not, it was said their intent was to destroy the Upper Country'. It gives us a glimpse of Wolfe's real feelings, saying, 'I afterwards heard Mr Wolfe lament his want of health that he could not execute his plan saying it was the only project that had any pith and marrow in it.'[124]

The senior British commanders were deeply negative in private. Townshend simply longed for home. Mackellar wrote in his journal that 'there was little or no appearance of making good a landing upon a coast so naturally strong, and so thoroughly fortified and defended by such superior numbers'.[125] Saunders' report to London was downbeat, never mentioning the possibility of capturing Quebec but saying simply that 'let the event be what it will, we shall remain here as long as the season of the year will permit, in order to prevent their detaching troops from hence against General Amherst'. To help a future campaign he tells the Admiralty that he will 'have cruisers at the mouth of the river to cut off any supplies that may be sent them, with strict orders to keep that station as long as possible'. Even though the weather required that 'I shall very soon send home the great ships.' Although Quebec would remain a possession of the French king, it was no longer the pride of North America; 'the town of Quebec,' he wrote, 'is not habitable, being almost entirely burnt and destroyed'.[126] No one, however, was more negative than Wolfe himself, the army's commander in chief. He wrote to a senior government official at the beginning of September that 'I am so far recovered as to do business, but my constitution is entirely ruined, without the consolation of having done any considerable service to the State, or without any prospect of it.'[127]

By the end of August Knox recorded in his diary that 'it blows fresh down the river. Mornings and evenings raw and cold.'[128] Canadians had always seen 20 October as the absolute end of navigation on the St Lawrence; traders raced to meet this deadline, getting their furs to the ships that would then depart for Europe. There was just over a month left to decide the fate of the town and the colony. Many believed, on both sides, that Wolfe would slink back down the St Lawrence without making one final attempt to take Quebec. Yet as the French heard from a deserter: 'notwithstanding' their weakened general, the British 'were preparing to make a last throw before returning'.[129]

TWELVE

'This man must finish with a great effort, and great thunder'

THOUSANDS OF MEN were hard at work at Montmorency. The sound of picks striking rock and thumping into earth was audible over the roar of the waterfall. Gangs of cursing soldiers and sailors hauled cannon and oxen bellowed as they were goaded while bearing heavy loads. At first glance the scene was typical of the industry shown by the British soldiers throughout the summer. But a seasoned eye would immediately have noticed something quite different. Rather than strengthening the ramparts, batteries, and strongpoints Wolfe's men were dismantling them. Rather than hauling more and more artillery up into the camp the guns were now being lowered down the slope, a task requiring as much skill and little less effort. Ditches were being filled in, ramparts flattened, and piles of tent floorboards burnt in heaps along with the superfluous detritus of an evacuating army. Montmorency, the rock on which Wolfe had anchored the flank of his army, the site of countless skirmishes, scalpings, and killings, and the focus of the commander in chief's strategy all summer, was being abandoned.

The sick and wounded hobbled and limped down to the St Lawrence at mid-morning on 1 September 1759, helped by the women. These were the first groups to be evacuated, after the camp colourmen and quartermasters who, as always, would go ahead to any new location and mark out where the regiments were to pitch their tents. Wolfe had issued detailed orders to his men. Two transports had been allocated for each regiment. The 'baggage that will not be absolutely necessary on board the transport appointed for the regiment' would be taken to

Point Lévis separately from the men.[1] The women, marines, and wounded, Saunders wrote to Townshend, would be taken off by 'eight flat bottomed boats'.[2] Montresor was in one of the first transports to leave, behind him he watched 'five hundred men employed in hauling all the heavy artillery to the beach and embarking them in boats'.[3]

Wolfe disguised his disappointment well. He had always seen Montmorency as a launch pad for assaults on the French army that did not rely on naval assistance. Now, weak with disease and demoralized by the immovable deadlock of the campaign, he had given in. At the prodding of his brigadiers he had agreed to a joint army–navy operation above the town of Quebec. By abandoning Montmorency he was placing himself in the hands of naval officers who he did not trust and increasingly despised. Wolfe had agreed to the brigadiers' plan on 31 August in a meeting with the three of them and Saunders. As soon as this decision was made, 'orders were immediately given out,' records Townshend's journal, 'for all the artillery and stores to be carried away from this camp'.[4]

Wolfe attempted to make a virtue of his retreat. The evacuation would be made without any pretence at disguise. Withdrawal was a notoriously risky enterprise; one that left an ever decreasing number of his troops vulnerable to enemy attacks. The last men to leave would be nervous that they would be abandoned while others made good their escape. A planned withdrawal could easily become a rout. Wolfe hoped that Montcalm would seize on this and attack. If his French counterpart did give in to temptation he would walk into a British trap. Wolfe ordered that

> as it is to be hoped that the enemy will attack us in our post, and as every advantage may be expected from such an attack if the troops are alert in getting to their alarm posts. It is Col Hale's [of Lascelles' 47th Regiment] orders that neither officer nor soldier put off their shoes, coats, or any part of their clothes while they remain in their camp.

To trick the French 'bell tents and drums, except one, are to be sent off this night. Every man is to load with two balls, and to have their arms with them in their tents, taking particular care to keep them dry and prevent accidents.' 'The tents of every company,' Wolfe continued, 'are to be struck at half an hour after one, and every thing is to be removed that may give an appearance of the regiments being on the ground.' Then under cover of darkness 'the grenadiers and battalion companies are to march into the redoubts ... carrying their tents, blankets, knapsacks etc with them, and are to keep themselves carefully concealed ... The commanding officers of companies will take care that this motion is made with as little noise and as much despatch as possible.'[5]

The French did not come the first night. The British troops lay behind redoubts, clutching their muskets as their commanders prayed for French aggression to get the better of their caution. One diarist recorded that 'our troops there expect an attack from the enemy this night, which is very desirable to all our gentlemen'.[6] The stubborn French failed to take the bait and the second night Wolfe redoubled his efforts. He ordered his men 'to conceal themselves entirely after daylight, so as to try to induce the enemy to attack them ... no fires to be made by the men in the alarm posts; all dogs to be sent off with the tents'.[7] Townshend recorded in his journal that 'the light infantry to lay concealed in the camp – great silence was to be observed and not a man to show himself on any account but to lay concealed in their posts to try once more in the enemy would attack us'.[8] Wolfe's 'Family Journal' hoped that the French would be lured 'into a scrape'. Their 'curiosity and love of plunder might induce them to explore the camp, supposing us to have stole away during the night'. Sadly for Wolfe, however, yet again 'the bait did not take'.[9]

Montcalm's men watched, but did not intervene. One French eyewitness commented that 'they seemed very busy at the English camp at the falls of Montmorency, and we could see them embarking their artillery, their baggage, and a part of their army, which landed at the Point de Lévis'. The next day was just as busy and he watched as they 'set fire to the épaulements of their batteries and to part of their entrenchments – insomuch, that the next day, nothing was to be seen there but a guard, not very numerous, to occupy the fortified post which still remained near the woods'.[10] French artillery blazed away at the flotilla of little boats as it crossed between the north shore and the Île d'Orléans. Knox tells us that 'they beat one of them to pieces'. A French cannonball scored a direct hit on a boat and six of the seven men in it were drowned.[11] The movement of ships and men certainly convinced the defenders of Quebec itself that an amphibious assault was imminent. Panet reports that the barges full of men 'caused an alert in the town'. He then describes how he, and no doubt many others, prepared himself psychologically for the coming battle: 'I got myself, after having drunk two shots of liquor, to ... the St. Jean gate, and we drank the third while on standby.'[12]

On the morning of 3 September a large barn near Townshend's headquarters was set on fire. It was the signal for the final withdrawal. The last four British battalions made their way to the shore of the St Lawrence. All houses, shacks, and wooden defences were burnt. Bragg's led the way to the St Lawrence, followed by Anstruther's, Lascelles', and then Otway's. Bringing up the rear were the indispensable light infantry. Townshend wrote that he was 'obliged to wait one hour after the houses was burnt and the redoubts evacuated as the howitzer and other column was so long marching down'. On the beach the force drew up in line as if willing the French to come and attack them, before embarking in the flat-bottomed boats and crossing the St Lawrence without the loss of a man. Townshend's lengthy wait with the rearguard had shaken his nerves. He confided to his journal that 'all the army got down to the boats without the enemy appearing to attack us which they might have done with great advantage'.[13] Knox reports that Monckton on Point Lévis thought that he saw two columns of French troops leave their positions along the Beauport shore and head inland to cross the ford and attack these last regiments. As a result he put Kennedy's 43rd and Fraser's 78th Highlanders into boats and made several feints along the Beauport shore. Knox reports that 'we remained near four hours on the water'.[14] Once the whole British force had been evacuated, they took a roundabout route to the south shore. Perhaps chastened by the previous day's direct hit on one of the boats, Townshend recorded that 'we was obliged to lay 3 hours until the tide made that our boats might row up at a greater distance from the enemy's batteries'. Even taking this longer route the French artillery 'kept up a perpetual cannonade at us all the way to Point Lévis'. It was to no avail, though, as the bombardment 'did not touch one boat'.[15]

Mackellar suspected that Montcalm must have seen something 'about our camp which gave him a suspicion of the affair, and made him decline the invitation'. The engineer regarded this as fortunate. 'It was a pretty general opinion,' he continued, 'that [Montcalm] might have made an attempt to great advantage at all events.'[16] French sources disagree on whether or not Montcalm had let slip yet another opportunity. One journal records that the British deception was too obvious 'to escape the vigilance of M de Montcalm', who suspected that 'some snare was intended'. The author concluded that 'Montcalm had judged well of their design.'[17] Others, however, thought Montcalm should have been more forward. One officer wrote that 'Montcalm and his principal officers, to try to justify themselves for having lost so fine an opportunity,' claimed with hindsight to have seen the 'more than 2,000 men ... lying on their faces behind the entrenchments'.[18] Panet's disgust for the French army grew. He noted with distaste that those families who returned to their homes in the vicinity of the British camp found 'their village intact, and less damaged than those that are near our soldiers'.[19]

When they landed on the south bank the British troops set up camp in the places that their quartermasters had laid out. Only the 2nd/60th Royal Americans and some marines stayed to guard the camp at the tip of the Île d'Orléans under the command of Carleton. The rest all arrived at Point Lévis and, according to Wolfe's 'Family Journal', 'encamped in the fields on the back of our batteries'.[20] The French cannon in the town fired on these large, new encampments and forced the commanders to resite them further up the slope. Despite this it was a safer environment than the near siege-like conditions at Montmorency.

Mackellar wrote that Wolfe himself 'now fixed his head-quarters at Point Lévis'.[21] Here he planned the next phase of the operation. Burton would stay at Lévis with one regiment. The rest would march upriver to the Etchemin River where they would board the ships in the upper St Lawrence. That fleet was now, according to its commander, Rear

Admiral Holmes, 'five sail of men of war and about eleven transports'. They had all passed the town, he boasted, 'in spite of all the fire of their batteries – a thing which they [the French] had thought impossible'.[22] On 4 September a fleet of flat-bottomed boats sped past the town on the flood tide. All thirty-two of them were loaded with tents for the soldiers and other pieces of heavy equipment. That day the men in the regiments had been told that they were going above the town and were to travel as light as possible. Monckton ordered that his brigade would sleep 'one tent to eight men', while four officers were told to share. They were to take '1 Shirt, 1 pair Shoes, 1 pair Stockings and a Blanket per man'. There was one other stern dictate: 'no women'. He ordered that 'if the men's superfluous necessaries can be left in security in their respective camps, they must be left'.[23] Even drums were to be left behind to save space. Only two drums per regiment were permitted, although the rest of the drummers, who fulfilled important roles as medical orderlies in battle, were allowed to go if the commanding officer wanted them.

While Wolfe's men prepared for the move upriver, news finally arrived from the commander of British forces in North America, Major General Amherst. Mackellar wrote in his journal that 'an officer and four rangers, brought a confirmation of the taking of Niagara, Carillon and Crown Point'.[24] Previously there had only been the jumbled rumours coming from French deserters and prisoners. Getting the message to Wolfe had been a Herculean task. A sergeant in the Louisbourg Grenadiers reports that 'they were 26 days on their journey'.[25] Ensign Benjamin Hutchins had come along the Kennebec River having made his way to Boston from Amherst's army on 7 August. Another messenger, Captain Quinton Kennedy, had attempted to run straight through to Wolfe along the south shore of the St Lawrence. He was a veteran of frontier fighting and was married to a Native American. It appears that Amherst had wanted Kennedy to test the loyalty of the Native tribes as he went and, if possible, wean them off their attachment to New France. Unfortunately for him that attachment was solid and he was captured. Since he was effectively spying, and was out of uniform, he was not protected by the protocols governing prisoners of war. Montcalm could have hanged him as a spy. As it was he and a fellow officer were roughly treated and their Mohawk companions tortured. Knox heard through a French deserter that 'two of these Mohawks were roasted to death by the French at Trois Rivières, in the presence of the other two, who were scalped alive, carried to Montréal and hanged in chains'. The officers were clapped in chains and 'very rigorously treated'.[26]

Ensign Hutchins' long-awaited message actually clarified very little. To start with the information it provided was a month old. It was also slightly ambiguous. Amherst gave no real timetable for his advance north. Wolfe had no idea how long it would take Amherst to move up Lake Champlain and drive Bourlamaque's army out of its positions at Île aux Noix. For all he knew Amherst could now be at the outskirts of Montreal. A letter written at around this time gives a fascinating impression of the feeling in the British camp. The soldier author says that 'various are the opinions concerning Quebec; some think it will fall others it will not'. He describes the town as 'entirely demolished' and 'the produce of the year spoiled'. Everyone was aware of the onset of winter which meant that it was 'thought the siege will continue six weeks longer if the place don't surrender'. Above all he is optimistic that 'Mr Amherst is expected every day and there are great hopes of the place surrendering.'[27] Knox reported that Wolfe said in public that 'he did not yet despair of seeing the commander in chief here before the end of the campaign'.[28]

In fact, Amherst was nowhere near Wolfe's army. Many at the time and since have linked the pedestrian speed of his advance to his weaknesses as a commander. Others go further and accuse him of timidity. But, as usual in North America, any advance was utterly dependent on complicated logistics. There were not enough specialist men or transport rafts, 'bateaux', to supply both Amherst's push and Prideaux's drive to Niagara simultaneously. Amherst had prioritized Prideaux which meant that he had to use unwilling soldiers to bring up his army's supplies from Albany. This was unpopular and inefficient. Heavy rain in May had turned the roads to mud. The colonial battalions, all nine of them composed of part-time volunteers, were late to the rendezvous. They were delayed by the roads and their refusal to leave their farms before planting their crops. In London Pitt had seen the presence of the colonials as a vital part of his mission to galvanize all the King's subjects in a giant war for empire. A war fought not by professional soldiers alone but by 'the people' themselves. Pitt always regarded this somewhat nebulous grouping of 'people' as his constituency and his power base. Amherst had been deliberately ordered to delay the start of his campaigning until these decidedly second-rate infantrymen arrived.

Lake Champlain had presented him with yet another challenge. Somewhat incongruously given that he was 150 miles inland from the Atlantic seaboard, Amherst was faced with a naval threat. The French had four small ships mounting, in all, thirty-two cannon on the lake. They were able to smash his flimsy bateaux to match wood, so before any advance could be made up the lake ships had to be built to wrest control of its waters from the French. He simply had to wait until the shipwrights could build and launch a brigantine, a sloop, and a floating gun platform.

Above all, Amherst was convinced that his priority was to avoid defeat and make any gains sustainable. Braddock and Abercrombie had both been routed and in both cases panic had proved as destructive as enemy musket balls. Their armies had fled back to their starting points having abandoned equipment and supplies, leaving no other option but to go into winter quarters. Amherst made sure that every stage of the modest advance was consolidated. Powerful forts were built in the wake of his army. It was better slowly to strangle Canada over two or three campaigns than try to rush through the nearly impenetrable country in search of a blitzkrieg victory only to be ambushed and sent reeling all the way back to the southern end of Lake George. Bourlamaque's position was a strong one. A French officer reported in his journal that 'M Bourlamaque assured that the advantageous post he had taken at Île aux Noix, the entrenchments he had had thrown up and the formidable artillery he had mounted there, placed him in a position not to fear the enemy, however numerous they might present themselves.' As well as artillery it had formidable natural defences: 'both banks of the river presented only deep swamps covered with timber, a passage across which could not be effected except with extreme difficulty'.[29] Above all Amherst had no idea of Wolfe's progress. With Canada's efficient internal waterways, Montcalm's army could move from Quebec to Lake Champlain in a few days. Amherst did not want to find himself facing the entire army of Canada if Wolfe had been forced to break off the siege.

Amherst's slow advance was understandable; failing to provide Wolfe with any constructive information, less so. His dispatch provided the latter with nothing of use. Wolfe had to continue as before, assuming that he and he alone would have to defeat Montcalm using only the resources he had available. It was a powerful reminder of the limitations of combined attacks in early modern warfare. A neat plan in Whitehall was proving wildly unrealistic in Canada. Wolfe immediately asked Hutchins to return to Amherst and the ensign gamely agreed. He left on 7 September but within days the information he carried was so out of date it was worthless.

Amherst's news was frustrating for Wolfe but was devastating for Townshend. One of the few items of solid information from Amherst was news of the death of Townshend's 28-year-old younger brother Roger. The keen young Adjutant General had gone forward on a reconnoitre during the brief siege of Fort Carillon. He and his companions had been fired on, but had escaped. Realizing he had dropped his telescope he crept back but was 'shot from the fort with a cannon ball through the body and lived about a minute'.[30] The young man was killed as he was on the threshold of professional fulfilment. He had seen his career blighted by his older brother George's feud with the Duke of Cumberland and he had been thrilled at the latter's fall and an offer to serve in the prestigious role of Adjutant General under the commander in chief in North America. In one of his last letters Roger wrote to George Townshend's wife, Lady Ferrers, he is ebullient; his only 'real concern' is 'not being employed on the same expedition' as his older brother. He signed off saying that 'believe me nobody can have a more real regard, affection and friendship for you and your family than your affectionate brother and real friend'.[31]

George Townshend was crushed. His brother's death unleashed a reservoir of vitriol in his letters home about Wolfe's generalship and the brutal campaign of terror against the Canadian people. He even questioned his decision to rejoin the army. 'The melancholy news I received the day before yesterday,' he wrote to his wife, 'upon my arrival here from the cursed camp of Montmorency of my poor brother's death has reproved me for not consulting my own nature more, when I asked you to [let me] return to the army.' He felt guilty for putting his wife through the agony of awaiting his safe return and also worried that his mother, 'now starts at every knock at the door'.[32]

A month later his letters are still dominated by his 'poor brother's death'. 'Accursed be this American tomb,' he wrote to his wife, 'so fatal to all those who have too much honour to refuse the service of their country in all climates.' He did not try to 'describe how much I feel poor Roger's loss' and considered these 'sufferings are meritorious and glorious, but too severe'. 'One can never,' he concluded, 'be so devoted to ones country but anxiety and death, envy and defamation may attend one.'[33]

Roger Townshend was buried in Albany. In the south aisle of the knave of Westminster Abbey in London is a fine monument to him, supported by a pair of life-size Native Americans, correct down to the scalps hanging at their waists. Nearby, just inside the main or 'Great' west door is a memorial to another promising, young aristocratic officer, George Augustus, Viscount Howe, the pioneering officer whose death the year before had so upset Abercrombie's campaign. Both these scions of illustrious families had been killed in operations against Fort Carillon. Both men had siblings now serving under Wolfe and both families would have a greater impact on Anglo–American relations than any others in history.

As George Townshend grieved for his brother the army continued to redeploy. On 5 and 6 September two waves of troops marched from Point Lévis over six miles along the south coast of the St Lawrence where they were met by the flat-bottomed boats that ferried them aboard the transports above the town.

There was little way to keep these movements hidden. Every French journal comments on the move, most of them with some trepidation. One French officer commented that 'this movement put it out of doubt, that the enemy had some design upon the north shore'.[34] Panet relates how the British 'made different marches in the south which have worried us'. He also reports a steady drip of casualties caused by the

British gunfire from Point Lévis.[35] It was disappointing for some in the French camp who had seen, in the abandonment of Montmorency, a precursor to the total evacuation of the St Lawrence. Montcalm always believed that Wolfe would not abandon the siege without another attack. 'It would be strange,' says his journal, 'if Mr. Wolfe would limit himself to the fires and ravages, and only one attempt, which cost him 400 grenadiers on the 31 July which bore no fruit. This man must finish with a great effort, and great thunder.'[36] He became increasingly nervous about the British change of posture. He wrote to Bougainville saying, 'I always worry that the English will seize a position somewhere to cut our communication. Be on your guard at Jacques Cartier and Deschambault.'[37]

One French journal agreed with Montcalm that the withdrawal from Montmorency was 'not calculated to indicate a retreat, but their seeking elsewhere for a place where they could make good a landing – or possibly, might be a snare in the hope of enticing us to abandon our position at Beauport, where we appeared to them invincible'. It describes the increased watchfulness above the town, 'detachments were sent from the camp at Beauport to Pointe aux Trembles – small posts were placed in all the most advantageous places from Quebec to where the English fleet was anchored, or could get up the river'. Above all there was Bougainville's force, 'formed to follow all the movements of the ships ... to move up or down the river, as did the English, and to be at hand to repulse them in case of their attempting a descent'.[38] Montcalm reinforced Bougainville as much as he dared. All five companies of grenadiers from his French army regiments were sent plus, according to Bougainville's journal, 'three light companies of our regulars, and a few militia light companies, which gave me a corps of fifteen hundred men, in addition to the various posts I had placed along the shore'.[39] All the Native Americans were likewise sent above the town. This force was around three thousand men in all and was, in the words of one French officer, 'the elite of the army'.[40] Bougainville based himself at Cap Rouge, which struck one French officer as being the place 'of the most consequence at this juncture'. This source believed that 'the north shore is nowhere accessible, especially for an army, but at Cap Rouge, Sillery, St Michel and Le Foulon, where a convenient road was made, wide enough even for carriages'.[41] These were the points at which the almost unbroken line of cliffs was penetrated by gullies which allowed access to the heights above from the river. Bougainville posted small detachments in these positions with orders to break up the roads and fortify them as best they could. Montcalm warned Bougainville that 'the continually embarrassing movements of the enemy may affect the communications, and tend to disperse our forces'; he was to 'watch sharply' and 'always keep ahead of the bateaux and barges with your flying camp'. He had sent him all the troops he could spare; from now on, 'Good luck is all I have to wish you.'[42]

The one huge, and presumably unintended, advantage of Wolfe's utter irresolution throughout the summer had been totally to befuddle the French commanders. Given that Wolfe had no idea where he was going to strike his decisive blow, it was too much to expect the French to work it out either. They were simply bewildered by ships moving constantly, hundreds of boats plying to and fro, feints, reconnoitres, and raids too numerous to mention. The letters of the French commanders are dominated by reports of interrogations of both prisoners and deserters. The British mood, intentions, numbers, and health are all the subject of detailed conjecture. Montcalm's journal illustrates his frustration. It states that 'three deserters' arrived in camp at the end of August. They 'tell stories and contradict themselves in what they are saying to the extent of not being able to conclude anything'.[43] Vaudreuil wrote to de Lévis on 4 September saying simply that 'it is very difficult to discern their plans'.[44] He was mainly focused on making sure his army had enough to eat until the middle of October. Ramezay neatly illustrates the French frustration: 'we saw their Barges sometimes full and sometimes empty. They moved continuously back and forth from shore to shore, in order to tire and confuse the troops observing them.'[45] It was near impossible to make a prediction based on 'observable intelligence' and 'human intelligence' was a worthless avalanche of gossip and hearsay. Besides not even Wolfe knew where exactly the blow was going to fall.

Montcalm seems to have remained convinced, rightly, that Wolfe was attached to the idea of a landing at Beauport; he wrote to

Bougainville saying that although he could see 'the large movement' of troops marching west from Point Lévis, 'M. Wolfe is just the man to double back under cover of darkness.'[46] Montcalm could not have guessed that Wolfe had capitulated to his brigadiers. He was certain that the Beauport shore would be the eventual battlefield and he himself remained stationed there. Wolfe's 'Family Journal' asked rhetorically 'why Mr Montcalm on our going above the town did not move more troops upwards'. The anonymous author of the journal assumed that 'he was of the opinion that he was inaccessible on that side by the precautions he had taken'. It was also true that the mobility that the navy offered meant that 'our being in the upper river did not make an attempt near Beauport less practicable, as the tide would set us there in an hour's time'. The British could still embark miles beyond Quebec and drift downriver to attack below the town. As a result says the mysterious diarist, Montcalm 'resolved not to diminish his force here as the tenderest part of his line'.[47] A French journal agrees: Montcalm was, apparently, 'invariably of the opinion that the position at Beauport was the essential point to maintain possession of, and the only one by which the enemy could hope to succeed in the conquest of the town of Quebec'.[48] Saunders made sure that Montcalm had plenty of evidence to maintain him in his conviction that the attack would come below the town. He regularly anchored '3 or 4 casks … to serve as buoys' off the shore as if to provide navigational markers for amphibious assault ships.[49] French boats would row out and remove them every time they appeared.

Like many of the French officers Vaudreuil regarded the upriver zone as inappropriate for a landing. They 'would not succeed', he wrote, taking rather more credit than he deserved, 'because, given the measures I've put into place, our retrenchments are well guarded, and, if they want to land above Quebec, they'll learn their lesson'.[50] Montcalm was cutting about this bluster. He told Bougainville that 'M. de Vaudreuil is more nervous than I am about the right' or upriver front.[51] Ramezay certainly claimed, after the event, to have been concerned. He said that he had 'given advice' to Montcalm on 6 September because Montcalm 'persists in acting with the sure assumption that the enemies cannot attack from anywhere except Beauport, and does not want to move any troops to this side of the city'.[52] It is impossible to know whether he actually raised his concerns during the fateful days of early September. In fact, Montcalm did move troops upriver to reinforce Bougainville. One French officer wrote in his journal that 'troops were drawn off from the left wing which was now no longer in danger of any attack'.[53] Another officer wrote that Montcalm 'stripped his left somewhat and removed the principal part of his forces to the right of his camp'. He moved one of his crack French regular army battalions, the Guyenne, to 'the heights of Quebec, whence it could repair, in case of need, equally to either Sillery or into the town, or towards the River St Charles'.[54] This regiment would act as a mobile reserve, throwing itself instantly at whichever point the British might make their landing.

The full potency of British naval supremacy was now brutally apparent. The river was not a barrier, it was a highway. Wolfe could strike at any point within a dozen miles. Exhausted French troops could only peer out at the ships, or listen on dark nights for the splash of oars and attempt to follow them and stop the landing of men. The situation was unbearably tense. A French journal described it as 'very critical' and realized that if the British could cut off 'the communication between Quebec and the upper country, we must resign ourselves to lose the fruits of three months' campaign, during which the enemy, notwithstanding his very large land and naval force, had not succeeded in gaining any material advantage'. Supplies in the city were running low. The daily ration was three-quarters of a pound of bread, 'with a very small portion of brandy'. There were sufficient provisions to last until near the end of September. The 1759 harvest of corn 'was ripening all over the country' and in 'those places where it was out of the reach of the English' it was 'the only resource that could save the colony'.[55] Montcalm noted in his journal that 'the people and the troops eat horse meat and every day we live with the threat of dying from hunger ... one must be a witness to such events to believe them'.[56] Another journal, rich in detail, comes to an end in early September. Its final words reflect the stress of the French position, waiting for an inevitable blow to fall but ignorant as to its place or timing: 'we do not know what they are looking for. It is to be wished for the good of everybody that they would make their landing as soon as possible. (They have only to come.)' The author confidently asserts that, 'I believe they would remember it a long time, from the forces which are preparing to give them a chance to land and then to be at them vigorously.'[57]

For two days British troops left the camp at Point Lévis and trudged west towards their rendezvous with the fleet of ships above Quebec. A sergeant major in the Louisbourg Grenadiers noted that he and his comrades were allowed 'to take only one shirt and one pair of stockings, besides what we had on'. He calculated that there were 3,349 men who embarked on the ships and as a result it was 'very much crowded on board the men of war and transports'.[58] Young Malcolm Fraser reported that 'we are much crowded: the ship I am in has about 600 on board, being only about two hundred and fifty tons'.[59] Knox counted his 43rd Regiment as 'particularly lucky' as they were 'put on board the *Seahorse* frigate where Captain Smith and his officers entertained us in a most princely manner, and very obligingly made it their principal care to render our crowded situation as agreeable as possible'.[60]

Bringing up the rear was Wolfe. He had not yet entirely shaken off his illness. Knox reported on 5 September that 'General Wolfe was much indisposed last night; he is better today, but the whole army are, nevertheless, very apprehensive lest his ill state of health should not permit him to command this grand enterprise in person.'[61] On the evening of 6 September, accompanied by a detachment of Highlanders, Wolfe made his way upriver and boarded Holmes' fleet. As he marched along the bank he would have witnessed a bizarre bit of bravado by a British schooner. The aptly named *Terror of France*, which, Knox reports, was 'of a most diminutive size', boldly passed the town in broad daylight, while tacking upwind. He goes on to say that 'the officers and gunners at the enemy's batteries were provoked at this small vessel's presumption in open daylight, which they ... looked upon as a contemptuous affront upon their formidable batteries'. They 'foolishly expended a number of shot at her, but she nevertheless got safe up, with her colours flying'.[62] Another eyewitness records that 'she received five of their shot; one in her jib, two in her mainsail and two in her foresail; but lost none of her hands, nor did she sustain any further damage'.[63] Panet wrote that 'we imagined it was a wager' because she was so small and seemed to be mainly crewed by officers. The French batteries fired 'around 100 cannon' which 'only pierced their sails'.[64] As she joined the fleet in the upper river she anchored and 'triumphantly saluted Admiral Holmes with a discharge' from all her little deck-mounted guns. Knox also reports that during the excitement a lucky British cannonball from Point Lévis knocked over a French cannon and careered into a rack of loaded muskets which fell over and discharged, killing two French officers and seven men and wounding four others.[65] By the evening of 6 September the men were embarked, Wolfe was well enough to join them, and the *Terror of France* had provided a morale-boosting display. One officer reported that 'the army is in great spirits'.[66]

Wolfe issued a general order to put fight into his men. He told them that he was 'too well acquainted with the valour and good inclination of the troop to doubt their behaviour'. However, he emphasized the need for 'vigilance' and for the men not to disperse 'and wander about the country' as soon as they landed. Nor were they to forget that the enemy were 'irregular, cowardly and cruel'. He finished with the warning that a landing was now days, if not hours, away.[67] Wolfe and his brigadiers met and drew up an order of battle. Ideally they would land and deploy as a front line and a reserve. Townshend would command the latter. If, however, they were forced to fight on an extended front all the regiments would line up abreast but keep a quarter of their strength in reserve behind each of them. Every battalion was assigned a carefully calculated number of flat-bottomed boats.

The following day the flotilla moved upriver. They worked their way up to Cap Rouge. Townshend thought it was a 'very good place for landing but the enemy had got at the mouth of the river that flanked the bay, 6 or 8 floating batteries and we saw great numbers of Canadians with some regulars come down and post themselves and immediately began to throw up a breastwork'.[68] Knox saw a 'spacious cove' with the 'lands all around us high and commanding'. The bay swarmed with floating batteries and 'a large body of the enemy are well entrenched' on the shore. The French forces 'appear very numerous'.

He spotted Montcalm's cavalry for the first time, 'clothed in blue, and mounted on neat light horses of different colours'. As soon as the British fleet had dropped anchor 'their whole detachment ran down the precipice with a ridiculous shout, and manned their works. I have often reflected upon the absurdity of this practice in the French.' Knox concluded that this kind of overt aggression 'must tend to defeat all regularity and good order among themselves, because their men are thereby confused and are rendered incapable of paying attention to their officers or their duty; – it is a false courage'. By contrast, he mused,

> how different, how nobly awful, and expressive of true valour is the custom of the British troops! They do not expend their ammunition at an immense distance; and, if they advance to engage, or stand to receive the charge, they are steady, profoundly silent and attentive, reserving their fire until they have received that of their adversaries, over whom they have a tenfold advantage.[69]

At two in the afternoon some of the warships pushed into the bay and tried to engage the floating batteries. Townshend reports that 'the tide was too far spent before they got up their anchor and could get in'.[70] There was some firing, though, as the *Squirrel*'s log reports that 'five floating batteries engaged us'. 'One of the enemy's shot went through our main mast' and parts of her rigging were shot away.[71] The infantry were sent into the flat-bottomed boats, which were rowed 'up and down, as if intending to land at different places, to amuse the enemy' according to Knox. He assumed that this was a feint, 'calculated to fix the attention of the enemy on that particular part while a descent is meditated elsewhere, perhaps lower down'.[72]

It is unclear whether or not the Cap Rouge demonstration was intended as a feint. Either way it was very clear that the French had the firepower and the defences to make any attack extremely costly. Later that afternoon, perhaps as a consequence of what he had witnessed, Wolfe went on a reconnoitre along the north coast. His 'Family Journal' suggests that he examined the coast 'at less than 200 yards distance all the way up to [Point aux Trembles] and there fixed on a place for the descent, and gave orders in consequence'.[73]

On the following day, 8 September, the weather collapsed. The rain poured. In the French camp nervousness about the moves Saunders was making off the Beauport shore meant that despite the awful weather troops were kept up all night in their positions rather than seeking shelter in tents and billets. On board the packed British men of war and transports the soldiers stoically endured the onset of a dampness that would last for days. The inclement weather brought with it some easterly winds which meant yet more transports and supply vessels swept past the batteries of the town that since the foundation of Quebec had been relied upon to seal off the interior of the continent. Ships were now passing at will; the batteries on shore had been seriously damaged by fire from ships and the British batteries on Point Lévis. One French journal reports that this further reinforcement brought the fleet above Quebec to around twenty ships, 'which created exceeding great anxiety, and the more, because no conjecture could be formed of what were their designs – whether they meant to ravage the country, or cut off the communication'. Either way, in the hopeful opinion of the author, 'they seemed to have renounced the hope of carrying the place'.[74]

Townshend wrote in his journal that 'it continued to rain all this day. The troops ordered to land tomorrow morning at 4 O'clock.'[75] Mackellar reported in his account of the campaign that Wolfe had chosen 'a place a little below Point aux Trembles for making a descent'.[76] Meanwhile the 2nd/60th Royal Americans and the light infantry would go to Pointe aux Trembles itself and pretend to land there. In the event neither the feint nor the real attack went ahead. The weather was still bad during the early morning of 9 September. The troops had made the now familiar climb down into the flat-bottomed boats at 0300 hours. They sat tightly packed together in the rain as the boats wallowed in the fast moving St Lawrence. They were in total ignorance of where and when the attack was to be made or even if the operation would go ahead at all. On board the *Adventure* transport, designated the hospital ship and told to raise her colours at her foretopmast head so that she was readily identifiable, surgeons prepared for the influx of casualties.

Wolfe and his senior commanders peered at the sky through dripping rigging at first light and made the decision to call off the attack.

At 0600 hours the men, with drenched clothes clinging to them, clambered back on board their transports.[77] Knox described the 'extreme wetness'.[78] Wolfe was now worried that the packed, soaking transports would prove a cradle for disease and he ordered around half of the men ashore to dry out and stretch their legs. They would leave their baggage aboard the ships and take only their blankets, kettles, and two days' provisions. The signal for getting them back on board ship, Knox reports, was 'two guns fired fast, and two slow, from the *Sutherland*; the signal by night will be three lights at the main-top-gallant mast head of the same ship and two guns'. Knox also reports that two officers from the 43rd were ill on board ship and when Wolfe found out, he offered the use of his own barge to take them to the camp at de Lévis where they could recuperate. The officers gallantly declined, 'assuring the general that no consideration could induce them to leave the army, until they should see the event of this expedition'.[79]

By the end of the day the wind had shifted, the weather was clear and Wolfe's fatalism had disappeared with the bad weather. He was again the aggressive, cocksure young commander. That day he had boarded a schooner and, as his 'Family Journal' says, 'reconnoitred close by the shore from Carrouge [Cap Rouge] down to the town of Quebec'. During his absence this fiercely loyal account of the campaign remarks that 'Mr Murray and Townshend came aboard the admiral and behaved very seditiously in respect of Mr Wolfe.'[80] Sadly the author does not enlarge on their activities. What is certain is that Wolfe returned from his exploring having had an epiphany. He was now very clear about where he wanted to land his army. Mackellar reported in his journal that he 'found another place more to his mind, and thereupon laid aside all further thoughts of that at Point aux Trembles'.[81]

Mackellar wrote in his journal that 'the place that the General fixed upon for the descent is called Foulon'.[82] The Anse au Foulon was, in fact, the cove Wolfe had mentioned to the engineering officer, Samuel Holland, back in July after his first reconnoitre upriver as a possible site for landing his army in the final resort. That eventuality having arrived, Wolfe took a closer look and decided it would indeed serve his purpose. Over the centuries myths, stories, and folklore have attached themselves to Wolfe's decision to attempt a landing at Foulon. Tourists are told that a careless laundry woman wandered down to wash clothes in the river and Wolfe caught sight of her and realized that this was a usable route up the cliffs that lined the St Lawrence. Other stories have, without any foundation, ascribed the decision to French agents who, for various corrupt reasons, wished their colony to fall to the British. These fanciful tales involve a web of conspirators, deserters, and even a beguiling lady who lured key French commanders into her bed at vital moments. Perhaps one day a smoking gun will be found to support such exciting theories but in the meantime it should be stated that Foulon was a rather obvious choice, a place Wolfe himself had contemplated throughout the summer and regularly mentioned in French sources as one of the few routes by which an army landing above Quebec could gain the high ground. There was an obvious break in the steep escarpment, where a road led down to the beach. At the top a force of at least a hundred men, encamped in highly visible tents, guarded it and had built an abatis across the road. This tangle of tree trunks with sharpened branches, if resolutely defended, was a serious and visible obstacle. This was no secret route nor was it given away by the much maligned, but thankfully anonymous, washerwoman. Another advantage to Foulon was that after the troops on the ships had been landed, the flat-bottomed boats could row across to the south shore where the rest of Wolfe's army would be waiting. Two battalions had stayed behind to guard the camps on Point Lévis and the Île d'Orléans and there were other troops for whom there was no space on Holmes' ships. Around a thousand men therefore would march two miles from the Point Lévis camp along the beach at low tide and wait to be ferried across. Added to Wolfe's force on the ships this would bring the total number of troops to something like four thousand five hundred. Foulon allowed Wolfe to maximize his chances of getting every single one of his infantrymen into the action.

Wolfe's restless energy returned. The following day he dragged all the key officers along the river to see his new suggested landing place. They were accompanied by an escort from Knox's own regiment, the 43rd. Mackellar reports that 'the General took with him Admiral Holmes, Brigadier Generals Monckton and Townshend, with some other officers, to reconnoitre the place he had fixed upon'. Among the other officers, as well as Mackellar were Colonel Howe, commander of the light infantry, and Captain Chads of the *Vesuvius*, who was the naval officer given the job of coordinating all the landing craft. They landed on the south side of the river at a place they had named Gorham's Post just below where the Etchemin River flowed into the St Lawrence. The group stood on a rise and stared across at the north bank. It was, and still is, an imposing sight. The shoreline is 'steep and woody'; in certain parts the topsoil has been unable to cling to the almost sheer slopes and patches of bare rock break up the otherwise uniform spread of trees. A mile and a half downriver from Foulon the smoking ruins of the Lower Town were just visible on the headland. Mackellar records that at Foulon itself the route up to the heights 'was thought so impracticable by the French themselves that they had only a single picket to defend it'. They guessed it was about a hundred men strong and they were camped 'near the top of a narrow winding path, which runs up from the shore'. Mackellar agreed with his commander's choice, 'the circumstances in conjunction with the distance of the place from succours seemed to promise a fair chance of success'.[83]

Holmes was less impressed. Later he wrote a letter saying that this 'alteration of the plan of operations was not I believe approved of by many, beside [Wolfe]'. Foulon was 'a very strong ground' with a steep slope, supplemented by a guard and an abatis. Wolfe 'thought that a sudden brisk attack, a little before day break', would overcome these difficulties and take his army up onto the plain above. Holmes was surprised that such a plan had been rejected in July when the area was undefended, only to be resurrected now when the French were waiting and considered it as 'highly improbable he should succeed'. Holmes believed it to be an act of desperation, he understood that 'the season was far spent, and it was necessary to strike some stroke'.[84]

The cabal of senior officers all peering at the opposite shore through telescopes was a very obvious signal to an observer that something important was brewing in that sector. Wolfe had thought of this and tried to disguise the group in 'grenadier's coats' borrowed from the 43rd Regiment. His dissimulation was not entirely successful. Rémigny, an efficient French officer at Sillery, spotted the British officers. He reported to Bougainville that 'yesterday at three in the afternoon three barges landed on the shore'. The sharp-eyed Rémigny spotted that one of the men was wearing a uniform 'under a blue overcoat [which] was heavily decorated'. It could well have been Townshend wearing his militia uniform of which he was so proud. Rémigny reported that the men waited until the flood tide when they embarked and headed back up the river.[85] This information was either lost or ignored. It was yet more activity to be added to the bewildering intelligence picture that the French were struggling to piece together. No extra units were sent to Foulon or Sillery. Instead, Bougainville's men continued to shadow Wolfe's fleet as it moved with the tide. They had no choice but to wait.

The same day as his reconnoitre, Wolfe wrote to his confidant and friend Lieutenant Colonel Burton, who was in command at the Lévis camp. He described how he had been forced to land many of his troops to relieve pressure on his crowded ships, saying that his army 'must have perished if they had continued forty eight hours longer on board'. He then laid out the plan. The fleet would sail upriver 'as if intending to land above upon the north shore' but all the while 'keeping a convenient distance for the boats and armed vessels to fall down to the Foulon'. He urged Burton to be 'careful not to drop it [the plan] to any, for fear of desertion'. He also mused on the state of the enemy force. French deserters were telling him that bread was being made from this year's wheat, which meant that 'scarcity in the colony' was 'excessive'. 'Their army,' Wolfe believed, 'is kept together by the violent strong hand of the government and by the terror of savages, joined to a situation which makes it difficult to evade. The Canadians have neither affection for their government, nor no tie so strong as their wives and children; they are a disjointed, discontented, dispirited peasantry, beat into cowardice' by their leaders. Returning to the subject of the landings Wolfe hoped that they 'may produce an action, which may produce the total conquest of Canada; in all cases it is our duty to try the most likely way, whatever may be the event'.[86]

Wolfe began drawing up the detailed plans. He fixed on dawn of 13 September for the attack. On 11 September the troops on the south shore, drying off and resting, were told to stand by to re-embark. They were to 'hold themselves in readiness to land and attack the enemy'.[87] Obviously, no more information was given to the men. They would have no idea where the attack was to be launched until they were delivered there in flat-bottomed boats. Rather more unorthodox was Wolfe's refusal to take even his brigadiers into his full confidence, despite outlining his thinking to Burton. On 12 September only hours before the start of the operation Monckton, Townshend, and Murray wrote a letter to their commander. In it these 'obedient, humble servants' told Wolfe that 'we do not think ourselves sufficiently informed of the several parts which may fall to our share in the execution of the descent you intend tomorrow'. They begged him to issue 'as distinct orders as the nature of the thing will admit of, particularly to the place or places we are to attack'. They would be 'very sorry no less for the public, than our own sakes, to commit any mistakes'. The scale of the breakdown in their relationship with their commander is illustrated by the fact that they are forced to assure him that 'we are persuaded you will see the necessity of this application which can proceed from nothing but a desire to execute your orders with the utmost punctuality'.[88]

Wolfe's reply was curt and addressed only to Monckton. 'My reason for desiring the honour of your company with me to Gorham's Post yesterday,' he wrote, 'was to show you, as well as the distance would permit, the situation of the enemy, and the place where I meant they should be attacked.' 'The place is called Foulon,' he continued, 'distant upon 2 miles or 2½ from Quebec, where you remember an encampment of 12 or 13 tents and an abatis below it.' He then quickly sketched out the plan: 'I have desired Mr Holmes to send the boats down, so that we may arrive about half an hour before day, as you desired to avoid the disorder of a night attack.' Wolfe did not let the imminence of the decisive clash of his entire career stop him from having a dig at his subordinates. 'It is not a usual thing to point out in the public orders the direct spot of our attack, nor for any inferior officers not charged with a particular duty to ask instructions upon that point.' The letter came to a haughty end:

I had the honour to inform you today that is my duty to attack the French army. To the best of my knowledge and abilities I have fixed upon that spot where we can act with the most force, and are most likely to succeed. If I am mistaken, I am sorry for it, and must be answerable to His Majesty and the public for the consequence.[89]

Townshend got the briefest of notes from his commander: 'General Monckton is charged with the first landing and attack at the Foulon, if he succeeds you will be pleased to give directions that the troops afloat be set on shore with the utmost expedition.' Wolfe finished by saying that, 'I have no manner of doubt but that we are able to fight and to beat the French army, in which I know you will give your best assistance.'[90] Murray, the junior brigadier and, in the opinion of Wolfe's 'Family Journal', senior troublemaker, was not sent a letter at all. Both letters end with the formal, 'I have the honour to be, Sir, etc, James Wolfe.' His note to Burton ended with the altogether more intimate, 'Yours affectionately.'

The indiscreet 'Family Journal' sheds more light on these strained relations. It recounts that 'orders were given to prepare for landing and attacking the enemy, when Mr Wolfe received a letter signed by each of the brigadiers, setting forth that they did not know where they were to land and attack the enemy'. On the morning of 12 September Monckton arrived on the *Sutherland* for a meeting with Wolfe, after which the commander told his close staff that 'the brigadiers had brought him up the river and now flinched. He did not hesitate to say that two of them were cowards and one a villain.'[91]

Wolfe had to deal with yet another concerned subordinate in these last few hours before the attack began. The 'Regulating Captain' of the boats, the man responsible for the coordination of the large flotilla of little vessels, Captain Chads, suddenly appeared in his cabin with serious reservations. He was worried that 'the heat of the tide would hurry the boats beyond the object'. Wolfe's 'Family Journal', with its entrenched hostility to all sailors, called Chads' objections 'frivolous'. Wolfe and his staff assumed 'someone had tampered with him'. Wolfe assured Chads that 'he should have made his objection earlier, that should the disembarkation miscarry, that he would shelter him from any blame, that all that could be done was to do his utmost'. Chads was still nervous. Wolfe's patience frayed and he told him that he 'would write any thing to testify that the miscarriage was General

Wolfe's and not Captain Chads' and that he would sign it'. None of this seemed to convince the naval officer: 'Chads persisted in his absurdity; the general told him he could do no more than lay his head to the block to save Chad and left the cabin.' Such was Wolfe's paranoia that he now saw a conspiracy lurking in the perfectly reasonable concerns of a naval officer. Events were to prove that Chads' worries were not as 'frivolous' or 'absurd' as Wolfe and his staff considered them.[92]

As throughout the campaign no mention of their generals' bickering appears in any account of it written by the officers and men who served under them. In blissful ignorance, the troops started to re-embark on the morning of 12 September. It immediately became clear that they would be involved in a last throw to seize victory after a long summer of disappointment. Knox reports in his journal that 'great preparations are making throughout the fleet and army, to surprise the enemy, and compel them to decide the fate of Quebec by a battle'.[93]

A few people were a good deal less bullish than the enthusiastic Knox. One man reported that 'by this day's orders it appears the General intends a most vigorous attack, supposed behind the town, where to appearance a landing is impracticable'.[94] The men would have had plenty of time to look at the north shore, from the south side of the river and from their various trips up and down the river by boat and ship. They were obviously not hugely encouraged by what they had seen. John Johnson reported that 'it was verily believed at the time, that no man, except the General Officers, or the Superior Officers of the regiments, had the least intimation of the duty we were going upon; although everyone believed it to be some very hazardous undertaking'.[95]

It was all too much for one Royal American who deserted during the twelfth. This could have been catastrophic had the landing place been widely circulated through the army. But he absconded, as Townshend wrote in his journal, 'before orders were given out to the men'.[96] This was lucky for the British, although one also suspects that after a summer which had seen deserters bringing information of a multitude of definite attacks that failed to happen the French would be rather jaded in their receipt of another such message. Either way the deserter did not compromise the secrecy to the operation.

Wolfe's inability to communicate with his senior officers was not reflected in his dealings with the mass of men in his army. During the afternoon of 12 September he delivered a short, upbeat, and quietly inspiring general order. He started by outlining the strategic picture. He told them of the miserable condition of the enemy, how they were 'now divided' and suffering from a 'great scarcity of provisions in their camp and universal discontent among the Canadians'. He encouraged the belief that Amherst was on his way to help and told them that 'a vigorous blow struck by the army at this juncture may determine the fall of Canada'. Like all great pre-battle exhortations Wolfe moves from the strategic to the tactical. He assured the men that they had the troops, artillery, and support to do the job: 'Our troops below are in readiness to join us. All the Light Artillery and tools are embarked at the Point of Levy, and the troops will land where the French seem least to expect them.' Technical advice followed. The first wave, as soon as it landed, was to 'march directly to the enemy, and drive them from any little post they may occupy'. Officers should look out that their soldiers did not fire on other British units while the light was low and the tension high. When all the supplies were landed Wolfe would endeavour 'to bring the French and Canadians to a battle'. In this event 'the officers and men will remember what their country expects from them, and what a determined body of soldiers, inured to war are capable of doing against five very weak French battalions, mingled in with a disorderly peasantry'. His final advice to the soldiers was to be 'attentive to their officers and resolute in the execution of their duty'.[97]

The order inspired John Johnson. Hearing these 'tender and expressive terms' about 'the nature of the undertaking, as well as the dangers and difficulties attending it; as also what it was our country expected from us', Johnson was certain that it was 'sufficient to inspire the most frozen constitution with a thirst for glory, and with a fervent desire to be a partaker in the event'.[98]

Many of the men were no doubt less moved than Johnson, but the majority of the army were keen to strike a blow against the French.

These men had been in and out of flat-bottomed boats all summer for a series of attacks, feints, raids, and aborted missions. New flints were fitted to the firing mechanism of their muskets. The sharper the edge of the flint, the better the chance of creating the all-important spark that would ignite the gunpowder. There were plenty of tasks to keep nervous hands and minds off the prospect of battle. Malcolm Fraser wrote that 'we were busied in cleaning our arms and distributing ammunition to our men'.[99] Muskets were burnished until they shone. Men mixed brick dust with sweet oil and then polished any patches of corrosion that had appeared in the damp conditions. They took great pains not to drizzle any oil into the touch-hole, which had to remain free from any obstruction. Then they worked the barrel with a series of wet and dry rags. Eighteenth-century soldiers had such affection for buffing the barrel that they thinned the metal and often dangerously weakened it. Men adjusted the straps holding their cartridge boxes in position and cleaned their long bayonets. Everyone was given two days' worth of ammunition, food, and rum. This meant they were carrying about seventy rounds; each one consisted of a paper cartridge containing powder and a musket ball. Rum was poured into the men's canteens, which were then topped up with water. No blankets or tents were to be brought onto the packed flat-bottomed boats. They would follow later on the transports.

After nightfall Colonel Howe summoned all eight gentlemen volunteers in the light infantry. Fitz-Gerald, Robertson, Stewart, McAllester, Mackenzie, MacPherson, Cameron, and Bell duly reported to their commander. He told them, in the words of one witness, that 'the General intends that a few men may land before the light infantry and army, and scramble up the rock'. It was a dangerous mission but 'if any of us survived, [we] might depend on our being recommended to the General'. Promotion was the common reward for demonstrating suicidal bravery in situations like this. The volunteers replied that they 'were sensible of the honour he did, in making us the first offer of an affair of such importance as our landing first, where an opportunity occurred to distinguish ourselves, assuring him his agreeable order would be put in execution with the greatest activity, care and vigour in our power'. Each of them was to take two men 'of our own choice from the three companies of light infantry which in all made 24 men'.[100]

At last light the French sentries saw the British fleet heading west, away from Quebec. Wolfe's 'Family Journal' explains that 'the ships moved up the river ... to draw their enemy's attention upriver'.[101] Wolfe wanted Bougainville to believe that the target of any landing would be Cap Rouge or Pointe aux Trembles.

At 2100 hours, near high water, the British soldiers started the laborious process of getting into the boats. Just before sunset there had been a burst of activity below the town as Saunders launched every longboat he had and filled them with seamen, marines, and any spare troops that could be found from the two camps in the Quebec basin. During the day six buoys had been laid off Beauport as if an attack was imminent. Cook wrote in his log that there was a sharp skirmish as the French tried to cut the buoys away and the *Richmond* fought them off. Knox explained that the boatloads of troops below Quebec were to make 'a feint of Beauport ... and engross the attention of the Sieur de Montcalm, while the army are to force a descent on this side of the town'.[102] The French remained bewildered. Récher reports that these moves convinced Quebecers: 'everyone expects that they are coming for the town,' he wrote.[103] Montcalm admitted in his journal that 'buoys are worrying us'. He had spent the whole day on the twelfth closely inspecting his entrenchments at Beauport, which even he now considered 'invincible'.[104] Vaudreuil wrote a letter to Lévis on the twelfth containing details of all the confusing activity above and below Quebec with ships and boats moving seemingly at random. He concluded: 'I foresee in every way possible that General Wolfe will fail if he attempts to try us before he leaves.'[105]

Within hours of these words being written, Wolfe's light infantry were the first men of his army into the flat-bottomed boats, with Howe's volunteers in the leading one. Fifty men squeezed onto one boat and when it was full it pushed away from the ship's side and another took its place. After the light infantry, the regiments embarked in strict seniority. Four boats were required to load the 200 men of Kennedy's 43rd Regiment from the transport *Employment*. Once full, the flat-bottomed boats rowed into a designated holding pattern, alongside the *Sutherland* between her and the south shore. She was showing a single light in her maintopmast shrouds to identify herself. There were thirty flat-bottomed boats in all (plus the feisty *Terror of France* schooner, which was packed with fifty Highlanders) and a few ship's boats. These vessels carried the first wave of 1,700 men. Another 1,900 stayed on the frigates, sloops and transports, which would bring them downriver before the empty flat-bottomed boats returned to take in this second wave. Absolute silence was to be observed in the boats. The light infantrymen who had been first into the boats found the anticipation difficult to tolerate. One wrote in his journal that he was 'waiting impatiently for the signal of proceeding'.[106]

At about 0200 hours a second light was hoisted into the *Sutherland*'s shrouds. It was the signal the light infantrymen had been so eagerly looking for. The tide was now ebbing fast, taking the fleet back towards Quebec. The naval officer in command of each boat saw the signal, muttered an order to his expectant men, and hundreds of oars dug into the water. Felt was wrapped around the rowlocks to muffle the groan made by the wooden shaft, and river water was splashed as lubricant on squeaking crutch plates. It was a perfect night. One of the volunteers in the first boat noted: 'Fine weather, the night calm, and silence over all.'[107] Knox remembered that it was a 'star-light night' and that the men around him were 'in high spirits'.[108] Johnson, with his flair for hyperbolic jingoism, describes the force as 'a handful of men' who 'were all resolutely determined to a single man to Die or Conquer'.[109]

THIRTEEN

The Landings

THE BOATS SPED ALONG on an increasingly fast ebbing tide. They had 'three leagues' or about ten miles to cover.[1] One account relates that they travelled the whole distance 'without striking with the oars', such was 'the force of the tide'.[2] At least some rowing would have been required to hold the boats in their respective positions. None of them were allowed to overtake the light infantry who led the flotilla. Wolfe specifically ordered that 'no officer must attempt to make the least alteration or interfere with Captain Chads' particular province, lest as the boats move in the night there be confusion and disorder among them'.[3] The eight lead boats contained the fit, enterprising light infantrymen who would spearhead the attack. Behind them were six boats with Bragg's 28th Regiment then four boats with Kennedy's 43rd Regiment. More boats containing Highlanders, Royal Americans, and others followed them. The men who were not rowing tried to grab a few minutes of uncomfortable sleep while sitting bolt upright in tight rows. They knew it would be the last chance for some time. The moon was in its last quarter, shining in the eastern part of the sky so that just enough light was available to see the north bank of the St Lawrence from the boats. It also meant that any sentries on shore would be looking into it. Just over ten miles away downstream the thunder of the British batteries on Point Lévis was audible. All night they blazed away, keeping the French defenders awake, distracted, and scared.

Around two hours after the flat-bottomed boats moved down the river the larger ships weighed anchor and followed them. Rear

Admiral Holmes left the *Sutherland* to keep an eye on enemy forces further up the river and transferred onto the *Lowestoft* in which he led the *Squirrel* and *Seahorse* and several transports. Each ship was packed with infantrymen, having a considerably more comfortable trip down the river than their comrades in the first wave. At the back of the little fleet were the ordnance vessels carrying artillery-men, cannon, and all their equipment. As soon as the infantry secured the beachhead they would get ashore and try to protect it from French counter-attacks. Mackellar recorded that all the ships and boats moved 'as silently as they could' and it appeared that 'the whole [were] seemingly unobserved by the enemy'.[4]

The soldiers sat quietly and thought of the battle that was to come. The naval officers, though, were wrestling with the greatest challenge of the campaign so far. Holmes later wrote that it was 'the most hazardous and difficult task I was ever engaged in'. 'The distance of the landing place,' he continued, 'the darkness of the night; and the chance of exactly hitting the very spot intended, without discovery or alarm; made the whole extremely difficult.' If he failed in his task it 'might have overset the general's plan', which 'would have brought upon me an imputation of being the cause of the miscarriage of the attack, and all the misfor-tune that might happen to the troops in attempting it'.[5]

Wolfe was blissfully ignorant of the challenges the expedition posed to his naval colleagues. He sat in the stern of one of the boats. Legend has it that Wolfe recited a verse of his favourite poem, Thomas Gray's 'Elegy in a Country Churchyard'. The midshipman who reported this said that Wolfe finished and commented that 'he would prefer being the author of that poem to the glory of beating the French tomorrow'.[6] It is unlikely, although not impossible, that Wolfe would have broken his own, very strict order not to talk. There would have been some communication. Chads adjusted the pace of the boats and the various coxswains had to speak up to control their rowers. The commander of the entire operation would certainly have felt able to give his aides-de-camp last minute instructions or messages. Wolfe had been given a copy of Gray's poem by his new fiancée before leaving Britain. He had made notes in the book and had underlined the last line of this partic-ular verse:

The boast of heraldry, the pomp of power,
And all that beauty, all that wealth e'er gave,
Awaits alike th' inevitable hour:–
The paths of glory lead but to the grave.

This particular path of glory did almost lead to a watery grave. As they crept along the north shore they passed the *Hunter* sloop which had been patrolling further downriver. One journal suggests that the commander of the sloop had not been 'apprised of our coming down' and as a result suspected the boats 'to be an enemy'.[7] A tense stand-off developed as the British soldiers attempted to stop the *Hunter* firing on them with muffled shouts. In the end, however, this near disaster had a very fortuitous conclusion for the British. At 2300 hours that night, just a few hours before, the *Hunter*'s log tells how the sloop received visitors: 'Came on board in a canoe two deserters from the French.'[8] They brought with them some very useful intelligence. They told the British that 'the enemy expected some boats down the river that night with provisions'.[9] The *Hunter* passed on this intelligence once they had established that the shadowy boats were British. This allowed the light infantry to answer any challenges that came from eagle-eyed sentries on the north shore by pretending that they were the French convoy.

On 12 September the French had been trying to organize this flotilla which the two deserters had reported. The French authorities needed to resupply Quebec and although it was possible by road it was considerably easier, cheaper, and quicker to do so by boat. A French officer wrote that among the men stationed along the river, 'the rumour circulated through all the posts in front of which it was to pass, without agreeing among themselves on any rallying cry'. However, 'some unforeseen event having prevented our bateaux taking advantage of the night tide to sail, their departure was postponed to the following day, and no attention had yet been paid to warn those same posts of the fact'. As a result when the French sentries saw the barges coming down with the ebb they thought they were friendlies. As there was no prearranged signal of passwords, the British were able to shout a hopeful 'France' in the direction of the shore and were allowed to pass.

Thus he concluded 'fortune appeared in this emergency to combine with the little order which prevailed among our troops, so as to facilitate the approach of those barges'.[10]

There are many variations on this story of responding to the French sentries. Historians have tried to piece together exactly who said what to whom, but it is more likely that various French-speaking officers in the British boats shouted replies to challenges from different watchmen throughout that busy night. Townshend reports that as the first wave was 'passing down the north side of the river and the French sentries on the bank challenged our boats, Captain Fraser who had been in the Dutch service and spoke French, answered, "La France" and "vive le Roi" on which the French sentinels ran along the shore in the dark crying, "let them pass, these are the men with the provisions"'.[11] One of the light infantrymen in the first boat confirms that a Captain Fraser answered a sentry 'in the French tongue' and he cautioned 'the sentry to be silent, otherwise he would expose us to the fire of the English man of war'.[12] There were three Captain Frasers serving in the 78th Highland Regiment; one of them, Simon, had fought for the Dutch, like so many other Highlanders when the British state deemed them untrustworthy rebels and denied them opportunities. He had seen action and had been wounded at the siege of Bergen-op-Zoom. During the Seven Years War, when Britain reversed its policy and began recruiting clansmen, he immediately joined the Highland Regiment. He had been made a captain in April of 1759 and served in the light infantry under Howe during the siege. He later had a successful military career and ended up a brigadier. His luck, and Britain's, would run out at that moment of imperial nemesis at Saratoga during the American Revolution.[13] Knox tells a similar story about a Captain Donald MacDonald who tricked a French sentry as the British troops landed. There was a Captain MacDonnell in the Highlanders who had served in the Royal Ecossois, a French regular army regiment that had served under the Jacobite banner at Culloden in 1746. He seems to have made good use of his French to trick enemy sentries as the two sides floundered around in the murky dawn light.[14]

With a luck and timing that had been so obviously absent from previous British attacks Wolfe's boats arrived off Foulon almost exactly on schedule at about 0400 hours as a faint light crept into the sky. The journey had taken them around two hours; there was about an hour till the sun actually rose. Saunders reported to London that 'considering the darkness of the night and the rapidity of the current, this was a very critical operation; and very properly and successfully conducted'.[15] Yet again the navy had overcome massive difficulties to land the army where it wanted.

Anse au Foulon was protected by a small force commanded by Captain Louis Dupont de Chambon de Vergor. He was illiterate, ugly, and avaricious, and in no way suited to independent command. Nevertheless, thanks to the fortunes of the French service, and some advantageous connections, he appeared again and again in the events of the Seven Years War. The 46-year-old had served in North America since he was 17. In October 1750 he had been in command of a brigantine which was attacked by a British sloop commanded by John Rous, the same man who now commanded the *Sutherland*. Vergor fought the British ship despite his inferior armament and after a full day of battle only seven of his fifty men were still able to operate the guns. The masts and rigging had been shot away and his little vessel was sinking. He surrendered but won acclaim in France and became a Knight of the Order of Saint Louis shortly after.

In 1754 he was in command of Fort Beauséjour on the Chignecto Isthmus protecting Nouvelle Acadie from the British forces in Nova Scotia. On the outbreak of war Monckton easily captured Beauséjour after a very poor attempt at defence by Vergor. The latter was court-martialled in Quebec, and although he performed badly on the stand he was acquitted, almost certainly thanks to his useful connections. During the siege he had watched over Quebec's back door with his small body of troops and some years later, in search of a pension, he gave the French government his version of what happened on the night of 12/13 September 1759. He began by blaming the confusion about the supply convoy. His sentries were told that the boats 'were on their way to Quebec with provisions'. But as they reached the sentry posts, he said, they did not continue their journey downstream, instead they turned and, to Vergor's horror, he 'noticed that they were coming round and trying to enter the cove'. The French levelled their muskets and, according to his own account, 'did their utmost to prevent the enemy coming ashore'.[16] Wolfe's 'Family Journal' agrees that not a shot was fired until the boats 'drew in towards the Foulon'.[17] Above the beach, on the Heights, was a five-gun battery at Samos that now opened fire as well. As the first shots rang out from musket and cannon the covert phase of the operation had come to an end. Now everything depended on both sides reacting; getting as many men as possible towards the beachhead as quickly as they could. Vergor's force occupied a strong natural position. A primitive road ran along a stream that over millennia had drained water off from the Heights above and had carved a canyon into the face of the steep escarpment. When people had complained to Montcalm about the lack of troops at Foulon, and a very similar position upriver at the next cove of Sillery, he had replied that 'I swear to you that 100 men, well posted, could stop the whole army and give us time to wait for daylight and then march to our right to that sector.'[18]

As the sailors pulled for the shore it became clear that the powerful tides of the St Lawrence had one more trick to play on the British that summer. Townshend later explained to Pitt that 'the rapidity of the ebb hurried the boats a little below the intended place of attack'. The light infantry in the leading boats had gone too far. They were totally unperturbed, however, and began their 'scramble up a woody precipice in order to secure the landing of the troops'.[19] Howe turned this accident into an advantage because it would allow his men to reach the Heights and then attack the rear of the French troops blocking the winding road up from the beach. So confidently did he and his men launch up this treacherous climb that it is possible that Townshend was wrong and the landing further down was deliberate. Mackellar had noted on his reconnoitre of the Foulon that there 'appeared to be a slope in the bank' which was 'about 200 yards to the right' of the Foulon road.[20] It is possible that Wolfe always intended Howe to land there and send his volunteers to outflank the defenders.

The slope up which Howe's men most probably scrambled is extremely steep and free from trees. In places shrubs and fissures provide handholds while in others the climber is forced to cling on to bare rock, after clearing away a loose covering of dry topsoil or shale.

To the right and the left are sections of sheer cliff and beyond them heavily wooded slopes which, despite the handholds provided by tree trunks, are even harder to climb. The men slung their muskets on their backs but it was impossible to stop them sliding around to their sides and getting the butts entangled in their legs. Water bottles, cartridge boxes, and the swords of the Highlanders thumped against legs. Feet slipped out from under them as their totally inappropriate footwear failed to grip the loose rock and scree. One soldier described it in a letter home that was printed in a local newspaper. He wrote that he had 'mounted a hill one hundred yards high, being forced to creep on our hands and knees up it, and hold by the bushes that grew on it'.[21]

Saunders later wrote that 'the difficulty of gaining the top of the hill is scarce credible, it was very steep in its ascent, and high, had no path where two could go abreast but they were obliged to pull themselves up by the stumps and boughs of trees that covered the declivity'.[22] High praise came from an enemy officer who wrote that they climbed up the 'immensely steep' slope with 'great difficulty and danger'.[23] The popping of muskets and the occasional thud of a cannon told them that the battle for Foulon had begun. Unless the light infantrymen could reach the top and drive the French guards off the road Wolfe's assault force might be penned in on the beach.

Those troops coming ashore in the cove itself a little further upstream were exposed to French fire and were taking casualties. Knox wrote that the French resistance was certainly not as effective as it could have been because surprise was almost total. The landing was a shock to the enemy, 'who from the natural strength of the place, did not suspect, and consequently were not prepared against so bold an attempt'. Even so the musket fire 'galled us a little, and picked off several men and some officers'. In a footnote he wrote that 'in the boat where I was, one man was killed; one seaman, with four soldiers, were slightly and two mortally wounded'.[24]

The situation was precarious. Groups of men fired at each other in the semi-darkness. The terrain was utterly unsuitable for traditional infantry tactics. If the French could maintain control of the narrow track up from the beach then it was possible they could delay the landings until reinforcements arrived and they could drive the British back into the river. Everything depended on Howe's men struggling up the loose rock of the near precipice. With an effort that was to become one of the most celebrated military achievements in British imperial history, his men made the summit. An eyewitness reported that 'the light infantry commanded by Lieutenant Colonel Howe … sustaining themselves by the stumps and branches of trees – bushes – roots and vines ascended – dislodged the guard and formed up on the height'. [25]

'On their gaining the summit,' wrote another witness, 'the signal was a loud huzza.' With a roar they burst into the midst of the French defences. The British light infantrymen ran through the camp in which half-awake Canadian militiamen were still looking for their weapons. It was the worst possible situation for the defenders. There was no chance at all of organizing any kind of effective response. Howe's men stormed down the road towards the abatis. Defenders were utterly shocked to find British troops behind them and scattered. One of Howe's volunteers wrote that 'after we got up we only received one fire, which we returned briskly, and took a prisoner, the remaining part of the enemy flying into a field of corn'. [26] The road to the Heights was open. Down on the beach, the British witness who had heard the huzzaing wrote that these cheers were 'joyfully answered'. [27] Knox relates the skirmishing came to an end when 'our light infantry got up to dislodge them'. [28]

Vergor, the French commander, later exaggerated the intensity of his defence. He wrote that the enemy was 'held back until daylight arrived' and only then were his men 'finally overpowered'. He reported that 'the greater part of his force was killed or wounded and this moreover was not until after having himself been twice wounded, once by a ball which broke his leg, and other in his hand'. The defence may have been less impressive, but he was wounded and captured. He was taken out to a British sloop 'where', he claimed, 'he found himself with 14 English officers who had been wounded in this action'. [29] This account was, to be sure, composed to justify the grant of a pension, and in that respect, at least, it was successful.

As the French defenders scattered into the woods or fled up the track towards the Heights, Knox and the other redcoats on the beach followed them up. 'We lost no time,' he wrote, and then, with no little exaggeration, 'scrambled up one of the steepest precipices that can be conceived, being almost perpendicular, and of an incredible height'.[30] One of Howe's volunteers was running down the track when he saw a shadowy force advancing up it, 'who we did not know (it being only daybreak),' he recounted. He and his comrades feared the worst; 'we put ourselves in the best posture of making a defence: two of us advanced, when they came close, and challenged them, when we found it was Captain Fraser with his company, who we joined'.[31] The two British thrusts had met halfway up the path. The Foulon road was theirs.

Minutes later, Knox reached the summit where 'all was quiet, and not a shot was heard, owing to the excellent conduct of the light infantry under Colonel Howe'. It was now daylight and the men halted, formed their ranks with their backs to the river and 'for a few minutes' they waited, looked around them and prepared themselves for the next phase.[32]

Below them more troops were streaming onto the beach. Knox had been very impressed with the efficiency of the amphibious side of the operation. 'As fast as we landed,' he wrote, 'the boats put off for reinforcements.'[33] These troops were on board the ships of Holmes' fleet which was now close at hand. They had swept down the river with the tide and the 1,700 soldiers on board were now clambering into the flat-bottomed boats as they returned from transporting the first wave. Some bore the scars of the skirmishing at the shore with splintered gunwales and blood slippery on the benches. Holmes had carefully prearranged the formation of his ships for when they arrived: 'the boats were to go close in shore and land the troops; the sloops were to lie next to them'; the frigates were to lie outside the sloops and on the outside the transports were to anchor, 'ready to disembark the troops when ordered'.[34]

The ships had all arrived at daybreak. This ensured that by the time the frigates added the fire support of their cannon to help the men ashore they could actually see what they were aiming at. Wolfe, suspicious of all things naval, ordered that 'officers of artillery and detachments of gunners are put on board the armed sloops to regulate their fire, that in the hurry our troops may not be hurt by our artillery ...

the officers will be particularly careful to distinguish the enemy and to point their fire against them ... Frigates will not fire till broad daylight, so no mistake can be made.'[35] The French battery at Samos, a few hundred yards upstream, blasted away at this wealth of new targets. The log of the *Squirrel* records that they had 'several shot fired at us which cut away part of our running rigging, two went through our flying jibb and one through our hull abaft the forechains'.[36] Most of the cannonballs screamed overhead as the flat-bottomed boats rowed into shore with the second wave.

Wolfe was ashore and pleased with his light infantry. His 'Family Journal' reported that

> Colonel Howe with the light infantry gained the heights with little loss, the enemy had a hundred men to guard the Foulon which were soon dispersed: Mr Wolfe was highly pleased with the measure Col Howe had taken to gain the heights, wished that Mr Howe might outlive the day that he might have an opportunity of stamping his merit to the government.[37]

There is some evidence, however, that Wolfe had an attack of nerves. Perhaps thinking it was all too easy, he sent his Adjutant General Isaac Barré down to the boats to 'stop them a little until he had an opportunity of knowing the enemy's strength ... and whether they might not be in numbers sufficient to prevent his establishing himself'.[38] Wolfe's 'Family Journal' agrees saying that the young general 'stopped a further debarkation of the troops until the first were well established above, saying if the post was to be carried there was enough ashore for that purpose, if they were repulsed a greater number would breed more confusion'.[39] Barré carried this message down from the Heights but on arriving at the beach he made an important decision. He saw the boats full of troops about to head for the shore. He later explained that 'thinking from the knowledge he had of Mr Wolfe's intentions' and knowing 'that the orders he had received were in consequence of [Wolfe's] not expecting the troops could be got landed so soon', he 'took the liberty seeing things thus situated, not to deliver the orders he had received, but suffered the Troops to land as fast as possible and went and reported it to General Wolfe, who was much pleased to find himself established on shore with his army sooner than he expected'.[40]

Barré's disobedience thus prevented a serious mistake by Wolfe. The General had made a terrible gamble landing his forces where he had and security lay in getting as many of them ashore as he could before the French arrived to drive him back. Barré ensured that this process continued. As more troops landed Wolfe's confidence grew. He dispatched Howe's light infantry to silence the Samos battery, which Mackellar reported 'annoyed both boats and shipping a good deal'.[41] One of these men wrote that 'this was effected without the loss of a man; the enemy placed one of the cannon to flank us crossing a bridge, which they fired, drew off, and got into the woods which was within forty yards of the battery. We demolished the powder and came away.'[42]

By now the second wave was ashore and drawn up at the top of the cliff. The sailors at the oars of the flat-bottomed boats struck out again, this time to collect the third wave. It consisted of the two regiments which had been concealed on the other bank of the St Lawrence. They were lying 'in the woods on the south shore opposite to the Foulon, and were soon brought over to join the army', reports the 'Family Journal'. When they finally joined the army it put the number of men at Wolfe's disposal at 4,400.[43]

By 0800 hours this small force was in neat ranks on the southern edge of the Heights of Abraham, with its back to the river, all eyes scanning the scrub and distant trees for any sign of the French. The amphibious landing had been a triumph because of the masterly coordination of the navy and the quick-witted initiative of the soldiers, who had attacked straight uphill, even though some of them found themselves further downstream than they were expecting. Behind the infantry heavier equipment was being manhandled up the narrow path. The sailors of the fleet were dragging two six-pound brass cannon up to give the British real firepower in the coming battle.

On the Heights all Wolfe cared about was the whereabouts of the French. Amphibious attacks are always terribly vulnerable to counterattacks and never more so than this one on the banks of the St

Lawrence in the early hours of 13 September 1759. Retreat was not an option. Wolfe had brought his army up a tiny, winding track, down which it would be impossible to conduct a fighting retreat. At the bottom lay the narrowest of beaches, too small to hold the thousands of men in his army. If disaster overtook them, a panicked mass of men would charge down the ravine, surge onto the beach, and many of them would be jostled into the St Lawrence and drowned. The boats could carry less than half the force so a quick evacuation was not possible. Wolfe had led his men into a situation from which there were two outcomes: victory or annihilation.

The first sign of the French was a light company from the Guyenne Regiment, the unit that was in limbo between Bougainville's force and Montcalm's. Mackellar reported that 'very soon' after Wolfe reached the summit, this company had appeared on some rising ground towards the town. 'Finding they were too late, they retired without making any attempt to molest us,' the engineer reported. Mackellar afterwards learnt that 'this battalion was to have come upon this ground the night before; but by some lucky accident their arrival was deferred; some say they were detained by the French General himself upon receiving intelligence by a deserter that there was a descent to be made that night upon the coast of Beauport'.[44]

The Guyenne had been encamped on the Heights for a few days in the first week of September. Its subsequent movements have kept historians arguing for centuries. Vaudreuil later tried to blame its absence from the Heights of Abraham squarely on Montcalm. He reported to the French government that 'I was counting much on the good [position] of the Guyenne Regiment, I thought it was still on the heights of Quebec, but Monsieur de Montcalm had recalled it, the same day at nightfall without warning me.'[45] This is not exactly the truth as letters written in those tense early September days show. On 6 September Vaudreuil had written to Bougainville saying 'after having conferred with M le Marquis de Montcalm ... we will hold back the Guyenne Regiment and have it return to its camp'. Based by the St Charles River it would then be 'in a position to give assistance at the Anse de Mères, to the town, and the Canardière [section of the Beauport shore immediately east of the St Charles River] alike'.[46] Montcalm's journal notes on 4 September that 'the Guyenne regiment is camped on the extreme right so that it can go wherever it is needed and even above Quebec if it is necessary.'[47]

The French leadership had remained sceptical about the likelihood of an attack in this sector. This had influenced their deployment of the troops and it also acted as a brake on their activity even when rumours of a landing started coming in at dawn on 13 September. Firing was heard, but this was hardly unusual after such a violent summer. The bells of Quebec rang but were ignored by the army at Beauport which had just spent the night in a state of high anxiety thanks to Saunders' complicated and realistic feints. Montcalm and the other senior officers were blinded by their preconceptions and what they could see in front of them. The British fleet in the basin looked threatening, and boats full of men swarmed to and fro. This perfectly matched Montcalm's expectations about where the British would attack and as a result he was convinced.

The French army at Beauport had been waiting in their trenches all night. Before dawn, Montcalm's journal written by one of his aides states that 'the town used the agreed signal to indicate that something had happened'. There was also the sound of firing: 'a little before daybreak we heard gunshots above Quebec. We did not doubt that a convoy of food that we had been expecting had been discovered and possibly taken.' As the first confused and inaccurate reports came in, Montcalm, who had been listening to false intelligence from enthusiastic but inexperienced Canadians all summer, was sceptical. Six weeks before he had tried to calm an edgy Vaudreuil who was nervous about an attack above the town. Montcalm had written, 'only God, sir, can do the impossible ... and we cannot believe that the enemy have wings that would allow them in one night to cross water, land, climb rugged slopes and scale walls'.[48]

It is unclear how and when Montcalm and Vaudreuil heard about the landings and, more importantly, when they realized that it was no false alarm. Montcalm's journal reports that a Canadian from Vergor's post arrived at daybreak, 'with all the marks of terror'. He claimed that 'he was the only one who had escaped and that the enemy was on the ground above'. Montcalm's aides were dismissive: 'we knew so well how difficult it was to penetrate by that route, if it was defended that we did not believe a word of what he was telling us and we thought that fear had made him mad'. The author 'went to have a rest'.[49]

Montcalm was quickly forced to revise this judgement, although Vaudreuil later claimed that Montcalm never informed him. Instead, he received a note written at 0545 hours from the commander of the forces in the Lower Town, Chevalier de Bernetz, which notified Vaudreuil of a landing at Foulon *and* one against the Lower Town which never, in fact, materialized. Bernetz could no longer hear musketry and assumed that the British had been beaten off. Even so he recommended that the Guyenne 'cannot make too much haste'.[50] The catastrophic dissonance at the top of the French forces was brought into stark relief in this great moment of crisis. Montcalm and Vaudreuil do not seem to have corresponded. It was unclear who was issuing orders or where final authority lay. An hour after Vaudreuil received Bernetz's note, he wrote to Bougainville: 'It seems fairly certain that the enemy has made a landing at the Anse au Foulon.' On the Beauport shore 'we have set a good number of troops in motion. We hear a certain amount of small arms fire ... I have the honour to wish you good day.'[51] He did not order Bougainville, posted with his men upriver, beyond the British landings, to march at full speed to the sounds of the fighting; instead, there were appeals for information and encouragement for the young man to stay 'attentive' to British movements. The great commanders have the ability to issue short, simple, and clear orders to their subordinates. This note might have been brief but it was neither of the other two. It left Bougainville none the wiser as to the unfolding crisis or what he could do, with his considerable force of crack troops, to assist his senior officers.

One French officer later wrote that

so badly established was the communication between each of M de Bougainville's posts and between the latter and M de Montcalm's camp that the English ... were already in order of battle on the heights of Quebec where they even had some field pieces of small calibre, before anyone in our camps was as yet aware that the enemy wished to attack us in that quarter.

The army, he reported, had just gone to their tents to grab some much needed sleep, after spending the night awake and waiting for an attack on their sector. Now 'the generale was beat; all the troops resumed their arms' and followed Montcalm to the west.[52]

Montcalm's aide-de-camp, the Chevalier Johnstone, had spent the morning chivvying the troops into action. He claimed later that Vaudreuil had ordered them all to stay put and he had to order them in the name of Montcalm to ignore their Governor General. He begged a senior French officer to march with all speed to the Plains of Abraham because 'it was evident that the English army – already landed near Quebec – could never think of making a second descent at Beauport'. Johnstone insisted that 'there would be in a few hours an engagement upon the heights which would immediately decide the fate of the colony'. He eventually won his argument.[53]

Another French officer wrote that initial reports suggested that the British had withdrawn after feigning a landing. But just after 0600 hours 'an express arrived with an account that the whole of the English army had landed and were advancing in good order'. 'Immediately our troops quitted their camp,' he continued, 'and filed off, leaving a guard of 1500 men only to defend it, and took post upon the heights of Abraham, waiting for the arrival of the enemy.'[54] The men trudged up the steep incline from the St Charles to the Plains. The certainties of defending their positions along the Beauport shore had been shattered, no one now knew what to expect.

By 0700 hours Montcalm was certain enough to send his forces streaming across the bridges over the St Charles River. They were finally leaving their Beauport positions which they had clung to so obstinately. Like the British troops taking their first tentative steps onto the Plains of Abraham above them, they had not slept that night. A summer of tension, of manoeuvre, of skirmishing and of waiting was over. The pitched battle which Montcalm had tried so hard to avoid, and Wolfe had been desperate to provoke, was now inevitable. Wolfe's men were threatening the poorly constructed western defences of

Quebec, which would not stand a serious siege. Montcalm could no longer rely on a passive defence. Now the British would have to be removed. He was going to have to fight a battle to save Quebec and New France.

FOURTEEN

The Battle of the Plains of Abraham

THE RED-COATED INFANTRY stood in neat ranks, properly dressed, gaps between each regiment, the unfurled colours flapping lazily above their heads. Grenadiers guarded the flank of each regiment. After the chaos and physical exertion of the landings and the climb there was a stillness, a chance to catch their breath and look about them. None of them had ever laid eyes on the Plains of Abraham before. It had always been out of sight at the top of the barricade of cliffs. Now this undulating stretch of open ground lay to their right, with some crops planted but used mainly for grazing. It is likely that it had once belonged to Abraham Martin who had arrived in New France as a 30-year-old in around 1620. He may have been of Scottish descent or, like so many other chancers who headed for the New World, he may have taken on a false identity to escape a dark past. He was known as 'the King's Pilot' and could have been an official pilot in addition to being a fisherman. He and his wife Marguerite had produced a brood of children, one of whom was the first French child ever born in Canada, and another the godchild of Samuel de Champlain himself. This did not stop Martin from behaving inappropriately with a young woman in Quebec, a crime for which he was imprisoned. His family no longer owned the land; it had been in the possession of the Ursuline nuns a century before it felt the tread of rough British boots.[1]

The army's back was to the river. In front of it in the distance was the road from Quebec to Ste Foy and Cap Rouge, to its left was thick woodland and Quebec itself lay off to the right although the men could not see it thanks to some higher ground known as the Buttes à Neveu. The visibility was good; the ships anchored off the Anse au Foulon and in the basin of Quebec recorded in their logs that the weather was 'fresh' but 'fair' and 'clear'.[2] Knox, however, remembers it being 'showery' as the morning progressed.[3]

There was still the popping of musketry, which rhythmically flared up and died away as pockets of resistance were found and dealt with by the light troops. The charismatic chaplain of the Highlanders, Robert MacPherson (*Caipal Mhor* in Gaelic) reported that 'there was perpetual hot skirmishing between our troops and the enemy who had full possession of every bush'.[4] Mackellar, the Chief Engineer, wrote in his journal that 'we found some of the enemy in a house and some Indians skulking in a coppice hard by'. Grenadiers were immediately detached to 'beat them off, which, after exchanging a few shots, they effected'.[5] Wolfe's 'Family Journal' says that from daybreak onwards, the 'enemy's light troops began to swarm in the bushes, and behind the hillocks, and perpetually thickened and kept a very hot fire on the troops'.[6] These attacks may have led to a trickle of casualties but they were no more than a nuisance for the British and there was still no sign of larger scale, more organized French counter-attacks.

Wolfe made his way to the right on a reconnoitre towards Quebec. There, beyond the higher ground, he caught his first glimpse of his enemy. His 'Family Journal' says that he watched as Montcalm's army 'formed under the cannon of the town'.[7] Wolfe hurried back to his men and marched them closer to the French. Both sides were now locked in the inexorable series of well-defined small steps that led to battle in the eighteenth century. During this so-called 'advance to contact' mistakes could prove lethal. If either side lost its shape and order, the enemy would see a clear advantage and launch its attack. Moving thousands of men across open countryside while keeping them under tight control was why drill was so central. A manual released during the Seven Years War told keen young officers that one of the maxims of the great Marshal Saxe, the brilliant French commander from the War of Austrian Succession, was that 'the principal and most material part of all exercise is the teaching soldiers to use their legs properly and not their arms'.[8] Saxe and Frederick the Great both spent much time encouraging the spread of the cadenced steps whereby men moved their limbs in time with each other rather than ambling along at their own pace. During the 1750s this cadenced marching was imposed throughout the British and Continental armies. Cumberland introduced fifes to help the men keep in time. By marching in time large numbers of men could be deployed over greater distances, making sure that when they arrived they were in tight formation and able to fire devastating musket volleys.

Wolfe's aides-de-camp would have carried the message along the line to prepare to form column and move off. The men in the regiments would have performed a smart right turn and, at the shouted command of 'March', pushed their left feet forward. They marched in time to the fifes and the drums. The men used the 'Prussian step' in which they carried 'foot directly forward with a straight knee, near and almost parallel to the ground'. They were told to leave a moment of pause with the forward knee in full extension before they sprang forward 'from the ball of the foot which you stood on' and let the other one fall to the ground. As they marched they constantly monitored the man to the right with whom they had to stay in line, while 'their steps should be exactly the same length'. There were three possible steps: the short, the long, and the double. The short was one foot and a half, the long was two feet, and the double was also two feet but performed in half the time.[9]

They were told not to look down at their feet or those of the men in front of them; they had to have confidence that if they all stepped off on the left and kept the same length of stride that they would not step on anyone. They had to 'assume themselves a soldier-like air'. That meant 'their breasts forward, and their shoulders back'. The importance of 'throwing back the shoulders and holding the head up high' was pounded into them, 'especially those who are used to follow the plough'. Above all they were 'to carry their arms well, pressing their piece against their body'.[10]

At the head of each company marched the captain; four feet behind him marched the drummers and another four feet behind them was the front rank of men; each successive rank was four feet back. On either flank subalterns kept station while sergeants marched along prodding, thumping, and encouraging men to stay in time. When Wolfe was ready, the lead regiment wheeled to the left and one by one the others followed. The men on the outside of the wheel lengthened their paces slightly to cover the greater distance on the outside of the bend while not losing their dressing. This brought the long column onto a north–south trajectory perpendicular to the river. At the command 'Halt', the army came to a stop, their heels level, about four inches apart. At the next command the men rotated through ninety degrees and the entire British line was now facing Quebec. Malcolm Fraser remembered that to the north, on his left, were 'a few houses and at some distance the low ground and wood above the General Hospital with the River St Charles'. In front he could see 'the town of Quebec, about a mile distant'.[11]

They were now in their line of battle. Great care was taken in presenting an impressive appearance to an attacking army. Every man had a preassigned place. 'The tallest men should be in the front rank,' stated a training manual, 'yet, if a man has a fine person, and is well made, he ought to be put into the front.'[12] This was not just a trick to intimidate the enemy or look neat on a parade ground. It fixed every man's position within the line which made it easier to rally and re-form the regiment in case it panicked or got scattered during a battle.

Wolfe stayed on a rise on the southern side of the battlefield near the cliffs that dropped off to the St Lawrence. Here on the very right of the British line were the three companies of Louisbourg Grenadiers, to their left was Bragg's 28th, then Kennedy's 43rd, Lascelles' 47th, Fraser's 78th Highlanders, and at the very left of the line Anstruther's 58th. Webb's 48th was in reserve, spread out in four separate 'subdivisions' which could reinforce the front line if required. To the north there were woods which were becoming increasingly occupied with Native Americans and Canadians who kept up a steady fire, sniping at the redcoats as they went through their evolutions. To protect this flank Townshend wheeled the three regiments which had been in the second line, Lawrence's 3rd/60th, Monckton's 2nd/60th, and Amherst's 15th, and formed them at right angles or *en potence* to the rest of the army facing north. A similar move on the extreme right of the army, between it and the St Lawrence, saw Otway's 35th Regiment placed at right angles facing south to counter any of the enemy's light troops that sought to sneak along the bushes and trees at the top of the cliff and get round behind Wolfe's army and between it and its landing place. Wolfe left Howe and his light infantry to secure houses and strongpoints to the rear of the whole army. One of the light infantrymen reported that 'we stood at about 800 paces from the line [and] were ordered to face outwards and cover the rear of our line as there was a body of enemy' in that direction.[13] This 'body of men' was Bougainville's powerful force, of which there was still no sign. Wolfe was obviously nervous as to their whereabouts, though; he sent Lawrence's 3rd/60th to join the light infantry in guarding the area around Foulon and the army's lines of communication. Wolfe's army was forced to protect itself from enemy forces on three sides and a steep cliff and river on its fourth.[14]

Each regiment was formed up only two ranks deep. Gone were formations ten men deep, bristling with pikes, which engaged in a giant shoving match. The advent of the musket meant that every man needed a clear view of the enemy so that he could bring his weapon to bear. Firepower now decided battles. The British army at the time still favoured a three-rank formation but assertive young commanders like Wolfe and Amherst believed that two ranks would deliver a sufficient weight of musketry and cover more ground. They were the pioneers of the famous 'thin red line' which a generation later Wellington, among others, would prove to be so impenetrably strong. Amherst had insisted that it was standard practice in North America. Wolfe echoed his commander in chief, ordering that 'the method is always to be practised ... as the enemy has very few regular troops to oppose us that no yelling Indians or fire of Canadians can possibly withstand two ranks'.[15] Adoption of the two ranks was the product of necessity as much as innovation. Wolfe's army was depleted. Sergeant Johnson later wrote that 'our line of battle would admit of us to be drawn up two deep only, from the smallness of our number, as well as the quantity of ground we had to cover to secure our flanks'. The men had three feet between them, and each regiment was around forty yards apart.[16] In all the line was about half a mile long.[17]

Behind Wolfe stood the Louisbourg Grenadiers. With only 216 men, four drummers, nine non-commissioned officers, and twelve officers, it was one of the smallest of his regiments that morning but even the largest were sadly understrength. Young Malcolm Fraser reported that the long summer had left the regiments 'very weak'.[18] Webb's 48th, in reserve, was the largest unit, with around six hundred and fifty men commanded by about thirty officers and thirty NCOs. Fraser's 78th mustered about six hundred Highlanders. In all Wolfe had 3,826 men, controlled by 230 officers and 239 NCOs and marshalled by 83 drummers. This figure does not include Howe's approximately six hundred light infantrymen who were guarding his rear. Meanwhile forty-six officers and men of the artillery handled the cannon when they arrived from the landing beach.[19]

Wolfe had been forced to detach the 3rd/60th to guard his rear and use the 15th, 2nd/60th, and the 35th to protect his flanks while the 48th was in reserve. That meant that the number of musket-wielding private soldiers who stood in his line of battle facing towards Quebec and the French was 1,800. As Wolfe watched the French mass in front of him he could see that these men were outnumbered.

The Plains of Abraham rang with noise: the thump of a thousand footfalls, the clatter of the drums, the opening salvoes by the artillery pieces still finding their range, the pop of muskets fired among the skirmishers around the fringes of the battlefield, and the roar of officers and NCOs as they attempted to keep their men in good order. There was also one distinctive sound which was quite new on a North American battlefield. Behind the 78th Highlanders the bagpipes were playing. No Highlander ever went to war without his piper. This included, of course, the 1745–6 rebellion. After it the pipes were defined as 'an instrument of war' and outlawed. Now, thirteen years later, they were only permitted when on British state business. They were attached to recruiting parties to inspire young men to join the colours and kept their spirits up on the battlefield. Pipers were born not made. It was a hereditary office. Sons of pipers would go and train for seven years at places like the MacCrimmon school on Skye. The piper for the grenadier company of the 78th was Alexander McIntyre, the latest in a long line of men who had piped for the Clan Menzies.[20] He and the other pipers of the regiment wore fine, silver-laced jackets and black bearskin hats. From the pipes themselves hung small banners with the regimental number and the royal cipher.

The British watched the French spread out across the Plains, and as more and more units arrived one redcoat compared them to swarming 'bees out of a hive'.[21] It took about two hours, until just before 1000 hours, to organize the French battle line. There is some disagreement as to the numbers of French troops present on the battlefield. Canadian sharpshooters and the Native Americans hovered on both flanks sniping at the British troops while the French army regiments, the colonial regulars, and some militia units all formed a battle line under the walls of Quebec. One French officer wrote that 'our army at Beauport had for some days been reduced, by the corps detached from it, to about 6000 men. To guard the camp were left the two battalions of Montreal, comprising about 1500 men, which nevertheless advanced as far as the river St Charles.' 'M de Montcalm,' he continued, 'could therefore, according to this calculation, muster only four thousand five hundred men.'[22] Montcalm had heard nothing from Bougainville and his force of around three thousand men.

To many of the British observers the French army appeared much bigger than their own. Malcolm Fraser wrote that 'I am certain they were greatly superior to us in numbers.'[23] Knox claims that it numbered seven and a half thousand men. Admiral Holmes heard from eyewitnesses that it was 'about 9000' strong.[24] Townshend gives the more realistic figure of 3,440. About two thousand, or just under half, of Montcalm's men were regular soldiers of the *troupes de terres* although their numbers had been bolstered by the inclusion of militiamen, whose ability to stand and deliver musket volley after musket volley while under fire themselves was unproven. Another 600 men were the colonial regulars of the *troupes de la marine* and the rest were militiamen and Native Americans. The French had more men overall and an advantage of numbers in terms of the two front lines that by mid-morning stretched across the Plains.

On the right of the French line proper was, according to Townshend, 'half the troops of the colony, the battalions of La Sarre, Languedoc and the remainder of their Canadians and Indians'. Next to them, in the centre of the line, was 'a column ... formed by the battalions of Béarn and Guyenne'. Their left wing, closest to the St Lawrence, was the other half of the colonial troops and the Royal Roussillon battalion.[25] The French were unable to exploit their vast reservoir of artillery in and around the town. Accounts differ but it is certain that at most Montcalm could only call upon three light cannon and possibly as little as one alone. On either flank hordes of sharpshooters and skirmishers hovered, making use of trees, bushes, and buildings to shelter behind as they picked off British targets.

The British waited silently for battle; each regiment in two straight lines. The officers stood in their customary positions. The commander was ahead of his men, in the dead centre. Company commanders likewise stood in front of their units, checking that all was as it should be. Subalterns and sergeants prowled behind the rear rank ready to remind men of their duty or drag them into gaps created by cannon and musket balls. Behind the centre of each regiment was the second in command and the adjutant. In Europe the former, at least, would have been on horseback to give him a view of the rest of the battle but here in North America the entire British army went into battle on foot.

At the centre of each regiment flapped the two unfurled colours. Each was carried by an ensign, the most junior of the officers, nearly always in their teens. The colours were six feet six inches wide and six feet high and mounted on a spear-tipped pole almost ten feet in length. To help the ensigns' boyish frames support the weight of them the foot of the pole rested in a leather pouch attached to a shoulder belt. One colour was the 'King's Colour', a Union Flag with a distinctive regimental badge at the centre surrounded by roses (or thistles, in the case of the 78th Highland Regiment). The other was particular to each unit, the 'Regimental Colour'. This had a Union Flag in the corner and then a design in the middle involving the regimental number and often some laurel leaves. These colours were the embodiment of the regiment's pride, fighting spirit, and honour. To lose them in battle was unthinkable; to capture them from an enemy guaranteed immortality. This value meant that the colours would witness the fiercest fighting. Behind the ensigns stood two sergeants, supposed to be armed with short pikes but probably carrying muskets and bayonets. Their grizzled presence reassured the young men charged with guarding the colours. When Wolfe had been a battalion commander he had ordered that one soldier from each of the ten companies in the regiment, who had a record unblemished by any disciplinary infractions, plus two corporals were to stand behind the sergeants and defend the colours, with their lives if required.

The grenadier company was split in two, each half taking up position on either extreme of their regiment. Their mitre caps made them look taller than the tricornes worn by the men of the other companies. By this stage of the campaign, though, the uniforms would have been a long way off Hyde Park parade standard. A long summer of skirmishing, amphibious landings, building, and digging had long since ruined their smart appearance. The men's hair was cropped short, their faces deeply suntanned. Their clothing and kit was just as worn. Their once bright coats were faded, patched, and stitched. Knapsacks and haversacks had been adjusted and modified. Tomahawks dangled from belts in place of swords. The only guarantee was that their muskets and bayonets were spotless and burnished bright as new.

Behind the two ranks were the musicians, whose regular drumming and fifing had brought the men to their current station in good order. Now they had laid aside most of their instruments and were preparing for their secondary, but equally important, role. They tied blankets between poles creating stretchers to carry the wounded back to receive the uncertain benefits of attention from the surgeon and his assistants who were setting out their equipment. The drummers always wore gaudy uniforms. The coats were made of the 'facing colour' of the regiment to which they belonged, that is the colour of the linings, lapels, and cuffs worn by the men of the unit. Thus the drummers and musicians of Knox's regiment, Kennedy's 43rd, wore white coats with red cuffs and lapels. The whole uniform was then decorated with plenty of white lace flecked with red and black.

The battalion commanders, the brigadiers, and Wolfe himself all took a close interest in the positioning of the men. Monckton, as the senior brigadier, took his place in battle on the right of the army. Near him Lieutenant Colonel Murray, one of Wolfe's only remaining friends in the army, commanded the Louisbourg Grenadiers, which were anchoring the army's right wing. They were particularly ragtag even among Wolfe's other motley regiments. Each company sported different facings because they were the grenadier company from three different regiments. One company had buff facings with white lace, another had buff facings with gold lace, and the third sported green facings with silver lace.

Townshend was in command of the left wing, but since that was now deployed at right angles to the line of battle, Murray, who had been in charge of the centre, now effectively commanded the left wing. The campaign had taken a heavy toll on the regimental commanders who had consistently put themselves at the heart of the action. Lieutenant Colonel Simon Fraser was off the field still recovering from the injuries that he had sustained during a skirmish in July, when he was wounded by a bullet that also hit his second in command, John MacPherson. As a result Fraser's men were commanded by a captain, John Campbell, who was still in his mid-thirties. Major Paulus Aemilius Irving, a veteran Scottish soldier, had also taken command of his unit, Amherst's 15th, described by Wolfe earlier in the summer as 'that excellent regiment'.[26] Irving was 44 years old and had seen plenty of action during the War of Austrian Succession in the Caribbean and in Flanders. He had been wounded on 8 August during a skirmish but his cool leadership had apparently warded off a sticky situation. Now he was keeping an eye on the threatening moves of the Native Americans and Canadian irregulars who waited for their chance to fall upon the British flank. The 48th Regiment, in reserve, was spread out and ready to respond to any weakening of the line in front. It was commanded by Colonel Burton. Wolfe's loyal companion was on the field even though Mackellar noted that he had 'scarcely recovered from his wound' which he had received during the attack at Montmorency.[27]

Wolfe was dressed in a simple red coat. It was faded and almost shabby. A black armband was still wrapped around his left arm in remembrance of his recently deceased father. He moved along the line, checking everything for himself and projecting competence and confidence. In a European battle he would have been mounted, with a raised, clear view of the battlefield and the ability to get from one side of his line to the other in under a minute. Here he was forced to walk the length of the line himself. Wolfe 'at first moved about everywhere', said Mackellar, and Townshend reported that 'General Wolfe came towards the left and finding all secure on there, he returned to the centre.'[28] He eventually settled on the higher ground with the Louisbourg Grenadiers that would allow him to survey the entire battlefield. There is a copy of a speech that he is purported to have made although transcripts of speeches by generals before battles are notoriously untrustworthy. It is certain, however, that he would have stopped often and shouted words of encouragement and the sentiments that appear in this surviving text do ring true. The story goes that he congratulated his men on scaling the cliffs and pointed out that Quebec, 'the object of all our toils', stood before them. He returned to one of his central themes, that of the cowardice of 'a perfidious enemy', who have 'dared to exasperate you by their cruelties, but not to oppose you on equal ground'. Now they were 'constrained to face you on the open plain, without ramparts or entrenchments to shelter them'. Wolfe warned his men not to fear their superior numbers; the French regulars were ill and hungry but even when fresh they 'were unable to withstand British soldiers'. As for the Canadians, as soon as their 'irregular ardour is damped by one firm fire, they will instantly turn their backs, and give you no further trouble'. The 'savage tribes of Indians, whose horrid yells in the forests have struck many a bold heart with affright' were, he told his men, easily dealt with by 'resolute men upon fair ground'. His hatred for the Native Americans burnt undimmed as he told his men 'to consider them as the just objects of a severe revenge for the unhappy fate of many slaughtered countrymen'. He finished the short speech with stirring words: 'The impossibility of a retreat makes no difference in the situation of men resolved to conquer or die: and, believe me, my friends if your conquest could be bought with the blood of your general, he would most cheerfully resign a life which he has long devoted to his country.'[29]

Wolfe's men were already paying for his desperate gamble. Native Americans and Canadian skirmishers were taking a steady toll on the British line. Johnson reported that so serious was this threat that Wolfe 'ordered us to lie flat on the ground on our arms; and which we did, for a considerable time'. This helped to protect him and his comrades from 'upwards of fifteen hundred of their best marksmen' who 'kept a continual fire upon our line for some time ... and which killed and wounded several of our officers and men'.[30] Knox reported that 'what galled us most was a body of Indians and other marksmen they had concealed in the corn opposite to the front of our right wing, and a coppice that stood opposite our centre'.[31] Townshend later reported that these skirmishers were 'most of their best marksmen' who kept up 'a very galling' fire. But he wrote that the British troops 'bore it with the greatest patience and good order'.[32]

To combat this threat the British deployed skirmishers of their own. All along the line picked groups of men were sent forward to contest no-man's-land with the French troops and push them back to distances at which their fire would not be as accurate or deadly. The problem, as one British account points out, was that 'since our light infantry were otherwise disposed of, we were obliged from time to time to advance platoons from the battalions to keep these at a distance'.[33] Normally the light infantry from each regiment would deal with the skirmishing but they were grouped together under Howe protecting the rear. It fell to men of the other companies for whom this type of fighting was less familiar.

Ideally skirmishers moved forward in pairs, one man reloading his musket, or in a few cases a rifle, the other keeping his head up looking for targets and threats. The ground between the two armies became the scene of a bloody, yet private battle as small groups of men wrestled for control. Mackellar reported that 'there were some clumps of high brush, which afforded good cover and brought on a skirmishing which was warmly kept up on both sides'. Bushes, hollows, shacks, and other buildings were vital cover. The wider context of battle was forgotten as these skirmishers focused exclusively on every friend, every enemy, and every fold of the ground in one 400-yard circle centred on themselves. The British efforts were successful. Mackellar comments on the far left of the line where Townshend ordered 'two pickets of the 15th to advance by turn and fire upon them, they hastily retired to a safe distance, from whence they kept up an intermittent and desultory fire'.[34] Johnson agreed that 'by keeping up a constant fire amongst them, their fire was greatly slackened'.[35] Knox wrote that a few rounds from the skirmishers 'obliged these skulkers to retire'.[36] Towards the left of the battlefield there was a fierce battle to control a few outlying houses. Possession of these buildings was useful to the defending side when the other attacked. The solid walls would protect those inside while they fired at close range on any troops that advanced past them, a harbinger of the concrete pillboxes of later conflicts. A French source records that Wolfe had 'ordered a company of highlanders to take possession of the house de Borgia'. French troops were sent to dislodge them, 'which brought on a brisk and obstinate attack; but all our efforts were to no purpose; as it was absolutely necessary to bring the cannon to drive them out'.[37]

As this source suggests, the popping of musketry in no-man's-land was soon joined by the louder boom of artillery. By mid-morning, both sides had managed to get a few cannon into action. Despite a good deal of confusion in reports of the day it is pretty certain that the British had manhandled two six pounder guns up the treacherous path from Foulon and onto the battlefield. Townshend wrote in his journal that the British guns were 'admirably well served' and 'galled their column exceedingly' as it formed up below the walls of the town.[38] Although he had incurred the artilleryman Williamson's displeasure by suggesting initially that only one gun had been brought into action. Williamson, in charge of the cannon during the battle, wrote to his superiors at the Board of Ordnance saying that, 'Brigadier Townshend acknowledged to me he was wrong informed in the account of field pieces at the battle ... and agrees to mine which is candid enough of him to confirm.'[39] He confirms that he had two guns on the battlefield and another four which the sailors were dragging up but did not reach him in time for the crisis. A French officer remembered that both sides 'were cannonading one another for about an hour, our artillery consisted only of three small field pieces'.[40]

With the armies hundreds of yards apart solid, round shot was used. Lighter brass cannon weighing about three-quarters of a ton were easier to get up the slope but could not withstand as much explosive force as heavier iron guns. As a result they had a more limited range. Even so a charge of a pound and a half of powder could fire a six-pound ball over half a mile, which was easily far enough to reach the

French ranks. Cannonballs could also skim off the ground and were still deadly after the second or third bounce. The gunners were practised at the 'laying' of guns. No artilleryman could buy the rank above him or rely on patronage to speed his promotion. Only time and experience could advance his career. As a result Williamson's gun layers were some of the most professional men on the battlefield. They only had crude sights and yet they could achieve impressive accuracy. They knew the precise performance of their gun from countless test firings and they took into account the atmospheric conditions and windspeed. On the barrel were various carved notches to help them lay the gun properly as well as a series of markings that gave the observer a great deal of information about the cannon at one glance. A broad arrow, usually carved near the vent, denoted British government ownership. Beyond that, between the stubby trunions, which were the fulcrum on which the barrel rested on the gun carriage, was the initial of the Master General of the Ordnance. Depending on how old the gun was it might have been 'M' for the Duke of Montagu who was Master General from 1740 to 1749 (with a short gap), or the same letter denoting the Duke of Marlborough, who held the post after 1755. In the most conspicuous position near the front of the barrel was the royal badge, 'GR2' surmounted by a crown and enclosed in a garter. The cannon might also have had the name of the founder, the man who made the gun, inscribed, usually around the base ring at the very back of the barrel.

A well-trained crew could clean out the barrel, load, and fire in a matter of seconds but all accuracy would have been sacrificed. It took much longer if the crew wanted to 'run up' the carriage after the gun had recoiled. On firing the cannon would typically jump back a couple of yards. It would have to be 'relaid' or re-aimed. Manuals from the time suggested that while eight rounds a minute might be possible, two rounds a minute was a safer, more accurate way. Overhasty sponging would leave traces of red-hot residue which would ignite the next charge as it was being rammed down. The stress of constant firing threatened to blast the barrel apart which would kill or horribly injure the crew. Safety was not the only concern, the rate of burn of gunpowder varied according to the amount of compression that it was put under. Consistency depended on ramming the charge in a deliberate fashion. Finally the gun layer had to wait for the substantial cloud of smoke from the previous discharge to clear before he could get a view of the target and lay the gun with any accuracy.

A steady well-aimed fire would do far more to the enemy than a random frenzy, however impressive that might sound. Soldiers hated being forced to stand still under an artillery bombardment. The terrified men could see the balls coming towards them; some Austrian veterans at Dettingen, Wolfe's first battle, impressed the British troops by dodging out of the way. They were wise to do so. Cannonballs did terrible damage if an expert crew could bounce one right through a densely packed group of men. At Waterloo, where identical cannon were used, there is a report that one ball killed or disabled an officer and twenty-five men of the 40th Regiment of Foot.[41]

As both armies formed, Montcalm was wrestling the greatest decision of his life. He had a bewildering array of options. He could attack immediately or stay on the defensive. He could wait for Bougainville to arrive before attacking or even march to meet his subordinate and join forces. If he attacked without delay he risked throwing his less well-trained army into expert British musket volleys and seeing them decimated. However, his other options were hardly better. Just as at Orléans and Montmorency he knew the British could land large numbers of cannon and fortify themselves in an impregnable base. From it they could begin siege operations against Quebec, the landward defences of which he thought worthless. It was late in the season but Wolfe would probably have enough time to push his trenches, snaking forward until his heavy guns could threaten the walls and open a breach. A French journal had recorded earlier in the summer that such was his low opinion of the fortifications that he had no confidence at all in the course of a siege. He believed, it reported, 'that the event of a battle alone could favourably decide the fate of Quebec'.[42]

His inclination not to let the British force settle in was reinforced by its position. The British now sat astride one of the main supply routes to the centre of the colony and his carefully husbanded reserve of food and gunpowder. There were three main roads running parallel to the St Lawrence. A couple ran close to the shore. These Wolfe now controlled. Another road ran three or four miles inland from Charlesbourg via Ancienne Lorette joining the coastal one two miles east of Pointe aux Trembles. This road was still open to the French. But while the British were not actually blockading all routes to the centre of the colony they were certainly in a position to threaten any communication or stop supply convoys along both these roads. Having blocked off the river, Wolfe was now tightening the noose around Montcalm's forces in and around the city.

But Montcalm knew that Wolfe's position was still deeply precarious. Bougainville was somewhere beyond the British with the finest troops in Montcalm's army. Later in the day Vaudreuil wrote to de Lévis, now in Montreal, telling him that he had sent a message to Bougainville as soon as he realized the scale of the threat on the Plains of Abraham.[43] If Bougainville could attack at the same time as Montcalm they would have Wolfe trapped between them with a cordon of Native Americans and Canadians to the north finishing the encirclement. One of his greatest frustrations was having no idea about where Bougainville was. One of Montcalm's staff officers wrote that 'the Marquis de Montcalm, not seeing him [Bougainville] arrive, could not but think he had not been notified at all'.[44]

If Bougainville had not even heard the news, he would not be on the battlefield for hours. Yet with every minute that passed, however, Montcalm believed Wolfe was getting stronger. He would have guessed that artillery was being hauled up the Foulon path. He would have seen troops arriving, deploying, and securing their position. He imagined shovels, fascines, and gabions being unloaded from the ships. Within hours the British army would be digging in and invulnerable to attack. His staff officer wrote that Montcalm saw 'his destruction certain, if he waited any longer', because of the 'impossibility of dislodging the enemy, should they once become masters of the height called the Côte d'Abraham, half a gun shot from Quebec'.[45] Another officer wrote that Montcalm was dismayed by a 'report he had received, which had not a shadow of a foundation, that the English were busy entrenching themselves'.[46] He did not have a clear picture of the enemy. He could see groups of men shuffling around while large numbers of troops were invisible to him thanks to Wolfe's order that they should lie down. Montcalm could not tell how many troops he faced or what state they were in. He could never have guessed at the stunning efficiency of the amphibious operation, which in around four hours had delivered every single available soldier in Wolfe's army to the Anse au Foulon. Admiral Holmes later wrote that Montcalm 'was deceived to the last; for he could not believe it was possible that we had so suddenly thrown over so large a body of forces: and the inequalities of the ground covered numbers of our men, and kept him from forming a just opinion of their strength'.[47] Montcalm no doubt believed that assembling his entire army on the Plains of Abraham would take a day at least. By waiting for Bougainville he probably suspected that he would only be increasing the men at Wolfe's disposal too.

Attacking sides had an advantage. They could choose where to strike and attempt to bring overwhelming numbers to bear on a weak part of the enemy's line. Soldiers liked to be moving forward, morale soared during a charge. The dead and wounded were left behind by the advance. Defenders stood beside piles of their own casualties; men were forced to go on fighting even with their lifeless or screaming comrade beside them. Taking the offensive was embedded deep in the professional DNA of a French officer. Montcalm's aide-de-camp, the Chevalier Johnstone, wrote that while they should perhaps in retrospect have marched around the British to Ancienne Lorette and joined with Bougainville, 'in short there was not a single member of the war council who was not of the opinion to charge ... immediately'.[48]

Montcalm had to make his decision in the face of a constantly shifting stream of information. He had suffered night after night of broken, insufficient sleep. He was unable to go to a quiet, private place to think, to separate himself from the minutiae of getting his men into formation and talk through his options with trusted staff and advisers. In fact, he had no trusted staff or advisers. Bougainville, his intimate protégé was miles away, de Lévis and Bourlamaque, the second and third most senior officers in the French army of North America, were on different fronts. He was, if possible, more isolated than Wolfe. An artillery officer, Montbelliard, afterwards wrote that he snatched a moment of conversation with Montcalm who said, 'We cannot avoid action; the enemy is digging in, he already has two pieces of cannon. If we give him time to establish himself, we shall never be able to attack him with the troops we have.' He apparently added 'with a shiver of disbelief', 'is it possible that Bougainville is not hearing this?'[49]

The eyes of the army were all focused on him. There is always a crushing expectation that commanders appear decisive. Pausing to reflect, to assess one's options, may be wise but it does not inspire confidence in men looking for leadership. There is an indefinable impulsion towards battle when two armies gather in sight of each other. Fighting this urge is the hallmark of only the very greatest commanders, men supremely confident in their standing. Other men, without mighty reputations for themselves, feel the tug of combat. Cowardice was the label most feared, worse even than incompetence and certainly worse than defeat.

Exhausted, surrounded by young, gallant, foolish officers who hid their terror behind aggression, taking the offensive was the easiest decision to make. All summer Montcalm had tried to ignore the inexorable gravitational pull of the enemy force, sought to hold back the weight of French martial tradition, and stifle the clamour for a decision. Now he gave in to it. A word to his aides sent them galloping away to notify the men: the French army would prepare to attack.

Many have sought to explain Montcalm's decision. A British officer speculated that Montcalm knew Wolfe was waiting for more artillery and chose to attack 'either willing to deprive us of this advantage or fearing that we might be reinforced; or perhaps from contempt of our numbers'.[50] Across the battlefield a French officer noted that 'our troops showed great eagerness to engage, and intrepidity, but kept it up a very little time only'. Montcalm, he supposed, wanted to harness this enthusiasm, and 'it was judged proper to take immediate advantage of this spirit; however it would have been more prudent to have waited the arrival of Monsieur de Bougainville, who was advancing with the flower of the army; but our generals thought they could do the business without him'.[51]

Perhaps there is yet another reason why Montcalm was keen to fight as soon as possible. One French officer wrote that such was his hatred of Vaudreuil that he wanted to win a victory before the latter had appeared on the field of battle. 'The rash haste with which M. de Montcalm had made his attack originated in jealousy,' wrote this officer. 'M. de Vaudreuil had in a note requested him to postpone the attack until he had reunited all his forces.' The officer concluded that Montcalm's 'ambition was that no person but himself should ever be named'.[52] Ramezay agreed. 'M. le Marquis de Montcalm allowed himself to be taken over by fervour, believing that he could overcome the enemy single-handedly,' wrote the Vaudreuil ally.[53] The Governor General himself later reported to the Minister for the Colonies that 'the Marquis de Montcalm, who was the first informed of the circumstance, supposed no doubt, that it was only a detachment. That general, carried away by his zeal and great vivacity, despatched the pickets of the different regiments, a part of the battalions and Canadians, and advanced himself without communicating his arrangements to me.' Vaudreuil then says that 'I ordered the remainder of our forces, with the exception of the posts of the line of Beauport and set out immediately to place myself at the head of the army.'[54] If Vaudreuil really did plan to 'place himself at the head of the army' then it is very possible that Montcalm was desperate to attack before the man he regarded as an amateur buffoon came to usurp his position.

Ultimately Montcalm was deeply pessimistic about the chance of the colony surviving whatever the outcome of this campaign. If he fought and lost a battle, Quebec would fall; but he clearly believed that if the British stayed where they were Quebec would certainly fall as well. At least this way King Louis' honour would be intact, the town's fate would be decided on the field of battle.

Like Wolfe, Montcalm moved along the battle line. He greeted officers and shouted words of encouragement. According to legend he wore a cuirass, or metal breast plate, which was a touch anachronistic even in the eighteenth century. Beneath it he wore the uniform of a general officer which was a single breasted blue coat, a red waistcoat beneath and a black cocked hat richly decorated with white trim and gold lace. Rather than walking like his British counterpart he rode on a powerful black charger with his sword drawn. Montcalm eventually took position in the centre at the head of the Béarn and Guyenne Regiments. These regular troops wore standard grey-white coats, their tails hitched up to secure them during the march, but underneath were distinctive red waistcoats. Mud covered their gaiters which attempted to protect the grey-white breeches beneath. Tricorne hats laced with metallic thread sat on the men's heads; the sergeants sported gold lace in theirs while some of the officers wore plumes. French troops were always shaved clean but wore their hair long, tied back in a tight plait with a black bow. Some had adopted the Canadian tradition of scarring their faces with tattoos, made by burning gunpowder into a pattern of small lacerations.

Montcalm formed the two battalions in his centre into a column. Colours fluttered above the regular companies. One was a plain white 'Colonel's Colour' and the other was a regimental colour, usually a white cross with colourful quarters. The Guyenne's colour had its first and third quarters green and the second and fourth quarters were buff.[55] This regiment now joined the Béarn in a narrow-fronted but deep battering ram, often favoured by attacking sides. Not all the men in the column could bring their muskets to bear on the enemy because they were packed in the middle of a dense mass of men, but the feeling of being surrounded by their comrades was comforting and bolstered the men's courage. Columns sought to punch through thin enemy lines by sheer weight of numbers and momentum. Montcalm aimed this column of his beloved regulars towards the very heart of Wolfe's position. He hoped to achieve an overwhelming superiority at just one point of the British line. Break it and rout would follow.

At 1000 hours the French drummers beat the signal to advance. They were dressed in their 'King's Livery', a blue coat with a red and white thread in a chain motif along the seams. Their drums were the same colours as their coats and richly decorated with fleurs-de-lis. Montcalm walked his horse at the head of the centre column. As the soldiers of France stepped off they held their muskets with the index finger of the right hand on the trigger guard and the thumb on top of the cock. Their left hands gripped the stock of their muskets at chin height, their thumb pointing upwards along the barrel. Knox remembers hearing their 'loud shouts'.[56] The unmistakable roar of *Vive le Roi!* reverberated across the battlefield. There was no doubt in any of the participants' minds that this would be a decisive clash for control of North America.

Mackellar watched the French attack and wrote that they came on 'briskly'.[57] Montcalm's journal reports that they 'ran, shouting loudly'.[58] They were perhaps a bit too keen. The pace of the advance quickly caused gaps between the men. Anne-Joseph-Hippolyte de Maurès de Malartic, the Comte de Malartic, a major in the Béarn, rode into battle just like his general. He later wrote to a fellow officer that the French set off 'much too fast'. 'We had not gone twenty paces,' he continued, 'when the left was too far in the rear and the centre was too far in front.'[59] De Lévis heard that 'our army started to move with plenty of ardour but little organization'. He also reported that the ground was rough and obstacles such as bushes and patches of wheat widened the gaps between the men as they got caught up in undergrowth or slowed down to clamber across an obstruction.[60]

British cannonballs tore through the centre column. The densely packed mass of men was a plum target and the British artillerymen were masters of their trade. Malcolm Fraser watched the effects of the British fire; the French seemed 'very much galled by our artillery', which was 'very well served'. As he watched the French advance it fell into 'some confusion'.[61]

At 600 yards a well-laid cannon had just under a 90 per cent chance of hitting a body of infantrymen. After a couple of minutes, at 300 yards range, the British artillerymen changed to firing canister shot. A tin container with around forty lead balls disintegrated as it left the muzzle. Its deadly payload sprayed in all directions, some balls hitting the ground and others going high and losing their speed, but around 30 per cent found the French column. As the attackers moved to within 150 yards that figure increased to around 50 per cent.[62] Charles-Joseph, the Prince of Ligne, a successful Austrian commander in Europe at the time, noticed a herding instinct among men when they became terrified as the projectiles tore through their ranks. 'I cannot recall an action,' he wrote after a lifetime on the battlefield, 'when I did not have to try to break up a multitude of such columns with blows with the flat of my sword, while my corporals were wading in with their sticks.'[63] Montcalm had filled the vacancies in his regular battalions with Canadian recruits when the army had gathered in the spring. But four months was not enough to make a hardened soldier. It took six months at the very least, if training time and ammunition were in plentiful supply which they had not been in the camp on the Beauport shore. Often a full year was required to turn a farm hand into a soldier.[64] These new recruits among the French regulars could not resist the urge to fire at the British line at extreme range and then, compounding their error, throw themselves on the ground to reload in the Canadian way. This might have made sense for the individuals but it was a death blow to the cohesion of the whole. Malartic wrote that these men 'fired without orders, and according to their custom threw themselves on the ground to reload. This false movement broke all the battalions.'[65]

Mackellar watched with glee. 'Their front began to fire before they got within range,' he wrote, 'and the firing immediately extended throughout the whole body; but in a very wild and scattered manner. They then began to waver, but still kept advancing with the same disorderly fire.'[66] Now was the moment that Montcalm needed the steadying presence of his elite grenadier units, tough veterans who could maintain the impetus of the attack. But they were all attached to Bougainville and to the west; where his considerable force should have been appearing at any moment, there was neither musket smoke nor sound of battle. They had not yet arrived.

Knox wrote that the French fired something approximating a full volley at about one hundred and thirty yards distance. Fraser wrote that it did 'very little execution'.[67] Many of the musket balls whistled over the heads of the British. Others found their targets but as one eyewitness reported, the French were 'firing at too great a distance' and as a result 'their balls were almost spent before they reached our men'. He wrote that 'several of our people having received contusions on parts where the blow must have been mortal, had they reserved their fire a little longer'.[68] Fraser was one of these lucky ones. 'I received a slight contusion,' he wrote, 'in the right shoulder or rather breast, before the action became general, which pained me a good deal, but it did not disable me from my duty then, or afterwards.'[69]

As the French advanced the British remained silent and still. 'General Wolfe had given positive orders,' wrote Sergeant Johnson, 'not to fire a shot until the enemy should be within forty yards.'[70] This was 'punctually obeyed' and there was hardly any movement, only the lazy flapping of the colours and a rare man tumbling to the ground killed or wounded. As the enemy neared every battalion commander gave one last look at his men and took up his position behind the colours in the very centre of his unit. Every word of command was given in a steady, calm voice, to project a confidence that the speaker may not have felt in the pit of his stomach. Frederick the Great was clear on the subject: 'the courage of the troops consists entirely in that of the officers: a brave colonel means a brave battalion'.[71] Some of the officers may have been a little amateur by modern standards but every one of them was scrupulously reckless in battle. They were under no account to duck or flinch. Besides, they knew that if they could hear the whoosh of a cannonball or the whine of a musket round then it was already past them anyway. They would never hear the ball that hit them.

The red-coated soldiers stood, immobile, impassive, as musket balls twitched at their clothes and knocked men to the floor next to them. After a long summer campaign in which skill at skirmishing was highly prized, and troops were rewarded for showing initiative, suddenly warfare had reverted to the type that they recognized. Here was war as they had trained for it. Years of drill on commons and heaths across Britain and Ireland and more recently in Halifax and Louisbourg had taught them to ignore death. A manual decreed that in the last few moments before battle the men must 'pay the greatest attention to the words of command, remaining perfectly silent and steady, not making the least motion with head, body, feet, or hands, but such as shall be ordered ... shoulders square to the front, and kept back; the body upright, the breast pressed forward'. Heads were erect and eyes forward, the men were 'not to be suffered to cast down their eyes, nor look on the ground'.[72]

Some armies needed infamous blocking detachments to shoot those who fled from the line of battle but Wolfe's men needed no such coercion. Unlike the scratch, demoralized battalions that Braddock had led into slaughter, Wolfe's regiments were communities bound by years of active campaigning. Every man stood between other men he knew, whose wives had cooked for him, whose children played together on the Île d'Orléans. To run in front of these comrades was unthinkable. Many wanted revenge; every man had lost a friend or mess mate to Native American ambush or French musket balls. They had grown to trust their officers who had kept them fed and watered and turned a blind eye to the looting of *habitants'* houses and never shied away from a fire fight. They seem to have had a genuine belief in the superiority of a Briton to Frenchman, Canadian or a despised Native American. But not all Wolfe's men were superhuman. Many of them smothered their terror in drink. Water bottles hung at the men's sides filled with carefully hoarded portions of powerful New England rum.[73]

Drunk or not, Knox remembered the 'uncommon steadiness' of the army. The French fire was tolerated with 'the greatest intrepidity and firmness' and the soldiers paid 'the strictest obedience to their officers'.[74] There was a perverse pleasure in receiving an enemy volley before firing one of your own. Lieutenant Colonel Murray wrote that his men were 'determined to conquer or die in their ranks rather than be scalped and hacked'.[75]

When the French got to forty yards a clear shout went up from each regimental commander: 'Make Ready!' The men of the rear rank smartly stepped right, into the gap between the men in front. At 'Present!' a thousand muskets whipped sharply through ninety degrees. Left hands slid about a third of the way down the long, forty-six-inch barrel, butts were forced, as the drill book said, into 'the hollow between your right breast and shoulder, pressing it close to you'. Callused right thumbs pulled back the cock and then slid off to rest on the smooth walnut top of the grip while the right index finger curled around the trigger. The men were told in training to keep 'both arms close to your body' and take 'good aim by leaning the head to the right and looking along the barrel'.[76] Time and again the men had been told to aim low; new recruits were made to aim at the ground just in front of them, to compensate for the tendency to fire high. Wolfe's more experienced infantrymen now pointed their weapons at the ankles of the advancing French infantry.[77]

The next command still echoes to this day. With all the clarity and volume they could muster the regimental commanders roared, 'Fire!'

Nearly as one, a thousand fingers pulled their triggers. Like a serpent strike the cock sprang forward and the new, sharp flint scraped down the steel frizzen. Sparks flew as the frizzen tipped back to reveal the pan, with its mound of gunpowder. The sparks ignited the powder with a puff of smoke and a shower of burning powder singed side whiskers and stung cheeks. The small explosion sent flames through the touch-hole in the side of the barrel where the main charge was ignited with a loud bang, sending the musket ball blasting out of the muzzle. The British line disappeared as an eruption of white smoke swallowed the men.

Knox wrote that the men fired with 'great calmness' and the resultant volley was 'as remarkable a close and heavy discharge, as I ever saw performed at a private field of exercise'. Talking to French officers after the battle he heard from them that 'they never opposed such a shock as they received from the centre of our line, for they believed every ball took place, and such regularity and discipline they had not experienced before; our troops in general and particularly the central corps, having levelled and fired, – *comme un coup de canon* [like the blast of a cannon]'.[78] The men had been ordered to load not one but two musket balls to achieve the maximum effect on the first massive volley. Thousands of lead balls, weighing 32 grams and a shade under two centimetres in diameter flew across the thirty- or forty-metre gap at over two hundred metres per second and slammed into the French infantrymen.

The Land Pattern Musket, better known by its later nickname, the 'Brown Bess', was one of the best infantry muskets in the world. The basic design survived from the 1730s to the 1850s. It was still, however, a deeply inaccurate weapon. In fact, some commanders like Frederick the Great trained their men to sacrifice any hope of accuracy for sheer volume of fire.[79] It also had a low muzzle velocity so even if the round was on target there was a good chance that it would not punch through the skin. To have any chance of hitting and killing somebody the target could not be more than eighty or possibly a hundred yards away. Most commanders tried to make their men wait, as Wolfe had done, until the enemy was very close indeed. The immortal, 'whites of their eyes' expression, attributed to William Prescott, a rebel American officer, was coined during one of the first engagements of the American Revolution at Bunker Hill, nearly sixteen years after Quebec, but could just as well have applied to the British policy on the Plains of Abraham. A letter from an eyewitness appeared in the British media saying that the French were so close that the British made 'them feel our bullets and bayonets almost at the same time'.[80] A conservative estimate is that perhaps 40 per cent of that first mighty discharge was on target. Some musket balls thudded into cartridge pouches and ricocheted off tomahawks and sword hilts but the rest hit French flesh.[81]

After just one crashing volley the front few ranks of the attacking column must have been utterly destroyed. Dead and wounded men lay in heaps on the ground. Any soldier whose enthusiasm to get to grips with the British was still intact after that pounding would have had to clamber over the shattered corpses of his comrades and find his feet on ground slick with blood. Worse still, he would have known that there was only the briefest of respites before the musketry resumed. Through the smoke he would have been able to hear the British officers shouting for the men to reload.

The British soldiers snatched a cartridge from their boxes and tore the end off with their teeth. There was the bitter taste of gunpowder as some inevitably tipped onto the tongue. The hydrosorbic black powder immediately absorbed any moisture in their mouths and within a couple of shots they were utterly parched. They tapped a little of the powder into the flash pan and brought down the frizzen to keep it there. Then the rest of the powder was poured into the muzzle, followed by the ball and then the paper cartridge to act as a wadding. Then there was a rasping sound as the ramrods were pulled out of their storage tube on the underside of the musket and plunged into the barrel to ensure that the powder was all collected at the very bottom and the ball was held snugly on top of it by the wadding. Most of the men had steel ramrods which required just one good downward thrust. Those unlucky enough to still be using wooden ramrods had to give it a couple of plunges. Too vigorous with the ramming, though, and the charge would fail to ignite.

The entire process was minutely controlled by a complex series of moves, all of them hammered into the men by the hours of training on the drill square and the firing range. Well-trained troops were capable of firing a shot every twenty seconds. The men were supposed to fire according to a preordained plan which meant that portions of the line would fire one after the other in a ripple that ensured that there were always some musket balls being sent towards the enemy. Traditionally the British army had practised 'platooning' whereby the regimental battle line was divided into platoons before the start of battle. Each platoon was assigned to a first, second, or third firing. This system worked very well in theory or on the parade grounds of London but was far too complicated for the field. Wolfe, among other young officers, introduced the Prussian method to the British army. He had once called platooning an 'impracticable chequer' and his preferred method was to use the existing companies as the fire unit and each one simply fired in turn from left to right or vice versa.[82]

In battle most observers agreed that all this discussion on firing was totally irrelevant. Once the shooting started men blazed away until they were told to stop. One veteran of Dettingen wrote that 'they were under no command by way of Hyde Park firing, but the whole three ranks made a running fire of their own accord, at the same time with great judgement and skill, stooping as low as they could, making almost every ball take place'. This was not unusual, the British general, Lord Stair, had 'seen many a battle, and never saw the infantry engage in any other manner'.[83]

After the first volley the next followed within twenty seconds. The British troops reloaded as quickly as they could. Ramrods were pushed into the ground for ease of use or simply abandoned altogether. Some men dropped the powder and ball into the barrel and hit the butt on the ground to force it down. This reduced the speed of the round when it was fired but the French were so close that it would still be travelling fast enough. This method of loading also lessened the kick of the musket and did less damage to the shoulders of the men, which by the end of several discharges would normally be black and blue with bruising.

Experienced officers would have tried to steady their men. Wolfe had told the 20th Regiment, when he had commanded it before the war, that 'there is no necessity for firing very fast; a cool well-levelled

371

fire, with the pieces carefully loaded, is much more destructive and formidable than the quickest fire in confusion'.[84] Many troops, though, just ignored this. Officers were hard to hear over the din of battle and the men would have been entirely absorbed in their own loading and firing. Flints would shatter every twenty or more shots. The British army's flints all came from Brandon in Suffolk and when one broke the men would reach into their pocket or pouch and pull out this little piece of England and go through the fiddly process of inserting it into the jaws of the cock. There were other running repairs that the men might be forced to make. The residue of the burnt powder clogged up the weapon. Somewhere on the men's equipment hung a steel pricker and a tiny brush on a chain. Soldiers used these to clear the charred mess from around the touch-hole to allow the flames from the pan to ignite the powder in the barrel.

After a couple of rounds the men's faces were smeared with blackened powder, their shoulders ached, their ears rang, and the smoke around them was totally opaque. They fired so fast that 'the smell of gun-powder became nauseous' according to one witness.[85] Only yards away the French were taking terrible punishment. Hundreds of musket balls flayed the column from its front, and obliquely from the British regiments to the right and left. Canister shot from the two cannon knocked down swathes of men. Johnson wrote that 'we poured in such a discharge ... which we continued, with such regular briskness, as was visible to all, by the good effect it produced; their seeming resolution was soon quelled, and their courage cooled'.[86] Robert MacPherson of the 78th Highland Regiment wrote that the musketry had been at 'so good a level and to such purpose the body of enemy were put in great confusion by the slaughter made among them, both from the front and flank'. After only 'four or five discharges, the enemy fire slackened, and halted'.[87]

The French attack stalled. All command and control broke down as the roar of the British volleys drowned out the shouts of their officers. If, indeed, there were any. Many of their officers had been the first to fall. The commander of the Guyenne, Louis Restoineau de Fontbonne, was killed. The commander of La Sarre, and Montcalm's second in command, Brigadier Étienne-Guillaume de Senezergues fell. Malartic had a lucky escape when his horse was shot dead under him. Many junior officers and NCOs followed their commanders to the grave. The grenadiers of each battalion, the steadiest men, who were attached to Bougainville's force, were sorely missed. Some of the Frenchmen attempted to return the fire through the blanket of smoke; others stumbled wildly away from the firing. They lunged wildly into the troops following on behind, spreading panic. Without leadership, without the backbone of veteran troops to rally around, the French force fell apart with every British discharge. A sergeant major in the Louisbourg Grenadiers wrote that 'a terrible slaughter ensued from the quick fire of our field pieces and musketry'.[88] Knox said it was so potent 'that better troops than we encountered could not possibly withstand it'.[89] In just a few minutes Montcalm's army broke, the well-ordered battalions now just a mass of fleeing, terrified men, shoving, running, and trying to save their own skins.

Wolfe had watched the thundering British volleys from the right wing. John Johnson, who fought with his 58th Regiment over on the left wing, heard that Wolfe was 'always where the attack was hottest', sometimes standing with the Louisbourg Grenadiers and occasionally walking over to the neighbouring Bragg's 28th Regiment. Johnson reports that 'he was often in imminent danger' but he would not be prevailed on to take more care over his own safety.[90]

He had always been brave to a fault. He had been miraculously unscathed at Montmorency, he had survived skirmishes in the woods that had killed and injured men only feet away from him, and that morning he had ignored the Canadian sharpshooters in the bushes beside his position. Now Wolfe's luck ran out. First a glancing blow struck him on the wrist. His 'Family Journal' notes that 'he took no notice of' this wound. He simply bound it up with a handkerchief. Next a bullet grazed his stomach, again he ignored the pain. But not even the coolest, most dispassionate Englishman could soldier on through the next wound. Two other musket balls, or possibly one larger ball from a canister, struck him 'in his body'.[91]

Command in the eighteenth century was a dangerous job. Braddock, Howe, and Prideaux had already fallen in North America at the head of armies or detachments. Montcalm's predecessor, Dieskau, had

been horribly mangled on the field of battle. In Europe von Browne
and von Schwerin, senior commanders of the Austrian and Prussian
forces respectively at the battle of Prague in 1757, were both killed.
How Frederick the Great survived his string of battles is something of
a mystery. Command of an army meant visible leadership, sharing the
dangers of the men in the front line. In this pre-industrial warfare the
presence of a commander at the critical melee, or his intervention with
fresh, reserve troops at a decisive moment, could swing the outcome
of a battle. The detached overview of later generals was less valuable
than dramatic appearances in the thick of the fighting. These leaders
were ostentatious with their lack of care for their own persons. Too
often they paid an awful price for glory.

Wolfe stumbled to the rear. After the battle Knox tells that many
men 'from a vanity of talking, claimed the honour of being his support-
ers'. Wolfe was, in fact, carried behind the lines by James Henderson,
a volunteer, and Lieutenant Henry Browne and an unnamed private
soldier, all from the Louisbourg Grenadiers. They were helped by an
artilleryman whose name Knox did not recollect; had he done so he
would have 'cheerfully recorded' it.[92] This little group was a distinctly
less glittering assembly of the great and the good which surrounds
Wolfe's broken but beatific body in the Benjamin West painting, one
of the classics of British imperial iconography. There were no senior
officers present, certainly no Native Americans and no massive flag
patriotically draped as a backdrop and a reminder of the cause for
which he was spilling his blood.

He remained conscious for some time. As he was hauled past
Otway's 35th who were still watching the right flank of the army, set
back from the main battle line, he 'waved his hat' at them, telling them
according to his 'Family Journal' to 'move up and flank the enemy'.[93]
Then his helpers laid him on the ground; the wound in his breast was
gushing blood and the front of his shirt was a deep red. They tried to
staunch the flow but the haemorrhaging continued. He waved away
offers of attention from a surgeon, saying 'it is needless; it is all over
with me'. When he noticed that Henderson was wounded he begged
him to see to his own injury. He drifted in and out of consciousness
but remained lucid. When he heard his companions talking about the

French breaking and running he snapped with 'great earnestness, like a person roused from sleep', 'Who runs?' One of the men replied, 'The enemy, Sir; Egad they give way every-where.' All the sources agree that despite the pain and his slipping grasp on life a broad smile broke out across Wolfe's face. Ever the soldier, he now gave his last order. 'Go one of you my lads, to Colonel Burton –; tell him to march Webb's regiment with all speed down to Charles's River, to cut off the retreat of the fugitives from the bridge.' Then, with only seconds of his life remaining, he turned on his side and said, 'Now, God be praised, I will die in peace.' He expired with the smile fixed on his face.[94]

The army was leaderless. Monckton, the second in command, who should have taken over, was badly injured at almost the same time as Wolfe fell. He had been by Lascelles' 47th Regiment, which had faced the central French column. Townshend wrote in his journal that the wound was 'in his right breast, by a ball that went through part of his lungs, and which was cut out under the blade bone of his shoulder, just as the French were giving way'.[95] He was taken to the *Lowestoft* for medical attention. Command now devolved to Townshend although it was some time before that became clear to anyone.

Along the line of battle the British soldiers peered into the murk. Some accounts suggest that the French were broken after just over a minute of crashing musket volleys. Malcolm Fraser remembered it as 'continuing very hot for about six, or (some say) eight minutes'.[96] Others suggest that 'the fire continued very hot indeed for about ten minutes when the French and the Canadians turned tail'.[97] The French may well have proved more tenacious along some parts of the line than others, but certainly after no more than ten minutes as the smoke cleared the British saw the fleeing backs of their enemy. With 'the smoke of the powder vanishing' Fraser watched 'the main body of the Enemy retreating in great confusion towards the town, and the rest towards the river St Charles'.[98]

Without waiting for instruction the commanders of the front line battalions prepared to chase down the enemy. Each of them roared, 'Fix Bayonets!' The men's right arms crossed their bodies to seize a seventeen-inch-long, thin isosceles triangle of steel. The edges of these bayonets were sharpened to such a fine degree that men could use them to shave. With a smart action the hollow ring at the base of the bayonet was thrust over the muzzle of the musket and then slotted down and turned snugly to fix it in position. The next command was 'Charge Your Bayonet!' At this the men's right feet stepped back and hundreds of muskets, now tipped with a bayonet, were brought back onto the horizontal, the right hand gripping the stock behind the trigger tightly at the level of their waists, their knuckles resting on the top of the hip bone.

When this was complete the officers led their men forward in pursuit of the enemy. At this point the men were finally allowed to roar a battle cry. Wolfe had written years before that 'when they are upon a point of rushing upon the enemy, the battalion may give a warlike shout and run in'.[99] Lascelles' 47th was the first to move off but was quickly overtaken by the Highlanders of the 78th who seem to have dispensed with their bayonet drills and reverted to a much older and more favoured weapon: the broadsword.

With a Gaelic scream the Highlanders drew their ancestral weapon and tore after the French. One eyewitness wrote that '450 Highlanders were let loose upon them'; as they caught them they 'made terrible havoc among the poor devils ... When these took their broadswords, my god! What a havoc they made! They drove everything before them and walls could not resist their fury – those breechless fellows are an honour to their country.' The author was particularly impressed that they were not motivated by financial incentive, 'praise and approbation the only reward (except half victuals and clothes) that a highlander demands, being prepossessed naturally with a kind of martial honour'.[100] Holmes agreed that the pursuit was 'carnage' as the Highlanders 'with their broad swords did great execution'.[101] Their chaplain reported to a fellow Scot that 'they rushed in sword in hand and some other regiments with bayonets. In a moment the rout was general. Your countrymen, led on by Brigadier Murray, were interspersed amongst the thick of them ... cutting and slashing every where about them.'[102]

Sergeant James Thompson was in the thick of it. He reported that 'If the French gave themselves quietly up, they had no harm done to them. But Faith! If they tried to outrun a Hielandmon [Highlander], they stood but a bad chance, for Whash! went the broadsword.' He looked around and 'the casualties lay on the field as thick as a flock of sheep and just as they had fallen, for the main body had been completely routed off the ground and had no opportunity of carrying away their dead and wounded'. One particular image seems to have stuck in his head, 'it was horrid to see the effect of blood and dust on their white coats'.[103]

John Johnson wrote that 'every man exerted himself, as if possessed with an extraordinary spirit, for the honour of old England, calling out aloud to one another, "Death or Victory!"' They chased the French with 'irresistible fury'.[104] Soon stories circulated about the deeds of certain berserk Highlanders, tales reminiscent of a distant past. One told of Ewan Cameron who killed nine men before losing his sword arm to a cannonball, and then picked up a bayonet and wounded several more before a bullet to the throat ended his rampage. The Highlander myth was born. They won a reputation during that charge that has endured beyond the existence of the true Highlander himself. It was the first time the Highlanders were portrayed in the army and in the British press with pride as the shock troops of empire. Until then the Highlander had been a deeply malignant, savage presence in the north of the island. Uncontrollable and capable, if properly mobilized, of threatening the very existence of the British state. On the Plains of Abraham they roared into the popular consciousness and established themselves as the elite of the British army. From Canada in 1759 to the Napoleonic Wars, the nineteenth-century wars of Empire, the global conflicts of the twentieth century and up to the craggy slopes of Tumbledown in the Falklands the Highland units advanced to the noise of their pipes and never surrendered the renown their forebears had won before the walls of Quebec.

Malcolm Fraser kept a cool enough head to realize that attacking with cold steel looked impressive but was an inefficient way of routing the enemy. The Highland charge, he wrote, 'I dare say increased their panic but saved many of their lives, whereas if the artillery had been allowed to play, and the army advanced regularly there would have been more of the enemy killed and wounded'. Even so, 'in advancing we passed over a great many dead and wounded, (French regulars mostly) lying in front of our regiment'. He, like all the other officers who left accounts, was generous in the praise of his men. 'To do them justice,' he wrote of the Highlanders, they 'behaved extremely well all day, as did the whole of our army.'[105]

Looking at the aftermath of the slaughter one eyewitness was appalled at the carnage. The Highlanders had 'made a havoc not to be described ... the bullet and bayonet are decent deaths, compared with the execution of their swords'. He stumbled across one corpse that had had its head removed with one blow from a broadsword.[106] Lieutenant Colonel Murray wrote to his wife that 'there was no restraining the men'. Several of his grenadiers returned from the charge with bayonets 'bent, and their muzzles dipped in gore'.[107]

As the French regulars fled off the battlefield, the Canadian troops, whom Montcalm and the other regular officers so despised, fought a gallant rearguard action that ironically saved King Louis' honour. Anchored in the bushes and houses around the north side of the battlefield the Canadians attacked the Highlanders and other pursuing troops and inflicted serious casualties, forcing them to back off and regroup. One French officer noted that 'the rout was total only among the Regulars; the Canadians accustomed to fall back Indian fashion (and like the ancient Parthians) and to turn afterwards on the enemy with more confidence than before, rallied in some places, and under cover of the brushwood, by which they were surrounded, forced divers corps to give way'. The Native Americans had been even more careful with their own skins: 'the Indians took scarcely any part in this affair. They kept themselves, for the most part at a distance, until the success of the battle should decide what part they should take. It is well known that they never face an enemy in open field.'[108] What they had just witnessed of European warfare was unlikely to have convinced them that their approach was mistaken.

Wolfe's 'Family Journal' recorded that 'the regular troops made but one effort and afterwards dispersed. The *troupes de Colonie* and Militia disputed the copse for some time afterwards.'[109] Vaudreuil attempted to take the credit for this fierce rearguard action. He wrote to the Minister of Marine in Paris saying that by the time he arrived on the battlefield, 'I could not stop a soldier. I rallied about 1000 Canadians, who by their bold front, arrested the enemy in his pursuit.'[110]

To de Lévis he reported that twice he 'rallied the army' and only ceded the battlefield when he saw 'the discouragement of the army would lead perhaps to an even worse outcome'.[111] In fact, the sharp fight bears all the hallmarks of a spontaneous stand by proud, gritty Canadians rather than a carefully orchestrated plan by Vaudreuil, but the reinforcements he brought across the St Charles may certainly have swelled the numbers of those who fought on.

Malcolm Fraser wrote that the Highlanders bore the brunt of this unexpected flaring up of fighting. With Brigadier Murray leading them on, they tried to drive the Canadians back. They found themselves plunged into bush fighting, similar to the skirmishing throughout July and August. Fraser recorded that casualties came from 'skulking fellows, with small arms, from the bushes and behind the houses in the suburbs of St Louis and St John's'. He claimed that 'they greatly exceeded us in numbers, they killed and wounded a great many of our men, and killed two Officers, which obliged us to retire a little, and form again'. To add to the British discomfort, the British ships' logs mention that the French hulks, anchored in the St Charles, 'fired several shots at our people'.[112] The Highlanders needed help; it appeared in the form of the '58th Regiment with the 2nd battalion of Royal Americans'. 'Having come up to our assistance,' reports Fraser, 'all three making about five hundred men, advanced against the enemy and drove them first down to the great meadow between the hospital and the town and afterwards over the river St Charles.' The fighting died down by midday. The fierce skirmishing had been an unwelcome sting in the tail of the battle for the British who had thought the fighting over when they saw the French regulars retreating. Fraser noted that 'it was at this time that our regiment suffered most'. The Highlanders had paid a high price for their aggression. Around a hundred and seventy of their 500 officers and men were casualties, eighteen of them killed outright. The officers suffered particularly badly as the sharpshooters singled them out. These included Thomas Ross of Calrossie, who was 'mortally wounded in the body, by a cannon ball from the hulks, in the mouth of the River St Charles, of which he died in great torment, but with great resolution, in about two hours thereafter'.[113] Simon Fraser of Inverallochy had been narrowly saved from facing the massed musketry of the British army at Culloden in 1746 by virtue of his youth. He had been 13 at the time of the battle but his older brother Charles had led the Frasers of Lovat as they fought for the Stuart Prince Charles and was killed by the British as he lay injured on the battlefield. Simon, now wearing both the red coat of King George and the kilt of his clan, was terribly wounded on the Plains of Abraham, but clung on to life for just over a month before joining his brother in the roll-call of Fraser heroes.

The French army fled into the city or across the bridges over the St Charles and back to the Beauport shore. The gates into the town were packed with a mass of panicking men and horses. Montcalm had watched his attack disintegrate. His beloved regular battalions had proved no match for the British and now his retreat was being covered by the Canadians who fought tenaciously along the wooded northern edge of the battlefield. Montcalm had no choice but to follow his broken men back to the city. As he waited in the crowd to get through the Saint-Louis gate he was wounded in the thigh and the stomach. He slumped in his saddle and had to be held upright in it by three soldiers. They threaded his horse through the town's streets. Onlookers screamed when they saw their general's shirt soaked in blood and he called out to these 'good friends' and told them 'it is nothing'. But on arriving at the Ursuline Convent it became clear that his wounds were, in fact, mortal. The battlefield had claimed another Montcalm.[114]

The Plains of Abraham had, in the space of no more than fifteen minutes, gone from being the scene of a tightly controlled manoeuvring by thousands of men to utter chaos. The most senior officers on either side had been killed or had left the field with mortal wounds. Whole units had disintegrated in flight or pursuit. Murray was leading the Highlanders against the Canadians and had lost all overview of the battle. In the midst of this mayhem Townshend's aide-de-camp, who had gone to Wolfe with a message from Townshend warning about his lack of troops, returned to tell his brigadier that Wolfe was dead, Monckton off the field, and that he was now in command of the army.

Townshend had spent the battle on the northern flank of the British position. Here the French had made a less spirited attack than in the centre and 'were soon repulsed' according to Townshend's report. To his wife he admitted that 'though I was not in the warmest part of the action; yet I had more shots near me than in any other action I've seen'. 'It has pleased god,' he continued, 'to preserve me for my Charlotte and my George and the rest and to restore me to you whom alone I have found good and grateful to me.'[115] The crisis was far from over, however. When Murray's brigade had all charged wildly after the retreating French, Townshend had been forced to move the 2nd/60th Royal Americans into the gap they had left. He worried that he was being spread too thin, especially because there was still 'a body of savages, which waited ... for an opportunity to fall upon our rear'.[116] Eighteenth-century battles were frequently lost when generals thought them won and vice versa. The Austrians won Kolin in 1757 despite being sure they had lost and were defeated at Torgau when they were certain of victory. Communication was haphazard, smoke obscured everything, noise was universal, and cheering could come from anyone.

Townshend had to be very careful that the British did not squander the winning position that musketry had brought them. He raced to the centre where he found that 'the pursuit had put part of the troops in great disorder'. While he struggled to impose some control and get the scattered men back into their ranks, a messenger brought him the news he had been dreading to hear: 'Monsieur de Bougainville with about 2000 men, the corps from Cap Rouge and that neighbourhood, appeared in our rear.'[117]

Forty-five minutes earlier and the history of North America may have been rather different. Bougainville later claimed that he had not been told about the landing until sometime after it had occurred. 'I was not informed of it until nine in the morning' he wrote in his journal. But, he claimed, he had begun marching 'at once'.[118] Given the impossibility of coordinating any joint attack before telegraph or radio, turning up ready to fight forty-five minutes apart was quite remarkable; however, in that brief flash of time the hopes of New France had been extinguished. Bougainville's 2,000 men were some of the finest in North America and would have acted as a hammer to Montcalm's anvil but alone they were not enough to defeat Townshend's army. He scrambled to redeploy his men. The reliable Burton and his 48th

Regiment who had stood in reserve all day were swung round to meet the threat as was the 3rd/60th who had been sent back to guard the landing zone. Williamson rushed his field pieces across to face the new threat.

The two British regiments, again outnumbered, called Bougainville's bluff. The young Frenchman, brilliantly gifted but experiencing independent command for the first time, looked desperately for any sign of Montcalm's forces. He also tried to gauge the strength of the troops blocking his way. He could see men swelling the British ranks with every minute that passed, running over from other parts of the battlefield. Williamson's guns fired a couple of shots at maximum elevation towards his position. Perhaps this decided him. Preferring caution to reckless abandon, he withdrew. In his journal he made his excuse: 'when I came within range of the battle, our army was beaten and in retreat. The entire English army advanced to attack me. I retreated before them and posted myself so as to cover the retreat of our army.'[119] If Montcalm and Bougainville had both made the other's decision the day might have ended with different results.

Townshend did not have the stomach to follow him. The army of New France had been soundly beaten. Hundreds of its men lay heaped on the field of battle. Townshend told Pitt that he did not want to 'risk the fruit of so decisive a day'. If he caught up with Bougainville he feared that he would have to fight 'upon his own terms and in the midst of woods and swamps'.[120] Failing to annihilate a broken and defeated enemy was common in this period. The process of battle seriously weakened the ties that bound the army. Mackellar wrote that 'our loss, though not great in numbers, was nevertheless severe'.[121] By this he meant that important men had been put out of action. Canadian sharpshooters had taken a toll on the British officers. Wolfe and Monckton were joined on the casualty list by Carleton, Barré, Spital (a 'Brigade Major' under Monckton), and Harvey Smythe, Wolfe's aide-de-camp. Units became lost and dispersed, totally out of touch. Officers could go for hours without knowing if the day was won or lost. Re-establishing some kind of centrifugal authority was almost more important than thrashing a beaten enemy. The men needed time to recover from huge emotional and physical strain. No one had slept for more than a few minutes in the previous thirty-six hours. Friends had been killed and horribly wounded beside them. Some men threw themselves to the ground and fell into a deep sleep straight after battle; others looted the corpses of the fallen. The Russian success at Gross-Jägersdorf in 1757 was not followed up because the Russian soldiers could not be stopped from killing the Prussian wounded, stripping their corpses, and downing any captured liquor. The men had survived; they were not overly enthusiastic about throwing themselves back into the fray. Commanders were just as exhausted. The intellectual effort required left nerves at breaking point. Townshend had a wood full of expert enemy bush fighters to his north, a city wall mounted with cannon to his front, and his two superior officers had been carried off the battlefield, one killed the other seriously wounded. Reassembling his army, clearing the battlefield, gauging French strength, and bringing up supplies would be more than enough work for the rest of the day. Townshend elected to stay put.

A summer of skirmishing and guerrilla warfare so typical of war in North America had culminated in a notably European battle. A thin red British line had trounced massed French columns in a tantalizing preview of the clashes that would become the symbol of a later and greater war between these two nations, when Napoleon Bonaparte would grasp at global hegemony. Monckton wrote to Pitt as he was convalescing from his wound trying to explain the causes of victory. Above all, he insisted that 'His Majesty's troops behaved with the greatest steadiness and bravery'.[122] Townshend wrote to Amherst echoing his colleague's sentiments: 'was I really to point out the most striking cause of this successful stroke I must attribute it to the admirable and determined firmness of every British soldier in the field'. 'Victory or no quarter,' he continued, 'was I may affirm in every man's face that day.'[123]

FIFTEEN

'Our rejoicings are not yet over'

QUEBEC'S WESTERN WALLS had been lined with onlookers during the battle. The townspeople watched helplessly as the future of their homeland was decided. They could see wounded men writhing on the ground and many other bodies who would move no more. Among them were friends, husbands, and relatives. As the French forces retreated the citizens knew that now the terrible trauma of a close siege beckoned, coming on top of a summer of shortages, fire, and bombardment. Others had an even closer view. The General Hospital was on the edge of the battlefield itself. It was packed with nuns from three different convents as well as many sheltering civilians. One of the nuns recorded that the atmosphere was one of 'terror and confusion'. The sisters peered out of the windows and 'witnessed the carnage'.

This seems to have had a bracing effect, one of them reports that 'it was in such a scene that charity triumphed, and caused us to forget self-preservation and the danger we were exposed to, in the immediate presence of the enemy'. There was a wave of casualties, brought to the hospital 'by hundreds, many of them our close connexions'. 'It was necessary,' she writes, 'to smother our grief and exert ourselves to relieve them.'[1]

The wounded and dead were collected during the truce that always followed pitched battles. Some of the British soldiers dragged or carried casualties to the rear. Sergeant Thompson wrote that 'our men had nothing better to carry them on, than a kind of hand barrow with canvas laid across it'. It was slow going and the strong Scotsman lost

384

his patience and threw one wounded Frenchman across his shoulder like a sack of coal and 'landed him safe at the temporary hospital'. With this kind of gentle treatment it is not surprising that 'the poor devils would cry out lustily when they were in an uneasy position, but one could not understand a word of what they said'. He reports one vivid memory of a man with 'one of his cheeks lying flat on his shoulder, which he got by attempting to run away though he had a highlander on his heels'.[2]

Slowly a picture emerged of the scale of the dead and wounded. The official British casualty return emphasizes that the regiments paid very different prices for the victory.[3] Fraser's 78th was cruelly battered with 170 reported casualties, just under one third of those who had taken part in the battle. Fifty-four Louisbourg Grenadiers, nearly a quarter of the unit, were killed or injured. One hundred men, about one in three, of Anstruther's 58th Regiment were also casualties. These three units had anchored both flanks and had borne the brunt of the sniping by the Canadians, and Fraser's had suffered for their enthusiastic pursuit of the broken French army. More than a third of the 2nd/60th were casualties, yet more evidence that Canadian fire from the woods had been effective. Other units that were not exposed to the full fury of Canadian skirmishing fared much better. Webb's 48th Regiment, held in reserve, had only three men wounded. Kennedy's 43rd and Lascelles' 47th which had faced the full force of the French column and blasted it with their muskets returned only twenty-six and thirty-eight casualties respectively. There is no doubting that in this battle it was the colonial sharpshooters who did the real damage to the British. The overall number of killed was very small. Just sixty-one officers and men died on the field whereas 592 were wounded. This is unusually disproportionate, the ratio of killed to wounded would normally be something in the order of 1:3 rather than the almost 1:10 that occurred on the Plains of Abraham. One explanation is that the French and Canadians were firing accurately but at too great a range to kill British soldiers. Many, like Malcolm Fraser, were hit, but not terminally. The casualty figures provide an indication of the danger associated with different jobs. Officers were almost twice as likely to be killed or injured as the men. If the two unengaged units are discounted, the

48th and the 3rd/60th, then two out of every seven officers who fought on the front line ended up as casualties. The figure for the men is one in six. Chaplain Robert MacPherson wrote grimly home that 'the volunteers of the army will be provided for'.[4] These eager young men who dreamt of being officers now found that French musket balls had created plenty of vacancies. Perhaps the most dangerous job of all was to be a general officer or on his staff. The British army on the Plains of Abraham had been virtually decapitated.

The French army had suffered even worse. 'We have just had an awful encounter,' Vaudreuil scribbled in a note to Lévis.[5] Montcalm, the French commander, his second in command, and a number of other senior figures such as the commander of the militia on the right wing, François-Xavier de Saint-Ours, had all been killed or mortally wounded. One French officer estimates that they lost 'between seven or eight hundred men killed and wounded'.[6] Mackellar writes that 200 'officers and men lay dead upon the field'. The British also took '13 officers and 350 men prisoners'. He noted that 'we could not exactly find out' the number of wounded 'but from what we could learn they must have been above 1000 or 1200 men'.[7] Townshend wrote in his official report that 'their loss is computed to have been about 1500 men, which fell chiefly upon their regulars'.[8]

Surgeons on both sides were busy. Unfortunately for the wounded the professional bar to becoming a surgeon could not have been lower. Few had degrees and there was certainly no requirement to have a medical qualification. The Royal College of Surgeons was only founded in 1800. There was no centralized army medical board, nor would there be until the end of the century, so each regimental commander made his own arrangements. Pay was poor, conditions usually awful and tools and medicines were basic and in short supply. Anyone with any skill was bound to regard a comfortable and well-paid practice in London, Bath, or Edinburgh as infinitely preferable to slogging around the mosquito-infested combat zones on the periphery of empire.[9]

Men undergoing surgery had around a 50 per cent chance of survival. The most common operation was an amputation. Strong liquor was poured down the throat of the patient, a blindfold put on, and a leather strap inserted between the upper and lower jaw to bite on. Then a screw tourniquet was applied above the wound and tightened to prevent haemorrhaging. The surgeon used a scalpel to slice the flesh away from his chosen point on the limb. Then he placed a blade up against the bone and started sawing. After a few amputations the saw grew dull and the cutting took longer and longer. Through the afternoon growing piles of severed limbs piled up behind the surgeon and his mates.

The wounded staggered or were carried down the track to the Anse au Foulon for transfer to the hospital on Île d'Orléans. They were forced to make way for bands of sailors dragging cannon up towards the Plains of Abraham. The *Hunter* alone sent 'an officer and 30 men', or just under a third of the ship's company to help with this task.[10] One witness watched this 'laborious employment which the honest tars set about with the greatest alacrity'. He reports that 'it was really diverting to hear the midshipmen cry out "Starboard, starboard, my brave boys."'[11]

On the Plains soldiers were setting to work fortifying their position. One British source describes how as soon as the fighting was over 'we received part of our entrenching tools, and began to make redoubts, not knowing but next morning we would have another [enemy force] to cut'.[12] At least one senior British officer regarded his army's position as very fragile. Murray, now second in command, wrote a year later that they had been 'surprised into a victory'. As he came to terms with the unexpected success he looked about him and realized that it had 'cost the conquered very little indeed'.[13] The French still had a considerable force on the other side of the St Charles River and Bougainville lurked to the rear.

With some alacrity, therefore, the ground was cleared, houses on the periphery of the battlefield were fortified, and, in the words of Chief Engineer Patrick Mackellar, 'we began to raise redoubts on the front and upon the flanks of our camp'.[14] Like the rest of the army young Malcolm Fraser and his men 'lay on our arms all the night of the 13th September'.[15] They slept rough, at the barricades, muskets in hand. If any one challenged a stranger the password was 'Victory'. Around them was the wreckage of battle. Dead bodies awaited burial and discarded kit lay in heaps. The battlefield smelt of burnt grass, gunpowder, and blood. Survivors were less moved than might be expected. They were all veterans and as an Austrian commander once wrote after a battle in Europe, 'it is not a question of being hard-hearted, unless you are an authentic villain. But you are so glad to have survived the day that you become a little insensitive.'[16]

The wary British troops would have been cheered if they had known what was afoot in the French camp across the St Charles. The confidence of the French regular troops, in particular, had been crushed by the day's fighting. One journal reports that 'after the battle ... diverse officers of the regular troops did not hesitate to say openly, in the presence of the soldier, that no other course remained for us than to capitulate promptly for the entire colony'.[17] Vaudreuil sent to a dying Montcalm for advice. The General wrote back that he had three options: surrender the colony, retire to the Jacques Cartier River, or attack. Montcalm's pessimism, now strengthened by his impending death, got the better of him and during the night he wrote to the British commander. The note is, as always, impeccably phrased: 'Sir, Obliged to cede Quebec to your arms I have the honour to beg your Excellency's kindness for our sick and wounded.' It ended: 'I have the honour to be, sir, your very humble and very obedient servant. Montcalm.'[18] After his somewhat premature surrender of Quebec Montcalm dictated a letter to his beloved family, praised his successor, de Lévis, and received the last rites from Bishop Pontbriand. Montcalm died as he watched his last dawn at 0500 hours. His corpse was lowered into a shell hole in the floor of the Ursulines' chapel where it remained until it was reburied with great pomp in 2001 in the cemetery of the General Hospital.[19]

But the town was not Montcalm's to surrender. There was still a garrison and an army licking its wounds on the Beauport shore. The previous evening Vaudreuil had called a council of war. It had been a bad-tempered affair. Vaudreuil and Bigot had urged an attack. A regular officer who watched the meeting wrote that the Governor General urged his subordinates to 'take their revenge the next morning and endeavour to wipe off the stains they had contracted the foregoing fatal day'. The witness believed that 'this proposal which seemed to carry a true sense of honour with it, ought never to have been rejected by those gentlemen who receive their sovereign's pay, in order to maintain his spirit of honour'.[20] However, reject it they did. The regular officers refused to follow Vaudreuil. Another witness was exasperated. 'All these gentlemen,' he wrote, were 'exaggerating somewhat the loss we had suffered, all voted unanimously that the army should retreat to Jacques Cartier.' This was madness according to the source, 'by concentrating M de Bougainville's corps, the Montréal Battalions and the garrison of the town we should still have remaining about nearly five thousand fresh troops, whom we might regard as the elite of the army'. In the end Vaudreuil was unable to convince the officers, reeling from their shocking defeat. He was simply outvoted.[21] At 2100, three hours after the meeting broke up, the French army fled north up the St Charles 'abandoning provisions, ammunition, baggage, and artillery and marched all night to gain the Point aux Trembles'.[22] One officer wrote that 'the disorder started when we left'. It was soon a 'melee'. Had the British intervened, '50 men could have destroyed the rest of our army'. The disconsolate author concluded that 'the French soldier does not know discipline any more, instead of training the Canadian he has taken all his bad faults'.[23] Johnstone, Montcalm's aide-de-camp, wrote that 'it was not a retreat but an abominable flight'.[24]

In the morning Mackellar inspected the abandoned Beauport shore. 'They left most of their tents standing,' he wrote, as well as 'all their artillery along that coast, and a considerable quantity of provisions which was plundered and carried off by the habitants'.[25] Vaudreuil had also left behind instructions to the commander of French forces in the city itself, Ramezay. He said that the British entrenchments made them 'every moment still more inaccessible' to French attack and as a result he was going to retreat upcountry. Ramezay was to defend the city until 'he shall fall short of provisions' at which point he was to send 'the most capable and intelligent officer of his garrison to propose its capitulation agreeably to the subjoined articles'. Vaudreuil enclosed these articles of capitulation in rough form.[26] On 14 September Ramezay reviewed his men. Three hundred and thirty French and colonial regulars formed a nucleus of professionals. They were joined by twenty artillerymen, 500 sailors, and around thirteen hundred militiamen, something like 2,200 in all. There were eight days' worth of rations to feed these men and the 4,000 civilian inhabitants of Quebec.

On 14 September Townshend ordered that the parole or challenge was 'Wolfe' and the countersign 'England'.[27] The imperial canonization of Wolfe had begun. His loss does seem to have profoundly affected his men. Knox reaches new heights of hyperbole and melodrama to describe his former commander in chief. 'Our joy at this success,' Knox insisted, 'is inexpressibly damped by the loss we sustained of one of the greatest heroes which this or any other age can boast of, – General James Wolfe, who received his mortal wound, as he was exerting himself at the head of the grenadiers of Louisbourg.' 'My pen is too feeble,' he continued, 'to draw the character of this British Achilles ... yet I may, with strict truth, advance that Major General James Wolfe, by his talents ... no means inferior to a Frederick [the Great], a Henry [*le grand* of France], or a Ferdinand [the successful commander of British and allied forces in Europe at the time].'[28] A volunteer with one of the regiments wrote that Wolfe had been a 'noble, a much loved, a much lamented officer'.[29] Malcolm Fraser wrote that 'we suffered an irreplaceable loss in the death of our commander the brave Major General James Wolfe, who was killed in the beginning of the general action; we had the good fortune not to hear of it till all was over'.[30]

It was not only the officers who grieved for their commander; the less audible voice of the men in the ranks was also in mourning. Iain Campbell composed a verse, in Gaelic, of his epic ballad which recorded the campaign in the memory of the clan Fraser:

> the flowing blood of our renowned general
> was soaking into the grass
> and it was a terrible loss
> though it is a great tale to tell ...
> He asked to be lifted, so that he could see
> the battle, while he was in that terrible plight
> he could not see the heroes
> as death took away his sight!

they said to him in high spirits
'we have suddenly won the battlefield
and the Gaels are among them
wounding them as they run downhill'.[31]

One officer wrote that 'the soldiers were inconsolable for the loss of their brave general as they loved him beyond measure; and well they might, for he was extremely tender to, and careful of, them, and was called, the Officer's Friend, and Soldier's Father'.[32] Lieutenant Browne who had shared Wolfe's final moments wrote to his father saying,

You can't imagine ... the sorrow of every individual in the army for so great a loss. Even the soldiers dropped tears, who were but the minute before driving their bayonets through the French. I can't compare it to anything better than to a family in tears and sorrow which had just lost their father, their friend and their whole dependence.[33]

Saunders and Townshend, who both had good cause to dislike Wolfe, behaved very correctly in their correspondence. Saunders wrote to Townshend saying that the 'loss of our friend General Wolfe gives me the greatest concern which in some measure is taken off by the great victory of today ... he was himself sensible of the weakness of his constitution, and determined to crowd into a few years actions that would have adorned length of life'.[34] Perhaps oddly the two men were the major beneficiaries of Wolfe's will. He had written it during the early summer during his long journey aboard the *Neptune* and left 'my light service of plate' to Saunders, 'in remembrance of his guest'. As for his 'camp equipage, kitchen furniture, table linen, wine and provisions', these were left to 'the officer who succeeds me in the command'. 'All my books and papers, both here and in England' were left to his keen fellow student of military history, Colonel Carleton. His linen and clothes were left to his servant François and his three footmen, and all the servants were paid up to the end of the year and their board looked after until they arrived in Britain or 'engage with other masters, or enter into some other profession'. On top of this he left '50 guineas to François, 20 to Ambrose and ten to each of the others'. Anything left 'I leave to my good mother, entirely at her disposal'.[35]

On 14 September Townshend issued a stirring General Order. It informed the men that 'the general officers remaining fit to act take the earliest opportunity to express the praise which is due to the conduct and bravery of the troops'. The nature of the victory 'sufficiently proves the superiority which this army has over any number of such troops as they engaged yesterday'. The men were told to bear the fatigues of the next few days with good cheer because 'this seems to be the period which will determine in all probability our American labours'. Tents were to be brought up to save the men from another night in the open while the army's pioneers were to start burying the heaps of dead.[36] Townshend instructed the engineers to widen the track from Anse au Foulon, to make it easier to bring tents and other supplies up. Once the tents were on the Plains, a heavy siege artillery train began the long, painful ascent to the higher ground where men were digging batteries to house it. Over the next few days, one journal reports, 'twelve heavy 24 pounders, six heavy 12 pounders, some large mortars and 4 inch howitzers' were brought up 'to play upon the town'.[37] Rear Admiral Holmes reported that 'the army and the fleet were incessantly employed in getting every thing ready for opening batteries against the town'. There was a good deal of hurry because 'it is now very late in the season and the utmost diligence was used and the greatest fatigue undergone, with spirit and cheerfulness by every body, to bring the campaign soon to an end'.[38] Townshend also appointed new brigadiers; Burton now finally won his promotion and Fraser, also recovering from a wound, was also elevated. The new commander was also careful to keep Monckton closely informed. Townshend wrote to his colleague upon hearing that the wound was not mortal, congratulating him on the fact and telling him that he was investing the town as closely as possible to complete the long siege. He finished the letter, 'Adieu, Dear Bob, no man wishes your health more than your obedient servant.'[39]

Inside Quebec the spirit of the townspeople was cracking. Militiamen slipped out of the town to avoid capture. Ramezay was astonished to receive a remonstrance on 15 September from the wealthiest citizens to capitulate on honourable terms rather than prolong the resistance and risk a violent assault on the city. The prospect of the British army sacking Quebec was far more terrible than even the bombardment that they had all endured for nearly two months. It was a fact of military life that when an eighteenth-century army had battered its way through ditches, breaches in the city wall, across barricades, and into the narrow streets of a town they could not nor would not be restrained. It was one of the few times that the mask of discipline was allowed to slip or, indeed, was discarded entirely. Captured cities were often subjected to obscene ravages, reminiscent of Attila's attacks on Roman cities at the end of the Western Empire. Not only did the chaotic, bloody, and ferocious nature of an assault make reimposing discipline a practical impossibility but also it was felt by many that the horrors visited on the townspeople punished them for their resistance and was the most effective encouragement for other towns to surrender quickly. This was certainly the case with Quebec. Men like Jean-Claude Panet, Jean Taché, a wealthy 61-year-old merchant and trader, and François Daine, de facto mayor of Quebec, had put up stoically with the destruction of their houses during the summer but to have their cellars plundered of all their worldly goods, their daughters raped, and their families murdered was too high a price to pay for patriotism.

Ramezay summoned his senior officers to a council of war. He later reported that 'we had lost all hope of being rescued'.[40] It was agreed that 'this place, little capable of defense, being enclosed partly by a mere palisade, might with its artillery and warlike stores, hold out, some time, against the efforts of the enemy, if provisions were in sufficient abundance'. However, those supplies were lacking. One option would have been to send out all the women and children, to ensure that only men who could bear arms were fed, and thus prolong the defence of the town. Townshend recorded in his journal that a messenger was sent to ask him to give safe passage to the women and children through British lines. He refused to give the French this assurance because it would clearly allow the men to hold out a good deal longer.[41] Knowing that he was unable to jettison 'useless' mouths, Ramezay went around the table and asked every officer for his view. All but one of the fourteen men present advised surrender. Bigot said that 'the extremity to which the place is reduced for provisions being considered, my opinion is, to demand a capitulation'. Another officer referred to the 'very bad, dilapidated fortifications'. One voice alone spoke up for heroic resistance. Louis-Thomas Jacau de Fiedmont was an artillery officer who had risen from the ranks. According to some he was the inventor of the floating batteries which were nicknamed 'Jacobites' after him. He had been captured twice during the war already and obviously did not relish another spell of British hospitality. He urged the council to 'reduce the ration and persevere in defending the place to the last extremity'. He failed to convince anyone else around the table but was made a Knight of the Order of Saint-Louis the following winter for his loyalty. Ramezay summarized the meeting: 'considering the instructions I have received from the Marquis de Vaudreuil and the scarcity of provisions, proved by the returns to me furnished and the searches I have had made, I conclude to endeavor to obtain from the enemy the most honorable capitulation'.[42]

Two days later Ramezay wrote to Vaudreuil excusing the step that he now felt forced to take. He explained that 'the precipitation of the retreat and the abandonment of the town has taken place without provision having been made for its sustenance'. The people were terrified of the 'dangers impending of its being taken by assault', while many of the sailors and militiamen were not interested in fighting. As he looked across the Plains of Abraham he could see two enemy batteries ready to 'fire at this moment'. He was not hopeful of help from Vaudreuil: 'your army all divided and separated offers me no prospect of prompt succour' while 'the arrival of the flour you promise is as difficult by land as by sea'. Above all Ramezay insisted that 'I must save my garrison and the people.'[43]

Vice Admiral Saunders struck fear into the hearts of the Quebecers by a well-timed demonstration with his mightiest warships. The very largest ships had waited throughout the summer further downstream and had played no part in the fighting. Now he moved seven of them into position off the Lower Town, their towering hulls bristling with cannon. These ships carried twice as many guns as the frigates that had been doing much of the fighting in the basin. Holmes reports that this highly aggressive move 'put the enemy in the utmost consternation'. The garrison now feared their 'coming up alongside of the lower town with the night tide, and that they would be stormed by sea and land'.[44]

It was too much for the French defenders. Ramezay was determined to surrender the town. As he made arrangements to do so, the return of de Lévis from Montreal to take control of the French army at Jacques Cartier had brought with it a new sense of purpose. He immediately insisted that the army march on Quebec and dislodge the British besiegers. Vaudreuil sent food on horseback to Ramezay and a messenger with instructions to 'encourage him by all means to hold out to the last extremity'.[45] The cavalryman, de la Rochebeaucourt led his men in a wild gallop around the British army and into Quebec with bags of biscuit lashed to their saddles. They arrived just after the departure of Armand de Joannès, an aide to Ramezay, to the British camp with a document of capitulation signed by his commander. It was not irreversible but the Quebec garrison had clearly lost their appetite for any further resistance. Daine wrote a letter to Versailles attempting to defend Ramezay's decision. He had surrendered, he insisted, 'in order not to expose the garrison and the people to a general assault, and thereby to the fury of the avenger, according to the laws of war'. Time had run out, 'the commandant judged that hesitation was no longer excusable'. Daine reported that he and his family were 'on the brink of dying of hunger'.[46]

Townshend accepted Ramezay's terms without hesitation. He was deeply nervous of the large French force operating upriver of him. His concern is apparent in one General Order in which he warned that 'the enemy is expected'. Officers were to 'keep lights in their tents and not lie down, but visit the men's tents and see that they are ready to turn out at a minute's warning, in case of alarm'. Two men in each tent were appointed to strike it as soon as the French were sighted.[47] The engineer, Montresor, wrote to his father saying that they had not had a chance to dig batteries to place the siege guns in because 'some advice [was] received that the enemy were making some motions seeming to attack us'. Defending the camp was more important than siege preparations and so cannon were parcelled out to the regiments and working parties 'cut down a quantity of brush in front of our encampment'.[48] Knox and his men remained 'very alert'.[49] Townshend's own journal shows a sense of relief that the French were giving in. It reports that 'before we had any batteries erected, or could have for two or three days', a messenger came out from the town on 17 September under a flag of truce 'with proposals of capitulation'.[50]

On the afternoon of 18 September the keys to the three gates into Quebec were handed over to Townshend. Before sunset Wolfe's close friend, Lieutenant Colonel Murray, led three companies of Louisbourg Grenadiers into the town to take possession of the gates. Small groups of men were sent to guard churches and the leading inhabitants. Next, fifty artillerymen ceremonially hauling a light cannon and a burning match, followed by Townshend and his aides, marched in to take possession of the town. Beside the shattered husk of the Governor General's palace the formal handover occurred. Immediately all bastions and storerooms were secured by British officers with small parties of troops. Careful lists were made of captured enemy supplies. The efficiency of the transition was intended to stand as a comparison to the slaughter and savagery of the French capture of Fort William Henry. Meanwhile Colonel Williamson of the artillery had the honour of hoisting the Union Flag of Great Britain on a prominent place on the south end of the city walls. Every company of Townshend's army had been given specific and immutable orders not to carry out 'acts of violence, pillage or cruelty'. Quebec, they were reminded, now belonged to 'his Britannic Majesty, and not to the French king'. Anyone who disobeyed this order could expect death and no mercy.[51] At 1800 hours, as these solemn proceedings went on in the Upper Town, Knox relates that Captain Palliser, commander of the seventy-four-gun ship of the line, *Shrewsbury*, led a 'large body of seamen and inferior officers' ashore to take possession of the Lower Town. They too raised a Union Flag on the road leading to the Upper Town. It could be seen from the basin and the banks of the St Lawrence below Quebec.[52] The capital of New France, the key to King Louis' North American empire, was now a British possession.

Townshend was generous to the garrison. The first article of the capitulation allowed the soldiers, sailors, and marines to 'march out with their arms and baggage, drums beating, lighted matches, with two pieces of cannon, and twelve rounds'. They would then be 'embarked as conveniently as possible, in order to be landed at the first port in France'.[53] The French were granted the so-called 'honours of war'. In return for a tenacious defence they were being allowed to leave with their colours flying, two symbolic cannon, and ammunition in their pouches. It meant they could return to France having demonstrated that they had done everything honour required of them to defend Quebec. Article Two dealt with the other great concern of eighteenth-century decision makers, the protection of property. Townshend agreed that 'the inhabitants shall be maintained in the possession of their houses, goods, effects and privileges'. Having thus preserved their personal honour, that of France, and the possessions of the propertied classes of Quebec, the following day French officers led their men down to four waiting transports and set sail for France.

There was obviously some grumbling in the British camp at this magnanimous treatment of the French who, many thought, did not deserve it. Townshend wrote to his wife telling her that 'the command of the army is as disagreeable as any other. Men are as mean here as in any other profession.'[54] The author of Wolfe's 'Family Journal' obviously led the whispering. 'We might have fixed our own terms as we knew by deserters the state of the place,' he criticized. Instead of which, he claimed, Townshend was far too lenient and missed an opportunity to rescue 'English prisoners taken in this campaign' from the 'hands of the enemy'.[55] Townshend knew the terms would not please everyone. In his dispatch to London he sought to pre-empt some of the criticism. A quick capitulation made military sense, he wrote, 'considering the enemy assembling in our rear, the inclemency of the season which would scarcely admit of our bringing a gun up the precipice, the critical situation of our fleet from the Equinoctial gales'. In addition he was keen to avoid battering down the walls; he wanted Quebec in 'a defensible state, against any attack which might otherwise be attempted against it in the winter'.[56] Holmes agreed; 'the defences of the town still entirely perfect,' he wrote in a letter, 'and the late season of the year, will account sufficiently for these terms'.[57] Above all Townshend was aware that King George's new French subjects could not be coerced into loyalty. He wrote to his mother saying that 'I have done all I could to reduce the Canadians by humanity. The only way I know of conciliating any people.'[58]

The invalid Monckton was unhappy with the capitulation. Townshend wrote to him on 19 September apologizing profusely for not having included him in the surrender discussions. 'I had no idea that you were well enough to attend to the business,' he told Monckton and assured him that it was 'far from my wish to gain credit with the newspapers'.[59] Monckton was generous in his next letter. 'You are one of the last men in the world that could give me offence,' he told Townshend. 'I do most sincerely assure you that I never said anything either pro or con, except that I did suppose I should see the capitulation before it was signed.' 'I hope my dear Townshend,' he warned, 'that malicious tongues will not be suffered – to hurt me in your opinion.'[60]

Ramezay's decision was closely scrutinized back in France and he came under vicious attack for surrendering the town. Vaudreuil, who had given him instructions to surrender as soon as supplies ran out, rounded on him and told Versailles that he had 'expected a more protracted resistance, having adopted the surest measures to convey provisions into the town'. He then hoped that the Minister would 'please express to the King the poignant regret I have felt at this occurrence in a moment so unexpected'.[61] De Lévis was desperate when he heard from his cavalry commander that Ramezay was about to surrender. According to Bougainville, the new French commander 'advanced the army to get within range of attacking the English'. Bougainville himself was leading an advanced guard and was only 'three quarters of a league from Quebec when I learned that the city had surrendered' after it had been 'bombarded for sixty-eight days'.[62] He blamed Ramezay. 'I even hoped to throw myself into Quebec to defend it,' Bougainville wrote, but Ramezay 'never wished to give me the opportunity, in spite of my several proposals … This man surrendered without having tried a cannon shot, and the enemy not even having started their trenches.'[63] The French had no choice but to fall back to Jacques Cartier. 'Such was the end of what up to this moment was the finest

campaign in the world,' wrote Bougainville. He was in no doubt of
the cause of their defeat. Always unswervingly loyal to Montcalm, he
believed that 'his death caused our misfortunes'.[64] In fact, Montcalm's
death had merely been a product of rather than a catalyst for the
French disaster.

Major combat operations for 1759 came to an end as de Lévis'
French army retreated for the last time. The British slowly fed their
troops into the town. Murray wrote in his journal for 19 September
that 'this day I marched into town, or more properly the ruins of it'.[65]
Mackellar wrote that 'we found the buildings in general in a most
ruinous condition, infinitely worse than we would have imagined, for
besides those burnt there was hardly a house in the town that was not
hurt by either shot or shell and scarcely habitable without some repairing'.[66] Williamson agreed that Quebec was 'more battered than I imagined'. He calculated that '535 [buildings] are burned down, besides
we have shattered most of the rest'.[67] Knox wrote that 'the havoc is
not to be conceived ... The low town is so great a ruin that its streets
are almost impassable.'[68] As the troops flooded into the city, despite
Townshend's strict instructions, there was, according to a French
source, 'considerable pillage'.[69] Men sifted through the ruins of the
once magnificent town, looking for wine, food, and a roof over their
heads. Knox reports that 'some soldiers ... committed disorders upon
the natives by robbing and plundering them'.[70] The nights were growing longer and colder. Malcolm Fraser looked about him as he entered
Quebec and realized that 'we have but a very dismal prospect for seven
or eight months' as 'most of the houses are destroyed' and 'fresh provisions are very scarce and every other thing exorbitantly dear'.[71] Other
soldiers were busy doing sightseeing of another kind. Jeremiah Pearson wrote that 'it is cloudy and wet weather today and I went about
the city and see some very likely French gals there'.[72]

Mackellar did a thorough investigation of the defences of the town
and stockpiles of food and military supplies. In his opinion the defences
were 'little more than half finished, and could have held out but for a
very few days after the opening of our batteries'. There was a considerable number of cannon in the town and along the Beauport shore;
he counted 234 in all with plenty of powder and round shot.

Poignantly thirty-seven of the guns had once belonged to General Braddock. They had been brought up from the Pennsylvania backcountry
where they had been captured at Monongahela but were now finally
restored to British masters. The pathetic stash of provisions which
Mackellar believed would have fed the town for no more than four
days was immediately 'distributed to the women and children of the
poorer inhabitants'. The engineer reports, remarkably, that 'there were
so many difficulties to struggle with that it was thought doubtful by
some what measures might be most advisable, whether to keep the
place or to demolish and abandon it'. Unsurprisingly the commanders quickly realized that abandoning the town that had been captured
with so much effort in time, sweat, and blood was politically unimaginable and 'it was therefore determined to keep Quebec at all hazards
and measures were immediately taken accordingly'.[73]

Townshend had had his fill of exotic foreign campaigning. As he told
his wife in a letter, 'do not think my Dear Life that any command tempts
me to stay. The troops will soon go into garrison and then I can set out
with the admiral.'[74] He told his mother that 'I know not what sleep or
a moment's retirement is, yet I am in perfect health.' His only real
concern was that those he was leaving in charge 'will give the French
but a poor idea of our humanity' and reverse much of his benign
work.[75] On the advice of the doctors Monckton was to head to New
York to recover from his wound. Murray would become Governor with
Burton as his second in command. Townshend left Murray his shaving
trunk and offered him the use of his chairs. He made it clear that he
expected to refight the campaign in Parliament and in the drawing
rooms of London. To arm himself he took a copy of all the letters sent
during the campaign, which had 'now become so interesting to us'. This
line was followed by the phrase, 'by the factious malignity of others'
which he thought better of and crossed out. 'I think I should have a
copy of the paper to General Wolfe concerning his intended landing at
first higher up the river,' he continued. 'Possession of such proofs,' he
assured Murray would allow them to 'escape the censure of rational and
upright men, though perhaps no authorities can secure a man from that
defamation which is the offspring of ignorance and faction'.[76] Murray
wrote back in an intimate tone. He refers to a joke they shared and says

he is sending a present for Townshend's wife. But he continues seriously, writing that 'since so black a lie was propagated I think myself very happy that you will be on the spot to contradict whatever ignorance or faction may suggest'. He was keen to show the world that Wolfe's orders 'throughout the campaign showed little stability, stratagem or fixed resolution'. He told Townshend that 'I wish his friends had not been so much our enemies', and admitted that thanks to this hostility the two of them were 'acting on the defensive'. Murray and Townshend obviously planned their strategy carefully. 'You have execution of the plan,' Murray told the London-bound Townshend, 'and I am well persuaded you will manage it with as much tenderness to the memory of the poor general as the nature of things will admit.'[77]

Murray would command the men who would stay in Quebec as a garrison over the winter and then attempt to finish the job of entirely conquering Canada in 1760. The vast majority of Wolfe's army stayed with him. Of the infantry, only the Louisbourg Grenadiers and many of the rangers would leave; the former returning to their regiments in the Louisbourg garrison. Williamson and many of the larger siege guns would winter in Boston. As for the naval contingent: Saunders could not risk his precious vessels in the St Lawrence over the winter. The ice would crush the hull of even his largest ships like an eggshell. He did leave the *Porcupine* and *Racehorse*, having pulled them up out of the water with four other small vessels. This, it was hoped, would give the British naval superiority on the river as soon as it melted the following spring. Lord Colville, Captain of the seventy-gun *Northumberland*, was made a commodore and left at Halifax in command of a strong squadron with orders to press into the St Lawrence as early as was physically possible after the ice started to melt. There was to be no repeat of Durell's failure to stop French reinforcements reaching Canada as they had done before the 1759 campaign.

Saunders departed on 18 October. The last naval detachments left on 26 October, as late as they dared. Townshend had been far more generous to his naval colleagues than Wolfe. In a dispatch to London he reported that 'I should be wanting in paying my due respects to the admirals and the naval service if I neglected this occasion to acknowledge how much we are indebted for our success to the constant assistance and support we have received.' He then told a diplomatic lie, referring to the 'perfect harmony and immediate corre- spondence which has prevailed throughout our operations in the uncommon difficulties which the nature of this country in particu- lar presents to military operations of a great extent and which no army can in itself solely supply'. With great generosity he concluded that 'it is my duty short as my command has been to acknowledge for that time how great a share the navy has had in this successful campaign'.[78] Saunders was no less generous; he credited Holmes with the 'very critical operation' and said that 'this tedious campaign' had been brought to a successful conclusion thanks to the fact that 'there has continued a perfect good understanding between the army and navy'.[79]

The voyage home was as difficult as the journey out. The ships were pounded by gales. Day after day they sped east under reefed topsails alone. By early December many of them, with 'provisions very short', limped into ports and bays on the west coast of Ireland, the Solent being simply too far.[80] Saunders and Townshend almost took part in a second decisive battle. In the first week of November a ferocious westerly gale had forced the British Channel fleet under Hawke to break off its relentless blockade of the French naval base at Brest. They scurried into the sheltered waters off Torbay, leaving the French fleet able to take advantage of an unusual easterly breeze to break out of Brest. The French admiral, Conflans, made for the invasion flotilla in the Morbihan on the south side of the Brittany peninsula. Admiral Hawke was chafing that he had not shared in the naval triumphs of the year which included Quebec and a smart victory off Lagos in Portu- gal at which his bitter rival Boscawen had captured or destroyed five French ships of the Mediterranean squadron that was on its way to rendezvous with the Channel fleet and invade Britain. As soon as the weather permitted Hawke set off down the Channel in hot pursuit. Saunders arrived in the Channel and heard from a British ship that Hawke was chasing Conflans. He gave Townshend the choice between heading back to Britain or altering course to help the Channel fleet. 'I preferred the latter having first wrote to Mr Pitt,' wrote Townshend.[81] They never caught up with the impatient Hawke. In one of the most dramatic naval encounters in British history Hawke led his fleet straight at the enemy who were attempting to escape into the dangerous waters of Quiberon Bay. Ignoring the fading light, an unknown and hazardous coastline, and a rising wind and sea Hawke fell upon the French rear. In the van of the British fleet was *Magnanime* commanded by Captain Richard Howe, older brother of William Howe who had commanded Wolfe's light infantry. In rough seas the British fell upon the confused French formation. Hawke's flagship, the *Royal George*, blasted two broadsides into the *Superbe*, which sank. Five other French ships were destroyed, including Conflans' flagship. One French ship was captured and the other fourteen were scattered along the coast; many had thrown their guns overboard in the panic to escape and their officers and men were utterly demoralized. The only British loss was two ships wrecked.

Rarely has the strategic balance been so radically altered. Louis XV's bold plan to save France's honour with an all or nothing attempt to invade Britain had collapsed. Quiberon was the final victory in an unprecedented year of British successes. Her forces in Germany had defeated a French army at Minden, Quebec had fallen and victories at Lagos, and now Quiberon Bay had effectively destroyed the French navy and ended any threat of invasion. It also meant that even had Louis wanted to send significant help to his rump empire in North America he was now unable to do so. For the rest of the Seven Years War the Atlantic was a British lake.

The autumn of 1759 was a glorious time for the British patriot. News of victories came in with such rapidity that there was barely time to restock ale houses and build another bonfire. Wolfe's dismal dispatch of 2 September had arrived in London on 14 October. Pitt was furious at Wolfe and both he and Newcastle assumed that Quebec would not fall in 1759. The King remained more positive, his mood bolstered by Anson, the First Lord of the Admiralty, whose good cheer was probably due to the fact that he had not bothered reading the dispatch. It was published, with the sensitive parts omitted, on 16 October. However, by a quirk of transatlantic communications news of the triumphant victory arrived that very night. Pitt scrawled a quick message to the Duke of Newcastle, his pen unable to keep up with his euphoria. 'Mr Secretary Pitt has the pleasure to send the Duke of Newcastle the joyful news,' he wrote, 'that Quebec is taken, after a signal and complete victory over the French army.' 'Mr Wolfe is killed,' he continued, 'Brig Monckton wounded but in a fair way – Brig Townshend perfectly well – Montcalm is killed + about 1500 French.'[82]

As the news raced through the population there was a universal, spontaneous outburst of celebration. In London there was 'riot and rapture' according to Tobias Smollett.[83] Candles lit every window and firecrackers exploded on the streets. Every village followed suit. A local clergyman, R. Leeke, wrote to Townshend's mother describing the local 'festival of joy'. 'Our bells were set a ringing forthwith,' he reported. 'A great bonfire was prepared' and two barrels of beer provided, while the sound of music and guns filled the air. The bonfire was seen for 'ten miles around, all of the parish assembled round it; men and women danced and drunk all night before it they danced and sung all the militia songs and dances'. 'The bells rung and guns fired,' he continued, 'and never ceased till daylight in the morning the field was full of people, of our own and strangers who came far and near to the new and wonderful sight.'[84] Another correspondent reported to Lady Townshend from Fakenham where 'bells have rang here since Thursday last and still continue, on Saturday when the gazette came we had public rejoicings feastings and illuminations of all kinds'. Four days later he wrote again reporting that 'our rejoicings are not yet over'. Sheep were roasted whole, 'barrels of beer are daily given away in every little village around us', and 'on Monday a bullock and a sheep were roasted whole on the beacon hill in the road'. At two other nearby towns there were 'better illuminations than ever known'.[85] At Bradbourne in Derbyshire George Burkston wrote that there was 'frequent shouting and hearty rejoicing'.[86] British troops serving with the allied army on the Continent lined up by battalion and fired a *feu de joie*.

The British colonies in North America more than matched the jubilation of the mother country. Candles were placed in windows, bonfires burnt in every open space, and towns rang with the peal of church bells. The twenty-fifth of October was set aside as a day of thanksgiving in Massachusetts Bay. Monuments were planned for Boston and one erected in New York. On Manhattan Island, just west of today's junction of 15th Street and Eighth Avenue, an obelisk stood for over a century. In the nineteenth century it was a popular destination for day-tripping New Yorkers.[87] When the news reached Philadelphia a full royal salute was fired; the next evening the town was illuminated and fireworks were let off. In Rhode Island one pastor scolded his flock over their 'carnal joy which degenerates into rioting and debauchery, into revelling and drunkenness'.[88] No one doubted that this was the end of New France. Generations of hostility, competition, ambushes, and outright war had bred a visceral hatred for the French empire. In his thanksgiving sermon on 16 October, Samuel Cooper, Pastor of Brattle Street church in Boston, painted a bright picture of a future in which British America could seize the opportunities presented by the near limitless continent now that vast and threatening entity was on the brink of extinction. The French had used 'savages to drench our borders with the blood of the unarmed'. Now the New World would see 'peace, prosperity and unhindered commercial expansion'.[89] Few did not think that they were witnessing the greatest strategic realignment of their lives and yet nobody could have guessed just how far reaching this change would be.

On both sides of the Atlantic the active press whipped their ever expanding pool of readers into paroxysms. A young Edmund Burke wrote that 'the effect of so joyful news, immediately on such a dejection, and then the mixture of grief and pity which attended the public congratulations and applauses, was very singular and affecting'. The loss of Wolfe was the only blemish: 'However glorious this victory was and however important in its consequences, it must be admitted that it was very dearly bought. Soldiers may be raised; officers will be formed by experience; but the loss of a genius in war is a loss that we know not how to repair.' In fact, his martyrdom gave the victory even more drama, and significance. In Britain panegyricists like Burke were already promoting Wolfe to the pantheon of British military greats. 'The death of Wolfe,' he wrote, 'was indeed grievous to his country, but to himself the most happy that can be imagined, and the most envied by all those who have a true relish for military glory.'[90]

Newspapers competed with melodramatic poetry spilling from their pages. Detailed accounts of the battle and of Wolfe's career filled special editions. Horace Walpole believed that the circumstances of the victory and the timing of Wolfe's death fired people's fascination. 'The incidents of dramatic fiction,' he wrote,

> could not be conducted with more address to lead an audience from despondency to sudden exaltation, than accident prepared to excite the passions of a whole people. They despaired, they triumphed and they wept, for Wolfe had fallen in the hour of victory. Joy, curiosity, astonishment, were painted on every countenance; the more they enquired the higher their admiration rose. Not an incident but was heroic and affecting.[91]

David Garrick's play *Harlequin's Invasion* played to packed houses in London and it featured a specially composed song, with words penned by the great thespian himself: 'Hearts of Oak'.

> Come, cheer up, my lads, 'tis to glory we steer,
> To add something more to this wonderful year;
> To honour we call you, as freemen not slaves,
> For who are as free as the sons of the waves?
>
> Heart of oak are our ships, jolly tars are our men,
> We always are ready;
> Steady, boys, steady!
> We'll fight and we'll conquer again and again.

It is still the official march of the British and Canadian navies. In Chatham a First Rate ship had been laid down on a sunny July day in 1759. Following the remarkable successes on land and sea in that year the decision was made to name her *Victory*. Many years later she too would take her place in British imperial folklore.

In two areas there were no bonfires, no shouts, and no muskets fired into the night sky. At Westerham in Kent and Blackheath local people mourned the fallen general. Wolfe had been born in Westerham and his mother now lived alone in Blackheath. Wolfe's death deprived her of the company of the last of her three men. Her husband had died earlier in the year and her only other child, her son Edward, was buried in Flanders, the victim of an earlier war.

Soon official praise was added to the spontaneous public outpourings. Parliament met in November and Pitt eulogized Wolfe's achievement by making comparisons with those of classical warriors. He painted a picture for the House of the dark night, the precipice, and the measureless empire that, he clearly assumed, would fall into Britain's lap following the taking of its capital. The thanks of the House were given to the admirals and generals for the 'glorious and successful expedition against Quebec' and an address made to the King, begging him to construct a monument in Westminster Abbey to the memory of Wolfe. 'Pardon us, most gracious sovereign,' it went, 'if we suspend awhile our otherwise unclouded joy, to lament the loss of that gallant general. How gloriously he finished his short, but brilliant career.'[92]

On Sunday, 17 November 1759, a stone casket was lowered down the side of the *Royal William* which was at anchor off Portsmouth having arrived from Canada the day before. She had left Canada on 25 September and had hit a rock in the St Lawrence that might well have sunk her had part of it not broken off and formed a neat plug. The casket had been removed from the ruins of one of the convents in Quebec and inside it were the remains of Wolfe. It was placed in a twelve-oared barge which was taken in tow by two others and slowly made its way towards the port accompanied by a formation of twelve other barges. The flotilla took an hour to get to shore. Every minute a cannon roared out from Spithead. At 0900 hours the body was landed, watched by the old and lame infantrymen who were given the task of garrisoning Portsmouth thus freeing younger and fresher men for active duty. The coffin was placed on a hearse and two of Wolfe's intimate friends and subordinates, both of them wounded, Captain Harvey Smyth and Captain Delaune (an officer of the light infantry that stormed up the slopes of the Anse au Foulon), accompanied it in a carriage behind as it set off for London. Through the city the soldiers accompanied the cortège with reversed arms. The muffled church bells tolled and thousands of spectators lined the route. They were bound for Blackheath where Wolfe would lie in his mother's hall under a black pall heaped with laurel leaves.

On 20 November his body was interred in St Alfege's church in Greenwich beside that of his father. There were just five mourners. His mother was left in dire financial straits partly as a result of her son's overgenerosity in his will. She made an appeal to both Pitt and the Duke of Newcastle but met with no success. The War Office even refused to pay her Wolfe's salary as a commander in chief. Katherine Lowther, Wolfe's fiancée, was sent the miniature that she had given Wolfe before he left for North America. His will had specified that it was to be set in precious stones and returned to her. She would go on to marry the Duke of Bolton but tradition has it that even late in life she always wore a pearl necklace given to her by her first fiancé.

Wolfe was canonized: the first truly British, as opposed to English, hero. In death he was more useful to the British imperial project than he had been alive. He became the personification of military virtue: strategic grasp, tactical brilliance, and compassion for his men. He was turned into a shining example to all those commanders who followed. No aspect of his short life was not rewritten; even his place of birth was fair game as pamphleteers from Yorkshire and Kent claimed him as a native son. Seven books about the Quebec campaign or Wolfe himself were published before the end of 1759, including the first of many Wolfe biographies. Poems, articles, and songs were soon followed by the visual art. Allegedly Wolfe's face was too decayed by the time his corpse arrived back in Britain to be much use to sculptors and portrait painters so a servant of Lord Gower that was said to look very like Wolfe posed instead. By the end of the eighteenth century this representation of Wolfe was the most recognized image in Britain, his collected writings sat in the luggage of all young officers, and the scene of his death had become the template for all subsequent martyrs of empire.

One image, in particular, was to become the most reproduced piece of art in the eighteenth century and arguably ignited a revolution in the way that British art dealt with historical events. Benjamin West was 35, American, and deeply ambitious when he arrived in England for the first time in 1763. He had just finished spending three years studying classical sculpture and neo-classicism in Italy. Over the next eight years he planned and painted the definitive representation of

Wolfe's death at the moment of victory. *The Death of General Wolfe* was a bold modernization of the traditional form of history painting. A reverence for Greece and Rome had dictated that all heroic scenes had to use the visual idiom of that golden age of virtue and heroism. Busts of Wolfe showed him in a Roman cuirass and toga, his eyes turned heavenward in imitation of the greatest of them all, Alexander. But West painted the scene with a new 'realism'. The figures were in contemporary dress, and though obviously idealized, there was a verity in the action and expressions. Critics suggested that this new fashion for accuracy might make it look dated when the costumes portrayed in it went out of fashion themselves. Roman dress was timeless; the central message of patriotic sacrifice could never be obscured. But their voices were ignored. By the late eighteenth century contemporary dress in paintings became the norm. West certainly took credit for this revolution, and while other artists had led the way his *Death of General Wolfe* was certainly the most popular expression of this new movement.

The painting built on the classical form rather than dispensed with it. Wolfe sprawls, near death, like the great Epaminondas surrounded by his band of brothers. Ships in the background and a noble-looking Native American in the foreground place the tableau squarely in America. The crowd around Wolfe is a curious mix of people, some, like Lieutenant Browne, who were almost certainly there, and others who were certainly not such as Fraser, who was recuperating from his wound far from the battlefield, Monckton, who had been dragged off wounded, and Barré, who was nowhere near Wolfe when he died. Townshend is curiously absent and Murray refused to sit for it, so great was his dislike of Wolfe. West was not looking for precise accuracy. There was, he believed, 'no other way of representing the death of a hero but by an epic representation of it'. A realistic painting of Wolfe, his body broken, slowly drowning in his own blood, in simple battle dress, supported by a grenadier and a lowly lieutenant would not support the Wolfe myth. 'To move the mind,' West insisted, 'there should be a spectacle presented to raise and warm the mind, and all should be proportioned to the highest idea conceived of the hero.'[93] What matters about West's painting is not the minute discussions by historians as to accuracies and inaccuracies but the effect it had on Britain, America, and the world. Like Shakespeare's rendering of so many characters from British history, West created a conception of Wolfe that has endured to this day despite determined attempts to correct it.

It was wildly popular. Lord Grosvenor snapped up the original for £400. George III joined the party late and bought a copy for £315. It was not universally popular though. David Garrick, who was one of the first to see the canvas, thought he could improve on a hero's death scene and acted one out in front of the painting to the delight of the considerable crowd. The engraving, when it was finally produced, was hugely successful. Around ten thousand prints were sold by 1790. European entrepreneurs issued pirated versions of the painting. Josiah Wedgwood mass-produced ceramic jugs with a version of Wolfe's death for a burgeoning middle class to augment their tea tables. They were even sold, remarkably, in France. There François-Louis-Joseph Watteau designed a print, *Mort de General Montcalm*, in the early 1780s that deliberately aped the composition of *The Death of General Wolfe* to reflect the shared sacrifice on that epic field of battle. According-ing to West the painting would eventually catch the eye of the great Horatio, Lord Nelson. West told Britain's greatest admiral that 'I fear your intrepidity will yet furnish me such another scene.' Nelson replied, 'Then I hope that I shall die in the next battle.' His wish was granted and West duly painted *The Death of Lord Nelson*, a visual paean to another of Britain's imperial heroes.[94]

Any voice that dissented from the wave of idolization was swept aside. Those who whispered of Wolfe's failings on the campaign were silenced by outraged commentators. A group around Townshend who agitated gently for a more realistic reappraisal of Wolfe's role was decried as jealous, unpatriotic ingrates. Townshend eventually even challenged the Duke of Albemarle to a duel, thinking him the author of a critical anonymous pamphlet. The siege could have claimed its last victim but the dispute was peacefully resolved.

The twenty-ninth of November 1759 was proclaimed a day of thanksgiving for Quebec; only a fortnight after another day was earmarked to celebrate the crushing naval victory at Quiberon Bay and the lifting of the threat of invasion. By year's end Horace Walpole wrote that the church bells of Britain were 'threadbare with ringing for victory'.[95] For Britain's enemies it was a year bereft of any comfort whatsoever. France's navy, empire, trade, and prospects were in tatters. Even the mighty French army had been categorically defeated on the Continent. King Charles of Spain, who had so far adopted an unfriendly neutrality and would soon declare for France, heard the news about Quebec and told the French Ambassador in Spain that his blood turned to ice.[96]

One British officer wrote to a friend pondering the year's momentous events. He believed that 'the kingdom of France perhaps was never more reduced in its naval power than at this era of time before us'. 'The French,' he continued, 'are at this instant but seldom seen upon the ocean, for this plain reason only, because they have been beat and burnt out of it by the English.' It was 'not for me to determine' where this 'superiority over the grand disturber of Europe' had suddenly sprung from. It could have been 'owing to the great increases of riches and commerce in England of late years'. Or it could be 'the people in general may have taken a more martial turn'. Either way Britain's sudden transformation into global hegemon was as welcome as it was unexpected. There was no such uncertainty about the 'most arduous undertaking, and the most important achievement that has taken place since the beginning of this war'. It was the 'extraordinary expedition' to capture Quebec.[97] A commemorative medal was issued, showing Britannia and her trident with 'Wolfe' and 'Saunders' written in the legend. The inclusion of Saunders' name suggests that contemporaries were happier to remember the role of the navy than posterity has been.

Amidst such celebrations many believed that the greatest danger now was overconfidence. Captain Augustus Hervey, who had covered himself with glory during the naval encounters of the Seven Years War thus far, hoped that the successes of the year 'will not elate us too much, and induce our leaders to carry on a very expensive war, which in the end is always doubtful – but let it incline us to close an honourable and lasting – though perhaps less advantageous peace than uncertain victories if obtained might give us'.[98]

While King George's American and British subjects imagined a new empire in the hinterland of the continent, replete with fertile river valleys, furs, and other raw materials, Murray's little army was on short rations, huddled among the wreckage of Quebec, trying to build shelters to protect themselves from the imminent winter freeze. Their writ did not extend beyond the range of the cannon on the battlements. The enemy army lay between them and the rest of the colony and foraging parties still needed close protection from the Canadians who lurked in the shadows. Murray issued order after order in an attempt to maintain discipline. 'No person whatsoever,' he announced on 30 September, 'is to molest or interrupt the French Inhabitants or people of the Country by taking their things or any other property of theirs, they be now subjects of his Majesty and under protection of the government.'[99]

The army had suffered badly over the summer. Only 250 men and twenty officers had been killed, but 1,200 were sick or wounded. Wolfe's army had lost around 15 per cent of its men.[100] Montresor spoke for those that were left: 'I think the desolation of this place exceeded Louisbourg,' he told his father, 'I'm quartered in a house that has no roof, not a single board.' He was jealous of the 48th Regiment which was billeted in the Intendant's Palace, which had survived the bombardment almost intact.[101] Sergeant Thompson 'made choice of a little house on the esplanade although it was scarcely inhabitable from the number of our shells that had fallen through it'. He 'contrived to get a number of little jobs done towards making it passably comfortable for the men, and for my own part I got Hector Munro, who was a joiner by trade to knock up a kind of cabinet (as the Canadians call it) in one corner of the house for myself'.[102] Like Wolfe before him, Murray had to deal with the scourge of women. He was forced to issue one order in which he 'desires the commanding officers of regiments will not suffer their men to marry with the French'.[103]

The men struggled to erect some form of shelter as well as working on the defences of the town and gathering enough firewood to last the winter. On top of this there was the threat of French attack. John Johnson wrote that 'from our first entrance in the town of Quebec, our orders were every night repeated, to lie on our arms: no officer, no soldier unless he was sick, was allowed to undress, or go to bed; nor were we on any pretence, allowed to put off our accoutrements during the night'.[104] No soldier was allowed to leave the town without specific permission from Murray himself.

As the weather got colder, survival became an ever greater challenge. It became harder to keep discipline among the half-starved and freezing men. An unnamed inhabitant wrote that 'Quebec is nothing but a shapeless mass of ruins. Confusion, disorder, pillage reign even among the inhabitants, although the English make examples of severity every day ... English and French, all is chaos alike. The inhabitants, famished and destitute, escape to the country. Never was seen such a sight.'[105] Pontbriand, the Bishop of Quebec, wrote just before he died in 1760 that 'Blessed are those who, without attributing it wrongly and rashly to secondary causes, recognize in it the avenging arm of the Lord and submit to it.' The Bishop blamed 'insulting talk', the 'continual grumbling', the 'little fidelity in the observance of feast-days and the Sabbath', and the 'ignominious passion of drunkenness' for the loss of Quebec.[106] The British were God's chosen instrument of punishment.

By mid-November Murray certainly did not feel that he was God's tool. He was growing desperate. On 13 November he wrote in his journal that 'a very unusual desertion at this time prevailed among the troops'. He blamed the 'plundering kind of war which had been carried on this last campaign had so debauched the soldier, that there was no putting a stop to these without very severe punishment; to avoid which, most probably, they deserted'. The next day he wrote that 'as drunkenness and theft continued to reign predominant vices in the garrison, highly prejudicial to the service, I recalled all licences, and ordered for the future every man who was found drunk to receive twenty lashes every morning till he acknowledged where he got it, and forfeit his proper allowance of rum for six weeks'.[107] Jean-Félix Récher was a victim of this growing anarchy. On 7 November he simply notes in his journal: 'I am burgled and wounded.'[108] After this brush with a British soldier he took shelter in the Ursuline Convent.

By December sentries were freezing to death on duty, parties of men who donned snow shoes to try to collect firewood were ambushed, and the first signs of scurvy were appearing among the soldiers. Fraser wrote in his journal on 1 December that 'it is thought we shall have a great deal of difficulty in supplying ourselves with fuel this winter. The winter is now very severe.' It was 'insupportably cold'; some of the sentries 'have been deprived of speech and sensation in a few minutes'. Frostbite was already taking men's toes and fingers and yet Fraser was alarmed that 'the country people tell us it is not yet the worst'. The garrison were 'but indifferently clothed' but the Highlander 'in particular is in a pitiful situation having no breeches, and the Philibeg is not at all calculated for this terrible climate'. The weather forced the proud Highlanders to part with their traditional dress. Malcolm Fraser noted that 'Colonel Fraser is doing all in his power to provide trousers for them, and we hope soon to be on a footing with other regiments in that respect.' The once neatly turned out redcoats now looked more like a band of marauding Siberians. Fraser wrote that 'the weather is such that they are obliged to have all covered but their eyes, and nothing but the last necessity obliged any men to go out of doors'.[109] The St Lawrence froze and the men had to stumble across the jagged ice to drag firewood and skirmish with enemy troops on Point Lévis.

A soldier in the 15th Regiment commented that 'we were totally unprepared for such a climate, neither fuel, forage, or indeed anything to make life tolerable. The troops were crowded into the vacant houses as well as possible. Numbers fell sick and the scurvy made a dreadful havoc among us.' Hauntingly, he wrote that the 'fatigues of winter was so great that the living almost envied the dead'.[110] There was an ever increasing number of the latter. By the end of the winter around a thousand British corpses were neatly stacked outside the walls. The ground was frozen solid and it was impossible to bury them.

As the snow eventually began to melt Murray could rely on only around 3,000 men to defend Quebec. Scurvy had, according to Fraser, made 'fierce havoc in the garrison'. He estimated that two and a half thousand men were sick with 'scarce a man of the army entirely free from it'. His own regiment, the 78th, had lost 106 men dead since the fall of Quebec and 580 of the survivors were in the sickbay.[111] It was deeply unfortunate that Murray now faced a daring enemy commander determined to make a bold strike to reverse the positions in Canada before the spring thaw brought the inevitable flow of British men and supplies up the St Lawrence.

De Lévis and Vaudreuil had scraped together a force of 7,000 men. As soon as the ice on the upper river started to crack de Lévis embarked this army. On 26 April the flotilla landed at St Augustin but one of his men fell overboard and was spotted by the British garrison at Quebec who rescued him and learnt about the movements of the French force. Murray quickly withdrew his men from Lorette and Ste Foy just before de Lévis could attack. Murray now faced exactly the same dilemma as that Montcalm had wrestled with in September. He believed, as he later wrote, that 'I could not hesitate a moment about giving the enemy battle. As everyone knows the place is not tenable against an army in possession of the heights.'[112] He had hoped to entrench his force on the Plains of Abraham but the ground was still too hard to dig trenches. Even so, like Montcalm, he believed that he had, at all costs, to deny the enemy the high ground outside the city walls, and he marched his shrivelled force out at 0700 hours on 28 April.

The force was composed, according to John Johnson, of 'a poor pitiful handful of half starved, scorbutic skeletons; many of whom had laid by their crutches on the occasion, and would not be prevailed on to stay behind'.[113] Around half of Fraser's Regiment had discharged themselves voluntarily from their hospital beds to join their comrades for the coming battle. Murray formed his men up on the same ground that Montcalm had chosen for his army in September. From there he could see the French force spilling out onto the Plains. After some skirmishing between his light troops and the French advance party, the latter seemed to give way hastily. Murray made a snap decision. Abandoning his defensive plan he ordered the army to attack the French. Like Montcalm, he gambled on an aggressive stroke to send the enemy reeling backwards before they could get their men, guns, and supplies onto the Plains of Abraham. Fraser wrote that 'the bait was too tempting, and his passion for glory [got] the better of his reason'.[114] Unfortunately Lévis' men, like Wolfe's, were ready to repel the attacks. The British retreated and the French formed their own columns and drove into Murray's line. Weak, sickly, and heavily outnumbered, the British line collapsed. Muskets were cast aside, artillery abandoned, and a mass of fugitives fled into the town. The defending general had fought on the same ground and used the same strategy as Montcalm had done the year before and the results had been virtually identical. The butcher's bill was even higher. Murray recorded just over a thousand casualties of whom 259 were killed. The long-suffering Highlanders of the 78th lost 100 men killed and wounded and twenty-seven of their thirty-nine officers. Colonel Fraser himself was wounded again and Malcolm Fraser was shot in the groin.[115] De Lévis lost over eight hundred men with 193 of them killed. Native Americans butchered and scalped many of the wounded.

The second siege of Quebec now commenced. Everything would depend on whether de Lévis could take the city before the British reinforcements arrived from the Atlantic. In the city the British force teetered on the brink of total anarchy. Murray hanged a man on the spot to try to discourage the endemic drunkenness and destroyed private alcohol stores. The siege works edged closer although the British artillery on the walls made them pay terribly for every yard gained, gunpowder being the one substance in the ruined town of which there was an abundance. Such was the shortage of men that British officers strapped themselves into harnesses to help haul cannon up from the Lower Town. Murray sent desperate appeals to Amherst for help. He began to load his sloops with equipment and stores in case he had to retreat.

On 9 May a ship appeared in the St Lawrence. Civilians and soldiers on both sides strained to decipher the colours at her masthead. As she neared Quebec a long pendant could be seen at the main truck, a sure sign that the ship bore the King's commission. The King of Britain's commission. Soon the ensign at the mizzen peak and the Union Flag on the jack staff confirmed her allegiance. Knox had stood on the shore as men around him argued as to whether she was French or British. As she dropped anchor the more perceptive among the soldiers would have recognized that she was the *Lowestoft*, which had been present at the landings at the Anse au Foulon the previous September. Knox watched as she blasted a twenty gun salute and her captain wasted no time in climbing down into his barge to give Murray his first report from the outside world since October. 'The gladness of the troops is not to be expressed,' Knox reports. 'Both officers and soldiers mounted the parapets in the face of the enemy, and huzzaed, with their hats in the air for almost an hour.' The countryside reverberated with musket and cannon fire as infantrymen and artillerymen alike blazed away in euphoria. 'The gunners were so elated, that they did nothing but fire and load for a considerable time.' Knox was certain that the 'garrison of Vienna, when closely besieged, and hard pressed … by the Turks, were not more rejoiced on sight of the Christian army … marching to their relief'.[116]

The French were disappointed but not dismayed. One ship did not mean the end. If a French fleet was in the St Lawrence it could swat the plucky *Lowestoft* aside, deliver troops and men to de Lévis, and force the town to surrender. Undaunted, the French commander commenced his bombardment on 11 May. He was short of powder and had to limit each cannon to only twenty rounds a day. Even so French cannon came close to opening a breach in the walls. In the end it was the sailors, not the engineers, that decided it. On 15 May two more British ships arrived, the *Vanguard* with seventy guns and the *Diana* with thirty-two. All the British ships had spent the previous summer in the St Lawrence and now they wasted no time in passing the narrows and scattering de Lévis' Canadian support vessels. One of his frigates hit a rock and sank as she fled; the other was driven ashore where her crew set her on fire. With no naval support, and his flank now threatened, de Lévis had to call off the siege. He sent a note to Murray requesting sympathy for the French wounded and then abandoned them and his heavy artillery as he retreated. On 17 May Murray led the garrison out hoping to pay his enemy back for his defeat at Ste Foy, but de Lévis was too quick and had already crossed the Cap Rouge River. There was nothing to be gained from further pursuit. Murray's exhausted men needed to recuperate.

British seapower had strangled New France; after Quiberon Bay the French navy effectively ceased to function. Money was so scarce that there was nothing to feed the dockyard cats. Versailles did send a token force, late in the season, to Canada of six ships and only 400 men. They never got near de Lévis. In July they anchored in the mouth of the Restigouche River, where despite batteries on either shore and a boom across the entrance British ships broke into the anchorage forcing the French sailors to burn their own ships. It now fell to the army to administer the final cut. During the summer three pincers advanced on Montreal. Murray led his army along the St Lawrence from Quebec. Brigadier William Haviland advanced up that ancient corridor of violence beside the Adirondacks: the Lake Champlain–Richelieu valley. Amherst approached Montreal along the St Lawrence from Lake Ontario. Remarkably all three armies reached Montreal from their three totally different directions within a day and a half of each other. De Lévis' force had almost disintegrated. The militia had gone home to protect their farms and families and try to salvage what they could of their lives under new masters. By 5 September even his regulars were deserting in droves. Montreal was indefensible and Lévis was outnumbered ten to one.

On 7 September Vaudreuil sent out his terms. Amherst accepted all of them but one. The French troops would not be allowed the honours of war. There would be no proud march past of French regulars, their colours unfurled, armed with a cannon and slow match burning. The British commander would not forgive French atrocities. De Lévis was appalled. He begged to be given permission to take his regulars and fight to the last on Île Ste Hélène 'in order to sustain there, in our own name, the honour of the King's arms, resolved to expose ourselves to every extremity rather than submit to conditions which appear to us so contrary thereto'.[117] Vaudreuil would not countenance this and ordered his general to surrender. De Lévis heaped up the colours of the army and set them ablaze; he would not have them thrown at the feet of George II. Finally he broke his own sword rather than surrender it. On 9 September a mere 2,100 men, the remnant of the army of Canada, laid down their arms in the Place d'Armes. Canada was under British occupation.

EPILOGUE

FOUR YEARS LATER, in 1763, that occupation was made annexation in the Treaty of Paris that ended the Seven Years War. Curiously it had actually been nine years after the first bloody encounter between Washington and Joseph Coulon de Jumonville. France's fortunes had not improved much after her crushing defeats in 1759. In January 1760 Colonel Eyre Coote crushed a French force at Wandiwash in south-east India. Following a close blockade by the Royal Navy; Pondicherry, the last major French possession in the Indian subcontinent, surrendered in 1761. Wolfe's army was sent from Canada to attack Martinique in the Caribbean, which fell in January 1762. Spain realized, far too late, that British global hegemony was not a welcome prospect and joined France in 1761. Her army and navy, which would have been so useful to France as allies a few years before, were now rounded on by the veteran British services. Her colonies in the Caribbean were stripped from her. Dominica, St Lucia, and St Vincent all fell. In the summer of 1762 a daring piece of navigation brought a British fleet through the Old Bahama Passage to stun the Spanish garrison of Havana, the cornerstone of Spanish power in the region. As on the St Lawrence a British fleet, with no previous knowledge of the navigation, felt its way through a treacherous channel, through waters which the Spanish assumed were impracticable for big ships. The disbelieving Spaniards defended the city with desperate bravery but it surrendered in August 1762. The British had been decimated by illness. Of 14,000 men who served in Cuba only 3,000 were fit for service when the surrender came; only 1,000 of these casualties were caused by enemy action. Wolfe's veterans died in Cuba. The army that had been blooded at Louisbourg, had poured musket volleys into the French on the Plains of Abraham, survived frostbite and scurvy to capture Montreal the following year were annihilated by disease before the walls of Havana. Captain Henry Moore commanded a company of the 48th Regiment. In December it consisted of one sergeant, one drummer, and four privates who were fit.[1] Men like Knox, Johnson, and Thompson did survive the war, due in large part to their staying in North America while their comrades headed south.

The shame of losing their Caribbean capital was compounded for the Spanish by the capture of Manila in October 1762, the heart of their Oriental empire, by a dashing operation launched by British forces in India. Unbeknownst to any of the belligerents in the Philippines, peace was being made in Europe at the time and so the Philippines were handed straight back. Despite this it had been the most successful war in British history. But this one-sided ascendancy brought with it grave difficulties in both the short and long term. Any peace that conceded anything to the defeated powers was bound to be unpopular with the more belligerent British politicians such as William Pitt. He had left the cabinet in disgust at his colleagues' refusal to declare war on Spain until it was absolutely certain that her king, Charles III, intended to fight. Men like the Duke of Bedford, who negotiated the eventual treaty, did not want Britain to so dominate the world that it would only drive her adversaries into a grand coalition to attempt to clip her wings. Louis XIV had brought just such an alliance together against him and France was still living with the consequences. Besides, the lawful acquisition of some colonies at the peace table was a good deal more satisfactory than temporary possession of all of them in times of war.

Britain had won but had paid a spectacular price. Britain's national debt had mushroomed, by early 1762 Newcastle was struggling to raise money on the financial markets even at interest rates of 5 per cent; dogged French armies still threatened Hanover and Spain had invaded Britain's ally, Portugal. Britain wanted a lasting peace; to attain one she would have to hand back some of her conquests. Belle Isle, an island off the south coast of Brittany which the British captured in 1761, was returned, as were Goree in West Africa, St Lucia, Martinique, and some settlements in India that were to remain unfortified. Perhaps most controversial of all was the debate around whether

Britain should keep Canada or the rich sugar-producing island of Guadeloupe. Although Canada is now the ninth largest economy in the world and site of the planet's second largest reserves of oil, in the mid-eighteenth century it had been a huge drain on the French crown and its climate and soil were thought to be unsuitable for huge expansions of agriculture and population. One British polemicist wrote that there was no economic reason for retaining it, 'for what does a few hats signify?'[2] Yet Americans overwhelmingly desired to see the removal of the only remaining hostile power on the continent, while many in Britain believed on economic and strategic grounds that a small rump of Canada should be returned to France and more lucrative conquests retained. Guadeloupe produced an estimated £300,000 of sugar per year; furs, the only Canadian export, brought in just £140,000 and the costs of running and protecting this vast space were obviously substantially higher. A more subtle British argument was that the balance of power in North America was desirable. It kept the Americans scared, and a scared subject is a loyal one. During the war the Americans had needed British guns, ships, leadership, and redcoats. With no French infantrymen in Canada, no violent raids along the frontier, and no men of war patrolling the St Lawrence the Americans would soon realize that they could shed their ties to the mother country. The same journalist wrote that the new enlarged British North America 'at such a distance, could never remain long subject to Britain'. 'They are always grumbling and complaining about Britain,' he continued, 'even while they have the French to dread. What may they not be expected to do if the French is no longer a check upon them?' In short, 'If we were to acquire all Canada, we should soon find North America itself too powerful and too populous to be long governed by us at this distance.'[3] Another journalist wrote that British North American colonies would become more 'licentious from their liberty, and more factious and turbulent from the power that rules them'.[4] A more vicious journalist sought to disparage Canada's climate, people, and prospects. It was a 'cold, barren, uncomfortable and uninviting country'. It had been peopled with the 'refuse' of French society, prostitutes and petty criminals. Now her national character was 'the united good qualities of a whore and a thief'.[5]

Benjamin Franklin weighed in to the debate. He decried talk of British and American positions instead insisting that their interests were indivisible. A population explosion in North America was 'fantastic' he wrote. Trade would increase and with it the power of the Royal Navy. The American colonies would never unite against Britain. They had been unable to coordinate their response to a violent foreign power in the mid-1750s as France made moves to seize the Ohio country. If attempts at union failed when faced with a bitter enemy then how could they ever unite 'against their own nation which protects and encourages them, with which they have ... ties of blood, interest, and affection, and which ... they all love much more than they love one another'. Such a threat was 'impossible'. Although Franklin cleverly added that the only chance of it coming about was if Britain insisted on ignoring American demands to the whole of New France. Canada was a vast domain, crying out for an influx of immigrants. As the population expanded there so would the market for British manufactured goods. He pointed out that Britain made more money exporting to North America than she did from imports of sugar from the Caribbean.[6]

In France the debate also raged. Enlightened opinion was hostile to colonies which they saw as a drain on the state and a nest of corruption and reactionary religious practices. Voltaire, who had described the war as being over 'a few acres of snow on the borders of Canada', wrote in *Candide* that 'they spend more money on this glorious war than the whole of Canada is worth'.[7] He regarded the entire war as 'a trifling quarrel' over 'a country to which neither had the least right'.[8] In November 1760 he wrote to François Claude Bernard Louis de Chauvelin, a close confidant of the King, saying 'would I dare, I would beg you on my knees to forever rid the government of France from Canada. If you lose it, you lose almost nothing; if you want it returned to you, all you will be returned is an eternal cause of war and humiliation. Consider that the English are at least fifty to one in northern America.'[9] The King's new leading minister, the Duc de Choiseul, was more than happy to cede Canada but determined to hold on to the fishing rights on the Newfoundland Banks, which was a nursery of sailors and shipping as well as a vast maritime larder. The St Malo

Chamber of Commerce petitioned Versailles begging them to insist on continued access to the fisheries. It was a 'branch of trade more precious to the state than all the gold of Peru, for gold cannot create a single sailor and it creates several thousand sailors every year'. Without these fishing grounds France would have no more sailors and no sailors meant 'no navy, no real power'.[10] Other Chambers of Commerce weighed in. Marseilles, La Rochelle, and, in particular, Bordeaux submitted, loyally but firmly, that Canada was a vital part of the French imperial project. They were also concerned that they would not be paid what they were owed by the Canadian government and individuals if it was ceded to Britain.

In the end Choiseul so desired to be rid of Canada and recover Guadeloupe that he refused to sign the treaty until this was agreed to. Britain returned Guadeloupe, Martinique, and Marie Galante in the Caribbean and conceded French access to the Newfoundland fisheries. The tiny islands of St Pierre and Miquelon off the coast of Newfoundland were retained by France as bolt-holes for their shipping to protect them from storms and places to dry their catch, and remain French to this day. Britain gained Canada, the Ohio country, and all of New France east of the Mississippi River with the exception of the town of New Orleans. The rest of France's vast domains in North America went to Spain as recompense for drawing her into a war against the British which had brought nothing but defeat. The Native American inhabitants of those lands were not present, nor were they consulted or, indeed, considered. Britain gained Florida in return for handing back Cuba; Spain also agreed to withdraw her troops from Britain's ally, Portugal. France also promised finally to end her flirtation with the exiled Stuart family and recognize the British Protestant succession.

Peace saw Britain reborn as the global hegemon. A network of trading outposts, footholds, and influence around the world, which had been slowly expanding for generations, was now transformed into a formal empire. It was a, if not the, defining moment in the rise of the British Empire, the largest and most populous the world has ever seen. Seventeen fifty-nine and the campaigns before and after it had resolved one of the greatest geopolitical questions in the history of the human race: the ethnic, religious, and political complexion of the North American continent.

Britain controlled the continent north and east of the Mississippi. Union flags flew over Detroit, Toronto, Montreal, Miami, and Pittsburgh. The English language, legal code, and political economy spread inexorably throughout and beyond this area through the course of the next two centuries. Despite a small minority largely concentrated in the province of Quebec clinging to their language, religion, and traditions, the North American continent would become a bastion for Anglo-Saxon values. In the twentieth century this area would first bolster and then supersede Britain as she fought yet more battles against other nations that sought global hegemony. When asked at the end of the nineteenth century by a journalist, an aged Otto von Bismarck said, 'The most significant event of the twentieth century will be the fact that the North Americans speak English.' He was absolutely right.

Unlike many seismic historical shifts there was an awareness of this at the time. Robert Kirk, a Highland soldier, who left a journal of his adventures during the Seven Years War in North America, travelled across New France as part of an expedition to take control of the furthest forts for the British crown. He wrote that 'this vast continent may be justly called, the new world, there being land enough to contain all the people in Europe, and part of Asia, and if there was people to be spared, to inhabit it, would become a more formidable world than ever was conquered by an Alexander'. It was, he believed, 'one of the finest countries in the universe'.[11]

The conquered French faced an uncertain future. Civil society was left shattered. Some in the elite had been killed; others returned to France, while many had been utterly ruined. British and American merchants bought up distressed assets at bargain prices. Quebec and Montreal became economically dominated by Anglophone gentry. The new French subjects of George III were, however, allowed to retain their religion and many of their customs. The British proved to be benign conquerors. An absence of the kind of vigorous expulsion and cultural extermination seen in Nova Scotia meant that French Canadians were not pushed into irreconcilable hostility to their British masters. Indeed, the protection given to the Francophones and their religion by the British imperial authorities helped to preserve their culture. It is significant that they sided overwhelmingly with the British against the rebel colonies during the American Revolution. The destruction of the old France following the revolution of 1789 led many social and religious conservatives in Quebec to conclude that they were better off under British rule. The motto of Quebec today is *Je me souviens*, 'I remember', usually understood to reflect Quebecers' pride in their distinct past. In fact, Eugène-Étienne Taché, the architect who had it carved over the door of the Quebec parliament building, may well have had a more ambiguous message. His granddaughter claimed that it was a shortened form of a longer phrase: 'I remember/ That born under the lily/ I grew under the rose.'[12]

It appeared that Britain had decisively won the centuries old battle with the Dutch, French, and Spanish for control of North America. Yet now, that victory is seen not as the end but as a beginning. British and American society fragmented as a result of the gigantic scale of their success. Britain's empire required policing. The British infatuation with low taxation and a minimal standing army was unsustainable now that she controlled a bigger area of land than King Louis. Garrisoning North America with 10,000 men in twenty regular battalions would cost £350,000 a year. The national debt had doubled to £135,000,000. Ironically, William Pitt had conquered by adopting the wild 'spend now, pay later' philosophy that would come to characterize the continent's attitude to credit. The interest on this unprecedented debt was £5,000,000 a year out of revenue of just £8,000,000. Attempts to make the colonies take their share of the fiscal burden of the new imperial project foundered on the determination of the Americans not to have their rights as British subjects infringed. They would not pay taxes voted on in distant London without the assent of their own representatives. The problem became acute when the Native Americans reminded the crown that they were yet to be conquered. A widespread assault on British forts and settlements, bearing the name of one of its leaders, Pontiac, began in May 1763. The war ended in stalemate. The British crown attempted to mollify the Native Americans by limiting American moves west, enraging their colonists who believed it their manifest destiny to settle all the land to the Pacific.

It gradually became clear that the removal of the French threat to the colonies had also reduced Britain's value as protector. A group in America emerged who argued strongly that British tyranny should also be cast off allowing Americans to trade with whoever they pleased, to tax themselves as they wished, and exploit the western lands at their own pace. This radical new philosophy tore apart both British and American society. Just fifteen years after the surrender of de Lévis and Vaudreuil at Montreal, as the sun rose on 19 April 1775 fighting broke out between American colonials and British redcoats at the village of Lexington near Boston. It was the start of a civil war. France and Spain saw the chance to win back some of what they had lost in the Seven Years War and intervened decisively on America's behalf. Larger navies with reformed and highly professional officer corps inflicted stunning defeats on the Royal Navy.[13] An unending guerrilla war and defeat at sea forced Britain to the negotiating table. America was given its independence; it was the most disastrous war in the history of the British state.

One man had foreseen this disaster. Montcalm had written to Versailles at the end of August 1759. As usual he says that the colony is lost and his life forfeit 'but I console myself,' he wrote, 'that the loss of this colony, this defeat will one day be of more service to my country than a victory'. 'The conqueror, in aggrandizing himself, will find a tomb even in that. The English must breathe the air of freedom, and these Americans more so; and the children of these are not degenerated from the republican principles of their parents. Their maxim is to obey as little as possible and when their interests are touched they will revolt. Can England send 300,000 men to oppose them at this distance?'[14]

Wolfe's antagonist had accurately predicted that his victory on the Plains of Abraham and the subsequent conquest of New France would produce not only Britain's imperial apogee but also its inevitable nadir.

BIBLIOGRAPHY

Manuscripts

National Maritime Museum (NMM)
  ADM/L Lieutenant's Logs

Public Record Office (PRO)
  ADM 2 Admiralty Out-Letters
  ADM 52 Master's Logs
  CO 5/51 Colonial Office, Correspondence of the Secretaries of State
    with the Governors and Commanders in America
  WO 34/46b Amherst's Correspondence

Public Record Office of Northern Ireland (PRONI)
  DOD 162/77 Wolfe's 'Family Journal'
  DOD 678

National Archives of Scotland
  GD 45/3/422 Anecdote of Wolfe's Army from Sergeant Thompson
  GD 216/213 Letter of Sir James Cockburn to Samuel Mitchelson
  GD 202/68/12 Letters of William Fraser to John Cameron

Library and Archives Canada (LAC)
  MG 1 Serie E, E 143 Petition of Captain Louis Dupont de Chambon de
    Vergor, 1761

  MG 18
  H54 Ramezay Papers
  L5 MS 2207 fols. 37–69 Letters from Wolfe to Captain William Rickson
  L6 Thomas Bell
  L7 George Townshend
  L9 Henry Parr

M1 Monckton Papers, including,
 XX: Documents Relating to the Preparation of the Expedition
 XXI: Documents Relating to the Expedition ...
 XXII: A Series of Twenty-eight Autograph Letters from General Wolfe
 to General Monckton
  XXVIII: 'Relation du siège de Québec, posé par les Anglois en l'anée
  1759'
  XXIX: 'Journal du siège de Québec'

N18 George Williamson Papers
N21 Williamson Papers
N43 Diary of Jeremiah Pearson
N45 Aemilius Irving
N51 Correspondence Relating to Wolfe. Miscellaneous Items Relating
 to Wolfe
N52 Journal of Colonel Laurence Holloran

MG 23
 GII 1 James Murray Collection

MG 24
 GII 1 James Murray Collection
 K2 vol. V James Thompson Journal

Royal Green Jackets Museum, Winchester
 'Order Book of the Royal American Regiment at Quebec from 24th
 September 1759 to 27th February 1760'

Printed Original Materials

*An Accurate and Authentic Journal of the Siege of Quebec, 1759, by a
 Gentleman in an Eminent Station on the Spot* (London, 1759)
Carver, P. L., ed., *Wolfe to the Duke of Richmond: Unpublished Letters*
 (Toronto, 1938)
Casgrain, H. R., ed., *Collection des manuscrits du Maréchal de Lévis* (12
 vols., Montreal and Quebec, 1889–95)
Doughty, A., ed., *An Historical Journal of the Campaigns in North
 America: For the Years 1757, 1758, 1759 and 1760 by Captain John
 Knox* (3 vols., Toronto, 1914–16)
Doughty, A. and G. Parmelee, eds., *The Siege of Quebec and the Battle of
 the Plains of Abraham* (6 vols., Quebec, 1901–2)

Bibliography

Foligné, Monsieur de, *Journal de faits arrivés a l'armé [sic] de Québec, capital [sic] dans l'Amérique septentrional[sic], pendant la campagne de l'année 1759* (Quebec, 1901)

General Wolfe's Instructions to Young Officers (London, 1778)

Hamilton, E. P., ed., *Adventure in the Wilderness: The American Journals of Louis Antoine de Bougainville, 1756–1760* (Norman, OK, 1990)

Hattendorf, J. B., R. J. B. Knight, A. W. H. Pearsall, N. A. M. Rodger, and G. Till, eds., *British Naval Documents 1204–1960* (Naval Records Society, CXXXI, Aldershot, 1993)

A Journal of the Expedition up the River St Lawrence (by a Sgt Major in Hopson's Grenadiers) (Boston, 1759)

Journal of the Particular Transactions during the Siege of Quebec by an Officer of Fraser's Regiment (Quebec, 1901)

Lebel, J.-M., *1759 Summer under Siege* (Quebec, 2001)

Léger, R., ed., *Le Journal de Montcalm* (Montreal, 2007)

——*Le Journal du Chevalier de Lévis* (Montreal, 2008)

Lincoln, C. H., ed., *Manuscript Records of the French and Indian War: In the Library of the American Antiquarian Society* (Worcester, MA, 1909)

Little, C. H., ed., *Despatches of Rear Admiral Philip Durell* (Halifax, NS, 1958)

——*Despatches of Vice Admiral Saunders* (Halifax, NS, 1958)

Manuscripts Relating to the Early History of Canada (Literary and Historical Society of Quebec)

    Second Series, Quebec, 1868–71

        Extract from a Manuscript Journal Relating to the Operations before Quebec in 1759, Kept by Colonel Malcolm Fraser, the Lt of the 78th (Fraser's Highlanders) and Serving in that Campaign.

        Governor Murray's Journal of Quebec, from 18th September 1759 to 25th May 1760

        Johnstone, Chevalier de, *The Campaign of Louisbourg 1750–58*

        Johnstone, Chevalier de, *A Dialogue in Hades*

        A Journal of the Expedition up the River St Lawrence

    Fourth Series, Quebec, 1875

        General Orders in Wolfe's Army during the Expedition up the River St Lawrence, 1759

McCulloch, I. and T. Todish, eds., *Through So Many Dangers: The Memoirs and Adventures of Robert Kirk, Late of the Royal Highland Regiment* (Toronto, 2004)

Memoirs of the Siege of Quebec, the Capital of all Canada, and of the Retreat of Monsieur de Bourlemaque (Quebec, 1901)

Major Moncrief, *A Short Account of the Expedition against Quebec Commanded by Major-General Wolfe in the Year 1759* (Quebec, 1901)

O'Callaghan, E. and B. Fernow, eds., *Documents Relative to the Colonial History of the State of New York; Procured in Holland, England and France* (15 vols., Albany, NY, 1853–87)

Orderly Book and Journal of Major John Hawks, on the Ticonderoga-Crown Point Campaign, under General Jeffrey Amherst, 1759–1760 (New York, 1911)

Panet, J.-C., *Précis de ce qui s'est passé au Canada depuis la nouvelle de la flotte de M. Canon* (Montreal, 1866)

Pargellis, S., *Lord Loudoun in North America* (New Haven, CT, 1933)

Pargellis, S., ed., *Military Affairs in North America, 1748–65: Selected Documents from the Cumberland Papers in Windsor Castle* (New York, 1936)

A Plan of Discipline Composed for the Use of the Militia of the County of Norfolk (2 vols., London, 1759)

Ramezay, J. B. N. R. de, *Mémoire du sieur de Ramezay, commandant à Québec, au sujet de la reddition de cette ville, le 18 septembre 1759* (Quebec, 1861)

Récher, J.-F., *Journal du siège de Québec en 1759* (Quebec, 1959)

Siege of Quebec and Conquest of Canada: in 1759. By a Nun of the General Hospital of Quebec (Quebec, 1855)

Sullivan, J., et al., eds., *The Papers of Sir William Johnson* (Albany, NY, 1921)

Walpole, H., *Memoirs of the Reign of George II* (2 vols., London, 1846)

Willson, B., ed., *The Life and Letters of James Wolfe* (New York, 1909)

Wood, W., ed., *The Logs of the Conquest of Canada* (Toronto, 1909)

Wylley, H. C., ed., *The Sherwood Foresters: Notts and Derby Regiment. Regimental Annual 1926* (London, 1927)

SECONDARY SOURCES

Books

Anderson, F., *The Crucible of War: The Seven Years War in North America, 1754–1766* (New York, 2001)

Bamfield, V., *On the Strength: The Story of the British Army Wife* (London, 1974)

Beaglehole, J. C., *The Life of Captain James Cook* (London, 1974)

Bernier, S., et al., *The Military History of Quebec City 1608–2008* (Montreal, 2008)

Black, J. and P. Woodfine, eds., *The British Navy and the Use of Naval Power in the Eighteenth Century* (Leicester, 1988)

Bibliography

Bothwell, R., *The Penguin History of Canada* (Toronto, 2006)

Bowen, H. V., *War and British Society, 1688–1815* (Cambridge, 1988)

Brumwell, S., *Paths of Glory: The Life and Death of General James Wolfe* (London, 2006)

——*Redcoats: The British Soldier and War in the Americas: 1755–63* (Cambridge, 2002)

——*White Devil: An Epic Story of Revenge from the Savage War that Inspired Last of the Mohicans* (London, 2004)

Casgrain, H. R., *Wolfe and Montcalm* (Toronto, 1911)

Chartrand, R., *French Fortresses in North America 1535–1763: Québec, Montréal, Louisbourg and New Orleans* (Oxford, 2005)

——*The French Soldier in Colonial America* (Bloomfield, ON, 1984)

——*Louis XV's Army*, vol. II, *French Infantry* (London, 1996)

——*Louisbourg and New Orleans* (Oxford, 2005)

Chénier, R., *Quebec: A French Colonial Town in America, 1660–1690* (Ottawa, 1991)

Clayton, T., *Tars* (London, 2007)

Dale, R. J., *The Fall of New France* (Toronto, 2004)

Dechêne, L., *Le Peuple, l'état et la guerre au Canada sous le régime français* (Quebec, 2008)

Dorn, W., *Competition for Empire 1740–63* (New York, 1965)

Duffy, C., *The Military Experience in the Age of Reason* (London, 1987)

Dull, J. R., *The French Navy and the Seven Years War* (Lincoln, NB, 2005)

Eccles, W. J., *Essays on New France* (Toronto, 1987)

——*The French in North America 1500–1783* (Lansing, MI, 1998)

Ferling, J. E., *A Wilderness of Miseries: War and Warriors in Early America* (Westport, CT, 1980)

Frégault, G., *Canada: The War of the Conquest* (Oxford, 1969)

Gardiner, R., ed., *Conway's History of the Ship: The Line of Battle* (London, 1992)

Guy, A., *Oeconomy and Discipline: Officership and Administration in the British Army 1714–1763* (Manchester, 1985)

Hargreaves, R., *The Bloodybacks: The British Serviceman in North America 1655–1783* (London, 1968)

Harper, J. R., *The Fraser Highlanders* (Montreal, 1979)

Holmes, R., *Redcoat: The British Soldier in the Age of Horse and Musket* (London, 2001)

Houlding, J., *Fit for Service: The Training of the British Army, 1715–1795* (Oxford, 1981)

Hughes, B. P., *British Smooth Bore Artillery: The Muzzle Loading Artillery of the 18th and 19th Centuries* (London, 1969)

——*Firepower: Weapons Effectiveness on the Battlefield, 1630–1850* (London, 1974)

James, L., *Warrior Race* (London, 2001)

Johnson, M., *American Woodland Indians* (Oxford, 1990)

—— *Indian Tribes of the New England Frontier* (Oxford, 2006)

Kennett, L., *The French Armies and the Seven Years War* (Durham, NC, 1967)

Lloyd, C., *The Capture of Quebec* (London, 1959)

Malone, P. M., *The Skulking Way of War: Technology and Tactics among the New England Indians* (Lanham, MD, 1991)

Matthew, H. C. G. and B. Harrison, eds., *Oxford Dictionary of National Biography* (Oxford, 2004); online edn ed. by L. Goldman, January 2008

May, R. and G. Embleton, *Wolfe's Army* (Reading, 1997)

McCulloch, I., *Highlander in the French–Indian War 1756–67* (Oxford, 2008)

——*Sons of the Mountain: The Highland Regiments in the French and Indian War, 1756–1767* (2 vols., Toronto, 2006)

McLennan, J. S., *Louisbourg from Its Foundation to Its Fall, 1713–1758* (London, 1918)

McNairn, A., *Behold the Hero: General Wolfe and the Arts in the Eighteenth Century* (Montreal, 1997)

Middleton, R., *The Bells of Victory: The Pitt-Newcastle Ministry and the Conduct of the Seven Years' War 1757–1762* (Cambridge, 1985)

O'Toole, F., *White Savage* (London, 2005)

Pease, T. C., ed., *Anglo-French Boundary Disputes in the West, 1749–1763* (Springfield, IL, 1936)

Pocock, T., *Battle for Empire* (London, 1988)

——*British Redcoat 1740–1793* (London, 1996)

——*King George's Army 1740–1793* (London, 1996)

——*Wolfe: The Career of General James Wolfe from Culloden to Quebec* (London, 2000)

Reid., S., *Quebec 1759: The Battle that Won Canada* (Oxford, 2003)

Reynolds, P. R., *Guy Carleton: A Biography* (Toronto, 1980)

Rodger, N. A. M., *The Command of the Ocean* (London, 2006)

——*The Wooden World: An Anatomy of the Georgian Navy* (London, 1986)

Rogers, H. C. B., *The British Army of the Eighteenth Century* (London, 1977)

Saint-Martin, G., *Québec 1759–1760! Les Plaines d'Abraham* (Paris, 2007)

Stacey, C. P., *Quebec 1759: The Siege and the Battle* (Toronto, 2002)

Steele, I., *Warpaths: Invasions of North America* (Oxford, 1994)

Bibliography

Townshend, C. V. F., *The Military Life of George First Marquess Townshend* (Toronto, 1907)

Ultee, M., ed., *Adapting to Conditions: War and Society in the Eighteenth Century* (Tuscaloosa, AL, 1986)

Voltaire, *Candide* (London, 1950)

Ward, M., *The Battle for Quebec, 1759* (Stroud, 2005)

Whitfield, C. M., *Tommy Atkins: The British Soldier in Canada, 1759–1870* (Ottawa, 1981)

Windrow, M., *Montcalm's Army* (Oxford, 1973)

Wood, W., *The Passing of New France* (Toronto, 1920)

Articles

Brumwell, S., 'Home from the Wars', *History Today*, 52, 3 (March 2002)

Charters, E. M., 'Disease, Wilderness Warfare, and Imperial Relations: The Battle for Quebec, 1759–1760', *War in History*, 16, 1 (2009)

Doughty, A., ed., 'A New Account of the Death of Wolfe', *Canadian Historical Review*, 4 (1923)

Eccles, W. J., 'Montcalm', *Dictionary of Canadian Biography*, (Toronto, 1974)

Harding, R., 'Sailors and Gentlemen of Parade: Some Professional and Technical Problems Concerning the Conduct of Combined Operations in the Eighteenth Century', *Historical Journal*, 32, 1 (1989)

Higginbotham, D., 'The Early American Way of War: Reconnaissance and Appraisal', in *William and Mary Quarterly* (Third Series), 44 (1987)

Kopperman, Paul E., 'The British High Command and Soldiers Wives in America, 1755–1783', *Journal of the Society for Army Historical Research*, 60, 241 (1982)

Lloyd, E. M., 'The Raising of the Highland Regiments in 1757', *English Historical Review*, 17 (1902)

MacKay Hitsman, J. and C. C. J. Bond, 'The Assault Landing at Louisbourg, 1758', *Canadian Historical Review*, 35 (1954)

Nicolai, M. L., 'A Different kind of courage: The French Military and the Canadian Irregular Soldier during the Seven Years' War', *Canadian Historical Review*, 70 (1989)

Olson, D. W., W. D. Liddle, R. L. Doescher, L. M. Behrends, T. D. Silakowski, and J. F. Saucier, 'Perfect Tide, Ideal Moon: An Unappreciated Aspect of Wolfe's Generalship at Québec, 1759', *William and Mary Quarterly* (Third Series), 59, 4 (2002)

Robson, E., 'British Light Infantry in the Eighteenth Century: The Effect of American Conditions', *Army and Defence Quarterly*, 62 (1952)

Saunders, R., 'A Forgotten Hero of British North America: Admiral Sir Charles Saunders', *Newfoundland Quarterly*, 62 (1963)

Smillie, E. A., 'The Achievement of Durell in 1759 (Facts Relating to Admiral Philip Durell and the St. Lawrence Expedition)', *Transactions of the Royal Society of Canada* (1925)

Stacey, C. P., 'The British Forces in North America during the Seven Years' War', *Dictionary of Canadian Biography*, vol. III (Toronto, 1974)

Steppler, G., 'British Military Law, Discipline, and the Conduct of Regimental Courts Martial in the Later Eighteenth Century', *English Historical Review*, 102 (1987)

Syrett, D., 'The Methodology of British Amphibious Operations during the Seven Years and American Wars', *Mariners Mirror*, 58 (1972)

Winstock, L., 'Hot Stuff', *Journal for the Society of Army Historical Research*, 43 (1955)

Web resources

Dictionary of Canadian Biography online
Dictionary of National Biography online
http://www.archive.org/details/correspondenceofo1pitt
http://www.fullbooks.com/The-Letters-of-Horace-Walpole-Volumex795615.html

NOTES

Prologue

1. Doughty, A., ed., *An Historical Journal of the Campaigns in North America: For the Years 1757, 1758, 1759 and 1760 by Captain John Knox* (3 vols., Toronto, 1914–16), I: 389–90.
2. Knox, *Journal*, I: 386.
3. *General Orders in Wolfe's Army*, 14.
4. Knox, *Journal*, I: 391.
5. Wolfe to Pitt, 2 September 1759, Montmorency, PRO, CO 5/51.
6. Quoted in I. McCulloch, *Sons of the Mountain: The Highland Regiments in the French and Indian War, 1756–1767* (2 vols., Toronto, 2006), I: 177.
7. *Extract from a Manuscript Journal Relating to the Operations before Quebec in 1759, Kept by Colonel Malcolm Fraser, the Lt of the 78th (Fraser's Highlanders) and Serving in that Campaign* (Literary and Historical Society of Quebec: Historical Documents, Second Series, Quebec, 1868), 4–5.
8. Quoted in McCulloch, *Sons of the Mountain*, I: 178.
9. 'Memoirs of the Siege of Quebec by John Johnson', in A. Doughty and G. Parmelee, eds., *The Siege of Quebec and the Battle of the Plains of Abraham* (6 vols., Quebec, 1901), V: 80.
10. Knox, *Journal*, I: 391.
11. Ibid., I: 394.

Chapter One: Assault on New France

1. W. Wood, ed., *The Logs of the Conquest of Canada* (Toronto, 1909), 90.
2. A. Doughty, ed., *An Historical Journal of the Campaigns in North America: For the Years 1757, 1758, 1759 and 1760 by Captain John Knox* (3 vols., Toronto, 1914–16), I: 362.
3. Ibid.
4. Newcastle to Albemarle, 5 September 1754, in T. C. Pease, ed., *Anglo-French Boundary Disputes in the West, 1749–1763* (Springfield, IL, 1936), 50–2.

5. Braddock quoted in F. Anderson, *The Crucible of War: The Seven Years War in North America, 1754–1766* (New York, 2001), 95.

6. T. Clayton, *Tars* (London, 2007), 99.

7. R. Middleton, *The Bells of Victory: The Pitt-Newcastle Ministry and the Conduct of the Seven Years' War 1757–1762* (Cambridge, 1985), 114–16.

8. Middleton, *The Bells of Victory*, 128.

9. Minutes of the meeting at Lord Anson's house, 19 February 1759, in Middleton, *The Bells of Victory*, 108

10. 'The Journal of Captain John Montresor', in A. Doughty and G. Parmelee, eds., *The Siege of Quebec and the Battle of the Plains of Abraham* (6 vols., Quebec, 1901), IV: 307.

11. *Dictionary of Canadian Biography* online see: http://www.biographi.ca/EN/ShowBio.asp?BioId=35452andquery=DURELL

12. Durell to Admiralty, 19 March 1759, Halifax harbour on the *Princess Amelia*, in C. H. Little, ed., *Despatches of Rear Admiral Philip Durell* (Halifax, NS, 1958), 7.

13. *Dictionary of Canadian Biography* online see: http://www.biographi.ca/EN/ShowBio.asp?BioId=35759andquery=john%20AND%20orous

14. 'Letter of James Gibson to Governor Lawrence', Basin of Quebec, 1 August 1759, in Doughty and Parmelee, *Siege of Quebec*, V: 61–2.

15. 'Extract of a Letter from an Officer in Major General Wolfe's Army, Island of Orleans, 10th August 1759', in S. Pargellis, ed., *Military Affairs in North America, 1748–65: Selected Documents from the Cumberland Papers in Windsor Castle* (New York, 1936), 433.

16. Clevland to Holburne, 1 January 1759, Adm 2/524, in Middleton, *The Bells of Victory*, 105.

17. Saunders to Pitt, 22 January 1759, PRO, CO 5/51 fol. 5.

18. Middleton, *The Bells of Victory*, 106.

19. Admiralty to Saunders, 9 January 1759, Adm 2/82; for the rough figures of British and French ships of the line see N. A. M. Rodger, *The Command of the Ocean* (London, 2006), 608.

20. A. Brice, *The Grand Gazetteer: or, Topographic Dictionary, Both General and Special, and Ancient as Well as Modern* (Exeter, 1759), 1058, in T. Clayton, *Tars* (London, 2007), 184.

21. 'Brigadier Townshend's Journal of the Voyage to America and Campaign against Quebec, 1759', in Doughty and Parmelee, *Siege of Quebec*, V: 225.

22. C. H. Little, ed., *Despatches of Vice Admiral Saunders* (Halifax, NS, 1958), 4.

23. A note on the colours associated with British admirals: in the seventeenth century the fleet fought as one long line in battle and was divided for command and control into three sections: the van, which flew the white ensign, the centre which flew the red, and the rear which flew the blue. The overall commander was in the centre and so became the 'Admiral of the Red'; the Vice Admiral of the Red commanded the front of the centre squadron and was, therefore, the senior Vice Admiral, and the Rear Admiral of the Red commanded the rear of the centre and was the senior Rear Admiral. The Admiral of the White commanded the van, the Vice Admiral of the White commanded the very front of the van, and the Rear Admiral of the White commanded the rear of the van. The rear had an Admiral, Vice Admiral, and Rear Admiral of the Blue who were the respective juniors of their ranks. At Quebec, Saunders was Vice Admiral of the Blue, i.e. the most junior Vice Admiral in the fleet, Holmes was a Rear Admiral of the White and Durell, Rear Admiral of the Red. By the Seven Years War the titles had lost their real meanings as the fleets grew in size and never fought as one giant formation. They remained only a mark of seniority.

24. Little, *Despatches of Vice Admiral Saunders*, 5.

25. 'Brigadier Townshend's Journal of the Voyage to America and Campaign against Quebec, 1759', in Doughty and Parmelee, *Siege of Quebec*, V: 226.

26. The *Cerberus* took thirty-four days to get from Spithead to Boston in 1775 and carried the three brigadiers for the North American campaign: Howe, Clinton, and Burgoyne. In R. Holmes, *Redcoat: The British Soldier in the Age of Horse and Musket* (London, 2001), 331.

27. Saunders to Admiralty, 28 February 1759, in Little, *Despatches of Vice Admiral Saunders*, 6.

28. Clayton, *Tars*, 211, 223.

29. 'Brigadier Townshend's Journal of the Voyage to America and Campaign against Quebec, 1759', in Doughty and Parmelee, *Siege of Quebec*, V: 227.

30. Durell to Admiralty, *Princess Amelia*, Halifax, 19 March 1759, in Little, *Despatches of Rear Admiral Philip Durell*, 7.

31. Saunders to Admiralty, Halifax, 2 May 1759, in Little, *Despatches of Vice Admiral Saunders*, 8. Interestingly a note on the reverse of the letter says it was received in London on 28 August.

32. J. C. Beaglehole, *The Life of Captain James Cook* (London, 1974), 32.

33. Wolfe to Father, Plymouth Sound, 22 February 1758, in B. Willson, *The Life and Letters of James Wolfe* (New York, 1909), 362.

34. Wolfe to Amherst, *Neptune*, 6 March 1759, in S. Brumwell, *Paths of Glory: The Life and Death of General James Wolfe* (London, 2006), 187.
35. Wolfe to Amherst, Halifax, 1 May 1759, in Willson, *The Life and Letters of James Wolfe*, 425.
36. Wolfe's 'Family Journal', PRONI, DOD 162/77 C, 29, 1–2, 28. Durell came in for much criticism subsequently that echoes this journal but it is hard to agree with the vitriol. The winter had been the worst on record and his ships awaited only a fair wind to leave Halifax. In 1760, despite all the harassment that the British army and state could bring to bear on Commodore Colville, he was only able to leave Halifax two weeks before Durell had done in 1759, on 22 April, and some of his ships were stuck fast in ice for twenty-four hours from 24 April. He too was beaten into the St Lawrence by ships sent from Europe. See Beaglehole, *The Life of Captain James Cook*, 52.
37. Saunders to Admiralty, Halifax, 2 May 1759, in Little, *Despatches of Vice Admiral Saunders*, 8.
38. Major Moncrief, *A Short Account of the Expedition against Quebec Commanded by Major-General Wolfe in the Year 1759* (Quebec, 1901), 5. All quotations throughout Moncrief are by Patrick Mackellar.
39. Wolfe to Pitt, Halifax, 1 May 1759, in Willson, *The Life and Letters of James Wolfe*, 423.
40. Middleton, *Bells of Victory*, 103.
41. Clayton, *Tars*, 242.
42. Brumwell, *Paths of Glory*, 155.
43. Wolfe to Lord George Sackville, Halifax, 24 May 1758, in Willson, *The Life and Letters of James Wolfe*, 368.
44. Wolfe to Pitt, Halifax, 1 May 1759, and Wolfe to Amherst, Halifax, 1 May 1759, in Willson, *The Life and Letters of James Wolfe*, 424, 425.
45. Wolfe to Major Walter Wolfe, London, 29 January 1759, in Willson, *The Life and Letters of James Wolfe*, 418.
46. A description by Lieutenant Henry Hamilton of the 15th Foot, in J. S. McLennan, *Louisbourg from Its Foundation to Its Fall, 1713–1758* (London, 1918), 315.
47. Wolfe to his mother, Bristol, 19 January 1753, in Willson, *The Life and Letters of James Wolfe*, 247.
48. Wolfe to Major Walter Wolfe, London, 29 January 1759, in Willson, *The Life and Letters of James Wolfe*, 418.
49. Description by Lieutenant Henry Hamilton of the 15th Foot, in McLennan, *Louisbourg from Its Foundation to Its Fall, 1713–1758*, 315.

50. *Sailing Orders by Mr Cobb, Commander of His Majesty's Province Sloop York,* in Wood, *Logs of the Conquest of Canada,* 93–4.
51. Moncrief, *A Short Account of the Expedition against Quebec,* 5.
52. Ibid.
53. Chevalier de Johnstone, *The Campaign of Louisbourg 1750–58* (Literary and Historical Society of Quebec: Historical Documents, Second Series, Quebec, 1868), 6.
54. R. Chartrand, *French Fortresses in North America 1535–1763: Québec, Montréal, Louisbourg and New Orleans* (Oxford, 2005), 47.
55. The figure and the quote from Amherst (who is writing to Governor Francis Bernard of New Jersey) are in S. Brumwell, *Redcoats: The British Soldier and War in the Americas: 1755–63* (Cambridge, 2002), 60.
56. Saunders to Pitt, 6 June 1759, PRO, CO 5/51 fol. 32; see also the description in *Extract from a Manuscript Journal Relating to the Operations before Quebec in 1759, Kept by Colonel Malcolm Fraser, the Lt of the 78th (Fraser's Highlanders) and Serving in that Campaign* (Literary and Historical Society of Quebec: Historical Documents, Second Series, Quebec, 1868), 1.
57. Moncrief, *A Short Account of the Expedition against Quebec,* 6.
58. Knox, *Journal,* I: 355.
59. Ibid., I: xiii.
60. Ibid., I: 99.
61. Moncrief, *A Short Account of the Expedition against Quebec,* 6.
62. Knox, *Journal,* I: 349.
63. There are different versions of Wolfe's Journal. One is in the McCord Museum in Montreal and runs from 10 May to 7 August 1759. It was originally believed that this journal was written by Wolfe but in 1987 a comparative handwriting study established that it was written by Wolfe's ADC, Thomas Bell, dictated by Wolfe. There is another copy in the archive of the Royal Military College in Kingston, Ontario, which seems to have been written during the campaign. A last version is a copy made by Thomas Bell which resides in LAC. The McCord copy is in C-173, box 1, MS 255 and the LAC is: Northcliffe collection, separate items, MG 18 M/rl C-370. I have used all of them where appropriate and will simply record the date of the entry. This one is 24 May 1759.
64. Knox, *Journal,* I: 349.
65. Ibid., I: 33–5, 38; for an excellent discussion on wartime training in the mid-eighteenth century see, J. Houlding, *Fit for Service: The Training of the British Army, 1715–1795* (Oxford, 1981), 335.

66. Fraser, *Journal*, 17 May 1759.
67. Knox, *Journal*, I: 358.
68. Wolfe to Brigadier Whitmore, Louisbourg, 19 May 1759, in LAC, MG 18 N 18, vol. IV, file 3.
69. Wolfe to Lord George Sackville, Louisbourg, 30 July 1758, in Willson, *The Life and Letters of James Wolfe*, 390; Wolfe to Lord George Sackville, Portsmouth, 7 February 1758, ibid., 358.
70. Wolfe to Pitt, *Neptune*, 6 June 1759, in Willson, *The Life and Letters of James Wolfe*, 432.
71. Logs: *Neptune*, 4 June 1759, in Wood, *The Logs of the Conquest of Canada*, 249.
72. *General Orders in Wolfe's Army during the Expedition up the River St Lawrence, 1759* (Literary and Historical Society of Quebec: Historical Documents, Fourth Series, Quebec, 1875), 5–9; Knox, *Journal*, I: 350–7.
73. *General Orders in Wolfe's Army during the Expedition up the River St Lawrence, 1759*, 9–10.
74. Ibid., 10; Saunders to Pitt, 6 June 1759, PRO, CO 5/51 fol. 32.
75. Knox, *Journal*, I: 356; Moncrief, *A Short Account of the Expedition against Quebec*, 7.
76. Knox, *Journal*, I: 357, 359.
77. Fraser, *Journal*, 2.
78. Wolfe to Pitt, *Neptune*, 6 June 1759, PRO, CO 5/51 fol. 63; Moncrief, *A Short Account of the Expedition against Quebec*, 6; the Embarkation Return, made on 5 June is PRO, CO 5/51, fol. 67.
79. Saunders to Pitt, 6 June 1759, CO 5/51 fol. 32; R. Gardiner, ed., *Conway's History of the Ship: The Line of Battle* (London, 1992), 182; J. R. Dull, *The French Navy and the Seven Years War* (Lincoln, NB, 2005), 149; C. P. Stacey, *Quebec 1759: The Siege and the Battle* (Toronto, 2002), Appendix F, 215–21.
80. Ordnance and ammunition supplies listed in Appendix E of Stacey, *Quebec 1759*, 214.
81. 'Sailing Orders and Instructions, By His Excellency Admiral Saunders', in Wood, *The Logs of the Conquest of Canada*, 97–106.
82. *General Orders in Wolfe's Army during the Expedition up the River St Lawrence, 1759*, 10; detail on transport organization is from General Townshend's Journal in C. V. F. Townshend, *The Military Life of George First Marquess Townshend* (Toronto, 1907), 150–1; 'Sailing Orders and Instructions, by His Excellency Admiral Saunders', *Neptune*, Louisbourg, 15 May 1759, in Wood, *The Logs of the Conquest of Canada*, 99, 104.

83. Twenty-sixth of May 1742 from an order book of the War of Austrian Succession, in Wood, *The Logs of the Conquest of Canada*, 5.

84. *General Orders in Wolfe's Army during the Expedition up the River St Lawrence, 1759*, 5.

85. Captain John Cremer quoted in N. A. M. Rodger, *The Wooden World: An Anatomy of the Georgian Navy* (London, 1986), 37.

86. Knox, *Journal*, I: 359.

87. Clayton, *Tars*, 11.

88. Knox, *Journal*, I: 31.

89. Wolfe to Sackville, 24 May 1758, Halifax, in Willson, *The Life and Letters of James Wolfe*, 369.

90. 'Journal of Captain Montresor', in Doughty and Parmelee, *Siege of Quebec*, IV: 303; 'Sailing Orders and Instructions, by His Excellency Admiral Saunders', *Neptune*, Louisbourg, 15 May 1759, in Wood, *The Logs of the Conquest of Canada*, 101.

91. Captain Richard Gardiner to the Honourable George Hobart Esq., 18 February 1761, in *Memoirs of the Siege of Quebec, the Capital of all Canada, and of the Retreat of Monsieur de Bourlemaque* (Quebec, 1901), 9–10.

92. Knox, *Journal*, I: 361; 'Journal of Captain Montresor', in Doughty and Parmelee, *Siege of Quebec*, IV: 303–4.

93. 'Journal of Captain Montresor', in Doughty and Parmelee, *Siege of Quebec*, IV: 304.

94. Wolfe's Journal, 10 June 1759.

95. *The Northcliffe Collection* (Ottawa, 1926), XXII: 145.

96. Knox, *Journal*, I: 361.

97. Wolfe's Journal, 18, 19 June 1759.

98. 'Journal of Captain Montresor', in Doughty and Parmelee, *Siege of Quebec*, IV: 304.

99. Moncrief, *A Short Account of the Expedition against Quebec*, 8.

100. Knox, *Journal*, I: 366.

101. 'Brigadier Townshend's Journal of the Voyage to America and Campaign against Quebec, 1759', in Doughty and Parmelee, *Siege of Quebec*, V: 236; 'Journal of Captain Montresor', in ibid., IV: 305; Knox, *Journal*, I: 364; 'Brigadier Townshend's Journal of the Voyage to America and Campaign against Quebec, 1759', in Doughty and Parmelee, *Siege of Quebec*, V: 234.

102. Wood, *The Logs of the Conquest of Canada*, 303.

103. Knox, *Journal*, I: 369.

Chapter Two: 'The enemy are out to destroy everything that calls itself Canada'

1. 'A Description of the Town of Quebec – Its Strength and Situation', in S. Pargellis, ed., *Military Affairs in North America, 1748–65: Selected Documents from the Cumberland Papers in Windsor Castle* (New York, 1936), 412–13; Chevalier de Johnstone, *The Campaign of 1760 in Canada* (Literary and Historical Society of Quebec: Historical Documents, Second Series, Quebec, 1868), 4.

2. Frontenac to Colbert, quoted in R. Chartrand, *French Fortresses in North America 1535–1763: Québec, Montréal, Louisbourg and New Orleans* (Oxford, 2005), 13.

3. H. R. Casgrain, *Montcalm and Wolfe* (Toronto, 1911), 7.

4. R. Léger, ed., *Le Journal de Montcalm* (Montreal, 2007), entry for 31 January 1756, 31.

5. Eccles, *Dictionary of Canadian Biography*, 459.

6. Montcalm to Cremille, 12 April 1759, in E. O'Callaghan and B. Fernow, eds., *Documents Relative to the Colonial History of the State of New York; Procured in Holland, England and France* (15 vols., Albany, NY, 1853–87), X: 961.

7. Léger, *Le Journal de Montcalm*, 460.

8. E. P. Hamilton, ed., *Adventure in the Wilderness: The American Journals of Louis Antoine de Bougainville, 1756–1760* (Norman, OK, 1990), 102, 51, 57.

9. Hamilton, *Bougainville*, 288.

10. O'Callaghan and Fernow, *Documents*, X: 959; Montcalm to Le Normand, 12 April 1759, in ibid., X: 966.

11. I. Steele, *Warpaths: Invasions of North America* (Oxford, 1994), 205.

12. Hamilton, *Bougainvillè*, 253.

13. Ibid., 193.

14. Ibid., 215.

15. Vaudreuil to Massiac, 4 September 1758, Montreal, in O'Callaghan and Fernow, *Documents*, X: 885.

16. Montcalm to Cremille, 12 April 1759, in ibid., X: 959.

17. Léger, *Le Journal de Montcalm*, entry for 15 April 1756, 33.

18. E. Taillemite, 'Bougainville', in *Dictionary of Canadian Biography* online-http://www.biographi.ca/EN/ShowBio.asp?BioId=36406 andquery=bougainville

19. Hamilton, *Bougainville*, 304–5.

20. Quoted by Alexis de Tocqueville, in G. Frégault, *Canada: The War of the Conquest* (Toronto, 1969), 10.

21. L. Kennett, *The French Armies and the Seven Years War* (Durham, NC, 1967), 3–4, 5, 6; J. R. Dull, *The French Navy and the Seven Years War* (Lincoln, NB, 2005), 23.
22. M. Windrow, *Montcalm's Army* (Oxford, 1973), 28.
23. 'Abstract of, and Ministerial Minutes on, the Despatches from Canada', in O'Callaghan and Fernow, *Documents*, X: 906–7.
24. Ibid.; Dull, *The French Navy*, 142–3.
25. Belle Isle to Montcalm, Versailles, 19 February 1759, in O'Callaghan and Fernow, *Documents*, X: 944.
26. Ibid., X: 943.
27. J.-C. Panet, *Précis de ce qui s'est passé au Canada depuis la nouvelle de la flotte de M. Canon* (Montreal, 1866), henceforth 'Panet's Journal', 14 May 1759.
28. Malartic to Cremille, Montreal, 9 April 1759, in O'Callaghan and Fernow, *Documents*, X: 957.
29. 'Summary of the Plan of General Operations for the Campaign of 1759', by Vaudreuil, in ibid., X: 953; Bigot to Berryer, 22 May 1759, quoted in Frégault, *Canada*, 240.
30. Quoted in Casgrain, *Wolfe and Montcalm*, 63.
31. Montcalm to Belle Isle, 8 May 1759, Montreal, in Callaghan and Fernow, *Documents*, X: 970.
32. 'Journal du siège de Québec', in *The Northcliffe Collection* (Ottawa, 1926), XXX: 223.
33. Montcalm to Belle Isle, 23/24 May 1759, Quebec, in O'Callaghan and Fernow, *Documents*, X: 971–2.
34. 'Narrative of the Siege of Quebec, Published by the French [Département de la Guerre]', in ibid., X: 994; *Memoirs of the Siege of Quebec, the Capital of all Canada, and of the Retreat of Monsieur de Bourlemaque* (Quebec, 1901), 15.
35. 'Summary of the Plan of General Operations for the Campaign of 1759', by Vaudreuil, in O'Callaghan and Fernow, *Documents*, X: 954; 'Journal du siège de Québec', in *The Northcliffe Collection*, XXX: 223–4.
36. 'Summary of the Plan of General Operations for the Campaign of 1759', by Vaudreuil, in O'Callaghan and Fernow, *Documents*, X: 955, signed on 1 April 1759.
37. Montcalm to de Lévis, in Casgrain, *Montcalm and Wolfe*, 83–4; 'Journal du siège de Québec', in *The Northcliffe Collection*, XXX: 224, 232–3.
38. Vaudreuil to de Léry, in ibid., XXIV: 185, 188.
39. Ibid., XXIV: 187.
40. 'Journal of de Léry', in ibid., XXV: 195–8.

41. Vaudreuil to de Léry, in ibid., XXIV: 192.
42. 'Journal du siège de Québec', in *The Northcliffe Collection*, XXX: 224.
43. Panet's Journal, 9 June 1759.
44. Marguerite Gosselin, quoted in J.-M. Lebel, *1759 Summer under Siege* (Quebec, 2001), 15.
45. 'Journal du siège de Québec', in *The Northcliffe Collection*, XXX: 224.
46. Montcalm to Cremille, 12 April 1759, in O'Callaghan and Fernow, *Documents*, X: 959.
47. Wolfe to Pitt, Halifax, 1 May 1759, in B. Willson, ed., *The Life and Letters of James Wolfe* (New York, 1909), 424.
48. Montcalm to Cremille, 12 April 1759, in O'Callaghan and Fernow, *Documents*, X: 962.
49. Hamilton, *Bougainville*, 14.
50. Dull, *The French Navy*, 144–5; 'Summary of the Plan of General Operations for the Campaign of 1759' by Vaudreuil, in O'Callaghan and Fernow, *Documents*, X: 954.
51. Captain Richard Gardiner to the Honourable George Hobart Esq., 18 February 1761, in *Memoirs of the Siege of Quebec, the Capital of all Canada, and of the Retreat of Monsieur de Bourlemaque*, 7–8.
52. Hamilton, *Bougainville*, 78.
53. 'Extract of a Journal Kept at the Army Commanded by the Late Lt Gen de Montcalm', in O'Callaghan and Fernow, *Documents*, X: 1017; Récher gives the figure of 1,800 Native Americans of which 162 were Christian. J.-F. Récher, *Journal du siège de Québec en 1759* (Quebec, 1959), entry for 9 September 1759.
54. J. B. N. R. de Ramezay, *Mémoire du sieur de Ramezay, commandant à Québec, au sujet de la reddition de cette ville, le 18 septembre 1759* (Quebec, 1861).
55. 'Memoir on the Position of the French and English in America', Département de la Guerre, Paris, in O'Callaghan and Fernow, *Documents*, X: 927.
56. Steele, *Warpaths*, 143.
57. Montresor to Colonel Montresor, 18 October 1759, Quebec, in A. Doughty and G. Parmelee, *The Siege of Quebec and the Battle of the Plains of Abraham* (6 vols., Quebec, 1901), IV: 332–3.
58. Montcalm to Cremille, 12 April 1759, in O'Callaghan and Fernow, *Documents*, X: 962; *Dictionary of Canadian Biography* online http://www.biographi.ca/EN/ShowBio.asp?BioId=36769andquery=pontleroy; Bougainville quoted in Chartrand, *French Fortresses*, 24.
59. 'Journal du siège de Québec', in *The Northcliffe Collection*, XXX: 229.

60. Montcalm to Le Normand, 12 April 1759, in O'Callaghan and Fernow, *Documents*, X: 963; Léger, *Le Journal de Montcalm*, entry for 10 October 1757, 262.
61. 'Memoir on Canada', in O'Callaghan and Fernow, *Documents*, X: 934.
62. 'Extract of a Journal Kept at the Army Commanded by the Late Lt Gen de Montcalm', in O'Callaghan and Fernow, *Documents*, X: 1016.
63. *Memoirs of the Siege of Quebec, the Capital of all Canada, and of the Retreat of Monsieur de Bourlemaque*, 16.
64. Major Moncrief, in Doughty and Parmelee, *Siege of Quebec*, V: 56.
65. Hamilton, *Bougainville*, 186-7.
66. Ramezay, *Mémoire du sieur de Ramezay, commandant à Québec, au sujet de la reddition de cette ville, le 18 septembre 1759*.
67. 'Memoir on the Position of the French and English in America', Département de la Guerre, Paris, in O'Callaghan and Fernow, *Document*, X: 927.
68. Marguerite Gosselin, quoted in Lebel, *1759 Summer under Siege*, 7.
69. Eccles, *The French in North America, 1500–1783*, p144.
70. *Siege of Quebec and Conquest of Canada: in 1759. By a Nun of the General Hospital of Quebec* (Quebec, 1855), 5.
71. *Memoirs of the Siege of Quebec, the Capital of all Canada, and of the Retreat of Monsieur de Bourlemaque*, 17.
72. 'Extract of a Journal Kept at the Army Commanded by the Late Lt Gen de Montcalm', in O'Callaghan and Fernow, *Documents*, X: 1017.
73. *Memoirs of the Siege of Quebec, the Capital of all Canada, and of the Retreat of Monsieur de Bourlemaque*, 17.
74. Chevalier de Johnstone, 'The Campaign of 1760 in Canada', 3-4.
75. Panet's Journal, 'end of May'.
76. 'Relation du siège de Québec, posé par les Anglois en l'anée 1759', in *The Northcliffe Collection*, XXVIII: 215; *Memoirs of the Siege of Quebec, the Capital of all Canada, and of the Retreat of Monsieur de Bourlemaque*, 17.
77. 'Journal du siège de Québec', in *The Northcliffe Collection*, XXX: 228.
78. Montcalm to Mercier, Quebec, 28 June 1759, quoted in Montcalm's Journal, 455.
79. The Plan of Operations for the campaign of 1759 is in the handwriting of de Lévis and is reprinted in 'French Documents Relating to Quebec', *The Northcliffe Collection*, XXVII: 209-14. On the far left of Montcalm's position 'following the crest of the

escarpment' and running all the way to the Montmorency River, he placed a regular unit, the 2nd battalion of the Royal Roussillon Regiment, with the militia drawn from the Montreal area and the Native Americans in support, all under the command of de Lévis. On the other flank by the St Charles River next to the city he placed the militia of Quebec and Trois Rivières and some of his *troupes de la marine* under the command of Vaudreuil, where Montcalm thought he could do the least harm. In the centre, where he expected the British landings to take place, he stationed the four remaining battalions of French regulars, Languedoc, La Sarre, Guyenne, Béarn, under his own command; 'Journal du siège de Québec', in *The Northcliffe Collection*, XXX: 240.

80. Ibid., 210–12.
81. De Lévis' orders in *The Northcliffe Collection*, XXVII: 209; *Memoirs of the Siege of Quebec, the Capital of all Canada, and of the Retreat of Monsieur de Bourlemaque, 19.*
82. De Lévis' orders in *The Northcliffe Collection*, XXVII: 210–11.
83. 'Journal du siège de Québec', in *The Northcliffe Collection*, XXX: 226, 228.
84. 'Extract of a Journal Kept at the Army Commanded by the Late Lt Gen de Montcalm', in O'Callaghan and Fernow, *Documents*, X: 1018; 'Journal du siège de Québec', in *The Northcliffe Collection*, XXX: 227; 'Relation du siège de Québec, posé par les Anglois en l'anée 1759', in *The Northcliffe Collection*, XXVIII: 215; Panet's Journal, 10 June 1759. Two British sources also mention the incident, but without comment on the relation between the Midshipman and the Admiral: Knox, *Journal*, I: 368; 'Letter of James Gibson to Governor Lawrence', of Quebec, 1 August 1759, in Doughty and Parmelee, *Siege of Quebec*, V: 63.
85. 'Journal du siège de Québec', in *The Northcliffe Collection*, XXX: 224.
86. Ibid., XXX: 230.
87. Ibid., XXX: 225.

Chapter Three: Mastering the St Lawrence

1. Quoted in J. C. Beaglehole, *The Life of Captain James Cook* (London, 1974), 36.
2. Quoted in *The Northcliffe Collection* (Ottawa, 1926), XXII: 145.
3. *Pembroke*'s Log, 4 June 1759, ADM 52/978 book 4.
4. Ibid., 263.

5. Cook's 'Directions for Sailing from the Harbour of Louisbourg to Quebec ...', in C. P. Stacey, *Quebec 1759: The Siege and the Battle* (Toronto, 2002), 65.

6. Ibid., 229.

7. 'Extract of a Journal Kept at the Army Commanded by the Late Lt Gen de Montcalm', in E. O'Callaghan and B. Fernow, eds., *Documents Relative to the Colonial History of the State of New York; Procured in Holland, England and France* (15 vols., Albany, NY, 1853–87), X: 1019; *Pembroke's* Log, 17 June 1759, ADM 52/978 book 4; *Centurion's* Log, 17 June 1759, in W. Wood, ed., *The Logs of the Conquest of Canada* (Toronto, 1909), 209; 'Journal du siège de Québec', in *The Northcliffe Collection*, XXX: 230.

8. 'The Journal of Captain John Montresor', in A. Doughty and G. Parmelee, eds., *The Siege of Quebec and the Battle of the Plains of Abraham* (6 vols., Quebec, 1901), IV: 307; A. Doughty, ed., *An Historical Journal of the Campaigns in North America: For the Years 1757, 1758, 1759 and 1760 by Captain John Knox* (3 vols., Toronto, 1914–16), I: 369; 'Letter of James Gibson to Governor Lawrence', Basin of Quebec, 1 August 1759, in Doughty and Parmelee, *Siege of Quebec*, V: 62.

9. Wolfe's Journal, 19, 22 June 1759.

10. Stacey, *Quebec 1759*, 66.

11. Wolfe's Journal, 25 June 1759.

12. *Hind's* Log, 24 June 1759, in Wood, *The Logs of the Conquest of Canada*, 227; *Stirling Castle's* Log, 27 June 1759, in ibid., 304.

13. Knox, *Journal*, I: 371.

14. It is difficult to know for sure how many pilots there were in all. One hint comes the following winter when the senior naval officer commanding the fleet at Halifax writes to London saying that he has eleven French pilots, with five more in Boston and three at Louisbourg. By December 1759 their main preoccupation was certainly not patriotic, as he writes that they 'are clamorous' for more money than the subsistence he has given them. He points out that 'their merits are very unequal as pilots, because some have much more skill than others'. Colville to Admiralty, 22 December 1759, *Northumberland*, Halifax, in C. H. Little, ed., *Despatches of Rear Admiral Philip Durell* (Halifax, NS, 1958), 13.

15. Knox, *Journal*, I: 371–2.

16. Ibid., I: 373–4.

17. *Lowestoft's* Log, 26 June 1759, in Wood, *The Logs of the Conquest of Canada*, 233; Knox, *Journal*, I: 374.

18. 'Journal of Captain Montresor', in Doughty and Parmelee, *Siege of Quebec*, IV: 309.
19. Major Moncrief, *A Short Account of the Expedition against Quebec Commanded by Major-General Wolfe in the Year 1759* (Quebec, 1901), 8.
20. Captain Richard Gardiner to the Honourable George Hobart Esq., 18 February 1761, in *Memoirs of the Siege of Quebec, the Capital of all Canada, and of the Retreat of Monsieur de Bourlemaque* (Quebec, 1901), 7.
21. Extract of a letter from an officer in Major General Wolfe's army, Island of Orleans, 10th August 1759, in S. Pargellis, ed., *Military Affairs in North America, 1748–65: Selected Documents from the Cumberland Papers in Windsor Castle* (New York, 1936), 433.
22. 'Letter of James Gibson to Governor Lawrence', of Quebec, 1 August 1759, in Doughty and Parmelee, *Siege of Quebec*, V: 62.
23. Knox, *Journal*, I: 368.
24. Wolfe's 'Family Journal', PRONI, DOD 162/77 C, 30.
25. Bougainville's Journal for 1756 in E. P. Hamilton, ed., *Adventure in the Wilderness: The American Journals of Louis Antoine de Bougainville, 1756–1760* (Norman, OK, 1990), 184.
26. *Memoirs of the Siege of Quebec, the Capital of all Canada, and of the Retreat of Monsieur de Bourlemaque*, 18.
27. 'Journal du siège de Québec', in *The Northcliffe Collection*, XXX: 231.
28. Quoted in B. Willson, ed., *The Life and Letters of James Wolfe* (London, 2006), 436.
29. Monsieur de Foligné, *Journal de faits arrivés a l'armé [sic] de Québec, capital [sic] dans l'Amérique septentrional [sic], pendant la campagne de l'année 1759* (Quebec, 1901), 10.
30. R. Léger, ed., *Le Journal de Montcalm* (Montreal, 2007), 457–8.
31. 'Journal du siège de Québec', in *The Northcliffe Collection*, XXX: 225.
32. Ibid., XXX: 232.
33. Ibid., XXX: 228.
34. 'Journal of Captain Montresor', in Doughty and Parmelee, *Siege of Quebec*, IV: 309; 'Genuine Letters from a Volunteer in the British Service at Quebec', in Doughty and Parmelee, *Siege of Quebec*, V: 14.
35. J. B. N. R. de Ramezay, *Mémoire du sieur de Ramezay, commandant à Québec, au sujet de la reddition de cette ville, le 18 septembre 1759* (Quebec, 1861), June 1759.

Chapter Four: Beachhead

1. Logs: *Richmond*, 27 June 1759, *Pembroke*, 27 June 1759, in W. Wood, ed., *The Logs of the Conquest of Canada* (Toronto, 1909), 282, 265; A. Doughty, ed., *An Historical Journal of the Campaigns in North America: For the Years 1757, 1758, 1759 and 1760 by Captain John Knox* (3 vols., Toronto, 1914–16), I: 376; *General Orders in Wolfe's Army during the Expedition up the River St Lawrence, 1759* (Literary and Historical Society of Quebec: Historical Documents, Fourth Series, Quebec, 1875), 11; 'The Journal of Captain John Montresor', in A. Doughty and G. Parmelee, eds., *The Siege of Quebec and the Battle of the Plains of Abraham* (6 vols., Quebec, 1901), IV: 309.
2. I. McCulloch, *Sons of the Mountain: The Highland Regiments in the French and Indian War, 1756–1767* (2 vols., Toronto, 2006), 35.
3. *London Evening Post*, 27–29 April 1758, in T. Clayton, *Tars* (London, 2007), 190; R. Middleton, *The Bells of Victory: The Pitt-Newcastle Ministry and the Conduct of the Seven Years' War 1757–1762* (Cambridge, 1985), 66.
4. General Monckton's Order Book, in *The Northcliffe Collection* (Ottawa, 1926), XXIII: 153.
5. *General Orders in Wolfe's Army*, 11, 12.
6. Knox, *Journal*, I: 377–8, 374–5.
7. Johnson's account of the campaign in reprinted in Doughty and Parmelee, *Siege of Quebec*, V: 71–166, this occurs on p. 80.
8. Iain Campbell's lyrical account of the campaign is published in I. McCulloch, *Sons of the Mountain: The Highland Regiments in the French and Indian War, 1756–1767* (2 vols., Toronto, 2006), I: 176.
9. Knox, *Journal*, I: 375.
10. 'Journal du siège de Québec', in *The Northcliffe Collection*, XXX: 234.
11. Ibid., XXX: 377; Wolfe's 'Family Journal', PRONI, DOD 162/77 C, 1–2.
12. *General Orders in Wolfe's Army*, 1.
13. Knox, *Journal*, I: 377–8.
14. 'Report on Quebec by Major Patrick Mackellar', 12 July 1757 is reprinted in full in Knox, *Journal*, III: 151–60, the quotes in this paragraph are from pp. 157, 160.
15. Wolfe to Major Walter Wolfe, 19 May 1759, Louisbourg, in B. Willson, ed., *The Life and Letters of James Wolfe* (London, 2006), 427–9.

16. Major Moncrief, *A Short Account of the Expedition against Quebec Commanded by Major-General Wolfe in the Year 1759* (Quebec, 1901), 9.

17. Wolfe's 'Family Journal', PRONI, DOD 162/77 C, 3.

18. Wolfe to Pitt, 2 September 1759, Montmorency, PRO, CO 5/51, reprinted in C. P. Stacey, *Quebec 1759: The Siege and the Battle* (Toronto, 2002), Appendix B.

19. Wolfe to Holderness, 9 September 1759, '*Sutherland* off Cap Rouge', in Willson, *The Life and Letters of James Wolfe*, 362.

20. Wolfe to Major Walter Wolfe, 19 May 1759, Louisbourg, in Willson, *The Life and Letters of James Wolfe*, 429.

21. Wolfe to Pitt, 2 September 1759, Montmorency, PRO, CO 5/51, reprinted in Stacey, *Quebec 1759*, Appendix B.

22. Knox, *Journal*, I: 378–9.

23. 'Extract of a Journal Kept at the Army Commanded by the Late Lt Gen de Montcalm', in E. O'Callaghan and B. Fernow, eds., *Documents Relative to the Colonial History of the State of New York; Procured in Holland, England and France* (15 vols., Albany, NY, 1853–87), X: 1019.

24. R. Léger, ed., *Le Journal de Montcalm* (Montreal, 2007), 460.

25. Moncrief, *A Short Account of the Expedition against Quebec Commanded by Major-General Wolfe in the Year 1759*, 10.

26. Knox, *Journal*, I: 379.

27. Ibid., I: 385.

28. Knox, I: 377.

29. *General Orders in Wolfe's Army*, 14.

30. Ibid., 11.

31. *General Wolfe's Instructions to Young Officers* (London, 1778), ix.

32. The battered copy in the British Library has a scribbled note inside the front cover, 'Henry Murray, Lt Colonel, 18th Hussars, Luz, Portugal, 26th February 1813.'

33. Wolfe to Major Walter Wolfe, 19 May 1759, Louisbourg, in Willson, *The Life and Letters of James Wolfe*, 429.

34. General Monckton's Order Book in *The Northcliffe Collection*, XXIII: 154.

35. Wolfe to Lord George Sackville, 30 July 1758, Louisbourg, in Willson, *The Life and Letters of James Wolfe*, 392.

36. Wolfe to Major Walter Wolfe, 19 May 1759, Louisbourg, in Willson, *The Life and Letters of James Wolfe*, 427; Wolfe to Pitt, 1 May 1759, Halifax, in ibid., 424.

37. Wolfe to Major Walter Wolfe, 19 May 1759, Louisbourg, in Willson, *The Life and Letters of James Wolfe*, 427.

38. Wolfe to Lord George Sackville, 30 July 1758, Louisbourg, in Willson, *The Life and Letters of James Wolfe*, 389.
39. Wolfe to Amherst, 29 December 1758, PRO, WO34/46b.
40. Wolfe to Monckton, 16 January 1759, London, in LAC, MG 18-M, Monckton Papers, XXII/rl C–366.
41. I. McCulloch and T. Todish, eds., *Through So Many Dangers: The Memoirs and Adventures of Robert Kirk, Late of the Royal Highland Regiment* (Toronto, 2004), 147.
42. Wolfe to Lord George Sackville, 30 July 1758, Louisbourg, in Willson, *The Life and Letters of James Wolfe*, 388.
43. Loudoun to Cumberland, 2 October 1756, Albany, NY, in S. Pargellis, ed., *Military Affairs in North America, 1748–65: Selected Documents from the Cumberland Papers in Windsor Castle* (New York, 1936), 235.
44. Wolfe's 'Family Journal', PRONI, DOD 162/77 C, 22.
45. M. J. Powell, 'Townshend, George, First Marquess Townshend (1724–1807)', in H. G. C. Matthew and B. Harrison, eds., *Oxford Dictionary of National Biography* (Oxford, 2004); online edn ed. by Lawrence Goldman, January 2008.
46. Walpole to Sir Horace Mann, 9 February 1759, Arlington Street, in *The Letters of Horace Walpole* http://www.fullbooks.com/The-Letters-of-Horace-Walpole-Volumex795615.html
47. Wolfe to Townshend, 6 January 1759, London, in C. V. F. Townshend, *The Life of Marquess Townshend* (Toronto, 1907), 143–4.
48. 'Journal of Captain Montresor', in Doughty and Parmelee, *Siege of Quebec*, IV: 309.
49. Montresor to Colonel James Montresor, 10 August 1759, Montmorency, in Doughty and Parmelee, *Siege of Quebec*, IV: 320.
50. Logs: *Lowestoft*, 28 June 1759, in Wood, *The Logs of the Conquest of Canada*, 235.
51. Lieutenant's Logs, ADM/L D/106B.
52. Wolfe's Journal, 27 June 1759.
53. 'A Journal of the Expedition up the River St Lawrence', in *A Journal of the Expedition up the River St Lawrence (by a Sgt Major in Hopson's Grenadiers)* (Boston, 1759).
54. Logs: *Pembroke*, 28 June 1759, ADM 52/978 book 4.
55. Moncrief, *A Short Account of the Expedition against Quebec Commanded by Major-General Wolfe in the Year 1759*, 10.
56. Wolfe's Journal, 27 June 1759.
57. Saunders to Admiralty, 5 September 1759, in C. H. Little, ed., *Despatches of Vice Admiral Saunders* (Halifax, NS, 1958), 14.
58. Léger, *Le Journal de Montcalm*, 459.

59. 'Journal du siège de Québec', in *The Northcliffe Collection*, XXX: 234–5.
60. 'A Journal of the Expedition up the River St Lawrence', in *Journal of the Expedition up the River St Lawrence (by a Sgt Major in Hopson's Grenadiers)*.

Chapter Five: First Skirmishes

1. Report on Quebec by Major Patrick Mackellar' 12 July 1757, in A. Doughty, ed., *An Historical Journal of the Campaigns in North America: For the Years 1757, 1758, 1759 and 1760 by Captain John Knox* (3 vols., Toronto, 1914–16), III: 159.
2. A notably successful attack occurred eleven years after Quebec when a Russian fleet carried out the most comprehensive destruction of any fleet in the eighteenth century. They incinerated eleven Turkish battleships after a fireship attack at Chesme.
3. R. Gardiner, ed., *Conway's History of the Ship: The Line of Battle* (London, 1992), 88.
4. 'Extract of a Journal Kept at the Army Commanded by the Late Lt Gen de Montcalm', in E. O'Callaghan and B. Fernow, eds., *Documents Relative to the Colonial History of the State of New York; Procured in Holland, England and France* (15 vols., Albany, NY, 1853–87), X: 1019.
5. 'Journal du siège de Québec', in *The Northcliffe Collection* (Ottawa, 1926), XXX: 228.
6. Knox, *Journal*, I: 381.
7. Ibid., XXX: 235.
8. Ibid., XXX: 236.
9. Wolfe's 'Family Journal', PRONI, DOD 162/77 C, 2.
10. Logs: *Centurion*, 29 June 1759, in W. Wood, ed., *The Logs of the Conquest of Canada* (Toronto, 1909), 210.
11. Logs: *Stirling Castle*, 29 June 1759, in Wood, *The Logs of the Conquest of Canada*, 304–5.
12. Knox, *Journal*, I: 381.
13. 'Genuine Letters from a Volunteer in the British Service at Quebec', in A. Doughty and G. Parmelee, eds., *The Siege of Quebec and the Battle of the Plains of Abraham* (6 vols., Quebec, 1901), V: 16.
14. Knox, *Journal*, I: 381.
15. Logs: *Stirling Castle*, 29 June 1759, in Wood, *The Logs of the Conquest of Canada*, 305.
16. Wolfe's Journal, 28 June 1759.
17. Wolfe's 'Family Journal', PRONI, DOD 162/77 C, 2.

18. Knox, *Journal*, I: 381–2.
19. Major Moncrief, *A Short Account of the Expedition against Quebec Commanded by Major-General Wolfe in the Year 1759* (Quebec, 1901), 11.
20. *A Journal of the Expedition up the River St Lawrence (by a Sgt Major in Hopson's Grenadiers)* (Boston, 1759), 1.
21. Knox, *Journal*, I: 383.
22. R. Léger, ed., *Le Journal de Montcalm* (Montreal, 2007), entry for 29 June 1759, 460.
23. 'Journal du siège de Québec', in *The Northcliffe Collection*, XXX: 236.
24. Panet's Journal, 29 June 1759.
25. 'Extract of a Journal Kept at the Army Commanded by the Late Lt Gen de Montcalm', in O'Callaghan and Fernow, *Documents*, X: 1019.
26. 'Relation du siège de Québec, posé par les Anglois en l'anée 1759', in *The Northcliffe Collection*, XXVII: 216.
27. 'Journal du siège de Québec', in *The Northcliffe Collection*, XXX: 236.
28. *General Orders in Wolfe's Army during the Expedition up the River St Lawrence, 1759* (Literary and Historical Society of Quebec: Historical Documents, Fourth Series, Quebec, 1875), 15.
29. Ibid., 13.
30. Ibid., 14.
31. Moncrief, *A Short Account of the Expedition against Quebec Commanded by Major-General Wolfe in the Year 1759*, 11; Wolfe to Pitt, 2 September 1759, Montmorency, PRO, CO 5/51.
32. Wolfe's 'Family Journal', PRONI, DOD 162/77 C, 2.
33. Wolfe to Pitt, 2 September 1759, Montmorency, PRO, CO 5/51.
34. P. L. Carver, ed., *Wolfe to the Duke of Richmond: Unpublished Letters* (Toronto, 1938), 26.
35. Wolfe's 'Family Journal', PRONI, DOD 162/77 C, 22.
36. Wolfe to his mother, 25 January 1758, in B. Willson, ed., *The Life and Letters of James Wolfe* (London, 2006), 353; Wolfe to his mother, 1 February 1758, Portsmouth, in ibid., 354.
37. Wolfe to Sackville, 24 May 1758, Halifax, in Willson, *The Life and Letters of James Wolfe*, 369.
38. Wolfe to Pitt, 2 September 1759, Montmorency, PRO, CO 5/51.
39. The last mention of grenades actually being used is in a drill manual from 1728. Houlding has identified their use for reviews in 1769 and 1777. See J. Houlding, *Fit for Service: The Training of the British Army, 1715–1795* (Oxford, 1981), 263.

40. In 1762 Lieutenant Alexander Baillie of the 1st/60th analysed a fully laden grenadier. His findings are in R. May and G. Embleton, *Wolfe's Army* (Reading, 1997), 35.

41. Moncrief, *A Short Account of the Expedition against Quebec Commanded by Major-General Wolfe in the Year 1759*, 11.

42. Knox, *Journal*, I: 386.

43. Lee to Miss Sidney Lee, Schenectady, 18 June 1756, in *NYSHC: Lee Papers*, I: 1–4, quoted in S. Brumwell, *Redcoats: The British Soldier and War in the Americas: 1755–63* (Cambridge, 2002).

44. Bougainville's Journal for 1756 in E. P. Hamilton, ed., *Adventure in the Wilderness: The American Journal of Louis Antoine de Bougainville, 1756–1760* (Norman, OK, 1990), 9, 40.

45. Hamilton, *Bougainville*, 103.

46. I. Steele, *Warpaths: Invasions of North America* (Oxford, 1994), 198.

47. 'Considerations upon the Site, Interests and Service of North America by Thomas Pownall, 1755', in S. Pargellis, ed., *Military Affairs in North America, 1748–65: Selected Documents from the Cumberland Papers in Windsor Castle* (New York, 1936), 163.

48. I. McCulloch and T. Todish, eds., *Through So Many Dangers: The Memoirs and Adventures of Robert Kirk, Late of the Royal Highland Regiment* (Toronto, 2004), 45.

49. I am very grateful to Andrew Birley for bringing this to my attention.

50. Wolfe's 'Family Journal', PRONI, DOD 162/77 C, 24.

51. Hamilton, *Bougainville*, 243.

52. Vaudreuil to Berryer, 30 March 1759, Montreal, in O'Callaghan and Fernow, *Documents*, X: 951.

53. Hamilton, *Bougainville*, 36.

54. Ibid., 9.

55. Ibid., 165.

56. Quoted in an exhibition on Native warfare at the Musée Canadien de la Guerre in Ottawa.

57. 'Journal of Cholmley's Batman', in C. Hamilton, ed., *Braddock's Defeat* (Norman, OK, 1959), 29.

58. Quoted in C. Duffy, *The Military Experience in the Age of Reason* (London, 1987), 281.

59. Hamilton, *Bougainville*, 142.

60. 'John Johnson's Journal', in Doughty and Parmelee, *Siege of Quebec*, V: 166.

61. Hamilton, *Bougainville*, 41, 143.

62. Knox, *Journal*, I: 74.

63. Hamilton, *Bougainville*, 149.

64. Wolfe's 'Family Journal', PRONI, DOD 162/77 C, 4.

65. 'Journal du siège de Québec', in *The Northcliffe Collection*, XXX: 237.
66. *Memoirs of the Siege of Quebec, the Capital of all Canada, and of the Retreat of Monsieur de Bourlemaque* (Quebec, 1901), 20.
67. Léger, *Le Journal de Montcalm*, 461.
68. 'Journal of Captain Montresor', in Doughty and Parmelee, *Siege of Quebec*, IV: 309–10.
69. 'Journal du siège de Québec', in *The Northcliffe Collection*, XXX: 237.
70. 'Extract of a Journal Kept at the Army Commanded by the Late Lt Gen de Montcalm', in O'Callaghan and Fernow, *Documents*, X: 1020; 'Narrative of the Siege of Quebec, Published by the French [Département de la Guerre]', in ibid., X: 995–6.
71. J.-F. Récher, *Journal du siège de Québec en 1759* (Quebec, 1959), entry for 30 June 1759.
72. Léger, *Le Journal de Montcalm*, 462.
73. Panet's Journal, 3 July 1759.
74. 'Extract of a Journal Kept at the Army Commanded by the Late Lt Gen de Montcalm', in O'Callaghan and Fernow, *Documents*, X: 1020.
75. Wolfe's Journal, 30 June 1759.
76. *Extract from a Manuscript Journal Relating to the Operations before Quebec in 1759, Kept by Colonel Malcolm Fraser, the Lt of the 78th (Fraser's Highlanders) and Serving in that Campaign* (Literary and Historical Society of Quebec: Historical Documents, Second Series, Quebec, 1868), 30 June 1759, 4.
77. Thompson's Journal quoted in McCulloch and Todish, *Sons of the Mountain*, I: 179.
78. Wolfe's Journal, 1 July 1759.
79. Wolfe's 'Family Journal', PRONI, DOD 162/77 C, 4, 20.
80. 'Journal of Captain Montresor', in Doughty and Parmelee, *Siege of Quebec*, IV: 310; Wolfe's Journal, 30 June 1759.
81. Knox, *Journal*, I: 393.
82. Wolfe's 'Family Journal', PRONI, DOD 162/77 C, 4.
83. P. D. G. Thomas, 'Barré, Isaac (1726–1802)', *Oxford Dictionary of National Biography* (Oxford, 2004); online edn, May 2006.
84. Wolfe's 'Family Journal', PRONI, DOD 162/77 C, 22.
85. Barré to Monckton, 1 July 1759, Point of Orleans, in Doughty and Parmelee, *Siege of Quebec*, VI: 63–4.
86. Wolfe's Journal, 1 July 1759.
87. Ibid., 2 July 1759.
88. 'Journal du siège de Québec', in *The Northcliffe Collection*, XXX: 238.

89. 'Narrative of the Siege of Quebec, Published by the French [Département de la Guerre]', in O'Callaghan and Fernow, *Documents*, X: 997.

90. Wolfe's Journal, 8 July 1759.

91. 'Journal of Captain Montresor', in Doughty and Parmelee, *Siege of Quebec*, IV: 310; see also 'Letter of Montresor to Father, Colonel James Montresor, Montmorency, 10 August 1759', ibid., 320.

92. Moncrief, *A Short Account of the Expedition against Quebec Commanded by Major-General Wolfe in the Year 1759*, 11–12.

93. *General Orders in Wolfe's Army*, 16.

94. Wolfe's 'Family Journal', PRONI, DOD 162/77 C, 5.

95. Wolfe's Journal, 3 July 1759.

96. Wolfe to Major Walter Wolfe, 19 May 1759, Louisbourg, in Willson, *The Life and Letters of James Wolfe*, 429.

97. Wolfe's Journal, 3 July 1759.

98. Moncrief, *A Short Account of the Expedition against Quebec Commanded by Major-General Wolfe in the Year 1759*, 12.

99. Wolfe's Journal, 4 July 1759.

100. Logs: *Stirling Castle*, 6 July, 7 July, 16 August 1759, in Wood, *The Logs of the Conquest of Canada*, 305, 306, 311.

101. Wolfe's Journal, 6 July 1759.

102. J. B. N. R. de Ramezay, *Mémoire du sieur de Ramezay, commandant à Québec, au sujet de la reddition de cette ville, le 18 septembre 1759* (Quebec, 1861).

103. Logs: *Stirling Castle*, 5 July 1759, in Wood, *The Logs of the Conquest of Canada*, 305.

104. This is a description by the French explorer Lahontan. It was plagiarized by Robert Kirk, a soldier in the Black Watch who published the story of his adventures in North America. Thus it appears in McCulloch and Todish, *Through So Many Dangers*, 71.

105. Hamilton, *Bougainville*, 246.

106. McCulloch and Todish, *Through So Many Dangers*, 71.

107. 'Relation du siège de Québec, posé par les Anglois en l'anée 1759', in *The Northcliffe Collection*, XXVII: 216.

108. 'Extracts from Journal of the Particular Transactions during the Siege of Quebec', in Doughty and Parmelee, *Siege of Quebec*, V: 169.

109. 'Relation du siège de Québec, posé par les Anglois en l'anée 1759', in *The Northcliffe Collection*, XXVII: 216.

110. Logs: *Stirling Castle*, 7 July 1759, in Wood, *The Logs of the Conquest of Canada*, 306.

111. Wolfe's 'Family Journal', PRONI, DOD 162/77 C, 5.

112. Bell's Journal, 7 July 1759.

113. Wolfe's Journal, 8 July 1759.
114. Wolfe's 'Family Journal', PRONI, DOD 162/77 C, 27.
115. Ibid., 27–8.
116. 'Journal du siège de Québec', in *The Northcliffe Collection*, XXX: 241.
117. Wolfe's Journal, 5 July 1759.
118. Moncrief, *A Short Account of the Expedition against Quebec Commanded by Major-General Wolfe in the Year 1759*, 12.
119. 'Journal du siège de Québec', in *The Northcliffe Collection*, XXX: 238.
120. 'Extracts from Journal of the Particular Transactions during the Siege of Quebec', in Doughty and Parmelee, *Siege of Quebec*, V: 169.
121. *Orderly Book and Journal of Major John Hawks, On the Ticonderoga-Crown Point Campaign, under General Jeffrey Amherst, 1759–1760* (New York, 1911), 16.
122. 'Journal du siège de Québec', in *The Northcliffe Collection*, XXX: 239; this is confirmed by Knox who was watching from the south shore. Knox, *Journal*, I: 398.
123. Récher, *Journal du siège*, entry for 4 July 1759.
124. Ibid.
125. 'Genuine Letters from a Volunteer in the British Service at Quebec', in Doughty and Parmelee, *Siege of Quebec*, V: 17.
126. Panet's Journal, 1 July.
127. 'Narrative of the Siege of Quebec, Published by the French [Département de la Guerre]', in O'Callaghan and Fernow, *Documents*, X: 996.
128. 'Journal du siège de Québec', in *The Northcliffe Collection*, XXX: 238.
129. 'Extract of a Journal Kept at the Army Commanded by the Late Lt Gen de Montcalm', in O'Callaghan and Fernow, *Documents*, X: 1020.
130. 'Journal du siège de Québec', in *The Northcliffe Collection*, XXX: 240, 238.
131. Knox, *Journal*, I: 396.

Chapter Six: A New Kind of War

1. Wolfe's 'Family Journal', PRONI, DOD 162/77 C, 5.
2. Ibid; Townshend made a detailed headcount of his brigade before the march and produced a figure of 1,487 men. Two hundred and forty-three of them were grenadiers, 160 of them were light infantry, and there were just over a thousand standard infantrymen. See 'Brigadier Townshend's

Journal of the Voyage to America and Campaign against Quebec, 1759',
in A. Doughty and G. Parmelee, eds., *The Siege of Quebec and the Battle
of the Plains of Abraham* (6 vols., Quebec, 1901), V: 241.

3. Wolfe to Captain Parr, 8 July 1759, 'Camp at the Island of Orleans',
   in Henry Parr Papers, LAC, MG 18 L 9.
4. Wolfe's 'Family Journal', PRONI, DOD 162/77 C, 5.
5. Ibid.
6. 'Journal du siège de Québec', in *The Northcliffe Collection* (Ottawa,
   1926), XXX: 240.
7. *Memoirs of the Siege of Quebec, the Capital of all Canada, and of the
   Retreat of Monsieur de Bourlemaque* (Quebec, 1901), 21.
8. 'Journal du siège de Québec', in *The Northcliffe Collection*, XXX: 241.
9. 'Journal of Captain Montresor', in Doughty and Parmelee, *Siege of
   Quebec*, IV: 311.
10. Although the 'Journal du siège' suggests that the mortars were landing
    on the right of the French army, which means by the St Charles River,
    possibly there were two bomb ketches operating that night. 'Journal
    du siège de Québec', in *The Northcliffe Collection*, XXX: 241.
11. Wolfe's 'Family Journal', PRONI, DOD 162/77 C, 5.
12. A. Doughty, ed., *An Historical Journal of the Campaigns in North
    America: For the Years 1757, 1758, 1759 and 1760 by Captain John
    Knox* (3 vols., Toronto, 1914–16), I: 375.
13. 'Extract of a Letter from an Officer in Major General Wolfe's Army,
    Island of Orleans, 10th August 1759', in S. Pargellis, ed., *Military
    Affairs in North America, 1748–65: Selected Documents from the
    Cumberland Papers in Windsor Castle* (New York, 1936), 433–4.
14. Wolfe's 'Family Journal', PRONI, DOD 162/77 C, 5.
15. 'Brigadier Townshend's Journal of the Voyage to America and
    Campaign against Quebec, 1759', in Doughty and Parmelee, *Siege of
    Quebec*, V: 242.
16. Townshend to Lady Ferrers, 5 October 1759, Quebec, LAC, MG 18
    L 7, fol. 122.
17. Wolfe's Journal, 7 July 1759.
18. Wolfe's 'Family Journal', PRONI, DOD 162/77 C, 21.
19. 'Brigadier Townshend's Journal of the Voyage to America and
    Campaign against Quebec, 1759', in Doughty and Parmelee, *Siege of
    Quebec*, V: 243.
20. C. V. F. Townshend, *The Military Life of George First Marquess
    Townshend* (Toronto, 1907), 178.
21. Ibid., 179; 'Brigadier Townshend's Journal of the Voyage to America
    and Campaign against Quebec, 1759', in Doughty and Parmelee,
    Siege of Quebec, V: 244–5.

22. Wolfe's 'Family Journal', PRONI, DOD 162/77 C, 7.
23. Panet's Journal, 7 July 1759.
24. Wolfe to Pitt, 2 September PRO, CO 5/51.
25. Townshend, *The Military Life of George First Marquess Townshend*, 176; other descriptions of the skirmish are in *A Journal of the Expedition up the River St Lawrence (by a Sgt Major in Hopson's Grenadiers)* (Boston, 1759), 2; 'A Journal of the Expedition up the River St Lawrence', in ibid.
26. Panet's Journal, 7 July 1759.
27. Ibid.; Wolfe's 'Family Journal', PRONI, DOD 162/77 C, 6.
28. Johnson's account of the campaign in reprinted in Doughty and Parmelee, *Siege of Quebec*, V: 71–166; this passage is on p. 97.
29. List of Medical Supplies is in LAC, Monckton Papers, XX, which are also on rl C-366.
30. 'John Johnson's Journal', in Doughty and Parmelee, *Siege of Quebec*, V: 72–3.
31. S. Brumwell, *White Devil: An Epic Story of Revenge from the Savage War that Inspired Last of the Mohicans* (London, 2004), 111; see also S. Brumwell, 'Home from the Wars', *History Today*, 52, 3 (March 2002), 41–7.
32. *Memoirs of the Siege of Quebec, the Capital of all Canada, and of the Retreat of Monsieur de Bourlemaque* (Quebec, 1901), 21–2.
33. 'Extract of a Journal Kept at the Army Commanded by the Late Lt Gen de Montcalm', in E. O'Callaghan and B. Fernow, eds., *Documents Relative to the Colonial History of the State of New York; Procured in Holland, England and France* (15 vols., Albany, NY, 1853–87), X: 1022.
34. *General Orders in Wolfe's Army during the Expedition up the River St Lawrence, 1759* (Literary and Historical Society of Quebec: Historical Documents, Fourth Series, Quebec, 1875), 19.
35. Major Moncrief, *A Short Account of the Expedition against Quebec Commanded by Major-General Wolfe in the Year 1759* (Quebec, 1901), 31.
36. Knox, *Journal*, I: 411.
37. *General Orders in Wolfe's Army*, 15, 19.
38. Wolfe's Proclamation, 27 June 1759, in O'Callaghan and Fernow, *Documents*, X: 1046–7.
39. Williamson to Sackville, 20 September 1759, Quebec, in LAC, MG 18 N 21 and rl A-573.
40. J. B. N. R. de Ramezay, *Mémoire du sieur de Ramezay, commandant à Québec, au sujet de la reddition de cette ville, le 18 septembre 1759* (Quebec, 1861).

41. 'Extracts from Journal of the Particular Transactions during the Siege of Quebec', in Doughty and Parmelee, *Siege of Quebec*, V: 168.
42. 'John Johnson's Journal', in Doughty and Parmelee, *Siege of Quebec*, V: 81–2.
43. *General Orders in Wolfe's Army*, 15, 18.
44. *Extract from a Manuscript Journal Relating to the Operations before Quebec in 1759, Kept by Colonel Malcolm Fraser, the Lt of the 78th (Fraser's Highlanders) and Serving in that Campaign* (Literary and Historical Society of Quebec: Historical Documents, Second Series, 1868), 6–7; Knox, *Journal*, I: 410.
45. Knox, *Journal*, I: 401.
46. Wolfe to Monckton, 12 July 1759, Montmorency, LAC, Monckton Papers, XXII, rl C-336.
47. Knox, *Journal*, I: 411.
48. Knox, *Journal*, I: 403–4.
49. At the battle of Minden, 1 August 1759, Prince Ferdinand commanded around one hundred and eighty cannon, very slightly more than these two ships. Even at the Marquess of Wellington's greatest victory, Vittoria, he only had around ninety-six guns.
50. Williamson to Sackville, 20 September 1759, Quebec, in LAC, MG 18 N 21 and rl A-573.
51. T. Clayton, *Tars* (London, 2007), 216–17.
52. Panet's Journal, 10 July 1759.
53. Knox, *Journal*, I: 412, 408; 'Journal of Captain Montresor', in Doughty and Parmelee, *Siege of Quebec*, IV: 312.
54. Quoted in A. McNairn, *Behold the Hero: General Wolfe and the Arts in the Eighteenth Century* (Montreal, 1997), 38.
55. 'Journal du siège de Québec', in *The Northcliffe Collection*, XXX: 241, 239.
56. Knox, *Journal*, I: 410.
57. 'Journal du siège de Québec', in *The Northcliffe Collection*, XXX: 242.
58. 'Narrative of the Siege of Quebec, Published by the French [Département de la Guerre]', in O'Callaghan and Fernow, *Documents*, X: 998.
59. 'Journal du siège de Québec', in *The Northcliffe Collection*, XXX: 242.
60. 'Narrative of the Siege of Quebec, Published by the French [Département de la Guerre]', in O'Callaghan and Fernow, *Documents*, X: 998; for the attitude of the regulars see R. Léger, ed., *Le Journal du Chevalier de Lévis* (Montreal, 2008), 136.

61. J. B. N. R. de Ramezay, *Mémoire du sieur de Ramezay, commandant à Québec, au sujet de la reddition de cette ville, le 18 septembre 1759*.

62. R. Léger, ed., *Le Journal de Montcalm* (Montreal, 2007), 468.

63. 'Extract of a Journal Kept at the Army Commanded by the Late Lt Gen de Montcalm', in O'Callaghan and Fernow, *Documents*, X: 1022.

64. Etienne Taillemite, 'Dumas, Jean Daniel (1721–1794)', in J. English and R. Bélanger, eds., *Dictionary of Canadian Biography* online, http://www.biographi.ca/EN/ShowBio.asp?BioId=35990andquery=Dumas.

65. 'Extract of a Journal Kept at the Army Commanded by the Late Lt Gen de Montcalm', in O'Callaghan and Fernow, *Documents*, X: 1023.

66. J. B. N. R. de Ramezay, *Mémoire du sieur de Ramezay, commandant à Québec, au sujet de la reddition de cette ville, le 18 septembre 1759*, July 1759.

67. 'Journal du siège de Québec', in *The Northcliffe Collection*, XXX: 243.

68. 'Relation du siège de Québec, posé par les Anglois en l'anée 1759', in *The Northcliffe Collection*, XXVII: 217.

69. Panet's Journal, 12 July 1759.

70. 'Extract of a Journal Kept at the Army Commanded by the Late Lt Gen de Montcalm', in O'Callaghan and Fernow, *Documents*, X: 1023.

71. Ibid.

72. Panet's Journal, 12 July 1759.

73. 'Journal du siège de Québec', in *The Northcliffe Collection*, XXX: 243.

74. 'Extract of a Journal Kept at the Army Commanded by the Late Lt Gen de Montcalm', in O'Callaghan and Fernow, *Documents*, X: 1023.

75. Ibid., X: 1023.

76. 'Journal du siège de Québec', in *The Northcliffe Collection*, XXX: 243.

Chapter Seven: 'Trust me, they shall feel us'

1. A. Doughty, *An Historical Journal of the Campaigns in North America: For the Years 1757, 1758, 1759 and 1760 by Captain John Knox* (3 vols., Toronto, 1914–16), I: 415.

2. Williamson to Sackville, 20 September 1759, Quebec, in LAC, MG 18 N 21 and rl A-573.

3. Knox, *Journal*, I: 415.
4. J.-F. Récher, *Journal du siège de Québec en 1759* (Quebec, 1959), entry for 12 July 1759.
5. 'Narrative of the Siege of Quebec, Published by the French [Département de la Guerre]', in E. O'Callaghan and B. Fernow, eds., *Documents Relative to the Colonial History of the State of New York; Procured in Holland, England and* France (15 vols., Albany, NY, 1853–87), X: 998.
6. J. B. N. R. de Ramezay, *Mémoire du sieur de Ramezay, commandant à Québec, au sujet de la reddition de cette ville, le 18 septembre 1759* (Quebec, 1861).
7. 'Journal du siège de Québec', in *The Northcliffe Collection* (Ottawa, 1926), XXX: 242.
8. Récher, *Journal du siège de Québec*, entry for 13 July 1759.
9. 'Journal du siège de Québec', in *The Northcliffe Collection*, XXX: 242.
10. R. Léger, ed., *Le Journal de Montcalm* (Montreal, 2007), 469.
11. Wolfe to Amherst, 1 May 1759, Halifax, in B. Willson, ed., *The Life and Letters of James Wolfe* (New York, 1909), 425.
12. Wolfe to Amherst, Battery Overlooking Louisbourg, 1 July 1758, in Willson, *The Life and Letters of James Wolfe*, 379.
13. Wolfe to the Duke of Richmond, 28 July 1758, Isle Royale, in P. L. Carver, ed., *Wolfe to the Duke of Richmond: Unpublished Letters* (Toronto, 1938), 23.
14. 'Brigadier Townshend's Journal of the Voyage to America and Campaign against Quebec, 1759', in A. Doughty and G. Parmelee, eds., *The Siege of Quebec and the Battle of the Plains of Abraham* (6 vols., Quebec, 1901), V: 262.
15. T. Clayton, *Tars* (London, 2007), 279.
16. Quoted in L. McCulloch, *Sons of the Mountain: The Highland Regiments in the French and Indian War, 1756–1767* (2 vols., Toronto, 2006), I: 179.
17. Panet's Journal, 15 July 1759.
18. Récher, *Journal du siège de Québec*, entry for 15 July 1759.
19. 'Journal du siège de Québec', in *The Northcliffe Collection*, XXX: 245.
20. Panet's Journal, 17 July 1759.
21. Wolfe's Journal, 12 July 1759.
22. 'Journal du siège de Québec', in *The Northcliffe Collection*, XXX: 244.
23. Major Moncrief, *A Short Account of the Expedition against Quebec Commanded by Major-General Wolfe in the Year 1759* (Quebec, 1901), 14.

24. Ibid., 15.
25. 'Journal du siège de Québec', in *The Northcliffe Collection*, XXX: 248.
26. Marguerite Gosselin, quoted inJ.-M. Lebel, *1759 Summer under Siege* (Quebec, 2001), 15.
27. Logs: *Stirling Castle*, 23 July 1759, in W. Wood, ed., *The Logs of the Conquest of Canada* (Toronto, 1909), 308.
28. *Siege of Quebec and Conquest of Canada: in 1759. By a Nun of the General Hospital of Quebec* (Quebec, 1855), 4–5.
29. 'Journal du siège de Québec', in *The Northcliffe Collection*, XXX: 246–7.
30. Récher, *Journal du siège de Québec*, entry for 30 July 1759.
31. 'Journal du siège de Québec', in *The Northcliffe Collection*, XXX: 246–7.
32. *A Journal of the Expedition up the River St Lawrence (by a Sgt Major in Hopson's Grenadiers)* (Boston, 1759), 4; See also Montresor to Colonel James Montresor, 10 August 1759, Montmorency, in Doughty and Parmelee, *Siege of Quebec*, IV: 323; *Journal of the Particular Transactions during the Siege of Quebec by an Officer of Fraser's Regiment* (Quebec, 1901), 12.
33. Récher, *Journal du siège de Québec*, entry for 23 July 1759.
34. 'Relation du siège de Québec, posé par les Anglois en l'anée 1759', in *The Northcliffe Collection*, XXVII: 218.
35. 'Journal du siège de Québec', in *The Northcliffe Collection*, XXX: 250.
36. Panet's Journal, 8 August 1759.
37. *A Journal of the Expedition up the River St Lawrence (by a Sgt Major in Hopson's Grenadiers)*, 6.
38. 'Relation du siège de Québec, posé par les Anglois en l'anéée 1759', in *The Northcliffe Collection*, XXVII: 219.
39. Moncrief, *A Short Account of the Expedition against Quebec Commanded by Major-General Wolfe in the Year 1759*, 24.
40. 'Journal du siège de Québec', in *The Northcliffe Collection*, XXX: 254.
41. Panet's Journal, 8 August 1759.
42. Knox, *Journal*, II: 22.
43. 'Extract of a Journal Kept at the Army Commanded by the Late Lt Gen de Montcalm', in O'Callaghan and Fernow, *Documents*, X: 1031; 'Journal du siège de Québec', in *The Northcliffe Collection*, XXX: 254.
44. Saunders to Pitt, 5 September 1759, PRO, CO 5/51 fol. 40.
45. 'Genuine Letters from a Volunteer in the British Service at Quebec', in Doughty and Parmelee, *Siege of Quebec*, V: 15.

46. Williamson to Ligonier, 12 August 1759, Point Lévis, in LAC, MG 18 N 21 and rl A-573.
47. 'Camp at Point Levis 18 August 1759 Expenditure and Remains of Ammunition', LAC, Monckton Papers, XX, which are on rl C-366. As a result of his calculations Williamson orders that only 15 large shells and 30 ten-inch shells will be fired with 300 shot per day.
48. Wolfe to Monckton, 16 July 1759, Montmorency, in LAC, MG 18 M 1, Monckton Papers, XXII, rl C-336.
49. *General Orders in Wolfe's Army during the Expedition up the River St Lawrence, 1759* (Literary and Historical Society of Quebec: Historical Documents, Fourth Series, Quebec, 1875), 23.
50. Wolfe's 'Family Journal', PRONI, DOD 162/77 C, 6–7.
51. *General Orders in Wolfe's Army*, 25.
52. Wolfe's Journal, 17 July 1759.
53. *A Journal of the Expedition up the River St Lawrence (by a Sgt Major in Hopson's Grenadiers)*, 3.
54. 'John Johnson's Journal', in Doughty and Parmelee, *Siege of Quebec*, V: 97.
55. J. B. N. R. de Ramezay, *Mémoire du sieur de Ramezay, commandant à Québec, au sujet de la reddition de cette ville, le 18 septembre 1759*, July 1759.
56. *General Orders in Wolfe's Army*, 12–13, 40–1.
57. 'Diary of Lt William Henshaw', in C. H. Lincoln, ed., *Manuscript Records of the French and Indian War: In the Library of the American Antiquarian Society* (Worcester, MA, 1909), 195–6.
58. The sheer volume of orders and threats issued by Wolfe during the summer suggests that the men could not be confined for long periods to the camps. On 6 August he was forced to send an officer and twenty men beyond the fortifications to lie in wait until dusk and 'take up all soldiers and others straggling beyond their posts'. Later in the month Wolfe ordered that 'the outposts and guards are to be more careful in the future in stopping all soldiers who are attempting to slip by them'. *General Orders in Wolfe's Army*, 35, 44.
59. 'Extract of a Journal Kept at the Army Commanded by the Late Lt Gen de Montcalm', in O'Callaghan and Fernow, *Documents*, X: 1036.
60. Knox, *Journal*, I: 413.
61. *General Orders in Wolfe's Army*, 25.
62. Ibid., 19, 26.
63. Ibid., 23.
64. General Monckton's Order Book, in *The Northcliffe Collection*, XXIII: 160.
65. *General Wolfe's Instructions to Young Officers* (London, 1778), 68.

66. Ibid., 30, 28, 30.
67. Ibid., 15.
68. See V. Bamfield, *On the Strength: The Story of the British Army Wife* (London, 1974), 45.
69. I am very grateful to Jon Nuttal at the Royal Hospital for this remarkable story.
70. S. Brumwell, *Redcoats: The British Soldier and War in the Americas: 1755–63* (Cambridge, 2002), 124.
71. *General Wolfe's Instructions to Young Officers*, 18.
72. LAC, MG 18 M 1, Monckton Papers, XXXII.
73. Knox, *Journal*, II: 18.
74. Quoted in A. McNairn, *Behold the Hero: General Wolfe and the Arts in the Eighteenth Century* (Montreal, 1997), 5.
75. Issued in Banff, 1750, in *General Wolfe's Instructions to Young Officers*, 26; see also A. Guy, *Oeconomy and Discipline: Officership and Administration in the British Army 1714–1763* (Manchester, 1985), 66 and R. Holmes, *Redcoat: The British Solider in the Age of Horse and Musket* (London, 2001), 282.
76. *Journal of the Particular Transactions during the Siege of Quebec by an Officer of Fraser's Regiment* (Quebec, 1901), 29.
77. In 1759 a brewer in Ireland signed a 9,000 year lease on a disused brewery, the St James's Gate Brewery, Dublin, and started brewing 'Extra Superior Porter'. His name was Arthur Guinness.
78. Knox, *Journal*, II: 19. The value of the colonial currency differed from colony to colony but was always slightly less valuable than the British pounds, shillings, and pence. Around 1750 the internationally approved Spanish Silver Dollar was appraised at 4*s*. 6*d*. in London, 5*s*. in Halifax, and 6*s*. in the New England colonies. Other ingredients included: Gloucester cheese 10*d*. for a pound, a pound of tobacco 22*d*. (1*s*. 10*d*.), soap, for which there was presumably great need, 10*d*. per pound.
79. 'Diary of Lt William Henshaw', in Lincoln, *Manuscript Records of the French and Indian War: In the Library of the American Antiquarian Society*, 197.
80. *General Orders in Wolfe's Army*, 19.
81. Knox, *Journal*, II: 18.
82. *General Orders in Wolfe's Army*, 37.
83. *Orderly Book and Journal of Major John Hawks, on the Ticonderoga-Crown Point Campaign, under General Jeffrey Amherst, 1759–1760* (New York, 1911), 45.
84. Montresor to Colonel James Montresor, 10 August 1759, Montmorency, in Doughty and Parmelee, *Siege of Quebec*, IV: 322.

85. *General Orders in Wolfe's Army*, 32.
86. *General Wolfe's Instructions to Young Officers*, 26.
87. *General Orders in Wolfe's Army*, 40.
88. Ibid., 35.
89. Ibid., 42.
90. General Monckton's Order Book, in *The Northcliffe Collection*, XXIII: 157.
91. *General Orders in Wolfe's Army*, 20.
92. Wolfe's Journal, 16 July 1759; Bell's Journal, 16 July 1759.
93. 'Journal of Captain Montresor', in Doughty and Parmelee, *Siege of Quebec*, IV: 314–15.
94. Wolfe's 'Family Journal', PRONI, DOD 162/77 C, 7–8.
95. 'Journal du siège de Québec', in *The Northcliffe Collection*, XXX: 246.
96. Léger, *Le Journal de Montcalm*, entry for 18 July 1759, 473.
97. Logs: *Sutherland*, 19 July 1759, in Wood, *The Logs of the Conquest of Canada*, 317; *Squirrel*, 19 July 1759, in ibid., 296.
98. 'Journal du siège de Québec', in *The Northcliffe Collection*, XXX: 246; see also 'Relation du siège de Québec, posé par les Anglois en l'anée 1759', in ibid., XXVIII, 217.
99. In 1758 one of the classic gunnery duels of the Seven Years War took place in which the *Monmouth* engaged and eventually defeated the *Foudroyant* after the two ships had blasted each other at a range of just forty yards. The *Monmouth* fired 520 12-pound balls and 435 24-pound balls in a battle that lasted over four hours. As British sailors examined their prize they discovered that more than a hundred British cannonballs were lodged in the side and 'several had gone right through'. In return sixteen shots had passed through the *Monmouth*'s side, eight of which were below the waterline. In Clayton, *Tars*, 24, 28, 44.
100. NMM, ADM/L D/106B, 19 July 1759.
101. Captain Schomberg to Admiral Forbes, 5 September 1759, Boston, in Doughty and Parmelee, *Siege of Quebec*, V: 59.
102. Panet's Journal, 18 July 1759.
103. Captain Schomberg to Admiral Forbes, 5 September 1759, Boston, in Doughty and Parmelee, *Siege of Quebec*, V: 59.
104. NMM, ADM/L D/106B, 19 July 1759.
105. Captain Schomberg to Admiral Forbes, 5 September 1759, Boston, in Doughty and Parmelee, *Siege of Quebec*, V, 59.
106. Logs: *Diana*, 19 July 1759, in Wood, *The Logs of the Conquest of Canada*, 212.
107. Léger, *Le Journal de Montcalm*, entry for 18 July 1759, 473.

Notes

Chapter Eight: Competing Ideas

1. Bell's Journal, 19 July 1759.
2. Wolfe's Journal, 19 July 1759.
3. Wolfe to Monckton, 20 July 1759, although in his agitated state Wolfe dated the note 20 May. It is in LAC, Monckton Papers, XXII, rl/C-336.
4. Samuel Holland to Lieutenant Governor John Graves Simcoe, near Quebec, 10 June 1792, in 'A New Account of the Death of Wolfe', *Canadian Historical Review* (1923), 48.
5. Wolfe to Monckton, 20 July 1759, 1300 hours, in LAC, Monckton Papers, XXII, rl/C-336.
6. 'Journal du siège de Québec', in *The Northcliffe Collection* (Ottawa, 1926), XXX: 247.
7. R. Léger, ed., *Le Journal de Montcalm* (Montreal, 2007), 474.
8. Logs: *Squirrel*, 20 July 1759, in W. Wood, ed., *The Logs of the Conquest of Canada* (Toronto, 1909), 296.
9. 'Relation du siège de Québec, posé par les Anglois en l'anée 1759', in *The Northcliffe Collection*, XXVII: 218.
10. Wolfe to Pitt, 2 September 1759, PRO, CO 5/51.
11. Murray to Wolfe, 22 July 1759, PRONI, DOD 678 2a–3a.
12. Wolfe to Murray, 22 July 1759, PRONI, DOD 678 3a–5a.
13. Logs: *Dublin*, 23 July 1759, in Wood, *The Logs of the Conquest of Canada*, 218–19.
14. Logs: *Hunter*, 23 July 1759, in Wood, *The Logs of the Conquest of Canada*, 229.
15. *Extract from a Manuscript Journal Relating to the Operations before Quebec in 1759, Kept by Colonel Malcolm Fraser, the Lt of the 78th (Fraser's Highlanders) and Serving in that Campaign* (Literary and Historical Society of Quebec: Historical Documents, Second Series, 1868), 8.
16. *A Journal of the Expedition up the River St Lawrence (by a Sgt Major in Hopson's Grenadiers)* (Boston, 1759), 4.
17. 'Extract of a Journal Kept at the Army Commanded by the Late Lt Gen de Montcalm', in E. O'Callaghan and B. Fernow, eds., *Documents Relative to the Colonial History of the State of New York; Procured in Holland, England and France* (15 vols., Albany, NY, 1853–87), X: 1026.
18. 'Journal du siège de Québec', in *The Northcliffe Collection*, XXX: 249.
19. Wolfe to Pitt, 2 September 1759, PRO, CO 5/51.

20. 'Narrative of the Siege of Quebec, Published by the French [Département de la Guerre]', in O'Callaghan and Fernow, *Documents*, X: 999.
21. Léger, *Le Journal de Montcalm*, 475.
22. I am grateful to Sir Christopher Prevost for much of this information about his ancestor.
23. *Memoirs of the Siege of Quebec, the Capital of all Canada, and of the Retreat of Monsieur de Bourlemaque* (Quebec, 1901), 23.
24. 'Extract of a Journal Kept at the Army Commanded by the Late Lt Gen de Montcalm', in O'Callaghan and Fernow, *Documents*, X: 1025–6.
25. Panet's Journal, 21 July 1759.
26. Ibid., 22 July 1759.
27. 'Extracts from Journal of the Particular Transactions during the Siege of Quebec', in A. Doughty and G. Parmelee, eds., *The Siege of Quebec and the Battle of the Plains of Abraham* (6 vols., Quebec, 1901–2), V: 173.
28. Panet's Journal, 25 and 31 July 1759.
29. Major Moncrief, *A Short Account of the Expedition against Quebec Commanded by Major-General Wolfe in the Year 1759* (Quebec, 1901), 15.
30. Vaudreuil to Lévis, 27 July 1759, in H. R. Casgrain, ed., *Collection des manuscrits du Maréchal de Lévis* (12 vols., Montreal and Quebec, 1889–95), VIII: 70–1.
31. Wolfe's 'Family Journal', PRONI, DOD 162/77 C, 8.
32. Moncrief, *A Short Account of the Expedition against Quebec Commanded by Major-General Wolfe in the Year 1759*, 16.
33. Wolfe's 'Family Journal', PRONI, DOD 162/77 C, 8.
34. Ibid.
35. The figure given by Don Higginbotham is 11,000 in D. Higginbotham, 'The Early American Way of War: Reconnaissance and Appraisal', *William and Mary Quarterly* (Third Series), 44 (1987), 235; there is an excellent discussion of this in S. Brumwell, *Redcoats: The British Soldier and War in the Americas: 1755–63* (Cambridge, 2002), 54–87.
36. D. J. Beattie, 'The Adaptation of the British Army to Wilderness Warfare, 1755–1763', in M. Ultee, ed., *Adapting to Conditions: War and Society in the Eighteenth Century* (Tuscaloosa, AL, 1986), 73.
37. A. Doughty, ed., *An Historical Journal of the Campaigns in North America: For the Years 1757, 1758, 1759 and 1760 by Captain John Knox* (3 vols., Toronto, 1914–16), I: 109.

38. Quoted in Beattie, 'The Adaptation of the British Army to Wilderness Warfare, 1755–1763', in Ultee, *Adapting to Conditions*, 72.

39. Ibid., 73.

40. Loudoun Papers, 2421, in S. Pargellis, *Lord Loudoun in North America* (New Haven, CT, 1933), 299–300.

41. I. McCulloch and T. Todish, eds., *Through So Many Dangers: The Memoirs and Adventures of Robert Kirk, Late of the Royal Highland Regiment* (Toronto, 2004), 132.

42. Instructions for 20 December 1755, Canterbury, in *General Wolfe's Instructions to Young Officers* (London, 1778), 51–2.

43. Knox, *Journal*, I: 468.

44. Loudoun Papers, 2421, in Pargellis, *Lord Loudoun in North America*, 300.

45. Chevalier de Johnstone, *A Dialogue in Hades* (Literary and Historical Society of Quebec: Historical Documents, Second Series, Quebec, 1868), 27.

46. Moncrief, *A Short Account of the Expedition against Quebec Commanded by Major-General Wolfe in the Year 1759*, 18; Townshend reports, very possibly unfairly, that the situation was so dire that Wolfe returned to camp to turn out his entire force. Townshend gives the credit for saving the day to his fellow brigadier, Murray. None of the other sources makes any reference to this but they all admit to having suffered heavy casualties. 'Brigadier Townshend's Journal of the Voyage to America and Campaign against Quebec, 1759', in Doughty and Parmelee, *Siege of Quebec*, V: 252.

47. Wolfe's Journal, 26 July 1759.

48. Thomas Bell's Journal, 26 July 1759.

49. 'Extract of a Journal Kept at the Army Commanded by the Late Lt Gen de Montcalm', in O'Callaghan and Fernow, *Documents*, X: 1028.

50. Panet's Journal, 26 July 1759.

51. Léger, *Le Journal de Montcalm*, 472.

52. Montcalm to de Lévis, 29 July 1759, in Casgrain, *Collection des manuscrits du Maréchal de Lévis*, VI: 206.

53. Johnstone, *A Dialogue in Hades*, 27.

54. Moncrief, *A Short Account of the Expedition against Quebec Commanded by Major-General Wolfe in the Year 1759*, 18.

55. J. B. N. R. de Ramezay, *Mémoire du sieur de Ramezay, commandant à Québec, au sujet de la reddition de cette ville, le 18 septembre 1759* (Quebec, 1861).

56. Wolfe to Monckton, 27 July 1759, in LAC, Monckton Papers, XXII, rl/C-336.

57. Wolfe to Pitt, 2 September 1759, PRO, CO 5/51.
58. 'Letter of James Gibson to Governor Lawrence', 1 August 1759, Basin of Quebec, in Doughty and Parmelee, *Siege of Quebec*, V: 65.
59. 'Brigadier Townshend's Journal of the Voyage to America and Campaign against Quebec, 1759', in Doughty and Parmelee, *Siege of Quebec*, V: 250.
60. Knox, *Journal*, I: 428.
61. Léger, *Le Journal de Montcalm*, 476.
62. Ibid., 474.
63. Logs: *Stirling Castle*, 28 July 1759, in Wood, *The Logs of the Conquest of Canada*, 309.
64. 'Letter of James Gibson to Governor Lawrence', 1 August 1759, Basin of Quebec, in Doughty and Parmelee, *Siege of Quebec*, V: 66.
65. Patrick Mackellar, 'A Description of the Town of Quebeck – Its Strength and Situation', in S. Pargellis, ed., *Military Affairs in North America, 1748–65: Selected Documents from the Cumberland Papers in Windsor Castle* (New York, 1936), 415.
66. Knox, *Journal*, I: 445.
67. 'Journal du siège de Québec', in *The Northcliffe Collection*, XXX: 250; 'Narrative of the Siege of Quebec, Published by the French [Département de la Guerre]', in O'Callaghan and Fernow, *Documents*, X: 1000.
68. Logs: *Lowestoft*, 28 July 1759, in Wood, *The Logs of the Conquest of Canada*, 235.
69. 'Copy of a Letter from on Board the *Lizard*, 5 September 1759 at Coudres, 17 Leagues from Quebec', in Pargellis, *Military Affairs in North America*, 436.
70. Logs: *Lowestoft*, 28 July 1759, in Wood, *The Logs of the Conquest of Canada*, 235.
71. 'Copy of a Letter from on Board the *Lizard*, 5 September 1759 at Coudres, 17 Leagues from Quebec', in Pargellis, *Military Affairs in North America*, 436.
72. Knox, *Journal*, I: 445.
73. 'Genuine Letters from a Volunteer in the British Service at Quebec', in Doughty and Parmelee, *Siege of Quebec*, V: 18.
74. Knox, *Journal*, I: 445.
75. 'Narrative of the Siege of Quebec, Published by the French [Département de la Guerre]', in O'Callaghan and Fernow, *Documents*, X: 1000; 'Journal du siège de Québec', in *The Northcliffe Collection*, XXX: 250.
76. Logs: *Stirling Castle*, 28 July 1759, in Wood, *The Logs of the Conquest of Canada*, 309.
77. Knox, *Journal*, I: 445.

78. Montcalm to Lévis, 29 July 1759, in Casgrain, *Collection des manuscrits du Maréchal de Lévis*, VI: 205.

Chapter Nine: Defeat at Montmorency

1. 'Brigadier Townshend's Journal of the Voyage to America and Campaign against Quebec, 1759', in A. Doughty and G. Parmelee, eds., *The Siege of Quebec and the Battle of the Plains of Abraham* (6 vols., Quebec, 1901), V: 254.
2. *Orderly Book and Journal of Major John Hawks, on the Ticonderoga-Crown Point Campaign, under General Jeffrey Amherst, 1759–1760* (New York, 1911), 7.
3. Ibid.
4. White cloth or linen breeches were becoming fashionable among all the ranks, and in the sweltering heat of midsummer they must have been preferable to the heavy red woollen ones they were issued.
5. Wolfe to Pitt, 2 September 1759, PRO, CO 5/51.
6. Major Moncrief, *A Short Account of the Expedition against Quebec Commanded by Major-General Wolfe in the Year 1759* (Quebec, 1901), 19.
7. *Universal Dictionary of the Marine*, 1789, quoted in J. C. Beaglehole, *The Life of Captain James Cook* (London, 1974), 9.
8. Wolfe's 'Family Journal', PRONI, DOD 162/77 C, 9.
9. Montresor to Colonel James Montresor, 10 August 1759, Montmorency, in Doughty and Parmelee, *Siege of Quebec*, IV: 325.
10. Wolfe to Pitt, 2 September 1759, PRO, CO 5/51.
11. Interestingly this mention of '1000 yards' belies Wolfe's later claim that he expected the Cats to get within spitting distance of the redoubt. Wolfe to Monckton, 28 July 1759, LAC, MG 18 M 1, Monckton Papers, XXII, rl C-336.
12. Wolfe to Monckton, undated but probably 29 July 1759, ibid.
13. Wolfe's 'Family Journal', PRONI, DOD 162/77 C, 26.
14. Montcalm to de Lévis, 25 July 1759, in H. R. Casgrain, ed., *Collection des manuscrits du Maréchal de Lévis* (12 vols., Montreal and Quebec, 1889–95), VI: 198.
15. Wolfe's Journal, 30 July 1759.
16. Moncrief, *A Short Account of the Expedition against Quebec Commanded by Major-General Wolfe in the Year 1759*, 20.
17. Published in the *Gentlemen's Magazine*, June 1801, in LAC, MG 18 N 18, vol. V.
18. Wolfe to Pitt, 2 September 1759, PRO, CO 5/51; see also Wolfe to Saunders, 30 August 1759, in B. Willson, ed., *The Life and Letters of James Wolfe* (New York, 1909), 460–3.

19. Wolfe's 'Family Journal', PRONI, DOD 162/77 C, 9.
20. *Extract from a Manuscript Journal Relating to the Operations before Quebec in 1759, Kept by Colonel Malcolm Fraser, the Lt of the 78th (Fraser's Highlanders) and Serving in that Campaign* (Literary and Historical Society of Quebec: Historical Documents, Second Series, 1868), 10.
21. Wolfe's 'Family Journal', PRONI, DOD 162/77 C, 10.
22. Wolfe to Pitt, 2 September 1759, PRO, CO 5/51.
23. 'Extract of a Letter from an Officer in Major General Wolfe's Army', 10 August 1759, Island of Orleans, in S. Pargellis, ed., *Military Affairs in North America, 1748–65: Selected Documents from the Cumberland Papers in Windsor Castle* (New York, 1936), 434.
24. A. Doughty, ed., *An Historical Journal of the Campaigns in North America: For the Years 1757, 1758, 1759 and 1760 by Captain John Knox* (3 vols., Toronto, 1914–16), I: 452.
25. Moncrief, *A Short Account of the Expedition against Quebec Commanded by Major-General Wolfe in the Year 1759*, 21.
26. 'Extract of a Journal Kept at the Army Commanded by the Late Lt Gen de Montcalm', in E. O'Callaghan and B. Fernow, eds., *Documents Relative to the Colonial History of the State of New York; Procured in Holland, England and France* (15 vols., Albany, NY, 1853–87), X: 1029.
27. *Memoirs of the Siege of Quebec, the Capital of all Canada, and of the Retreat of Monsieur de Bourlemaque* (Quebec, 1901), 25.
28. R. Léger, ed., *Le Journal de Montcalm* (Montreal, 2007), 478.
29. 'Journal du siège de Québec', in *The Northcliffe Collection* (Ottawa, 1926), XXX: 251–2.
30. Panet's Journal, 31 July 1759.
31. *Memoirs of the Siege of Quebec, the Capital of all Canada, and of the Retreat of Monsieur de Bourlemaque*, 25.
32. 'John Johnson's Journal', in Doughty and Parmelee, *Siege of Quebec*, V: 93.
33. Montresor to Colonel James Montresor, 10 August 1759, Montmorency, in Doughty and Parmelee, *Siege of* Quebec, IV: 325.
34. 'Extract of a Letter from an Officer in Major General Wolfe's Army', 10 August 1759, Island of Orleans, in Pargellis, *Military Affairs in North America*, 434.
35. Knox, *Journal*, I: 452.
36. Wolfe to Pitt, 2 September 1759, PRO, CO 5/51.
37. 'John Johnson's Journal', in Doughty and Parmelee, *Siege of Quebec*, V: 89.

38. 'Hot Stuff' was published 5 May 1774 in *Rivington's New York Gazetteer* reprinted in C. P. Stacey, *Quebec 1759: The Siege and the Battle* (Toronto, 2002), Appendix J, 236. The curious reference to Montcalm misidentifying Lascelles' for Shirley's stems from the fact that Lascelles' had been forced to borrow Shirley's uniforms for the campaign, theirs having been lost the year before.

39. Lieutenant James Grant to Colonel Bouquet, 15 September 1759, Crown Point, LAC, MG 18 N 18, vol. VII.

40. *A Journal of the Expedition up the River St Lawrence (by a Sgt Major in Hopson's Grenadiers)* (Boston, 1759), 5.

41. Panet's Journal, 31 July 1759.

42. 'Genuine Letters from a Volunteer in the British Service at Quebec', in Doughty and Parmelee, *Siege of* Quebec, V: 19.

43. 'Copy of a Letter from on Board the *Lizard* September 5th 1759, at Coudres 17 Leagues from Quebec', in Pargellis, *Military Affairs in North America*, 435.

44. Knox, *Journal*, I: 452.

45. Journal of Sergeant James Thompson quoted in I. McCulloch, *Sons of the Mountain: The Highland Regiments in the French and Indian War, 1756–1767* (2 vols., Toronto, 2006), I: 183.

46. Wolfe to Saunders, 30 August 1759, in B. Willson, ed., *The Life and Letters of James Wolfe* (New York, 1909), 460.

47. Wolfe to Pitt, 2 September 1759, PRO, CO 5/51.

48. Letter of Captain Schomberg of the *Diana* to Admiral Forbes, Boston, 5 September 1759, in Doughty and Parmelee, *Siege of Quebec*, V: 60.

49. Logs: *Stirling Castle*, 1 August 1759, in W. Wood, ed., *The Logs of the Conquest of Canada* (Toronto, 1909), 309.

50. Knox, *Journal*, I: 453.

51. Wolfe to Pitt, 2 September 1759, PRO, CO 5/51.

52. Wolfe's 'Family Journal', PRONI, DOD 162/77 C, 11.

53. Panet's Journal, 31 July 1759.

54. *Extract from a Manuscript Journal Relating to the Operations before Quebec in 1759, Kept by Colonel Malcolm Fraser, the Lt of the 78th*, 11.

55. 'John Johnson's Journal', in Doughty and Parmelee, *Siege of Quebec*, V: 89–90.

56. *Siege of Quebec and Conquest of Canada: in 1759. By a Nun of the General Hospital of Quebec* (Quebec, 1855), 7.

57. 'Townshend's Rough Notes', in *Northcliffe Collection*, 423.

58. Letter of Captain Schomberg of the *Diana* to Admiral Forbes, Boston, 5 September 1759, in Doughty and Parmelee, *Siege of Quebec*, V: 60.

59. Montresor to Colonel James Montresor, 10 August 1759, Montmorency, in Doughty and Parmelee, *Siege of Quebec*, IV: 326.
60. 'Return of the Dead and Wounded' by Barré, in *The Northcliffe Collection*, XXI: 136.
61. Wolfe's Journal, 31 July 1759.
62. Moncrief, *A Short Account of the Expedition against Quebec Commanded by Major-General Wolfe in the Year 1759*, 23.
63. 'Brigadier Townshend's Journal of the Voyage to America and Campaign against Quebec, 1759', in Doughty and Parmelee, *Siege of Quebec*, V: 255.
64. *Memoirs of the Siege of Quebec, the Capital of all Canada, and of the Retreat of Monsieur de Bourlemaque*, 26.
65. 'Extract of a Journal Kept at the Army Commanded by the Late Lt Gen de Montcalm', in O'Callaghan and Fernow, *Documents*, X: 1029.
66. *Memoirs of the Siege of Quebec, the Capital of all Canada, and of the Retreat of Monsieur de Bourlemaque*, 26.
67. 'Journal du siège de Québec', in *The Northcliffe Collection*, XXX: 252.
68. Panet's Journal, 31 July 1759.
69. J.-F. Récher, *Journal du siège de Québec en 1759* (Quebec, 1959), entry for 31 July 1759.
70. Vaudreuil to Lévis, 1 August 1759, in Casgrain, *Collection des manuscrits du Maréchal de Lévis*, VIII: 74–5.
71. R. Léger, ed., *Le Journal du Chevalier de Lévis* (Montreal, 2008), 140.
72. Léger, *Le Journal de Montcalm*, 478–9.
73. 'Narrative of the Siege of Quebec, Published by the French [Département de la Guerre]', in O'Callaghan and Fernow, *Documents*, X: 1000; 'Extract of a Journal Kept at the Army Commanded by the Late Lt Gen de Montcalm', in ibid., X: 1029.
74. Vaudreuil to Lévis, 2 August 1759, in Casgrain, *Manuscrits du Maréchal de Lévis*, VIII: 75.
75. *General Orders in Wolfe's Army during the Expedition up the River St Lawrence, 1759* (Literary and Historical Society of Quebec: Historical Documents, Fourth Series, Quebec, 1875), 31–2.
76. Wolfe to Pitt, 2 September 1759, PRO, CO 5/51.
77. Wolfe to Saunders, Banks of the St Lawrence, 30 August 1759, in Willson, *The Life and Letters of James Wolfe*, 462.
78. Wolfe's 'Family Journal', PRONI, DOD 162/77 C, 10–11.
79. Moncrief, *A Short Account of the Expedition against Quebec Commanded by Major-General Wolfe in the Year 1759*, 25.

Chapter Ten: 'It is war of the worst shape'

1. Wolfe's 'Family Journal', PRONI, DOD 162/77 C, 8.
2. *General Orders in Wolfe's Army during the Expedition up the River St Lawrence, 1759* (Literary and Historical Society of Quebec: Historical Documents, Fourth Series, Quebec, 1875), 37.
3. V. Bamfield, *On the Strength: The Story of the British Army Wife* (London, 1974), 52; P. E. Kopperman, 'The British High Command and Soldiers' Wives in America 1755–1783', *Journal of the Society for Army Historical Research*, 60, 241 (Spring 1982).
4. Wolfe's Journal, 1 August 1759.
5. Wolfe to Monckton, 1 August 1759, LAC, Monckton Papers, XXII, rl C-336.
6. 'Brigadier Townshend's Journal of the Voyage to America and Campaign against Quebec, 1759', in A. Doughty and G. Parmelee, eds., *The Siege of Quebec and the Battle of the Plains of Abraham* (6 vols., Quebec, 1901), V: 255.
7. Vaudreuil to Wolfe, 2 August 1759, in *The Northcliffe Collection* (Ottawa, 1926), XXI: 137.
8. 'Relation du siège de Québec, posé par les Anglois en l'anée 1759', in *The Northcliffe Collection*, XXVIII: 219.
9. Montcalm to Lévis, 2 August 1759, in H. R. Casgrain, ed., *Collection des manuscrits du Maréchal de Lévis* (12 vols., Montreal and Quebec, 1889–95), VI: 214.
10. Panet's Journal, 24 August 1759.
11. 'Journal du siège de Québec', in *The Northcliffe Collection*, XXX: 253.
12. Ibid.
13. 'Narrative of the Siege of Quebec, Published by the French [Département de la Guerre]', in E. O'Callaghan and B. Fernow, eds., *Documents Relative to the Colonial History of the State of New York; Procured in Holland, England and France* (15 vols., Albany, NY, 1853–87), X: 1001.
14. E. P. Hamilton, ed., *Adventure in the Wilderness: The American Journals of Louis Antoine de Bougainville, 1756–1760* (Norman, OK, 1990), 282.
15. Panet's Journal, 16 August 1759.
16. J.-F. Récher, *Journal du siège de Québec en 1759* (Quebec, 1959), entry for 12 August 1759.
17. Wolfe's Journal, 3 August 1759; Wolfe to Murray, *Stirling Castle*, 5 August 1759, PRONI, DOD 678 11a–14a.

18. A. Doughty, ed., *An Historical Journal of the Campaigns in North America: For the Years 1757, 1758, 1759 and 1760 by Captain John Knox* (3 vols., Toronto, 1914–16), II: 10.

19. Vaudreuil to Lévis, 20 July 1759, in Casgrain, *Collection des manuscrits du Maréchal de Lévis*, VIII: 66–7.

20. Bougainville's Journal for 1759–60, in Hamilton, *Adventure in the Wilderness*, 319.

21. Montreuil to Belle Isle, Camp at Pointe aux Trembles, 22 September 1759, in O'Callaghan and Fernow, *Documents*, X: 1013.

22. 'Extract of a Journal Kept at the Army Commanded by the Late Lt Gen de Montcalm', in O'Callaghan and Fernow, *Documents*, X: 1029.

23. LAC, James Murray Collection, MG 23 GII 1, rl A-1992. Bundle 1, letter 1.

24. 'Extracts from Journal of the Particular Transactions during the Siege of Quebec', in Doughty and Parmelee, *Siege of Quebec*, V: 177.

25. Ibid., V: 178.

26. *Journals of Louis Antoine de Bougainville*, 319.

27. LAC, James Murray Collection, MG 23 GII 1, rl A-1992. Bundle 1, letter 1.

28. Ibid.

29. Major Moncrief, *A Short Account of the Expedition against Quebec Commanded by Major-General Wolfe in the Year 1759* (Quebec, 1901), 26.

30. LAC, James Murray Collection, MG 23 GII 1, rl A-1992. Bundle 1, letter 1.

31. 'Extracts from Journal of the Particular Transactions during the Siege of Quebec', in Doughty and Parmelee, *Siege of Quebec*, V: 179.

32. Moncrief, *A Short Account of the Expedition against Quebec Commanded by Major-General Wolfe in the Year 1759*, 26–7; LAC, James Murray Collection, MG 23 GII 1, rl A-1992. Bundle 1, letter 1; 'Extracts from Journal of the Particular Transactions during the Siege of Quebec', in Doughty and Parmelee, *Siege of Quebec*, V: 179.

33. Panet's Journal, 7 August 1759.

34. 'Relation du siège de Québec, posé par les Anglois en l'anée 1759', in *The Northcliffe Collection*, XXVII: 219.

35. 'Journal of the Siege of Niagara', in O'Callaghan and Fernow, *Documents*, X: 975–90; 'Journal du siège de Québec', in *The Northcliffe Collection*, XXX: 255.

36. 'Extract of a Journal Kept at the Army Commanded by the Late Lt Gen de Montcalm', in O'Callaghan and Fernow, *Documents*, X: 1031.

37. J. B. N. R. de Ramezay, *Mémoire du sieur de Ramezay, commandant à Québec, au sujet de la reddition de cette ville, le 18 septembre 1759* (Quebec, 1861).

38. 'Journal du siège de Québec', in *The Northcliffe Collection*, XXX: 256.

39. 'Extract of a Journal Kept at the Army Commanded by the Late Lt Gen de Montcalm', in O'Callaghan and Fernow, *Documents*, X: 1032.

40. 'Journal du siège de Québec', in *The Northcliffe Collection*, XXX: 256.

41. 'Extract of a Journal Kept at the Army Commanded by the Late Lt Gen de Montcalm', in O'Callaghan and Fernow, *Documents*, X: 1030.

42. 'Canada Campaign from the 1st of June to the 15th September, 1759 [Département de la Guerre]', in O'Callaghan and Fernow, *Documents*, X: 1003.

43. R. Léger, ed., *Le Journal du Chevalier de Lévis* (Montreal, 2008), 144.

44. LAC, James Murray Collection, MG 23 GII 1, rl A-1992. Bundle 1, letter 3.

45. Moncrief, *A Short Account of the Expedition against Quebec Commanded by Major-General Wolfe in the Year 1759*, 28.

46. Wolfe to Monckton, 25 July 1759, LAC, Monckton Papers, vol. XXII, rl C-336.

47. 'Extract of a Journal Kept at the Army Commanded by the Late Lt Gen de Montcalm', in O'Callaghan and Fernow, *Documents*, X: 1027.

48. Ibid., X: 1028.

49. Wolfe's Proclamation 25 July 1759 reprinted in O'Callaghan and Fernow, *Documents*, X: 1047.

50. *Memoirs of the Siege of Quebec, the Capital of all Canada, and of the Retreat of Monsieur de Bourlemaque* (Quebec, 1901), 26–7.

51. Vaudreuil to de Lévis, 18 August 1759, Casgrain, *Lettres de Vaudreuil à Levis*, 86, in M. Ward, *The Battle for Quebec, 1759* (Stroud, 2005), 118, 121.

52. Wolfe's 'Family Journal', PRONI, DOD 162/77 C, 13.

53. Wolfe to Pitt, 2 September 1759, PRO, CO 5/51.

54. The Tsarina's Cossack horsemen came in for terrible criticism after their devastation of Pomerania during the Seven Years War.

55. 'John Johnson's Journal', in Doughty and Parmelee, *Siege of Quebec*, V: 82.

56. Moncrief, *A Short Account of the Expedition against Quebec Commanded by Major-General Wolfe in the Year 1759*, 25.

57. Montresor to Colonel James Montresor, 10 August 1759, Montmorency, in Doughty and Parmelee, *Siege of Quebec*, IV: 319.

58. Wolfe to Sackville, 30 July 1759, in B. Willson, ed., *The Life and Letters of James Wolfe* (New York, 1909), 389.

59. 'John Johnson's Journal', in Doughty and Parmelee, *Siege of Quebec*, V: 97.

60. 'Appendices of the Nova Scotia Papers of the Northcliffe Collection', in *The Northcliffe Collection*, 100.

61. Knox, *Journal*, II: 17; the return for Gorham's men in LAC, Monckton Papers, XX, rl C-366 says he had three officers, seven NCOs and sixty-seven privates from the regulars. In addition he had 8 ranger officers, ten NCOs, 136 privates and forty marines.

62. *A Journal of the Expedition up the River St Lawrence (by a Sgt Major in Hopson's Grenadiers)* (Boston, 1759), 7.

63. Knox, *Journal*, II: 38–9.

64. Ibid., II: 23.

65. *A Journal of the Expedition up the River St Lawrence (by a Sgt Major in Hopson's Grenadiers)*, 7–8.

66. Wolfe to Monckton, 14 August, in LAC, Monckton Papers, XXII, rl C-336.

67. Wolfe to Monckton, 15 August, in ibid., XXII, rl C-336.

68. Knox, *Journal*, II: 55.

69. Panet's Journal, 21, 23 August 1759.

70. C. P. Stacey, *Canadian Dictionary Biography* online: http://www.biographi.ca/EN/ShowBio.asp?BioId=35775andquery=scott.

71. Knox, *Journal*, II: 57.

72. 'French Documents Relating to Quebec', in *The Northcliffe Collection*, XXVII: 214.

73. Knox, *Journal*, II: 42.

74. Ibid., II: 44.

75. *Extract from a Manuscript Journal Relating to the Operations before Quebec in 1759, Kept by Colonel Malcolm Fraser, the Lt of the 78th (Fraser's Highlanders) and Serving in that Campaign* (Literary and Historical Society of Quebec: Historical Documents, Second Series, 1868), 13–14.

76. *Mémoire du sieur de Ramezay, commandant à Québec, au sujet de la reddition de cette ville, le 18 septembre 1759*.

77. *Canadian Dictionary of Biography* online: http://www.biographi.ca/EN/ShowBio.asp?BioId=35746andquery=portneuf.

78. *General Orders in Wolfe's Army during the Expedition up the River St Lawrence, 1759* (Literary and Historical Society of Quebec: Historical Documents, Fourth Series, Quebec, 1875), 29.

79. Knox, *Journal*, II: 45.
80. 'The Townshend Papers', in Doughty and Parmelee, *Siege of Quebec*, V: 258.
81. 'Genuine Letters from a Volunteer in the British Service at Quebec: 2 September 1759, 2 Miles below Quebec', in Doughty and Parmelee, *Siege of Quebec*, V: 19.
82. *Orderly Book and Journal of Major John Hawks, on the Ticonderoga-Crown Point Campaign, under General Jeffrey Amherst, 1759–1760* (New York, 1911), 11.
83. Léger, *Le Journal de Montcalm*, entry for 1 September 1759, 491.
84. Knox, *Journal*, II: 21.
85. Hamilton, *Bougainville*, 11.
86. *General Orders in Wolfe's Army*, 35.
87. 'Brigadier Townshend's Journal of the Voyage to America and Campaign against Quebec, 1759', in Doughty and Parmelee, *Siege of Quebec*, V: 257.
88. Knox, *Journal*, II: 40.
89. 'Journal du siège de Québec', in *The Northcliffe Collection*, XXX: 260.
90. *A Journal of the Expedition up the River St Lawrence (by a Sgt Major in Hopson's Grenadiers)*, 13.
91. W. J. Eccles, *Essays on New France* (Toronto, 1987), 127.
92. Robert MacPherson to Andrew MacPherson, Camp before Quebec, 16 September 1759, James Grant Papers, Library of Congress, reprinted in full in I. McCulloch, *Sons of the Mountain: The Highland Regiments in the French and Indian War, 1756–1767* (2 vols., Toronto, 2006), I: 185–6.
93. Townshend to Lady Ferrers, 6 September 1759, Camp Lévis, from 'Letters and Papers Relating to the Siege of Quebec in the Possession of the Marquess of Townshend', in Doughty and Parmelee, *Siege of Quebec*, V: 194–5.

Chapter Eleven: 'We find ourselves outnumbered and we fear, out generaled'

1. Major Moncrief, *A Short Account of the Expedition against Quebec Commanded by Major-General Wolfe in the Year 1759* (Quebec, 1901), 28.
2. 'Extracts from Journal of the Particular Transactions during the Siege of Quebec', in A. Doughty and G. Parmelee, eds., *The Siege of Quebec and the Battle of the Plains of Abraham* (6 vols., Quebec, 1901), V: 181.
3. 'Extracts from Journal of the Particular Transactions during the siege of Quebec', in Doughty and Parmelee, *Siege of Quebec*, V: 181.

4. LAC, James Murray Collection, MG 23 GII 1, rl A-1992. Bundle 1, letter 2.

5. Moncrief, *A Short Account of the Expedition against Quebec Commanded by Major-General Wolfe in the Year 1759*, 29.

6. 'Journal du siège de Québec', in *The Northcliffe Collection* (Ottawa, 1926), XXX: 258.

7. R. Léger, ed., *Le Journal de Montcalm* (Montreal, 2007), entry for 17 August 1759, 484.

8. Bougainville's Journal for 1759–60 in E. P. Hamilton, ed., *Adventure in the Wilderness: The American Journals of Louis Antoine de Bougainville, 1756–1760* (Norman, OK, 1990), 320.

9. LAC, James Murray Collection, MG 23 GII 1, rl A-1992. Bundle 1, letter 2.

10. *Memoirs of the Siege of Quebec, the Capital of all Canada, and of the Retreat of Monsieur de Bourlemaque* (Quebec, 1901), 24.

11. 'Journal du siège de Québec', in *The Northcliffe Collection*, XXX: 258–9.

12. Wolfe to Monckton, 19 August 1759, LAC, Monckton Papers, XXII, rl C-336.

13. Wolfe to Murray, 13 August 1759, Montmorency, PRONI, DOD 678 14a.

14. Wolfe to Monckton, 22 August 1759, LAC, Monckton Papers, XXII, rl C-336.

15. A. Doughty, ed., *An Historical Journal of the Campaigns in North America: For the Years 1757, 1758, 1759 and 1760 by Captain John Knox* (3 vols., Toronto, 1914–16), II: 33.

16. 'Journal du siège de Québec', in *The Northcliffe Collection*, XXX: 259.

17. Knox, *Journal*, II: 34.

18. Barré to Monckton, 24 August 1759, LAC, MG 18 N 18, vol. IV, file 1, fol. 13.

19. Wolfe to Holderness, 'on board the *Sutherland* off Cape Rouge', 9 September 1759, in B. Willson, ed., *The Life and Letters of James Wolfe* (New York, 1909), 474.

20. Wolfe to Monckton, 4 August 1759, LAC, Monckton Papers, XXII, rl C-336.

21. Knox, *Journal*, II: 43.

22. 'Brigadier Townshend's Journal of the Voyage to America and Campaign against Quebec, 1759', in Doughty and Parmelee, *Siege of Quebec*, V: 259.

23. Knox, *Journal*, II: 26.

24. *General Orders in Wolfe's Army during the Expedition up the River St Lawrence, 1759* (Literary and Historical Society of Quebec: Historical Documents, Fourth Series, Quebec, 1875), 38.
25. *General Wolfe's Instructions to Young Officers* (London, 1778), 46–55.
26. *General Orders in Wolfe's Army*, 43.
27. Knox, *Journal*, I: 129.
28. Perth, 1 January 1750, in *General Wolfe's Instructions to Young Officers*, 19.
29. Wolfe to Monckton, 16 August 1759, LAC, Monckton Papers, XXII, rl C-336; Wolfe's 'Family Journal', PRONI, DOD 162/77 C, 11–12; 'Extract of a Journal Kept at the Army Commanded by the Late Lt Gen de Montcalm', in E. O'Callaghan and B. Fernow, eds., *Documents Relative to the Colonial History of the State of New York; Procured in Holland, England and France* (15 vols., Albany, NY, 1853–87), X: 1032.
30. *General Orders in Wolfe's Army*, 41.
31. Wolfe's 'Family Journal', PRONI, DOD 162/77 C, 12.
32. Wolfe to Monckton, 16 August 1759, LAC, Monckton Papers, XXII, rl C-336.
33. Ibid.
34. Wolfe to Monckton, 22 August 1759, in Willson, *Life and Letters of James Wolfe*, 466.
35. R. Holmes, *Redcoat: The British Soldier in the Age of Horse and Musket* (London, 2001), 177; J. Houlding, *Fit for Service: The Training of the British Army, 1715–1795* (Oxford, 1981), 104.
36. Houlding, *Fit for Service*, 107.
37. 'Brigadier Townshend's Journal of the Voyage to America and Campaign against Quebec, 1759', in Doughty and Parmelee, *Siege of Quebec*, V: 255.
38. 'Journal du siège de Québec', in *The Northcliffe Collection*, XXX: 255.
39. 'Extract of a Journal Kept at the Army Commanded by the Late Lt Gen de Montcalm', in O'Callaghan and Fernow, *Documents*, X: 1030.
40. 'Brigadier Townshend's Journal of the Voyage to America and Campaign against Quebec, 1759', in Doughty and Parmelee, *Siege of Quebec*, V: 259.
41. Knox, *Journal*, II: 34.
42. *General Orders in Wolfe's Army*, 44.
43. *A Journal of the Expedition up the River St Lawrence (by a Sgt Major in Hopson's Grenadiers)* (Boston, 1759), 9.

44. *A Journal of the Expedition up the River St Lawrence (by a Sgt Major in Hopson's Grenadiers)*, 7.
45. 'Diary of Lt William Henshaw', in C. H. Lincoln, ed., *Manuscript Records of the French and Indian War: In the Library of the American Antiquarian Society* (Worcester, MA, 1909), 191.
46. *Orderly Book and Journal of Major John Hawks, on the Ticonderoga-Crown Point Campaign, under General Jeffrey Amherst, 1759–1760* (New York, 1911), 55.
47. *General Orders in Wolfe's Army*, 34.
48. Wolfe's Journal, 11 August 1759.
49. Moncrief, *A Short Account of the Expedition against Quebec Commanded by Major-General Wolfe in the Year 1759*, 25.
50. Knox, *Journal*, II: 36–7.
51. Wolfe to Pitt, 2 September 1759, PRO, C 5/51.
52. Knox, *Journal*, II: 40.
53. Ibid.
54. Wolfe to Pitt, 2 September 1759, PRO, C 5/51.
55. *General Orders in Wolfe's Army*, 42, 44.
56. James Gibson to Governor Lawrence, 1 August 1759, in Doughty and Parmelee, *Siege of Quebec*, V: 65–8.
57. Captain Schomberg to Admiral Forbes, Boston, 5 September 1759, in Doughty and Parmelee, *Siege of Quebec*, V: 60.
58. Bell's Journal, 31 July 1759.
59. Wolfe's 'Family Journal', PRONI, DOD 162/77 C, 28–9.
60. Ibid., 21.
61. Ibid., 29.
62. Townshend to Lady Townshend, Point Lévis, 6 September 1759, LAC, MG 18 L 7, fol. 18.
63. Lieutenant Colonel Murray to 'Manie', Montmorency, 8 August 1759, in 'Letters of Colonel Murray', in H. C. Wylley, ed., *The Sherwood Foresters: Notts and Derby Regiment. Regimental Annual 1926* (London, 1927), 212.
64. Wolfe to Monckton, 15 August 1759 and 16 August 1759, LAC, Monckton Papers, vol. XXII, rl C-336.
65. Williamson to Ligonier, Point Lévis, 12 August 1759, in LAC, rl A-573.
66. 'Extract of a Journal Kept at the Army Commanded by the Late Lt Gen de Montcalm', in O'Callaghan and Fernow, *Documents*, X: 1033.
67. Knox, *Journal*, II: 7.
68. 'Return of the Marines at the Camp at the Point de Lévis 9 August 1759', LAC, Monckton Papers, XX, rl C-366.
69. 'Extract of a Journal Kept at the Army Commanded by the Late Lt Gen de Montcalm', in O'Callaghan and Fernow, *Documents*, X: 1033.

70. *General Orders in Wolfe's Army*, 22.
71. Ibid., 28, 30.
72. Major Clephane, quoted in I. McCulloch, *Highlander in the French-Indian War 1756–67* (Oxford, 2008), 44.
73. *Orderly Book and Journal of Major John Hawks, on the Ticonderoga-Crown Point Campaign, under General Jeffrey Amherst, 1759–1760*, 24, 25.
74. Montresor to Colonel James Montresor, Quebec, 5 October 1759, in Doughty and Parmelee, *Siege of Quebec*, IV: 329.
75. *General Orders in Wolfe's Army*, 28.
76. Knox, *Journal*, I: 412.
77. Ibid., II: 53.
78. *General Orders in Wolfe's Army*, 27.
79. Ibid., 42–3.
80. Ibid., 30.
81. Knox, *Journal*, II: 16.
82. 'John Johnson's Journal', in Doughty and Parmelee, *Siege of Quebec*, V: 99.
83. Wolfe's 'Family Journal', PRONI, DOD 162/77 C, 13.
84. Wolfe to Holderness, in B. Willson, ed., *The Life and Letters of James Wolfe* (New York, 1909), 474.
85. 'John Johnson's Journal', in Doughty and Parmelee, *Siege of Quebec*, V: 95.
86. Knox, *Journal*, II: 40.
87. Ibid., II: 42.
88. Willson, *The Life and Letters of James Wolfe*, 483–4.
89. Wolfe's 'Family Journal', PRONI, DOD 162/77 C, 13.
90. Wolfe's Instructions to Brigadiers, PRONI, DOD 678 5a–6a.
91. Ibid., 7a.
92. C. V. F. Townshend, *The Military Life of George First Marquess Townshend* (Toronto, 1907), 210.
93. 'Brigadier Townshend's Journal of the Voyage to America and Campaign against Quebec, 1759', in Doughty and Parmelee, *Siege of Quebec*, V: 262.
94. 'At a Council of War at Point Levy, 29 August 1759', PRONI, DOD 678 8a.
95. Ibid., 8a–9a.
96. Ibid., 9a–10a.
97. 'Plan of Operations in Consequence of the Preceding Answer'.
98. Wolfe to Monckton, 13 August 1759, LAC, Monckton Papers, XXII, rl C-336.

99. Saunders to Admiralty, 5 September 1759, in C. H. Little, ed., *Despatches of Vice Admiral Saunders* (Halifax, NS, 1958), 15.

100. 'Extracts from Journal of the Particular Transactions during the Siege of Quebec', in Doughty and Parmelee, *Siege of Quebec*, V: 183.

101. *A Journal of the Expedition up the River St Lawrence (by a Sgt Major in Hopson's Grenadiers)*, 9.

102. Logs: *Hunter*, 28 August 1759, *Lowestoft*, 28 August 1759, in W. Wood, ed., *The Logs of the Conquest of Canada* (Toronto, 1909), 230, 237.

103. *A Journal of the Expedition up the River St Lawrence (by a Sgt Major in Hopson's Grenadiers)*, 9.

104. J. B. N. R. de Ramezay, *Mémoire du sieur de Ramezay, commandant à Québec, au sujet de la reddition de cette ville, le 18 septembre 1759* (Quebec, 1861).

105. 'Journal du siège de Québec', in *The Northcliffe Collection*, XXX: 253.

106. Ibid., 262.

107. Montcalm to Bougainville, quoted in Wood, *The Logs of the Conquest of Canada*, 149.

108. 'Journal du siège de Québec', in *The Northcliffe Collection*, XXX: 260.

109. 'Relation du siège de Québec, posé par les Anglois en l'anée 1759', in *The Northcliffe Collection*, XXVIII: 220.

110. Panet's Journal, 17 August 1759.

111. 'Journal du siège de Québec', in *The Northcliffe Collection*, XXX: 261.

112. Panet's Journal, 4 September 1759; J.-F. Récher, *Journal du siège de Québec en 1759* (Quebec, 1959), entry for 24 August 1759.

113. Vaudreuil's ceaseless courting of de Lévis is illustrated by the opening sentence of the second letter: 'Even though I have absolutely nothing interesting to tell you, I could not refuse myself the pleasure of writing you this letter.' Vaudreuil to de Lévis, 10, 11 August 1759, in H. R. Casgrain, ed., *Collection des manuscrits du Maréchal de Lévis* (12 vols., Montreal and Quebec, 1889–95), VIII: 79–82.

114. Vaudreuil to de Lévis, 28 August 1759, in ibid., VIII: 93–5.

115. Récher, *Journal du siège de Québec en 1759*, entry for 13 August 1759.

116. Léger, *Le Journal de Montcalm*, entry for 20 August 1759, 485.

117. Montcalm to de la Molé, Quebec, 24 August 1759, LAC, MG 18 N 18, vol. VII.

118. Knox, *Journal*, II: 42, 55.

119. Wolfe to Saunders, 30 August 1759, *Gentlemen's Magazine*, June 1801, in LAC, MG 18 N 18, vol. V.
120. This new concoction was 'held in the highest esteem by the Quality and Gentry of France who constantly carry it in their pockets a smelling bottle ... it recovers immediately from either fainting or hysteric fits, and is a most admirable remedy in the head ache, lowness of spirits, hypochondriacal, and nervous disorders'. No doubt Montcalm's officers had vials of the liquid about their persons at all times.
121. Wolfe to Pitt, 2 September 1759, PRO, C 5/51.
122. William Corry to Sir William Johnson, 23 August 1759, Albany, NY, 23 August 1759, in J. Sullivan et al., eds., *Sir William Johnson Papers* (Albany, NY, 1921), 128.
123. Wolfe to Mrs Wolfe, 31 August 1759, in Willson, *The Life and Letters of James Wolfe*, 468–9.
124. Wolfe's 'Family Journal', PRONI, DOD 162/77 C, 14.
125. Moncrief, *A Short Account of the Expedition against Quebec Commanded by Major-General Wolfe in the Year 1759*, 25.
126. Saunders to Admiralty, 5 September 1759, in Little, *Despatches of Vice Admiral Saunders*, 16.
127. Wolfe to Holderness, 'on board the *Sutherland* off Cape Rouge', 9 September 1759, in Willson, *The Life and Letters of James Wolfe*, 475.
128. Knox, *Journal*, II: 41.
129. 'Relation du siège de Québec, posé par les Anglois en l'anée 1759', in *The Northcliffe Collection*, XXVIII: 220.

Chapter Twelve: 'This man must finish with a great effort, and great thunder'

1. *General Orders in Wolfe's Army during the Expedition up the River St Lawrence, 1759* (Literary and Historical Society of Quebec: Historical Documents, Fourth Series, Quebec, 1875), 45.
2. Saunders to Townshend, 1 September 1759, in A. Doughty and G. Parmelee, eds., *The Siege of Quebec and the Battle of the Plains of Abraham* (6 vols., Quebec, 1901), V: 275.
3. Montresor to Colonel James Montresor, Quebec, 5 October 1759, in Doughty and Parmelee, *Siege of Quebec*, IV: 330.
4. 'Brigadier Townshend's Journal of the Voyage to America and Campaign against Quebec, 1759', in Doughty and Parmelee, *Siege of Quebec*, V: 262.
5. *General Orders in Wolfe's Army*, 45–6.
6. 'Extracts from Journal of the Particular Transactions during the Siege of Quebec', in Doughty and Parmelee, *Siege of Quebec*, V: 184.

7. *General Orders in Wolfe's Army*, 47.
8. 'Brigadier Townshend's Journal of the Voyage to America and Campaign against Quebec, 1759', in Doughty and Parmelee, *Siege of Quebec*, V: 263.
9. Wolfe's 'Family Journal', PRONI, DOD 162/77 C, 14.
10. 'Journal du siège de Québec', in *The Northcliffe Collection* (Ottawa, 1926), XXX: 262.
11. A. Doughty, ed., *An Historical Journal of the Campaigns in North America: For the Years 1757, 1758, 1759 and 1760 by Captain John Knox* (3 vols., Toronto, 1914–16), II: 59.
12. Panet's Journal, 2 September 1759.
13. 'Brigadier Townshend's Journal of the Voyage to America and Campaign against Quebec, 1759', in Doughty and Parmelee, *Siege of Quebec*, V: 264.
14. Knox, *Journal*, II: 70.
15. 'Brigadier Townshend's Journal of the Voyage to America and Campaign against Quebec, 1759', in Doughty and Parmelee, *Siege of Quebec,* V: 264.
16. Major Moncrief, *A Short Account of the Expedition against Quebec Commanded by Major-General Wolfe in the Year 1759* (Quebec, 1901), 30.
17. 'Journal du siège de Québec', in *The Northcliffe Collection*, XXX: 264.
18. 'Extract of a Journal Kept at the Army Commanded by the Late Lt Gen de Montcalm', in E. O'Callaghan and B. Fernow, eds., *Documents Relative to the Colonial History of the State of New York; Procured in Holland, England and France* (15 vols., Albany, NY, 1853–87), X: 1035–6.
19. Panet's Journal, 4 September 1759.
20. Wolfe's 'Family Journal', PRONI, DOD 162/77 C, 15.
21. Moncrief, *A Short Account of the Expedition against Quebec Commanded by Major-General Wolfe in the Year 1759*, 31.
22. 'Letter of Admiral Holmes', *Lowestoft*, River above Quebec, 18 September 1759, in Doughty and Parmelee, *Siege of Quebec*, IV: 295.
23. Robert Monckton's Order Book, in *The Northcliffe Collection*, XXIII: 162.
24. Moncrief, *A Short Account of the Expedition against Quebec Commanded by Major-General Wolfe in the Year 1759*, 31.
25. *A Journal of the Expedition up the River St Lawrence (by a Sgt Major in Hopson's Grenadiers)* (Boston, 1759), 9.
26. Knox, *Journal*, II: 55.
27. 'Copy of a Letter from on Board the *Lizard* September 5th 1759 at Coudres, 17 Leagues from Quebec', in S. Pargellis, ed., *Military*

Affairs in North America, 1748–65: Selected Documents from the Cumberland Papers in Windsor Castle (New York, 1936), 436–7.

28. Knox, *Journal*, II: 71.
29. 'Extract of a Journal Kept at the Army Commanded by the Late Lt Gen de Montcalm', in O'Callaghan and Fernow, *Documents*, X: 1035.
30. 'Diary of Lt William Henshaw', in C. H. Lincoln, ed., *Manuscript Records of the French and Indian War: In the Library of the American Antiquarian Society* (Worcester, MA, 1909), 216.
31. The Hon. Roger Townshend to Lady Ferrers, 'Camp Fort Edward', 7 June 1759, in 'Letters and Papers Relating to the Siege of Quebec in the Possession of the Marquess of Townshend', in Doughty and Parmelee, *Siege of Quebec*, V: 191.
32. Townshend to Lady Ferrers, Camp Lévis, 6 September 1759, in C. V. F. Townshend, *The Military Life of George First Marquess Townshend* (Toronto, 1907), 210.
33. Townshend to Lady Ferrers, Quebec, 5 October 1759, LAC, MG 18 L 7, fols. 122–3.
34. *Memoirs of the Siege of Quebec, the Capital of all Canada, and of the Retreat of Monsieur de Bourlemaque* (Quebec, 1901), 27–8.
35. Panet's Journal, 7 September 1759.
36. R. Léger, ed., *Le Journal de Montcalm* (Montreal, 2007), entry for 26 August 1759, 488–9.
37. Montcalm to Bougainville, in Doughty and Parmelee, *Siege of Quebec*, IV: 84.
38. 'Journal du siège de Québec', in *The Northcliffe Collection*, XXX: 263.
39. Bougainville's Journal for 1759–60 in E. P. Hamilton, ed., *Adventure in the Wilderness: The American Journals of Louis Antoine de Bougainville, 1756–1760* (Norman, OK, 1990), 320.
40. 'Extract of a Journal Kept at the Army Commanded by the Late Lt Gen de Montcalm', in O'Callaghan and Fernow, *Documents*, X: 1038.
41. *Memoirs of the Siege of Quebec, the Capital of all Canada, and of the Retreat of Monsieur de Bourlemaque*, 28.
42. Montcalm to Bougainville, 5 September 1759, in *The Northcliffe Collection*, 433.
43. Léger, *Le Journal de Montcalm*, entry for 18 August 1759, 484.
44. Vaudreuil to de Lévis, 4 September 1759, in H. R. Casgrain, ed., *Collection des manuscrits du Maréchal de Lévis* (12 vols., Montreal and Quebec, 1889–95), VIII: 99.
45. J. B. N. R. de Ramezay, *Mémoire du sieur de Ramezay, commandant à Québec, au sujet de la reddition de cette ville, le 18 septembre 1759* (Quebec, 1861).

46. Montcalm to Bougainville, 5 September 1759, 'à 4 heures', in Doughty and Parmelee, *Siege of Quebec*, IV: 94.
47. Wolfe's 'Family Journal', PRONI, DOD 162/77 C, 26.
48. 'Journal du siège de Québec', in *The Northcliffe Collection*, XXX: 265.
49. 'Relation du siège de Québec, posé par les Anglois en l'anée 1759', in *The Northcliffe Collection*, XXVIII: 221.
50. Vaudreuil to de Lévis, 7 September 1759, in Casgrain, *Collection des manuscrits du Maréchal de Lévis*, VIII: 101.
51. Montcalm to Bougainville, 10 September 1759, in Doughty and Parmelee, *Siege of Quebec*, IV: 116–17.
52. Ramezay, *Mémoire du sieur de Ramezay, commandant à Québec, au sujet de la reddition de cette ville, le 18 septembre 1759*.
53. *Memoirs of the Siege of Quebec, the Capital of all Canada, and of the Retreat of Monsieur de Bourlemaque*, 27.
54. 'Extract of a Journal Kept at the Army Commanded by the Late Lt Gen de Montcalm', in O'Callaghan and Fernow, *Documents*, X: 1036.
55. 'Journal du siège de Québec', in *The Northcliffe Collection*, XXX: 263–4.
56. Léger, *Le Journal de Montcalm*, entry for 9 September 1759, 495–6.
57. 'Relation du siège de Québec, posé par les Anglois en l'anée 1759', in *The Northcliffe Collection*, XXVIII: 221.
58. *A Journal of the Expedition up the River St Lawrence (by a Sgt Major in Hopson's Grenadiers)*, 10.
59. *Extract from a Manuscript Journal Relating to the Operations before Quebec in 1759, Kept by Colonel Malcolm Fraser, the Lt of the 78th (Fraser's Highlanders) and Serving in that Campaign* (Literary and Historical Society of Quebec: Historical Documents, Second Series, 1868), 16.
60. Knox, *Journal*, II: 76.
61. Ibid., II: 74.
62. Ibid., II: 75.
63. *A Journal of the Expedition up the River St Lawrence (by a Sgt Major in Hopson's Grenadiers)*, 10.
64. Panet's Journal, 7 September 1759.
65. Knox, *Journal*, II: 75.
66. *Journal of the Particular Transactions during the Siege of Quebec by an Officer of Fraser's Regiment* (Quebec, 1901), 32.
67. *General Orders in Wolfe's Army*, 48.
68. 'Brigadier Townshend's Journal of the Voyage to America and Campaign against Quebec, 1759', in Doughty and Parmelee, *Siege of Quebec*, V: 265.

69. Knox, *Journal*, II: 79.
70. 'Brigadier Townshend's Journal of the Voyage to America and Campaign against Quebec, 1759', in Doughty and Parmelee, *Siege of Quebec*, V: 266.
71. Log: *Squirrel*, 6 September 1759, in W. Wood, ed., *The Logs of the Conquest of Canada* (Toronto, 1909), 299.
72. Knox, *Journal*, II: 79.
73. Wolfe's 'Family Journal', PRONI, DOD 162/77 C, 15.
74. 'Journal du siège de Québec', in *The Northcliffe Collection*, XXX: 265.
75. 'Brigadier Townshend's Journal of the Voyage to America and Campaign against Quebec, 1759', in Doughty and Parmelee, *Siege of Quebec*, V: 266.
76. Moncrief, *A Short Account of the Expedition against Quebec Commanded by Major-General Wolfe in the Year 1759*, 32–3.
77. Log: *Squirrel*, 8 September 1759, in Wood, *The Logs of the Conquest of Canada*, 299.
78. Knox, *Journal*, II: 83.
79. Ibid., II, 82–3, 85.
80. Wolfe's 'Family Journal', PRONI, DOD 162/77 C, 15.
81. Moncrief, *A Short Account of the Expedition against Quebec Commanded by Major-General Wolfe in the Year 1759*, 33.
82. Ibid., 33.
83. Ibid., 33–4.
84. 'Letter of Admiral Holmes, *Lowestoft,* off Foulon in the River St Lawrence, above Quebec, 18 September 1759', in Doughty and Parmelee, *Siege of Quebec*, IV: 295–6.
85. Rémigny to Bougainville, 11 September 1759, in Doughty and Parmelee, *Siege of Quebec*, IV: 121.
86. Wolfe to Burton, '*Sutherland* above Cap Rouge', 10 September 1759, LAC, MG 18 N 51, vol. I.
87. Knox, *Journal*, II: 86.
88. Monckton, Murray, and Townshend to Wolfe, 12 September 1759, in *The Northcliffe Collection*, 425.
89. Wolfe to Monckton, 12 September 1759, '*Sutherland*, 8½ O'clock', LAC, MG 18 N 18, vol. IV, file 1.
90. Wolfe to Townshend, 12 September 1759, ibid.
91. Wolfe's 'Family Journal', PRONI, DOD 162/77 C, 15–16.
92. Ibid., 16.
93. Knox, *Journal*, II: 90.
94. 'Extracts from Journal of the Particular Transactions during the Siege of Quebec', in Doughty and Parmelee, *Siege of Quebec*, V: 186.

95. 'John Johnson's Journal', in Doughty and Parmelee, *Siege of Quebec*, V: 101.

96. 'Brigadier Townshend's Journal of the Voyage to America and Campaign against Quebec, 1759', in Doughty and Parmelee, *Siege of Quebec*, V: 267.

97. 'From an Officer at Quebec', *Scots Magazine*, 21 (October 1759), 552, LAC, MG 18 N 18, vol. V. The talk of expectation and duty has a distinctly Nelsonian ring to it. Fifty years later Vice Admiral Lord Horatio Nelson, a keen student of Wolfe, made the famous signal at Trafalgar, 'England expects every man will do his duty.' It was flown from his flagship, HMS *Victory*. Work had begun on this vast warship in July 1759 in the Old Single Dock at Chatham dockyard on the Medway in Kent.

98. 'John Johnson's Journal', in Doughty and Parmelee, *Siege of Quebec*, V: 101.

99. Fraser, *Journal*, 12 September 1959, 18.

100. 'Extracts from Journal of the Particular Transactions during the Siege of Quebec', in Doughty and Parmelee, *Siege of Quebec*, V: 187.

101. Wolfe's 'Family Journal', PRONI, DOD 162/77 C, 16.

102. Knox, *Journal*, II: 90.

103. J.-F. Récher, *Journal du siège de Québec en 1759* (Quebec, 1959), entry for 2 September 1759.

104. Léger, *Le Journal de Montcalm*, entry for 11 September 1759, 497.

105. Vaudreuil to de Lévis, 7 September 1759, in Casgrain, *Collection des manuscrits du Maréchal de Lévis*, VIII: 105.

106. 'Extracts from Journal of the Particular Transactions during the Siege of Quebec', in Doughty and Parmelee, *Siege of Quebec*, V: 187.

107. Ibid.

108. Knox, *Journal*, II: 94.

109. 'John Johnson's Journal', in Doughty and Parmelee, *Siege of Quebec*, V: 100–1.

Chapter Thirteen: The Landings

1. Saunders to Clevland, Secretary to the Admiralty, 21 September 1759, in J. B. Hattendorf, R. J. B. Knight, A. W. H. Pearsall, N. A. M. Rodger, and G. Till, eds., *British Naval Documents 1204–1960* (Naval Records Society, CXXI, Aldershot, 1993), no. 225, p. 393.

2. Wolfe's 'Family Journal', PRONI, DOD 162/77 C, 16.

3. *General Orders in Wolfe's Army during the Expedition up the River St Lawrence, 1759* (Literary and Historical Society of Quebec: Historical Documents, Fourth Series, Quebec, 1875), 52.

4. Major Moncrief, *A Short Account of the Expedition against Quebec Commanded by Major-General Wolfe in the Year 1759* (Quebec, 1901), 36.

5. 'Letter of Holmes, *Lowestoft* off Foulon in the River St. Laurence, above Quebec 18 September 1759', in A. Doughty and G. Parmelee, eds., *The Siege of Quebec and the Battle of the Plains of Abraham* (6 vols., Quebec, 1901), IV: 296.

6. For a full discussion of this oft-quoted story see Stephen Brumwell's excellent *Paths of Glory: The Life and Death of General James Wolfe* (London, 2006), 272.

7. 'Extracts from Journal of the Particular Transactions during the Siege of Quebec', in Doughty and Parmelee, *Siege of Quebec*, V: 187.

8. Log: *Hunter*, 12 September 1759, in W. Wood, ed., *The Logs of the Conquest of Canada* (Toronto, 1909), 232.

9. Moncrief, *A Short Account of the Expedition against Quebec Commanded by Major-General Wolfe in the Year 1759*, 36.

10. 'Extract of a Journal Kept at the Army Commanded by the Late Lt Gen de Montcalm', in E. O'Callaghan and B. Fernow, eds., *Documents Relative to the Colonial History of the State of New York; Procured in Holland, England and France* (15 vols., Albany, NY, 1853–87), X: 1038.

11. Rough notes on the siege in 'Letters and Papers Relating to the Siege of Quebec in the Possession of the Marquess of Townshend', in Doughty and Parmelee, *Siege of Quebec*, V: 214.

12. 'Extracts from Journal of the Particular Transactions during the Siege of Quebec', in Doughty and Parmelee, *Siege of Quebec*, V: 187.

13. I. McCulloch, *Sons of the Mountain: The Highland Regiments in the French and Indian War, 1756–1767* (2 vols., Toronto, 2006), 88.

14. A Doughty, ed., *An Historical Journal of the Campaigns in North America: For the Years 1757, 1758, 1759 and 1760 by Captain John Knox* (3 vols., Toronto, 1914–16), II: 96.

15. Saunders to Pitt, Quebec, 21 September 1759, PRO, CO 5/51 fol. 45.

16. Vergor to Duc de Choiseul, Secretary of State for Marine and the Colonies, reprinted in full in C. P. Stacey, *Quebec 1759: The Siege and the Battle* (Toronto, 2002), Appendix D, 211–12.

17. Wolfe's 'Family Journal', PRONI, DOD 162/77 C, 17.

18. This phrase is contained in an undated letter attached to Vaudeuil's Report to the Minister, 5 October 1759, in Stacey, *Quebec 1759*, Appendix C, 200.

19. Townshend to Pitt, 'Camp before Quebec', 20 September 1759, PRO, CO 5/51 fol. 90.

20. Moncrief, *A Short Account of the Expedition against Quebec Commanded by Major-General Wolfe in the Year 1759*, 34.
21. 'Letter from Quebec, 7 October 1759', in *Derby Mercury*, 30 November to 7 December 1759, in Brumwell, *Paths of Glory: The Life and Death of General James Wolfe*, 275.
22. Saunders to Pitt, Quebec, 21 September 1759, PRO, CO5/51 fol. 45.
23. *Memoirs of the Siege of Quebec, the Capital of all Canada, and of the Retreat of Monsieur de Bourlemaque* (Quebec, 1901), 28–9.
24. Knox, *Journal*, II: 95–6.
25. 'Fragment of a Journal of the Siege from the Original in the Library of Congress at Washington', LAC, MG 18 N 18, vol. IV, file 7.
26. 'Extracts from Journal of the Particular Transactions during the Siege of Quebec', in Doughty and Parmelee, *Siege of Quebec*, V: 187–8.
27. 'A Journal of the Expedition up the River St Lawrence', in *A Journal of the Expedition up the River St Lawrence (by a Sgt Major in Hopson's Grenadiers)* (Boston, 1759), 17–18.
28. Knox, *Journal*, II: 96.
29. Vergor to Duc de Choiseul, Secretary of State for Marine and the Colonies, reprinted in full in Stacey, *Quebec 1759*, Appendix D, 211–12.
30. Knox, *Journal*, II: 96. This 'precipice' was actually a track. It was not nearly as steep as the route taken by Howe's men.
31. 'Extracts from Journal of the Particular Transactions during the Siege of Quebec', in Doughty and Parmelee, *Siege of Quebec*, V: 188.
32. Knox, *Journal*, II: 96.
33. Ibid.
34. 'Letter of Holmes, *Lowestoft* off Foulon in the River St. Laurence, above Quebec 18 September 1759', in Doughty and Parmelee, *Siege of Quebec*, IV: 296.
35. *General Orders in Wolfe's Army*, 53.
36. Log: *Squirrel*, 13 September 1759, in Wood, *The Logs of the Conquest of Canada*, 300.
37. Wolfe's 'Family Journal', PRONI, DOD 162/77 C, 17.
38. Barré's comments were made to Henry Caldwell over a decade later; he in turn reported them to Murray. See Henry Caldwell to Murray, 1 November 1772, quoted in Stacey, *Quebec 1759*, 146.
39. Wolfe's 'Family Journal', PRONI, DOD 162/77 C, 17.
40. Henry Caldwell to Murray, 1 November 1772, quoted in Stacey, *Quebec 1759*, 146.
41. Moncrief, *A Short Account of the Expedition against Quebec Commanded by Major-General Wolfe in the Year 1759*, 38.

42. 'Extracts from Journal of the Particular Transactions during the Siege of Quebec', in Doughty and Parmelee, *Siege of Quebec*, V: 188.
43. Wolfe's 'Family Journal', PRONI, DOD 162/77 C, 17.
44. Moncrief, *A Short Account of the Expedition against Quebec Commanded by Major-General Wolfe in the Year 1759*, 37–8.
45. Vaudreuil to Minister, 5 October 1759, in Stacey, *Quebec 1759*, Appendix C, 199.
46. Vaudreuil to Bougainville, 6 September 1759, 11 o'clock, in Doughty and Parmelee, *Siege of Quebec*, IV: 100.
47. R. Léger, ed., *Le Journal de Montcalm* (Montreal, 2007), 493.
48. Montcalm to Vaudreuil, 29 July 1759, in G. Frégault, *Canada: The War of Conquest* (Oxford, 1969), 253.
49. Léger, *Le Journal de Montcalm*, entry for 13 September 1759, 498–9.
50. Bernetz to Vaudreuil, in Stacey, *Quebec 1759*, 148.
51. Vaudreuil to Bougainville, 13 September 1759, 0645 hours, in Doughty and Parmelee, *Siege of Quebec*, IV: 126–7.
52. 'Extract of a Journal Kept at the Army Commanded by the Late Lt Gen de Montcalm', in O'Callaghan and Fernow, *Documents Relative to the Colonial History of the State of New York; Procured in Holland, England and France*, X: 1038.
53. Chevalier de Johnstone, *A Dialogue in Hades* (Literary and Historical Society of Quebec: Historical Documents, Second Series, Quebec, 1868), 40. Needless to say Vaudreuil claimed, in a letter written that night to de Lévis, that he 'did not tarry' in sending men to meet the threat on the Plains; see Vaudreuil to de Lévis, 13 September 1759, in H. R. Casgrain, ed., *Collection des manuscrits du Maréchal de Lévis* (12 vols., Montreal and Quebec, 1889–95), VIII: 106.
54. *Memoirs of the Siege of Quebec, the Capital of all Canada, and of the Retreat of Monsieur de Bourlemaque* (Quebec, 1901), 29.

Chapter Fourteen: The Battle of the Plains of Abraham

1. H. B. M. Best, 'Martin, Abraham', in *Dictionary of Canadian Biography* online.
2. Logs: *Dublin, Centurion, Hunter*, 12 September 1759, in W. Wood, ed., *The Logs of the Conquest of Canada* (Toronto, 1909), 222, 211, 232.
3. A. Doughty, ed., *An Historical Journal of the Campaigns in North America: For the Years 1757, 1758, 1759 and 1760 by Captain John Knox* (3 vols., Toronto, 1914–16), II: 98.
4. Robert MacPherson to Andrew MacPherson, Camp before Quebec, 16 September 1759, James Grant Papers, Library of Congress,

reprinted in full in I. McCulloch, *Sons of the Mountain: The Highland Regiments in the French and Indian War, 1756–1767* (2 vols., Toronto, 2006), I: 185.

5. Major Moncrief, *A Short Account of the Expedition against Quebec Commanded by Major-General Wolfe in the Year 1759* (Quebec, 1901), 38–9.

6. Wolfe's 'Family Journal', PRONI, DOD 162/77 C, 17.

7. Ibid.

8. *A Plan of Discipline Composed for the Use of the Militia of the County of Norfolk* (2 vols, London, 1759) II: 19.

9. Ibid., II: 21–3.

10. *A Plan of Discipline Composed for the Use of the Militia of the County of Norfolk*, II: 22, 39.

11. *Extract from a Manuscript Journal Relating to the Operations before Quebec in 1759, Kept by Colonel Malcolm Fraser, the Lt of the 78th (Fraser's Highlanders) and Serving in that Campaign* (Literary and Historical Society of Quebec: Historical Documents, Second Series, 1868), 20.

12. Ibid., II: 43.

13. 'Extracts from Journal of the Particular Transactions during the Siege of Quebec', in A. Doughty and G. Parmelee, eds., *The Siege of Quebec and the Battle of the Plains of Abraham* (6 vols., Quebec, 1901), V: 188.

14. Townshend to Pitt, Camp before Quebec, 20 September 1759, 'Letters and Papers Relating to the Siege of Quebec in the Possession of the Marquess of Townshend', in Doughty and Parmelee, *Siege of Quebec*, V: 216–17.

15. Knox, *Journal*, I: 488.

16. 'John Johnson's Journal', in Doughty and Parmelee, *Siege of Quebec*, V: 107.

17. Stuart Reid has pointed out that had they been drawn up on the usual frontage of twenty-four inches per file as laid down in 1756 *Regulations* then it ought to have been about eight hundred yards. Instead Johnson says they were thirty-six inches apart.

18. *Extract from a Manuscript Journal Relating to the Operations before Quebec in 1759, Kept by Colonel Malcolm Fraser, the Lt of the 78th*, 24.

19. 'Morning State, 13 September 1759', PRO, CO 5/51, fol. 102.

20. McCulloch, *Sons of the Mountain*, II: 168. Many of the 78th pipe reels and airs have survived because they were written down in 1816 by Simon Fraser of Knockie, the son of a 78th officer who had an extensive knowledge of Gaelic tunes.

21. 'Letter from Quebec, 7 October 1759', from the *Derby Mercury*, 30 November to 7 December 1759, quoted in S. Brumwell, *Paths of Glory: The Life and Death of General James Wolfe* (London, 2006), 279.
22. 'Extract of a Journal Kept at the Army Commanded by the Late Lt Gen de Montcalm', in O'Callaghan and Fernow, *Documents*, X: 1039.
23. *Extract from a Manuscript Journal Relating to the Operations before Quebec in 1759, Kept by Colonel Malcolm Fraser, the Lt of the 78th*, 23.
24. 'Letter of Holmes, *Lowestoft* off Foulon in the River St. Laurence, above Quebec 18 September 1759', in Doughty and Parmelee, *Siege of Quebec*, IV: 297.
25. 'A Journal of the Siege of Quebec by Brigadier Townshend', in Doughty and Parmelee, *Siege of Quebec*, IV: 269.
26. Wolfe to Monckton, 6 August 1759, LAC, Monckton Papers, XXII, rl C-336.
27. Moncrief, *A Short Account of the Expedition against Quebec Commanded by Major-General Wolfe in the Year 1759*, 41.
28. Ibid., 41; 'Letters and Papers Relating to the Siege of Quebec in the Possession of the Marquess of Townshend', in Doughty and Parmelee, *Siege of Quebec*, V: 214.
29. 'General Wolfe to his Army', in the appendix to the Murray Journal, printed in Knox, *Journal*, III: 335–6.
30. 'John Johnson's Journal', in Doughty and Parmelee, *Siege of Quebec*, V: 102, 103–4.
31. Knox, *Journal*, II: 99.
32. 'A Journal of the Siege of Quebec by Brigadier Townshend', in Doughty and Parmelee, *Siege of Quebec*, IV: 269.
33. 'An Account of the Action which Happened near Quebec 13th September 1759', in S. Pargellis, ed., *Military Affairs in North America, 1748–65: Selected Documents from the Cumberland Papers in Windsor Castle* (New York, 1936), 438.
34. Moncrief, *A Short Account of the Expedition against Quebec Commanded by Major-General Wolfe in the Year 1759*, 40, 42.
35. 'John Johnson's Journal', in Doughty and Parmelee, *Siege of Quebec*, V: 104.
36. Knox, *Journal*, II: 99.
37. *Memoirs of the Siege of Quebec, the Capital of all Canada, and of the Retreat of Monsieur de Bourlemaque*, 29–30.
38. 'A Journal of the Siege of Quebec by Brigadier Townshend', in Doughty and Parmelee, *Siege of Quebec*, IV: 269.

39. Williamson to Board of Ordnance, Quebec, 20 September 1759, LAC, rl A-573.
40. 'Extract of a Journal Kept at the Army Commanded by the Late Lt Gen de Montcalm', in O'Callaghan and Fernow, *Documents*, X: 1039.
41. R. Holmes, *Redcoat: The British Solider in the Age of Horse and Musket* (London, 2001), 241.
42. 'Journal du siège de Québec', in *The Northcliffe Collection* (Ottawa, 1926), XXX: 229.
43. Vaudreuil to Lévis, 13 September 1759, in H. R. Casgrain, eds., *Collection des manuscrits du Maréchal de Lévis* (12 vols., Montreal and Quebec, 1889–95), VIII: 106.
44. Montreuil to Belle Isle, Pointe aux Trembles, 22 September 1759, in O'Callaghan and Fernow, *Documents*, X: 1014.
45. Ibid.
46. 'Extract of a Journal Kept at the Army Commanded by the Late Lt Gen de Montcalm', in O'Callaghan and Fernow, *Documents*, X: 1039.
47. 'Letter of Admiral Holmes, *Lowestoft*, River above Quebec, 18 September 1759', in Doughty and Parmelee, *Siege of Quebec*, IV: 297.
48. Chevalier de Johnstone, *A Dialogue in Hades* (Literary and Historical Society of Quebec: Second Series, Quebec, 1868–71), 43.
49. R. Léger, ed., *Le Journal de Montcalm* (Montreal, 2007), entry for 13 September 1759, 500.
50. 'An Account of the Action which Happened near Quebec 13th September 1759', in Pargellis, *Military Affairs in North America*, 438.
51. *Memoirs of the Siege of Quebec, the Capital of all Canada, and of the Retreat of Monsieur de Bourlemaque*, 30.
52. 'Extract of a Journal Kept at the Army Commanded by the Late Lt Gen de Montcalm', in O'Callaghan and Fernow, *Documents*, X: 1039.
53. J. B. N. R. de Ramezay, *Mémoire du sieur de Ramezay, commandant à Québec, au sujet de la reddition de cette ville, le 18 septembre 1759* (Quebec, 1861).
54. Vaudreuil to Berryer, HQ St Augustin, 4 Leagues from Quebec, 21 September 1759, in O'Callaghan and Fernow, *Documents*, X: 1010.
55. A royal regiment like the Royal Roussillon had permission to use fleurs-de-lis. Its colour had quarters of blue, scarlet, buff, and green and in the white cross between them, a scattering of fleurs-de-lis. The connection of lilies with the royal house of France stretched back to the conversion of the Frankish king Clovis in 493; they were adopted as a symbol by Charlemagne and all subsequent French monarchs.

56. Knox, *Journal*, II: 101.
57. Moncrief, *A Short Account of the Expedition against Quebec Commanded by Major-General Wolfe in the Year 1759*, 42.
58. Léger, *Le Journal de Montcalm*, entry for 13 September 1759, 500.
59. Malartic to Bourlamaque, 28 September 1759, in C. P. Stacey, *Quebec 1759: The Siege and the Battle* (Toronto, 2002), 162.
60. R. Léger, ed., *Le Journal du Chevalier de Lévis* (Montreal, 2008), 156.
61. *Extract from a Manuscript Journal Relating to the Operations before Quebec in 1759, Kept by Colonel Malcolm Fraser, the Lt of the 78th*, 20–1.
62. B. P. Hughes, *British Smooth Bore Artillery: The Muzzle Loading Artillery of the 18th and 19th Centuries* (London, 1969), 52–3. The figures he cites are from a later period although the equipment remained essentially unchanged. They are corroborated by studies made by the Prussian army during the Seven Years War.
63. Charles-Joseph Fürst von Ligne, quoted in C. Duffy, *The Military Experience in the Age of Reason* (London, 1987), 199–200.
64. If a regiment was too full of raw recruits it was not 'fit for service'. In 1755 the 5th and 7th Foot were brought to England and put on the British establishment from Ireland. After a few months around 50 per cent of both were recruits and both were reported 'too full of recruits to be as yet fit for service'. They would remain unfit for a year to come. J. Houlding, *Fit for Service: The Training of the British Army, 1715–1795* (Oxford, 1981), 133.
65. Malartic to Bourlamaque, 28 September 1759, in Stacey, *Quebec 1759*, 162.
66. Moncrief, *A Short Account of the Expedition against Quebec Commanded by Major-General Wolfe in the Year 1759*, 42.
67. *Extract from a Manuscript Journal Relating to the Operations before Quebec in 1759, Kept by Colonel Malcolm Fraser, the Lt of the 78th*, 20.
68. *An Accurate and Authentic Journal of the Siege of Quebec, 1759, by a Gentleman in an Eminent Station on the Spot* (London, 1759), 41.
69. *Extract from a Manuscript Journal Relating to the Operations before Quebec in 1759, Kept by Colonel Malcolm Fraser, the Lt of the 78th*, 24.
70. 'John Johnson's Journal', in Doughty and Parmelee, *Siege of Quebec*, V: 104.
71. Frederick the Great, *Règles de ce qu'on exige d'un bon commandeur de battalion* (1773), in Duffy, *The Military Experience in the Age of Reason*, 240.

72. *A Plan of Discipline Composed for the Use of the Militia of the County of Norfolk*, I: 1; II: 6.
73. The temptation to dull fear with alcoholic befuddlement was nothing new. 'Dutch courage' was an expression born in the seventeenth century when English troops campaigned in the Low Countries. The local tipple provided inspiration when the men's patriotism or sense of Protestant solidarity fell short.
74. Knox, *Journal*, II: 101.
75. 'Battle of Quebec, 20 September 1759, Quebec', in Letters of Colonel Alexander Murray 1742–59, in H. C. Wylley, ed., *The Sherwood Foresters: Notts and Derby Regiment. Regimental Annual 1926* (London, 1927), 216.
76. *A Plan of Discipline Composed for the Use of the Militia of the County of Norfolk*, I: 16.
77. Two of the most senior officers on the field that day, Mackellar and Lieutenant Colonel Murray, both suggest that the British line, in the words of Murray, 'advanced very slowly and resolutely' towards the French attack and started platoon firing when they were in range. When the two sides were very close then they stopped and gave one massive battalion volley. See 'Battle of Quebec, 20 September 1759, Quebec', in Letters of Colonel Alexander Murray 1742–59 in Wylley, *The Sherwood Foresters: Notts and Derby Regiment. Regimental Annual 1926*, 216 and Moncrief, *A Short Account of the Expedition against Quebec Commanded by Major-General Wolfe in the Year 1759*, 42. Other accounts emphasize the unmoving wait for the French attack and the scale of the opening volley when it came.
78. Knox, *Journal*, II: 101.
79. The Prussian musket issued a generation after the Seven Years War was designed in such a way as to make it virtually impossible to aim.
80. 'From an Officer at Quebec', *Scots Magazine*, 21 (October 1759), 552 in LAC, MG 18 N18, vol. V.
81. The Prussians reckoned on 60 per cent of their musket balls hitting a line of enemy troops at seventy-five yards. A Norfolk militia regiment conducted the same experiment and only 20 per cent of their shots hit the target. At half that distance the well-drilled regiments of Wolfe's army would have achieved significantly better results. For the figures from these two experiments see Houlding, *Fit for Service: The Training of the British Army, 1715–1795*, 262 and Holmes, *Redcoat: The British Solider in the Age of Horse and Musket*, 198. At the battle of Fontenoy in May 1745 the British foot guards, after much saluting and mutual insistence that the other side fire first, poured a

volley into two battalions of the *gardes françaises* at fifty yards. Four hundred French guardsmen were hit.

82. Houlding, *Fit for Service*, 318.

83. Holmes, *Redcoat*, 219.

84. 'Instructions for the 20th Regiment', Canterbury, December 1755, *General Wolfe's Instructions to Young Officers* (London, 1778), 49.

85. 'Extracts from Journal of the Particular Transactions during the Siege of Quebec', in Doughty and Parmelee, *Siege of Quebec*, V: 188.

86. 'John Johnson's Journal', in Doughty and Parmelee, *Siege of Quebec*, V: 104.

87. Robert MacPherson (*Caipal Mhor*) to Andrew MacPherson, Camp before Quebec, 16 September 1759, James Grant Papers, Library of Congress, reprinted in full in McCulloch, *Sons of the Mountain*, I: 185–6.

88. *A Journal of the Expedition up the River St Lawrence (by a Sgt Major in Hopson's Grenadiers)* (Boston, 1759), 11.

89. Knox, *Journal*, II: 101.

90. 'John Johnson's Journal', in Doughty and Parmelee, *Siege of Quebec*, V: 104.

91. Wolfe's 'Family Journal', PRONI, DOD 162/77 C, 18.

92. Knox, *Journal*, II: 114.

93. Wolfe's 'Family Journal', PRONI, DOD 162/77 C, 18; Johnson, Knox, and Henderson all left descriptions of the next few minutes which chime with Wolfe's 'Family Journal'.

94. Knox's description is in Knox, *Journal*, II: 114. Henderson was rewarded for his service to the General with a commission in Bragg's 28th Regiment. John Johnson claimed that Wolfe's last words were 'Do they run already: then I shall die happy'; in Doughty and Parmelee, *Siege of Quebec*, V: 105. There are several other versions such as Holmes' letter on Doughty and Parmelee, *Siege of Quebec*, IV: 298; his 'Family Journal' reports that on being given the news of the French retreat he 'smiled and said 'twas as expected'; PRONI, DOD 162/77 C, 18.

95. 'A Journal of the Siege of Quebec by Brigadier Townshend', in Doughty and Parmelee, *Siege of Quebec*, IV: 269.

96. *Extract from a Manuscript Journal Relating to the Operations before Quebec in 1759, Kept by Colonel Malcolm Fraser, the Lt of the 78th*, 20.

97. 'From an Officer at Quebec', *Scots Magazine*, 21 (October 1759), 552, LAC, MG 18 N 18, vol. V.

98. *Extract from a Manuscript Journal Relating to the Operations before Quebec in 1759, Kept by Colonel Malcolm Fraser, the Lt of the 78th*, 20.

99. *General Wolfe's Instructions to Young Officers*, 47.
100. 'From an Officer at Quebec', *Scots Magazine*, 21 (October 1759), 552 in LAC, MG 18 N 18, vol. V.
101. 'Letter of Holmes, *Lowestoft* off Foulon in the River St. Laurence, above Quebec 18 September 1759', in Doughty and Parmelee, *Siege of Quebec*, IV: 298.
102. Robert MacPherson (*Caipal Mhor*) to Andrew MacPherson, Camp before Quebec, 16 September 1759, James Grant Papers, Library of Congress, reprinted in full in McCulloch, *Sons of the Mountain*, I: 186.
103. Sergeant James Thompson Journal, quoted in McCulloch, *Sons of the Mountain*, I: 189.
104. 'John Johnson's Journal', in Doughty and Parmelee, *Siege of Quebec*, V: 105.
105. *Extract from a Manuscript Journal Relating to the Operations before Quebec in 1759, Kept by Colonel Malcolm Fraser, the Lt of the 78th*, 21.
106. 'Genuine Letters from a Volunteer in the British Service at Quebec', in Doughty and Parmelee, *Siege of Quebec*, V: 23.
107. 'Battle of Quebec, 20 September 1759, Quebec', in Letters of Colonel Alexander Murray 1742–59 in Wylley, *The Sherwood Foresters: Notts and Derby Regiment. Regimental Annual 1926*, 216.
108. 'Extract of a Journal Kept at the Army Commanded by the Late Lt Gen de Montcalm', in O'Callaghan and Fernow, *Documents*, X: 1039.
109. Wolfe's 'Family Journal', PRONI, DOD 162/77 C, 18.
110. Vaudreuil to Berryer, HQ St Augustin, 4 Leagues from Quebec, 21 September 1759, in O'Callaghan and Fernow, *Documents*, X: 1011.
111. Vaudreuil to de Lévis, 13 September 1759, in Casgrain, *Collection des manuscrits du Maréchal de Lévis*, VIII: 107.
112. Logs: *Stirling Castle*, 13 September 1759, in Wood, *The Logs of the Conquest of Canada*, 315.
113. *Extract from a Manuscript Journal Relating to the Operations before Quebec in 1759, Kept by Colonel Malcolm Fraser, the Lt of the 78th*, 22–4.
114. Wolfe's artilleryman Colonel Williamson claimed that the French commander was hit by some rounds from a canister fired by one of his six pounders. It capped what he regarded as a victory won entirely by his men and guns. He wrote to a senior British officer that 'we fired our cannon so briskly seconded by the regiments that we fairly

beat them in the open field'. Williamson to Sackville, 20 September 1759, in LAC, rl A-573.

115. Townshend to Lady Ferrers, Camp before Quebec, 20 September 1759, in 'Letters and Papers Relating to the Siege of Quebec in the Possession of the Marquess of Townshend', in Doughty and Parmelee, *Siege of Quebec*, V: 202.

116. 'A Journal of the Siege of Quebec by Brigadier Townshend', in Doughty and Parmelee, *Siege of Quebec*, IV: 270.

117. Townshend to Pitt, Camp before Quebec, 20 September 1759, in 'Letters and Papers Relating to the Siege of Quebec in the Possession of the Marquess of Townshend', in Doughty and Parmelee, *Siege of Quebec*, V: 218.

118. Bougainville's Journal for 1759–60 in E. P. Hamilton, ed., *Adventure in the Wilderness: The American Journals of Louis Antoine de Bougainville, 1756–1760* (Norman, OK, 1990), 320–1.

119. Bougainville's Journal for 1759–60 in ibid., 321.

120. Townshend to Pitt, Camp before Quebec, 20 September 1759, in 'Letters and Papers Relating to the Siege of Quebec in the Possession of the Marquess of Townshend', in Doughty and Parmelee, *Siege of Quebec*, V: 218.

121. Moncrief, *A Short Account of the Expedition against Quebec Commanded by Major-General Wolfe in the Year 1759*, 43.

122. Monckton to Pitt, River St Lawrence, Camp at Point Lévis, 15 September 1759, PRO, CO 5/51 fol. 88.

123. Townshend to Amherst, Camp before Quebec, 26 September 1759, 'Letters and Papers Relating to the Siege of Quebec in the Possession of the Marquess of Townshend', in Doughty and Parmelee, *Siege of Quebec*, V: 221.

Chapter Fifteen: 'Our rejoicings are not yet over'

1. *Siege of Quebec and Conquest of Canada: in 1759. By a Nun of the General Hospital of Quebec* (Quebec, 1855), 9.

2. Sergeant James Thompson Journal, quoted in I. McCulloch, *Sons of the Mountain: The Highland Regiments in the French and Indian War, 1756–1767* (2 vols., Toronto, 2006), I: 189.

3. PRO, CO 5/51 fol. 97.

4. Robert MacPherson (*Caipal Mhor*) to Andrew MacPherson, Camp before Quebec, 16 September 1759, James Grant Papers, Library of Congress, reprinted in full in McCulloch, *Sons of the Mountain*, I: 186.

5. Vaudreuil to de Lévis, 13 September 1759, in H. R. Casgrain, ed., *Collection des manuscrits du Maréchal de Lévis* (12 vols., Montreal and Quebec, 1889–95), VIII: 106.

6. *Memoirs of the Siege of Quebec, the Capital of all Canada, and of the Retreat of Monsieur de Bourlemaque* (Quebec, 1901), 31.

7. Major Moncrief, *A Short Account of the Expedition against Quebec Commanded by Major-General Wolfe in the Year 1759* (Quebec, 1901), 44.

8. 'A Journal of the Siege of Quebec by Brigadier Townshend', in A. Doughty and G. Parmelee, eds., *The Siege of Quebec and the Battle of the Plains of Abraham* (6 vols., Quebec, 1901), IV: 270.

9. R. Holmes, *Redcoat: The British Solider in the Age of Horse and Musket* (London, 2001), 95–6, 260.

10. Logs: *Hunter*, 13 September 1759, in W. Wood, ed., *The Logs of the Conquest of Canada* (Toronto, 1909), 232.

11. 'From an Officer at Quebec', *Scots Magazine*, 21 (October 1759) 552, LAC, MG 18 N 18, vol. V.

12. 'Extracts from Journal of the Particular Transactions during the Siege of Quebec', in Doughty and Parmelee, *Siege of Quebec*, V: 189.

13. Murray to Amherst, Quebec, 19 May 1760, in A. Doughty, ed., *An Historical Journal of the Campaigns in North America: For the Years 1757, 1758, 1759 and 1760 by Captain John Knox* (3 vols., Toronto, 1914–16), III: 439.

14. Moncrief, *A Short Account of the Expedition against Quebec Commanded by Major-General Wolfe in the Year 1759*, 45.

15. *Extract from a Manuscript Journal Relating to the Operations before Quebec in 1759, Kept by Colonel Malcolm Fraser, the Lt of the 78th (Fraser's Highlanders) and Serving in that Campaign* (Literary and Historical Society of Quebec: Historical Documents, Second Series, 1868), 25.

16. Charles-Joseph Fürst von Ligne, quoted in C. Duffy, *The Military Experience in the Age of Reason* (London, 1987), 260.

17. 'Extract of a Journal Kept at the Army Commanded by the Late Lt Gen de Montcalm', in E. O'Callaghan and B. Fernow, eds., *Documents Relative to the Colonial History of the State of New York; Procured in Holland, England and France* (15 vols., Albany, NY, 1853–87), X: 1040.

18. Printed in Knox, *Journal*, II: 109.

19. Knox reports one exchange that has become widely repeated. This is slightly curious given that the excellent Knox is at his weakest when describing relations within the French high command. Here his source for the last moments of Montcalm is very obscure.

Nevertheless he reports that Montcalm told the officers who pressed him for orders, 'I'll neither give orders nor interfere any farther; I have much business that must be attended to, of greater moment than your ruined garrison and this wretched country: my time is very short, – therefore pray leave me – I wish you all comfort, and to be happily extricated from your present perplexities.' Knox, *Journal*, II: 112.

20. *Memoirs of the Siege of Quebec, the Capital of all Canada, and of the Retreat of Monsieur de Bourlemaque* (Quebec, 1901), 31.
21. 'Extract of a Journal Kept at the Army Commanded by the Late Lt Gen de Montcalm', in O'Callaghan and Fernow, *Documents*, X: 1040.
22. *Memoirs of the Siege of Quebec, the Capital of all Canada, and of the Retreat of Monsieur de Bourlemaque*, 32.
23. R. Léger, ed., *Le Journal de Montcalm* (Montreal, 2007), 502.
24. Quoted in C. Lloyd, *The Capture of Quebec* (London, 1959), 143.
25. Moncrief, *A Short Account of the Expedition against Quebec Commanded by Major-General Wolfe in the Year 1759*, 46.
26. 'M de Vaudreuil's Instructions to M de Ramezay, 13 September, at Nine o'Clock at Night', in O'Callaghan and Fernow, *Documents*, X: 1004.
27. Monckton's Order Book, in *The Northcliffe Collection* (Ottawa, 1926), XXIII: 167.
28. Knox, *Journal*, II: 102–4.
29. 'Genuine Letters from a Volunteer in the British Service at Quebec', in Doughty and Parmelee, *Siege of Quebec*, V: 23.
30. *Extract from a Manuscript Journal Relating to the Operations before Quebec in 1759, Kept by Colonel Malcolm Fraser, the Lt of the 78th*, 24.
31. Iain Campbell's Gaelic song is transcribed in McCulloch, *Sons of the Mountain*, I: 189.
32. *New York Gazette*, 3 December 1759, under 'Philadelphia, November 29', citing letter from Quebec, 14 September 1759, quoted in S. Brumwell, *Paths of Glory: The Life and Death of General James Wolfe* (London, 2006), 287.
33. Browne to his father, Louisbourg, 17 November 1759, in Brumwell, *Paths of Glory*, 287.
34. Saunders to Townshend, *Stirling Castle*, 13 September 1759, in C. V. F. Townshend, *The Military Life of George First Marquess Townshend* (Toronto, 1907), 242.
35. '*Neptune* at Sea', 4 June 1759, in B. Willson, ed., *The Life and Letters of James Wolfe* (New York, 1909), 483–4.

36. *General Orders in Wolfe's Army during the Expedition up the River St Lawrence, 1759* (Literary and Historical Society of Quebec: Historical Documents, Fourth Series, Quebec, 1875), 54.

37. *A Journal of the Expedition up the River St Lawrence* (Literary and Historical Society of Quebec: Historical Documents, Second Series, Quebec, 1868), 12–13. Holmes reports that there were '17 pieces of battering cannon from below, besides other of a smaller calibre, mortars, shells, shots, powder, plank etc' brought up by the 17th. See 'Letter of Admiral Holmes, *Lowestoft*, River above Quebec, 18 September 1759', in Doughty and Parmelee, *Siege of Quebec*, IV: 298.

38. 'Letter of Admiral Holmes, *Lowestoft*, River above Quebec, 18 September 1759', in Doughty and Parmelee, *Siege of Quebec*, IV: 298.

39. Townshend to Monckton, 14 September 1759, LAC, MG 18 M 1, vol. XXXI.

40. J. B. N. R. de Ramezay, *Mémoire du sieur de Ramezay, commandant à Québec, au sujet de la reddition de cette ville, le 18 septembre 1759* (Quebec, 1861).

41. 'Brigadier Townshend's Journal of the Voyage to America and Campaign against Quebec, 1759', in Doughty and Parmelee, *Siege of Quebec*, V: 270.

42. 'Minutes of the Council of War Previous to the Surrender of Quebec', Quebec, 15 September 1759, in O'Callaghan and Fernow, *Documents*, X: 1007–9.

43. Ramezay to Vaudreuil, 17 September 1759, in *The Northcliffe Collection*, 441.

44. Saunders to Clevland, 21 September 1759, in J. B. Hattendorf, R. J. B. Knight, A. W. H. Pearsall, N. A. M. Rodger, and G. Till, eds., *British Naval Documents 1204–1960* (Naval Records Society CXXI, 1993), No. 225, p. 393; 'Letter of Admiral Holmes, *Lowestoft*, River above Quebec, 18 September 1759', in Doughty and Parmelee, *Siege of Quebec*, IV: 299.

45. *Memoirs of the Siege of Quebec, the Capital of all Canada, and of the Retreat of Monsieur de Bourlemaque*, 33.

46. Daine to Belle Isle, Quebec, 8 October 1759, in O'Callaghan and Fernow, *Documents*, X: 1015.

47. 'Monckton's Order Book', in *The Northcliffe Collection*, XXIII: 171. The tone of Wolfe's 'Family Journal' was not ameliorated by the death of its hero. Spiteful criticism of Townshend and Murray reached new heights now that they were actually the two most senior officers in the army. The author claimed that 'opposition to Mr Wolfe had linked Townshend and Murray ... [but with] Mr Wolfe dead,

opposition to each other went so far, that they parted with irreconcilable hatred'. It states that 'Murray had persuaded Mr Townshend that the remains of the enemy's army were still dangerous and that great precautions were necessary towards fortifying the rear of the camp which was an occupation that became the commander in chief, and in the meantime that he would carry on the works against the place: Townshend consented, and Murray having gained his ends, made the other the subject of ridicule at his table and insinuated things to dishonour on that very account'. Wolfe's 'Family Journal', PRONI, DOD 162/77 C, 19.

48. Montresor to Colonel Montresor, Quebec, 18 October 1759, in Doughty and Parmelee, *Siege of Quebec*, IV: 333.
49. Knox, *Journal*, II: 121.
50. 'A Journal of the Siege of Quebec by Brigadier Townshend', in Doughty and Parmelee, *Siege of Quebec*, IV: 273.
51. *General Orders in Wolfe's Army*, 55–6.
52. Knox, *Journal*, II: 125.
53. Articles printed in full in 'A Journal of the Siege of Quebec by Brigadier Townshend', in Doughty and Parmelee, *Siege of Quebec*, IV: 273ff.
54. Townshend to Lady Ferrers, 'Camp before Quebec', 20 September 1759, in 'Letters and Papers Relating to the Siege of Quebec in the Possession of the Marquess of Townshend', in Doughty and Parmelee, *Siege of Quebec*, V: 202.
55. Wolfe's 'Family Journal', PRONI, DOD 162/77 C, 20. It is worth noting that the draft surrender terms drawn up by Wolfe earlier in the summer and copied in *The Northcliffe Collection*, XXVI: 203–4 make no mention of prisoners taken and are very similar indeed to Townshend's eventual terms.
56. Townshend to Pitt, 20 September 1759, PRO, CO 5/51, fol. 92.
57. 'Letter of Admiral Holmes, Lowestoft, River above Quebec, 18 September 1759', in Doughty and Parmelee, *Siege of Quebec*, IV: 299.
58. Townshend to his mother, Lady Townshend, 'Camp before Quebec', 20 September 1759, in LAC, MG 18 L 7, fols. 20–1.
59. Townshend to Monckton, Quebec, 19 September 1759, LAC, MG 18 M 1, vol. XXXI.
60. Monckton to Townshend, 18 September 1759, *Medway*, in C. V. F. Townshend, *The Military Life of George First Marquess Townshend* (Toronto, 1907), 248–9.
61. 'Vaudreuil to Berryer, St Augustin, 4 Leagues from Quebec, 21 September, 1759', in O'Callaghan and Fernow, *Documents*, X: 1011.
62. Hamilton, *Bougainville*, 321.

63. Ibid., 325.
64. Ibid., 321.
65. *Governor Murray's Journal of Quebec, from 18th September 1759 to 25th May 1760* (Literary and Historical Society of Quebec: Historical Documents, Second Series, 1868), 2.
66. Moncrief, *A Short Account of the Expedition against Quebec Commanded by Major-General Wolfe in the Year 1759*, 50.
67. Colonel Williamson to the Principal Officers of His Majesty's Ordnance, 20 September 1759, Quebec, LAC, MG 18 L 5, IV and rl: A-573.
68. Knox, *Journal*, II: 135.
69. 'Extract of a Journal Kept at the Army Commanded by the Late Lt Gen de Montcalm', in O'Callaghan and Fernow, *Documents*, X: 1042.
70. Knox, *Journal*, II: 134.
71. *Extract from a Manuscript Journal Relating to the Operations before Quebec in 1759, Kept by Colonel Malcolm Fraser, the Lt of the 78th*, 25.
72. 'Jeremiah Pearson His Book 1759', LAC, MG 18 N 43.
73. Moncrief, *A Short Account of the Expedition against Quebec Commanded by Major-General Wolfe in the Year 1759*, 51, 53–4.
74. Townshend to Lady Ferrers, 'Camp before Quebec', 20 September 1759, in 'Letters and Papers Relating to the Siege of Quebec in the Possession of the Marquess of Townshend', in Doughty and Parmelee, *Siege of Quebec*, V: 202.
75. Townshend to his mother, Lady Townshend, 'Camp before Quebec', 20 September 1759, in LAC, MG 18 L 7, fols. 20–1.
76. Townshend to Murray, 5 October 1759, LAC, James Murray Collection, MG 23 GII 1, also microfilm A-1992. Bundle 1 letter 5.
77. Murray to Townshend, 5 October 1759, in 'Letters and Papers Relating to the Siege of Quebec in the Possession of the Marquess of Townshend', in Doughty and Parmelee, *Siege of Quebec*, V: 205–6.
78. Townshend to Pitt, 20 September 1759, PRO, CO 5/51, fol. 92.
79. Hattendorf, Knight, Pearsall, Rodger, and Till, *British Naval Documents 1204–1960*, 393; on the dispatch John Clevland, Secretary to the Admiralty, wrote that the Lords 'have the highest satisfaction in the account he gives them ... and the more so that it appears to Brig Townshend's letters that the officers and men belonging to his Majesty's ships contributed so much to the reduction of the place'.
80. Saunders to Admiralty, Cork, 11 December 1759, in C. H. Little, ed., *Despatches of Vice Admiral Saunders* (Halifax, NS, 1958), 27.

81. Townshend, *The Military Life of George First Marquess Townshend*, 251.
82. Pitt to Newcastle, 'Tuesday night past eleven', 16 October 1759, reprinted in *Jackdaw* No. 23, collection of contemporary documents compiled by Richard Howard.
83. Quoted in A. McNairn, *Behold the Hero: General Wolfe and the Arts in the Eighteenth Century* (Montreal, 1997), 10.
84. R. Leeke to Lady Townshend, LAC, MG 18 L 7, fols. 23–4.
85. John Jones to Lady Townshend, Fakenham, 22 October 1759, LAC, MG 18 L 7, fol. 44; John Jones to Lady Townshend, Fakenham, 26 October 1759, LAC, MG 18 L 7, fol. 52.
86. George Burkston to Lady Townshend, Bradbourne, 22 October 1759, LAC, MG 18 L 7, fol. 45.
87. *Evening Post*, 4 February 1882, LAC, MG 18 N 51, I.
88. McNairn, *Behold the Hero*, 18.
89. Ibid.
90. Burke, *Annual Register*, 1759, 43, in B. Willson, ed., *The Life and Letters of James Wolfe* (New York, 1909), 499–500.
91. Walpole, *Memoirs of George II*, II: 385, quoted in Willson, *The Life and Letters of James Wolfe*, 500.
92. McNairn, *Behold the Hero*, 8. A monument was raised. It took a decade to complete and consists of a large bronze relief showing the landings at Anse au Foulon, on top of which sit two lions and a neoclassical sarcophagus. The top of the pyramid is Wolfe's death scene. The hero is naked and muscle bound, while angels wait to escort him to heaven and under his feet is the flag of France.
93. McNairn, *Behold the Hero*, 138–9.
94. Ibid., 182.
95. R. Middleton, *The Bells of Victory: The Pitt-Newcastle Ministry and the Conduct of the Seven Years' War 1757–1762* (Cambridge, 1985), 146.
96. J. R. Dull, *The French Navy and the Seven Years War* (Lincoln, NB, 2005), 155.
97. Captain Richard Gardiner to the Honourable George Hobart Esq., 18 February 1761, in *Memoirs of the Siege of Quebec, the Capital of all Canada, and of the Retreat of Monsieur de Bourlemaque*, 3–8.
98. T. Clayton, *Tars* (London, 2007), 150.
99. 'Order Book of the Royal American Regiment at Quebec from 24th September 1759 to 27th February 1760', in Royal Green Jackets Museum.
100. 'Return of Killed, Wounded, Missing, during the Campaign', in *The Northcliffe Collection*, XXI: 144; Moncrief, *A Short Account of the*

Expedition against Quebec Commanded by Major-General Wolfe in the Year 1759, 52.

101. Montresor to Colonel Montresor, Quebec, 18 October 1759, in Doughty and Parmelee, *Siege of Quebec*, IV: 331-2.

102. I. McCulloch, *Highlander in the French–Indian War 1756–67* (Oxford, 2008), 35.

103. 'Order Book of the Royal American Regiment at Quebec from 24th September 1759 to 27th February 1760', 6 October 1759.

104. John Johnson, 'Memoirs of the Siege of Quebec', in Doughty and Parmelee, *Siege of Quebec*, V: 117.

105. C. Lloyd, *The Capture of Quebec* (London, 1959), 149.

106. *Canadian Dictionary of Biography* online http://www. biographi.ca/EN/ShowBio.asp?BioId=35446andquery=pontbriand.

107. *Governor Murray's Journal of Quebec, from 18th September 1759 to 25th May 1760* (Literary and Historical Society of Quebec: Historical Documents, Second Series, 1868), 8–9.

108. J.-F. Récher, *Journal du siège de Québec en 1759* (Quebec, 1959), entry for 7 November 1759. Perhaps it was John Lord who was executed on 16 November 1759 for 'robbing a French inhabitant'. 'Order Book of the Royal American Regiment at Quebec from 24th September 1759 to 27th February 1760'.

109. *Extract from a Manuscript Journal Relating to the Operations before Quebec in 1759, Kept by Colonel Malcolm Fraser, the Lt of the 78th*, 26–7. Murray issued orders on how to deal with cases of frostbite: 'Doctor Russell recommends that every person to whom this accident should happen should be particularly careful to avoid going near fire and to have ye parts so frost bit immediately rubbed with snow by one who has a warm hand, and as soon as can be afterwards put into a blanket or something of that kind that will restore heat to the part.' 'Order Book of the Royal American Regiment at Quebec from 24th September 1759 to 27th February 1760'.

110. McCulloch, *Sons of the Mountain*, I: 192.

111. *Extract from a Manuscript Journal Relating to the Operations before Quebec in 1759, Kept by Colonel Malcolm Fraser, the Lt of the 78th*, 29.

112. 'Murray's Account of Ste Foy', in Townshend, *The Military Life of George First Marquess Townshend*, 277.

113. John Johnson, 'Memoirs of the Siege of Quebec', in Doughty and Parmelee, *Siege of Quebec*, V: 120.

114. *Extract from a Manuscript Journal Relating to the Operations before Quebec in 1759, Kept by Colonel Malcolm Fraser, the Lt of the 78th*, 34.

115. Ibid., 32.
116. Knox, *Journal*, II: 415.
117. Quoted in M. Ward, *The Battle for Quebec, 1759* (Stroud, 2005), 235.

Epilogue

1. S. Brumwell, *Redcoats: The British Soldier and War in the Americas: 1755–63* (Cambridge, 2002), 157.
2. *Reasons for Keeping Guadeloupe at a Peace, Preferable to Canada, Explained in Five Letters, from a Gentleman in Guadeloupe to his Friend in London* (London, 1761), quoted in G. Frégault, *Canada: The War of Conquest* (Oxford, 1969), 309.
3. Ibid., 309–10.
4. Quoted in A. McNairn, *Behold the Hero: General Wolfe and the Arts in the Eighteenth Century* (Montreal, 1997), 27.
5. A letter to a Great M——r, on the Prospect of Peace ... By an Unprejudiced Observer (London, 1761), in Frégault, *Canada: The War of Conquest*, 313–14.
6. *The Interests of Great Britain Considered with Regard to her Colonies, and the Acquisitions of Canada and Guadeloupe. To which are Added, Observations Concerning the Increase of Mankind, Peopling of Countries, and* (London, 1760), quoted in Frégault, *Canada: The War of Conquest*, 304–5.
7. Voltaire, *Candide* (London, 1950), 110.
8. McNairn, *Behold the Hero*, 18.
9. Voltaire to Chauvelin, 3 November 1760, Les Delices, in The Voltaire Foundation, *The Complete Works of Voltaire*, vol. CVI, Correspondence XXII, 1968, letter D9378.
10. Quoted in Frégault, *Canada: The War of Conquest*, 321.
11. I. McCulloch and T. Todish, eds., *Through So Many Dangers: The Memoirs and Adventures of Robert Kirk, Late of the Royal Highland Regiment* (Toronto, 2004), 85, 104.
12. Either way Francophone Quebecers have remained as a homogeneous linguistic group which flourished in the twentieth century and recently has come very close to secession from Canada. A referendum in 1995 saw the independence vote at 49.4 per cent.
13. France's lust for revenge forced her tottering state into bankruptcy and despite victories over her nemesis, it was the beginning of the end for the absolutist monarchical state. Under a decade later it collapsed completely into near anarchy. Place Louis XV, the incompetent monarch who had been the author of her defeats, was renamed Place

de la Révolution and on 21 January 1793 his grandson and successor, Citoyen Louis Capet, formerly Louis XVI, went to the guillotine as a mob howled their approval.

14. Montcalm to de la Molé, 24 August 1759, Quebec, in LAC, MG 18 N 18, VII.

INDEX

forts *see under individual fort
name*
Fortitude 96
Foxes (Native Americans) 130
France: defeat in Quebec, effect
upon 403, 411, 417–18, 419,
422–3, 424–6; Canada, attitude
towards 55–8; Seven Years War
and xviii, 2, 3–9, 410–11,
417–18, 419–26
Franklin, Benjamin 5
Fraser, Captain Simon 332, 337
Fraser, Lieutenant-Colonel Simon
354, 416
Fraser, Malcolm 30, 226, 314;
brutality of British troops,
shocked by 163, 259; family and
history 25, 26; floating batteries,
on French 135; Foulon landings,
role in 326, 332; Plains of
Abraham, role in battle of 348,
350, 351, 365, 366, 375, 377–8,
385, 387; promoted 392;
Quebec, time inside 399, 414,
415, 416; Quebec batteries, on
French 206; sails from
Louisbourg to St Lawrence 32;
78th Regiment of Foot and 27,
105, 221, 263, 271, 348; *The
Death of General Wolfe*,
appearance in 409; wounded
366, 385, 392, 409, 416
Fraser, Simon 379–80
Frederick II of Prussia, King 6, 7,
56, 346–7, 367, 374
French army: Béarn battalion 352,
363–4, 365; British, relations
with 52, 146–7, 208, 219,
240–1, 242, 252–3; Canadian
allies and *see* Canadian

troops/militia; Canadian
habitants and 47, 50, 62, 162,
321; casualties, number of 370,
372–3, 382, 384–5, 386–7, 404,
416, commanders and tactics
44–58, 133, 134, 147–8,
214–15, 216–17 *see also under
individual commander name*;
*Compagnies franches de la
marine* 64; Deschambault, fight
Murray at 263–6; fail to follow
up successes of small-scale raids
158–60; first attack British
moving up St Lawrence 41,
84–6; Fort Niagara, loss to
British of 248–50; Foulon
landings, attempt to stop British
331–44; Guyenne Regiment 227,
313, 340, 341, 342, 363–4, 372;
La Sarre battalion 351, 372;
Languedoc battalion 351;
Montmorency, defeat British at
220–38; Montmorency, reaction
to British move to 150, 151–2,
155–7; Native Americans allies
and *see* Native Americans; North
American warfare, style of
47–50, 51–2; Plains of Abraham,
battle of 345–83, 384, 385, 386;
Plains of Abraham, reaction to
defeat on 388–90, 392–5; plan
for defeat 77–8; Plan of
Operations 76–7; Point Lévis,
fight British at xxiv–xxv, 126,
133–4, 136, 169–72; Pointe aux
Trembles 243–7; prepare for
British attack on Quebec 53–80;
prisoners, treatment of 133–4;
retreat to Jacques Cartier River
389, 395; second siege of